INDIA in SEARCH of GLORY

ADVANCE PRAISE FOR *INDIA IN SEARCH OF GLORY*

'It is said that democracy enables a nation to make amends for its own mistakes. Through the unbiased lens of the eminent economist Ashok Lahiri, the book examines how geopolitical conflicts, economic compulsions and political landscapes have shaped our policies, some of which have worked more successfully than others. Dr Lahiri presents a compelling case that our electorate is maturing as India steadily improves its legacy shortcomings in areas like education, health, physical infrastructure and ethnic polarization. This timely and intellectual "tour de force" reaffirms India's unwavering faith in democracy and is a must-read for policymakers who need to take India's past into account while deciding upon growth-oriented and inclusive measures'—Deepak Parekh, Indian businessman and chairman, Housing Development Finance Corporation, India

'Ashok Lahiri brings extraordinary domain knowledge and compelling analytical skills in this outstanding book. The book combines his understanding on the evolution of both the Indian and international context reflecting periodic paradigm shifts in policy approaches. A compelling read enhancing our understanding of the past, present and future in India's abiding quest as a global economic powerhouse'—N.K. Singh, Indian politician, economist, former IAS officer, former revenue and expenditure secretary, Ministry of Finance and former secretary to PM Vajpayee, PMO and chairperson of the Fifteenth Finance Commission

'Ashok Lahiri has written the Mahabharata of India's political economy. As it was said of the epic, what is not here did not happen. Lahiri displays a deep knowledge of political economy as well as of the economics of politics which is comprehensive as well as analytical. He has brought to this account all his knowledge and skill pertaining to the economic theory and economic history of India, along with an account of political history such as we have not seen before and are unlikely to see again'—Meghnad (Lord) Desai, India-born naturalized British economist and former Labour politician

'Ashok Lahiri has written an excellent book which describes how democracy has served India well in building the nation. Socio-economic progress may have been tepid so far, but as democracy matures, he convincingly argues that such progress should accelerate'—Bimal Jalan, former governor, Reserve Bank of India

INDIA *in* SEARCH *of* GLORY

POLITICAL CALCULUS AND ECONOMY

ASHOK K. LAHIRI

BUSINESS

An imprint of Penguin Random House

PENGUIN BUSINESS

USA | Canada | UK | Ireland | Australia
New Zealand | India | South Africa | China | Singapore

Penguin Business is part of the Penguin Random House group of companies
whose addresses can be found at global.penguinrandomhouse.com

Published by Penguin Random House India Pvt. Ltd
4th Floor, Capital Tower 1, MG Road,
Gurugram 122 002, Haryana, India

First published in Penguin Business by Penguin Random House India 2022
This edition published in Penguin Business by Penguin Random House India 2025
Copyright © Ashok K. Lahiri 2022

10 9 8 7 6 5 4 3 2 1

ISBN 9780670092079

Typeset in Adobe Garamond Pro by Manipal Technologies Limited, Manipal
Printed at Replika Press Pvt. Ltd, India

www.penguin.co.in

This is a legitimate digitally printed version of the book and therefore might not
have certain extra finishing on the cover.

To
Gita, my mother, who against heavy odds, nurtured
and taught me to fly towards my dreams,
and
Rita (aka Dolly), my wife, who fully supported all my ventures
and also tried to teach me that happiness is as important as glory

Contents

Figures

Contents

Boxes

Abbreviations

AAIFR	Appellate Authority for Industrial and Financial Reconstruction
ACA	Additional Central Assistance
AIADMK	All India Anna Dravida Munnetra Kazhagam
AIBP	Accelerated Irrigation Benefit Programme
AICC	All-India Congress Committee
AIMTC	All-India Motor Transport Congress
AITC	All-India Trinamool Congress
AJGAR	Ahir, Jat, Gujar and Rajputs
APDP	Accelerated Power Development Programme
APDRP	Accelerated Power Development and Reform Programme
APHC	All Parties Hurriyat Conference
APHLC	All-Party Hill Leaders Conference
APL	Above the Poverty Line
APM	Administered Pricing Mechanism
ARDC	Agricultural Refinance and Development Corporation
AREP	Accelerated Rural Electrification Programme
ASHA	Accredited Social Health Activist
AT&C	Aggregate Technical and Commercial
AYUSH	Ayurveda, Yoga and Naturopathy, Unani, Siddha and Homeopathy
BCBS	Basel Committee on Banking Supervision

BCCT	Banking Cash Transaction Tax
BCR	Balance of Current Revenues
BEPS	Base Erosion and Profit Shifting
BICP	Bureau of Industrial Costs and Prices
BIFR	Board for Industrial and Financial Reconstruction
BIS	Bank for International Settlements
BIT	Bilateral Investment Treaty
BJD	Biju Janata Dal
BJP	Bharatiya Janata Party
BMS	Basic Minimum Services
BPCL	Bharat Petroleum Corporation Limited
BPL	Below the Poverty Line
BSE	Bombay Stock Exchange
BSP	Bahujan Samaj Party
C&AG	Comptroller and Auditor General
CACP	Commission for Agricultural Costs and Prices
CBI	Central Bureau of Investigation
CEO	Chief Executive Officer
CERC	Central Electricity Regulatory Commission
CFSA	Congress Forum for Socialist Action
CGST	Central Goods and Services Tax
CIC	Credit Information Company
CIF	Cost including Insurance and Freight
CIL	Coal India Limited
CIP	Central Issue Price
CMNAP	Common Minimum National Action Plan for Power
COC	Committee of Creditors
ComPI	Communist Party of India
CPC	Centralized Processing Centre
CPI	Consumer Price Index
CPI(M)	Communist Party of India (Marxist)
CPP	Congress Parliamentary Party
CPSE	Central Public Sector Enterprises
CRAR	Capital to Risk (Weighted) Assets Ratio
CRR	Cash Reserve Ratio
CRSP	Centrally sponsored Rural Sanitation Programme

CSP	Congress Socialist Party
CSRE	Crash Scheme for Rural Employment
CSS	Centrally Sponsored Schemes
CST	Central Sales Tax
CTT	Commodities Transaction Tax
CVC	Central Vigilance Commission
CWC	Congress Working Committee
CWG-2010	Commonwealth Games in 2010
DDA	Delhi Development Authority
DDP	Desert Development Programme
DDUGJY	Deen Dayal Upadhyay Gram Jyoti Yojana
DEPB	Duty Entitlement Passbook Scheme
DGFT	Director General of Foreign Trade
DGTD	Directorate General of Technical Development
DISCOM	Distribution Company (power)
DMK	Dravida Munnetra Kazhagam
DoT	Department of Telecommunications
DP	Depository Participant
DPC	Dabhol Power Company
DPAP	Drought Prone Areas Programme
DPEP	District Primary Education Programme
DPCO	Drug Price Control Order
DRDA	District Rural Development Authority
DRI	Differential Rate of Interest
DRAT	Debts Recovery Appellate Tribunal
DRT	Debts Recovery Tribunal
EAG	Empowered Action Group
EAS	Employment Assurance Scheme
ECB	External Commercial Borrowing
ED	Enforcement Directorate
EDI	Electronic Data Interchange
EGS	Employment Guarantee Scheme
EFF	Extended Fund Facility
ELF	Ethno-Linguistics Fractionalization
EW	East-West
FBT	Fringe Benefit Tax

FCI	Food Corporation of India
FDI	Foreign Direct Investment
FEMA	Foreign Exchange Management Act
FERA	Foreign Exchange Regulation Act
FII	Foreign Institutional Investors
FIPB	Foreign Investment Promotion Board
FIR	First Information Report
FIU-IND	Financial Intelligence Unit—India
FPS	Fair Price Shop
FWP	Food for Work Programme
G-10	Group of Ten
GATT	General Agreement on Tariffs and Trade
GDP	Gross Domestic Product
GIC	General Insurance Corporation of India
GSDP	Gross State Domestic Product
GST	Goods and Services Tax
HINDALCO	Hindustan Aluminium Corporation Ltd.
HPCL	Hindustan Petroleum Corporation Limited
HVP	Haryana Vikas Party
IAAP	Intensive Agricultural Area Programme
IADP	Intensive Agricultural Development Programme
IAEA	International Atomic Energy Agency
IAS	Indian Administrative Service
IAY	Indira Awaas Yojana
IBA	Indian Banks' Association
IBC	Insolvency and Bankruptcy Code
ICDS	Integrated Child Development Services
ICEGATE	Indian Customs Electronic Gateway
ICICI	Industrial Credit and Investment Corporation of India
ICMR	Indian Council of Medical Research
ICS	Indian Civil Service
ICSSR	Indian Council of Social Science Research
IDBI	Industrial Development Bank of India
IDFC	Infrastructure Development Finance Company
IDRA	Industries (Development and Regulation) Act
IFCI	Industrial Finance Corporation of India

IGST	Integrated Goods and Services Tax
IIFCL	India Infrastructure Finance Company Limited
IMF	International Monetary Fund
INLD	Indian National Lok Dal
IOA	Indian Olympic Association
IOC	Indian Oil Corporation
IPKF	Indian Peace Keeping Force
IPR	Industrial Policy Resolution
IRDA	Insurance Regulatory and Development Authority
IRDP	Integrated Rural Development Programme
IREP	Integrated Rural Energy Programme
ISD	International Subscriber Dialling
IT	Information Technology
ITA	Information Technology Agreement
ITI	Indian Telephone Industries
IWDP	Integrated Watershed Development Programme
JD(S)	Janata Dal (Secular)
JD(U)	Janata Dal (United)
JGSY	Jawahar Gram Samridhi Yojana
JKLF	Jammu Kashmir Liberation Front
JKNLF	Jammu and Kashmir National Liberation Front
JMM	Jharkhand Mukti Morcha
JNNURM	Jawaharlal Nehru National Urban Renewal Mission
JPC	Joint Parliamentary Committee
JPRGY	Jaya Prakash Rozgar Guarantee Yojana
JRY	Jawahar Rozgar Yojana
JSY	Janani Suraksha Yojana
KHAM	Kshatriya, Harijan, Adivasi, Muslim
KMPP	Kisan Mazdoor Praja Party
KYC	Know Your Customer
LAF	Liquidity Adjustment Facility
LARR	Land Acquisition, Rehabilitation and Resettlement Act
LIC	Life Insurance Corporation
LJP	Lok Janashakti Party
LNG	Liquified Natural Gas
LPG	Liquid Petroleum Gas

MAT	Minimum Alternate Tax
MCAA	Multilateral Competent Authority Agreement
MCD	Municipal Corporation of Delhi
MDG	Millennium Development Goals
MLA	Member of Legislative Assembly
MMPO	Milk and Milk Product Order
MMTC	Minerals and Metals Trading Corporation
MNREGA	Mahatma Gandhi National Rural Employment Guarantee Act
MoU	Memorandum of Understanding
MP	Member of Parliament
MRP	Maximum Retail Price
MRTP	Monopolies and Restrictive Trade Practices
MRTPA	Monopolies and Restrictive Trade Practices Act
MSDE	Ministry of Skill Development and Entrepreneurship
MSEB	Maharashtra State Electricity Board
MSME	Micro, Small and Medium Enterprise
MSP	Minimum Support Price
MTNL	Mahanagar Telephone Nigam Limited
MUDRA	Micro Units Development and Refinance Agency Ltd.
NABARD	National Bank for Agriculture and Rural Development
NAV	Net Asset Value
NBA	Nirmal Bharat Abhiyan
NCC	National Credit Council
NCDC	National Coal Development Corporation
NCMP	National Common Minimum Programme
NCP	Nationalist Congress Party
NDA	National Democratic Alliance
NDDB	National Dairy Development Board
NDMC	New Delhi Municipal Corporation
NFBS	National Family Benefit Scheme
NFL	National Fertilizers Limited
NH	National Highway
NHAI	National Highways Authority of India
NHB	National Housing Bank
NHPC	National Hydroelectric Power Corporation

NIDC	National Industrial Development Corporation
NIPFP	National Institute of Public Finance and Policy
NITI	National Institution for Transforming India
NMDC	National Mineral Development Corporation
NNP	Net National Product
NOAPS	National Old Age Pension Scheme
NMBS	National Maternity Benefit Scheme
NPA	Non-Performing Assets
NPS	New Pension Scheme
NREGA	National Rural Employment Guarantee Act
NREGS	National Rural Employment Guarantee Scheme
NREP	National Rural Employment Programme
NRHM	National Rural Health Mission
NRI	Non-Resident Indian
NRLM	National Rural Livelihood Mission
NS	North-South
NSAP	National Social Assistance Programme
NSDA	National Skill Development Agency
NSDC	National Skill Development Corporation
NSDCB	National Skill Development Coordination Board
NSDF	National Skill Development Fund
NSDL	National Securities Depository Limited
NSE	National Stock Exchange
NSS	National Sample Survey
NSSF	National Small Savings Fund
NSSO	National Sample Survey Organization
NTC	National Textile Corporation
NTPC	National Thermal Power Corporation
OAPEC	Organization of Arab Petroleum Exporting Countries
OCB	Overseas Corporate Bodies
OCC	Oil Coordination Committee
OGL	Open General Licensing
OIL	Oil India Limited
ONGC	Oil and Natural Gas Corporation
OPEC	Organization of the Petroleum Exporting Countries
PDO	Public Debt Office

PDP	People's Democratic Party
PDS	Public Distribution System
PEPSU	Patiala and East Punjab States Union
PFC	Power Finance Corporation
PFRDA	Pension Fund Regulatory and Development Authority
PHC	Primary Health Care
PIL	Public Interest Litigation
PIO	Persons of Indian Origin
PIREP	Pilot Intensive Rural Employment Project
PMGKY	Pradhan Mantri Garib Kalyan Yojana
PMGY	Pradhan Mantri Gramodya Yojana
PMGSY	Pradhan Mantri Gram Sadak Yojana
PMIUPEP	Prime Minister's Integrated Urban Poverty Eradication Programme
PMJAY	Ayushman Bharat-Pradhan Mantri Jan Arogya Yojana
PMJDY	Pradhan Mantri Jan Dhan Yojana
PMJJBY	Pradhan Mantri Jeevan Jyoti Bima Yojana
PMKSY	Pradhan Mantri Krishi Sinchayee Yojana
PMKVY	Pradhan Mantri Kaushal Vikas Yojana
PMLA	Prevention of Money Laundering Act
PMMY	Pradhan Mantri MUDRA Yojana
PMSBY	Pradhan Mantri Suraksha Bima Yojana
POTA	Prevention of Terrorism Act
PPA	Power Purchase Agreement
PSP	Praja Socialist Party
QR	Quantitative Restriction
R-APDRP	Restructured Accelerated Power Development and Reform Programme
RBI	Reserve Bank of India
REC	Rural Electrification Corporation
RF	Ready Forward
RGGVY	Rajiv Gandhi Grameen Vidyutikaran Yojana
RIDF	Rural Infrastructure Development Fund
RJD	Rashtriya Janata Dal
RLEGP	Rural Landless Employment Guarantee Programme
RPI	Republican Party of India

RPS	Retention Price Cum Subsidy Scheme
RRB	Regional Rural Banks
RRP	Akhil Bharatiya Ram Rajya Parishad
RSBY	Rashtriya Swasthya Bima Yojana
RSP	Revolutionary Socialist Party
RTI	Right to Information
SAD	Shiromani Akali Dal
SAIL	Steel Authority of India Ltd
SAP	State Advised Price
SARFAESI	Securitization and Reconstruction of Financial Assets and Enforcement of Securities Interest
SASB	Sri Amarnathji Shrine Board
SAUBHAGYA	Pradhan Mantri Sahaj Bijli Har Ghar Yojana
SBA	Swachh Bharat Abhiyan
SCF	All India Scheduled Caste Federation
SDI	Social Diversity Index
SDL	State Development Loan
SEB	State Electricity Board
SEBI	Securities and Exchange Board of India
SECC	Socio-Economic and Caste Census
SERC	State Electricity Regulatory Commission
SFC	State Finance Corporation
SGL	Subsidiary General Ledger
SGRY	Sampoorna Grameen Rozgar Yojana
SGSY	Swarnajayanti Grameen Swarojgar Yojana
SHG	Self-Help Group
SJSRY	Swarna Jayanti Shahari Rozgar Yojana
SIA	Secretariat of Industrial Approvals
SICA	Sick Industrial Companies Act
SIDBI	Small Industries Development Bank of India
SIT	Special Investigation Team
SJP	Samajwadi Party
SLR	Statutory Liquidity Ratio
SMP	Statutory Minimum Price
SP	Socialist Party
SSI	Small Scale Industry

SSP	Samyukta Socialist Party
STC	State Trading Corporation
STD	Subscriber Trunk Dialling
STT	Securities Transaction Tax
SUCI	Socialist Unity Centre of India
T&D	Transmission and Distribution
TDP	Telugu Desam Party
TDS	Tax Deduction at Source
TFR	Total Fertility Rate
TINXSYS	Tax Information Exchange System
TMC	Tamil Maanila Congress
TRAI	Telecom Regulatory Authority of India
TRIPS	Trade-Related Aspects of Intellectual Property Rights
TRS	Telangana Rashtra Samithi
TRYSEM	Training Rural Youth for Self-Employment
TSC	Total Sanitation Campaign
UASL	Unified Access Service Licence
UBSP	Urban Basic Services Programme
UDAY	Ujwal DISCOM Assurance Yojana
UF	United Front
UID	Unique Identification Number
UIDAI	Unique Identification Authority of India
UIP	Universal Immunization Programme
UN	United Nations
UT	Union Territory
UTGST	Union Territory Goods and Services Tax
UTI	Unit Trust of India
VAAY	Valmiki Ambedkar Awas Yojana
VDIS	Voluntary Disclosure of Income Scheme
VHP	Vishwa Hindu Parishad
VRS	Voluntary Retirement Scheme
VSNL	Videsh Sanchar Nigam Limited
WPI	Wholesale Price Index
WTO	World Trade Organization

Introduction

I

India in Search of Glory

On 9 October 2012, in the Swat Valley in north-west Pakistan, Malala Yousafzai, a fifteen-year-old girl and advocate for female education, had been shot in the head and injured badly by the Taliban. After a gap of ten days, some members of the executive board of the Asian Development Bank (ADB), of which I was one, called on President Asif Ali Zardari in Islamabad to elicit his views on ADB's effectiveness in helping Pakistan pursue its developmental agenda. The genesis of this book lies in what followed, after a brief discussion about Malala.

Upon learning that I was from India, the President asked me how I viewed the region's prospects. I told him that there was wide agreement that we were in the Asian century. In terms of spectacular growth and rapid development, Japan had successfully paved the way in the 1960s, and was succeeded by the neighbouring Asian tigers and most recently, by China. I was not fully confident about South Asia, as its leaders tended to promise much and deliver less, I added. Nevertheless, I was hopeful, I said, because of democracy, not only in India but also in Bangladesh, Pakistan and the other states. After all, it is a well-proven adage that politicians do not win elections to formulate policies but formulate policies to win elections. With people demanding growth, politicians will be forced to deliver even in South Asia, if only to ensure their political perpetuation. The President pointed out that in 2004, the Bharatiya Janata Party (BJP)-led National Democratic Alliance (NDA)-led coalition, was thrown out of power despite its 'India Shining'

3

campaign, which had some merit in its claims. Why did that happen, he wondered.

'India Shining,' which Zardari was referring to, was an advertising campaign at home and abroad from early December 2003. It was intended not only to promote the country internationally but also to publicize the considerable economic achievements under the NDA, led by Prime Minister Atal Bihari Vajpayee. The jumbo outreach highlighted the steps the NDA government had taken to boost economic growth, slash interest rates, stabilize prices, expand road and telecommunication and health networks, and offer free basic education. The campaign created a controversy about whether it was a ruse for promoting the 'feel good' factor and attracting votes to the ruling NDA in general and to the BJP in particular.

Our brief exchange ended, like most such dialogues, without resolution. But ever since then I have been trying to formulate a cogent answer to President Zardari's question. Do Indian voters reward leaders and parties that promise and deliver growth? Or do they vote only emotionally and along more traditional caste and community lines, with the dice loaded against incumbents?

In the postcolonial period, India was an exception in choosing the steadfast and almost uninterrupted pursuit of democracy not only as an end in itself but perhaps as an instrument for its socio-economic development and for reclaiming its past glory. It was in sharp contrast to the model of 'development first and democracy later' followed by India's more successful neighbours to the east, namely the East Asian Tigers and also China. India has lagged behind its neighbours to the east so far, but as India develops and people become better educated, healthier and better informed, are there signs of economic policies in democratic India being better aligned with what is needed to deliver higher growth and faster development, and further its search of past glory? Indian democracy may have suffered limitations because of the social 'backwardness' of the people, such as illiteracy and caste, religious and other ethno-linguistic cleavages. The 'backwardness' has not disappeared but is on the wane.

In a democracy, politicians and their parties, who aspire to capture positions of governance and formulate policies, must carry the people along with them. Doubtless, they can sway public opinion to some extent, and some charismatic leaders can do that better than others, but within finite and region-specific limitations. Policies that can be carried in Belgium, for instance, may not be practical in Burkina Faso. But there is also an interlocked corollary: policies for attaining universal literacy, or industrialization and urbanization, when implemented with reasonable efficiency, can change peoples' lives and, in turn, increase the scope for refashioning goals. Simply put, a symbiosis of appropriate policies and how these change people's lives constitute a singularly powerful force in economic development.

This book is an attempt to decipher improvements in the political calculus, as the country develops and the backwardness of the people diminishes, for democracy to start yielding better dividends in the Indian search for glory. The challenge of building such a narrative of Indian economic evolution and political developments for a wide readership with interest in the subject but not necessarily a background in economics appeared both daunting and exciting. The task appeared even more stimulating with the complete ascendance of the BJP under Narendra Modi for two successive five-year terms in 2014 and 2019. What follows is an attempt to build such a narrative of the interplay between politics and economic policies by giving only a brief description of the historical events since Independence without getting into their quotidian diversity. This chapter starts with a stocktaking—a broad-brush picture of how India has done overall, politically and in securing democratic rule, and on the economic front.

I.1 Elusive Search for Glory So Far

Underlying the freedom movement was always a celebration of the past, when India occupied pride of place among nations in terms of civilization, including intellectual achievements and economic development. Freedom was expected to enable the country to reclaim its past glory. On the eve of Independence in 1947, Jawaharlal Nehru, the first Prime Minister, pledged to do so in his iconic 'Tryst with Destiny' speech. On 25 January 2013, in his address to the nation on the eve of the sixty-fourth Republic Day, Pranab Mukherjee, the thirteenth president of India, summed it up succinctly when he said, 'India has changed more in last six decades than in six previous centuries. This is neither accidental nor providential; history shifts its pace when touched by vision.'[1]

According to the pioneering work by economic historian Angus Maddison, Indian per capita income in real terms (that is, the income an average Indian would receive if all incomes were distributed equally among the people, adjusted for the increase in prices) increased by only a little over 12 per cent in the 447 years between 1500 and 1947. In the sixty-nine years between 1950–51 and 2019–20, per capita income, at constant prices, increased by 697 per cent! Indeed, India and Indians have changed significantly after Independence, but not enough to reclaim their past glory, especially vis-a-vis some of India's not-so-distant eastern neighbours.

Amartya Sen, a Nobel Laureate, and Jean Dreze, a Belgian economist who has become an Indian citizen and dedicated his life to the upliftment of the Indian poor, have described in detail how, in terms of social indicators like infant mortality or female literacy, India compares unfavourably even with some South Asian countries such as Bangladesh. Indians have been searching for ways to regain their past glory among the comity of nations. In one of their books, Sen and Dreze have pointed out several shortcomings of economic policies pursued so far to name their book in 2013, *An Uncertain Glory—India and Its Contradictions*.

India's socio-economic indicators have lagged behind those of its not-so-distant neighbours in the east. Gross domestic product (GDP) is a summary measure of the goods and services produced by a country and constitutes a first proxy for its aggregate income. In the 1960s, relative to India, per capita GDP at constant 2010 US dollars for South Korea was only 2.8 times higher, while Singapore and Hong Kong's were 10 times higher, and Japan's 26 times. The corresponding figures in 1990 were South Korea's 14.6 times, Singapore's 38.8 times, Hong Kong's 31.4 times and Japan's 65.5 times (Figure I.1). Between 1960 and 1990, while India increased its per capita GDP at constant 2010 US dollars by only a factor of 1.8, the East Asian Tigers or Newly Industrializing Countries (NICs), namely Hong Kong, South Korea, Singapore and Taiwan, increased theirs by a factor of over 5.5 and totally transformed the very nature of living for most of their population.

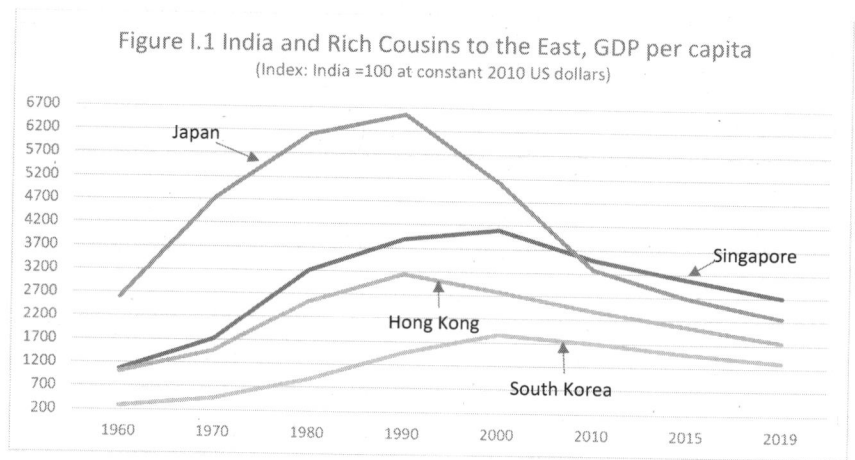

Figure I.1 India and Rich Cousins to the East, GDP per capita
(Index: India =100 at constant 2010 US dollars)

Source: World Development Report 2020. Per capita GDP derived by dividing GDP by population in the same year.

Just as the gap between Indian per capita GDP and that of the East Asian Tigers started narrowing, the gap between Indian and Chinese per capita GDP started exploding. The much smaller 'tigers'—both in area and in population—could be dismissed from the argument by saying that a mouse could not be the model for an elephant. But the Chinese dragon was not a mouse. While China's per capita income was lower than that of India's between 1960 and 1983, it grew 19.5-fold from $423 (2010 US dollars) in 1983 to $8,254 in 2019; India grew only 4.7 times from $464 to $2,169 (Figure I.2). With its comparable population, China's rapid growth has taken the sheen away from India's performance.

In the 1970s, Prof. Raj Krishna of the Delhi School of Economics used to say: no matter what India did, on average, it tended to grow annually only at the 'Hindu' rate of around 3.5 per cent! With such a low aggregate income growth and population growing by about 2 per cent per year, India's per capita income would double only in about forty-six years. The eastern neighbours were growing much faster and doubling their per capita income in ten to fifteen years. Thus, a succinct way to describe India's growth performance is 'Good, but not good enough!'

A major reason for slow growth was the abysmally poor literacy rate at Independence and the sluggish progress thereafter. Inability to read and write seriously handicaps skill formation.

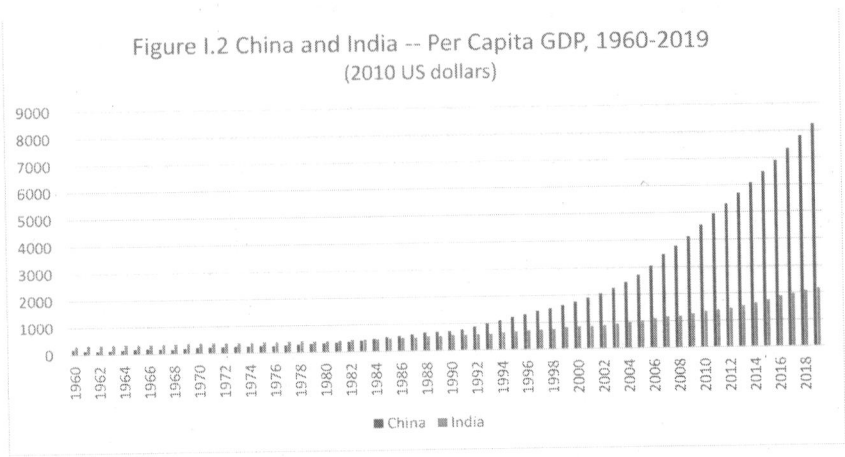

Source: World Development Report 2020. Per capita GDP derived by dividing GDP by population in the same year.

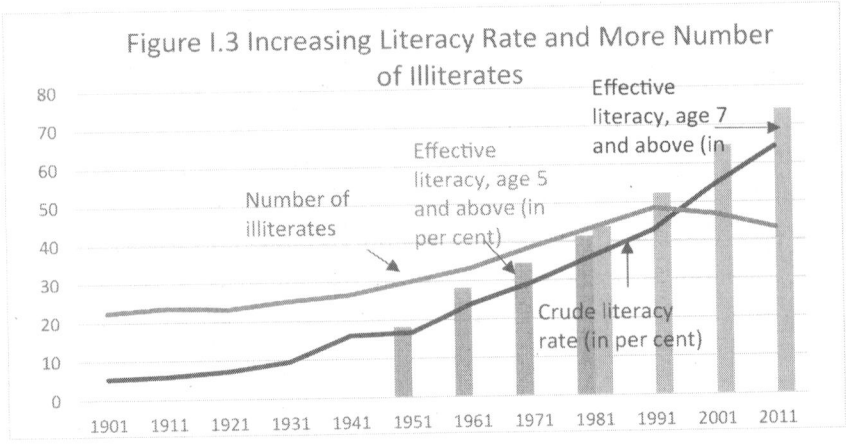

Source: Statements 20 and 21. State of Literacy. http://censusindia.gov.in/2011-prov-results/data_files/india/Final_PPT_2011_chapter6.pdf

Like education, health was another dimension where India lagged. Health, like education, is not only a critical component of human welfare but also an important determinant of economic growth. In 2004, Robert Fogel, the American economic historian who had won the Nobel Prize for economics in 1993, argued that a healthier population, bigger and stronger, had accounted for around half of the growth in national income in Britain since 1790. Good health is a necessary condition for people to provide efficient labour services. A healthy person may be expected to live longer than an unhealthy one, and thus, rising life expectancy is generally taken as a proxy for improving health status. With spectacular breakthroughs in medical sciences, particularly in childhood immunization, life expectancy at birth, or the number of years a newborn could expect to live, increased rapidly from forty-four to forty-nine in 1881 to fifty-nine to sixty-three in 1931 in the UK. Unfortunately, in its Indian colony, it fluctuated between twenty-three and twenty-seven during the same period, with significant changes in the interim because of famines and epidemics. A healthy population needs adequate nutrition, good sanitation and healthcare, aspects which were neglected by the imperial government.

There was a rapid increase of about ten years in life expectancy right in the first post-Independence decade. By 1991, life expectancy, at around fifty-eight years (57.9 years, to be exact), was more than double that of about twenty-seven years in 1931. With mortality steadily declining through improvements in child immunization, medical care, sanitation, housing and education, by 2010, an average Indian's life expectancy, at around sixty-seven years, was twice that of 1951! Yet, improvements were not rapid enough to match the progress in India's neighbours to the east (Figure I.4). Indian life expectancy at birth in 2010 fell short of the world average by about four years.

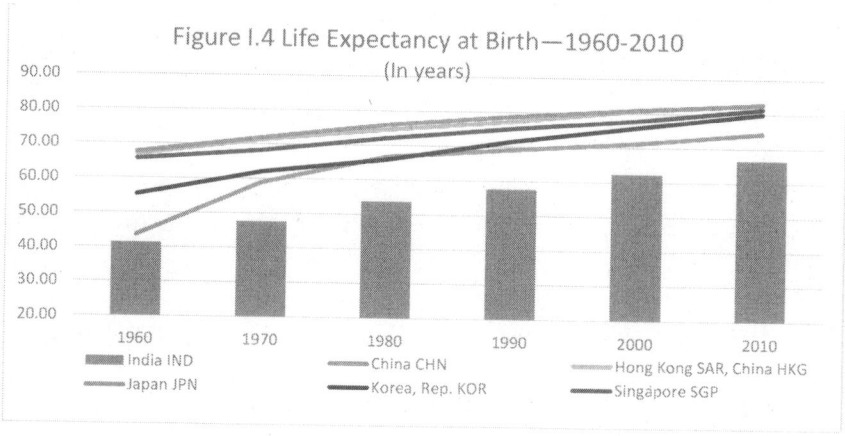

Figure I.4 Life Expectancy at Birth—1960-2010
(In years)

Source: World Development Indicators, World Bank. https://data.worldbank.org/indicator/SP.DYN. LE00.IN?view=chart

On physical infrastructure, the famous economist Rosenstein-Rodan has observed '. . . that before building consumer goods factories, a major indivisible block of social overhead capital or infrastructure must be built and sponsored because private market initiatives will not create it in time. Low wages should have been a sufficient incentive to create a textile industry in India in the post-Napoleonic era and not in Lancashire, England. Indian wages were 50 or 60 per cent lower than the low wages in England . . . the prospect of building a textile mill in Bombay instead of Manchester or Coventry seemed most attractive . . . however, that in order to build a factory one would have to build a bridge or finish a road or a railway line or later an electric power station. Each of these elements in the so-called social overhead capital requires a minimum high quantum of investment which could serve, say, fifty factories but would cost far too much for one. One cannot build a bridge small enough to allow only a hundred crossings a day. Lower wages are not a sufficient incentive for investment.'[2] Apart from insufficient progress in education and health, a reason for the elusive search for glory was also the poor state of physical infrastructure, including roads, railways, water and electricity supply, and civic amenities in urban areas.

I.2 The Poor, Fewer in Proportion but Still Too Many

The pursuit of glory also looks elusive when we examine poverty in India. India, the jewel of the British Crown, was notorious for its killer famines, e.g., the Great Bengal Famine of 1770 with 10 million deaths, which is still etched deep in public memory. During colonial times, famines were only the most stark and ungainly demonstration of pervasive poverty which was silent, sustained and invidious. Poverty was invisible to the colonial masters; they noticed the Indian poor only when they died in millions. The Grand Old Man of Indian nationalism, Dadabhai Naoroji, was the first to focus on the issue of poverty in a methodical way. In 1876, before the East India Association in Bombay, in a paper entitled 'Poverty in India,' he presented the first estimate of a 'poverty line' for India and compared it with per capita GDPs in the different provinces to assess the severity of their poverty problem. Naoroji established the extensive nature of poverty in India in 1867–68 by showing that production per head fell short by three-fourths of the cost of maintaining inmates in prison in all provinces but Punjab.

Measurement of poverty attracted adequate attention only after Independence, from the early 1970s onwards (Table I.1). After Independence, India's progress in the removal of poverty, relative to that of its neighbours to the east, looks particularly unsatisfactory. With rapid growth and vigorous welfare measures, poverty was over by the 1960s in Japan, the unquestioned leader in Asia in charting a path to development. The four NICs, namely Hong Kong, Singapore, South Korea and Taiwan, followed soon, and the three relatively large ASEAN countries of Indonesia, Malaysia and Thailand were not far behind.

Table I.1. Percentage and Number of Poor based on Lakdawala Committee's Methodology

Year	NSS Round	Poverty Ratio (in per cent)			Number of Poor (in million)		
		Rural	Urban	Total	Rural	Urban	Total
1973-74	28	56.4	49.0	54.9	261.3	60.0	321.3
1977-78	32	53.1	45.2	51.3	264.3	64.6	328.9
1983	38	45.7	40.8	44.5	252.0	70.9	322.9
1987-88	43	39.1	38.2	38.9	231.9	75.2	307.1
1993-94	50	37.3	32.4	36.0	244.0	76.3	320.3
1999-2000*	55	27.1	23.6	26.1	193.2	67.0	260.3
2004-05*	61	28.3	25.7	27.5	220.9	80.8	301.7

Source: 'Report of the Expert Group to Review the Methodology for Measurement of Poverty,' Planning Commission, Government of India, June 2014. Table 2.1, p. 14 and Table A.8 p. 26.
* Until 1993-94, NSSO collected consumption expenditure data on all items based on a uniform recall period (URP) of 30 days. In 1999–2000, it switched to a mixed recall period—for five low-frequency items of purchase (clothing, footwear, education, institutional medical care and durables) on a 365-day recall basis, and for the rest on a 30-day recall period.

A meaningful inter-country comparison of poverty requires a common yardstick. But even a common poverty line in terms of a currency, say the US dollar, leaves us with the problem of conversion into domestic currencies of various countries. Unfortunately, the market exchange rates, which are determined in the currency markets by including speculative forces, do not provide a satisfactory solution. They do not equalize prices of any but a few standardized commodities and services that are widely traded in the international market. The relativities of prices of different commodities and services in two countries can differ significantly from the market exchange rate. For example, by multiplying the prices of a kilogram of fish or of a haircut, or the rent of a two-bedroom apartment in the US suburbs in dollars by the rupee-dollar exchange rate, we do not get the corresponding prices in India. Hence, exchange rates do not reflect purchasing powers of different currencies in the respective domestic markets.

The World Bank's poverty lines in purchasing power parity (PPP) dollars ($) are useful in this context. PPP can be calculated for any product, and has most famously been done for the Big Mac in 'Burgernomics' by *The Economist* magazine. Big Mac PPP is defined as 'the exchange rate that would mean hamburgers cost the same in America as abroad'. The PPP$ equivalent of a country's currency used by the World Bank is not limited to a single commodity, such as a Big Mac, but covers hundreds of commodities and services. The basket of commodities and services considered is not identical across countries. The basket varies according to tastes and cultural backgrounds but provides equivalent satisfaction or utility in principle. For example, PPP$1 at 1985 prices, is the amount required in domestic currency to buy more or less the same bundle of goods and services as $1 could buy in the US in 1985.

With their dramatic growth, eight countries—Japan, the four NICs, Thailand, Malaysia and Indonesia—have come to be known as the 'East Asian miracle'. Japan had abolished poverty long ago. By the World Bank's PPP$1 at 1985 prices yardstick, the four NICs banished poverty by the early 1980s. Thailand did so by the late 1990s, and Malaysia by the early 2000s. That leaves only two—Indonesia among the East Asian miracle countries, and China, the late entrant in the race to prosperity— to compare with India in poverty amelioration. Indonesia and China, with populations in 2010 of 238 million and 1340 million, respectively, are large countries like India (population of 1211 million in 2011) and appropriate as comparators (Figure I.5).

With PPP$1.90 at 2011–12 prices as the yardstick, in a comparison of 1986–1990, India shows up in an unfavourable light (right-most panel). By the same yardstick, between 1990 and 2015, China and Indonesia

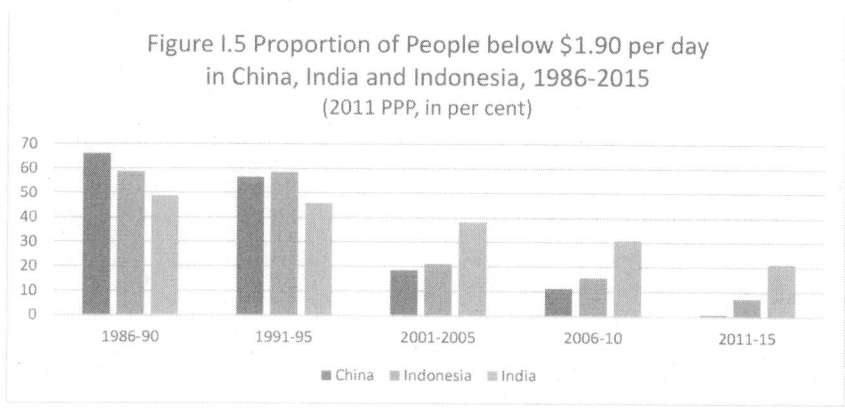

Figure I.5 Proportion of People below $1.90 per day in China, India and Indonesia, 1986-2015 (2011 PPP, in per cent)

Source: World Bank.

reduced the proportion of below the poverty line (BPL) people from 66.2 per cent and 58.8 per cent, to 0.7 per cent and 7.2 per cent, respectively. By contrast, between 1987 and 2011, the reduction in India was from 66.2 per cent to 21.2 per cent. Good, but not good enough.

I.3 Democracy—An Instrument of Governance

After Independence, India adopted the Westminster model of parliamentary democracy for the country as well as its constituent provinces, called 'states'. In 1947, women were still deprived of universal and equal voting rights in many 'developed' countries such as Belgium, Canada, Switzerland and the US. From its first general election in 1951–1952, India gave full voting rights to women and launched a new experiment in the world—the practice of a full-throttled parliamentary democracy in a large developing country. Even in the mid-1970s, outside Western Europe, North America, Australia and New Zealand, India was the only major country, apart from Japan, to sustain democratic governments in a continued way. Democracy is widely, and rightly, considered to be an end in itself. But what we are interested in is the effectiveness of democracy as an instrument of governance.

Inter-party competition in a democratic political arena looks remarkably like competition among producers in markets in the economic sphere. In neo-classical economics, individuals maximize their satisfaction and firms or producers maximize their profits by competitively interacting in the institutional setting of markets. Under certain market conditions, e.g., the absence of market power or collusion and increasing returns to scale, such interactions produce optimal outcomes where no one can be made better off without making someone else worse off. Even in practice, competition and functioning markets have tended to deliver better results in terms of economic outcomes. So why do competitive politics in a democratic set-up, with voters expressing their demands through the ballot, not result in optimum policies?

As Gary Becker, a Nobel Laureate in economics, pointed out in 1958, ignorance and the large scale required of political organizations, periodic rather than continuous elections, and different preferences among members of the electorate can produce imperfections in competitive democratic politics. Unlike in the market for goods and services, where people have more power as buyers and as sellers if they are rich, and have incentives to act wisely, in political democracies, with 'one person, one vote', the incentives to act wisely are lacking. Similarly, the large scale, along with the resources required for political organizations and for winning a seat in the Lok Sabha (the lower house of the bicameral national parliament) or Vidhan Sabha (state-level legislative assembly) election, can result in limited competition. Periodic elections only every five years lead to a lack of voters' control over the elected representative. Furthermore, the diversity of what different segments of the electorate want creates an added complication. These deficiencies typically result in four observable problems.

First, a poor and illiterate household, for legitimate reasons, prefers the certainty of a few additional kilograms of subsidized rice or wheat today to the uncertain promise of an educated daughter or a prosperous village with proper infrastructure a decade later. Thus, there is pressure on public consumption in a democracy, particularly a poor one. It manifests itself in the preponderance of subsidies and transfers at the cost of public expenditure on education, health and physical infrastructure such as roads, and power and water supply. These pressures tend to be greater in cleft societies with fractures along language, religion and caste characteristics.

Second, there is the tension between property rights and democracy with universal adult suffrage. Property rights are essential for incentives to work hard, save, invest and innovate. Under universal democracy, the poor with insufficient income and no wealth, who are a majority, can threaten property and even confiscate it. While this tension was uppermost in the minds of economists such as David Ricardo and Karl Marx in the nineteenth century, the experience of the second half of the twentieth century demonstrated how several democratic countries, including India, succeeded in safeguarding property rights, partly through constitutional provisions.

Third, narrow sectarian divisions may lead to identity politics—a tendency of people sharing a racial, religious, ethnic, social or cultural identity to form exclusive political alliances, instead of engaging in traditional broad-based party politics focused on issues. Divisive identity politics can dampen the pursuit of reforms and hinder development in a democracy with low levels of socio-economic development. So we ask the question: how has democracy served India as an instrument of governance?

Building a nation

Many countries have a diversity of people. For example, in the US, not only are there whites, but also whites of different extractions such as Irish, Italian etc., and blacks, Hispanics and Asians. Furthermore, southerners, with their history of segregationist practices, differ from those in the north. In India, such differences can be even more pronounced, with a bewildering diversity in people's ethnicity, language, caste and tribe-non-tribe characteristics, and religion. According to the ethno-linguistics fractionalization (ELF) index measuring this diversity, in the 1970s, India ranked at the top of sixty-seven countries, and in 2005, by the expanded social diversity index (SDI) incorporating linguistic, racial and religious aspects, it was in the two top deciles.

After Independence, the commitment to democratic ideals helped the leadership in building an integrated India from the British Indian provinces and over 560 princely states. The pro-integration Praja Mandals or people's organizations in the princely states were demanding democratic rights and abolition of iniquitous feudal monarchical systems, and acted as pressure groups on some of the recalcitrant rulers. Around 1947, Indians got their own 'state'—a defined territory and permanent population under their own sovereign or supreme authority duly recognized by other states.

It was different from a nation, which can be taken to mean people who, amid their diversity, share a unity and sufficient commonality of interests, goals and preferences to transcend their social fragmentation and not to wish to separate from each other as Indians. The 'state' and 'nation' support each other, and the nation had to be built and reinforced. India was not the first in having to embark on nation-building. The challenge was similar to that in Italy in 1860, when, after the northern elite in Italy succeeded in the country's unification, Massimo d'Azeglio, one of the founders of unified Italy, famously remarked: 'Italy has been made; now it remains to make Italians.'

'Nation-building' in the eighteenth and nineteenth centuries played an important role in the emergence of many established European nations of today. For example, from the French Revolution onwards and throughout the nineteenth century, there were concerted attempts 'to form French citizens'. *Peasants into Frenchmen* is the title of the book by the American historian Eugen Weber, in which he describes how it is only through roads and railways, and an expanding school system, that traditional attitudes and practices crumbled under the forces of modernization, it was only by 1914 that France became *la patrie* or the fatherland for its inhabitants.

Nation-building can be done by brute force, such as prohibiting local language or culture—or even genocide—or by benevolent means. Benevolent means include establishing a common education system and language, connecting places by roads and railways, promoting a common market for goods, services, capital and labour, and devolving government's powers across jurisdictions in a federal arrangement. Benevolent also means an accommodative stance at times to some groups' vigorous demands that prima facie do not appear consistent with the efficient functioning of a unified nation. Often, nation-building is a combination of coercive and benevolent means, with one dominating the other. Benevolence tends to dominate coercion in a democratic polity.

India's accommodative stance on nation-building was manifest in its linguistic reorganization of the states of Madras, Bombay and Punjab within a decade of Independence. India managed the fracture along caste lines and along tribal-non-tribal lines through special provisions of affirmative action, and the religious cleavages by the pursuit of secularism. Democratic India not only survived fractures along linguistic, caste and tribal-non-tribal lines, but slowly changed the depth of the fractures. Perhaps, it is fair to say that the process of 'making Indians' continues.

India joined others, such as Belgium, Singapore and Switzerland, to demonstrate that a nation need not be a single ethnic, cultural or linguistic group. India's case was particularly noteworthy because it was much larger, both in area and population, than any of these three, and also had considerably more social fragmentation in cultural, religious, racial, ethnic and linguistic terms. Furthermore, nation-building in many large countries with social fragmentation failed in the twentieth century, for example in Pakistan, Yugoslavia and the Soviet Union. The two large countries that survived and thrived in nation-building are China and India, but with different strategies. The Indian strategy differed from the Chinese in two important ways—first, it was more accommodative rather than assimilative, and second, it has been with the simultaneous pursuit of full-throttled democracy. While nation-building has not been smooth in some areas, like in Nagaland, Jammu and Kashmir, and Punjab, India has been more accommodative than coercive.

Would the assimilative iron rule of a benevolent dictator have accelerated nation-building in an underdeveloped country with widespread illiteracy and social cleavages? The counterfactual needs to be weighed against three relevant factors. First, the risk of the dictator turning out to be less than benevolent. Second, the assimilative approach even under a 'competent' dictator, like in the former Soviet Union under Joseph Stalin, might have failed in the medium to long run. Third, the short-run costs may disappear as democracy matures and people become better educated, better informed and have access to better economic opportunities.

For rapid development

As far as economic growth is concerned, did India prematurely choose democracy, which many believed was a luxury a poor country with widespread illiteracy could ill afford? It is difficult to draw any clear-cut conclusions from the scholarly debate on the relative merits of democracy and dictatorship in a poor illiterate country. For example, if democracies in such countries with very unequal distribution of income pose a threat to property rights, such rights are not secure under a less than benevolent dictator either. Similarly, if democracies in a poor country prefer present consumption to future growth, it is not obvious that even a benevolent dictator would necessarily do otherwise. Even the empirical evidence on the relative growth performance of democracies and dictatorial regimes is inconclusive.

Without the democratic checks and balances, a benevolent and enlightened dictator can, in principle, produce better outcomes than a democracy. It is analogous to central planning with perfect information, where an efficient government can produce better outcomes than markets. Like perfect information and efficient governments in centrally planned economies, benevolent dictators with enlightened self-interest are hard to come by under authoritarian regimes. For one Deng Xiaoping of China, there is an Idi Amin of Uganda, and a General Oswaldo López Arellano of Honduras to match. While the vulnerability of economic development to poor or venal leadership under authoritarian regimes makes democracy a safer bet, Nehru, the first Prime Minister of India, did enjoy almost unbridled powers and policy autonomy because of the overwhelming electoral dominance of the Indian National Congress Party (sometimes Congress henceforth) in the country and the unquestioned loyalty of his partymen to him. After Nehru's demise, an upsurge in popular participation in the late 1960s resulted in unsettled politics, the rise of regional parties, a brief period of internal Emergency with fundamental rights suspended, short-lived coalition governments, and the assassination of a sitting and a former Prime Minister.

In Part III, the rise of identity politics based on caste, religion or regional affiliation detracted from the full socio-economic benefits that democracy could have delivered in the country. Political scientist Pratap Bhanu Mehta, in his short and crisp book *Burden of Democracy*, has pointed out the immense difficulties of pursuing democratic policies in an inegalitarian society riven by caste, religion, class and patriarchy, where there is scant recognition of the moral worth of individuals. Democratic politics in such a society leads to inter-group conflicts and such conflicts can be interpreted as intense struggles for power, resulting in the breach of many democratic norms. Mehta prefers to look at such conflicts as resulting in greater empowerment of the people and 'through that medium produce a more lasting and just politics'. 'What we are witnessing is something more akin to a transitional stage, a process of churning of old injustice is necessary to produce a politics with more credible moral convictions. Whether or not this claim is credible only time will tell,' Mehta adds. This book supports this interpretation, and notes that after the second stage until the 1980s, slowly but surely, Indian democratic politics moved to a more stable and reformist mode from the 1990s (Part IV). As the country developed and the people got educated and better informed, democracy started showing an underlying broad trend of functioning with greater effectiveness. After all, all developed countries today are democratic.

I.4 Root of the Good-but-Not-Good-Enough Performance and Political Calculus

Under the British, the country was poor and the people backward because the colonial government spent little on health, education and infrastructure. The colonial government by design was a 'small' government with limited state capacity and it only tried to maintain peace and perpetuate the status quo to maximize what the 'home' country could 'drain' or get out of its empire. Development of the Indian economy was low, if at all, in their list of priorities.

Things changed after Independence. The framers of the Indian Constitution understood the importance of education and health. Article 45 stipulated that education for all children until they attained the age of fourteen would not only be free but compulsory within a period of ten years and Article 47 specified that, among other things, the State would regard the raising of the level of nutrition and the standard of living of its people and the improvement of public health as among its primary duties. 'State' referred to both the Centre and the states. Because of resource constraints and implementation issues, both the Articles were Directive Principles and not enforceable in courts.

In the initial years, the role of the people in the design of state activities was limited at best. With the glow of having steered the freedom struggle to success, the leadership, particularly Prime Minister Jawaharlal Nehru, enjoyed considerable policy autonomy and freedom from public pulls and pressures. The leadership's development strategy was strongly motivated by socialist planning, with the state at the commanding heights of the economy. After Independence, Indian leadership rapidly expanded the state's role in the promotion of development activities and management of public sector enterprises, perhaps even ahead of what it could successfully implement and society could sustain. The idea most probably was to develop the industrial base, create employment, mobilize more revenues and then get on with the job of creating social overheads and physical infrastructure. Post-Independence, social change quickened under a developmental state.

Over time, as the country developed, different groups became more efficient at different times in producing political pressure and channelling public expenditure and subsidies to themselves and/or reducing their taxes. For example, during the Nehru era, the middle and upper classes did well in getting the exemption limits raised on personal income tax and expanding opportunities for higher education, which would primarily benefit young men and women from their families. Independent India became an evolving story of the state changing itself and society changing in response, and changing society, through feedback, changing the state and so on.

By the end of the Nehru era, doubts had arisen about the efficacy of the command-and-control planned model of development and the state at the commanding heights of the economy. But there was policy hysteresis, an unwillingness to accept the mistake and make amends, because of the suspected popular reaction to such a course correction. The end of the Nehru era saw the electoral dominance of the Congress Party getting decimated and even the leadership within the party becoming a matter of contest. The state, wittingly or otherwise, had unleashed various societal forces. In the 1960s, various caste and regional groups coalesced to form political parties and capture power in their relevant states, and, through coalitions, attempt to exercise control even at the Union level. Policies had to be designed to 'buy' popular support, and in a democracy with social fragmentation, their formulation involved many compromises to satisfy people divided along multiple criteria. Politics overtook economics in policymaking. Prime Minister Indira Gandhi turned left and decided to follow her father's socialist policies with a populist twist (Chapters XIV and XV). The slogan was '*Garibi Hatao*' or abolish poverty here and now. Poverty on such a large scale could be removed on a sustained basis, not by doles or subsidies, but by providing better education and health facilities and physical infrastructure, such as rural roads, to improve the poor's earning capacity. Providing handouts for immediate succour won votes for some time but did not remove poverty on a lasting basis. The need for handouts increased over time and subsidies started exceeding the government's resources. It resulted in fiscal unsustainability and a government out of control. With repeated balance of payments crises—in 1957, 1962, 1965 and 1981—the country had to seek exceptional support from the International Monetary Fund (IMF). Furthermore, the popular upsurge in the mid-1970s overwhelmed the state, and the state had to even suspend democracy and declare an Emergency from 26 June 1975 onwards. Fortunately, in nineteen months, the state-society balance was restored, and democracy was back.

After the emergency, in Indian democracy, despite the signs of its growing maturity, the challenge of rationalizing subsidies continued. In any democracy, subsidies, once given, are difficult to withdraw even after the reason for giving them disappears. Some beneficiary group with enough political influence will try and block their discontinuation. Eminent economist Pranab Bardhan aptly compares India with 'a battered, bulging and extremely slow-moving'[3] public bus, commonly found on Indian roads, in which every passenger gets to decide the stops. Food subsidy provides a good example.

Facing a dire food shortage in the mid-1960s, the Union or central government intervened in agricultural input markets through subsidies and in output markets of mainly wheat and rice through minimum support price (MSP), public procurement and public distribution system (PDS). Government support and improved hybrid seeds led to the Green Revolution, and India moved from an era of shortage to an era of surpluses in food grains. Beyond promoting food production, MSP soon became a political instrument for mobilizing farmers' support. MSP was determined without reference to demand conditions and led to enormous surplus stocks of food grains, particularly wheat, which could be exported only with more subsidies. How agricultural policy had become a hostage to the farm lobby in the northern states became evident in September 2020, when three liberal farm laws were passed by the Union. Farmers—mainly Jats belonging to Haryana, Madhya Pradesh, Punjab, Rajasthan and western Uttar Pradesh—organized a 'Bharat Bandh' on 25 September, and intensified their agitation thereafter. In the face of stubborn protests, Prime Minister Modi announced their repeal on 19 November 2021.

Simultaneously, while mounting subsidies from premature welfarism ate up fiscal space, the government did not try and mobilize more tax revenues to please the taxpayers. Increasing the exemption limit of personal income tax or reducing the income tax rate for a particular income slab or granting an exemption to a commodity from, or reducing the rate of, excise or customs duty on it could always be justified as an incentive for promoting a particular sector or giving a fiscal stimulus. A tax cut or exemption invites much less scrutiny than an increase in expenditure and often benefits a very selected group of beneficiaries. For a long period of over six decades, tax cuts proved to be very attractive to politicians. Such cuts pleased a select group of their supporters at the cost of many others who did not understand the implications for them or even when they did, did not lobby enough to prevent such cuts.

While Indian democracy, like many others, has continued to struggle against its 'deficit bias', its almost sustained pursuit of economic reforms since 1991 has attested to its growing maturity. This was particularly the case with several reform measures, which the government that proposed it could not push through before its term was over, and was implemented by its successor government belonging to a different political party or combination of parties. Examples include Fiscal Responsibility and Budget Management Act 2003, Value Added Tax, and Goods and Services Tax. Does this mean that from the 1990s onwards, the political calculus in Indian democracy has been driven only by economic considerations in general and the promise and delivery of rapid economic development? The answer appears to be somewhat mixed.

I.5 Political Calculus in a Maturing Democracy and Rapid Development

Prima facie, the maturity of Indian democracy is not immediately obvious from the economic performance and electoral fortunes of incumbent governments since 1991 (Figure I.6). For example, in his five-year rule from 1991, Prime Minister Narasimha Rao had become the father of economic reforms and steered the economy out of crisis mode, with growth at only 1.4 per cent in 1991–92 to accelerating growth with macroeconomic stability. Yet, the Congress under the leadership of Narasimha Rao lost the 1996 Lok Sabha election. Similarly, from 1999 to 2004, under the BJP or Indian People's Party-led NDA with Prime Minister Atal Bihari Vajpayee at the helm, the average rate of growth of GDP at factor cost at constant prices of 5.8 per cent during 2004–09 had been higher than the 5.2 per cent during the preceding Narasimha Rao government (1991–96) or under Rajiv Gandhi (1984–89). Before the 2004 Lok Sabha polls, the NDA even had the 'India Shining' campaign, which had some merit in its claims. Nevertheless, the NDA was thrown out of power in 2004. But the electoral setback for a reformist government delivering higher growth also has to be alongside the competitive politics of identity assertion in the various regions of the country and the flexible coalitions of political parties which formed and dissolved, often with little connection to economic policies.

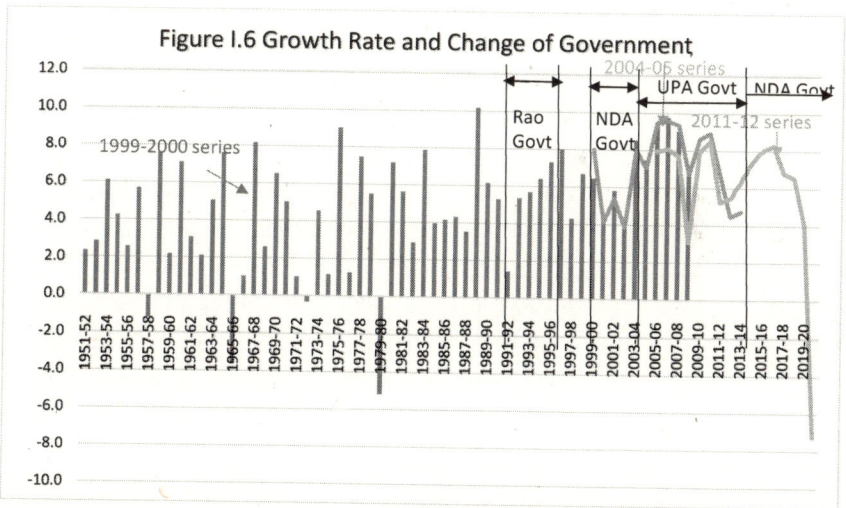

Source: RBI Handbook of Statistics on the Indian Economy, Table No. 02, Macroeconomic Aggregates at constant prices.
Note: The figures for growth rates for the 2004–05 series is the same as those of 1999–2000 series until 1998–99.

Evidently, political fortunes of incumbent governments continued to be determined not by their economic performance alone; the interplay of politics and economic policy was a variegated one, with multiple layers.

Democratic politics in India was, and still is, constrained by its social cleavages in terms of ascriptive group identities such as language, caste and tribe. These cleavages have not disappeared but, with the spread of literacy, higher incomes and urbanization, only blurred. People are increasingly casting their votes and not voting their castes, but the salience of regional parties based on caste, for example, has not vanished.

In-group loyalties can bias electoral responses to not only inappropriate policies but also to corruption of elected representatives. People's changing attitude to corruption at high places illustrates the changing in-group loyalties as well. Corruption had plagued India right from the early 1950s and 1960s, but allegations of corruption did not affect electoral results significantly in the beginning. A perceptible change in people's tolerance of corruption came from the late 1980s. Alleged corruption is likely to have contributed to the defeat of the Congress under Rajiv Gandhi in 1989 and under Narasimha Rao in 1996, and All India Anna Dravida Munnetra Kazhagam (AIADMK) under Jayalalitha in Tamil Nadu in 1996. After the Bihar fodder scam, Chief Minister Lalu Prasad Yadav had to resign and hand over the post to his wife Rabri Devi.[4] The fodder scam may have effectively ended Lalu's political career, including, by his own admission, his dream of becoming the Prime Minister. Corruption issues are likely to have contributed to the defeat of the United Progressive Alliance (UPA) in the 2014 Lok Sabha election. People have become less forgiving of corruption, irrespective of the perpetrator's caste, tribe, religion, region or group, and information about alleged corruption has become easier to obtain with the RTI Act. Proving such allegations and getting the perpetrators convicted, however, continue to be problematic.

Admittedly, communal riots break out at times and raise questions about how far India has succeeded in its nation-building endeavour. This book argues that with caste consolidation among the Hindus—which is a welcome development on its own—religion-based conflicts and politics may increase for some time before starting to decline. Managing the religious cleavages in India will continue to be a challenge for Indian democracy in the short to medium run until caste consolidation nears completion among Hindus. The good news is also that communal conflicts are likely to go down as caste consolidation nears completion. It argues that the process of establishing communal harmony is a work in progress. While there are ups and downs, with economic growth, the spread of education and urbanization, the prospect of communal amity in the long term looks bright.

At the root of the lack of emphasis on collecting enough revenues and spending enough on, and implementing schemes of, social and physical infrastructure is the compulsion of democratic politics. In a democracy, to mobilize votes and win elections, politicians respond to what people demand, and politics through promise of subsidies has not disappeared. The iconic populist All-India Trinamool Congress (AITC) leader and chief minister of West Bengal, Mamata Banerjee, had resolutely rallied against rationalization of petroleum prices in 2000 and of railway passenger fares in 2012. As a UPA ally, in 2012, she had also demanded that the number of subsidized 14.2 kg liquid petroleum gas (LPG) cylinders be raised to twenty-four. She swept the 2021 Vidhan Sabha polls in West Bengal on the promise of free food, housing and monetary allowance for all. Ahead of the Vidhan Sabha polls in Uttar Pradesh, which he swept, Chief Minister Yogi Adityanath (from BJP) slashed the power rate for farmers by half.

Social fragmentation is known to result in higher subsidies and lower demand for public goods such as education, health and physical infrastructure. Such fragmentation is getting blurred with economic development and migration. Furthermore, slowly and surely, the fact that subsidies are not manna from heaven and any subsidy to a particular group has to be paid for or financed by the others have become clearer to people. There are already indications of democracy and democratic norms taking root, people asking not for doles and subsidies for their special groups but for education, health, and physical infrastructure such as uninterrupted quality power supply, roads, and supply of safe drinking water. The demand for 'roti, kapda, makaan' (bread, clothing and shelter) has slowly been replaced by the demand for 'bijli, sadak, paani' (electricity, roads and water). Electoral politics is moving away from identity politics and into debates about serious economic and policy reforms.

This book argues that Indian democracy will start delivering better outcomes as ethnic identities lose their relevance. The many-faceted Arun Shourie, economist, journalist, author and politician, famously said, 'Governance is not golf: that we are a democracy does not entitle us to a handicap.' We may appear to be dangerously close to justifying India's painfully slow pace of economic progress by adducing her democratic system as an excuse. But we are not. The economic development of a poor country is not a 100-metre race but a 42-km marathon. What we argue is that democracy may have led to a slow start, but it is premature to pass a final judgement on the likely outcome in India. India lacks the strong physical infrastructure, such as roads, power and water supply, that authoritarian China has built up, but what it has developed and sustained is a strong institutional infrastructure in terms of separation of powers among legislature, executive and judiciary, rule of law, and freedom of press. Policies in India will increasingly reflect the progress of the average Indian in terms of education, health and awareness about the effectiveness of policies, not only in India but in other countries as well.

When the Voting Rights Act of 1965, to give black Americans in the USA the 'weapon—the vote', was passed after the Civil Rights Act of 1964, an elated President Lyndon Johnson said this would give the power to the African Americans to 'do the rest for themselves'.[5] Did it solve all the problems for the African Americans in the USA overnight? No. But, 'Forty-three years later, a mere blink of history's eye, a black American, Barack Obama, was sitting behind the desk in the Oval Office.'[6] Similarly, pluralist politics and adult franchise has not only reinforced Indian nationhood, but gradually ushering in progressive policies also irrevocably changed Indians themselves, allowing democracy to work better and deliver appropriate development outcomes.

In India, while democracy has served well in building the nation, socio-economic development has been somewhat tepid in the first seven decades after Independence. But, as Indian democracy matures and people benefit from higher incomes, less poverty, more education and urbanization, such development is likely to accelerate. This book argues that as democracy matures in India, the political calculus of attracting electoral support from these changed Indians is likely to help the country in its search for glory.

I.6 Plan of the Book

Economists are described by some as more storytellers than scientists. What follows is an attempt to build a narrative of the interplay between politics and economic policies in India, with a brief description of the historical events since Independence. It is not only the story of India's development since Independence and the policies followed, but also of the electoral logic of that policy, and how the electoral logic is changing with a gradual transformation of Indians themselves. The story has implications for India's search for glory.

The book is in three parts. It is a chronological account of the evolution of economic policies, divided into three parts. After this introductory chapter, Part I deals with challenges confronting the newly independent country and how they were met in the Nehruvian period (1947-64). With Nehru like a 'colossus' dominating the politics and economics in the country, it was a period of policy autonomy, pluralist politics and socialist economics. Part II deals with the twenty-seven years post-Nehru (1964–1991) when, with the transformation of society in the Nehruvian period, there was an upsurge in popular participation. It was a period when, rather than being led by the state, society started leading the state. This is followed by Part III, covering the period from 1991 to 2019, when the balance between the state and society was back, and when reforms, albeit with their ups and downs, continued and were accelerated.

Part I

The Backdrop

II

Post-Independence Integration

After Independence, the first thing the Indian government attended to was the task of building an integrated India out of the British Indian provinces and over 560 princely states, and establishing a secular state in the aftermath of the communal carnage that had rocked the subcontinent. Pluralist politics was the instrument for building an integrated India and the secular promise of equal treatment of all religions for soothing the misgivings of religious minorities about their future in India. In economic policy, the principle was socialism.

Robin Meredith recounts an Indian joke about Deng Xiaoping, the next supreme leader of China after Mao Zedong (also, Mao Dzedong[1]). Deng is in his car and is reading a newspaper. His driver interrupts and asks, 'Comrade, there's a problem. The sign says turn Left for communism, turn Right for capitalism. Which way should I go?' Deng tells his driver, 'No problem. Just signal left and go right.'[2] Apocryphal, no doubt, but it succinctly captured 'Communist' China after Mao's death and Deng's rise—a rare combination of communist politics, such as one-party rule and severe restrictions on fundamental rights, with capitalist economics. Pluralist politics with socialist economics, which India followed after Independence, was just the reverse of what Deng Xiaoping, after Mao, would be following in China three decades later. To get on with the story, let us start with the first government of independent India under Prime Minister Nehru.

II.1 The Challenge of Integration

Around Independence, there were hundreds of princely states under rulers known by various names such as Maharaja, Raja, Nizam, Raje, Deshmukh, Nawab, Mirza, Baig, Chhatrapati, Khan, Thakur Saheb and Darbar Saheb. Monarchies and feudalism did not fit in with the India of the people's dream. Their integration was at the top of the priorities, and in achieving this priority, the country was blessed with the leadership of Sardar Patel as the deputy prime minister, ably assisted by the adroit bureaucrat V.P. Menon as his secretary in the ministry of states.

The Government of India Act 1935, after transferring all subjects at the provincial level to the provincial ministers, and making them responsible to the elected provincial legislature, had proposed a 'Federation of India' made up of the provinces of British India and Indian princely states which might accede to be united. It could be established only when at least half of the Indian states, in terms of population and seats in the Council of State or Rajya Sabha, voluntarily acceded to the Federation. With the Second World War intervening, and the opposition of their rulers, the Indian states never did and the Federation of India never came into operation under British rule. Many experts had prophesied this to be impossible without violent revolution. Indian leadership after Independence would prove them wrong.

The princely states were under the 'paramountcy' and 'suzerainty' of the British Crown through treaties of subsidiary alliances. Under paramountcy, they were supposed to act in subordinate cooperation with the British Crown and acknowledge its supremacy. Queen Victoria had been proclaimed as Kaisar-i-Hind or Empress of India at the Delhi Durbar of 1877, and sanction from the Crown was necessary in all matters of succession. With its suzerainty, the British Crown had exclusive control over their foreign affairs. The British, by the Indian Independence Act 1947, while granting independence to British India by dividing it into India and Pakistan, were giving up their paramountcy and suzerainty over the princely states. They left the states free to choose their future, including whether or not to join the newly independent successor states of India or Pakistan.

Sardar Patel, in charge of the ministry of states in the interim cabinet, appealed to the patriotic feeling of rulers to join the Indian dominion in matters of defence, communication and external affairs—the three areas which had been part of the paramountcy of the Crown and over which the states anyway had no control. Beyond appeals to their patriotism, Patel and V.P. Menon reportedly used all the four tools of *'saam, daam, danda, bhed'*—cajoling, financial incentive, punitive action and divide and rule— to accomplish this 'impossible' task and integrate almost all the territories within the current Indian borders.

The Praja Mandals in the princely states, which were demanding democratic rights, abolition of iniquitous feudal monarchical systems and integration with India, were allies in this building of an integrated democratic India. They acted as pressure groups on some of the recalcitrant princes. The offer of a privy purse to the princes, with size determined by revenues of the state, the right to retain their palaces, personal properties and titles, also helped. Louis Mountbatten, 1st Earl Mountbatten of Burma, the last Viceroy and first Governor-General of India, played an important role by insisting that though the princely states were theoretically free to choose independence, to maintain unity, they should join either India or Pakistan based on geographical continuity as well as people's aspirations, resource availability and administrative ability.

The Government of India Act 1935 defined three categories— Governor's provinces, Chief Commissioner's provinces and federated states. Most princes voluntarily merged their states with adjacent Indian provinces, or after joining a union of princely states, such as Saurashtra, Madhya Bharat or expand acronym, eventually merged with Indian provinces. Between May and 15 August 1947, most princely states had signed the standstill agreement confirming the continuation of the agreements and administrative practices that existed between them and the British Indian Government as well as the Instrument of Accession. Some, for a short while, did explore other possibilities, including independence. But, by the time King George VI gave up his title of 'Emperor of India' by a royal proclamation on 22 June 1948, a united India was well on its way to being born. Three large princely states that created a flutter before acceding by 15 August 1947 were Travancore, Bhopal and Jodhpur.

II.2 The Three That Caused a Flutter before Signing By 15 August 1947

The two princely states of Travancore and Jodhpur had access to the outside world through either neighbouring Pakistan or the Arabian Sea, and long and proud histories of continuous rules by the respective royal families. Bhopal, the second largest after the Nizam's Hyderabad, was a different category. It was set up by Dost Mohammad Khan, a Pashtun mercenary, in the first decade of the eighteenth century. In 1947, it was ruled by Nawab Sir Hamidullah, an active member of the Indian Muslim League and a close ally of Jinnah. Anticipating the problems of Muslims outside East and West Pakistan, the Nawab was against partition of the country and in favour of Muslim autonomy within India. The story of the integration of these three princely states attests to the finesse with which Sardar Patel and V.P. Menon avoided the balkanization of India and the supporting role that a commitment to democratic principles played in the process.

Travancore

Travancore in the southern-most part of the country—today called Kerala, 'God's own country'—had a long coastline, an educated population, a long tradition of thriving maritime trade and some rare earth from which thorium could be extracted for atomic energy. Legend has it that Parasurama, or Rama with the *parasu* or axe, the sixth incarnation of Lord Vishnu, delivered the world from the oppressive Kshatriyas by killing them all with his axe. After expiating for all his sins, he threw the axe in the sea, and where his axe fell, Parasuramkshetra or Parasuram's area of Konkan, of which Kerala is a part, emerged from the sea.

Travancore followed a matrilineal system, with inheritance and succession passing through the sister's children in the female line. The monarch ruled on behalf of Padmanabhaswamy, the deity in the form of Anantashayi Vishnu or Vishnu lying (*shayi*) on *Ananta* (endless), the king of snakes, in the temple by the same name. It is the same temple that in 2011 was discovered to be one of the richest temples in the world, with an estimated wealth of over $22 billion, or perhaps even $1 trillion, according to some estimates.

Travancore was proud of having stood up to the European colonial powers much before the First War of Independence in 1857. 'In 1741, Travancore was the only Asian power to defeat the Dutch when they arrived here. After the battle, all the Dutch soldiers kneeled before my ancestors. One Dutchman, Benedictus Eustachius, even joined our army. We called him the Great Kapitan,' boasted Uthradam Thirunal Marthanda Verma, the former king of Travancore, in 2011.[3] Before Independence, Travancore was ruled by Maharaja Chithira Thirunal Balarama Varma. He enjoyed a ten-gun salute, and Sir C.P. Ramaswamy Aiyar was his famous Diwan from 1936 onwards.

A brilliant and ambitious lawyer, Sir C.P. was a member of the Executive Council of the Viceroy of India for many years. 'Maharani Sethu Parvathi Bai, mother of the Maharaja of Travancore, was a well-known beauty. Sir C.P. Ramaswamy Iyer came to Trivandrum to plead an important judicial case on behalf of the Christian Association and . . . fell in love with Maharani Parvathi Bai at first sight and later, with the help of the Viceroy of India, managed to get himself appointed as Diwan of Travancore.'[4] He wielded enormous power and was a great reformer as well. During the very first year of his premiership, he abolished the ban on the entry of so-called 'low caste people' or *avarnas* into Hindu temples in Travancore. Also, he '. . . abolished the traditional custom of women untying brassiere from their breasts when seeing the Maharaja, Diwan or a Brahmin. It is a common and popular story in Trivandrum that whenever Sir C.P. appeared in the presence of women whose breasts were not covered, they lifted up their skirts to cover their breasts to obey the orders of the Diwan.'[5]

As early as February 1946, Sir C. P. had declared that as soon as the British left, Travancore would become a 'perfectly independent unit'. In the summer of 1947, he tried to rally the people of Travancore in favour of independence. Jinnah welcomed this bid, and so did some politicians in London, lured by the monazite deposits containing thorium in Travancore.

On 21 July 1947, Sir C.P. met Viceroy Mountbatten and V.P. Menon and made it clear that instead of the Instrument of Accession, Travancore would like to have a treaty with independent India. After returning to Travancore, when he was on his way to a music concert on 27 July, he was attacked by a 'man in military shorts, knifed in the face and body and taken off for emergency surgery.' The attacker most likely was a Praja

Parishad member or supporter. 'The consequences were immediate . . .
From his hospital bed, Sir C.P. advised his Maharaja to "follow the path
of conciliation and compromise" which he, "being autocratic and over-
decisive", had not himself followed. On 30 July, the Maharaja wired the
viceroy of his decision to accede to the Indian Union.'[6] Indian commitment
to democracy won the day in integrating Travancore.

Bhopal

Close to Jinnah and a bitter opponent of the Mahatma and his Congress,
Nawab Hamidullah Khan was a polo-playing close friend of Viceroy
Mountbatten. He looked at the British Indian Independence Act 1947 as a
great betrayal, a lapse in British justice. He asked his friend Mountbatten:
'Are we to write out a blank cheque and leave it to the leaders of the Congress
Party to fill in the amount?'[7] He also saw the danger of India, without the
princely states, being overrun by the communists. Mountbatten reminded
the Nawab that leaders like Sardar Patel were 'as frightened of communism'
as the Nawab himself and needed the help of the princes.[8] He also said that
no ruler could 'run away from the dominion closest to him'.[9] With most
princes falling in line by the end of July 1947, he asked for a small sop to his
pride in an extension of the timeline to 15 August. Sardar Patel refused, and
Mountbatten offered a halfway solution. Bhopal could sign the instrument
of accession on 14 August; Mountbatten would keep it safe under lock and
key and hand it over to Sardar Patel on 15 August.

Jodhpur

Jodhpur, bordering Pakistan, was ruled by the flamboyant Raj Rajeshwar
Maharajadhiraj Shri Hanwant Singh Rathore, still in his early twenties.
Already married twice, the Maharaja, popularly known as Hanwant
Singh, was having an affair with Zubeida, a Bohra Muslim film actress
from Mumbai. He was strongly anti-Congress. Persuaded perhaps by the
Nawab of Bhopal, he met Jinnah at his residence at 10, Aurangzeb Road
(now Dr A.P.J. Abdul Kalam Road) on 6 August 1947.

In the meeting, Jinnah offered him a signed blank sheet of paper,
asking him to enter whatever conditions he wished for joining Pakistan!

When Jinnah asked the Maharajkumar of Jaisalmer, Giridhar Singh, who had accompanied Hanwant Singh, whether he would also prefer to join Pakistan like Jodhpur, he raised his doubts regarding Jinnah's neutrality on issues of communal differences between Hindus of Jaisalmer and Muslims of Pakistan. Zafarullah, political advisor to Jinnah, ruled out communal differences leading to violence and rioting in Pakistan and, since Jinnah was travelling to Karachi the next day, pressed Hanwant Singh to sign the Instrument of Accession. As soon as Hanwant Singh asked for more time to consult his more than fifty sardars or feudal heads and his mother, the dowager Maharani Sri Badan Kunwar Saheba, Jinnah brusquely pulled away the blank paper with his signature from Hanwant Singh.

Hanwant Singh met Lord Mountbatten and Sardar Patel in Delhi on 9 and 10 August. Sardar Patel asked him to take into consideration the possible revolt of the people in case he decided to join Pakistan. He also agreed to connect Jodhpur with the port of Kutch in case it joined India. Hanwant Singh visited the Viceroy's house the next day to sign the Instrument of Accession. Along with Mountbatten, V.P. Menon was also present at the ceremony. Hanwant Singh had a pen-pistol that he had made to order. When Mountbatten was absent for a while, there are alternative accounts of how Hanwant Singh opened the cap of the pen, took out the pistol and threatened to shoot V.P. Menon. According to one account, after signing the Instrument of Accession with his pen-pistol, the Maharaja told Menon that he could even kill him with the same pen. Just as Menon got scared, Mountbatten entered and dismissed the whole episode as a joke. Hanwant Singh gave the pen-pistol to Mountbatten, who took it to London and gifted it to the Magic Circle Gift Museum in London, where it is still on display.

After Travancore, Bhopal and Jodhpur, what remained was the integration of the two major princely states of Jammu and Kashmir and Hyderabad, and the small but significant princely state of Junagadh. Their integration is what is taken up in the next section.

II.3 The Three Thorns in the Flesh

The integration of the three princely states of Jammu and Kashmir, Hyderabad and Junagadh had remained pending on 15 August 1947.

In Muslim-majority Jammu and Kashmir in the north, the Dogra king Maharaja Hari Singh, a Hindu, ruled over his three provinces of Kashmir, Jammu and the Frontier Districts. Jammu and Kashmir had the largest territory among the princely states and a long land border with not only India and Pakistan, but also with Afghanistan, China and Tibet. In the Pamir mountains, the narrow Wakhan Corridor separated the state's Gilgit-Baltistan from Tajikistan in the former Soviet Union.

In Hindu-majority Hyderabad in the south, the seventh Nizam, Mir Osman Ali, was a Muslim. Both Jammu and Kashmir and Hyderabad were large princely states whose rulers were entitled to twenty-one-gun salutes, but with an important difference: Hyderabad in the south-east, unlike Jammu and Kashmir, was not contiguous to Pakistan. Neither did it have access to the Bay of Bengal.

The princely state of Junagadh in the west, ruled by Nawab Mahabat Khan, was small relative to Jammu and Kashmir and Hyderabad. The Nawab was entitled to thirteen hereditary and fifteen personal and local gun salutes. While surrounded to the north, east and south by Indian provinces or princely states, unlike Hyderabad, it had access to the Arabian Sea, particularly through the port of Veraval.

All the three 'excellencies' had their own hallmark signs of a mix of grandeur, flamboyance, eccentricities and decadence. Maharaja Pratap Singh of Jammu and Kashmir had sent his young nephew Hari Singh, the prince regent, on a tour of Europe. In 1921, only 26 and already married twice, Hari Singh was caught in flagrante delicto in a Paris hotel with a jockey's wife. He was blackmailed for money and dragged through the courts. The case, with his identity concealed as 'Mr. A', was splashed across the newspapers of Europe and America.

Nizam Osman Ali's portrait was featured on the cover of the *Time* magazine on 12 February 1937. Inside, the cover story, entitled 'Hyderabad: Silver Jubilee Durbar,' described him as the richest man in the world! But he was also known for his miserliness. Once, Osman Ali offered a cigarette to Sir Tej Bahadur Sapru, the Nizam's legal advisor, and when Sapru accepted it, he politely took it back, clipped it into two with a clipper he had in his pocket and offered one half to Sapru! He had unusual interests, including photography. 'After his death a cache of bizarre photographs were found that had been taken with a hidden camera inside his guest bathroom. They provide a candid record of his famous visitors performing their toilet.'[10]

Junagadh's Nawab Mahabat Khan had a passion for dogs. He owned 800 dogs, each with its own room, a telephone, and a servant. He got his favourite bitch Roshana married to a handsome golden retriever named Bobby in a state ceremony attended by 50,000 guests. In the context of the annexation of princely states to India and Pakistan, Junagadh, a small relative to both Jammu and Kashmir and Hyderabad, has been described by some as the 'joker in the pack'.[11] So, let us first turn to the accession of Junagadh to India.

II.4 Junagadh

Situated in the erstwhile Saurashtra at the foot of Mount Girnar and the northern fringes of the Gir forest, Junagadh had a history dating back to ancient times. It was a famous place for pilgrimage due to its link with Girnar, which is holy for Hindus, according to *Girnar Mahatmya*. The Somnath temple in Prabhas Patan near Veraval, revered by Hindus as the first among the twelve *jyotirlinga* or radiant signs of Lord Shiva, was also in Junagadh. The Saurashtra peninsula was also called Kathiawar after the Kathi Durbar that once ruled the area. Junagadh was the 'premier' princely state in Kathiawar! Unlike the Nizam of Hyderabad, the Nawab of Junagadh did not possess the resources to go it alone, so he was inclined to accede to Pakistan. In May 1947, the acting Diwan was Sir Shah Nawaz Bhutto, father of Zulfikar Ali Bhutto and grandfather of Benazir Bhutto, two future Prime Ministers of Pakistan. Shah Nawaz was a Muslim League politician in close touch with Jinnah.

On the advice of Shah Nawaz, Nawab Mahabat Khan waited until the day of transfer of power and announced its accession to Pakistan only on 15 August 1947. Jinnah accepted the Instrument of Accession only on 16 September 1948! Speculation is that Jinnah, a believer in the two-nation theory, never really thought that Junagadh would be allowed to join Pakistan, so he tried to use Junagadh in a strategic way. For Jinnah, Junagadh, by setting a precedent, would help Pakistan to get either Jammu and Kashmir or Hyderabad, if not both. If India accepted Junagadh's accession to Pakistan, then it would set a precedent favourable for the accession of Hyderabad to Pakistan. If India rejected Junagadh's accession to Pakistan and asked for a plebiscite, it would set a precedent for a plebiscite in Jammu and Kashmir and, hopefully for Pakistan, perhaps a favourable outcome. India rejecting Junagadh's accession to Pakistan and storming it by force would justify Pakistan doing the same in Jammu and Kashmir.

India was committed to democracy, and Sardar Patel demanded that the state's accession should be decided by the people through a plebiscite, and not by the ruler. Indian nationalists formed an *'Aarzee Hukumat'*, a caretaker government in exile under Samaldas Gandhi, the son of the Mahatma's elder brother Laxmidas Gandhi. Nehru agreed to negotiate with Junagadh. There were allegations of an Indian economic blockade of Junagadh, surrounded as it was by princely states that had already acceded to India, and reports of Hindu-Muslim riots. By mid-October, the Nawab had almost lost his grip on Junagadh. In the last week of October 1947, '. . . the Nawab decided the game was up and made a hasty departure for Karachi, taking with him all the cash and negotiable assets of the treasury, his family and many of his dogs (though his consort, the Begum, forgot her youngest child in the royal nursery and had to turn back to collect the infant).'[12] On 1 November 1947, Indian troops took over the enclaves of Babariawad and Mangrol without bloodshed. On 8 November 1947, Junagadh's State Council asked India to intervene to prevent the situation from descending into chaos. Delhi was only too happy to send in its troops.

Pakistan raised the issue of Junagadh in the UN (the erstwhile UNO or UN Organization) Security Council on 15 January 1948. In a plebiscite held on 20 February 1948, out of a population of 7,20,000 in Junagadh and its feudatories, India polled 2,22,184 and Pakistan 130. A month later, 217 princely states, including Junagadh, were merged to form the United State of Kathiawar. By then, even in Pakistan, Junagadh, the 'joker in the pack,' had faded into irrelevance, with significant developments in Jammu and Kashmir and Hyderabad. On 27 October 1947, four days before the Indian takeover of Junagadh's administration at the request of its State Council, Maharaja Hari Singh had signed Jammu and Kashmir's accession to India. 'The understanding of Junagadh thus became limited as a "curtain-raiser to a problem which was to find its climax" in Jammu

& Kashmir and Hyderabad.'[13] Let us first deal with what happened to Jammu and Kashmir.

II.5 Jammu and Kashmir

Muslims constituted 77 per cent of Jammu and Kashmir's population, but there was also a sizeable section of Hindus. Furthermore, Hindus had a long historic connection with Kashmir. The name 'Kashmir' itself is derived from sage Kashyapa, one of the seven great sages or *saptarshis* of the Rgveda. Kashmir is a shortened form of 'Kashyapa Mir' or the 'lake of the sage Kashyapa', or alternatively derived from 'Kashyapa Meru' or the sacred mountains of Kashyapa. While many Muslims wanted Maharaja Hari Singh to join Pakistan, the non-Muslims wanted him to join India. So did Sheikh Abdullah and his secular National Conference, an ally of the Congress and a strong rival of the pro-Pakistan Muslim Conference. Sheikh Abdullah, the son of a shawl trader and a self-made man, had set up the Muslim Conference in October 1932 and changed it to the National Conference on 11 June 1939 after meeting Pandit Nehru in 1938. Nehru, a friend of Sheikh Abdullah, strongly supported him and his secular National Conference. Nehru had even been imprisoned by Hari Singh in June 1946.

Cradled in the Himalayas, the Kashmir valley was renowned for its picturesque and enchanting natural beauty. And with his large state esteemed as the Switzerland of the East and with its international borders, the Maharaja preferred the option of independence and continued autocracy. In July 1947, trouble had started with the anti-Maharaja stir on excessive taxation in Poonch, alleged embezzlement of the money promised by the British Indian Government to Second World War veterans, and disarming of the population, particularly Muslims. The rebels had blockaded the roads, disrupting supplies meant for Jammu and Kashmir's army. The rebellion was put down by a heavy hand. Furthermore, with passions inflamed by the transit of Hindu and Sikh refugees from Pakistan, there was communal trouble in Jammu.

All of Jammu and Kashmir's important geographic, economic and transport links were with areas in newly formed Pakistan. Hari Singh had not signed any Instrument of Accession, with either India or Pakistan, till

15 August 1947, but sent instead a standstill agreement on 12 August, which Pakistan accepted on 15 August. Jinnah and his countrymen had taken it for granted that Muslim-majority Jammu and Kashmir would join Pakistan. Unwell from his deteriorating lung disease and exhausted after the victory in his one-man crusade for Pakistan, Jinnah, some-time around 24 August, sent his secretary, Col William Birnie, to go and arrange a two-week rest and relaxation stint in Kashmir in late September. Birnie came back to report that the Maharaja did not want Jinnah in Kashmir, not even as a tourist. Jinnah and his Pakistan sensed trouble. On 9 September 1947, Pakistan cut off supplies of sugar and petroleum to Jammu and Kashmir, which, by mid-October 1947, was complaining to Pakistan and the UK about the violation of the standstill agreement.

On 20 October, on the eve of the Hindu Navaratri festival, tribesmen from NWFP, egged on by Pakistan, started pouring into Muzaffarabad, and from there into Poonch, Domel and Baramulla. Hari Singh sent a formal appeal for help to India on 24 October, and the following day escaped from Srinagar to the safety of Jammu. V.P. Menon went and had discussions with Hari Singh, and on 27 October, as Jammu and Kashmir signed the Instrument of Accession to India, the Indian army started landing at Srinagar airport.

The first mover advantage that the raiders had gained in areas such as Baramulla, Uri, Jhangar, Naoshera and Kotli was neutralized by the Indian army in November and December. On 1 January 1948, at the United Nations (UN), India requested a meeting of the Security Council to consider the situation between India and Pakistan, which was likely to endanger international peace and security. India said that invaders were drawing aid from Pakistan for operations against the state of Jammu and Kashmir. The Security Council called for restraint on both sides and a ceasefire agreement, but the fighting continued. On 5 March 1948, Sheikh Abdullah was sworn in as the Wazir-e-Azam or Prime Minister of Jammu and Kashmir. A ceasefire agreement between India and Pakistan could be reached only on 1 January 1949. The Security Council recommended a free and fair plebiscite after demilitarization of Jammu and Kashmir. Such a plebiscite could not be held because demilitarization had not been achieved. Why India went to the Security Council without throwing the raiders completely out of Jammu and Kashmir continues to be debated even today.

On 20 June 1949, Maharaja Hari Singh stepped down as the ruler, and handed over the reins to his only child, Karan Singh, appointing him the prince regent of Jammu and Kashmir. On 17 October 1949, the Indian Constituent Assembly adopted Article 370, granting Kashmir special status, thereby integrating Jammu and Kashmir into the Indian Constitution. In the elections to the Jammu and Kashmir Constituent Assembly, based on adult franchise by a secret ballot held in September–October 1951, twenty-five seats were left vacant for the territory forcibly occupied by Pakistan. The slogan of the National Conference was 'One Leader, One Party, One Programme'. With some other parties boycotting the polls and some candidates' nominations rejected under controversial circumstances, National Conference (NC) won all the seventy-five seats. According to political scientist Sumantra Bose, 'The circumstances of formation of the Constituent Assembly revealed that the NC elite wished to govern Kashmir as a party-state, in which they would have a monopoly on political power.'[14] On 24 July 1952, in Delhi, an agreement—which came to be known as the Delhi Agreement—was signed between Pandit Nehru and Sheikh Abdullah, delineating some of the features of the special status of Jammu and Kashmir in the Indian Union. Under this Agreement, the Dogra monarchy was formally abolished, Jammu and Kashmir proclaimed a 'republic' on 15 November 1952, and prince regent Karan Singh elected by the Constituent Assembly as Sadr-i-Riyasat or Head of State.

II.6 Hyderabad

Even till 15 August 1947, Nizam Osman Ali of Hyderabad had not signed the Instrument of Accession. Hyderabad was not only a large state but also among the most prosperous of the princely states. The family of Osman Ali, who had been Nizam from 1911 onwards, had ruled the state since 1724. Qamruddin, the first Nizam-ul-Mulk, had risen from a loyal soldier to become one of the most successful rulers of eighteenth-century India and, with his empire, filled a void left by the disintegration of the Mughal dynasty. In comparison, many of his successors were pale shadows and after his death in 1748, in the twenty-year-long succession struggle among his three sons and grandson, first the French and then the East India Company got involved through subsidiary alliances with the warring parties. By 1768, Governor-General Lord Wellesley had managed to get Hyderabad to sign the Treaty of Masulipatnam, lease the coastal region to the East India Company on an annual rent, and, in 1798, also sign a subsidiary alliance. Under the subsidiary alliance, the Company's Army could occupy Bolarum (modern Secunderabad) to protect the state's borders in return for an annual maintenance charge from the Nizam.

Soon after Prime Minister Clement Attlee, on 15 March 1946, had told the House of Commons of the need for India to gain independence, Osman Ali had started dreaming about full freedom for Hyderabad. The Indian Independence Act of 1947 only reinforced his dreams of an independent Osmanistan. On 12 May 1946, he sent a telegram to the Viceroy that Hyderabad would not join any federation. While he would settle outstanding issues with the successor government, he would not give up the 'historical connection with the British Crown'. The time had come, he said, for Britain to 'boldly protect the interests and integrity of the Faithful Ally's Dynasty and State'. Majlis Ittehad-ul-Muslimeen (MIM), or Movement for Muslim Unity, had been formed in 1927 to bring together Muslims of different sects, and its leader Qasim Razvi, a lawyer from UP, who believed that Hyderabad should be declared a sovereign Muslim state, organized a private militia called the Razakars, or the volunteers, to support the rule of the Nizam. V.P. Menon thought Qasim Razvi had 'fanaticism bordering on frenzy'. 'Death with the sword in hand is always preferable to extinction by a mere stroke of the pen', he told his followers. The waters of the Bay of Bengal, he promised, would wash the feet of the Nizam. 'We are the grandsons of Mahmood Ghaznavi and the sons of Babur. When determined, we shall fly the Asaf Jahi Flag on the Red fort.'[15]

Many prominent Muslim personalities such as Nawab Mehadi Nawaz Jung, Barrister Akbar Ali Khan, famous editor Sohaibulla Khan, Nawab Ali Yavar Jung and some of the Nizam's Diwans like Sir Mirza Ismail, the highly respected former Diwan of Mysore and Jaipur, were in favour of Hyderabad's accession to India. But Osman Ali vacillated about integration with India. On 29 November 1947, Laik Ali, a wealthy Hyderabadi industrialist and one of the main financial backers of the MIM, became the Diwan of Hyderabad. On his first day in office, he signed a standstill agreement with India. He elevated the Nizam above all other

Indian princes, demanded that the British address him as 'His Majesty' and began referring to him as the 'King of the Dekkan'. On 10 January 1948, presumably to muster support for its cause of 'independence, it was announced that Nizam's Government had lent $60 million to Pakistan, which was suffering serious shortage of foreign exchange'.[16]

Laik Ali also enlisted the services of Sidney Cotton, an Australian pilot who had flown combat missions over Germany in World War I, and also worked for MI6, the British espionage agency. In January 1948, Cotton, a wannabe businessman, had come to Hyderabad to explore opportunities for sourcing groundnuts for the US market. He met Laik Ali and struck a £20 million deal to do some gunrunning, using five second-hand Lancaster Bombers converted into civilian aircraft and eight three-men crews. He agreed to supply 500 tonnes of machine guns, grenades, mortars and anti-aircraft guns, and started his secret flights with supplies from Pakistan on 4 June 1948. Indian intelligence agencies became aware of the operation.

The government of India protested Cotton's airlifts. It was equally concerned by the rising communal tension and the communist insurgency. In Hyderabad state, with its very unequal land holdings, the banned Communist Party was stoking the largest peasant uprising in Asia outside China. In a desperate act, Nizam Osman Ali removed the ban on the Communist Party in early May. Mountbatten sent his press attaché, Alan Campbell-Johnson, in May 1948 to the Nizam to negotiate an amicable settlement with India. It failed. Osman Ali, in a reference to the biblical Israelite judge Samson who pushed apart the pillars of a Philistine temple, bringing down the roof and killing himself and thousands of Philistines who had captured him, threatened to commit the 'Samson Act' and take down Hyderabad with himself in case he went under.

'On 15 June 1948, just six days before Mountbatten was to leave India for good and Rajaji was to take over as the new Governor-General, the Nehru Government presented the Nizam with its final offer. The question of accession would be determined by a plebiscite and a responsible government would be introduced following the establishment of a Constituent Assembly . . .'[17] The Nizam rejected the offer. Charges and counter-charges of Razakars oppressing the Hindus and trying to change the state's demographic pattern by settling Muslims from outside, and India fomenting trouble and imposing an undeclared economic blockade, flew. By end-August, while the standstill agreement was still valid, the Indian army surrounded the princely state. On 21 August, at the UN, Hyderabad's external affairs representative, Zahir Ahmed, asked the Security Council for mediation. Before the Security Council could take it up on 16 September, after a final warning of intervention to put down the disorder in the state, India launched 'Operation Polo', its 'police action.' In a radio address on 17 September, Laik Ali announced the recapitulation of Hyderabad. The formal surrender by Maj. Gen. El Edroos to Maj. Gen. Jayanto Nath Chaudhuri took place on 18 September 1948. Jinnah did not live to hear of the police action; he had died on 11 September 1948. On 16 September 1948, before the UN Security Council could take it up, the Nizam withdrew Hyderabad's request for mediation.

On 6 December 1948, by a *farman*, Nizam Osman Ali dissolved the Hyderabad Legislative Assembly and called upon all officers and subjects of the state to assist in the preparation of electoral rolls for a new Constituent Assembly. By another farman on 24 November 1949, he declared that the Constitution of India should be the Constitution of the State of Hyderabad. The integration of Hyderabad into the Union of India was over. Laik Ali and Qasim Razvi were imprisoned, Cotton flew away, but Nizam Osman Ali remained as the figurehead.

II.7 Manipur

Manipur was an ancient kingdom whose domain, at the height of its rule in the seventeenth century, extended to the Kabaw valley in northern Myanmar. After its defeat in the Anglo-Manipur War in 1891, Manipur became a princely state under British rule. It was an eleven-gun salute state and a member of the Chamber of Princes. The large valley in the state around its capital Imphal was dominated by the Meiteis, which included its royal family, while the surrounding hills were populated by hill tribes such as Nagas in the areas bordering Nagaland, and Kukis and Mizos in the areas bordering Mizoram. The Meiteis were mostly Hindu Vaishnavites, while the hill tribes were Christians. Their relationship was considerably strained.

Anticipating the British departure, Maharaja Bodhchandra Singh had set up a committee under his chief minister, Sir Francis Fenwick Pearson, a British civil servant, to draft a constitution for Manipur. The draft was passed as the Manipur State Constitution Act in May 1947. When the British, by the Indian Independence Act 1947, were giving up paramountcy and suzerainty over princely states, Sir Akbar Hydari, governor of Assam, came to Imphal at the end of June 1947, and explained the position of Manipur to the maharaja. Some Manipur Darbur members thought independence an impractical idea and wanted Manipur to join India. By an agreement with Governor Hydari signed on 1 July, Manipur Darbar agreed to join the Indian Constituent Assembly through the common representative of Tripura and Khasi and Jayantia Hills.

The maharaja finally signed the standstill agreement and the Instrument of Accession on 11 August, four days before Independence. The standstill agreement confirmed that the agreements and administrative practices that existed between Manipur and the British would be continued by India. By the instrument of accession, the maharaja agreed to the accession of his kingdom to independent India and to granting India control over specified subject matters as under British rule. For integration into India, what was needed was the merger agreement. In the meantime, in June 1948, Manipur as a constitutional monarchy even held elections with universal adult franchise. The pro-integration Manipur India Congress fared poorly in the elections.

The merger agreement was not made available for a little over two years. Reportedly, it was finally obtained under duress. In September 1949, Maharaja Bodhchandra Singh was invited to Shillong, the capital of erstwhile undivided Assam, for talks on integration. In Shillong, he was kept under house arrest in his summer residence and not released till he signed the agreement on 21 September. The merger agreement was put into force from 15 October 1949 onwards.

II.8 The Liberation of Dadra and Nagar Haveli and Goa

Then there were also the French (Puducherry, Chandernagore, Mahe, Karaikal and Yanaon) and Portuguese (Goa, Dadra and Nagar Haveli, and Daman and Diu) colonies, which were called French India and Portuguese India, and were ruled from Puducherry and Goa, respectively. The integration of French India through peaceful negotiations is briefly described in Box II.1. The story of integration of Portuguese India, which happened only in 1961, follows. Sardar Patel as home minister and Nehru as Prime Minister and external affairs minister was a win-win combination for Indian integration. Unfortunately, Sardar Patel passed away on 15 December 1950, when the liberation of the Portuguese colonies of Dadra and Nagar Haveli, Goa, Daman and Diu, and the French colonies of Puducherry, Chandernagore, Mahe, Karaikal and Yanaon, were still pending. The integration of the French colonies looked like a relatively easier affair than that of the Portuguese.

Box II.1 Integration of French India

India signed an agreement with France in June 1948 giving power to the people of the French colonies to determine their own future. Accordingly, the French government held a plebiscite in Chandannagore, in which 97 per cent voted in favour of becoming a part of India.[18] In May 1950, the French handed over de facto control over Chandannagore to the Indian government. The plebiscite in erstwhile Pondicherry (now Puducherry), Karaikal and Yanam (erstwhile Yanaon) followed in October 1948, along with municipal elections. The French had offered autonomy within the French system, and the verdict, this time, was pro-French. Keen to integrate Puducherry, Karaikal and Yanam into India, the Government of India promised special status to Puducherry. Slowly, opinions turned. There were demonstrations in favour of a merger with India. On 18 March 1954, the members of the executive council and mayors of Pondicherry and seven adjoining communes proclaimed their decision to merge with India without a referendum.

India and France agreed to decide the issue by a 'referendum' among elected members of the Representative Assembly and the municipal councillors of Puducherry and Karaikal. Yanam was left out because it had been liberated by a coup d'état on 13 June 1954. In this referendum, held on 18 October 1954, of the 178 members voting, an overwhelming majority of 170 members favoured the merger of French Indian territories with the Republic of India. Three days later, an agreement on the de facto transfer of the French territories to India was signed in New Delhi between the two countries. A treaty of cession was signed by the two countries in May 1956. It was ratified by the French parliament in May 1962. On 16 August 1962, India and France exchanged the instruments of ratification under which France ceded to India full sovereignty over the territories it held. Pondicherry and the other enclaves of Karaikal, Mahe and Yanam came to be administered as the UT of Puducherry from 1 July 1963.

Vasco da Gama, the Portuguese explorer, discovered the sea route to India via the Cape of Good Hope in Africa, and reached Calicut in May 1498. Soon thereafter, the Portuguese came to India and set up a mini empire. Because of their location on the sea trade route from East to West Asia, Diu and Daman were of strategic importance. In 1510, Alfonso de Albuquerque, the conquistador, laid the foundation of Portuguese power in India by capturing the seaport of Goa from the sultan of Bijapur. The importance of Goa lay in the fact that it was a centre for the import of horses into the region. Goa became the seat of the Portuguese viceroyalty for Asia and the 'Rome of the Orient,' the centre of missionary operations in Asia. It was also the place from where the Portuguese controlled their pepper trade. Apart from Goa, the Portuguese acquired four other small colonies, separated from each other—Daman (1559) and Diu (1535), and Dadra (1785) and Nagar Haveli (1783).

In 1946, Nehru had said, 'Goa is a small pimple on the beautiful face of India and it would not take much time to pinch after India gained independence.'[19] The Goa Congress Committee, founded in 1928, was active in demanding an end to foreign rule. The Portuguese imprisonment of Ram Manohar Lohia, the Indian socialist leader, who had joined the Goan satyagrahis in June 1946, had solidified the Indian support for Goa's liberation. From 1947 onwards, India made repeated efforts to peacefully negotiate the transfer of Indian territories under Portuguese rule, but Portugal stubbornly refused. In 1947, India, because of Portugal's violation of basic UN principles, opposed its membership in the UN.

The Portuguese saw their imperialism as different from that of the other European powers. They had captured colonies because of their altruistic concern, to convert the heathens to Christianity and salvage their souls. Dr António de Oliveira Salazar, the dictator who ruled Portugal from 1932 onwards, had introduced the Estado Novo (New State), or the Second Republic, and installed a corporatist far-right regime, which was opposed to communism, socialism, anarchism, liberalism and anti-colonialism, in 1933. Portugal was supposed to be a 'pluricontinental' nation with Angola, Mozambique, Goa and other Portuguese colonies as extensions of Portugal, and a source of 'civilization and stability'. The idea was to perpetuate their vast, centuries-old empire. Portugal joined the North Atlantic Treaty Organization (NATO) as a founding member in 1949, winning them new allies and friends among the western powers. In 1951, Portugal amended its constitution to change the status of its overseas colonies to provinces, 'styling her pockets in India as "State of India"'.[20] Global calls for self-determination and independence, including Article 73 of the UN Charter, or the UN Declaration on the Granting of Independence to Colonial Countries and Peoples in 1960, fell on the Portuguese's deaf ears.

For the Portuguese, landlocked Dadra and Nagar Haveli were the most vulnerable. Between 22 July and 2 August 1954, armed freedom fighters, assisted by the RSS, forced the surrender of Portuguese forces and Dadra and Nagar Haveli became integral parts of India. An economic blockade imposed on Goa in 1954 failed because of Goa's access to the sea and because of smuggling. Diplomatic relations were discontinued in 1955 after Portuguese soldiers, on 15 August, fired at and killed 70 Indian satyagrahis who had marched into Goa from Patradevi and Pollem in the north and south.

On 13 August 1961, referring to the satyagrahis in Goa, Nehru said that a time may come when India may send the army and not unarmed people. In October, the Indian Council for Africa organized a seminar in Delhi to discuss the problems of Portuguese colonies. The delegates spoke of the discontent of the colonial people against ruthless Portuguese oppression. They said that the Indian insistence on non-violence had prejudiced the freedom movement in Portuguese colonies outside India and declared that the Portuguese empire would collapse once Goa was free. Tensions were mounting, with one Indian naval personnel injured and one fisherman killed by Portuguese firing, in two separate incidents on 17 and 24 November 1961. On 15 December, in response to a letter by UN Secretary-General U. Thant, Salazar agreed to negotiate with India. But it was already too late. At midnight on 18 December, 'Operation Vijay' commenced. With little resistance from the Portuguese forces, the liberation of Goa, Daman and Diu was complete in no time. On the afternoon of 18 December at Mormugao, with the formal surrender of the governor-general of Goa, the Portuguese empire in India was over.

Nehru, the protagonist of peace and non-violent methods, came under severe criticism from the western powers for Operation Vijay in Goa. However, Henry Kissinger, special assistant to US President Kennedy on international affairs, said he 'fully supported India's claims on Goa and also felt that no amount of negotiation with the Portuguese would have persuaded them to leave their former colony'.[21]

III

Linguistic Identities

If you happen to bump into two unrelated Indians, it is more than likely that you will find they belong to different 'groups' in terms of mother tongue, religion, caste and tribal affiliation. The ELF index measures this diversity—the probability or likelihood of two persons you meet at random in a country *not* belonging to the same ethno-linguistic group. In the 1970s, India ranked at the top of sixty-seven countries in terms of the ELF index. According to an expanded SDI incorporating linguistic, racial and religious aspects, in 2005, it was in the two top deciles. Newly independent India faced the challenge of building a nation by consolidating the populace's fundamental unity beneath this bewildering diversity.

India continued the federal architecture of the nation crafted in colonial times, contained in the Government of India Act of 1935. It was a Union of States, with sovereign functions, funds and functionaries devolved between the Union (the Centre in popular parlance) and the states. It allowed combining the advantages of being a big country with those of being many small countries at the same time. But, with a mixed population of multiple identities at various places, even a federal structure could not address all the cleavages along linguistic, religious, caste and tribal lines.

Emotive issues stirred up by clashing identities sometimes led to demonstrations, strikes and even riots, and complicated governance. Policies had to be managed carefully to meet the twin goals of development and nation-building. A workable structure evolved through time, with the number of territorial units reducing from twenty-seven states in four parts, Parts A, B, C and D, in 1947, to fourteen states and 7 centrally administered territories or Union Territories (UT) in 1956, and then increasing over time to reach twenty-eight states and eight UTs in 2020 (Table III.1).

III.1 Impact of Social Cleavages

Population heterogeneity even in a small locality, scholars suggest, impacts everything, even criminal activity. A straightforward theory is that 'people are inclined to feel antagonistic to, and act abusively toward, others who are physiologically or culturally different from themselves'.[1] Group norms and sanctions tend to break down in the presence of conflicting cultures.

Long-standing ascriptive ethnic identities (or social cleavages in short) in terms of language, religion and caste focus not on the characteristics or personalities of different individuals, but on categories such as Malayali (by language), Muslim (by religion) or Mahar (by caste). Social identities involve exclusivity, the construction of the category *us* and a feeling of superiority vis-a-vis *others*. Such identities can take an ominous turn when associated with a narrative of competitive 'victimology'—or how one has been victimized by the other perhaps in the distant past—and, in extreme cases, can lead to violent conflict and even civil war, as in Iraq, Northern Ireland and Sudan. Even without a civil war, such conflicts tend to perpetuate. Violence segregates communities in search of safety into different quarters of a town or a village.

While the root of the conflict is in mutual misunderstanding, its more immediate cause is either greed or grievance or a combination of the two. Such conflicts can be triggered by desecrating the statue of the hero of a community, planting a cow's head in a temple or a pig's head in a mosque, burning the holy book of a religion, planting a scurrilous piece about a community in the media, or spreading news of or rumours about the abduction of a girl by a member of the other community. Miscreants or criminal elements can pull such a trigger and whip up feelings among the masses to benefit from looting and capture of real estate belonging to the other community.

Table III.1. Indian States and Union Territories
(Year of Creation and Principal Languages)

State/Union Territory	Creation	Change/further division	Three principal languages
States:			
Andhra Pradesh	1956	1956, 1959, 2014	Telugu, Urdu, Hindi
Arunachal Pradesh	1971		Nyishi, Adi, Bengali
Assam	1951	1962, 1971	Assamese, Bengali, Hindi
Bihar	1950	1950, 1956, 1968, 2000	Hindi, Maithili, Urdu
Chhattisgarh	2000	2000	Hindi, Odia, Bengali
Goa	1967	1967	Konkani, Marathi, Hindi
Gujarat	1960	1960	Gujarati, Hindi, Sindhi
Haryana	1966	1966, 1979	Hindi, Punjabi, Urdu
Himachal Pradesh	1971		Hindi, Punjabi, Nepali
Jammu and Kashmir	1950	2019 (became a Union Territory)	Kashmiri, Hindi, Dogri
Jharkhand	2000		Hindi, Santhali, Bengali
Karnataka	1950	1956 (Mysore), 1968	Kannada, Urdu, Telugu
Kerala	1956		Malayalam, Tamil, Tulu
Madhya Pradesh	1950	1956, 2000	Hindi, Marathi, Urdu
Maharashtra	1950	1960 (Gujarat)	Marathi, Hindi, Urdu
Manipur	1971		Manipuri, Nepali, Hindi
Meghalaya	1971		Khasi, Garo, Bengali
Mizoram	1971		Mizo, English, Hindi
Nagaland	1963		Naga languages, English, Hindi
Odisha	1950	1960	Odia, Bengali, Telugu
Punjab	1950	1956,1960, 1966	Punjabi, Hindi, Urdu
Rajasthan	1950	1956, 1959	Hindi, Punjabi, Urdu
Sikkim	1975		Nepali, Hindi, Bengali
Tamil Nadu	1950	1953, 1959	Tamil, Telugu, Kannada
Telangana	2014		Telugu, Urdu, Hindi
Tripura	1950		Bengali, Kokborok, Assamese
Uttar Pradesh	1950	1968, 1979, 2000	Hindi, Urdu, Punjabi
Uttaranchal	2000		Hindi, Urdu, Punjabi

West Bengal	1950	1954, 1956	Bengali, Hindi, Santhali
Union Territories			
Andaman and Nicobar Islands	1950	1956	Bengali, Hindi, Tamil
Chandigarh	1966		Hindi, Punjabi, Urdu
Dadra and Nagar Haveli	1961		Hindi, Gujarati, Marathi
Daman and Diu	1967		Gujarati, Hindi, Marathi
Jammu and Kashmir	1950	2019	Kashmiri, Hindi, Dogri
Ladakh	2019		Ladakhi, Purgi, Hindi, English
Lakshadweep	1956		Malayalam, Tamil, Hindi
National Capital Territory/ Delhi	1950	1956	Hindi, Punjabi, Urdu
Puducherry	1962		Tamil, Telugu, Malayalam

Businesspersons wishing to eliminate competitors from the other community may provide the finances while the poor, particularly the unemployed youth, at the vanguard provide the 'labour' for the conflict. Some believe that people of means might even conspire to instigate such conflicts between social communities to keep the danger of class conflict at bay. Political leaders or parties may instigate conflict to mobilize a community in their favour and win elections. Perhaps, relative to greed, grievance plays a more important role in conflicts between social groups. The narrative of social conflict in terms of evil politicians or greedy businesspersons and innocent masses is too simplistic to explain the emotional intensity of crowd behaviour or the enormous personal risks that they take in a conflict. Grievances stem from memories, real or imagined, of being 'wronged' in the past. These can be the destruction of a place of worship hundreds of years ago, like in Jerusalem or Ayodhya, invasion and capture of a country by the forbears—biological or cultural—of the other group, conversions by the sword, changing demographics because of in-migration or differential fertility rates, loss of the status of the ruling group after the British conquest of India, or unfair treatment by the ruling dispensation or the other group.

Conflicts directly affect the economy through damage to houses, properties and business establishments, death and the cost of medical treatment of injuries. Then there is income foregone from workdays lost because of insecurity, fear or imposition of curfew. The poor tend to be the main victims of such violence. Loss of the breadwinner sends an entire household into chronic poverty. The danger of conflict itself leads to indirect losses through excessive public expenditure on an expanded police force, higher interest rates because of risk premium and higher prices because of supply disruptions. Violence acts like a tax and deters investment. Conflict retards growth. Maintenance of law and order is an essential prerequisite for macroeconomic stability and growth. In the computation of its Global Peace Index, the Institute for Economics and Peace, based in Sydney, found that in the last seventy years, per capita growth has been three times higher in highly peaceful countries when compared to countries with low levels of peace.

Even without conflict, social cleavages can hurt economic development. Demanding and securing public goods, such as a good elementary school in the village, requires collective action. Such collective action can be a casualty of social fragmentation. For example, under-provisioning of water supply through tube wells can arise from the unwillingness of the upper castes to share the water source with the formerly 'untouchable' castes. This may result in poor quality infrastructure, low literacy and school attainment and higher infant mortality. Unlike public goods such as education and health, salaries and wages, and subsidies, do not have to be shared with the 'others'. Thus, a war of attrition among interest groups may tilt the balance in favour of salaries and wages to government employees and subsidies to special groups. Economists, including the Nobel laureate Abhijit Banerjee, have shown how regions in India with higher social fragmentation have lower access to public goods such as educational institutions, healthcare centres, and availability of water sources and electricity, transportation facilities and communication infrastructure.

Complementary skills of individuals from diverse groups, however, can also be a rich resource for increasing productivity and accelerating growth. Cities like Los Angeles, Mumbai and New York, with their rich diversity, have produced a splendid variety of cognitive abilities, experiences and cultures leading to innovation and creativity. The challenge for India was and is to unleash the immense potential for innovation and creativity that lies hidden in its rich diversity.

III.2 Linguistic Divisions

Social fragmentation in India can be divided into three categories: (i) linguistic, (ii) religious, and (iii) caste- and tribe-based divisions. This chapter contains a brief description of the complications that arose from linguistic fragmentation in the first two decades after Independence. Issues of religious and caste- and tribe-based complications in brief follow in Chapters IV and V.

In polyglot India, many speak two, if not three, languages—their mother tongue, Hindi and English. This rich diversity is reflected in India's 'official' languages. The Constitution of 1950 included fourteen languages in its Eighth Schedule. Beyond these fourteen, there were others with claims to be included. More additions followed, bringing the tally to twenty-two. Of all these twenty-two, Hindi is the language spoken by most. None is declared as the national language, and the Constitution only designates Hindi written in the Devanagari—from the *nagar* or abode of the *deva* or divinity—script and English as the official languages of the government of India. States are free to specify their own official languages through legislation.

In the colonial period, the division into provinces was determined not by economic logic or linguistic homogeneity, but purely by the growth of British power in India and the colonial capture of territory. The only exceptions were the separation of Bihar and Orissa (now known as Odisha) as one unit from the united province of Bengal in 1912 and subsequently of Orissa from 'Bihar and Orissa' in 1936. The British did no rationalization of the provinces under the Government of India Act of 1919. Originally, the Constitution had divided India into twenty-seven territorial units: (i) nine Part A states (like Madras and West Bengal), which were former provinces directly under British rule with a governor, (ii) eight Part B states (like Hyderabad and Mysore), which were former princely states with elected legislatures, and (iii) ten Part C states (like Ajmer and Manipur), which were former Chief Commissioner's provinces and some small princely states, apart from the Part D territory of Andaman and Nicobar Islands.

People's needs and preferences may vary across jurisdictions. Such variations and the lower-level governments' information advantage about them, particularly public goods, motivate the division of a country into provinces under a federal or decentralized arrangement. Provision of public goods and services such as education, health, roads and water supply can be better designed and sequenced to conform to the needs and preferences of the people in a smaller territory. Whether needs and preferences for public goods and services differ across linguistic groups in India can be a matter of debate, but admittedly, the division on a linguistic basis provides an informational advantage to the local governments.

For conveying its message to people in their own languages, the Congress had already set up its Provincial Committees on a linguistic basis from 1920 onwards. In 1927, it had declared its commitment to redrawing the provinces on a linguistic basis. In 1928, the Simon Commission came to India to study and recommend Constitutional reforms. It did not include any Indian representative, and Indians greeted it with 'Go Back Simon' placards. The Congress set up an All-Party Conference headed by Motilal Nehru and eight other members. For preparing its report, the Conference was ably assisted by Motilal's young son, the thirty-eight-year-old Jawaharlal Nehru. The report, which quite appropriately came to be known as the Nehru Report, noted the need for a reorganization of provinces and emphasized how the principles governing it should be 'Partly geographical and partly economic and financial, but the main considerations must necessarily be the wishes of the people and the linguistic unity of the area concerned. It is well recognized that rapid progress in education as well as general culture and in most departments of life depends on language . . . A democracy must be well informed and must be able to understand and follow public affairs in order to take an effective part in them . . . It becomes essential therefore to conduct business and politics of a country in a language which is understood by the masses. So far as the provinces are concerned this must be the provincial language.'[2] In 1930, the Simon Commission noted the Nehru report but recommended no reorganization of states.

After the Partition of the country, there came a perceptible change in its attitude to linguistic states. Redemption of old pledges in the new conditions looked difficult. In the Constituent Assembly, on 27 November 1947, the Prime Minister, while conceding the linguistic principle, remarked: 'First things must come first, and the first thing is the security and stability of India.'[3] The Constituent Assembly appointed the

Linguistic Provinces Commission under the chairmanship of Justice S.K. Dar. In its report in December 1948, 'to check fissiparous tendencies and strengthen national feeling',[4] the Commission did not favour creation of linguistic provinces.

Soon after the Dar Commission had submitted its report, the Congress appointed a committee comprising Jawaharlal Nehru, Vallabhbhai Patel and Congress President Pattabhi Sitaramayya—known as the JVP Committee—to review the issue of linguistic provinces. In April 1949, the JVP Committee reported that the Congress's linguistic principle of organizing states needed to factor in the consequences of its practical application. A case-by-case approach was necessary to avoid the emergence of language as a separating force and mutual conflict, administrative dislocation and any threat to the security, unity and economic prosperity of the country. In case of insistent and overwhelming public sentiment, the committee recommended a careful balancing of the practicability of satisfying public demand with its implications and consequences, and applying the principle only to well-defined areas about which there was mutual agreement. It cautioned against the simultaneous implementation of all the proposals with merit and said that a beginning could be made with the creation of Andhra from the Telugu-speaking areas in the Madras state. In the same month, the Congress Working Committee (CWC) adopted the JVP recommendations, and the government started following them. But there was a groundswell of public opinion for linguistic states, and soon the government had to bifurcate three states, namely Madras, Bombay and Punjab, to accommodate the demands of diverse linguistic groups.

III.3 Tamil versus Telugu—Madras State and Andhra Pradesh

There had been demands for a separate province for Telugu speakers since the 1910s. Much of the Telugu-speaking areas were either in the erstwhile Madras state or in the princely state of Hyderabad. After Independence, in the Madras Vidhan Sabha, all the legislators from the Telugu-speaking areas, cutting across party lines, were united in their demand for a separate province. The Tamil speakers, a majority in Madras state, were against any division. Furthermore, the city of Madras was claimed by both the Telugu and the Tamil speakers.

Potti Sriramulu was a well-respected freedom fighter, a devoted Gandhian and a Dalit, or formerly 'untouchable', activist. With the negative verdict from the Dar Commission and the JVP Committee, on 19 October 1952, he started a fast unto death on the demand for a separate Andhra Pradesh. With demonstrations, angry protests and strikes in the eighth week of the fast, Prime Minister Nehru wrote to Madras Chief Minister C. Rajagopalachari, popularly known as Rajaji, suggesting that the time had come to accept the Andhra demand. But before the decision was formally announced, Sriramulu died during his fast, on 15 December. People's anger burst out in attacks on government property and disruption of railway traffic. Police fired to restrain the mobs. There were multiple fatalities.

The very next day, Nehru declared that there would be a state of Andhra. On 1 October 1953, eleven districts in the Telugu-speaking portion of Madras state became the new Andhra state, with Kurnool as the capital. T. Prakasam, who had become the premier of the Madras state after the 1946 provincial election, became the chief minister of the new Andhra state. After its boundaries were decided by an independent commission, a new state of Andhra Pradesh was formed on 1 November 1956. It was an amalgam of the Telugu districts of Madras and the Telugu-speaking areas of the erstwhile princely state of Hyderabad.

Following the recommendations of the States Reorganization Commission of the previous year, in 1956, by the Seventh Amendment to the Constitution, the distinction between A, B and C States was abolished, and by the States Reorganization Act 1956, India was made into fourteen states. One of the fourteen states was the newly created Andhra Pradesh. After agreeing to the creation of Telugu-speaking Andhra Pradesh, Nehru had written to a colleague: '. . . we have disturbed the hornet's nest and I believe all of us are likely to be stung.'[5] He proved to be prescient. Demands for linguistic states became increasingly forceful in the Bombay state, in Punjab and in PEPSU.

III.4 Marathi versus Gujarati—Maharashtra and Gujarat

Around 1951, Marathi-speakers, numbering a little over 27 million, were spread out mostly in thirty-five districts of three provinces—Bombay state (twelve), Vidarbha region in Madhya Bharat (eighteen), and the Marathwada region of erstwhile Hyderabad State (five). Sixty per cent of the population was in Bombay state, and the state itself was multilingual. In Bombay state, 44 per cent spoke Marathi, 32 per cent Gujarati and 12 per cent Kannada. Like the demand for a Telugu-speaking Andhra, the Marathi-speakers wanted a Maharashtra state formed by consolidating the relevant areas in the three provinces. It had been a long-standing demand since the late 1910s.

Before Independence, what constitutes the current state of Gujarat consisted of: (i) the southern part ruled directly by the British—districts of Ahmedabad, Bharuch (erstwhile Broach), Kheda (erstwhile Kaira), Panchmahal and Surat in the Bombay state; (ii) thirty-two 'salute' states—including Baroda, Kutch, Idar, Bhavnagar, Junagadh and Dhrangadhra—where the ruler exercised full criminal and civil jurisdiction over his own subjects; and (iii) 337 'non-salute' states and estates, where the princes held partial jurisdiction, usually only in civil matters. The Mahagujarat movement in the early 1950s aimed at the integration of these 369 princely states.

On 15 February 1948, 217 princely states, including Junagadh, merged to form the United State of Kathiawar. Kathiawar was a historic area that produced the fathers of both India and Pakistan—Mahatma Gandhi from Porbandar, and Quaid-e-Azam or Great Leader Muhammad Ali Jinnah from a family in Gondal! Its name was changed to Saurashtra in November 1948. The princely state of Kutch signed the merger agreement and became a Chief Commissioner's Province. The rest of the smaller princely states and estates merged with the adjoining erstwhile British-ruled territory. After the integration of the 369 princely states, the Gujarati speakers in the Bombay state were not too enthusiastic about its division along linguistic lines. The main reason was the risk that the city of Bombay, 'the product of Gujarati capital and Maharashtrian labour',[6] might pass out of control. The Mahagujarat movement was more of the reactive variety.

In case of a split of the Bombay state into Maharashtra and Gujarat, the recommendation of the State Reorganization Commission in September 1955, of constituting Bombay city as a separate unit and creating a new state to be known as Vidarbha out of the Marathi-speaking districts of Madhya Pradesh, was not acceptable to the Marathi speakers.

On 16 January 1956, when Prime Minister Nehru, in a radio broadcast, confirmed the three-way split into Maharashtra, Gujarat and Bombay city, Bombay erupted with widespread violence, police firing and loss of lives and property. The government stuck to its decision, and the decision was embodied in the State Reorganization Bill published on 16 March. The bill contained the new terminology of UT for what was called centrally administered territory or area. Feelings were strong. Sir C.D. Deshmukh, the first Indian to be appointed as Governor, Reserve Bank of India (RBI), before Independence in 1943, was from Maharashtra. He was the finance minister in Nehru's cabinet from 29 May 1950 onwards. On 24 July 1956, he sent in his resignation as finance minister. Protests continued in Bombay.

The Bill was passed with one significant amendment—Vidarbha, Marathwada, Kutch and Saurashtra were included in the composite Bombay state. The struggle—sometimes violent—for linguistic Maharashtra and Gujarat continued. After a period of four years, on 1 May 1960, the Bombay state faded away and was replaced by Maharashtra and Gujarat. The city of Bombay was not only a part of Maharashtra, but the capital of Maharashtra as well. Resolution of the Gujarat-Maharashtra dispute was not the end of the battle for linguistic states, because farther north, Punjab was waiting in the wings.

III.5 Punjabi versus Hindi—Punjab and Haryana

At Independence, the British province of Punjab was partitioned into West and East Punjab. In India, East Punjab came to be known as Punjab. Simla (renamed Shimla in 1972) was its capital. On 15 July 1948, the eight princely states of Faridkot, Jind, Kalsia, Kapurthala, Malerkotla, Nabha, Nalagarh and Patiala, which had acceded to India, were merged into PEPSU; Patiala city was its capital. Though the most immediate challenge for Punjab and PEPSU was the rehabilitation of refugees from West Pakistan, the linguistic divide in both remained a crucial complication.

Punjabi written in the Gurmukhi—literally meaning from the mouth of the guru—script had emerged as the sacred language of the Sikhs sometime in the twentieth century. The holy book of Sikhs, Guru Granth Sahib, is written in Gurmukhi. Prior to Partition, with Muslims constituting a slight majority over the Hindus in united Punjab, Urdu had been the medium of school instruction and administration at the lower and middle levels. With the Muslims migrating to Pakistan, post-Independence, the choice for a language of education and administration was either Punjabi or Hindi. With the exhortation of Swami Dayanand, founder of the Arya Samaj, the Hindus' emphasis on Hindi had already started in the 1880s. According to the 1951 census, in Punjab, Hindus, with 63 per cent of the population, constituted a majority. The Sikhs were in the majority in the seven districts in the north-west, and Hindus dominated the six districts in the south-east. As Hindus started cultivating Hindi, Punjabi became a symbol of the Sikhs' cultural and political identity. The coincidence of the Hindi-Punjabi and Hindu-Sikh fault lines became a highly volatile cocktail.

Gurdwaras are Sikh places of worship, literally the *dwar* or door to the Guru. The Shiromani Akali Dal (SAD)—meaning the supreme akali (followers of the timeless or eternal one) party—was the political wing of the central gurdwara board known as the Shiromani Gurdwara Prabandhak (Organizational) Committee (SGPC). SAD, popularly known as Akali Dal, claimed to represent the Sikhs. The executive committee of the SAD passed a resolution on 22 March 1946 demanding 'for the preservation and protection of the religious, cultural, and economic and political rights of the Sikh nation, the creation of a Sikh state which would include a substantial majority of the Sikh population and their sacred shrines and historical gurdwaras with provision for the transfer and exchange of population and property'.[7]

On 2 October 1949, Chief Minister Bhim Sen Sachar had introduced the famous Sachar formula in schools in Punjab by which, in Sikh-dominated areas, Punjabi in Gurmukhi script became the medium of instruction and Hindi in Devanagari script a compulsory subject of study. In the Hindi-speaking areas, Hindi in Devanagari script became the medium of instruction and Punjabi in Gurmukhi script a compulsory subject. The Sachar formula, which aimed to retain the bilingual character of Punjab, ended up sharpening the state's divide into Hindu and Sikh areas. It became controversial, and after factional fights, Sachar was replaced by Gopi Chand Bhargava as chief minister after a little over six months. The factional fights continued. Under Article 356 of the Constitution,

President's rule had to be imposed in Punjab on 20 June 1951, earning Punjab the distinction of being not only the first Indian state to come under President's rule, but also a rare case of a government at the Centre dismissing its own party government in a state.

Knowing that religion could not be the basis for state reorganization, many Sikh leaders decided to strive for an area where they would be a majority to protect and develop their language and culture. Akali leader Master Tara Singh decided to activate the SAD and agitate for a Punjabi *suba*, or a province for the Punjabis. In April 1948, as president of SAD, he raised the demand for a Punjabi suba. While SAD continued with the Punjabi Suba agitation, Congress, particularly under Pratap Singh Kairon as president during 1950–52, vigorously opposed the demand. When the government accepted the recommendations of the States Reorganization Commission in 1955 with a few exceptions, these exceptions included the creation of a Maha Punjab or Great Punjab consisting of Punjab, PEPSU and Himachal Pradesh. With stiff opposition to Maha Punjab from SAD, a compromise was struck, creating a new Punjab by joining PEPSU with erstwhile Punjab, implementing the Sachar formula on language with minor changes, and SAD eschewing political activity and confining itself to cultural and religious aspects of the Sikh community. Only PEPSU, and not Himachal Pradesh, was merged with Punjab in 1956.

By the early 1960s, the SAD was back in electoral politics, and the Congress was torn apart by factionalism. Even as the SAD intensified the Punjabi Suba movement, in a factional feud, Sant Fateh Singh broke up with his mentor Master Tara Singh in 1963 and emerged as the majority leader of the Akalis. On 16 August 1965, from the holy Akal Takht in Golden Temple, he announced his resolve to go on a fast unto death from 10 September 1965 onwards and, if he did not die in fifteen days, self-immolate on the sixteenth day. The threat coincided with the launch of Pakistan's 'Operation Gibraltar' on 5 August 1965. Pakistan, after mounting hostilities along the ceasefire line, infiltrated Jammu and Kashmir with around 30,000 army guerrillas to foment insurgency. India retaliated by crossing the international border into West Pakistan on 6 September 1965. In view of the war, the Sant postponed his fast unto death.

After the war, a Cabinet Committee under Indira Gandhi, minister of information and broadcasting, and a twenty-two-member Parliamentary

Committee under the Speaker of the Lok Sabha Sardar Hukam Singh, were set up to consider the issue of reorganization of Punjab on linguistic lines. On 11 January 1966, Prime Minister Lal Bahadur Shastri passed away in Tashkent, and after about a fortnight of Gulzarilal Nanda's caretaker government, Indira Gandhi became Prime Minister on 24 January. The Parliamentary Committee submitted its report to Parliament on 18 March. Three days later, in the Lok Sabha, Home Minister Gulzarilal Nanda announced the acceptance of the Parliamentary Committee's recommendation for linguistic reorganization of the Punjab state. Punjab was bifurcated into Punjabi Suba and Haryana from 1 November 1966. Chandigarh, the capital city of erstwhile Punjab (East), was declared as a UT, and served as the capital of both the Punjabi Suba and Haryana.

No estimates of economic losses from the Punjabi Suba agitation or the Tamil versus Telugu or Marathi versus Gujarati movements are readily available. But analysts agree that the undercurrent of fear and instability deterred entrepreneurs from starting new industries or expanding existing ones. Religious and linguistic issues replaced economic issues in the political discourse. Despite the creation of the Punjabi Suba, the separatist movement would continue for over two more decades. Language remained an extremely divisive issue between Punjab and Haryana. Upset with Punjab on the myriad issues dividing the two states, the third chief minister of Haryana, Bansi Lal, in 1969, instituted Telugu as the second language to be taught in schools. It was primarily to avoid introducing Punjabi as a second language, but the official justification was to show that if a northern state could adopt a south Indian language, the southern states should not object to learning Hindi. After more than three decades, in December 2004, with Om Prakash Chautala as the chief minister, Punjabi was declared Haryana's second official language.

III.6 Integration versus Accommodation

With the trauma of Partition still fresh after Independence, the Indian leadership was unanimous about the need for integrating the people and the country. Diversity in the private realm was welcome, not its public recognition. The integrating tendency was manifest in the quasi-federal nature of the Indian Constitution, with the 'quasi' part reflected most prominently in Article 3,[8] giving Parliament the power to, among other things, form a 'new State by separation of territory from any State or by uniting two or more States or parts of States or by uniting any territory to a part of any State; and alter the name of any State'.

The creation of Andhra Pradesh out of the Madras state and Haryana out of Punjab, and the bifurcation of the Bombay state into Maharashtra and Gujarat, signified concessions only after persistent and mounting popular pressures. All the three cases had four remarkable similarities. First, while they were motivated by agitations of linguistic groups— minorities in the case of Andhra and Punjab, and a majority in the case of Maharashtra—they were vigorously opposed by the 'other' linguistic group. Second, in all these three cases, the battle invariably involved rival claims to the capital city, Madras (now Chennai), Bombay (now Mumbai) and Chandigarh. Third, even leaders of the ruling Congress Party were divided on the issues. Time has proved that those asking for linguistic states were no less nationalistic than those who opposed them. Last and not the least, the demands for new states in the first two decades after Independence were conceded only when disruptions in the form of agitations, strikes and breakdowns in law and order, and nuisance violence, thrust these issues onto the national stage.

Why did the government of India wait for violence to erupt and disrupt society and the economy before accepting the demand for the new states in the 1950s and early 1960s? Some scholars explain it as 'voters' myopia', which lead to phenomena such as voters rewarding governments for disaster relief but not disaster mitigation and for famine relief but not for fighting chronic hunger or malnutrition.[9] The average voter outside the affected area did not pay attention to the demands for a new state until nuisance violence of some intensity compelled them to do so. Furthermore, the situation was complicated by a pro- and an anti-reorganization camp among the people in a concerned state. The government of India accepted the demand for new states in the 1950s and early 1960s only when the law and order machinery failed to cope with the rising level of violence associated with the demand for new states.

Gradually, as the fear of secessionist tendencies in subnational identity diminished, India became more assured of its unity and more accommodative of such demands. The expanded list of states in India is in

Table III.1. Comparisons of India with Pakistan and China are illuminating in this context. Pakistan was formed in 1947, with two wings on the west and the east separated not only geographically by about 2,000 kms of Indian territory, but also in terms of language and culture. While East Pakistan had mainly Bengalis, West Pakistan had a bewildering diversity of Punjabis, Sindhis, Balochis and others. When India was securing its federal structure by reorganizing the states in the mid-1950s, Pakistan, under General Sahibzada Iskander Ali Mirza, first as interior minister and then as president, was moving in the opposite direction.

Mirza, from East Pakistan, had a distinguished lineage, and descended from Nawab Syed Mir Jafar Ali Khan Bahadur, better known as Mir Jafar, the general of Siraj-ud-Daulah, the last independent Nawab of Bengal. Mir Jafar, in 1757, at the Battle of Plassey, betrayed Siraj, defected to Robert Clive of the East India Company, laid the foundation of the British empire in India and became the Nawab of Bengal as a puppet of the Company. If Mir Jafar destroyed the independent kingdom of Bengal, two centuries later, in 1955, Iskander Mirza sowed the seeds of Pakistan's destruction by moving the bill for its 'One Unit' policy.

Under the 'One Unit' policy of 1955, Pakistan would be one unit, with no Bengalis, Punjabis, Sindhis, Pathans, Balochis, Bahawalpuris or Khairpuris, but only Pakistanis. This was expected to strengthen its integrity. The policy failed in less than a decade and a half. Its reversal became a critical necessity. In 1970, President Yahya Khan created the four provinces of Balochistan, North-West Frontier Province (NWFP), Punjab and Sindh in West Pakistan. And, instead of there being no Bengalis and only Pakistanis in East Pakistan, in December 1971, East Pakistan itself became the Newly (adverb) independent state of Bangladesh. While Pakistan pursued its One Unit policy, India continued creating new provinces or states. After Andhra Pradesh in 1956, Gujarat and Maharashtra in 1960, Nagaland followed in 1963, Haryana in 1966 and Himachal Pradesh in 1971. By 1972, the number of Indian states had gone up from fourteen to twenty-one.

With the separation of Bangladesh, the new Pakistan in 1971 was what the poet-philosopher Muhammad Iqbal, as president of the Muslim League in 1930, had wanted—an independent Muslim state consisting of Sindh, Balochistan, Punjab and NWFP. While Pakistan means 'land of the pure,' Choudhary Rahmat Ali, a young student studying at Cambridge in England, in a pamphlet titled 'Now or Never' published in 1933, coined the term Pakistan as an acronym for only **P**unjab, **A**fghania (NWFP), **K**ashmir and **I**ndus-Sindh, combined with the ***-stan*** suffix from Balochistan. Rahmat Ali's Pakistan never included Bengal or Bangladesh in Pakistan.

It is interesting to compare India with China as well, particularly their relative successes in developing their own lingua francas. The languages of China are as varied as those in India. The Han Chinese, who constitute more than 90 per cent of China's population, speak and use the 'Chinese' language, while the non-Han minorities speak about 300 other languages. But even the 'Chinese' used by the Hans is not one but a family of the Sinitic branch of Sino-Tibetan languages in East Asia. Except for their written versions, which use the same logographic characters, varieties of Chinese—for example, Shanghainese, Cantonese and Mandarin—are not mutually intelligible when spoken. The Hans alone speak as many as 1,500 dialects.

Mandarin, the form of Chinese spoken in Beijing and called Putonghua (common speech), was a standardized form of Chinese and had been one of its official languages right since 1913. The Chinese Constitution granted freedom to the people of all nationalities—under Article 4 (3), to use and develop their own spoken and written languages, and under Article 134, to have court proceedings in their own languages. After promoting Putonghua as its national language for a long time, China, from 1 January 2001, made Putonghua the national language and decreed its compulsory use in all mass media, government offices and schools, besides imposing a bar on the overuse of other forms of Chinese language in movies and broadcasting. In sharp contrast to integrationist China, accommodative India, even after seventy-three years of Independence, still does not have an Indian language as its national language and continues to use Hindi, as well as English, only as its official languages at the national level.

IV

Fractured Identities: Scheduled Tribes and Castes

The diversity of India has been charted along multiple cross-cutting axes, for example, linguistic, regional and religious, and two of the important axes are based on tribe and caste. Approximately one in every dozen Indians belongs to the Scheduled Tribes (STs) and one in every six belongs to the Scheduled Castes (SCs). Castes may be defined as endogamous groups of people determined hereditarily, ranked hierarchically and tied to occupations. There are four caste categories—SCs, STs, Other Backward Caste (OBCs) and Others—in almost all religious groups. Originally, OBCs stood for Other Backward *Classes*, but for identification purposes at the ground level became Other Backward or intermediate *Castes*. After Independence, democratic India faced the challenge of integrating the STs and SCs, the two large and historically most socio-economically disadvantaged segments, into the mainstream.

Caste was a 'cage of norms' to straitjacket people. Traditional Hindu society had *chatur* (four) *varnas* (orders, classes, colours or types): Brahmins, Kshatriyas, Vaishyas or Baniyas and Shudras, and many castes or *jatis* within each varna. The upper castes or the elite have dominated and exploited the lower castes for centuries. Some of the lowest castes were even considered 'untouchables'. In the twentieth century, similar castes aligned themselves into jati clusters to gain salience. But with the caste system differing across states, jati clusters were generally restricted to individual states.

Under British rule, the lowest castes—the avarnas or Hindus beyond the chaturvarnas—were called Depressed Classes in the second half of

69

the nineteenth century, SCs since the Government of India Act 1935, and Dalits, meaning 'oppressed' in Sanskrit, at various times. In March 1933, a white paper prepared under Prime Minister Ramsay MacDonald proposed provincial autonomy, an All-India Federation of British India and the native states. One of its lasting contributions was the listing of SCs in its Appendix VIII and including 'primitive tribes' (PTs) within it as well. It contributed the concepts of SCs and STs to the Indian Constitution.

On the eve of Independence, elevated hopes for redressal and optimism about the future were summed up well in the Constituent Assembly by two of the doyens of the STs and SCs, Jaipal Singh Munda and Babasaheb Ambedkar, respectively. Jaipal Singh, from the Munda tribe, was a man of many parts. An economist by training at Oxford, he was selected as an Indian Civil Service (ICS) probationer and had also led the first victorious Indian hockey team in the 1928 Olympics in Amsterdam. To the tribals of Chota Nagpur, he was Marang Gomke or 'Great Leader'. On 19 December 1946, speaking on Nehru's Objective Resolution, he said that his people '. . . have been disgracefully treated, neglected for the last 6,000 years. The history of the Indus Valley civilisation, a child of which I am, shows quite clearly that it is the newcomers—most of you here are intruders as far as I am concerned . . . who have driven away my people from the Indus Valley to the jungle fastness . . . The whole history of my people is one of continuous exploitation and dispossession by the non-aboriginals of India punctuated by rebellions and disorder . . .'[1] After the tongue-in-cheek remark 'As a *jungli*, an Adibasi, I am not expected to understand the legal intricacies of the Resolution,' he added, 'But my common sense tells me that every one of us should march in that road to freedom and fight together.'

In the other group, namely the SCs, the feeling of estrangement and deprivation was strong. So strong that, at the first London Round Table Conference in 1930, they, like the Muslims, had demanded a separate electorate. Leading them was Ambedkar, a fellow 'untouchable' from the Mahar community and a brilliant young lawyer in his late thirties. Traditionally employed as soldiers, the Mahars also had to clear cow carcasses. After getting the separate electorate under the British Prime Minister Ramsey MacDonald's August 1932 communal award, a month later, they relented and withdrew their demand only to prevent Mahatma Gandhi from fasting unto death in Pune. Later, the same Ambedkar proved to be a moving spirit behind the Indian Constitution. In the Constituent Assembly, speaking on the same Objective Resolution that Jaipal Singh spoke on two days later, Ambedkar had said, 'I know today we are divided politically, socially and economically. We are in warring camps, and I am probably one of the leaders of a warring camp. But with all this I am convinced that given time and circumstances, nothing in the world will prevent this country from becoming one, and with all our castes and creeds, I have not slightest hesitation in saying that we shall in some form be a united people.'[2]

Table IV.1 Some social characteristics of the SCs and STs, 2011 (All in per cent, except sex ratio which is females per 1,000 males)

Caste category	Share in population	Proportion of population in the respective category		Literacy rate			Sex ratio
		Rural	Urban	Total	Male	Female	
Aggregate	100.0	68.86	31.14	73.0	80.9	64.6	943
Scheduled Castes	16.6	76.40	23.60	66.1	75.2	56.5	945
Scheduled Tribes	8.6	89.99	10.01	59.0	68.5	49.4	990

Source: Handbook on Social Welfare Statistics, Ministry of Justice and Social Empowerment, Government of India, 2018 and Statistical Profile of Scheduled Tribes in India, Ministry of Tribal Affairs, Government of India, 2013.

Post-Independence, the STs and SCs have been marching ahead but have not yet caught up with the rest. In 2011, in both urbanization and literacy, the STs were at the bottom of the rung, with the SCs just above (Table IV.1). Only in terms of the sex ratio was the order reversed. In a sad reflection of the questionable quality of social progress, the most disadvantaged group had the least number of 'missing women' for 1,000 males!

The ranking of the four groups of ST, SC, OBC and 'others' in terms of per capita monthly income or proxy monthly consumer expenditure is also the same as urbanization and literacy. Most socio-economic indicators reflect this relative lack of progress among the STs and the SCs. With more than a quarter of the population belonging to SCs and STs together, the rapid advancement of these two groups is not only a necessity for the country's overall progress but also a moral imperative because of the centuries of neglect and oppression that they have suffered.

The oppression of the SCs has diminished but not disappeared. 'Gujarat Dalit groom rides horse, his community faces social boycott' ran the headline of a media report on 10 May 2019.[3] In July 2020, in Agra's Kakarpura village in UP, the body of a twenty-six-year-old woman Dalit woman from the Nat community was taken off the funeral pyre after the Thakur community objected and forced the family to cremate her 4 km away at grounds meant for the Dalit community.[4]

IV.1 Special Provisions for Scheduled Tribes and Scheduled Castes

In the Constituent Assembly, after narrating the travails his adivasi people have suffered for the last 6,000 years, Jaipal Singh Munda had said '. . . and yet I take Pandit Jawahar Lal Nehru at his word. I take you all at your word that now we are going to start a new chapter, a new chapter of independent India where there is equality of opportunity, where no one would be neglected.'[5] Jaipal Singh Munda's expectations were met at least in legal provisions and constitutional safeguards. There were similar provisions and safeguards for the SCs as well. Articles 341 and 342 of the Indian Constitution[6] empowered the President, after due consultations with the governors of the states, to specify which 'castes, races or tribes or parts of or groups within castes, races or tribes' qualify as SCs, and which 'tribes or tribal communities or parts of or groups within tribes or tribal communities' qualify as STs. According to the Presidential Constitution (SC) Order, 1950 and Constitution (ST) Order, 1950, after due amendments over time up to the Census of 2011, across States and UTs, there were 1,108 castes which were SCs and 1222 tribes which were STs.

For electoral purposes, following Article 330 of the Constitution, the SC and ST are recognized as distinct categories. As of 2018, of the 543 Lok Sabha constituencies, eighty-four and forty-seven constituencies were 'reserved' for SC and ST candidates, respectively. In these 'reserved' constituencies, the electorate included non-SC or non-ST members, but only SC or ST candidates were eligible to contest. The number of seats reserved is based on the proportion of SCs and STs in the total population of the country, and such seats are allocated among states roughly in terms of the proportion of SCs and STs in the population of the states. There is similar reservation of seats for SCs and STs in the legislative assemblies of states under Article 332 and in government jobs under Article 335. Reservations also apply in educational institutions, particularly institutions of higher education such as colleges and universities. It is interesting to note that the Indian Constitution has more safeguards for the STs than for the SCs. Reservations for SCs and STs were initially made for ten years, but have been extended in stages to January 2030.

IV.2 Scheduled Tribes

The colonial rulers used the term 'tribes' to describe people different from 'mainstream' civilization. The term 'tribes' was convenient and 'neat' to capture a very heterogeneous group of people with different 'physical and linguistic traits, demographic size, ecological conditions of living, regions inhabited, or stages of social formation and level of acculturation and development'.[7] Tribes were seen as lying outside or at the fringes of the larger Indian society, and in various stages of 'acculturation' or interaction with the broader society.

The wide variation of tribals in acculturation and interaction with the broader society has not disappeared even with more than seven decades of Independence. For example, North Sentinel Island in the Bay of Bengal is a tribal reserve, with travel prohibited to within 4.8 km of the island. It is the home of the North Sentinelese, numbering somewhere between forty and 100, one of the world's last uncontacted people. In mid-November 2018, John Allen Chau, an American tourist, made an illegal visit to the North Sentinel Island in the Andaman Sea to declare Jesus to the Sentinelese and convert them to Christianity, and was killed. By contrast, the Meenas from Rajasthan, another tribe, have produced Indian Institutes of Technology (IITs)-educated engineers, top bureaucrats and Union ministers.

The relative isolation of the STs over several centuries raises some troubling questions about the historic problem of castes in Hindu society. Ambedkar, a stalwart among thinkers on social cleavages in Hindu society, in his classic 'Annihilation of Caste' in 1936, wrote, 'Thirteen millions (sic) of people living in the midst of civilisation are still in a savage state, and are leading the life of hereditary criminals!! But the Hindus have never felt ashamed of it. This is a phenomenon which in my view is quite unparalleled.' He asked: 'What is the cause of this shameful state of affairs? Why has no attempt been made to civilise these aborigines and to lead them to take to a more honourable way of making a living?'

Ambedkar added, 'The Hindus will probably seek to account for this savage state of the aborigines by attributing to them congenital stupidity. They will probably not admit that the aborigines have remained savages because they had made no effort to civilize them, to give them medical aid, to reform them, to make them good citizens. But supposing a Hindu wished to do what the Christian missionary is doing for these aborigines, could he have done it? I submit not. Civilising the aborigines means adopting them as your own, living in their midst, and cultivating fellow-feeling—in short, loving them. How is it possible for a Hindu to do this? His whole life is one anxious effort to preserve his caste. Caste is his precious possession which he must save at any cost. He cannot consent to lose it by establishing contact with the aborigines, the remnants of the hateful Anaryas of the Vedic days.'

The colonial rulers had apprehensions about the 'effect of a sudden inrush of modernism in the form of a new democratic Provincial Government on aboriginal tribes'.[8] They had passed a Scheduled Districts Act in 1874 to keep districts inhabited by 'primitive' tribes beyond the operation of the general acts and regulations and the jurisdiction of the ordinary courts of judicature. While the Montagu-Chelmsford Reforms of 1919 treated these areas as 'backward tracts', these were renamed as excluded and partially excluded areas in the Government of India Act 1935, to indicate such exclusion. In the Constituent Assembly, Gopinath Bardoloi, the premier of Assam, cogently explained the asymmetry in Indian federalism: 'It is true that some of these tribal people sometimes indulge in head hunting, but it should be clearly understood that this is only when there is enmity of one clan against another. These people nurtured a spirit of collective hatred in them for generations. The point therefore that presented itself to us was whether we should raise in their (them) a spirit of enmity and hatred by application of force or whether we should bring them up under the broad principle of government by good will and love. The Advisory Committee thought that the latter course was the course that should be adopted.'[9]

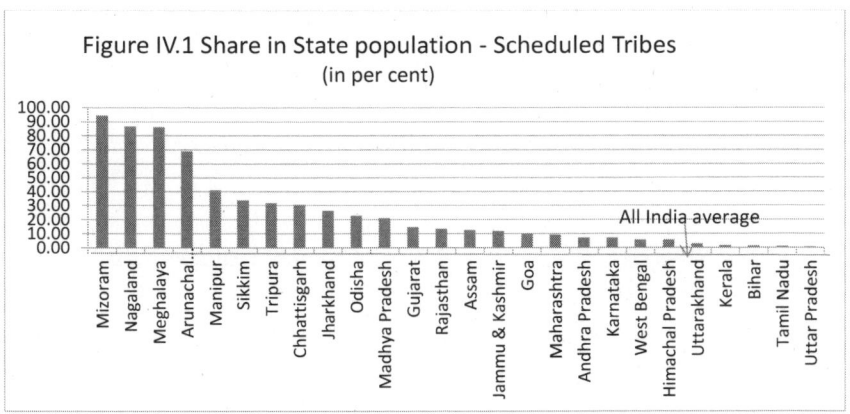

Figure IV.1 Share in State population - Scheduled Tribes (in per cent)

Source: 2011 Census Data; http://www.censusindia.gov.in/2011census/population_enumeration.html. Before bifurcation of erstwhile undivided Andhra Pradesh into Andhra Pradesh and Telangana, there were only twenty-eight states in 2011. All-India total may not add up to 100 because of rounding errors.

Article 342 of the Constitution provided for the specification of tribes or tribal communities or parts of groups within tribes or tribal communities which are deemed to be STs in relation to that state or UT. The Constitution enjoined the state to promote the ST's educational and economic interests and protect them from social injustice and exploitation. It provided for a form of self-government to the STs through the creation of autonomous district councils. Every state enacted laws to prevent the alienation of tribal land.

According to the Census of India 2011, the proportion of the Indian population belonging to STs was 8.6 per cent (Figure IV.1). There were sixteen states with more than 10 per cent of the population consisting of STs, and these states together had a little more than half the population of India. As a proportion of total Indian population, the STs have increased from 6.9 per cent in 1961 to 8.2 per cent in 2001 and further to 8.6 per cent in 2011.

The well-known and age-old social cleavage in terms of tribes and castes has been changing in India. But progress with the STs has been slower than with the SCs. Furthermore, because of their so-called 'primitive' traits, geographical isolation, shyness of contact with the community at large and divisions in terms of language, culture and tradition, the STs have not been as successful as the SCs in mobilizing themselves politically.

STs have made progress in education, health and income. Their literacy rate went up from 8.5 per cent in 1961 to 29.6 per cent in 1991 and further to 59.0 per cent in 2011.[10] The increase in literacy was particularly sharp for females among STs; it rose from 3.2 per cent in 1961 to 49.4 per cent in 2011. Between 1993-94 and 2004-05, the proportion of ST population living below the poverty line declined from 51.94 per cent to 47.3 per cent in rural areas and from 41.14 per cent to 33.3 per cent in urban areas. Yet, the incidence of poverty was extremely high at more than 50 per cent in Jharkhand, Madhya Pradesh (including Chhattisgarh) and Odisha.

The colonial administration in India had difficulties understanding people who lived in the jungles or were nomadic in nature. After eradicating the problem of plunder and murder of travellers by *thuggees*—from the Hindi word *thag* meaning 'swindler' or 'deceiver' in the mid-nineteenth century, the colonial rulers enacted the Criminal Tribes Act in 1871 and included several tribes and castes under its purview. They believed that since people from time immemorial have been pursuing the caste system defining job positions, such as weaving and carpentry, on a hereditary basis, there must have been hereditary criminals who also pursued their forefathers' profession. Every individual of the 'notified' tribes was considered as a potential criminal and subjected to severe reporting requirements and restrictions on movement beyond a prescribed area. After Independence, the Criminal Tribes Act was repealed in 1949 and the criminal tribes denotified in 1952. Nevertheless, suspicion and prejudice against tribals have not disappeared.

There are cases of conflicts among different STs or between STs and others. Such conflicts are particularly pronounced in the north-eastern parts of the country. For example, Kukis and Nagas in Manipur have conflicting demands regarding the four hill districts of Chandel, Senapati, Tamenglong and Ukhrul. In Changlang district of Arunachal Pradesh, there are conflicts over granting of citizenship rights between the Singhpos and the predominantly Buddhist Chakma and the Hindu Hajong refugees, who came from the Chittagong Hill Tracts of erstwhile East Pakistan in the 1960s. In this context, the north-eastern parts of India beyond West Bengal, for convenience referred to as the North-East, merit special mention.

IV.3 The North-East

In 1951, about 10 per cent of India's total tribal population of 19.1 million were in the undivided state of Assam in the North-East. This figure did not include tribals like Mundas, Oraons and Santhals, who had come from outside Assam to work in the tea plantations and were called tea tribes. These tea tribes were about a fifth of Assam's population in 2011 and were not—indeed, are still not—recognized as STs in Assam. Except for the eight major tribes of the Bodos, Miris, Mikirs, Rabhas, Kacharis (Sonwals), Lalungs, Dimasas and Deoris, or parts thereof, most of the tribes were in the hill districts of Assam. In the North-East, outside of Assam, there were the two erstwhile princely states of Manipur and Tripura. The entire population was tribal in Manipur and there were also tribes in Tripura.

Tripura and Mizoram in India, along with the Chittagong Hill Tracts in Bangladesh, form a sort of triangle marking the western end of Asia's largest stretch of tribal populations.[11] From this triangle, the tribal stretch extends through Manipur, Nagaland, upper Myanmar (erstwhile Burma), Thailand and Lao. Under-administered during colonial times, it had limited contact with the societies on the plains. Tribes in these thickly wooded hilly terrains shared 'neither a common tradition of culture or faith nor the legacy of a united anti-colonial movement with the plains-dwellers whose states . . . controlled (their) long hilly jungle stretch since decolonisation.' Sharp edges of ethnicity along with religious divides resulted in a highly complex relationship, pithily captured by the States Reorganization Commission in 1955 as: 'Racially, linguistically and culturally, even the tribes which are described compendiously under a single name, for example, the Nagas, are in reality different each (sic) from the other.'[12] The diversity was reflected in the constant reorganization of the North-East over two and a half centuries.

At the time of Independence, undivided Assam consisted of four parts: (i) the Brahmaputra valley; (ii) the Lushai or Mizo Hills and the North Cachar Hills, which were 'excluded areas' where the government of Assam had no jurisdiction and which were ruled by the special powers of the Governor; (iii) United Khasi and Jayantia Hills (with the exception of Shillong, which was then the capital of undivided Assam), the Garo hills, the Naga hills and the Mikir Hills (renamed Karbi Anglong in 1976), which were 'partially excluded areas'; and (iv) the northern hill areas, which was also an 'excluded area' known as the North-East Frontier Tract and later as the North-East Frontier Agency (NEFA), administered by the ministry of external affairs with the Governor of Assam acting as an agent to the President of India.

In the Constituent Assembly, like Gopinath Bardoloi, Ambedkar argued how the tribal communities of the North-East were different from the tribals in the rest of the country and needed a different administrative structure. Article 244 of the Constitution included the Sixth Schedule, which had provisions for the administration of tribal areas in Assam, Meghalaya, Tripura and Mizoram, and for safeguarding the rights of tribal populations through the formation of Autonomous District Councils (ADC). Under the Sixth Schedule, there are three ADCs each in Assam, Meghalaya and Mizoram, and one in Tripura.

In 1957, the Naga Hills District and Tuensang Frontier Division were separated from Assam to create Naga Hills Tuensang Area (NHTA) as a UT. NHTA became the Nagaland state in 1960. In 1972, the two districts of Khasi and Jayantia Hills, and the Garo Hills, were made into the state of Meghalaya, or the *alaya* (abode) of *megh* (clouds), and statehood was also accorded to the two UTs of Manipur and Tripura. In the same year, NEFA was renamed Arunachal Pradesh, or the land of the dawn-lit mountains, and converted into a UT. Arunachal became a state in 1987. Thus, starting from a single state of Assam and two princely Part C states of Manipur and Tripura, in forty years, the North-East had become the seven states of Arunachal Pradesh, Assam, Manipur, Meghalaya, Mizoram, Nagaland and Tripura.

In the North-East, one of the aggravating factors was the break-up of a natural economic space by the Partition of the country. Shanmukham Chetty, in his budget speech in November 1947, noted: 'Regions which have functioned for centuries on a complementary basis have been suddenly cut asunder.' For the North-East, rail and road links with Kolkata were through East Bengal, which became East Pakistan. The Partition cut off the established links from the rest of the country. A new rail link quickly established from Takiagram to Siliguri in West Bengal through the Himalayan foothills mitigated the difficulties of the Assam plains to some extent. But there was no satisfactory alternative to the flourishing trade in cotton, lac, timber and other forest produce to East Pakistan, or from East Pakistan to the North-East of other essential supplies. Partly because of this connectivity problem, all the seven states of the North-East have lagged behind and remained mostly on the left tail of the distribution of states according to per capita net state domestic product (NSDP) at current prices in 2018–19 (Figure IV.2).

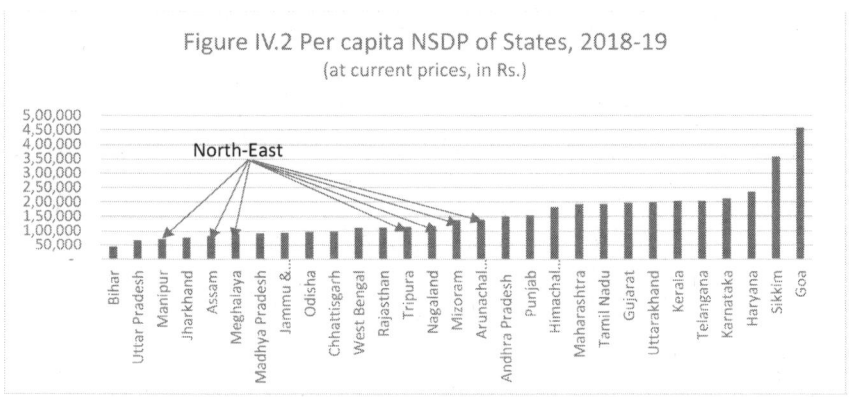

Figure IV.2 Per capita NSDP of States, 2018-19
(at current prices, in Rs.)

Source: Ministry of Statistics and Programme Implementation, Government of India

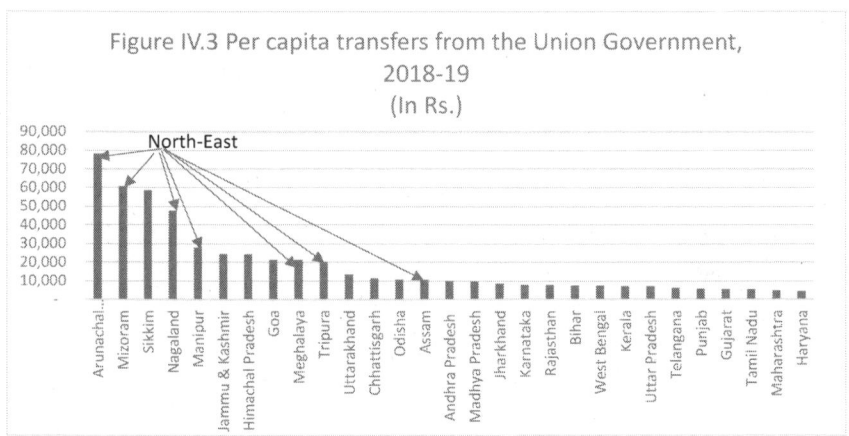

Figure IV.3 Per capita transfers from the Union Government, 2018-19
(In Rs.)

On a per capita basis, transfers from the Union government through devolution of its tax proceeds and other grants have been higher for the states in the North-East than for most others (Figure IV.3). The absence of commensurate development outcomes in the North-East is mostly because of political turbulence persisting right from the time of Independence. Many of the tribes in these parts started vigorous identity movements, which turned violent at times. Nation-building continues in these parts of the country by dealing with the depth and intensity of their subnational feelings.

IV.4 Scheduled Castes

In 2011, SCs constituted 16.6 per cent of India's population (Figures IV.4). Relative to the STs, they were numerically twice as many and also more concentrated in different populous states.

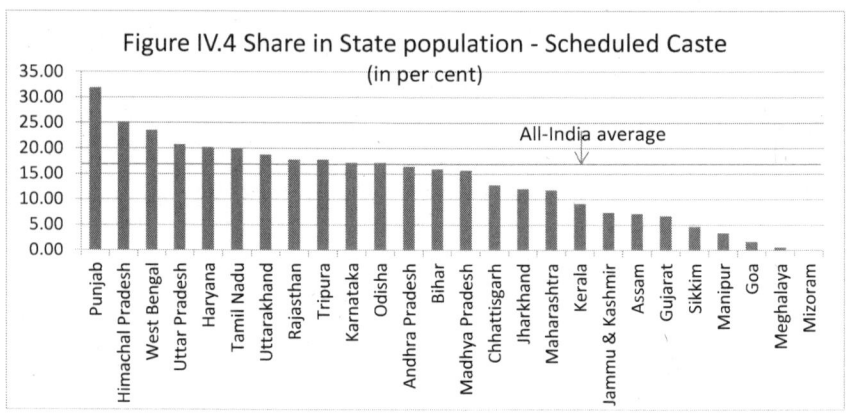

Figure IV.4 Share in State population - Scheduled Caste (in per cent)

Source: 2011 Census Data; http://www.censusindia.gov.in/2011census/population_enumeration. html. There are only twenty-eight states because the 2011 Census was conducted before the bifurcation of erstwhile undivided Andhra Pradesh into Andhra Pradesh and Telangana. All-India total may not add up to 100 because of rounding errors.

The seventeen states that had SCs constituting more than 10 per cent of the population in each accounted for as much as 85.95 per cent of the total Indian population. But unlike the STs, they did not constitute a majority in any of India's states. In contrast to many STs, the SCs were in the same locality as the OBCs and upper castes, and suffered less isolation from the rest of the society.

Around Independence, apart from Ambedkar, the other notable leader of the erstwhile Depressed Classes, now the SCs, was Babu Jagjivan Ram. Also called Babuji, he was from the so-called 'untouchable' caste of Chamar, linked to leatherworks and agriculture. Ambedkar and Jagjivan Ram represented two contrasting strands of confrontational and integrationist SC politics.

Ambedkar was a brilliant student and had gone to study at Columbia University in 1913. He had moved to London in 1916 to enrol for the Bar and also to study at the London School of Economics. But with his scholarship from the Princely State of Baroda running out, he had to return to India in June 1917. In fulfilment of his obligations for the scholarship with which he had gone to Columbia, Ambedkar entered Baroda State service. Later, in 1935–36, in 'Waiting for a Visa', a twenty-page autobiographical life story, he reminisced about his experiences with untouchability, including how he had to leave Baroda for Mumbai as he could not find residential accommodation because of his caste. His two years as a professor at Sydenham College, Mumbai, saw the beginning of his socio-political activities.

Separate representation of the minorities in the legislature was a contentious issue during the freedom struggle. On 20 July 1906, in the House of Commons, Lord Morley, the secretary of state for India, announced reforms concerning the Indian Constitution, and on 1 October 1906, some Indian Muslim leaders organized the Simla Deputation and met Governor-General and Viceroy Lord Minto in Simla. Shortly thereafter, in December 1906, the Muslim League was formed, and it started demanding separate electorates for the Muslims. In 1916, the Congress and the Muslin League, after their simultaneous annual sessions in Lucknow, drew up the 'Lucknow Pact' to provide for Muslim representation through a separate electorate. The question of a separate electorate for the Depressed Classes remained open.

In Mumbai, in January 1919, before the Southborough Committee on Franchise, Ambedkar strongly advocated reserved seats in the legislature for the Depressed Classes. He argued that each caste group tends to create its own distinctive type of like-mindedness which depends on its 'extent of communication, participation or endosmosis'. Endosmosis, or the tendency of osmosis towards the inside of a cell or a vessel, like in biology, was most pronounced between touchable and untouchable Hindus, more than between the religious communities such as Hindus, Muslims and Parsis, he argued. Between 30 May and 1 June 1920, Ambedkar actively participated in the first All-India Conference of the Depressed Classes in Nagpur, presided over by Shahu Chhatrapati I. Shortly thereafter, he was back in London to get his doctorate in economics, and also to complete his legal training and become a barrister. He came back to India in 1924 and was soon recognized as a famous lawyer and intellectual leader of the Depressed Classes. In Mahad in Raigad district of Maharashtra, he led the Chavdar Lake Satyagraha—literally, firmly holding on to truth, a non-violent protest—on 20 March 1927 to establish the rights of untouchables to use the water in a public tank.

He, along with Rettamalai Srinivasan, represented the Depressed Classes in negotiations with the colonial government and other political parties. Ramsey MacDonald, the British prime minister, announced his Communal Award on 16 August 1932. It included a separate electorate for the Depressed Classes. Gandhiji had repeatedly declared that he would resist with his life any attempt to rend the Depressed Classes from the main body of the Hindus by means of separate electorates. Accordingly, he wrote to the prime minister that, if the Award relating to Depressed Classes was not changed, he would undertake a fast unto death. He claimed that the Communal Award was the '. . . injection of a poison that is calculated to destroy Hinduism and do no good whatever to the Depressed Classes'. In Yervada Jail in Pune, he started his fast unto death on 16 September 1932. There was grave concern about his health. On 24 September, Ambedkar and his Depressed Classes associates signed the 'Poona Pact' with some upper-caste Hindu leaders such as Madan Mohan Malaviya, Tej Bahadur Sapru, Rajendra Prasad and Rajaji. The pact urged the British government to withdraw the decision on separate electorates for the Depressed Classes in favour of reserved seats for them and to end untouchability by statutory provisions. On 26 September, the British government announced that it would recommend the Poona Pact for parliamentary endorsement. The Mahatma broke his fast.

The Government of India Act 1935, while introducing a federal structure with greater powers for self-rule in the provinces, as we know, also instituted reservation of seats in the legislatures for the Depressed Classes. The Act introduced the term Scheduled Caste (SC) to indicate groups of 'such castes, parts of groups within castes, which appear to His Majesty in Council to correspond to the classes of persons formerly known as the "Depressed Classes", as His Majesty in Council may prefer.'[13] The Government of India (Scheduled Castes) Order, 1936 contained a list or 'Schedule' of castes throughout the British-administered provinces.

Ambedkar set up the Independent Labour Party in August 1936 to fight against the Brahmanical and capitalist societal structures. It fought the 1937 Bombay election to the Central Legislative Assembly for thirteen reserved and four general seats, and won eleven and three seats, respectively.

Six years later, he changed the name of the party to All India Scheduled Caste Federation (SCF). SCF became the Republican Party of India (RPI) in 1957.

Ambedkar's role in the freedom struggle has been the most controversial aspect of his otherwise brilliant career. Critics point out that it is hard to find 'one instance, not one single, solitary instance in which Ambedkar participated in any activity connected with that struggle to free the country'.[14] In 1931, he had explicitly stated, 'The depressed classes are not anxious, they are not clamorous, they have not started any movement for claiming that there shall be an immediate transfer of power from the British to the Indian people.' He was also highly critical of Mahatma Gandhi. For example, at the Second Round Table, while the Mahatma did not have '. . . a shadow of doubt that the iceberg of communal differences will melt under the warmth of the sun of freedom', Ambedkar was not sure. Some suggest that Ambedkar, not so inadvertently, helped the British to divide and rule India. He even joined the Viceroy's Executive Council as member labour—or effectively as minister of labour—in 1942 and continued until 1946.

After the elections to the Constituent Assembly in August 1946, an interim government under Nehru was installed in September 1946. In this interim government, as minister of labour, Ambedkar was succeeded by the other SC stalwart, Babu Jagjivan Ram. While both were sons of soldiers in the colonial army, Jagjivan Ram, in his dhoti-kurta, was quite a contrast to Dr Ambedkar in his western suits, and in more ways than one. Ambedkar was focused only on the upliftment of the SCs, while Jagjivan Ram had the twin goals of uplifting the SCs and the freedom of the country. He believed that the SCs should be involved in the freedom struggle and rally together for social reform and greater political representation at the same time. He believed that self-rule would benefit all Indians. Inspired by Gandhiji, he was deeply involved in the freedom struggle and suffered imprisonment several times.

Like Ambedkar, Jagjivan Ram had experienced the pain and inequities, prejudices and superstitions associated with the caste system. In Arrah Town School in Bihar, where he studied, there used to be two water pitchers marked for Hindus and Muslims. When there was a complaint about his drinking water from the pitcher marked for Hindus, he had told the principal that he did so because he was a Hindu! Pundit Madan Mohan Malaviya, the founder of Benaras Hindu University (BHU), was so impressed by young Jagjivan Ram's proficiency in Sanskrit that he had invited him to come and join BHU! From BHU, after his intermediate degree, he went to Vidyasagar College in Kolkata for his bachelor's degree in science and got involved in agitations against British rule in January 1930, the same year he joined the Congress.

Jagjivan Ram came from a deeply religious family and was a devout Hindu. In 1928, while studying in Kolkata, he had set up the Ravidas Sabha, an organization of the followers of Sant Ravidas, the mystic poet-saint from the Bhakti movement in the fifteenth and sixteenth centuries, and a Chamar himself. He was against the attempts by Muslims and Christians to convert the SCs from Hinduism. He was an integrationist with the aim of achieving a free India joined in the ties of unity, equality and fraternity. Liberation of the SCs, he believed, could be realized only by the economic and social upliftment of the whole of Indian society. By contrast, on 13 October 1935, at the Yeola Conversion Conference in Nasik district, Ambedkar had told the assembled 10,000 SCs to change their religion and to choose any that gave them 'equality of status and treatment', and publicly proclaimed, 'I was born a Hindu because I had no control over this but I shall not die a Hindu.' True to his word, Ambedkar converted to Buddhism less than two months before his death in December 1956.

The Mahatma's Harijan Movement—with Hari (God's) *jan* (people) translating to 'children of god'—became a major national campaign between 1932 and 1936. It aimed at providing the Depressed Classes access to public places such as temples, schools, roads and water resources, and encouraging inter-dining and inter-caste marriages. Jagjivan Ram became a part of this movement. He became the secretary of the Congress Party in Bihar and also an important leader and founder member of the League of Depressed Classes, an associate of the Congress. The league's objectives included promotion of understanding and cooperation between the Depressed Classes and other sections of society, developing healthy nationalism, evolving a well-knit and compact body of Hindus and improving the Depressed Classes' religious, moral, educational, social and political rights. For the Congress, Jagjivan Ram and his league were the nationalists who could counteract Ambedkar and the separatists among the Depressed Classes.

In the election to the Central Legislative Assembly in the winter of 1936–37, while Ambedkar's Independent Labour Party did well in Bombay Province and the Central Provinces and Berar, outside of western India, its victories were limited. Of the 151 reserved seats all over India, the Congress won seventy-three and the balance went to a variety of other parties and independent candidates. It showed the fragmented nature of the SCs'—which the Depressed Classes had been rechristened by then—movement at that time. The results of the 1945–46 elections were even more disastrous for Ambedkar's SCF, which the Independent Labour Party had become by 1942. It won only two out of the 151 reserved seats all over India – one each in Bengal and the Central Province. The results partly reflected the limited franchise, available to only to 35.5 million or about a fifth of the adult population, based on factors such as property, education and white-collared occupational qualifications. Nevertheless, for Ambedkar and his party, it was a representational crisis. The Congress did well in the constituencies reserved for the SCs and Jagjivan Ram emerged as the most prominent SC leader in the party.

Ambedkar, who would play a prominent role in the Constituent Assembly, could not be elected to it from the Provincial Assembly of Bombay, as the SCF had won only one seat. Sardar Patel had proclaimed that 'apart from the doors, even the windows of the Constituent Assembly are closed for Dr Ambedkar. Let us see how he enters into the Constituent Assembly'.[15] He got elected to it only with the help of Jogendra Nath Mandal, from the Muslim League-ruled Bengal, one or two independent SC MLAs and 'one or perhaps two Anglo-Indian votes in addition'.[16] Mandal, along with Ambedkar, was one of the founders of the SCF. A controversial figure, he would make common cause with the Muslim League in their demand for Pakistan, temporarily migrate to Pakistan, and play a key role in swinging the 1947 plebiscite in favour of the Sylhet district of Assam going to East Pakistan. He would become one of Pakistan's ninety-six founding fathers and its first labour and law minister, only to resign and migrate to India in 1950.

On 15 July 1947, the British Parliament passed the Act of Indian Independence and declared that the country, along with Bengal, would be partitioned. It led to two Constituent Assemblies, one for India and one for Pakistan. Many of the members, including Ambedkar, from Bengal lost their membership of the Constituent Assembly of India. A vacancy from Bombay arose because of M.R. Jayakar's resignation after some disagreements with the Congress. Rajendra Prasad, Chairman of the Constituent Assembly, wrote to B.G. Kher, then prime minister of Bombay, and said, 'Apart from any other consideration we have found Dr. Ambedkar's work both in Constituent Assembly and the various committees to which he was appointed to be of such an order as to require that we should not be deprived of his services. As you know, he was elected from Bengal and after the division of the province he has ceased to be a member of the Constituent Assembly commencing from the 14th July 1947 and it is therefore necessary that he should be elected immediately.'[17]Even Sardar Patel stepped in to persuade both Kher and G.P. Mavalankar, who was otherwise slated to fill in the vacancy caused by Jayakar.

Ambedkar was back in the Constituent Assembly of India and went on to play a critical role in the drafting of the Constitution. In his remarkable prose, he summed it up by saying, 'The Hindus wanted the Vedas, and they sent for Vyasa who was not a caste Hindu. The Hindus wanted an epic Ramayana and they sent for Valmiki who was an untouchable. The Hindus want a Constitution and they have sent for me.'[18] Independent India started off with high expectations about according their rightful place to the SCs. Among the SCs, there were alternate strands of confrontational and integrationist politics, which continue even today. But the integrationist strand seems to be ascendant. It can be argued that even Ambedkar, the Vyasa of the Indian Constitution, had turned less confrontational and more integrationist after Independence.

Socio-economic empowerment of the SCs and ensuring them social justice have been pursued through: (i) reservation policy in legislature and local bodies, educational institutions and public sector jobs, (ii) implementation of the Indian Penal Code, the Protection of Civil Rights Act, 1955, the Scheduled Castes and Scheduled Tribes (Prevention of Atrocities) Act, 1989 and Prohibition of Employment as Manual Scavengers and Their Rehabilitation Act, 2013, and setting up of the National Commission for Scheduled Castes and Scheduled Tribes (1990), and (iii) targeted intervention in the provision of public goods and services and financial assistance.

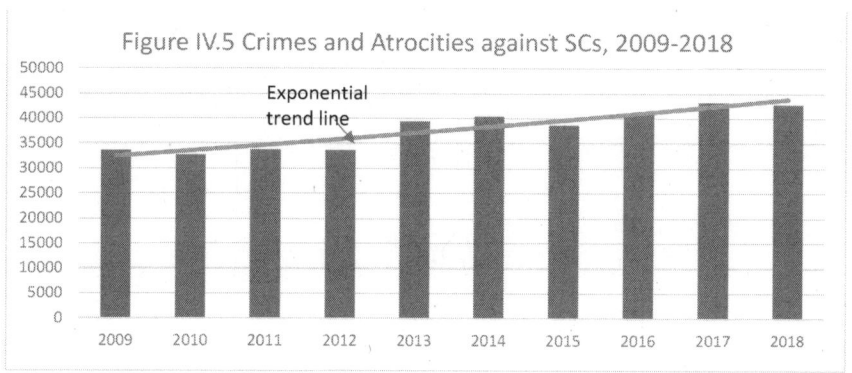

Figure IV.5 Crimes and Atrocities against SCs, 2009-2018

Source: Crime in India, 2013, 2016 and 2018. National Crime Records Bureau (NCRB), Ministry of Home Affairs, Government of India.

The number of crimes and atrocities committed against SCs reported in official statistics grew from 33,594 in 2009 to 42,793 in 2018 (Figure IV.5). The rate of growth of such crimes at 3.3 per cent was faster than the growth in the SC population. While reporting of such cases may have increased in recent times with greater awareness among the SCs about their rights, and their increasing unwillingness to take such crimes lying down, it is not a picture of the rapid elimination of their social oppression and discrimination. The literacy rate among SCs went up from 10.27 per cent in 1961 to 66.10 per cent in 2011, but it was still short of the overall literacy rate of 74.04 per cent in 2011. Economists Suresh Tendulkar and K. Sundaram estimated that between 1993–94 and 1999–2000, the headcount ratio of poverty—that is, the proportion of the relevant population below the poverty line—for SCs came down from 45.69 per cent to 38.39 per cent. The decline of 7.30 percentage points was higher than the corresponding decline of the headcount ratio for the entire country, of 5.27 percentage points, from 34.20 per cent to 28.93 per cent. Yet, at 38.39 per cent, the still higher incidence of poverty among the SCs indicates that economic upliftment of the SCs to bring them at par with the rest of the society remains an unfinished story.

V

Religious Conflicts

In Jew Town, in Kerala's coastal city of Kochi, Sarah Cohen, an elderly widow, would have turned 97 in a few days. She died in late August 2019 and the news made it to the Indian newspapers.[1] The reason: among the three of the surviving '*paradesi* (foreign) Jews' in Kochi, she was the one who stayed in Jew Town all through the year. According to some, Jews had come to south India on the ships of King Solomon thousands of years ago. There had been a sizable and well-to-do Jewish community in India

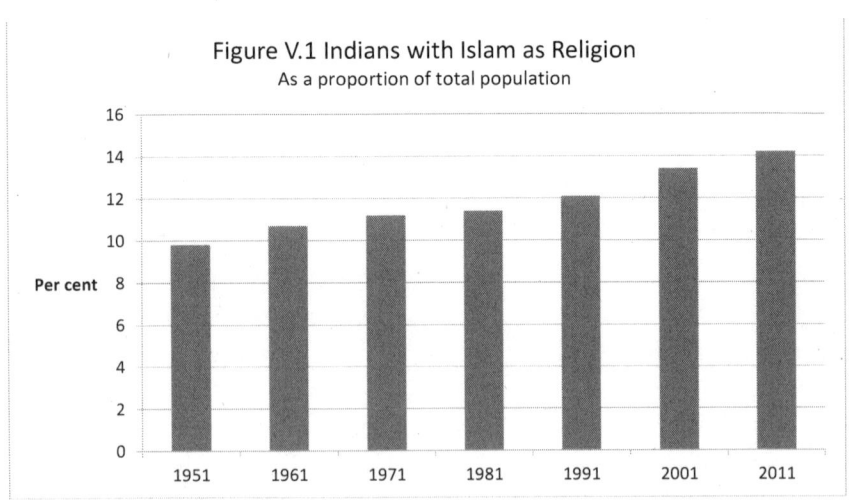

Figure V.1 Indians with Islam as Religion
As a proportion of total population

Source: Census of India http://www.censusindia.gov.in/data/Census_2001/Publication/India/41020_2001_REL.pdf for 1961–2001, http://www.censusindia.gov.in/2011census/C-01.html for 2011

88

even before the creation of Israel. From the 1950s onwards, they made *aliya*—immigration from the diaspora to Israel—by the thousands, and their numbers elsewhere started dwindling. Sarah Cohen's demise was mourned. It symbolized the end of the collective history of Jew Town and a part of India's rich religious diversity.

India has Hinduism as the faith of the majority, and Islam, Christianity, Sikhism, Buddhism and Jainism as the other major faiths. In 2011, according to the Census, of the 1.21 billion population, 79.8 per cent (966.3 million) were Hindus, 14.2 per cent (172.2 million) Muslims, 2.3 per cent (27.8 million) Christians, 1.7 per cent (20.8 million) Sikhs, 0.7 per cent (8.4 million) Buddhists and 0.4 per cent (4.5 million) Jains. The religious composition of the population has remained stable between 1951 and 2011, except for a mild increase in the proportion of Muslims (Figure V.1) and a corresponding decrease in the share of Hindus.

V.1 Diverse Religions—A Long History of Relatively Peaceful Coexistence

Hinduism is the religion that a preponderant majority of Indians follow. In the absence of a single founder and a single holy book, the term 'Hindu' itself poses considerable challenge. In July 2015, in response to an enquiry under the RTI Act, the country's Central Public Information Officer stated that the government did not have information on the definition of 'Hindu'! The term 'Hinduism' as a religion comparable to other world religions was not invented until the late nineteenth century. The colonials used to refer to the people as Hindoos or even Gentoos, not Hindus. Raja Rammohun Roy (1772–1833), described as the Father of Modern India, identified himself as a 'Hindoo' in his book *A Defense of Hindoo Theism* (1817). In 1893, when Swami Vivekananda went to the World Parliament of Religion in Chicago in the US, he was described as a 'Hindoo' monk. With multiple fractures along castes and denominations, originally, the term 'Hindu'—an exonym, or a term used by outsiders—described not a religion but the people living in today's India and its neighbouring regions. Since the beginning of the Census in 1872, an individual's religion was recorded as the religion that they claimed they belonged to. You were a Hindu if you called yourself so.

Apart from Hinduism, India is the birthplace of three other major religions, namely Buddhism, Jainism and Sikhism. Jainism and Buddhism (fifth to fourth century BCE) are ancient Indian religions, with Jainism predating Buddhism and even the Hindu Vedas. Sikhism is another 'Indian' religion which has been there since it was founded in the north-western part of the country by Guru Nanak, sometime in the late fifteenth or early sixteenth century, as a reformed version of Hinduism to create a spiritual, social and political platform based on equality, fraternal love, goodness and virtue.

Christianity is believed to have been introduced into the country first by Thomas the Apostle, when he reached the Malabar coast in Kerala in 52 CE, and simultaneously by Bartholomew the Apostle along the Konkan coast. Legend has it that in Kerala, the first group to be converted to Christianity by St Thomas—obviously, not by the sword—were a group of upper-caste Brahmins! According to the 2011 Census, apart from in Kerala, where they accounted for 18.4 per cent of the total, Christians constituted more than a fifth to almost nine-tenths of the population in Nagaland (87.9 per cent), Mizoram (87.2 per cent), Meghalaya (74.6 per cent), Manipur (41.3 per cent), Arunachal Pradesh (30.3 per cent), Goa (25.1 per cent) and Andaman and Nicobar Islands (21.3 per cent).

Islam came to some of the coastal parts of India in the seventh century CE with the seafaring Arabs, though its spread remained limited till the Islamic conquest of north India in the twelfth century CE. India has the third largest population of Muslims in the world after Indonesia and Pakistan. The country has had a small and successful community of Zoroastrians for at least 1100 years. They are commonly known as Parsis as their ancestors came as refugees during the Islamic Arab conquest of Persia. Interestingly, Quaid-i-Azam Jinnah himself had a Parsi wife. Their only daughter, Dina, stayed back in India and married a Parsi who had become a Christian! India is where His Holiness the Dalai Lama and the Tibetan government in exile reside.

In olden times, communal violence resulting in loss of lives and destruction or looting of sacred places of worship were not unknown. But, until the Partition in the run up to Independence, their duration and severity were limited and there was little significant change in numbers through extermination. Over centuries, competition and royal patronage changed the ranks of the faithful of different religions, mainly through peaceful conversion and reconversion. The royal house of Ashoka the Great, whose Dharma Chakra or Wheel of the Law is at the centre of the Indian national flag, symbolizes the peaceful fluidity of religious affiliations around the third century BCE. Ashoka's grandfather, Chandragupta Maurya, the founder of the Mauryan empire, was born a Hindu, renounced his empire and became a Jain monk in his later years. Ashoka was a great promoter of Buddhism, while his grandson Samprati is said to have converted to Jainism.

Similarly, Maharaja Ranjit Singh, the founder of the Sikh empire, donated gold not only for the world-famous gurdwara in Amritsar, Sri Harimandir Sahib, also known as the Golden Temple, but also to the Hindu Kashi Vishwanath Shiva temple in Varanasi. He is also claimed to have bequeathed the world-famous Kohinoor diamond to the celebrated Hindu Lord Jagannath in Puri, Odisha.[2] The British crown has sported the Kohinoor for more than 170 years and refuses to restore it to Lord Jagannath.

People of different religious faiths have vigorously participated in the national endeavour. For example, Jains have produced many extraordinarily successful individuals in business. In 2011, Buddhists constituted a significant proportion of the population in Ladakh (39.7 per cent), Sikkim (27.4 per cent), Arunachal Pradesh (11.8 per cent) and Mizoram (8.5 per cent). Arunachal is where Tsangyang Gyatso, the sixth Dalai Lama, was born in the late seventeenth century and where the Tawang Monastery— the second largest Buddhist monastery in the world, after Potala Palace in Tibet—is located. Tawang is a tourist hotspot. Competition among the different religions was observed most spectacularly when, protesting against the caste system, Babasaheb Ambedkar, a Dalit himself, argued that Buddhism was the only way for the Dalits to attain equality and, on 14 October 1956, embraced Buddhism and went on to convert half a million Dalits to his neo-Buddhist faith, mostly in today's Maharashtra.

Christians have played a major role in the propagation of education and health facilities all over the country, especially in tribal areas. St Xavier, the Jesuit from the sixteenth century, lives on through the highly regarded educational institutions named after him all over the country. The community has produced political leaders such as George Fernandes,

Chandrababu Naidu, Oomen Chandy and Purno Sangma, eminent sportspersons such as Leander Paes and Mary Kom, and business houses such as the Muthoot Group. The Congress Party, during its decade-long rule in 2004–14, was headed by Sonia Gandhi, a Catholic of Italian origin.

No history of the freedom movement in India is complete without mention of Maulana Abul Kalam Azad, who also went to become the education minister of the country and to inaugurate the first IIT at Kharagpur on 18 August 1951. In 1948, Brig Mohammad Usman, recipient of the Maha Vir Chakra for gallantry, was instrumental in foiling the Pakistani attempt to capture Jammu and Kashmir. The most recent of the three Muslim presidents of India, A.P.J. Abdul Kalam, was a rocket scientist and is considered the 'Missile Man' of India. Mughlai dishes are an integral and indispensable part of the rich Indian cuisine. Indian classical music has been enriched by the contribution of stalwarts such as Baba Allauddin Khan and Abdul Karim Khan. Many of the leading actors in Bollywood, like the late Dilip Kumar, the late Meena Kumari, Shah Rukh Khan, Aamir Khan and Salman Khan, were and are Muslims.

Many martyrs in the freedom struggle, including the charismatic Bhagat Singh, were Sikhs. The community has produced one president and one prime minister. Apart from many brave soldiers and generals, the community has also produced outstanding sports personalities such as Milkha Singh, Bishen Singh Bedi, Pragat Singh, Dara Singh and Jeev Milkha Singh.

The successful integration of people of diverse faiths into the mainstream is best illustrated by the dramatis personae of the events that took place around 16 December 1971, when Pakistan finally surrendered and Bangladesh de facto became an independent country. In the Indian blitzkrieg, it was Maj. Gen. Jacob-Farj-Rafael Jacob, a Jew, who entered Dhaka with only 3,000 troops and persuaded Pakistan's Lt Gen. Amir Abdullah Khan Niazi to surrender without a fight! While the chief of the Indian Army, Gen. Sam Manekshaw, a Parsi, orchestrated the overall military strategy, the Indian Foreign Minister Sardar Swaran Singh, a Sikh, continued to explain to the UN Security Council the historic background of Bangladesh's liberation struggle through a long speech over two days until he could announce that Lt Gen. Niazi, heading the Eastern

Command of the Pakistan Army, had signed the instrument of surrender in Dacca and given it to Lt Gen. Jagjit Singh Aurora, the General Officer-in-Command of the Eastern Command, another Sikh!

Parsis provide another good example of religious amity in the Indian tradition. The story goes that when the Zoroastrian refugees from Iran, escaping religious persecution, landed on the shores of Gujarat, the local king, Jadi Rana, sent them a cup of milk filled to the brim to hint that the kingdom had no place for more people. The Zoroastrian head priest added a pinch of sugar to the milk to signify that their arrival would not add to problems for the population but only make their lives sweeter. The king provided them sanctuary in exchange for a few promises. The Zoroastrians consented to and adopted Gujarati as their language, local customs such as wedding after sunset and local attire, put down their weapons and promised not to proselytize. True to their word, the Zoroastrians have continued to adhere to their vows. Numbering only 57,264 in 2011, the small community has produced stalwarts in diverse fields, such as Dadabhai Naoroji, Jamsetji Tata, the founder of the Tata group of industries, nuclear scientists Homi Bhabha and Homi Sethna, Field Marshal Sam Manekshaw and Nani Palkhivala, the prominent lawyer. Perhaps India would have been better off if the Parsis were less punctilious in sticking to their vow, taken more than a thousand years ago, of not taking spouses from other religious communities!

V.2 Secularism

Even though Jinnah had created Pakistan based on religious separatist arguments, he did not want a theocratic or religious state. He had said that religion is a matter purely between man and God and should not be allowed to come into politics. On 11 August 1947, in Pakistan's Constituent Assembly, Jinnah had told the people, 'You are free; you are free to go to your temples, you are free to go to your mosques or to any other place or worship in this state of Pakistan. You may belong to any religion or caste or creed that has nothing to do with the business of the state.'[3] Jinnah did not survive more than thirteen months after the birth of Pakistan, and neither for much longer did his dream of a non-theocratic Pakistan. India was different.

In India, the Constitution itself—until the Forty-Second Amendment in 1976—did not call the country a secular republic. Secularism was enshrined instead in no discrimination on the basis of religion in Article 15 and the right to freedom of religion in Articles 25, 26, 27 and 28 of the Indian Constitution. Unlike in the west, religion and state were not separated in the Indian Constitution; Article 30(2) made educational institutions set up by religious groups eligible to receive aid from the state. Indian secularism was more like multi-culturalism, under which the state honours all faiths equally and gives them equal opportunities. This multi-culturalism was evident in independent India's approach to the applicability of a universal civil code.

Personal laws were different, hence divisive, for the Hindus and Muslims, with a long history going back to the Slave dynasty (1206–1290 AD). The East India Company, the de facto ruler of extensive parts of India after the Battle of Plassey in 1757, ruled in the name of the Mughal emperor, the titular sovereign. The farman of Mughal Emperor Shah Alam bound the company to decide cases 'agreeably to the rules of Mohomet and the laws of the Empire.'[4] The company abided by the farman through its famous Regulation 11 of 1772, which by Sec. 27 enacted that 'in all suits regarding inheritance, succession, marriage and caste and other religious usages or institutions, the laws of the Quran with respect of Mohamedan and those of the Shastras with respect to Gentoos (Hindus) shall be invariably adhered to'.[5] The British colonial government continued to deal with civil matters, particularly marriage and succession, by the laws of the respective religious communities.

Under the British, until 1937, the Muslims continued to be governed by the Shariat or the Court of Canon Law, though different sections, like the Khojas and Cutchi Memons, could be following different customary laws. Similarly, all Muslims in the North-West Frontier Province were not subject to the Shariat law. In response to Muslim leaders' demand for express legislation superseding custom with Islamic law came the Muslim Personal Law (Shariat) Application Act, 1937, dealing with marriage, succession, inheritance and charities among Muslims, and the Dissolution of Muslim Marriages Act, 1939, dealing with the circumstances in which Muslim women could obtain divorce.

For the Hindus came Dr G.D. Deshmukh's Hindu Women's Right to Property Bill in 1937. A four-member Hindu Law Committee appointed in 1941 under the chairmanship of B.N. Rau, a former judge of the Calcutta High Court, had prepared a Draft Code dealing with succession, maintenance, marriage (including banning of polygamy) and divorce, minority and guardianship, and adoption. This code, which was translated into twelve regional languages and widely circulated, came to be known as the Hindu Code Bill. The nationalists wanted religious reforms, but not enacted by an alien power. Its enactment had to await Independence.

In the run-up to Independence, there were extensive debates in the Constituent Assembly on whether to replace these disparate and divisive personal laws with a Uniform Civil Code for all Indians. What was incorporated in the Indian Constitution was Article 44, which stated, 'The state shall endeavour to secure for the citizens a uniform civil code throughout the territory of India.' Even this Article 44 and the Hindu Code Bill created apprehensions among many Muslims. For example, Pocker Sahib Bahadur, a lawyer in Malabar, from the Muslim League and a leading figure of the Khilafat Movement, argued against uniform personal laws because 'it is a tyrannous provision which ought not to be tolerated; and let it not be taken that I am only voicing forth the feelings of the Mussalmans. In saying this, I am voicing forth the feelings of ever so many sections in this country who feel that it would be really tyrannous to interfere with the religious practices, and with the religious laws, by which they are governed now.'[6]

The Indian Constitution, in its seventh schedule, placed religious institutions, charities and trusts in the Concurrent List, which means that both the Union Government and various state governments could make their own laws about them. Many states intervened in Hindu religious customs and practices. For example, soon after Independence, Madras state enacted the Madras Devadasis (Prevention of Dedication) and Madras Temple Entry Authorization Act in 1947, Madras Animal and Bird Sacrifices Abolition Act in 1950 and Madras Hindu Religious and Charitable Endowment Act in 1951. In India, it was expected that though religiosity was unlikely to decline rapidly, the secularization process would continue with religion progressively becoming an individual's private business as opposed to a communal social mandate and there would be institutional differentiation of secular spheres from religious institutions.

The Indian brand of secularism was strongly contested even by many Hindus. Two groups against its pursuit were the Hindu nationalists and the Hindu right or traditionalists. 'The Hindu nationalists held that Indian identity was embodied in Hinduism because Hindus formed the country's majority community and were sons of the soil. By contrast, Hindu traditionalists were less interested in such a stark ethnic view and paid more attention to cultural features, like the defense of traditional Hindu (or Ayurveda) holistic medicine and the linguistic pre-eminence of Hindi over Urdu, which many Indians regarded as a foreign language.'[7] The most potent reaction to the Indian brand of secularism came from the Hindu right, who criticized it as pseudo-secularism that tolerated religious obscurantism and the bigotry of religions such as Islam.

The Hindu right did not find any justification for continuing with the colonial policy of non-interference in religious areas that were unreasonable and against the development of a common citizenship. After the enactment of the Hindu Code Bill in 1955–56, even the much-respected socialist leader Acharya Kripalani protested the communalism of the government. He said: 'If they (the MPs) single out the Hindu community for their reforming zeal, they cannot escape the charge of being communalists in the sense that they favour the Hindu community and are indifferent to the good of the Muslim community or the Catholic community.'[8] What is more consistent with secularism: a universal civil code, or different personal laws for different communities, was the question. Around Independence, the opinion of most leaders appears to have been that reforms of personal laws should be led by the leaders of the respective communities and not imposed by others. The debate continues to this day.

Like many socio-economic developments in India, even about secularization it is possible to ask both 'why so little' and 'how so much'. With deadly Hindu-Muslim riots and the arrival of thousands of Hindu and Sikh refugees from Pakistan around Independence, the odds were heavily in favour of consolidation of majoritarian Hindu politics. So let us first address the question 'how so much secularization?' Apart from the Hindu Mahasabha from 1915 onwards and the RSS from 1925 onwards, one other Hindu party, the Akhil Bharatiya Ram Rajya Parishad (RRP), or the All-India Council for Establishment of an Ideal State as under Lord Rama, founded by Swami Karpatri, had appeared on the scene in 1948.

At Prime Minister Nehru's invitation, Dr Shyama Prasad Mookerjee, a barrister, a former Vice Chancellor of Calcutta University, and a politician from the Hindu Mahasabha, had joined independent India's first interim government as minister of industries and supply.

With the outbreak of communal violence in 1949–50, a large influx of Hindu refugees from East Pakistan to India, and a corresponding—albeit smaller—outflow of Muslims into East Pakistan, Nehru went for a negotiated settlement with Prime Minister Liaquat Ali Khan of Pakistan. It came to be known as the Nehru-Liaquat Ali Pact of 8 April 1950. Among other things, it promised restitution of property to refugees returning by 31 December 1950, and the right to sell or exchange such property to or with a refugee from the other side even without returning. Sardar Patel wanted a harder stand with Pakistan. Agreeing with Patel, Shyama Prasad Mookerjee resigned from the Cabinet on 1 April 1950, and founded the Akhil Bharatiya Jana Sangh or All India People's Party, popularly known as Jana Sangh, on 21 October 1951. Jana Sangh is the predecessor of the BJP and had close links with the RSS.

In the first three general elections to the Lok Sabha, the total number of seats won by the three Hindu-oriented parties declined from ten in 1952 to five in 1957 before increasing to seventeen in 1962. The corresponding improvement in the share of votes polled was marginal, from 6 per cent to 7.2 per cent and further to 7.7 per cent. What the period saw was the rise of the Jana Sangh and gradual decimation of the Hindu Mahasabha and the RRP. Even though the Hindu Mahasabha and the RSS were already there to act as catalysts, the consolidation of majoritarian politics did not happen in any effective manner and did not pose any palpable threat to Nehru and his Congress, mostly because of the deep influence of the Mahatma and his principle of 'sarva dharma sama bhava' or all paths lead to the same destination in the religious sense. Besides, there could have been three further reasons.

First, the attributes, charisma, and irresistible popular appeal of Nehru, often described as the prime builder of modern India. His attributes are summarized well in an article in the *Economic and Political Weekly*: 'An aristocrat whose wealth and status could be traced to the decaying days of the Moghul Empire; a social and intellectual background almost self-consciously patrician, the acquired veneer of Westernisation happily coexisting with the native priestly heritage; reasonably authentic socialist credentials too, going back to a period when describing oneself as socialist was not merely not modish, but was slightly disreputable; even a limited familiarity with socialist and Marxist theory; and all these civilised graces embedded, as it were, within a larger framework which, for want of a better word, can be described as agnostic-humanist, admittedly possessing a certain period flavour of early, very early Bertrand Russell and George Bernard Shaw. Such were the intellectual and political (not to speak of class) counters that Jawaharlal Nehru possessed when he arrived on the political scene.'[9]

Second, Nathuram Godse's assassination of the Mahatma on 30 January 1948. Godse claimed that he killed the Mahatma because he had 'weakened' the Hindu nation 'by his doctrine of ahimsa' or non-violence.[10] Godse was immediately arrested after the murder, tried on camera from 27 May, sentenced to death on 8 November 1949, and the death penalty was carried out a week later. The Mahatma's assassination had widespread repercussions for both the Hindu Mahasabha and the RSS. Leaders of the Mahasabha, including Veer Savarkar, were arrested following the assassination, and so was Golwalkar, the supreme leader or *sarsanghchalak* of the RSS. The RSS was banned on 4 February 1948. The RSS, which was non-political, was shocked by the ban. Many in the RSS felt that it had to transform itself into a political party. To prevent this transformation, Sardar Patel wanted to recruit the RSS cadre into the Congress.

Third, the possibility of a rapprochement between the RSS and Congress. After the ban on RSS, Golwalkar wrote to Prime Minister Nehru, asking him to lift the ban on the RSS, and claimed that the RSS was one effective check on the 'de-nationalising' activities of the communists. Golwalkar, '. . . worried at the waves of victory of that foreign "ism" which are sweeping over our neighbouring countries', offered to combine RSS's organized cultural force with Government's power to eliminate the menace of communism. In the event, the ban continued.[11] The RSS prepared a constitutional document in line with the discussions that Golwalkar had with Sardar Patel in October 1948. Speculation is that Sardar Patel, recognizing the value of the committed cadre of the RSS, which the Congress lacked, wanted to absorb it into the Congress. The constitutional document prepared by Deendayal Upadhyay—the future all-India general secretary and president of the Jana Sangh—among others, was accepted by the government, and the ban on the RSS was lifted on 11 July 1949. With the deteriorating India-Pakistan relationship, in October 1949, the CWC ruled that RSS members could join the Congress. The decision, which was opposed by Nehru, was reversed in November 1949. The Congress allowed RSS members to join only if they gave up their membership of the RSS. The possibility of integrating the RSS and Congress lapsed after Sardar Patel's demise on 15 December 1950.

V.3 De Jure Secularism and Growth

Admittedly, to be a religious tolerant does not necessarily require a person to be irreligious. The Mahatma was a devout Hindu, and it is difficult to argue that he was not tolerant of other religions. Religion can be useful as a source of solace for the poor, the deprived and the ailing. Belief in supernatural compensation for the non-fulfilment of worldly needs or desires helps. Similarly, religions promoting the traits of hard work, honesty and thrift, in the absence of excessively organized religion, can help economic development and contribute to growth. However, in a multi-religious country, a high level of religiosity, particularly of the organized variety, among the masses may intensify religious influence on public life, result in inter-religious conflicts, distract focus from economic problems and retard development.

International evidence suggests that religiosity as measured by attendance at religious services, personal prayers, belief in hell and afterlife, and even considering oneself as a religious person, goes down with the growth of per capita income. While the definition of religiosity and the impact of socio-economic development on religiosity or belief in the sacred are controversial issues, there is more unanimity about the effect of socio-economic development on the nature and manifestation of religiosity. Opportunity cost of time spent on organized religion – that is the cost in terms of what you could have earned by doing something else—increase with rising wages. The secularisation hypothesis posits that economic progress weakens the influence of religion on politico-economic decision-making and in other social and legal processes. But the problem is, how soon?

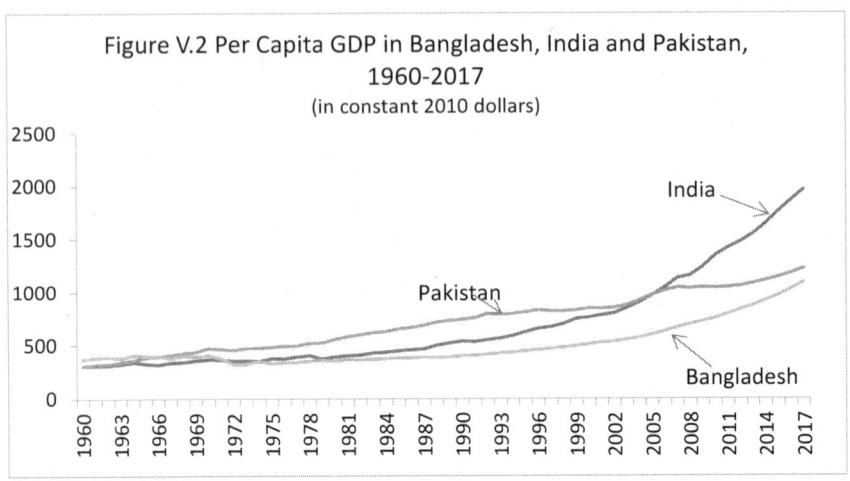

Figure V.2 Per Capita GDP in Bangladesh, India and Pakistan, 1960-2017 (in constant 2010 dollars)

Source: http://databank.worldbank.org/data/reports.aspx?source=2&series=NY.GDP.PCAP.KD&country=#

The growth trajectories in post-colonial South Asia corroborate the strong correlation between secularism and economic growth observed in many countries in the world. Like for many other principles and policies, even for secularism, practice and preaching can differ. Verification of how secular a country is in practice is a difficult empirical exercise. Furthermore, the causality between de facto secularism and growth can run either way. While all the limitations of not considering other relevant factors such as education and investment ratio remain, we mitigate these problems by focusing on de jure secularism and growth in three important countries in South Asia, namely Bangladesh, India and Pakistan (figure V.2). All three were part of undivided India under British rule until 14 August 1947.

Secularist India started off with a per capita GDP lower than that of theocratic Pakistan but overtook it in the middle of the first decade of the new millennium. Bangladesh was a part of Pakistan until 1971. In its chequered history, secularism was one of the four fundamental principles of the original Bangladesh Constitution of 1972. After the assassination of its founder Sheikh Mujibur Rahman, Ziaur Rahman, former freedom fighter and deputy chief of the Bangladesh Army, became the President on 21 April 1977, and by the Fifth Amendment in 1979, removed secularism from the Constitution and replaced it with a statement of 'absolute trust and faith in Almighty Allah'. Also, '*Bismillah-ar-Rahman-ar-Rahim*' (in the name of Allah, the Beneficent and Merciful) preceded the preamble. Islam was declared the state religion in 1988. In 2010, the Bangladesh Supreme Court restored secularism as one of the basic tenets of the Constitution but Islam remained the state religion. A comparison of Islamic Pakistan and Bangladesh, with its chequered secularist history, is interesting in this context. In 1991, per capita GDP in Bangladesh was only about 52 per cent of that in Pakistan. But thereafter, its economy started growing much faster than Pakistan's. By 2017, Bangladesh had done quite a bit of catching up, and its per capita income was as much as 89 per cent of that of Pakistan. By 2020, Bangladesh's per capita income was 60 per cent higher that of Pakistan.

V.4 Religious Minorities

International law commonly accepts that 'A minority is a group which is numerically inferior to the rest of the population of a State, in a non-dominant position, whose members—being nationals of the state—possess ethnic, religious or linguistic characteristics differing from those of the rest of the population, and show, if not implicitly, a sense of solidarity, directed towards preserving that culture, traditions, religion, or language.'[12] The Indian Constitution defined minority rights and recognized religious and linguistic minorities without defining the term minorities.

A Minorities Commission set up in 1978 was given a statutory basis by the National Commission for Minorites (NCM) Act in 1992 and renamed NCM in 1993. NCM Act declared the minorities to be Muslims, Christians, Sikhs, Buddhists and Zoroastrians (Parsis) by a gazette notification only in October 1993. After a prolonged controversy about whether Jainism was a part of the Hindu religion, in 2006, the Supreme Court categorically recognized Jainism as not a part of Hindu religion. The original notification of 1993 was duly modified in January 2014 to add Jains as the sixth minority group.

In India, in popular parlance, the term 'minorities' refers to those who are not Hindus, with its implication that the dominant core of Indian identity is Hinduism. However, it is both problematic and inconsistent with ground reality. For practical purposes, the majority or minority status of a community, whether linguistic or religious, is determinable only by reference to demography of the state and not of the entire country. While Muslims, Christians, Sikhs, Buddhists, Zoroastrians and Jains are minorities at the all-India level, even Hindus are a minority in specific states (Figure V.3). In 2005, the Supreme Court of India left it to the respective states to decide on the minority status of a religion within their own jurisdictions.

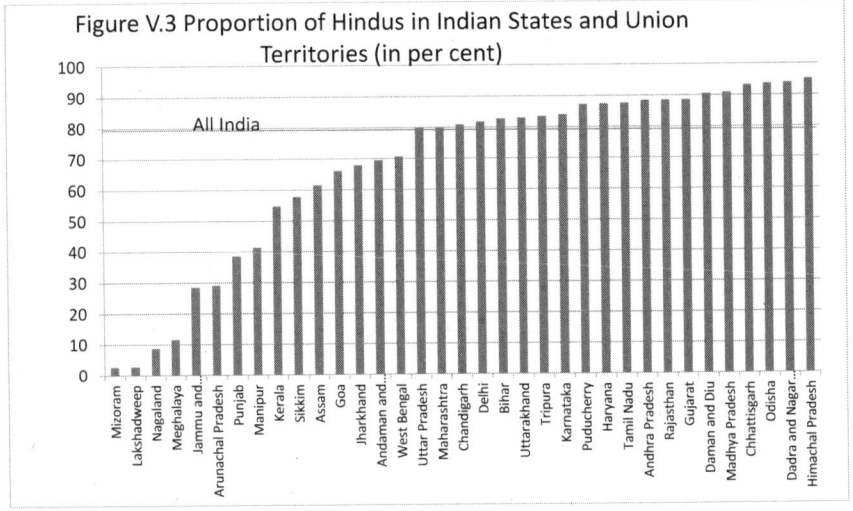

Figure V.3 Proportion of Hindus in Indian States and Union Territories (in per cent)

Source: Religion-wise Census Data, Census of India, 2011.
https://www.census2011.co.in/religion.php

The application of this numerical test with reference to religion in states or UTs makes Sikhism, Islam and Christianity the majority religions in Punjab, Jammu and Kashmir and Nagaland, respectively. According to the 2011 Census, Hindus are in a minority in the eight states of Mizoram (2.75 per cent), Nagaland (8.75 per cent), Meghalaya (11.53 per cent), Jammu and Kashmir (28.44 per cent), Arunachal Pradesh (29 per cent), Manipur (31.39 per cent) and Punjab (38.40 per cent), and in the UT of Lakshadweep (2.5 per cent). However, more than 95 per cent of India's population resides outside these nine. In all the other states and UTs, the Hindus are an overwhelming majority with a share of 79.8 per cent of the population in the country.

V.5 Hindu–Muslim Conflicts

Religious conflicts signify not only a breakdown of law and order and serious miscarriage of justice, but a serious threat to property rights. Almost three centuries ago, Adam Smith, the pioneer of political economy, had emphasized how 'Little else is requisite to carry a state to the highest degree of opulence from the lowest barbarism, but peace, easy taxes, and a tolerable administration of justice; all the rest being brought about by the natural course of things'.[13]

Violent conflicts, or what are commonly called riots, between various religious groups have marred India's syncretic tradition, its leadership's vision and the expectations from the secular Constitution. Some riots have involved religious communities other than just Hindus and Muslims—for example, Hindus and Sikhs in the mid-1980s, and Christians in the tribal-dominated Dang district in Gujarat around Christmas of 1998. Most riots, however, have been between Hindus and Muslims.

Hindus and Muslims share a troublesome history of Islamic invasions on India stretching over a thousand years. For example, the Turkic slave king Mahmud of Ghazni (997–1030 CE) launched seventeen raids against India, plundering and looting temples. The Afghan king Muhammad Ghori (1176–1206 CE) launched several attacks and ultimately succeeded in establishing Muslim rule in India under one of his slave generals, Qutb-ud-din Aibak, whose name survives in Delhi's iconic twelfth century Qutub Minar. Ahmad Shah Durrani, also known as Ahmad Shah Abdali (1747–1772), during his rule in Afghanistan, raided India eight times and is notorious for his campaigns of rape, murder and the plunder of Delhi in 1756, and the massacres of Sikhs, known as the Wadda and Chhota Ghallughara. Ghazni, Ghori and Abdali, much reviled in India, particularly by the Hindus and Sikhs, are revered in Pakistan as heroes who helped in the propagation of Islam and are honoured by missiles named after them. The history of Islamic invasions in India divided, and continues to divide people along religious lines.

The Partition of the country based on the two-nation theory proved its impracticality almost immediately. With people of different faiths intermixed in most habitations, wholesale transfer of population was never in the realm of possibility. Only two-thirds of the Muslims in undivided

India found themselves in Pakistan, while a third continued in India. According to the 1951 Census, the Muslim population of India, at 35.4 million, exceeded the whole population of West Pakistan. The Partition, rather than resolving, only exacerbated the communal or 'minority' problem in both countries. With uncanny precision, Maulana Abul Kalam Azad had foreseen it all—hopefully, for a long period only, and not permanently—to predict: 'Partition would not solve the communal problem but would make it a permanent feature of the country.'[14]

Soon after accomplishing his dream of Pakistan, even Jinnah, its designated Governor-General and President of its Constituent Assembly, may have had second thoughts. On 11 August 1947, he said: 'I know there are people who do not quite agree with the division of India and the partition . . . On both sides, in Hindustan and Pakistan, there are sections of people who may not agree with it, who may not like it, but in my judgement, there was no other solution and I am sure future history will record is (sic) verdict in favour of it. And what is more, it will be proved by actual experience as we go on that was the only solution of India's constitutional problem. Any idea of a united India could never have worked and in my judgement, it would have led us to terrific disaster. Maybe that view is correct; maybe it is not; that remains to be seen.'[15]

Partition came with barbaric religious riots. The tragedy, with hundreds of thousands killed and 'blood trains' carrying refugees killed en route, has been documented by numerous chroniclers and needs no repetition. The subcontinent saw the largest migration in human history, with India receiving more than seven million Hindu and Sikh refugees from Pakistan and Pakistan an almost equivalent number of Muslim refugees from India. Building a secular society after such trauma was an enormous challenge.

Ernest Renan, the nineteenth-century French scholar, had said, 'Forgetting, I would even say historical error, is an essential factor in the creation of a nation and it is for this reason that the progress of historical studies often poses a threat to nationality. Historical inquiry, in effect, throws light on the violent acts that have taken place at the origin of every political formation, even those that have been the most benevolent in their consequences.'[16] Many fundamentalist Hindus in India have difficulties in coming to terms with history. For example, they believe that

Ayodhya, on the banks of the river Saryu in the northern state of UP, is the birthplace of Rama, the divine avatar of Vishnu. They believe that the place of Rama's birth, the Ramjanmabhumi, was marked with a splendid temple which was destroyed in the sixteenth century by a nobleman in the first Mughal emperor Babur's court and replaced by the Babri Masjid or mosque in honour of the emperor. The Babri Masjid-Ramjanmabhumi controversy has been compared with the struggle for Jerusalem's *Har Ha Bayit*/*Al-Haram al-Sharif*, Temple Mount or Noble Sanctuary, between the Muslims and the Jews.

Demolition of the Babri Masjid on 6 December 1992 visibly displayed the trouble in exercising amnesia. Communal riots followed. After a long and tortuous legal battle, on 9 November 2019, the Supreme Court of India handed over the site to the protagonists of Ramjanmabhumi and ordered the government to provide an alternative five-acre site to the Sunni Waqf Board.

While God's demise is sufficient for religious conflicts to vanish, it is not a necessary condition for such disappearance. Belief in the supernatural can coexist with a lack of religiosity in the public sphere. The focus of this book is neither on the legitimacy of religious beliefs nor the details of religious riots, on which a lot has been written, but only briefly on how economic development in India promotes secularization and affects religious conflicts, and hence growth itself.

V.6 How Is Economic Development Impacting Religious Conflicts?

Data on religious riots for the period until the 1990s, painstakingly collated from newspaper reports by political scientists Ashutosh Varshney and Steven Wilkinson, show that between 1950 and 1995, over 7,000 people were killed in such riots. With fatalities during the fourteen years between 1982 and 1995 numbering 4500, compared to around 2500 in the thirty-two years between 1950 and 1981, there were no signs of such riots diminishing over time with economic development. The riots in Gujarat in 2002 and in Muzaffarnagar, UP, in 2012 in more recent times caused a lot of concern. According to answers to parliamentary questions, on average, between 2010 and 2017, the annual number of riots was 712, with 103 deaths and 2164 injured. Most recently, on the eve of former US President Donald Trump's visit to Delhi, riots broke out in its north-western part on 23 February 2020, lasted for three days, and involved the loss of fifty-two lives, with 526 injured and 371 shops and 142 houses set on fire.

Religions may continue with economic development, but the important question is why religious conflicts are not disappearing in India? In many countries, development is known to reduce organized religions' appeal to the people, particularly to a better educated populace. When the income from extra time devoted to work goes up, people spend less time on associational activities such as cultural groups, local clubs, trade unions and political parties, and also on organized religion. Is India an exception to this secularization hypothesis? Is Indian secularism under threat? Can secularism succeed only in the Christian west? It appears that a hasty conclusion may be unwarranted for four reasons.

First, while the macro-level figures on communal riots in India show no clear downward trend, the sporadic Hindu-Muslim conflicts tend to recur in some specific states, and within these states, in some specific cities. There are no wars of all Hindus against all Muslims or vice versa. Political scientist Ashutosh Varshney has noted how highly concentrated the riots were between 1950 and 1995: eight cities, with only about 5 per cent of the country's population, accounted for nearly 46 per cent of all deaths in Hindu-Muslim violence.[17] Varshney explains this concentration in terms of the absence of inter-ethnic civic organizations in these specific cities.

Second, some scholars point out that a state-wise analysis of data on religious riots between 1982 and 1995 indicates that 1 per cent increase in growth rate decreases the probability of riots by 5 per cent.[18] States in the north, particularly Bihar and UP, which are believed to be some of the worst affected by the riots, are also the states that have not done as well in economic growth as the relatively peaceful states in the south. One riot elevates the risk of another, and the underlying declining macro trend in riots may be concealed by the recurring incidence of riots in some specific cities in some states because of either the state's low growth or specific local conditions, such as segregated living and memories of riots in the not-too-distant past, or both.

Third, Muslims in India lag behind other religious communities in socio-economic terms, such as in education, health and income. Their rapid upliftment is an urgent necessity for the country to make progress in economic terms and in population control. However, changes in relative income can upset the social ranking of religious communities and cause resentment. Economists Anirban Mitra and Debraj Ray have demonstrated—both theoretically as well as empirically—that riots may in fact be increasing in some places, not for the lack of economic progress of the Muslims, but because of their economic progress. According to them, '. . . economic progress of one's enemies may heighten the resentment and spite that one feels . . . if a group is relatively poor to begin with, an increase in the average incomes of the group—controlling for changes in inequality—must raise violence perpetrated against that group. In contrast, the effect on violence perpetrated by that group on members of the other group is generally negative . . . a 1 percent increase in Hindu per capita expenditure is predicted to decrease casualties by anywhere between 3 percent and 7 percent, while the same increase in Muslim per capita expenditure increases casualties by 3–5 percent. We conclude that an increase in Hindu prosperity is negatively associated with greater religious fatalities in the near future, while the opposite is true of Muslim prosperity.'[19] From this finding, the conclusion that follows is that riots will decrease when there is balanced growth of both the communities.

Fourth, religious conflicts need to be seen in the context of the loosening grip of the caste system, a predominant characteristic of traditional Hindu society. Even the Indian Constitution, for affirmative action, has come to recognize not only the SCs, but also the OBCs. Formally, most non-Hindu religions do not recognize castes, and the Constitution Scheduled Caste Order 1950, issued under Article 341, postulated that only those who profess Hinduism as their religion could be deemed as SCs. But the Hindu caste system cast its long shadow on the other religious communities as well. So much so that the SC order of 1950 was amended in 1956 and 1960 to qualify those professing Sikhism and Buddhism and belonging to specified castes in the SC order to qualify as SCs. There are many Muslims and Christians who claim to belong to the same castes as the Hindu, Sikh or Buddhist SCs, but are not entitled to the affirmative benefits.

Table V.1. Distribution of Religious Groups by Caste Categories 2004–05

(In per cent)

Religion/Caste	SCs	STs	OBCs	Others	All
Hindu	22.2	9.1	42.8	26.0	100.0
Muslim	0.8	0.5	39.2	59.5	100.0
Christians	9.0	32.8	24.8	33.3	100.0
Sikhs	30.7	0.9	22.4	46.1	100.0
Jains	0.0	2.6	3.0	94.3	100.0
Buddhists	89.5	7.4	0.4	2.7	100.0
Zoroastrians	0.0	15.9	13.7	70.4	100.0
Others	2.6	82.5	6.2	8.7	100.0
Total	**19.7**	**8.5**	**41.1**	**30.8**	**100.0**

Source: 'Report on Social, Economic and Educational Status of the Muslim Community of India—Prime Minister's High-Level Committee', Cabinet Secretariat, Government of India, November, 2006, pp. 6-7

Similarly, in most religious communities in India, there are STs. The balance, who are not SCs, OBCs or STs, are called 'others', 'general' or 'upper' or 'forward' castes in different communities. The four categories—ST, SC, OBC and others or general—exist among practically all the religious communities in India. There is no caste breakdown of the population in Census 2011. What is readily available are the data on caste breakdown of the different religious communities from the National Sample Survey Organization's (NSSO) Sixty-First (2004-05) Round (Table V.1), compiled by the high-level committee under Chief Justice Rajinder Sachar of the Delhi High Court, appointed by Prime Minister Manmohan Singh.

Comparison with figures from NSSO's Fifty-Fifth (1999–2000) Round shows quite a bit of churning in the caste composition of both Hindus and Muslims in the five years to 2004–05. The share of the OBCs among Hindus went up by almost 5 percentage points, from 38.3 per cent to 43.0 per cent, with a compensating decline in the category of others from 30.5 per cent to 25.9 per cent. Muslims experienced an even greater shift of 9 percentage points in favour of the OBCs, from 31.7 per cent to 40.7 per cent, at the expense of an equivalent decline in the share of the others from 68.3 per cent to 59.3 per cent. Differentials in natural growth rates of population among the OBCs and others cannot account for such large changes in five years. Significantly, since classification of caste status is by self-declaration of respondents, it is more than likely that the caste system is blurring. The bulging of the intermediate castes reflects the process of rapid consolidation among both the Hindus and the Muslims. The salience of caste is on the decline. In Tamil Nadu, for example, the AIADMK, an offshoot of the anti-Brahmin DMK, chose Jayalalitha, a Brahmin lady, as its leader to rule the state as its chief minister for well over fifteen years! The emergence of strong caste-based parties, such as the Samajwadi Party (SJP), the Bahujan Samaj Party (BSP), the Rashtriya Janata Dal (RJD) and the Janata Dal (United) (JD(U)) in UP and Bihar, also appears to be proving itself a temporary phenomenon, with the ascendance of the BJP in these states.

'Caste has ruined the Hindus,' declared Ambedkar in *Annihilation of Caste* in 1936. He was not alone; the deleterious impact of the caste system on every religious community has been noted by many scholars. The analysis of the underlying forces at work, like secularism, urbanization, literacy, the Sanskritization process—the process by which caste or tribes placed lower in the caste hierarchy seek upward mobility by emulating the rituals and practices of the dominant or upper castes—and Hindutva politics, or among the Muslims, stricter adherence to Islamic scriptures, is beyond the scope of this book. What we offer instead is a hypothesis that while the blurring of the caste system is a welcome development, one of its possible temporary fallouts may have been an elevated risk of Hindu-Muslim conflicts.

In the context of ethno-linguistic diversity, fractionalization is the probability or likelihood of choosing two persons at random and finding them belonging to two different groups. For a population with 'm' ethnic groups, one measure of fractionalization (F) is

$$F = \sum_{j=1}^{m} p_j (1 - p_j) = 1 - \sum_{j=1}^{m} p_j^2 \qquad (5.1)$$

where p_j is the proportion of population belonging to the jth group, and $\sum_{j=1}^{m} p_j = 1$. Note that p_j is the probability of choosing a person from group 'j' and $(1 - p_j)$ is the probability of choosing another person who is not from group 'j'. Thus, $p_j (1 - p_j)$ gives the probability of choosing two persons of whom one is from group 'j' and the other is not. The sum of such probabilities for all the groups is F. Clearly, fractionalization is zero when there is no diversity and everyone belongs to the same group, m = 1 and p_1 = 1. And fractionalization is almost 1 when there are very many groups of equal size. The more diverse the country, the higher is the fractionalization. It is possible to argue that fractionalization should increase when a religion is riven by more caste divisions.

Applying the caste breakdown of the religious groups in 2004–05 to the religious composition of the population in Census 2011, we get the approximate religion-cum-caste composition of the population in Table V.2. Applying (5.1) to the data in Table V.2, we get fractionalization of 0.79, indicating considerable caste-cum-religious diversity.

Table V.2. India—Estimated Share of Religious-cum-Caste Groups Hybrid of 2004–05 and 2011

					(In per cent)
Religion/Caste	SCs	STs	OBCs	Others	All
Hindu	17.7	7.3	34.2	20.7	79.9
Muslim	0.1	0.1	5.6	8.5	14.2
Christians	0.2	0.8	0.6	0.8	2.3
Sikhs	0.5	0.0	0.4	0.8	1.7
Jains	0.0	0.0	0.0	0.3	0.4
Buddhists	0.6	0.1	0.0	0.0	0.7
Others	. . .	. . .	. . .	0.8	0.8

Source: Table V.1 and Census 2011 https://censusindia.gov.in/2011census/Religion_PCA.html
The proportion of SCs in the total population at 19.2 per cent and of STs at 8.2 per cent differ from 16.6 per cent and 8.6 per cent, respectively, reported in Census 2011 because of hybridization of sources. Also, the figure for the Others (under 'Religion/Caste') 'Others' (in per cent) have been adjusted downwards by 0.0789 to make the total add up to 100.

As religious groups become less differentiated along caste lines, fractionalization in effective terms goes down. If all of them consolidate across caste lines within their own respective communities, fractionalization reduces by more than a half point, from 0.79 to 0.34. Almost all this reduction is from the consolidation of the Hindus, who account for almost 80 per cent of the population. The effect of consolidation across castes in a religious community depends on its relative size. The greater the relative size of a religious community, the greater is the reduction in fractionalization from its caste consolidation. Thus, consolidation of all the caste groups into one only among the Hindus, while all the other religious groups remain as fractured as before, results in fractionalization reducing from 0.79 to 0.35. Similar consolidation among only the Muslims, accounting for only 14.2 per cent of the population, reduces fractionalization only marginally, from 0.79 to 0.78. The effect of consolidation of all the other religious groups is an even smaller and negligible reduction.

We know how the caste system has adversely affected the country by, for example, in Ambedkar's words, 'not a division of labour but division of labourers based not on aptitude or choice but by birth' and an 'artificial chopping off of the population into fixed and definite units, each one prevented from fusing into another through the custom of endogamy'.[20] Fractionalization is known to be at the root of many social conflicts. Should we expect consolidation across castes within a religious community, particularly the Hindus, to deliver, together with all the other well-known benefits, lessened religious conflicts and also fewer riots? The answer is less than straightforward.

Following the fundamental theoretical contribution of economists Joan-Maria Esteban and Debraj Ray in 1994, many social scientists analyse ethnic conflicts in terms of 'fractionalization' and 'polarization'.[21] In our context of religious conflicts, while fractionalization (F) is an important determinant of such conflicts, it does not capture the intensity of animosity between different pairs of religious groups. Such animosity may in fact increase when diverse groups form different clusters, or even one group forms a cluster when the others remain as they were. Fractionalization may decrease, but intra-group identification and inter-group alienation may increase and create a more 'polarized' situation contributing to conflict. Esteban and Ray's index of polarization (P) provides a summary measure of the intensity of the intra-group identification and inter-group alienation with all the known desirable and reasonable properties. It is defined as:

$$P = K \sum_{i=1}^{m} \sum_{j=1}^{m} \delta_{ij} p_i^{1+\alpha} p_j \qquad (5.2)$$

where K is a constant to ensure $0 \leq P \leq 1$, $\partial_{ij} = \partial_{ji} > 0$ is the alienation between groups 'i' and 'j', and $0 < \alpha \leq 1.6$. For our purposes, the details of the mathematical intricacies need not detract, and it is sufficient to note some of the essential features of the measure of polarization P.

Note that we can rewrite (5.2) as:

$$P = K \sum_{i=1}^{m} \sum_{j=1}^{m} (\delta_{ij} p_i^{\alpha}) p_i p_j \qquad (5.2a)$$

Polarization depends on how the members of a religious group feel 'similar' to each other and 'dissimilar' from members of another group. Identification is the similarity that a person feels with the other members of the group, and it can be expected to increase with the group size p_i. Alienation between groups 'i' and 'j' is represented by $\partial_{ij} = \partial_{ji} > 0$. Polarization is measured as the sum of the pair-wise identification and alienation of groups weighted by their shares in the population. Note that fractionalization and polarization are different because of the presence of $\delta_{ij} p_i^{\alpha}$ in polarization. Size matters in polarization—groups of insignificant size contribute little to polarization. For this reason, in the Indian context, most conflicts are of the Hindu-Muslim variety.

Clearly, in a country with half a dozen medium and many small ethnic groups, fractionalization may be high, but even with high inter-group alienation, polarization can be low because of the low salience of identification in groups of medium size. When two groups coalesce to form a single group, while, with fewer groups around, fractionalization declines, polarization may increase with greater salience of the identification factor from a larger group size. Let us illustrate this possibility of reducing fractionalization and increasing polarization in India with the data in Table V.2.

For estimating polarization, we need the values of δ_{ij} and α. Note that all δ_{ij} is the same irrespective of which two groups we are considering or whether the two groups come from the same religion or otherwise is a very bold and simplifying assumption. But for want of a ready and better alternative, let us assume both to be equal to unity. Then, (5.2) can be written as:

$$P = 4 \sum_{i=1}^{m} \sum_{j \neq 1}^{m} p_i^2 p_j = 4 \sum_{i=1}^{m} p_i^2 (1 - p_i) \qquad (5.3)$$

as $\sum_{j\neq i}^{m} p_j = \sum_{j=1}^{m} p_j - p_i = (1 - p_i)$. $P \approx 0$ when there is only one or one exceptionally large and many small groups, and $P \approx 1$ when there are only two more or less equally sized groups.

Applying (5.3) to the data in Table V.2, we find that the measure of polarization is 0.60. Furthermore, like in the case of fractionalization, polarization does not change significantly when there is full consolidation across castes in communities other than Hindus and Muslims. Full consolidation in the case of only Hindus reduces polarization from 0.60 to 0.55, while for only the Muslims, such consolidation increases polarization from 0.60 to only 0.64. If only the Hindus and the Muslims consolidate their caste categories within their respective folds, polarization comes down from 0.60 to 0.58. For Christians, Sikhs, Jains, Buddhists and others, because of their relatively limited size, full consolidation across caste categories in each of these five groups at the same time increases polarization from 0.60 to only 0.61. Size matters in polarization and the limited impact of consolidation across religious groups other than the Hindus and Muslims on polarization reflects their limited population shares.

Box V.1. Polarization

One measure of polarization proposed by Montalvo and Reynal-Querol, a special case of a more general measure suggested by Esteban and Ray, is

$$P = 4 \sum_{j=1}^{m} p_j^2 (1 - p_j) \qquad \text{(BIV.1.1)}$$

Consider $P' = \sum_{j=1}^{m} p_j^2 (1 - p_j)$, $0 < p_i < a < 1$, and $p_j = a - p_i$, that is $p_i + p_j = a$, and contribution Δ of p_i and p_j to p'. Note that $P' = \frac{P}{4}$, and P' and P move in the same direction. We are going to consider what happens to polarization when we change the share of the bigger group 'i' and reduce that of group 'j' while keeping their combined share unchanged as 'a'. One of the limitations of (BIV.1.1) for considering the effect of a shift between two caste categories of specified sizes is that the result is the same irrespective of whether such a shift is within a particular religious group or from one religious group to another. Note that for the bigger group 'i,' $p_i > \frac{a}{2}$. Now,

$$\Delta = p_i^2(1 - p_i) + (a - p_i)^2(1 - a + p_i)$$
$$= (2 - 3a)p_i^2 - a(2 - 3a)p_i + a^2(1 - a) \qquad \text{(BIV.1.2)}$$

Thus,

$$\frac{d\Delta}{dp_i} = 2(2 - 3a)\left(p_i - \frac{a}{2}\right) \qquad \text{(BIV.1.3)}$$

And

$$\frac{d^2\Delta}{dp_i^2} = 2(2 - 3a) \qquad \text{(BIV.1.4)}$$

Therefore, Δ is a minimum when $\frac{d\Delta}{dp_i} = 0$, that is:

$$p_i = \frac{a}{2}$$

and $\frac{d^2\Delta}{dp_i^2} > 0$ that is $a < \frac{2}{3}$. In other words, in two groups whose combined share is less than two-thirds of the population, polarization is a minimum when both the groups are of equal size and decreases with consolidation when population from the smaller group shifts to the bigger group. By contrast, polarization increases when, in two groups whose combined share is more than two-thirds of the population, population shifts from the smaller group to the bigger group and is a minimum when both the groups are of equal size.

Why does consolidation across caste categories among the Hindus reduce polarization, while such consolidation among the other religious groups increase it? Again, size matters; consolidation of groups with more than two-thirds' share of population reduces polarization; such consolidation for groups with a total size less than two-thirds increases it. Only Hindus have a population share higher than two-thirds. Readers interested in a proof of the two-third rule may refer to Box V.1.

A consolidated group that is 'too large' relative to the others may feel greatly assured of its pre-eminence while a consolidated group that is not 'too large' but 'large enough' may feel greater need and capacity for assertion. Consistent with this rule of two-thirds, we find that with full consolidation across caste lines in all the religious groups, polarization reduces from 0.60 to only 0.59, which is less than the reduction in polarization from only the consolidation among the Hindus. The beneficial impact of full consolidation among the Hindus on polarization is partly neutralized by an increase in polarization among the other religious groups.

The important question that arises in this context is: if full consolidation across caste categories, particularly among the Hindus, reduces polarization, and such consolidation is ongoing, why are religious conflicts and riots not coming down more rapidly in India? In the framework of fragmentation and polarization, the answer again lies in the critical threshold of two-thirds. While fragmentation is coming down with the ongoing consolidation, polarization will go down only after two-thirds or roughly 67 per cent or more of the population among the Hindus—which is about 83 per cent of the Hindu population—are consolidated into a single category. Until that happens, partial caste consolidation among the Hindus can elevate rather than reduce polarization and enhance the risk of riots. Furthermore, the role of religious conflicts as a strategic facilitator of caste consolidation, at least in its initial stages, needs investigation.

In this context, it is interesting to note what Pratap Bhanu Mehta has said about unity in diversity and diversity in unity in India: 'India has worked not because of "unity and diversity", the presence of a locus of identity beneath differences, as the state is fond of telling us. We have flourished rather because we are "diverse in our unities", each able to imagine the connection with others in his/her own way.'[22] By Mehta's logic, a partial decline in this diversity in unity among the Hindus is likely to lead to conflict.

The upshot of the story is that while the blurring of the caste system, particularly among the Hindus, is a very welcome development, in the interim, until such consolidation covers about 80 per cent of the Hindus, its beneficial impact through decreased religious conflicts and riots may not be realized. Until such a beneficial impact kicks in, there is a need to work on reducing the alienation between groups 'i' and 'j', represented by

$\delta_{ij} = \delta_{ji}$, which conveniently and too simplistically we have assumed to be unity. The ways of reducing it, for example checking the criminalization of politics, and improving the efficiency of the law-and-order machinery, particularly in urban areas most susceptible to religious riots, is beyond the scope of this book.

Part II

1947–1964—Policy Autonomy

Pluralist Politics, Socialist Economics, Integration and the Colossus

VI

Pursuit of Democratic Socialism

The post-Partition upheaval in terms of communal rioting and large-scale migration was massive. A natural economic space had been artificially divided up into two separate sovereign countries, potentially disrupting trade between the two and hurting economic activity in both. Newly independent India also had to divvy up the assets and liabilities of the undivided country between itself and the successor state of Pakistan. Furthermore, the Second World War had just ended, and it had to expeditiously ease the wartime scarcities and carry out post-war demobilization. In his budget speech in November 1947, the first finance minister of independent India, R.K. Shanmukham Chetty, had complained that the tragic developments had diverted the attention of the government almost completely from normal activities. As if that was not enough, the conflict with Pakistan over Jammu and Kashmir altered the strategic needs of newly independent India, resulting in the shelving of post-war demobilization plans and considerable stepping up of budgeted expenditure on defence services.

VI.1 The Shadow of Partition and Indo-Pak Conflict on the Economy

In the shadow of the Indo-Pak conflict, provisions made for extension of cooperation between the two countries in the fields of defence, currency and public finance and communication did not last for long. For example,

Field Marshall Sir Claude Auchinlek, commander-in-chief of the British Indian army since June 1943, had become the British supreme commander of India and Pakistan on 15 August 1947. But this supreme commander's office did not last after November 1947, when the two countries appointed their separate defence chiefs without any common supreme commander. Similarly, Pakistan did not have a central bank of its own, and the RBI was supposed to function as the central banker to not only India but also to Pakistan until September 1948. The arrangement did not last beyond May 1948.

Like in a divorce proceeding, all the assets, including cash balances, of the undivided country had to be distributed between the two successor states. At the time of Partition, the Indian and Pakistani governments' cash balances were determined at a little under ₹400 crore and ₹75 crore, respectively. Of the ₹75 crore, ₹20 crore was made available to Pakistan as a working balance on 15 August 1947. By January 1948, India had complained to the UN Security Council about Pakistan's invasion in Jammu and Kashmir and there was trouble when Pakistan asked for accommodation, through ways and means advances and transfer, of its share of ₹55 crore cash balances. RBI proposed a limit on ways and means advances to Pakistan of ₹5 crore and indicated its inability to release the balance of ₹55 crore because of the objections of the government of India. While the Indian government had apprehensions that Pakistan would use the proceeds to purchase arms and ammunition for use against India, Pakistan objected to the treatment of the financial issues and the Kashmir question together. Mahatma Gandhi, very unhappy about the balances not being released to Pakistan, intervened and even undertook a fast. After a review of its decision, on 15 January 1948, a fortnight before the Mahatma's assassination, India decided to transfer ₹55 crore to Pakistan. Soon after this imbroglio, from 30 June 1948, Pakistan decided to stop the RBI from functioning in Pakistan and let the State Bank of Pakistan, based in Karachi, take over the RBI's functions from 1 July 1948.

The Partition fractured what had been a unified economic space and the strained relationship between the two countries did not help. Before 1948, '70 per cent of Pakistan's trade was with India and India's exports to Pakistan made 63 per cent of its total exports'.[1] Almost within a year of Independence, Indo-Pak commercial relations also became a victim of their territorial disputes. Traditionally, areas in Pakistan depended on areas in India for their supply of cloth and yarn, coal, iron and steel, paper and paper board, jute manufactures, mustard oil and sugar. In exchange, these areas in Pakistan exported to the areas of India raw jute, raw cotton, gypsum, rock salt, raw hides and skins, potassium nitrate, cattle and food grains. More importantly, areas in India had been critically dependent on areas in Pakistan as their primary supply source for wheat and such imports of wheat soon became a major drain on India's foreign exchange reserves. After Independence, this trade was maintained under a general standstill agreement signed between the two countries, followed by the Indo-Pakistan Customs Agreement, providing for duty-free trade. The free trade agreement unravelled when India put an export duty on jute; Pakistan demanded a share of the duty and India denied it.

Friction between the two intensified when the UK devalued its pound sterling by 30.5 per cent in September 1949. India and most other countries in the sterling area devalued their currencies vis-à-vis currencies outside the sterling area in line with the pound's devaluation, but Pakistan did not. It made Pakistan's exports to India costlier and imports from India cheaper. Pakistan started demanding ₹144 for every 100 of its own rupees. 'As under the Payments Agreement between India and Pakistan, the exchange rate between the two countries was to be at par and was not to be altered without due notice and mutual consultation, controversy started between the two Governments as to which of them acted contrary to the Agreement, and trade relations between the two countries were disrupted for quite some time.'[2]

Trade was severely affected after 1948. But it continued at a slower pace until the 1965 war between the two countries, and then came to a halt for ten long years before resuming in 1975. Intense difficulties arose with disruption of backward and forward linkages. The South Asian Association for Regional Cooperation (SAARC), established in 1985, and its successor, the South Asian Preferential Trade Agreement (SAPTA), established in 1993, have not made much tangible progress because of strained Indo-Pak relations. India gave most-favoured nation (MFN) status to Pakistan in 1995–96, but Pakistan denied it to India on the plea that India had a complex web of non-tariff barriers. Beyond the official channels, quite a bit of Indo-Pak trade continued through illegal routes across long land borders and third country routes, mainly Dubai, and involved additional costs, inefficiencies and losses to both the exchequers. Stringent visa conditions discourage inter-country movement of people and harm trade.

Hardliners in both countries are against liberalization of trade. They know the basics of commercial peace theory, namely that trade between two countries will enhance their economic interdependence and prevent them from going to war. In both, there are also vested interest groups, both in agriculture and industry, who do not want enhanced competition from across the border.

VI.2 Democratic Socialism—1947–1964

The Indian freedom movement had little explicit economic content. There was confusion about what was to be achieved in independent India. First, there was 'rural communitarianism', which was against laissez-faire and capitalistic industrialism. It wanted to achieve economic progress while eliminating the excesses of wealth and poverty, as well as the alienation between human beings and between town and country. This nostalgic vision of idyllic and unchanging rural life was also reflected in the Mahatma's *Hind Swaraj*. Gandhiji wrote about the dangers of indulging our passions and substituting our hands and feet with machines. These views had a large following and even Rajaji, the future founder of the Swatantra Party—the first major Indian political party with an openly pro-market and anti-statist ideology—supported the view that civilization consisted not in the multiplication but in the deliberate and voluntary restriction of wants.

Opposition to modern technology and industry had disappeared by the time of Independence. In the almost four decades after his *Hind Swaraj*, even the Mahatma had modified his views about mechanization and urbanization somewhat. The remaining strains of the nostalgic vision of idyllic, simple and unchanging rural life were mostly overwhelmed by the vision of a new India industrializing fast. While India's leadership wanted the state to lead the charge in a 'planned' way, they were against orthodox socialism. Early in 1919, Nehru had clarified why he was as against it as against capitalistic manipulation of democracy. He said,

'Orthodox socialism does not give us much hope. The war has shown that an all-powerful state is no lover of individual liberty. It is the breeding ground of the bureaucrat . . . life under socialism would be a joyless and soulless thing, regulated to the minutest detail by rules and orders framed by the all-powerful official.'[3] From the mid-1920s onwards, he played a critical role in the evolution of the Indian brand of democratic socialism. He said '. . . I suppose I am temperamentally and by training an individualist, and intellectually a socialist . . .'[4] The utopian socialists in the early nineteenth century believed that society would accept socialism voluntarily once the idea was presented convincingly to everyone. In 1929, in Lahore, after succeeding his father Motilal as Congress president, Nehru had '. . . categorically declared himself as a socialist, and in 1936, again as Congress president, he claimed that he spoke of socialism in an economic, and not merely in a humanitarian sense. He regarded his socialism as scientific and differentiated it from the utopian socialism of St. Simon, Owen and Fourier.'[5]

The first economic and social programme of the Congress, which Nehru helped draft and which was adopted at the Karachi session in 1931, suggested—along with civic liberties, universal adult suffrage, and free and compulsory education—the nationalization of key industries. The state would own or control key industries and services, mineral resources, railways, waterways, shipping and other means of public transport. By 1933, Nehru had become convinced about the need for planning, in which according to him, 'the Soviets have put magic'.[6] An inveterate democrat, Nehru believed that India should follow pluralist politics and socialist economics. In 1933, in his writings provocatively titled 'Whither India', he clearly stated that the socialist goal was the ending of vested interest in land and industry. The sentiments of the times were in sympathy with him.

Nehru grew more and more radical between 1933 and 1936, partly because of what he saw as the impact of the Great Depression on the capitalist world. This period has been described as '. . . his most Marxist phase, the Indian summer of leftism'. Within the Congress Party, there were heated debates on socialism. In May 1934, the Congress Socialist Party (CSP), more a caucus than a party, was formed within the Congress and Gandhi resigned from the Congress citing it as one of the reasons and alleging Jawaharlal's open sympathy for the group. The CWC passed a resolution on 18 June 1934, indirectly condemning socialism and socialists for practising 'the necessity of class war' and 'confiscation of private property'.

Elected as president of the Congress Party in Lucknow in 1936, Nehru gave a fiery speech obliquely asking for a renunciation of the constitutional approach, or the process of gaining independence without a violent revolution.[7] This was the apogee of socialist Nehru, also granting direct affiliation of trade unions and Kisan Sabhas, or peasant unions, to the Congress. On both, with leaders such as Sardar Patel, Rajaji and Rajendra Prasad playing an important part, he was overruled. With the democrat in Nehru getting the better of his revolutionary zeal, he followed the party decision and in the Faizpur session of the Congress on 26 December 1936, announced, 'The Congress stands to-day for full democracy in India and fights for a democratic State, not for socialism. It is anti-imperialist and strives for great changes in our political and economic structure. I hope that the logic of events will lead it to socialism for that seems to me the only remedy for India's ills. But the urgent and vital problem for us today is political independence and the establishment of a democratic State.'[8]

It has been famously said that 'the centre never exists in politics'. Congress, during the freedom struggle, was a centrist party, sufficiently amorphous to absorb various groups differing in ideologies. After Independence, with the challenges of governing India and formulating economic policies, it could not remain so anymore. Nehru's retreat from 'socialism' in 1936 was only temporary, and his commitment to socialism revealed itself again, right after Independence, in the report of his Economic Programme Committee of January 1948. Under Nehru, Congress turned left to democratic socialism, an exotic blend of socialism and democracy that was the favourite of that time in many countries, including in Europe. The ideological distances among its various Congress factions did come to the fore. But Nehru, as the *primus sol*, could maintain cohesion and defections could not pose a credible threat to the Congress's hold on power.

India embarked on a liberal democracy and the pursuit of socialist economics. The blueprint for economic policy, as it developed before Independence, was a broad-brush picture with considerable ambivalence. Missing were the details, such as the role of private enterprise in socialist

India and the difference between communism and socialism. The preponderant majority of the Indian electorate had little idea about this brand of socialist economics the country was embarking on. Interestingly, the Indian Constitution of 1950 did not include the word 'socialism'. In the Constituent Assembly, on 15 November 1948, Ambedkar had rejected K.T. Shah's proposed amendment to include 'socialist' in the Preamble to describe the Indian state. Socialism was a way of organizing society, and Ambedkar wanted to leave the people free to choose their ideology.

The socialist part of democratic socialism had two pillars: the state actively promoting development through a plan framework, and the pursuit of 'socialism'. Laissez-faire or the 'hands-off policy' of the colonial government in economic matters had only resulted in chronic underdevelopment. Independent India wanted the state to be active in the economic domain and promote development. The Indian brand of socialism was akin to a mixed economy, with the private sector coexisting with the public sector, accepting the objective of the national plan and fitting into it. Two landmark nationalizations that followed were of the RBI and the railways (Box VI.1), but both were in a way unrelated to the pursuit of socialism.

Box VI.1. Nationalization of the RBI and Railways

The RBI had been set up under the RBI Act, 1934, whose preamble stated its objective as 'to regulate the issue of Bank notes and the keeping of reserves with a view to securing monetary stability in India and generally to operate the currency and credit system of the country to its advantage'. Despite a strong demand by nationalists for a wholly government-owned RBI, it was set up as a shareholders' organization in 1935. The British government's view of keeping the RBI free from active political control in its day-to-day management had prevailed. It had 44,400 shareholders on 30 June 1948.

Demand for nationalization of the RBI had become stronger after the installation of the interim government at the Centre in September 1946. A non-official resolution urging the nationalization of the bank was moved in the Legislative Assembly in February 1947. Both the British government and the RBI were not in favour of such a move. They did not want to commit 'to the sole charge of an irresponsible Executive an institution which plays such an important part in the economic life of India'.[9] Nevertheless, Liaquat Ali Khan, the finance member of the interim government, reportedly without the concurrence of the Governor RBI, in his budget speech on 28 February 1947, announced the government's decision to nationalize the RBI. The RBI was nationalized on 1 January 1949 by paying compensation to the non-government shareholders. This, however, was not a march towards socialism but more a following of the trend in other developed countries immediately before and after the Second World War. Denmark and New Zealand had converted their central banks into wholly state-owned institutions in 1936; Canada did that in 1938; France and UK followed in 1946, and the Netherlands in 1948.

Similarly, from 1854 onwards, the railways had been built up in various parts of British India by private British companies, with the East India Company and its successor British government providing land free of cost and a scandalously high guaranteed rate of return of 4.5 to 5 per cent, when the interest on long-term government bonds in London was around 3.5 per cent or less. There was provision for the government to purchase the lines after twenty-five or fifty years on payment of the companies' capital at par. There was a public outcry against the level of service by the private railway companies as well as the extra-generous guarantees provided. As a result, the government terminated the contracts and took over the private railway companies in batches between 1879 and 1907, and in 1925, 1942 and 1944. After Independence, with the accession of the princely states to India, the railways owned and managed by states such as Baroda, Bikaner and Hyderabad came under the control of the Indian government on 1 August 1949 and 1 August 1950. Thus, the Indian Railways became a major government organization by 1 August 1950. In a way, though, in the railways, independent India only continued with the policies that the colonial rulers had established before their departure.

Industrial Policy Resolution divided industries into four categories: (i) reserved for the public sector—defence and strategic industries such as manufacture of arms and ammunition, production and control of atomic energy and ownership and management of railways; (ii) all-new units to be in the public sector but existing private sector units to continue at least for ten years—basic and key industries such as coal, iron and steel, aircraft manufacture, ship building, manufacture of telephone, telegraph and wireless apparatus and mineral oils; (iii) eighteen industries under private ownership but subject to overall regulation and government control, such as salt, automobiles and tractors, prime movers, sugar, cement, cotton and woollen textiles; and (iv) the rest in the private sector subject to import restrictions and government's overall general control. Industries that were soon impacted by socialism and IPR through nationalization were electricity and banking.

Nationalization of the electricity industry

The consumption of electricity, which is essential for many activities, especially manufacturing, and for lighting up homes, is a good barometer of development. India's annual consumption per capita was abysmally low at only 16-18 kWh between 1947 and 1950. The corresponding figure for the US was 1990 kWh in 1950! The Electricity Act of 1910 was administered by the provincial governments, and a licence was required to operate an electricity company. The suppliers, mostly owned by provincial governments and in urban areas, were vertically integrated entities handling all the three functions of generation, transmission and distribution.

Thirteen months after Independence, the Electricity Act 1948 was passed to make the provinces, soon to be called states, responsible for managing the power sector through state-owned, autonomous bodies on the lines of the Central Electricity Generating Board in the UK. The states were extremely reluctant to lose their direct control over the sector, and the autonomous State Electricity Boards (SEBs) came into being only from the mid-1950s onwards, starting with West Bengal on 1 May 1955. Furthermore, private companies in the sector, except for three, namely, Ahmedabad Electric Company, Calcutta Electricity Supply Corporation and Tata Power Company serving Mumbai, were nationalized. With only 0.5 per cent of the villages having electricity connections, the Electricity Act of 1948 stipulated that the benefits of electricity would be extended to semi-urban and rural areas.

Nationalization of the Imperial Bank of India

The Imperial Bank of India was the largest bank in the country around Independence, and the de facto central bank before the RBI was set up in 1935. There were complaints about its bias towards European businesses and the slow pace of the Indianization of its senior staff and management. What clinched the issue of its nationalization was the report of the Rural Credit Survey Committee in 1954. It recommended that the Imperial Bank should play a key part in rural credit and be a 'part of a wider effort to direct the funds of the banking system into certain neglected, but important, sectors of the economy such as agriculture, and spread banking facilities in rural areas'.[10] It was nationalized and converted into the State Bank of India (SBI) on 1 July 1955, with a controlling stake in its shares transferred to the RBI.

VI.3 Constitution and Socialism—The Case of Zamindari Abolition

In the Mughal empire, land revenue was collected by intermediaries called zamindars. Zamindari—literally from *zamin* (land) and *dar* (holder) in Persian—was a system of revenue farming. It was an office rather than a property. The heir had to obtain a certificate of succession from the government to confirm their claim. By the time of the East India Company's Permanent Settlement of 1793, in many parts of eastern and northern India—Bihar, United Provinces and West Bengal, and in parts of Andhra Pradesh, Assam, Madhya Pradesh, Madras and Orissa—zamindars had become owners of properties transferable without the permission of the government. Even under the other main system of *ryotwari*—*ryot* meaning the peasant—where the tillers were recognized as the owners and paid their taxes directly to the government, many of the peasants, especially the wealthier ones, had leased their lands and become virtual zamindars. By the time of Independence, the difference between the zamindari and ryotwari systems had become 'mainly historical'. With tremendous population pressure on land, zamindari or tenant farming had become a major source of exploitation and led to small, scattered holdings and inefficiencies.

The Congress had been advocating land reforms, including in its election manifesto for 1945–46. In the Constitution, states had jurisdiction over land and hence on legislations regarding land reforms. Many such laws followed, for example in Madras, Hyderabad, Bihar, Uttar Pradesh and Madhya Pradesh. But the right to property was also a fundamental right in the Constitution. Article 19 guaranteed to all citizens the right to acquire, hold and dispose of property, and Article 31 provided that 'no person shall be deprived of his property save by authority of law', and compensation had to be paid for property taken over for public purposes. Furthermore, Article 14 promised to all 'equality before the law or the equal protection of the laws within the territory of India', and had implications for differential payment of compensation to different people whose properties had been taken over. With the urgent need for land reforms, the fundamental right to property was socialism's first Constitutional casualty, precipitating a legal challenge.

It all started with a legal challenge to the Bihar Land Reforms Act 1950 from Maharajadhiraj Sir Kameshwar Singh Bahadur of Darbhanga, his brother Raja Bahadur Visheshwar Singh and Raja Kamakhya Narain Singh of Ramgarh, Bihar's three largest zamindars. Kameshwar Singh was the zamindar in Bihar's Mithila region, famous as the birthplace of Lord Rama's wife Sita, also known as Maithili, in the epic Ramayana. Kamakhya Narain Singh was the zamindar in the mineral-rich and mainly tribal Chota Nagpur region of Bihar. Under the Bihar Land Reforms Act 1950, by a notification on 24 September 1950, theirs were the first three zamindaris that were to be taken over the following day. The three zamindars immediately challenged the order in a court of law.

Compensation had to be provided to acquire the rights of the proprietors and tenure holders. Its total amount and funding were major concerns. In general, the basis of compensation was net annual income after appropriate market adjustments and that too on a sliding scale. Compensation upfront in cash was beyond the government's fiscal capacity, and payment in negotiable bonds was feared for its inflationary consequences. So the decision was to pay a part in the form of non-negotiable bonds and/or annuities. In Bihar, for example, the bonds carried 2.5 per cent annual interest and were repayable in forty equal instalments. The compensation was on a sliding progressive scale as a proportion of net income. Some details of the compensation scheme in Bihar are described in Box VI.2. Furthermore, with many million zamindars—for example, more than two million in UP alone—there were problems in taking over all zamindari estates at the same time. Thus, for example in Bihar, on the recommendations of subordinate government officials, the zamindaris of the Maharaja of Darbhanga and his brother and of the Raja of Ramgarh were the first to be taken over. And this resulted in a judicial challenge to the decision.

Box VI.2. Zamindari Compensation Scheme in Bihar, 1950

Under Section 24 of the Bihar Land Reforms Act of 1950, compensation as a multiple of annual net income was payable at: (i) twenty times for net income not exceeding ₹500, (ii) nineteen times for such income between ₹500 and ₹1250, (iii) eighteen times for such income between ₹1250 and ₹2000, (iv) seventeen times for such income between ₹2000 and ₹2750, (v) sixteen times for such income between ₹2750 and ₹3500, (vi) fifteen times for such income between ₹3500 and ₹4250, (vii) fourteen times for such income between ₹4250 and ₹5000, (viii) ten times for such income between ₹5000 and ₹10,000, (ix) eight times for such income between ₹10,000 and ₹20,000, (x) six times for such income between ₹20,000 and ₹50,000, (xi) four times for such income between ₹50,000 and ₹1,00,000, and (ix) three times for such income exceeding ₹1,00,000. This sliding scale was an important issue in the case before the Patna High Court.

Furthermore, net income was to be calculated by deducting from the aggregate of the rents, including all cesses, income from 'fisheries trees, jalkars, ferries, hats, bazars (melas) and sairati interests', and forests, the cost of works for the benefit of ryots and cost of management. Cost of works per annum to benefit the ryots as a proportion of gross assets were taken as: (i) 4 per cent for gross assets not exceeding ₹5000, (ii) 6 per cent for such assets between ₹5000 and ₹10,000, (iii) 8 per cent for such assets between ₹10,000 and ₹15,000, (iv) 10 per cent for such assets between ₹15,000 and ₹20,000, and (v) 12.5 per cent for such assets exceeding ₹20,000. For large zamindars, whether 12.5 per cent of their gross assets as cost of works per annum to benefit the ryots was excessive or not was also a matter of contention in the case before the Patna High Court.

The cost of management per annum as a proportion of gross assets was calculated as: (i) 5 per cent for gross assets not exceeding ₹2000, (ii) 7.5 per cent for such assets between ₹2000 and ₹5000, (iii) 10 per cent for such assets between ₹5000 and ₹10,000, (iv) 12 per cent for such assets between ₹10,000 and ₹15,000, and (v) 15–20 per cent for such assets exceeding ₹15,000. Apart from the cost of works for the benefit of ryots and the cost of management, other items to be deducted were land revenue, agricultural income tax, income tax with respect to income from the estate and municipal tax.

On 12 March 1951, the Patna High Court held the Bihar Land Reforms Act 1950 unconstitutional, mainly because of its transgression of Article 14 of the Constitution promising equality before the law. It did not agree that progressive rates for compensation could be justified on the same grounds as progressive taxation of income and held that compensation should be the monetary value of the property. The judgment came as a major blow to the socialist agenda of the government. Prime Minister Nehru used to write to the chief ministers every fortnight. On 1 February 1951, in the context of injunctions from the High Courts obtained by a large number of zamindars in both UP and Bihar to stop the implementation of the zamindari abolition acts, he said, 'This raises very important points. Parliament, representing the will of the people decides on certain essential social reforms. These are then, by a process of interpretation of the Constitution, held up by the judiciary. The result may well be trouble in the rural areas of the states concerned. It is the right of the judiciary to interpret the Constitution and to apply it and none of us can or should challenge that. But if the Constitution itself comes in our way, then surely it is time to change the Constitution to that extent. It is impossible to hang up urgent social changes because the Constitution comes in the way, according to the interpretation of courts.'[11]

An elected Parliament had not yet been convened, and the same Constituent Assembly which had drafted the Constitution was continuing in a legislative capacity. If the Constitution were to be amended, Ambedkar, the chairman of the Constitution Drafting Committee, would be drafting the amendment as the law minister. Moving the First Amendment Bill to be referred to a Standing Committee of Parliament, on 16 May 1951, Nehru said, 'Somehow we have found that this magnificent Constitution that we had framed was later kidnapped and purloined by lawyers.'[12] One scholar describes the days until its passage on 2 June 1951 as *Sixteen Stormy Days*, the title of his book. He notes, 'The battle raged for two weeks, in Parliament and outside, across the columns and opinion pages of newspapers, in bar associations and courtrooms, through protest meetings and angry letters to editors. The bill was eventually passed after a bitterly acrimonious debate on 2 June 1951, with 228 ayes, twenty noes and a large number of abstentions, the final numbers obscuring the intensity of the battle.' The First Amendment nullified the judicial restrictions on not only zamindari abolition, but also curtailment of freedom of speech and reservation for SCs and STs. 'The First Amendment implied, according to apocryphal statement by a later chief justice, that the Indian Constitution became the only one that contained a provision providing for protection against itself.' There are speculations about why the First Amendment did not grant exemption to all cases of 'nationalization' or eminent domain by the newly added Articles 31-A and 31-B. According to one '. . . neither the government nor the Congress party at that time was fully wedded to the socialist ideology involving large scale reforms and measures of expropriation of property.'

VI.4 Planning Commission—Institutional Structure

Planning, which would follow technocratic advice and take the country towards a modern industrial society, was an integral part of India's democratic socialism. It was expected to make up for what the colonial state had not done for almost two centuries to bring about material progress through scientific means and share such progress equitably among all citizens. But the Constitution did not provide for a planning body and there was opposition within the party to a planned economy. In January 1950, Nehru succeeded in getting the CWC to adopt a resolution to create a Planning Commission. In March 1950, by a Cabinet Resolution, the Planning Commission was set up as an advisory and specialized institution with the declared objectives of promoting a rapid rise in the standard of living of the people by efficient exploitation of the resources of the country, increasing production and offering opportunities to all for employment in the service of the community. With Prime Minister Nehru as its first chairman, it was charged with the responsibility of making an assessment of all resources of the country, augmenting deficient resources, formulating plans for the most effective and balanced utilization of resources and determining priorities. Setting up such a commission with considerable powers was controversial. Finance Minister John Mathai resigned in protest.

VI.5 First Five-Year Plan (1951–56)

Veteran economist V.K.R.V. Rao, the founder of the Delhi School of Economics, describes India's First Five-Year Plan as '. . . not a plan in the normally accepted sense of the term. It does not offer a description and assessment of national resources, either natural or human, nor does it contain a survey of the extent to which these resources have been utilised so far or of the full range of the task that is still to be done . . . (it) does not lay down targets for achievement in terms of national income or specified over-all increases in national standards of living. Nor does it contemplate the planned production, distribution and exchange of the entire economic output of the country. Thus, the analogy with the Soviet First Five-Year Plan is more in name than in actual content or ideology. There is neither a revolutionary background nor a totalitarian regime behind the Indian Plan. In truth, it is altogether a more modest venture.'[13]

A part of the reason for the 'modest venture' was that many projects that had already been started by the colonial government for post-war economic reconstruction and development needed to be completed or restructured. Furthermore, with shortages of not only food grains but other agricultural inputs such as cotton and jute, which before Independence used to come from parts that became parts of Pakistan, agriculture needed intensive care. Also, inflation was dangerously high, and the members had a conservative outlook on deficit financing. According to Rao: 'The five years following the termination of the war had borne ample evidence to the fallacy of the wartime myth that money did not matter and that deficit financing could do the trick of building bricks without straw.'[14]

The First Plan followed the practical approach of listing various investment projects, ranked in order of basic priorities, with emphasis on agriculture and social overhead capital. But it also contained a macro model exercise, which emphasized the output-capital and savings ratios and showed that the cut-off point on the investment projects list and the growth rate as functions of the marginal propensity to save and the output-capital ratio. The plan also stressed the need to increase savings and capital formation to foster economic growth. It implicitly followed the Harrod-Domar model, named after the English economist Roy Harrod and American-Russian economist Evsey Domar in the late 1930s and early 1940s.

In simple terms, the model postulated that growth depended on investment or addition to capital stock, and investment must be financed by savings. Two critical factors determining growth in the model are: how much additional capital is needed to produce an extra unit of output and what proportion of income people save. The less capital needed for producing a unit of extra output, the higher the growth. Similarly, the higher the proportion of income that people save, the higher the growth. This can be seen as follows: with ₹4 of extra capital needed to generate ₹1 of extra income, and people saving a fifth of their income, an income of ₹100 would generate ₹20 of savings and investment, and such investment of ₹20 would generate ₹5 of extra income, or a growth of 5 per cent. With people saving a fifth of their income, if only ₹3 of extra capital generated ₹1 of extra income, growth would be about 6.7 per cent. And, with ₹4 of extra capital needed to generate ₹1 of extra income, if people saved a fourth of their income, growth would be about 6.3 per cent. Thus, ways to increase the rate of growth would be to increase the savings rate and/or to reduce the capital-output ratio by increasing efficiency and/or deploying capital in sectors that are less capital-intensive.

Food production, which had grown at an annual average rate of 0.3 per cent between 1901 and 1947, grew at an annual average rate of over 7.5 per cent, from 50.8 million tonnes in 1950–51 to 68 million tonnes in 1954–55, under the First Five-Year Plan, mainly due to an increase in irrigated land, new acreage and favourable monsoon. With good agricultural performance overall, the annual average growth target of 2.1 per cent for national income was surpassed with an actual rate of 3.6 per cent (Figure

VI.1). During the First Plan, in fifty-five pilot projects, Prime Minister Nehru also introduced the Community Development Programme (CDP) on Gandhi Jayanti (2 October) 1952 to bring about a social and economic transformation of village life through the efforts of the people themselves.

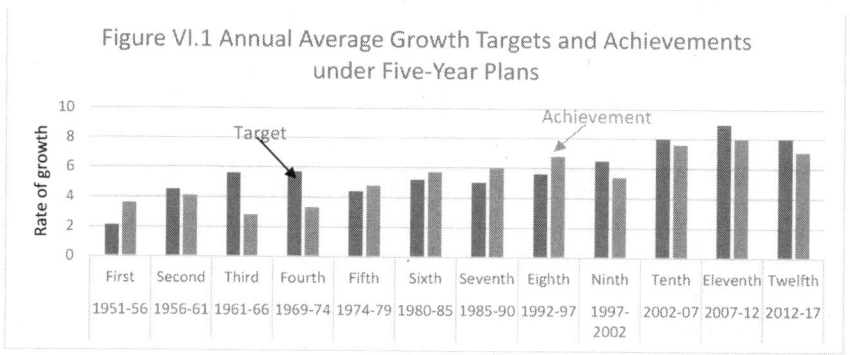

Figure VI.1 Annual Average Growth Targets and Achievements under Five-Year Plans

Source: http://mospi.nic.in/sites/default/files/Statistical_year_book_india_chapters/Five%20Year%20Plan%20writeup_0.pdf

Growth targets for the first three Plans were set with respect to National Income. In the Fourth Plan it was Net Domestic Product. In all the plans thereafter, Gross Domestic Product has been used. See http://14.139.60.153/bitstream/123456789/1488/1/India%20Planning%20Experience.pdf

VI.6 Second Five-Year Plan (1956–61)

The belief that the food problem had been solved led to a change in emphasis from agriculture under the First Plan to industry under the Second Plan. Furthermore, the First Plan had ignored the real structural constraints in the economy in transforming savings into investments because of a shortage of capital goods. For transforming savings into investment, the necessary steel, cement and capital goods had to be available. The Second Plan emphasized this supply side of capital goods in the economy. How much investment can be made depends on how much capital goods are produced in the economy. And how much capital goods can be produced depends on how much investment went into the capital goods industry in the past. While at least some capital goods could be imported from other countries, the Second Five-Year Plan effectively assumed a 'closed' economy or very limited scope for foreign trade.

The Second Plan, drawn up primarily by Professor Prasanta Chandra Mahalanobis in the Planning Commission, addressed the problem of transforming savings into investments by distinguishing between investment in the capital goods and in the consumer goods sectors. It emphasized the build-up of capacity in hydroelectric power generation and the production of coal and steel, and railways to ease structural constraints. Promotion of heavy industries such as steel, to produce the capital goods needed to produce machines needed to produce consumer goods, was expected to maximize growth in the medium to long run. Diversion of resources for building up the machine-building industry meant some postponement of current consumption, but only to result in higher consumption potential in the future. Grigory Alexandrovich Feldman, a Russian mathematician and economist, had developed a similar model for the Soviet Union's Gosplan in the 1920s. The model underlying the Second Five-Year Plan came to be known as the Mahalanobis or Feldman-Mahalanobis model.

The model contained what came to be known as the famous Mahalanobis paradox, namely the preference for capital goods investment over consumption goods investment, even in violation of the simple-minded productivity criterion. The Mahalanobis model showed that extra investment in the capital goods sector, even if it yields lower growth initially because of the capital-intensive nature of the capital goods industry, is likely to result in faster growth of not only output but also consumption in the medium to long run.

The Mahalanobis model for the Second Five-Year Plan went beyond the two-sector framework with just consumer goods and capital goods, and had four sectors: Sector 1—investment goods industries; Sector 2—factory-organized, consumers' goods industries; Sector 3—small-scale, household industries producing consumers' goods; and Sector 4—service industries, including health and education. For the four sectors, the capital-output ratios were stipulated as 5, 2.86, 0.80 and 2.22, respectively. The planning problem was essentially one of how to distribute a limited amount of investment funds among the various sectors to maximize rate of growth and also achieve full employment. In distributing investment funds, Sector 1 was given special priority with allocation of a third of the investment funds. As Ryutaro Komiya, a Japanese economist, demonstrated in an important paper in 1959, the Mahalanobis–model for the Second Plan neglected the demand side of the economy and factor prices, and it could have increased the growth rate of the economy by devoting more investments to Sector 3, that is, small-scale, household industries producing consumer goods.[15]

During the Second Plan, the economic scenario underwent a few important changes. First, the good crop years of 1952–55, which saw food prices declining, were followed by the bad years of 1955–57. In May 1955, India had started negotiating with the US for imports of food grains, under Title I of the US Agricultural Trade Development and Assistance Act of 1954, also known as Public Law 480 or PL480. There was immediate need for such imports when the protracted negotiations ended in an agreement in August 1956. PL480 imports become a major source of urban food supply from late 1956 onwards. Second, the policy emphasis shifted to a 'socialist pattern of society' through industrial licensing and promotion of central public sector enterprises (CPSE). The practice of setting industrial targets, both in terms of capacity and production, for the organized sector became common from the Second Plan onwards.

Third, there was the policy of freight equalization to make available, through long-distance railway freight subsidies, certain key manufacturing inputs such as iron, steel, fertilizers and cement at the same rates all over the country to secure a balanced and coordinated development of the industrial and agricultural economy in each region. This freight equalization policy, introduced in 1956, would be followed till 1991 and benefit the relatively rich western and southern states at the cost of the resource-rich eastern states, such as Bihar and West Bengal.

Third, in early 1956, when the need for investible surpluses was paramount, came the report of a survey on Indian Tax Reform by the famous British economist Nicholas Kaldor. Fourth, the First Plan was basically an agricultural development plan limited in scope, and it was only with the Second Plan that the contradiction between the Finance Commission and the Planning Commission came to the fore. Under Article 280 of the Constitution, the core responsibility of the Finance Commission is to evaluate the state of finances of the Union and state governments, recommend the sharing of taxes between them, and lay down the principles determining the distribution of these taxes among states. What would the Finance Commission distribute to the states from the revenues of the Union government, and how much of the distribution would be under the Planning Commission's jurisdiction? This distribution of powers, which had political implications, needed more clarity. The Constitution does not make any distinction between 'plan' and 'non-plan' expenditure, but the presidential terms of reference started 'to restrict the Finance Commissions to confine themselves to making transfers only to meet the non-plan requirements of the states'.[16] This eventual resolution of the problem produced a workable scheme, but not without controversies.

Major opponents of the Mahalanobis plan framework were the wage-goods model proponents, led by Professors C.N. Vakil and P.R. Brahmananda. In sharp contrast to Mahalanobis, Brahmananda and Vakil emphasized not the role of fixed capital but that of wage goods, mainly food. They focused on the 'disguised' unemployed—'the sons, cousins, uncles and aunts, who live on a farm and pretend to do something since they are there, but whose labour is really not necessary'.[17] This reserve army of disguised unemployed could be deployed in higher productivity industrial activity, particularly of producing capital goods, and they could be supplied with food by procuring what they consumed on the farm.

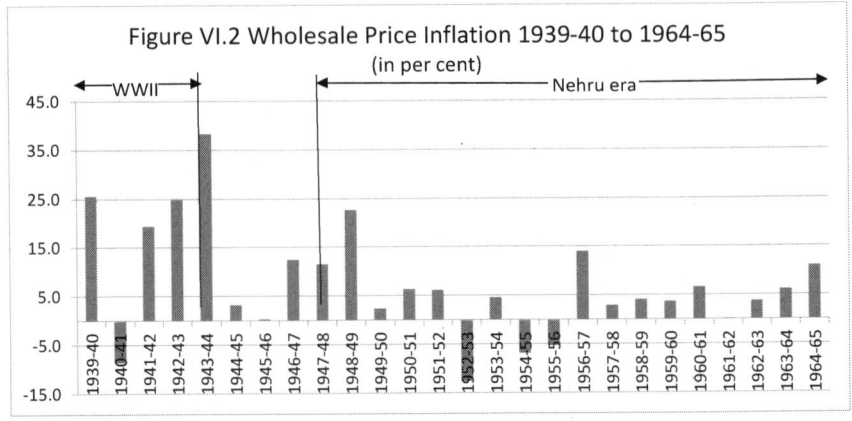

Figure VI.2 Wholesale Price Inflation 1939-40 to 1964-65 (in per cent)

Source: RBI Handbook of Statistics on the Indian Economy. https://m.rbi.org.in/Scripts/PublicationsView.aspx?id=8241 Figures for 1953-54 to 1961-62 based on series with base 1952-53, from 1962-63 that with base 1961-62

Relative to its target of 4.5 per cent annual average growth of national income, the Second Plan achieved a rate of 4.1 per cent (Figure VI.1). The main difficulty was on the inflation and balance of payments fronts. Inflation, as measured by the Wholesale Price Index (WPI), after remaining benign during the First Plan, had shot up to 14 per cent in the first year of the Second Plan (Figure VI.2). It did come down to below 5 per cent in the next three years, only to raise its head above 5 per cent in the last year of the Second Plan.

The current account of the balance of payments includes the balance of exports and imports of both goods and services along with that of unrequited transfers. The country had generated current account surpluses for the First Plan's last four years between 1952–53 and 1955–56. This surplus turned into a deficit of $657 million in 1956–57, the first year of the Second Five-Year Plan, and remained a sizeable deficit averaging an annual $693 million during the Second Plan (Figure VI.3). The current account deficit, as a proportion of GDP at current market prices, was 2.2 on average during the Second Plan. Foreign currency assets, in months of import cover, declined from a comfortable 12.2 in 1955–56 before the commencement of the Second Plan to only 2.0 at the end of it. As we shall discuss, it would trigger a vigorous debate on the role of deficit finance, but the majority view in favour would prevail.

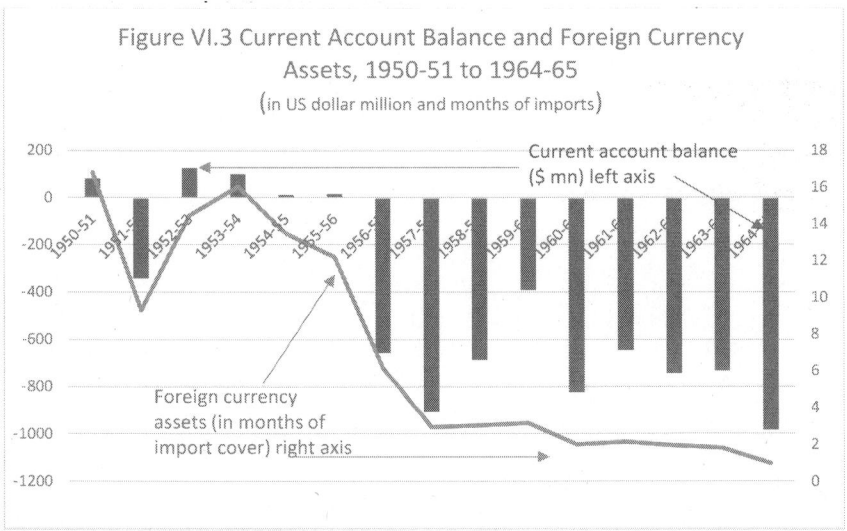

Figure VI.3 Current Account Balance and Foreign Currency Assets, 1950-51 to 1964-65

(in US dollar million and months of imports)

Source: RBI Handbook of Statistics on the Indian Economy.

With the 'big push theory' advocated by the famous economists Paul Rosenstein-Rodan and Ragnar Nurkse, the Vakil-Brahmananda model shared 'disguised unemployment' as a critical building block. But Vakil-

Brahmananda appear to have not paid enough attention to the problems of indivisibilities, externalities and information failures emphasized by the advocates of the big push theory.[18] The mere availability of labour would not allow industrialization without the necessary capital goods and social overhead capital. Questions could also be raised about the implicit objective of full employment now and here in the Vakil-Brahmananda model. Furthermore, wage goods comprised not only food but non-food items such as clothing. Thus, what was needed was a more elaborate planning model than what Mahalanobis produced.

VI.7 Third Five-Year Plan (1961–66)

In an economy, for the supply of its machinery, semi-processed inputs and raw materials, every sector is dependent on many other sectors. For example, agriculture depends on fertilizers and industrial products such as pesticides and tractors, among others. You cannot increase agricultural output without augmenting production in these associated sectors or industries. The Third Plan built an elaborate framework with emphasis on maintenance of inter-sectoral consistency. It targeted maximizing aggregate consumption in the terminal year 1970 while focusing on multi-sectoral balances for achieving consistency.

Furthermore, the Third Plan explicitly built upon exports and imports, and the role that foreign aid could play in augmenting investment as well as supplies of other goods. Policy shifted from import substitution to efficient import substitution by a transition from quantitative restrictions (QR) to duties on imports. Exports were incentivized by reducing export duties on a few products such as jute goods, tea and raw cotton, giving drawback on import duties on raw materials and inputs utilized for the manufacture of exports, and providing import entitlement schemes, including for capital goods, to exporters. The government also started to give cash subsidies on selected exports, such as sugar, in 1961–62.

Despite the focus on promoting exports and efficient import substitution, insufficient foreign aid resulted in scarcity of foreign exchange, slowed down the implementation of projects and programmes because of lack of imported inputs, and resulted in shortages of power, transport, coal and steel in 1961–62, the first year of the Third Plan. The logjam in terms of coal not being mined because of power shortage and power not being produced because of shortage of pithead stock or such coal not being brought to the power stations because of transportation problems, which were to continue for decades, revealed that all was not well with planning, and the public sector at the commanding heights was not delivering the expected outcomes.

The Third Plan was greatly concerned with the distribution of economic power and the ability of well-established firms to expand their capacity, to utilize economies of scale and also to enter new areas of activity. Apart from balanced industrialization, reducing concentration of economic power was added to the goals of licensing from the Third Plan onwards. It recommended 'considerable vigilance' in not only licensing new units but also in sanctioning the expansion of existing units.

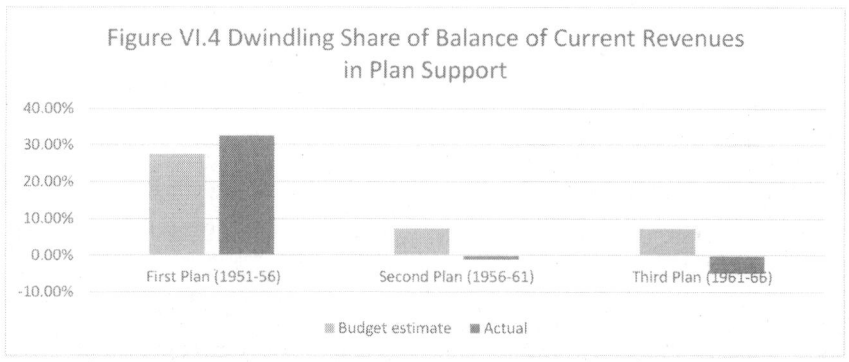

Source: Plan documents, Planning Commission

The fiscal problem from the Second Plan was accentuated during the Third Plan. Balance of current revenues (BCR) is the excess of current revenues of the Union government, after meeting its current non-plan expenditure. The First Plan had started with a bang by planning to generate as much as over a quarter of the aggregate planned resource deployment from this BCR and actually surpassing this target by generating almost a third of the total resources required (Figure VI.4). But with inadequate revenues as well as mounting non-plan revenue expenditure, such BCRs were planned to generate only less than a thirteenth of the aggregate plan expenditure in the subsequent Second and Third Five-Year Plans that Nehru lived to see. And, in the event, such BCR turned out to be negative in these two plans. A silent fiscal crisis was in the making.

The Chinese aggression in 1962 changed India's security perspective and increased its defence outlay by almost 1 per cent of GDP for a long time to come. That left fewer resources for development, upsetting the Third Five-Year Plan and leading to large shortfalls in achievements relative to targets. After the Nehru era, it even resulted in the government declaring a plan holiday and having Annual Plans during 1966–67, 1967–68 and 1968–69, and the Fourth Five-Year Plan starting only from 1969–70. Revenues could not be enhanced appropriately, or expenditure restructured to accommodate the elevated defence outlay, and fiscal deficit as a proportion of GDP jumped up from 3.9 per cent in 1961–62 to 4.8 per cent in 1962–63 and 1963–64. After remaining at 4.7 per cent or less during the next two years, it jumped to 5.2 per cent in 1966–67 and, as we shall see, precipitated a full-blown balance of payments crisis.

The Third Five-Year Plan was a disappointment. Growth in five years had been a bit less than 15 per cent compared to almost 22 per cent in the Second Plan. From 0.2 per cent in 1961–62, WPI inflation had climbed up every year to reach 11 per cent in 1964–65 before declining to 7.6 per cent in the terminal year of the Third Plan. Vulnerability on the external front continued with the current account deficit in 1965–66 exceeding $1 billion for the first time and foreign currency assets in months of imports deteriorating from 3.16 in 1960–61 to less than 1 in 1964–65 before rising to 1.60 in the terminal year of the Third Plan.

VI.8 Rural Development, Agriculture and Cooperatives

In 1951, 82.7 per cent of the population was living in rural areas and more than 50 per cent of GDP came from agriculture, fisheries and forests. Thus, despite the emphasis on industrialization, rural and agricultural development also was the government's focus. In a way, the government under Nehru, despite its political autonomy, did what any democratic government with electoral pressure would have done under the circumstances.

Rural development

The CDP, launched in October 1952 (Section VI.5), was an ambitious project for the overall development of the people, for the people and by the people themselves. It covered all aspects of village life including agriculture, health, education, rural industries, transport, communications and social welfare of women and children. Given the popular enthusiasm about CDP and insufficient resources, in April 1953, in other parts of the country, the government launched the National Extension Service (NES), a less intensive version of CDP. By 1956, a full-fledged ministry of community development was launched.

Under the First Five-Year Plan, 7.75 crore people were covered by the CDP for an expenditure of ₹46 crore. According to some scholars, CDP was appealing because it had the great potential of reaching millions of people as a symbol of the Congress government's dedication to achieving progress and of its concern for the hitherto neglected villager.[19] But beyond politics, if any, CDP had wide-ranging aims encompassing the setting up of rural industrial estates, improving health, education, youth and women's welfare, adult literacy and organization of recreation centres, all of which could not be achieved simultaneously. With only about ₹6 spent per beneficiary over the First Five-Year Plan, the results were unsatisfactory. With the CDP informing 'the villager of the possibilities of improvement without at the same time providing the wherewithal for their fruition', there may not have been any electoral dividends from CDP for the Congress in the Second Lok Sabha elections in 1957. For political reasons, the rapid expansion of projects without testing their implementation efficiency would become an endemic feature of democratic governments in India over time. By 1964, CDP had covered the entire country but it was judged to be a failure, primarily because of poor performance of its officials. In January 1966, the ministry of community development and cooperation was merged with the ministry of food and agriculture to form a ministry of food, agriculture, community development and cooperation. Though there was disillusionment about the CDP, some scholars argue that it played an important role in the democratization of rural India.

In November 1957 came the report of the Team for the Study of Community Projects and National Extension Service headed by Balwantrai

Mehta, the freedom fighter and future chief minister of Gujarat. One of its most important conclusions was the need for an immediate shift of emphasis of community development from welfare to increased production needs in pure drinking water, agriculture and animal husbandry, cooperative activities, rural industry and health projects.

After the relevant decision at the Sixty-Fourth Plenary Session of the Congress Party at Nagpur in 1959, a three-tier plan of democratic decentralization within each state—called the 'panchayati raj'—involving directly elected gram panchayats or village councils, and two indirectly elected higher-level bodies, namely the block panchayats and zila or district panchayats, was launched. Starting with Rajasthan from 2 October 1959, the states started implementing the plan, which was according to the Directive Principles of the Constitution embodied in Article 40. Devolution to the third tier on a secure basis, however, started only in the early 1990s after the Seventy-Third and Seventy-Fourth Constitutional Amendments.

After the shockingly bad crop years of 1955–1957, in 1959 came the report of the Expert Committee of the Ford Foundation on 'India's Food Crises and Steps to Meet It'.[20] All efforts were concentrated to 'grow more food grains'. The Intensive Agricultural Development Programme (IADP) was launched in 1960–61 to rapidly increase production by integrated and intensive use of improved techniques, such as improved seeds, fertilizer, pesticides, implements and proper soil and water management, and providing sufficient production incentives to farmers. Based on the principle of maximum irrigation facilities and minimum natural hazard, it was introduced in 1960–61 in one district each of seven states: rice-producing Andhra Pradesh, Bihar, Madhya Pradesh and Tamil Nadu, wheat-producing Punjab and Uttar Pradesh, and millet-producing Rajasthan. By 1963–64, it was extended to eight more districts in different states. Food grains output increased from 82 million tonnes in 1960–61 to 95 million tonnes in 1967–68. The story of how IADP succeeded in ushering in the green revolution and how the country moved from food shortage to self-sufficiency is too well-known to repeat. The direct benefit of the increased yield, however, accrued mostly to the relatively affluent and landed peasants, who had the resources to buy the necessary inputs for technological innovation and that too in selected parts of the country.

Slowly, the CDP was overshadowed by the 'grow more food' campaign. Encouraged by the results of IADP, after the mid-term appraisal of the Third Plan, the Intensive Agricultural Area Programme (IAAP) was introduced in 1964 over 114 districts and extended to 150 districts later. IAAP was less intensive than IADP. The idea was to cover 20–25 per cent of the cultivated area of the country and select districts based on assured irrigation and predominant crops.

Utilising '. . . to the fullest extent possible the manpower resources of the country and to ensure a substantial expansion in employment opportunities' was one of the basic objectives of the Third Plan.[21] For this objective, almost simultaneously with IADP, the Rural Works Programme was launched in 1961. Because of resource constraints, only a fraction of what was planned was finally spent on the programme. Eight years later, the programme was given an unceremonious burial in the Draft Fourth Plan, released in March 1969, on the grounds that it had not yielded results commensurate with the expenditure.

Agricultural credit and cooperatives

The RBI Act 1934 (Section 54) assigns RBI the responsibility 'to study various aspects of rural credit and development' and have an Agricultural Credit Department. Even before Independence, RBI's refinance facility was available to commercial banks for agricultural loans, but there was limited buy-in. The focus gradually, and particularly after Independence and nationalization of RBI, shifted to the agricultural cooperative movement. The RBI Act was amended in 1955 to provide for the establishment of two funds, namely the National Agricultural Credit (Long-Term Operations) Fund and National Agricultural Credit (Stabilization) Fund. But the dominance of the private moneylenders in rural credit continued.

Traditionally, commercial banks and other credit institutions shied away from agricultural loans because of the smallness of individual loans, the poor value of the securities offered, the difficulties involved in the marketing of the collaterals and, consequently, the greater risk involved in such loans. In the absence of institutional credit, agriculturists and rural artisans were left to the mercy of moneylenders, who more often than not were usurious and far from transparent in their dealings. To increase farmers' access to institutional credit, in July 1963, the RBI also set up the Agricultural Refinance Corporation, with a paid-up share capital of ₹5 crore, for supplementing banks' resources. It was later called the Agricultural Refinance and Development Corporation (ARDC).

The decennial all-India rural credit surveys showed progress in extending the reach of cooperative credit to agriculture and rural artisans during the Nehru era, and their borrowings from co-operatives as a proportion of their total borrowings increased from 3.1 per cent in 1951 to 15.5 per cent in 1961 and further to 22.7 per cent in 1971. The report of the All-India Rural Credit Review Committee in 1969 pointed out that the integrated scheme of rural credit envisaged by the Rural Credit Survey (1954) with state participation at every level of the cooperative structure was not pursued vigorously in all the states. Furthermore, there were problems of poor recovery and poor financial conditions of cooperative credit societies.

VII

Industrial Licensing, Public Sector Undertakings and Commanding Heights

Even before the republic came into being in 1950, the Industries (Development and Control) Bill in April 1949 stipulated that existing industries had to register with the government and apply for a licence before any new facility could be built. An exasperated Ghanshyam Das Birla (G.D. Birla, or simply Birla henceforth), widely acknowledged as a genius among the Indian business community in the period between 1940 and 1970, complained to Finance Minister John Mathai: 'It seems as if we businessmen with all our experience have forgotten all about our art. The order will now come from the Secretariat as to how to produce, when to produce, what to produce, where to produce.'[1]

Birla had set up the Hindustan Aluminium Corporation Ltd (HINDALCO) in 1958, and after obtaining the necessary approvals, started production in October 1962. Over time, HINDALCO grew to be the world's largest aluminium rolling company and one of Asia's biggest producers of primary aluminium. Birla had foreseen a rapid expansion in the demand for steel and had also wanted to get into iron and steel in the 1950s. The West Bengal government had been proposing to set up a coke oven and gas production plant in Durgapur. As Birla drew up detailed plans for setting up a pig iron plant initially, later to be expanded into a full-fledged steel mill, in 1951, West Bengal Chief Minister Dr Bidhan Chandra Roy suggested Durgapur as the location. In Durgapur, the government's coke oven plant could complement Birla's steel mill.

Birla's initial feedback from ministers for industry and for finance was positive. After getting the necessary approvals, he registered the Durgapur Iron and Steel Co. with an authorized capital of ₹50 crore. But it all came to nought. In the autumn of 1954, the West Bengal government's proposed coke oven project was turned down by the Planning Commission. Soon thereafter, Nehru himself turned down Birla's proposal as it went against IPR 1948's stipulation that future expansion of steel should be in the public sector. Had Birla been given the approval to set up a steel plant in Durgapur, even if it did not match the performance of HINDALCO in aluminium, would the outcome have been better than what was obtained under the publicly-owned Steel Authority of India Ltd's (SAIL) Durgapur steel plant? What would have happened without the widespread controls and restrictions on economic activity in the private sector is a matter of speculation, but it is useful to summarize the restrictions inherited from wartime, which only increased with the introduction of the planning framework.

VII.1 Widespread Controls and Restrictions on Real Economic Activity

Around Independence, many of the widespread controls and restrictions on economic activity in the real sector from the Second World War were compounded by new restrictions necessitated by the planning framework.

Continuation of Wartime Restrictions

During the Second World War, to address the problem of severe shortages of many commodities, the British rulers added certain rules to the India Act in 1939. These continued up to 1946, when the Essential Supplies (Temporary Powers) Act was passed. After Independence, with the expectation that wartime scarcities would ease, the government announced a gradual dismantling of controls on prices, movement, procurement and distribution of food grains. In 1947, a foodgrain policy committee headed by Sir Purushotamdas Thakurdas recommended liquidation of the rationing commitments as well as food imports in a gradual manner, building up of a reserve stock of 0.5 to 1 million tons of food grains, and steps to increase annual production by 10 million tonnes. But, by September 1948, particularly with the disruption of supplies of wheat from West Pakistan, prices failed to decline. Controls were back. In agriculture, this was one of the many policy reversals that were to follow. India continued with a mainly urban-centric PDS for food that it had inherited from wartime. Under a social policy of planned development with distributive justice, it was extended to rural areas with chronic food shortages. There were two types of ration areas—statutory with only ration shops as sources of supply, and non-statutory with ration shops supplementing private shops as sources of supply.

The Essential Supplies (Temporary Powers) Act 1946 remained in force till 26 January 1955. With shortages continuing, a permanent measure for control of supply and prices of essential commodities was considered necessary. The Constitution was suitably amended for this purpose in 1954 by adding entry No.33 to list 3 (concurrent list with jurisdiction of both the Centre and the States) of its Seventh Schedule. The Essential Commodities Act came into effect on 1 April 1955 to provide the legal framework for the government to extend price controls, or remove them, on commodities that it deemed 'essential' by notification. The list eventually included steel, cement, drugs, nonferrous metals, chemicals, fertilizer, coal, automobiles, tires and tubes, cotton textiles, food grains, bread, butter and vegetable oils, among others. Both the Central and state governments acquired the power to control production, supply and distribution of such commodities and impose punitive measures, including confiscation of stocks.

With good crop output between 1952 and 1955, prices started declining and 1954 saw the lowest food prices in post-Independence India. Controls on food grains were no longer seen to be necessary, were relaxed in 1953 and then completely removed, except for on rice, in 1954. The bad crop years of 1955–1957 saw the controls come back, and in 1958, the restarting of procurement of cereals. PDS was reintroduced with other essential commodities—sugar, cooking coal and kerosene oil—added to it. By the end of the Second Five-Year Plan, 'PDS had changed from the typical rationing system to a social safety system, making available food grains at a "fair price" so that access of households to food grains could be improved and such distribution could keep a check on the speculative tendencies in the market. The concept of buffer stocks was also incorporated in the overall food policy, although no buffer worth the name got created in view of easy and continuous availability of food grains under . . . PL480.'[2] Ration shops started to be called 'fair price shops' (FPS) and their number went up from 18,000 in 1957 to 51,000 in 1961.

Planning-related restrictions on industrial activity

If the Industrial Policy Resolution of April 1948 had laid the foundation of the mixed economy, the manifesto of the Congress for the first general election in 1952 had clearly spelt out its vision. In industry, beyond investments in public sector enterprises, the state would direct private sector investments by physical controls operating through an exhaustive licensing system. The licensing system would not only tally with detailed targets set by the Planning Commission in successive Five-Year Plans but also specify the pattern of investment down to the product level, together with the choice of technology, scale, location, import content and foreign collaboration in finance and know-how.

The Industries (Development and Regulation) Act (IDRA) 1951 was a diluted version of the April 1949 Industries (Development and Control) Bill, with, significantly, the name changed from Development and Control to Development and Regulation. But even this diluted version gave powers to the government to exercise control over production, distribution and prices. Many of the pervasive wartime controls over prices, production and use of foreign exchange could continue under IDRA 1951 and the Essential Commodities Act of 1955. A significant item in the controlled list was fertilizers, which in 1957 was brought under Fertilizer Control Order (FCO) to regulate its sale, price and quality. Over time, subsidies on fertilizers, particularly nitrogenous fertilizers, would become a major drain on the exchequer as well as a major cause of excessive use of urea, leading to not only an imbalance in the use of nitrogen-phosphorus-potassium mix and soil degradation but also groundwater pollution. Successive governments would struggle to correct the problem, but with limited success.

Selective credit control

The RBI traditionally distinguished between the post-kharif harvest busy season (October-March) and the slack season (April-September). Conditions in the market for funds tended to be tight during the busy season because of the money required to purchase and store the harvest, withdrawal of funds for year-end disbursement, for transfer to government by corporates and public sector enterprises, and flotation of loans by state governments and the railways. The Banking Regulation Act 1949 gave wide-ranging powers to the RBI to discourage credit for inessential purposes. The RBI issued its first directive for selective credit control on 17 May 1956 to restrict advances against paddy and rice, and later extended it to food grains, pulses, oil seeds, vegetables and sugar. In 1956, the RBI also started to fix margin requirements, namely the part of the funds required that could not be borrowed from the banks and were to be met only by the borrower's own funds. It started to control credit by varying the margin requirements—raising them in inflationary periods and lowering them when prices were soft.

The RBI stipulated specific restrictions on bank advances against specified sensitive commodities to prevent their speculative holding with the help of bank credit. For curbing inflation, from the mid-1960s, by selective credit controls, RBI tried to restrict agricultural commodity financing to trade and industry by raising interest and margin requirements on such loans and also prescribing low aggregate ceilings on such advances. In 1965, the RBI also introduced the credit authorization scheme, whereunder commercial banks had to obtain its prior approval for giving any fresh credit of ₹1 crore or more to any single party. Some argue that such restrictions were counterproductive, as trade and industry borrowed at usurious rates from the informal market and the higher cost of stock holding led to higher prices in the future.

Five months before Independence, Foreign Exchange Regulation Act (FERA), 1947 had been passed to put exchange control regulations on a statutory footing. Initially, it was valid for five years. But in 1952, it was extended for another five years, and put on a permanent footing in 1957. RBI, to which the Government delegated the authority for day-to-day administration of FERA, created the Exchange Control Department and it became a 'striking presence' in the RBI, 'both in size and importance.' The Enforcement Directorate (ED) was set up as an independent entity in the Economic Affairs Department of the Finance Ministry in May 1956. It had the powers of search, seizure, and arrest, and could adjudicate contraventions of FERA and impose penalties up to three times the sum involved, and upon conviction, imprison the guilty up to two years.

VII.2 Industrial Licensing—The Key to Planned Development

With IDRA 1951, licensing was on in the Indian economy. A licence was a document issued by the ministry of industry, permitting a plant to begin or continue production in an industry. It told the relevant establishments what, how much and how to produce, and where. It gave the state the power to ensure private establishments invested in 'desirable industries and locations'. It could also, at least theoretically, reduce the concentration of economic power.

IDRA 1951 listed thirty-eight broad industries and specific products thereunder in its first schedule, called them scheduled industries and subjected them to registration, licensing requirements and permission for establishment and start of operations, expansion of operations in terms of scale or new products, and change of location and maintenance of quality and output levels. For some time, licensing applied even to small-scale establishments in the scheduled industries. Box VII.1 contains some details of the wide reach of and elaborate procedure under industrial licensing.

Box VII.1 Wide Reach and Elaborate Procedure of Industrial Licensing

Of the three schedules attached to IDRA 1951, the first contained a list of thirty-eight broad industries, including a group called miscellaneous industries. Industries included in the first schedule were described as scheduled industry and: (i) had to be registered with the government within a prescribed period; (ii) where no new industrial unit could be established

---

or existing units substantially expanded without a license; (iii) where the government could order an investigation in respect of any scheduled industry or undertaking if, in its opinion, there had been or was likely to be an unjustifiable fall in the volume of production in the industry or undertaking or if there was a marked deterioration in quality or an increase in price for which there was no justification; and (iv) in the event of an entity not carrying out the directions issued after such an investigation, the government could take over its management.

Licenses were of five types: (i) new undertaking, (ii) substantial expansion of an existing licensed undertaking, (iii) production of a new article, (iv) change of location, and (v) carrying on business by an undertaking to which the provisions of the IDRA did not originally apply but became applicable subsequently. Initially, the idea was to exempt small-scale units, even in Scheduled Industries, from the provisions of IDRA. But the original exemption for investment below ₹1 lakh was removed in 1953 and replaced by an explicit provision empowering the government to exempt scheduled industries or industrial undertakings from the provisions of the Act. Between 1953 and 1960, all undertakings satisfying the criterion of a 'factory' were subject to the provisions of the Act. After 1960, the criteria for exemption kept changing.

For implementation, Industrial Policy Resolution 1956 emphasized the institutions created under IDRA 1951, namely the Central Advisory Council for Industries and, more important, the Development Council. It also mentioned the availability of the control of capital issues together with financial and other types of assistance and incentives to ensure that private industry developed according to plan priorities. The resolution also stated the possibility of using the provisions of IDRA for regulating locations to help the development of the backward states and regions.

A Directorate General of Technical Development (DGTD) was set up to examine the technical angle of the application for licences, including prospects for import substitution and export promotion, technological soundness, indigenous content and location of the plant. All licences, after they had been recommended by the relevant administrative ministry such as steel and chemicals, were cleared by an Inter-Ministerial Licensing Committee, which was set up in 1952.

In case the Licensing Committee did not approve the application, it went to the Rejection Committee for reconsideration. The final decision on the issuance of the licence was taken on the advice of these committees, by the minister for industrial development. Apart from DGTD controls, there were several physical controls, including capital goods licenses, import licenses, terms and conditions of the foreign collaborations and local finance clearances.

In 1956, by the revised IPR, the state encroached further on industrial decisions. List A of industries exclusively reserved for the public sector was expanded from six in 1951 to seventeen categories. List B included a dozen industries which would be progressively state-owned. It covered categories such as all minerals (except minor minerals), and aluminium and other non-ferrous metals not included in List A. These industries would be progressively state-owned, with private enterprises supplementing the efforts of the state. List C was an omnibus category of all industries not under Lists A and B.

An administered and overvalued exchange rate regime, with shortages of foreign exchange and import restrictions, operated simultaneously with industrial licensing. QRs on imports avoided the uncertainty involved in trying to control imports through tariffs. Canalization of imports through government-owned entities, especially the State Trading Corporation (STC) established in 1956, provided another lever of control. Exporters were required to surrender all their foreign exchange earnings at the official exchange rate. Importers were regulated by the requirement of having a licence to import. Open General Licensing (OGL), except in the case of items such as poultry, fish and vegetables from Pakistan, had been discontinued in 1957. Only limited quotas for essential commodities were granted to importers based on their actual imports during 1952–56. There was little authorization for imports to traders. Most import licences went directly to producers, in the form of Actual User Licences for intermediates and of Capital Goods Licences for equipment. To protect domestic suppliers of import substitutes, the licences had numerous restrictions on import specification, transferability and 'indigenous clearance'.

This extreme protectionist policy was rooted in the pre-Independence period's widespread belief that, with severe British competition, industrialization in India could not be promoted under free trade. Even the Indian Fiscal Commission in 1922 had recommended 'discriminating protection'. Lala Harkissen Lal, an Indian businessman, was the author of the oft-quoted imperative 'Nurse the baby, protect the child and free the adult'.[3] While there was general support for discriminating protection, there were economists like Jehangir Coyajee who cautioned against such policies becoming 'the breeding ground for fallacies like the home market argument, indiscriminate protection and autarky', and wanted protective duties only 'when no other means (were) available to bring national resources to the aid of a particular backward industry'. Unfortunately, for at least three decades after Independence, what India followed was indiscriminate protection through not even high tariffs but QRs.

There was little opposition to the introduction of licensing as an integral part of planned development. Licensing was supposed to ensure that private industry furthered true social need, including the development of industry in backward areas, and prevent the emergence of private monopolies and concentration of economic power in the hands of a few. Licensing was the *Brahmastra* or Zeus's thunderbolt for achieving planned industrialization. What was not foreseen is that while licensing could prevent industries from coming up in forbidden sectors or places, it could not ensure that they actually came up in sectors or locations that the planners wanted. Indeed, as Gary Becker had pointed out in 1958, there are many situations where government intervention *could* improve matters, but that does not imply that government decisions *actually would improve* them.[4] There can be 'government failures'. Few anticipated how, with the limited capacity of the government to administer industrial licensing, the regime would deteriorate into what, in 1961, Rajaji, known as the Kautilya of Indian politics during the independence struggle, called the 'Permit-quota-license Raj'.[5]

VII.3 Arduous Process of Industrial Licensing

Apart from doubtful capacity and desirability, a crucial problem of the licensing system was the arduous nature of the process involved. In IDRA

1951, there was a provision for a Development Council for industries, but clear directions about how the council would operate within the framework were missing. Furthermore, the Companies Act in 1956 provided an additional instrument to regulate the organization and functioning of the private sector. The private sector was to develop and expand as an agency for planned national development, but in the event, IDRA 1951 worked more for its regulation than for its development.

In 1952, rules under IDRA laid down how licensing would be administered. This included the constitution of a Licensing Committee, forms of applications calling for information, procedure for review of licences, monitoring progress and revocation of licence. For a licence, an application in prescribed form had to be made to the empowered ministry in charge of licensing. Rule 14 prescribed that government could invite applications through a notice published in the gazette for the grant of licences for the establishment of new industrial undertakings. But it was rarely done. Furthermore, apart from IDRA, there were mutually reinforcing controls on the import of capital goods, the issue of capital, and on foreign investment and foreign collaboration. Controls were not always in complete synchrony, but to set up an industrial unit, all the hurdles had to be crossed.

The arduous process of how a licence could be obtained was described well in the Dutt Committee's Report on Industrial Licensing Policy in 1969. Licensing applications on receipt were marked for comments to the DGTD, the Department of Economic Affairs, the Planning Commission, the concerned ministries and the state governments. State governments were required to comment on the availability of land, power and water required for the proposed unit and on the indigenous availability of raw material where such a source had been indicated by the applicant as located within their control. Other ministries and departments, for example, the Coal Controller, the Textile and Jute Commissioners, the Iron and Steel Controller, and the railways, were selected according to the requirements of the case. The Department of Company Affairs was consulted from 1963 onwards; it was expected to comment if anything adverse about the applicant had come to its notice and to examine the proposal from the point of view of diversification of activities. From 1964 onwards, a copy was sent to the Council of Scientific and Industrial Research (CSIR) for advice regarding the availability of indigenous know-how, especially with reference to foreign collaboration. From 1966 onwards, whether the product proposed was already being manufactured in the small-scale sector or deserved to be reserved for such development was ascertained by the Development Commissioner (Small Scale Industries). The Planning Commission used to be consulted on matters affecting the overall development problems such as targets set out in the plans. Comments received from all authorities were included in the agenda notes for the Licensing Committee.

With such complexities, the practice of industrial licensing turned out to be quite out of sync with what it intended to achieve. Not only in retrospect, but even contemporaneously, problems were revealed. But such problems, instead of being identified as inherent problems with the licensing system itself, were considered implementation failures which could be redressed by more rigorous administrative action. This was well before the 'ease of doing business' became a priority. There were a few voices of discord, but too few to bring about a change.

VII.4 Development Banks for Promoting Industry

The lack of finance, of both loans and equity, can be a major impediment to industrialization in a developing country. An entrepreneur with a bright idea for a business venture may not have the financial strength to provide the equity and/or access to the organized financial sector to obtain the credit and start the project. Finance from the unorganized or informal sector of family, friends and moneylenders may be inadequate and/or exorbitantly expensive.

After Independence, for long-term finance, the Industrial Finance Corporation of India (IFCI) was set up in 1948. Many state governments set up their own State Finance Corporations (SFCs) in the next five years. The IFCI and SFCs were to extend loans to small and medium enterprises above and below ₹10 lakh, respectively. The National Industrial Development Corporation (NIDC) was set up in 1954 to promote entrepreneurship and provide finance to the industrial sector, especially for modernization of the cotton textile, jute and sugar sectors. The Industrial Credit and Investment Corporation of India (ICICI) was floated in January 1955 as a public limited company, with the World Bank and the government of India's support as well as that of representatives of the public sector banks and insurance companies, to provide project finance. It soon emerged as a major source of foreign currency loans and an institution for underwriting loans. In 1964, the Industrial Development Bank of India (IDBI) was set up as a wholly owned subsidiary of the RBI and an apex institution in the sphere of medium- and long-term finance.

With licences issued by the government on the basis of anticipated demand, and trade restrictions assuring no foreign competition, business ventures were considerably de-risked under the planning regime, with widespread controls and restrictions. The lender had to only keep a watch on the ineptness or venality of its management. The end of this comfortable role of development banks, with the ushering in of market-based reforms in 1991, as we shall see, would also end the era of development banks in India.

VII.5 Financial Repression—Interest Rate Controls and Pre-Emption of Funds

In the market for loanable funds, interest rates play a role similar to prices in the market for goods and services. In any market, if you fix the price too low, too little supply relative to demand will result in shortages, the need for 'rationing' and even the emergence of black markets. On the other hand, too high a price will lead to insufficient demand relative to supply, build-up of stocks and unsold inventories. Like in commodities, in the market for funds, too low an interest rate will result in too many borrowers chasing too few lenders with limited funds. Too high an interest rate, on the other hand, will lead to deposits piling up in banks and financial institutions without adequate demand for credit from borrowers. Of course, with rationing, those with preferential access, for example the government, can gain in terms of cheaper credit.

Until October 1958, interest rates on deposits were more or less free. From October 1958 onwards, there were ceilings on the deposit rates of various maturities at commercial banks through the voluntary agreement between some Indian and foreign banks. In September 1964 came the RBI's regulation of deposit rates of Scheduled Commercial Banks (banks henceforth)—banks that are listed in the Second Schedule of the RBI

Act 1934 and have to abide by the RBI's regulatory restrictions regarding paid-up capital, cash and other reserve requirements. A maximum rate was prescribed for deposits of maturities up to ninety days, and a minimum for deposits of maturities beyond ninety days. The RBI also started to regulate the banks' lending rates from 1 October 1960 onwards, and gradually, started prescribing minimum, maximum, dual and differential interest rates.

The Banking Regulation Act 1949 also required banks to maintain a minimum of cash with themselves or as interest-free deposits with the RBI. The sum thereof as a proportion of net deposit liabilities was called the cash reserve ratio or CRR. From 5 July 1935 onwards, all banks were to maintain minimum CRR amounting to 5 per cent and 2 per cent of their demand and time liabilities, respectively. Banks were also required to maintain a minimum share of their net deposit liabilities in the form of liquid instruments—cash, gold and approved securities. This minimum was specified by the RBI as the statutory liquidity ratio or SLR, and introduced for the first time on 16 March 1949. The rate was 20 per cent. With mounting pressures on the fiscal front, the SLR was raised to 25 per cent on 16 September 1964. An amendment to the RBI Act in 1956 empowered the RBI to vary the reserve requirement between 5 per cent and 20 per cent of banks' demand liabilities and between 2 per cent and 8 per cent of their time liabilities in India. The higher the CRR and SLR, the less money the banks have for lending and the more contractionary is the monetary policy. Thus, for example, for three consecutive years until 1959, when deposits were growing fast at an annual 17-23 per cent, the RBI sensed a build-up of inflationary pressures, particularly in the commodity segments, and from 6 March 1960, required banks to maintain additional reserves equivalent to 25 per cent of the increase in their deposit liabilities. An amendment to the RBI Act in 1962 fixed the reserve requirement uniformly at 3 per cent of banks' total demand and time liabilities in India (doing away with the distinction between demand and time liabilities) and allowed the CRR to vary between 3 per cent and 15 per cent.

While CRR and SLR are important tools for providing a cushion in times of emergency and maintaining the soundness of the banking system, they can also be instruments for pre-empting funds from or taxing the banking system for purposes such as financing the fiscal deficit. Often, too high a CRR and/or SLR, like in India during the Nehru era, are seen as signs of financial repression. Despite such financial repression and pre-emption of funds, problems on the fiscal front would spill over to the balance of payments.

VII.6 Public Sector at the 'Commanding Heights'

In 1956 came the revised Industrial Policy Resolution—IPR 1956—based on a socialist pattern of society. It emphasized an acceleration of economic growth by speeding up industrialization, with attention to heavy and machine-building industries, expanding the public sector and developing a large and growing co-operative sector. For speedy industrialization as well as for preventing private monopolies and concentration of economic power in the hands of a few, the state would progressively assume a predominant and direct responsibility for setting up new industrial undertakings. The government owned and controlled not only the defence industry but also the bulk of the steel industry, almost the entire heavy electrical and other machinery sectors, civil aviation and aircraft production, and power generation. The electricity industry and the Imperial Bank of India had already been nationalized in 1948 and 1955, and airlines, life insurance companies and provident societies would follow.

The echo of Soviet Union-style state-sponsored growth in the Indian model was striking. After the civil war between 1918 and 1922, when the Soviet economy was flagging, Vladimir Lenin had initiated his New Economic Policy to replace war communism with a mixed economy, allowing individuals to own small enterprises, with the state controlling banks, foreign trade and large industries. Many Bolsheviks were shocked by this compromise. In a convention of the Communist Party in 1922, Lenin had assured them that the reforms were relatively modest, and the state would always retain control of the 'commanding heights' of the economy. The 'commanding heights' consisted of critical sectors of the economy, such as power generation, heavy manufacturing, mining and transportation, which dominated economic activity and were the essential growth sectors in a modernizing economy. Control of these critical sectors, which were at the heart of the economy, would enable control of the whole economy.

The public sector did not produce consumer goods (at least in the first two decades), and through licensing, the private sector was discouraged from producing them. Together with QRs on imports, this ensured that there was no excessive consumption by the upper or middle classes, and enough resources were left to produce capital goods essential for economic development. The manufactured consumer goods industry did not come up, and the choice of such goods was also extremely limited. In the 1960s and even early 1970s, it was difficult to find good quality refrigerators, toasters and electric irons in the market. The Hindustan Ambassador, a car based on the Morris Oxford series III model, first made by Morris Motors Limited in the UK in the late 1950s, remained the 'king of Indian Roads' for decades. The 'aspirers'—just above the poverty line—such as small shopkeepers, marginal farmers and semi-skilled workers, did not have much to aspire to in terms of consumption.

VII.7 Voices of Discord

While socialist leaders of the Congress, with Prime Minister Nehru in the lead, carried the day in implementing the socialist vision with industrial licensing and the public sector at the commanding heights, there were a few voices of discord. Such discord came out in exchanges within the party as well as the government about the role of the public sector vis-à-vis the private sector, both domestic as well as foreign. The debate was beyond the reach of the average voter and their opinions, if any, hardly mattered.

For example, Natural Resources Minister K.D. Malaviya and Planning Commission Deputy Chairman V.T. Krishnamachari had a serious exchange. In 1957, Malaviya, with some others, had started the Congress Socialist Forum with Nehru's approval. He was unhappy about the meagre funding and low priority attached to the oil sector. With oil accounting for only 5 per cent of India's energy consumption, V.T. Krishnamachari and the finance ministry did not attach that much importance to the oil sector and found Malaviya's approach too public sector-oriented. Malaviya accused V.T. Krishnamachari of relying too much on foreign oil magnates in a 'blind way'. V.T. Krishnamachari hit back by calling Malaviya a 'Bolshevik'.

The mid- to late-1950s was an exciting period of Indian economic policymaking. With the brilliant statistician and founder of the famous Indian Statistical Institute Prasanta Chandra Mahalanobis at the

Planning Commission, many outstanding economists—Ragnar Frisch, Jan Tinbergen, Gunnar Myrdal, and Oscar Lange—from abroad visited India and gave their views. To neutralize the influence of the left-leaning economists around Mahalanobis, the US government sent Milton Friedman from Chicago as an adviser. Friedman, like Frisch, Tinbergen and Myrdal, went on to receive the Nobel Prize for economics in later years.

Friedman argued against the Soviet-style emphasis on physical investment, and investment alone, in large industry and handicrafts, and in the public sector. He tried to convince the policymakers about the virtues of the free market. Arguing against overemphasis on investment and capital-output ratios, he said, 'The cathedrals of medieval Europe, the pyramids of Egypt, the monuments of the Moghul empire in India are all testimony to the possibility of a high rate of investment in physical capital without a growth in the standard of living of the masses of the people'.[6]

Friedman observed 'the tendency to concentrate investment in heavy industry at one extreme and handicrafts at the other, at the expense of small and moderate size industry' and emphasized the need for a widely diversified and much more expanded light industry. He pointed out how, in the post-war period, country after country in Europe moved in the direction of expanding the public sector and how 'the results were, in every case, disappointing'. Pointing out the pitfalls of planning in general and directed investment in particular, he said, 'It is impossible to predict in advance the lines of investment that will turn out to be the most productive—as the failure of so many private enterprises amply demonstrates. There is therefore great need for a system that is flexible and can change easily.' But Friedman's arguing was all in vain.

VII.8 Problems Revealed

In the meantime, there was public disillusionment with investments in CPSEs not paying off, and until 1963–64, annual dividend and profit payments by CPSEs to the Union government were less than ₹5 crore. Then there was the problem of corruption in transactions involving CPSEs. Defined as the abuse of public office for private gain, corruption lowered investment, and affected the quality of public investment and of public services such as education and health.

In 1955, in Parliament, Feroze Gandhi, an outstanding Congress parliamentarian who was married to Indira, the only child of Prime Minister Nehru, had raised the issue of Ramkrishna Dalmia, a leading industrialist, siphoning off money from a bank and insurance company to acquire Bennet Coleman and Co. Ltd, the media conglomerate. On 19 January 1956, through an ordinance, the government had taken over, mostly through forty-three nominated custodians, the management of 245 Indian and foreign life insurance companies and provident societies. Through a separate act, these companies had been consolidated under the government-owned Life Insurance Corporation (LIC) in September 1956.

In June 1957, LIC had invested ₹1.24 crore in fraudulent stocks of six companies owned by Haridas Mundhra, a Kolkata-based businessman. This investment, the largest in LIC's short history, was contrary to regulations. Its investment committee had not been consulted on the decision. It was a conspiracy to beguile the LIC of its funds. On 4 September 1957, Feroze Gandhi started his attack on the government for the Mundhra scandal, the first major scandal to break into public almost within a year of the consolidation of the nationalized life insurance business under the LIC. A commission of inquiry headed by Justice M.C. Chagla found that Finance Secretary H.M. Patel had ordered the deal. Finance Minister T.T. Krishnamachari was forced to quit. Most disturbingly, Mundhra, whom Feroze called the 'mystery man of India's business underworld', revealed he had contributed to the Congress party coffers.

Interestingly, the Mundhra scandal was not the first of the corruption scandals in independent India. In 1950, there was the scandal involving Rao Shiv Bahadur Singh, the twenty-sixth 'Rao' of Churhat in Madhya Pradesh, a distinguished Congress leader, a descendant of a branch of the Rewa royal family and a minister in Nehru's cabinet. Shiv Bahadur Singh was convicted in 1950 of taking bribes to issue a forged document to a diamond mining firm and sentenced to three years' imprisonment. The Mundhra scandal was the first high-profile revelation of the corruption problems associated with the government's strategy involving industrial licensing and CPSEs. These problems had started to come to the fore in the late 1950s. In retrospect, the strategy was brilliant as long as it was just an idea. Its implementation was problematic because of the limited capacity of the government machinery not only in newly independent India, but also in the former Soviet Union and in Mao's China. Quite a few opportunities of industrialization were missed because of licensing.

By 1961, Rajaji had coined the term 'Permit-quota-license Raj'. With its arduous process involving informational, monitoring and enforcement issues, the industrial licensing system was not only holding up industrialization, but also resulting in regulatory capture and subversion, defeating the purpose of reducing concentration. Books were being published with titles such as *The Quiet Crisis in India.*[7] Even the government became aware of the difficulties in implementing such a complex licensing system with the limited government capacity.

First was the delay in issuing the industrial licences. Rules prescribed that an application for an industrial license had to be disposed of in three months. But it seldom was. Until 1959, many times, a Condition Letter was issued providing an indication that government would grant a licence provided certain conditions were satisfied. The conditions related to matters like arrangements for import of capital goods and the requisite finance in terms of foreign exchange, proposals for foreign collaboration and methods of raising capital. After 1959, capacity was licensed without any conditions and the entrepreneur with the licence had to take up the authorization for items such as foreign exchange and raising capital with the relevant authorities. The gap between obtaining such authorization and the grant of the licence often resulted in long delays in issuing the licence.

Second was the monitoring of the implementation of the licences issued. There was a system of licensees filing half-yearly returns regarding progress in implementing the licence, but the maintenance and scrutiny of these returns, and action on that basis, was half-hearted at best. Often, installed capacity and output produced were far larger than what was licensed. 'The Report of the Industrial Licensing Committee,' 1969, chaired by Subimal Dutt, p. 193. What follows about problems revealed relies heavily on the same report.

Third was the problem of interpreting the implementation of a licence. Was it to be interpreted as creation of licensed capacity or actual enhanced production through utilization of such capacity? The answer was far from clear. The Second Five-Year Plan document had added the '. . . need for evolving a better definition of the "effective steps" required to be taken by licensing within the periods prescribed in advance'.[8]

Fourth was capture of the licensing system by established industrial houses. Without a system of inviting applications for new industrial undertakings, applications could be considered as and when received. The principle of 'first come, first served' was difficult to follow, with comments from the different agencies to which the applications were referred for scrutiny not received in the same order in which they were submitted. Sometimes, applications received within a certain period were also bunched together for consideration. Often, rejected applications were revived and reconsidered without any definite rule or procedure for doing this. Furthermore, consideration of applications out of turn, or in respect of which expected comments had not been received, was not unknown. No specific guidelines for enabling potential applicants to understand the criteria for successful applications were issued. Applicants became increasingly aware of the relationship between targets laid down in the Plans and licensing policy. Sometimes, additional capacity beyond licensed was considered in anticipation of the finalization of targets by the Planning Commission. 'All this resulted in knowledge about such thinking in Government being at a premium and entrepreneurs, who were in a position to obtain inside information, were at an advantage as compared to others.'[9]

The government was aware of the slow speed and inefficiency of the industrial approval process and from the late 1950s onwards, started to appoint committees to examine the working of the licensing system and to recommend corrective action. Also, there were misgivings about how far industrial licensing had been helping in achieving the desired goal of a more equitable distribution of benefits from planned development. In October 1960, the Planning Commission had appointed an Expert Committee under the chairmanship of Mahalanobis to examine how 'the operation of the economic system has resulted in the concentration of wealth and means of production'. In its report submitted in February 1964, the Committee concluded 'that the working of the planned economy has contributed to (the) growth of big companies in Indian industry'.[10] It also observed that industrial licensing was an important instrument for preventing the emergence of industrial monopolies 'though this objective has to be constantly balanced against the equally imperative need of promoting efficiency and productivity'. It had recommended a more detailed study of economic power and controls in the private sector. Accordingly, the Monopolies Enquiry Commission, with Justice K.C. Das Gupta as chairman, was appointed in April 1964.

The government was aware of how the permit-quota-licence raj was spawning lobbying as well as corruption. In June 1962, Lal Bahadur Shastri as the home minister had announced the decision to set up a committee to address the growing menace of corruption in administration. The 'Report of the Committee on Prevention of Corruption', prepared under the chairmanship of Congress leader K. Santhanam in March 1964, noted how the sudden extension of the government's role in the economy through a large armoury of regulations, controls, licences and permits had provided new and large opportunities for corruption. 'Speed money' to expedite the process had become common, with sections of the staff getting 'into the habit of not doing anything in the matter till they are suitably persuaded'.

In September 1963, the government appointed a committee with T. Swaminathan, Secretary, Department of Supply and Technical Development, as chairman, to examine the operation of controls applicable to the establishment of additional industrial capacity under IDRA 1951, the import of capital goods, the issue of capital and foreign investment and collaboration, and suggest such modifications as would reduce delays in decisions. This committee noted that Rule 15 of the Registration and Licensing of Industrial Undertakings Rules, 1952, which stipulated a period of three months within which decisions should be taken on applications for industrial licenses, had remained inoperative. 'In fact, in respect of 8 cases selected at random for case study, the time taken ranged from 61 to 396 days, and in 6 out of the 8 cases, the period involved was more than 150 days.'[11] To redress this delay, as recommended by the Swaminathan Committee, in February 1964, the government started issuing Letters of Intent specifying time limits for steps to be taken, and its automatic lapse in case of default.

By the early 1960s, Japan had already demonstrated the possibilities of rapid industrialization (Figure VII.1). While the East Asian Tigers were yet to 'take off', the nascent dynamism of the manufacturing sector in expanding its share in value added to the economies, such as the

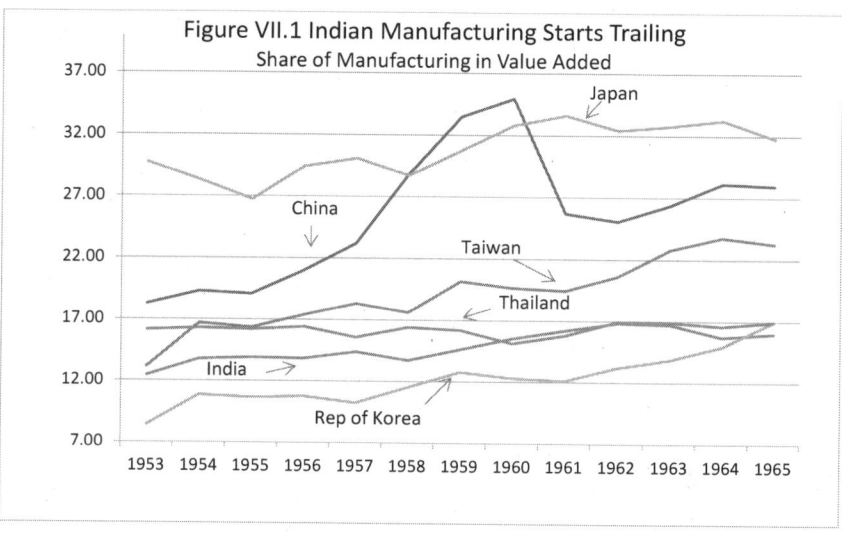

Figure VII.1 Indian Manufacturing Starts Trailing
Share of Manufacturing in Value Added

Source: Groningen Growth and Development Centre, GGDC 10-Sector Database, http://www.rug.nl/ggdc/productivity/10-sector/

Republic of Korea and Taiwan, was already visible. Korea had doubled this share from 8.4 per cent in 1953 to 16.9 per cent in 1965, while the corresponding increase in Taiwan was from 13.1 per cent to 23.3 per cent. By 1965, India was trailing behind the dynamic East Asian countries in industrialization and a large part of the reason could be the permit-quota-licence raj. But there was an unwillingness to look around and see what or how other countries were doing. Recourse to Indian exceptionalism was rampant when India's performance was compared to that of other countries. The argument inevitably was that 'India is unique'.

The government faced a growing dilemma. In a mixed economy, planning and industrial licensing complemented each other. Detailed planning was necessary for coordinated and planned development and avoiding discretion and ad-hoc decisions relating to applications for licences, whether in terms of size, technical process or location. Allowing the private industry a free hand to decide what, when and how much to produce could frustrate the planned development of the economy and result in scarcity or glut of particular commodities. The problems revealed, however, were enormous.

VIII

Tax Regime and Fiscal Devolution

The imperial rulers spent little on developmental activities, and were averse to mobilizing unpopular taxes. Lord Canning, India's first viceroy, is reported to have said, 'Danger for danger, I would rather risk governing India with an army of only 40,000 Europeans than I would risk having to impose unpopular taxation.'[1] Under the British crown, except during the two wars of the twentieth century, tax revenues were no more than 5-7 per cent of national income. A major challenge after Independence was transforming the colonial state into a developmental state with adequate resources as well as implementation capacity. The resources had to come primarily from taxes, both direct and indirect.

Direct taxes refer to taxes such as income tax or property tax collected by the government directly from the taxpayer on whom these are imposed. Indirect taxes, by contrast, are collected from an intermediary such as a retail store, which in turn collects it from the person, for example, a final consumer, who buys the product or the service. Examples of indirect taxes are sales tax or Goods and Services Tax (GST), customs duty and excise. Independent India inherited from the colonial times a federal fiscal arrangement under the Government of India Act 1935, but loss of revenue from the two most important traditional sources—land revenue and salt tax—was imminent.

In olden times, from the Mauryas down to the British, land revenue was by far the largest item of public income. In 1856–57, for example, in total receipts of about £33 million, land revenue of £17.5 million was the largest contributor, followed by opium! During the freedom movement, there had been several protests against excessive land revenue demands by the government or its representative zamindars. For example, after the poor harvest in 1917–18, Mahatma Gandhi, assisted by Sardar Patel, advised the peasants in Gujarat's Kheda district to stop paying land revenue. Similarly, there were the Champaran Indigo Satyagraha (1917) and Bardoloi Satyagraha (1928). In its Faizpur session in 1936, the Congress had identified land reforms and reduction in land revenue demands as a solution to the poverty and indebtedness of peasants. Land revenue, a State subject in the Constitution and a major source of revenue for the states, stagnated without revision of the rates and periodic surveys, assessments and settlements.

Similarly, roughly about a tenth of the colonial government's revenues came from salt. Every human, poor or rich, needs salt for survival. A salt tax is almost like a poll tax covering the entire population. The colonial government's salt monopoly facilitated its collection and the iconic Dandi March of Mahatma Gandhi in 1930 was against this monopoly. In the run-up to Independence, Liaquat Ali Khan, the finance minister in the interim government, in his 'poor man's budget' on 28 February 1947, abolished the customs duty on imported salt and excise duty on indigenous salt with effect from 1 April 1947.

The Indian Constitution of 1950 continued with most features of the Government of India Act 1935 in regard to taxation powers. Its Article 246 and the Seventh Schedule assigned taxation powers between the two levels of government in terms of List I and List II (Box VIII.1) with three notable features. First, both the Union and state governments had concurrent jurisdictions over domestic goods: in the form of excise duties on their production for the Union and taxes on sales for the states. This, as we shall see, would later complicate the introduction of the Value Added Tax (VAT) and the GST. Second, taxes on services (except a few such as entertainment and freight and passenger services delegated to states), as opposed to goods which were tangible and movable, were not explicitly mentioned in either of the lists. Third, entry ninety-seven delegated any other matter not enumerated in List II or List III (which is the concurrent list with jurisdiction of both Union and state governments) to the central government.

Box VIII.1 Constitutional Assignment of Taxation between Union and States

Eleven items under List I for the Union are: (i) taxes on income other than agricultural income, (ii) customs duties, (iii) excise duty on tobacco and other goods except alcohol for human consumption and narcotics, (iv) corporation tax, (v) taxes on capital value of assets, exclusive of agricultural land, (vi) estate duty in respect of property other than agricultural land, (vii) duties in respect of succession to property other than agricultural land, (viii) taxes on goods or passengers, carried by railway, sea or air, (ix) taxes other than stamp duties on transactions in stock exchanges and futures markets, (x) stamp duty in respect of financial instruments, and (xi) taxes on the sale or purchase of newspapers and on advertisements published therein.

List II contained eighteen categories for the States: (i) land revenue, (ii) taxes on agricultural income, (iii) duties in respect of succession to agricultural land, (iv) estate duty in respect of agricultural land. (v) taxes on lands and buildings, (vi) taxes on mineral rights subject to any limitations imposed by Parliament by law relating to mineral development, (vii) duties of excise on alcohol for human consumption and narcotics, (viii) taxes on the entry of goods into a local area for consumption, use or sale therein, (ix) taxes on the consumption or sale of electricity, (x) taxes on advertisements other than advertisements published in the newspapers, (xi) taxes on goods and passengers carried by road or on inland waterways, (xii) taxes on vehicles, (xiii) taxes on animals and boats, (xiv) tolls, (xv) taxes on professions, trades, callings and employments, (xvi) capitation taxes, (xvii) taxes on luxuries, including on entertainments, amusements, betting and gambling, and (xviii) stamp duty in respect of documents other than those specified in item (x) above under List I.

The Nehru era started with direct taxes accounting for about 45 per cent of gross (that is before sharing it with provinces) tax revenues, and indirect taxes accounting for the balance 55 per cent. It ended in the mid-1960s with the share of direct taxes down to around 30 per cent with a corresponding increase in the share of indirect taxes.

VIII.1 Union's Direct Taxes

India was one of the pioneers in introducing the income tax in 1860, shortly after the First War of Independence. The Income Tax Act of 1886 excluded agricultural income from its ambit, as it does even now. This act granted partial exemption of personal savings in the form of life insurance premiums, and such exemption was extended to other savings instruments like provident fund contributions from 1918 onwards. Certain public religious and charitable institutions, agricultural income, yield of Post Office cash certificates, the privy purses of the rulers of the former princely states were also exempt from income tax. An additional income tax called the super tax was introduced in 1917, mainly to raise more revenues after World War I.

With a standard rate of 5 pies (192 pies in a rupee) applicable to all incomes above ₹2000, there was no progressivity in income tax until 1916. Introduction of various slabs and higher rates for higher slabs thereafter resulted in the rate—together with super tax—rising from 6.25 per cent for the first non-exempt slab to 96.875 per cent for the top slab of ₹1.5 lakh and above in 1946–47. At Independence, the rates were lower than that of many other countries for income between ₹15,000 and ₹25,000, but considerably higher in the top-most income bracket. For example, the top rate in Japan was only 55 per cent, and only the UK had a similarly high rate. It seems that unlike industrialized countries, India started to impose highly progressive taxes much before a large fund of private capital had been accumulated and enterprise was flourishing.

Income tax was originally introduced as a tax to be administered by the provincial governments. It was only in 1922 that the Indian Income-tax Act XI made it a tax administered by the central government and shared with the provinces. Similarly, the rates of income tax were originally specified in the basic act itself, and only the Income Tax Act XI of 1922 made the specification of the rates a part of the Finance Act presented along with the Annual Budget. The act also made the charge, that is the liability, in the year of assessment relate to the income of the previous year, and incorporated the super tax, which was till then a separate tax, as an additional duty of income tax. Until 1939, super tax was on a slab system, while income tax was on a step basis. Under the step system, a single average rate was charged on each taxpayer's total income, with the rate increasing with income. Under the superior 'slab system', which was introduced 1939, total income was split into slabs and progressively higher rates were charged on successive slabs of income.

Individuals, Hindu undivided families, companies, firms and other associations of individuals could be charged income tax in India. Rates applicable differed across categories, but until 1960–61, there was no distinction between personal income tax and corporation tax. Independence ended the preferential treatment previously accorded to the European business community and to European civil servants. Distinction between earned (for example, wages and salaries) and unearned incomes (for example, from properties) for tax treatment, introduced in 1945, continued during the Nehru era and ended only on 1 April 1968. The system also had incentives, like concessions for new undertakings, to promote capital formation and economic development.

Liaquat Ali Khan, the finance minister in the interim government, in his 'poor man's budget' on 28 February 1947, increased the exemption limit for personal income tax from ₹2000 to ₹2500. Simultaneously, Khan also lowered the income limit so that the super tax for the rich kicked in and doubled the rate of corporate tax from one anna to two annas (i.e., from 1/16 to 1/8 of a rupee).

Rates of income tax were left unchanged during 1948–50. In the next four years, 1951–52 to 1954–55, while the maximum rate per rupee was reduced from 15.5 annas to 12.5 annas, with a surcharge of 5 per cent, the rates were in the range of 4.922–82.031 per cent. The surcharge, which looked like a temporary measure and did not have to be shared with states under fiscal devolution, would continue, except for nine years, with variations in the rate almost continuously until 2020–21! It caused problems in the realm of Centre-state relations.

Apart from income tax, from 1953, there was also an estate duty—a death duty levied on property—with rates progressing from 4 per cent at the threshold to as much as 85 per cent for estates above ₹20 lakh. Furthermore, this was only a brief interlude before a major change in the direct tax structure. In early 1956 came the report on Indian Tax Reform by the famous British economist Nicholas Kaldor. Already engaged with the Royal Commission on Taxation of Profits and Income in the UK,

Kaldor had come to India to teach a refresher course for university teachers of economics. The Second Plan was just starting, and with tax revenues at around only 7 per cent of GDP, planning was in trouble. Because of his abiding interest in the field of taxation and suggestion from 'influential circles', Kaldor investigated the design of direct taxation in India. The report was published in early 1956.

Kaldor recommended four new taxes: (i) a tax on capital gains, (ii) a tax on wealth, (iii) a progressive personal expenditure tax, and (iv) a tax on all gratuitous transfers. Simultaneously, he recommended a comprehensive reporting system for transactions of a capital nature and lowering of the maximum rate of income tax to 45 per cent. T.T. Krishnamachari had become the finance minister on 30 August 1956 and was in favour of implementing the recommendations. In the face of severe resistance from vested interests as well as implementation risks, T.T. Krishnamachari managed to bring in a capital gains tax in 1956, a net wealth tax and an expenditure tax in 1957, and a gift tax in 1958. The Kaldor recommendations were implemented, but in a truncated fashion. Three of the important components missing were a reduction in the high rates of income tax, the filing of comprehensive returns and removal of exemptions. Furthermore, the expenditure tax rates were not only much lower than what Kaldor had recommended, but also had generous exemptions for expenditures such as own marriage or marriages of dependents. The introduction of an expenditure tax without a reduction in the rates of income tax increased the incentive for understating both income and expenditure. The highest marginal rate, inclusive of surcharge, went up from 82.03 per cent in 1954–55 to 88.6 per cent in 1955–56 and further to 91.88 per cent in 1956–57 before coming down to 84.0 per cent during the next five years of 1957–62. It started going up again from the following year of 1962–63 to 87.0 per cent, and further to 88.04 per cent in 1963–64 and 88.13 per cent in 1964–65.

The expenditure tax, after its introduction in 1957, was suspended in 1962, reintroduced in 1964 and repealed in 1966. During its operation, it never raised more than ₹1 crore in revenues or 0.125 per cent of total tax revenues of the Union government. I.G. Patel, the former Chief Economic Adviser to Government of India, Governor RBI and Director London School of Economics, notes how with '. . . a high expenditure tax superimposed on a high income tax combined with a new wealth-tax and gift tax . . . total incidence was crushing, exceeding 100% in some cases. The Expenditure Tax proved short-lived . . . But its short-term consequences were grave.'[2] Economist G. Thimmaiah believes that the piecemeal way of introducing the Kaldor reforms encouraged the emergence of the black economy.[3]

The three main features of the direct tax regime in independent India until 1980–81 and even till 1991 were the lack of stability in the tax structure, proliferation of concessions and exemptions to counteract the adverse impact of high tax rates on capital formation and exports, and evasion and low compliance.

High rates of income tax looked good for socialism but, with loopholes in administration, led to problems of low compliance and evasions. From 1951 onwards, India started experimenting with tax amnesty schemes, which were limited time opportunities to pay a concessional amount in exchange of forgiveness of an unpaid tax liability in the past. In 1951, Mahavir Tyagi, who was the minister for revenue and expenditure, introduced the first Voluntary Disclosure Scheme, also known as the Tyagi Scheme, to bring into the open incomes which had not been revealed to the imperial government prior to Independence. It allowed income tax assesses to bring into books unaccounted cash before 31 August 1951 after giving intimation to the Income Tax Officer and paying tax on it without any fear of penalty or prosecution under the law. It resulted in disclosure of ₹70 crore and collection of tax of ₹11 crore. Reportedly, it failed because of the lack of confidence in the assurances of immunity from penalties and prosecution.

Corporation tax is a term which does find a mention in the Income Tax law, but is popularly used to describe income tax, super tax, excess profits tax, business profits tax, super profits tax, advance payments of tax, surtax etc., levied on income of companies from all sources. Until 1966–67, there was no exemption limit, the rates of corporate tax were higher for foreign companies than for Indian companies, and higher for closely held Indian companies than for widely held Indian companies, but the rate was uniform across companies within a specific category. The rate for widely held domestic companies, which was 40.6 per cent in 1950–51, increased gradually to 43.4 per cent in 1951–52, 51.5 per cent in 1957–58, 50 per cent in 1962–63 and 81 per cent in 1964–65. Until 1959, corporation tax was based on the grossing up concept, that is, those receiving dividends or profits from the company could claim rebate for the taxes paid by the company. Equality between the corporate tax rate and the maximum rate of personal income tax is desirable to avoid any distortionary tax bias in favour of or against forms of business organization. But by 1964–65, the maximum rate of personal income tax along with super tax was 75 per cent with 17.5 per cent surcharge, that is, effectively 88.125 per cent, which was considerably higher than the corporate rate of 70 per cent.

The Nehru era started with revenue from corporation tax at about 20 per cent lower than that from personal income tax, and ended with such revenues almost 20 per cent higher than personal income tax revenue. With serious compliance issues and significant exemptions and incentives, the progressivity of the personal income tax failed to produce the intended redistributive effects, and personal income tax as a proportion of total tax revenue of the Union government declined from 24.2 per cent in 1948–49 to 14.2 per cent in 1964–65. The corresponding decline in the share of corporation tax was from 19.4 per cent to 17.2 per cent.

In the first fifteen years, income tax in independent India was based on the Income Tax Act of 1922. Following the recommendations of the Law Commission in 1958 and the Direct Taxes Administration Enquiry Committee under Mahavir Tyagi in 1959, the government enacted a new Income Tax Act in 1961. The new act brought in the concept of the 'assessment year' (AY), which is the financial year following the immediately preceding financial year (FY) for which the tax is being assessed. For example, AY 2020–21 assesses the tax liability on income for FY 2019–20. The new law came into force on 1 April 1962. It also introduced a scheme of self-assessment to gradually replace the scheme of provisional assessment. From 1964, for improving administration, the Central Board of Revenue was bifurcated into Central Board for Direct Taxes (CBDT) and Central Board of Excise and Customs (CBEC).

VIII.2 States' Direct Taxes

For the states, land revenue and agricultural income tax were two sources of direct tax revenues. After Independence, the abolition of zamindari and land reforms increased the number of farmers with smaller holdings and lower ability to pay. Land revenue slowly became an insignificant part of the government's revenues. For example, in Odisha, the share of land revenue in the state's own tax revenue came down from 48.7 per cent in 1936–37 to 15.9 per cent in 1964–65. A casualty of declining land revenue was the land records. Starting from Raja Todarmal, Akbar's minister of finance, right up to British colonial times, record of land rights was important primarily for collection of revenues. After Independence, with land revenue becoming an insignificant source of revenue, there was no financial incentive in maintaining land records. Furthermore, the decline in land revenue for the states created pressure on the Union government to bridge their revenue shortfalls.

On agricultural income tax, the Taxation Enquiry Commission 1953–54 reported that twelve states—six Part A states, namely Assam, Bihar, Madras, Orissa, UP and West Bengal; three Part B states, namely Hyderabad, Rajasthan and Travancore-Cochin; and three Part C states, namely Bhopal, Coorg and Vindhya Pradesh—were levying it. The tax was repealed in Hyderabad and UP in 1957 and in Rajasthan in 1960. After the reorganization of states in 1956, Kerala and Mysore introduced the tax in 1957 for land under commercial crops only. In 1961, only seven states, namely Assam, Bihar, Kerala, Madras (now Tamil Nadu), Mysore (now Karnataka), Odisha and West Bengal were levying the tax, but some on plantations only. Maharashtra introduced an agricultural income tax in 1962. The powerful farm lobby, and the argument that in an under-developed country like India with smaller size of holdings, lower average incomes, greater own-consumption of agro-produce and illiteracy, agricultural income tax could only be collected with some degree of efficiency from a very small minority of the rural population, won the day and agricultural income tax, except for on plantations, faded away over time.

VIII.3 Union's Indirect Taxes

The share of indirect taxes in total tax revenues of the Union, which was around 55 per cent at Independence, became almost 67 per cent by the end of the Nehru era in 1964–65. In seventeen years, indirect taxes, which included customs and union excise duties, became twice as important as direct taxes. Furthermore, excise became far more important than customs under indirect taxes. While customs duties on imports applied to goods produced in other countries and brought to India, excise duties applied to goods manufactured within India. Excise duties applied to mainly non-agricultural goods which came into existence because of 'manufacture' within the country – for example, iron ore into steel, or steel into buckets. Excise was collected at the factory gate before the goods were taken out from the production facility under the supervision of the Central Excise Officer. Revenue from customs, which was almost 2.5 times that from excise in 1948–49, became a little less than a half of that from excise in 1964–65. Apart from the development of the domestic industry, which contributed to the growth of excise revenues, primary reliance on QRs rather than tariff to regulate imports contributed to loss of customs revenues.

Though the salt tax was completely abolished on 28 February 1947, the relevant act, called the Central Excise and Salt Act, 1944, continued with the same name for another half a century, and was renamed only after the 1996–97 Budget! The Indian Tariff Act 1934, which governed basic customs duty rates, was amended in 1954. In 1962, the Customs Act repealed the Sea Customs Act 1878, the Inland Bonded Warehouses Act of 1896, the Land Customs Act, 1924 and the Aircraft Act of 1934, and consolidated them, with suitable amendments, under one enactment. The Union government had and has the power to reduce this rate on any good or exempt it from duty. Thus, applied rates could be considerably less than the basic rates for many goods and within the bounds of the basic rates, the excise and customs duty rates could be changed through notification any time during the year. Duty rates varied widely across commodities, leading to classification problems and economic distortions. There was no 'harmonized system nomenclature' (HSN); HSN by the World Customs Organization was introduced much later in 1988.

Three significant features of the customs duty regime during the Nehru era are worth noting. First was the existence of many specific rather than ad valorem duties. The Act of 1944 provided for duties other than ad valorem by specifying that this duty may be with reference to the value, weight, volume, unit, length or area of the excisable goods. The excise duties under the 1944 Act were called basic excise duties, which again, like under customs, the Union government had and has the power to reduce or grant exemption from. Apart from the basic excise duty, there were additional ones under Salt Cess Act 1953, the Tea Act 1953, the Medicinal and Toilet Preparation (Excise Duties) Act 1955, the Additional Duties of Excise (Goods of Special Importance) Act 1957, the Mineral Products (Additional Duties of Excise and Customs) Act, 1958 and the Sugar (Special Duty) Act 1959. Specific duties are stipulated, for example as ₹X per kg of steel or per bag of cement, and are independent of the valuation of the commodity in question. Specific duties avoid the vexing question of assessment of value of the commodity to be taxed, but when prices change and specific duties are not revised, either the government loses revenue or the product is overtaxed.

Second was the existence of export duties on India's traditional exports of jute, tea, raw cotton and manganese ore. Export duties on raw materials were common in the first half of the twentieth century, for example in the form of British preferential export taxes, to promote industries in their own jurisdiction. Illustratively, to promote the domestic leather industry, India under colonial rule had an export duty of 15 per cent on raw hides and skins for a few years around the First World War. After Independence, restrictions were imposed on the export of raw hides and skins from the mid-1950s, an export duty was levied on semi-finished leather from the mid-1970s, and the duty continues to this date.

Third was the absence of countervailing duty or additional duty of customs equivalent to the excise duty (and also sales tax levied by the states) on similar goods manufactured in India. High excise duty and low customs duty on a particular good could coexist and create a bias in favour of the foreign manufacturer vis-a-vis their domestic counterpart.

Before Independence, excise duties were governed by the Central Excise and Salt Act 1944, which included many more items than what had been under excise before. Yet, by 1947, only about fourteen commodities were covered under excise. To compensate for the loss of revenue from the abolition of the duty on salt, and to help the handloom industry, excise duty on mill cloth was introduced in 1949. Independence gave a new fillip to indigenous industry and production multiplied rapidly. The Taxation Enquiry Commission 1953–54 pointed out the need to 'extend excise and sales taxation to the consumption of lower income groups and of goods which are commonly classed as necessaries' for 'any substantial receipts from commodity taxation and appreciable restraint on consumption in the economy as a whole'.[4] Following this recommendation, within ten years of Independence, the number of items under excise more than doubled to thirty-three. The list of excisable items continued to expand with the addition of items such as cigarettes, mill cloth, woollen fabrics, electric fans, paper, soaps, synthetic fibres and motor cars.

A major problem with excise duty was 'tax on tax'. There was no rebate for excise duties when one excise duty-paid capital or intermediate good, say steel, was used for producing another manufactured good, say buckets. This led to cascading of taxes—or 'tax on tax' in popular parlance. Excise duty on buckets levied on its ex-factory price would include the cost of steel including excise duty paid on the steel. The 'tax on tax' problem was also part of the sales tax levied by the states, which is discussed below. Such sales taxes were charged on the sale price, which included the excise duty levied by the Union government. This lack of rebate for taxes paid on inputs at earlier stages was one of the main shortcomings of the extant excise regime. Furthermore, this complicated the estimation of incidence of the excise duty on various goods because such calculation had to include not only the excise duty on the final product, but also the excise duty paid at the input stage. Problems with the estimation of incidence also introduced difficulties in judging the progressivity of the excise duty structure in terms of the incidence on goods consumed by the poor vis-à-vis those consumed by the affluent.

VIII.4 States' Indirect Taxes

Consolidated data for states for the period earlier than 1970–71 are not readily available, but for the later period, the structure of revenues in states may be described by the two-thirds rule: (1) total tax revenues accounted for about two-thirds of total revenues; (2) own tax revenues accounted for about two-thirds of total tax revenues; and (3) sales tax revenue accounted for a little less than two-thirds of own tax revenues. It is interesting to note in this context that no state had imposed a sales tax before 1938! The Constitution empowered states to levy sales tax on the sale of all commodities except newspapers and on the sale of some selected services such as transportation (road and inland waterways) and entertainment. The UTs, like the states, have the power to levy such taxes.

Being a state subject, sales tax across states was levied in a variety of ways including differing points of levy (both single- as well as multi-point levies), with or without surcharges and turnover tax, multiplicity of rates with varying ranges, and differing lists of exemptions and incentive provisions. With such a variety of sales taxes across states, India was far from a single market. This complexity led economist Amaresh Bagchi, in his famous 1994 National Institute of Public Finance and Policy (NIPFP) report on 'Reform of Domestic Trade Taxes in India, Issues and Options', to comment, 'It would not be an exaggeration to say that the States sales tax systems in India are one of the most complex around the world.'[5]

Article 286 of the Constitution forbids taxation by states of: (a) imports into or exports from the territory of India, (b) inter-state trade and (c) sales of goods declared by Parliament by law to be essential for the life of the community. Prohibition of taxation of inter-state sales created a problem—the purchaser of an inter-state transaction was found serving notices for payment of tax to dealers who sold the commodity in the other states. Furthermore, since the Constitution did not distinguish between registered and unregistered dealers, inter-state sales became a major source of tax evasion. To circumvent this problem, following the recommendation of the Taxation Enquiry Commission 1953–54, the Constitution was suitably amended, and the Central Sales Tax (CST) Act 1956 promulgated. The Constitutional Amendment also enabled Parliament to formulate principles for determining when the sale or purchase of goods takes place in the course of interstate trade or commerce.

The Union government retained the power to levy CST on inter-state sales but authorized the states to levy the CST on such sales originating in their territories and retain the proceeds with effect from January 1957. The rate of tax, which was originally 1 per cent, was increased to 2 per cent from 1963. The CST rate applied to sales to registered dealers from outside the state. Sales to an unregistered dealer (such as consumer of final product) attracted tax at 10 per cent or the rate applicable on local sales including additional sales tax and surcharge, whichever was higher.

The Indian market became even more fractured with the introduction of CST and progressive increases in the CST rate over time. One additional feature of the CST Act 1956 was the introduction of the category of goods of special importance—a category that came to be known as declared goods—on which sales tax imposed for within-state sale was subject to the 4 per cent ceiling of the CST rate and the sales tax on inter-state sales was reimbursable. Such declared goods included a range of products, from cereals to jute and iron and steel, and decreased the intensity of fracturing in the Indian market to some extent.

If the CST was a tax rental arrangement whereby the Union authorized the states to collect the CST and retain its proceeds, there was another tax rental agreement whereby the states authorized the Union to levy excise duty on mill-made textile, sugar and tobacco in lieu of sales tax, and distribute the proceeds appropriately among the states. The logic in favour of this arrangement stemmed from the relative ease with which excise duty could be collected from and paid by the producers at the production site itself rather than the myriad points of sales across states, as well as having a uniform system of taxation and rates across the country. The Second Finance Commission was asked to work out how the proceeds should be distributed among the states to compensate for their loss of sales tax revenues from these items, and this distribution formula along with the rates were specified in the Act itself.

For persuading the states to accept the introduction of the additional excise duty in lieu of sales tax, the Union government had to guarantee that the shares accruing to each state would not be less than the revenue realized by the state in the year 1956–57 from the levy of sales tax on the commodities which were brought under the new regime of additional duties of excise in lieu of sales tax. As we shall see, there would be repeats of a similar scheme of guaranteed revenues for the states when value added tax (VAT) would replace sales tax after 1 April 2003, and also when GST would replace VAT in 2017. Coming back to the introduction of additional excise duties in lieu of sales tax, there was a demand from trade and other interests to expand its coverage to more commodities, but the states claimed that they had lost out in the arrangement and resisted such an expansion. They also complained that while the rate of additional excise duty in lieu of sales tax continued unchanged, the Union government had continued to put additional levies in the form of special excise duty and cesses on these relevant commodities.

Apart from the multiplicity of state sales tax rates and CST, there was also the levy of entry tax and octroi by local self-governments like municipal corporations and gram panchayats on goods entering their jurisdiction. While entry tax is account-based, octroi is based on a physical control mechanism, where the levy is collected after inspection of the goods and the relevant documents of every transport vehicle at the time of entry into the area. Octroi duties were an important revenue source for the local governments and, in the absence of an alternative viable revenue model for the local bodies, continued in large parts of the country.

Taxes on motor vehicles were levied under item 57 of List II and contributed about 5.5 per cent of the states' own tax revenue, but would increase in significance over time. Stamp duties and registration fees (discussed below) constituted another important source, contributing sometimes more and sometimes less than taxes on motor vehicles in recent times. Other indirect taxes such as entertainment tax, taxes on passengers and goods and electricity duty contributed the rest.

By virtue of powers conferred upon states by entry 51 of List II of the Seventh Schedule to the Constitution, the states levied excise duty on alcoholic liquors for human consumption and some narcotic drugs. From 1970 to 2020, it contributed between 11 per cent and 16 per cent of the own tax revenues of the states. The major sources of such excise revenue were arrack (a distilled alcoholic drink produced from fermented fruits, cashew apple, sugar or jaggery, coconut flower, grains etc.), toddy (an alcoholic beverage created from the sap of various species of palm such as the palmyra, date palms and coconut), Indian Made Foreign Liquor (IMFL) and beer and various licence fees. Rates of excise duty on IMFL and beer were higher than the rate on country liquor, and the rates varied across states.

Revenues from state excise duties for the fifteen states that existed in the early 1960s—excluding Nagaland, which was created in 1962 and had negligible revenue of only around ₹1 lakh in 1964–65—increased from ₹58.64 crore in 1961–62 to ₹79.38 crore in 1964–65. In the aggregate, excise duties constituted around 11–12 per cent of the states' tax revenues, but the share, without taking into account the states implementing prohibition, varied widely from around 10 per cent in Karnataka to about 20 per cent in Rajasthan. Apart from the variation in tax base because of income, customs and traditions, reasons for the variation in revenues were the differing procedures and rates. The methods of collection varied across states and included direct production and distribution by the government, bid-cum-tender system for distribution rights, rentals and tree tax on palm trees allotted and licence fee on manufacture/sale of alcohol.

The temperance—in reality, abstinence rather than moderation— agitation in India started in the late nineteenth century, shortly after a similar movement had started in England. Many—not all—Brahmins in Hindu society were vegetarians and teetotallers. Sanskritization, a term coined by the famous sociologist M.N. Srinivas, refers to a process wherein a low caste, tribe or other groups collectively change their customs, rituals, ideology and way of life in the direction of some upper dominant caste to acquire higher status in society. The controversy over whether the Indian temperance agitation was because of Sanskritization or western influence is beyond the scope of this book.

What is not controversial, however, is that given the interest that the colonial government had in excise revenue from liquor, the social reform programme was also rich in terms of payoffs for the nationalist movement. The anti-liquor movement was supported by the Congress and got a special fillip from the Mahatma after 1921. In 1937, Rajaji, as premier heading a Congress government, introduced prohibition in the Madras province. In the United Provinces, the Congress government introduced prohibition in six hill districts in 1938, but after its resignation in 1939, it was promptly withdrawn. The Bombay Prohibition Act came into force in 1949 and the Indian Constitution, under Directive Principles of State Policy, in Article 47, stipulated '. . . the State shall endeavour to bring about prohibition of the consumption except for medicinal purposes of intoxicating drinks and of drugs which are injurious to health'. Prohibition and its practical implications have been a controversial subject ever since. Bihar's prohibition policy from 2016 raked up a controversy after the deaths caused by illicit and poisonous liquor consumption in late 2021.[6]

From the colonial times, India employed a system of collecting duty through the requirement of affixing stamps to official documents and various transaction instruments. The Constitution divided the power to levy stamp duty between the Union and the states. The stamp duties assigned to the Union are levied by the Centre but assigned for collection and retention by the states where they are levied. The stamp duties in the State List are levied and collected by the states. Stamp duties are of two types, judicial and non-judicial, with the latter being the more significant one in terms of revenue.

Revenues from stamp duties for the fifteen states (except Nagaland) that existed in the early 1960s increased from ₹39.45 crore in 1961–62 to ₹55.36 crore in 1964–65. In the aggregate, stamp duties constituted around 8 per cent of the states' tax revenues, but the share varied widely across states, from 3-6 per cent in Andhra Pradesh, Assam and Madhya Pradesh to 13–16 per cent in Rajasthan. Apart from differing tax bases, reasons for the variation in revenues were the differing procedures and rates. In some states, the rates were too low, and in some others, the rates were too high and procedures too cumbersome, leading to low compliance.

VIII.5 Fiscal Devolution

As the First Finance Commission 1952 pointed out in its report, the pre-Independence period starting from 1858, when the British crown took India over from the East India Company, can be divided into three subperiods: (i) about six decades before the Government of India Act of 1919, (ii) the period from 1921 to 1937 under the Government of India Act 1919, and (iii) from 1937, under the Government of India Act 1935 and then the Indian Constitution.

In the first period, together with fixed financial grants, there was some decentralization, giving provincial governments financial control over limited services such as jails, registration, police, education, medical services, printing, roads, miscellaneous public improvements and civil buildings. Certain heads of revenue, such as excise and income tax (which was then called licence tax), and more heads of expenditure were transferred to the provinces. Customs, posts and telegraphs, and railways, which required uniformity of policy and whose locale was no guide to its true incidence, were reserved for the Centre; other heads of revenue such as receipts from civil departments and public works were made entirely provincial. The heads divided in all or some of the provinces were land revenue, stamps, excises, income tax and irrigation receipts. Whichever were not assigned to the provinces were to be divided between the Centre and the provinces in conformity with settlements made every five years, a system that came to be known as one of divided heads. Under Lord Curzon (1899–1905), these five-yearly settlements became quasi-permanent settlements, and under Lord Hardinge (1910–16), permanent settlements in 1912. Under the system, the central government suffered an insufficiency of revenue. With the provinces under its strict supervision, the central government retained a proportion—fixed in the case of each province, but not uniform across provinces—of the proceeds of the main heads of revenue collected by the provinces, based on their respective needs.

Under Lord Chelmsford (1916–21), the Montagu-Chelmsford Report on Constitutional Reforms led to the Government of India Act of 1919. It abolished the divided heads and made a clear separation of responsibilities and powers regarding heads of expenditure and revenues between the Centre and the states. Of the erstwhile divided heads, income tax and commercial stamps were made into central receipts, and excise, judicial stamps, land revenue and irrigation receipts were given entirely to the provinces. The provinces gained considerable additional revenues under the new arrangement and the deficit of the Centre increased. The Montagu-Chelmsford Report proposed that provinces should make contributions to the Centre.

A Finance Relations Committee was appointed under Lord Meston, the finance member—equivalent to the finance minister in later times—of the Viceroy's executive council. This Meston Committee, in its report in March 1920, recognized that it would not be possible permanently to exclude provincial governments from some form of direct taxation upon the industrial and commercial earnings of their people, but advised against division of the proceeds of income tax with the provinces. It recommended that all stamps be made a provincial subject, for financial and administrative reasons. It proposed a scheme of initial contributions and of standard contributions by the provinces to be made over a period of seven years. The standard contributions were based on the relative taxable capacity and other economic factors of the provinces. The provinces protested against the Meston award, and it was never implemented.

The Devolution Rules promulgated in December 1920 under the Government of India Act 1919 provided, for a province, 3 pies (192 pies in a rupee) in each rupee of the amount by which the assessed income in any year exceeded that of the year 1920–21. The complete division of revenue heads did not work, and income tax had to be used as a balancing factor. The trends in central and provincial budgets did not conform to what the Meston Committee had based its recommendations on, and the provincial contributions were suspended in 1927–28 and abolished in 1928–29. The financial needs of the provinces were far greater than what the committee had anticipated.

The Indian Taxation Enquiry Committee 1924–25—the first systematic enquiry in the field of Indian taxation—recommended that general stamps, excises on foreign liquor manufactured in the country, and the whole of the revenue from opium, should be transferred to the Centre. Furthermore, if any revenue head was to be shared at all, it should be that from income tax. Apart from income tax, the balancing could be done as a last resort by the sharing of export duties, restrictive excises, duties on foreign liquor and opium, and probate duties. After a few other important committees' reports, the Joint Parliamentary Committee on Indian Constitutional Reforms 1933–34 followed. It recommended, among other things, that the provincial share of income tax be prescribed by an Order-in-Council—orders approved personally by the Queen at a meeting of the Privy Council. These recommendations were incorporated in the Government of India Act 1935.

In 1936, Sir Otto Niemeyer, the British banker and civil servant, was appointed to recommend on matters which had been left to be determined by an Order-in-Council. He recommended that half of the revenue from income tax should be shared with the provinces and distributed among them according to percentages that he derived based on the residence of the taxpayers and population. He also recommended sharing of 62.5 per cent of the net revenue from export duty on jute with the jute-growing provinces. There were a few other recommendations, such as of annual grants to the relatively backward United Provinces, Assam, NWFP, Orissa and Sind, and the cancellation of the outstanding debt to the centre of Bengal, Bihar, Assam, NWFP and Orissa contracted prior to 1 April 1936. These recommendations were accepted and embodied in the Government of India (Distribution of Revenues) order 1936, which continued to operate until Independence.

The Partition of the country in 1947 required an adjustment in the sharing of the proceeds of income tax and duty on jute exports among the provinces. Regarding income tax, the government of newly independent India reduced the shares of the divided provinces of Bengal and Punjab in proportion to the population. For export duty on jute, the provincial share was reduced from 62.5 per cent to 20 per cent, in recognition of the proportion of the jute-growing area included in Pakistan. The financial provisions of the proposed new Constitution were referred to an expert committee under the chairmanship of Nalini Ranjan Sarkar. The committee recommended that 60 per cent of income tax, both personal and corporate, should be shared with the provinces on the following basis: 20 per cent on the basis of population, 35 per cent on the basis of collection and 5 per cent for mitigating hardship that may result from the application of this specified formula. It recommended an end to the sharing of export duty on jute and replacing it with fixed grants-in-aid until the duty itself was abolished for seven years, whichever was earlier. In response to persistent demands by provinces for sharing of excise duties, the committee recommended sharing of the excise duty on tobacco based on their consumption. It also recommended the setting up of a Finance Commission to deal with the problem of fiscal devolution.

India became a republic on 26 January 1950 after the Constitution came into effect. Assignment of expenditure responsibilities and power to tax among the Centre and the provinces under the Constitution remained unchanged from the post-war period. So did the asymmetry between the Union and states in terms of relative mismatch between revenues and expenditure. Between 1950–51 and 1964–65, for example, between 62.5 per cent (1952–53) and 70.1 per cent (1964–65) of total tax revenues accrued to the Union, whereas its share of total expenditure was considerably lower. Thus, the Constitution specified a system of fiscal devolution from the Union to the states based on the recommendations of Finance Commissions constituted every five years.

For the award period of the first ten Finance Commissions (until 1999–2000), devolution was restricted to the Union's revenues only from personal income tax and excise duties. Under Nehru, in the award period of the first three Finance Commissions, the states' share of income tax increased from 55 per cent in 1952–57 to 60 per cent in 1957–62 and 66.7 per cent in 1962–66, but as the coverage of excise duties increased from 3 to 8 to 35 per cent, the share of excise duties for the states came down from 40 per cent to 25 per cent and further to 20 per cent. The devolution was restricted to tax revenues net of collection costs; cesses and surcharges were excluded. There was a built-in incentive for the Union to increase cesses and surcharges rather than the basic rates, a trend that many states point out only intensified over time.

In summary, during the Nehru era, there were attempts to improve the legacy tax system inherited from the colonial times. The Income Tax Act 1961 was a landmark; other reform efforts were more piecemeal than comprehensive. Changes at the Union level were motivated by the twin objectives of mobilizing additional revenues while furthering social justice. The motivation for mobilizing more revenues increased with the need for additional defence outlays with the Chinese aggression in 1962. The combined tax revenue of the Union and the states as a proportion of GDP at current market prices (2004–05 series) declined from 6.7 per cent in 1951–52 to a low of 5.7 per cent in 1953–54, increased thereafter with some fluctuations to a high of 9.9 per cent in 1963–64 before declining to 9.5 per cent in 1964–65. The increase in tax revenues relative to GDP in the concluding years of Pandit Nehru's era was higher due to additional levies. It was a strategy of tax-deepening by taxing those entities and commodities already in the tax net rather than broadening the net by taxing a wider clientele and commodities and services. India remained far from a comprehensive reform of the tax system.

Resource Constraint and Neglect of Taxation, Education and Health, and Physical Infrastructure

With the benefit of hindsight, we know now that the pursuit of socialist planning with industrial licensing and public sector at the commanding heights of the economy during the Nehru era held the Indian economy back from realizing its full growth potential between 1947 and 1964. But if it was an error in the design of policy, it was an error committed in great intellectual company. Two celebrated economists—Joseph Schumpeter in 1942 and Nobel laureate Paul Samuelson in 1967—had predicted the victory of socialism over capitalism. What is intriguing, however, is the neglect of primary education, primary health and physical infrastructure during the Nehru era. And this requires a bit more analysis.

IX.1 Relative Neglect of Education, Health and Physical Infrastructure

Primary education

Thomas Babington Macaulay, a British historian, before becoming the secretary at war in the UK between 1839 and 1841, was the first law member in the Governor General's Council in India under the East India Company. He is famous for his 'Minute on Indian Education' in 1835, which determined the course of the colonial government's education policy during the imperial days. The emphasis was not on education for the people, but in Macaulay's words, on developing a set of people as interpreters between the British rulers and the millions they governed— 'a class of persons Indians in blood and colour but English in taste, in opinions, in morals and in intellect'.[1] Macaulay's notorious Minute in 1835, together with an unwillingness to raise resources for education, had left India at Independence with widespread illiteracy. This was despite the fact that ever since the Forster's Education Act, 1870 was passed in the UK, Indian leaders had demanded similar compulsory education acts for India.

Some of the princely states, like Baroda, Travancore and Manipur, had introduced compulsory education well before Independence. Before Independence, even in provinces of British India, there were at least twenty-two such acts starting from 1917. But their implementation was tardy because of resource constraints. The framers of the Indian Constitution understood the importance of health and education and made appropriate provisions under Articles 45 and 47. But because of resource constraints and other implementation issues, both the Articles were Directive Principles and not enforceable in courts.

By the early 1960s, Theodore Schultz, the economics professor at the University of Chicago, had already started his pathbreaking work on human capital and the importance of education in economic development, for which and for his contribution to agricultural economics, he was awarded the Nobel Prize in economics in 1979. With John Kenneth Galbraith, the 6 ft 7 in tall Harvard economist, as the US ambassador to India during 1961–63, it is very unlikely that Indian policymakers were completely unaware of the importance of education and literacy in economic development. Galbraith is famous for having said '(n)o where in the world is there an illiterate peasantry that is progressive. Nowhere is there a literate peasantry that is not'[2]. He also said: 'There is no place in the world where a well-educated population is really poor.'[3]

The First Five-Year Plan had almost completely ignored education. In 1956, Education Minister Maulana Abul Kalam Azad, in his chairman's speech at the twenty-third meeting of the Central Advisory Board of Education (CABE), had said that '. . . I am continuing with my endeavours and it is my resolve that we must provide a reasonable allocation for education in the Second Plan . . .' In 1958, at CABE's twenty-fifth meeting, he ruefully added, 'I may add that one of our difficulties has been that some of our colleagues have regarded education to be a purely provincial subject and did not therefore think it necessary that the central government should provide adequate funds for education . . . There seemed to be a general view that we should take up only subjects, which would give quick returns . . . they held that education could not do this . . .' In the finance ministers' budget speeches between 1951 and 1961, there was not even a passing reference to education.

Until 1970–71, many states had attendance officers, and served notices to and prosecuted parents who did not send their children to school. In 1965–66, for example, more than 13 lakh notices were served on parents not sending their children to school, and ₹11,403 was realized as fines in 1966–67. Without the availability of schools in nearby locations, which was a failure of the government, it was difficult for the poor to send their wards to schools, and from 1963–64, enforcement of compulsory education was deliberately discouraged. Collection of data on compulsory education enforcement ceased from 1972. There was also a problem of quality in primary education. With widespread teacher absenteeism and an already high pupil-teacher ratio, many surveys described the primary schools as little more than child-minding centres.

Primary health

Like education, health remained a neglected area in the Union government's agenda in the first three decades after Independence. Admittedly, in the Seventh Schedule to the Constitution, like education (part of entry 3), 'public health and sanitation; hospitals and dispensaries' (entry 6) was in List II under the jurisdiction of the state governments. But with the benefit of the reports of the Bhore Committee (1946), Sokhey Sub-Committee (1948), and Mudaliar Committee (1962), the government could not have been unaware of the importance of public health for socio-economic development, or of what was happening at the ground level.

The Health Survey and Development Committee, popularly known as the Bhore Committee, had recommended establishing an effective rural health services infrastructure by creating a network of primary health centres, provision of integrated preventive, promotive and curative services with people's participation, educating the people about health matters, providing adequate health and medical care even to those who are unable to pay and training of necessary health manpower, including medical, nursing, paramedical and auxiliary personnel. In 1952, under CDP, there was a start in setting up primary health centres to provide integrated promotive, preventive, curative and rehabilitative services to the entire rural population. But it was not sustained. The First Five-Year Plan noted that only 3 per cent of households in India had toilets, and that much of the population lacked basic water, drainage and waste disposal services, yet it did little in ameliorating the problem. The healthcare problem was particularly acute in rural areas, where, for example, in 1961, on average, there was only one doctor for 18,751 people compared to one doctor for 1720 people in urban areas. The expenditure on health, as a proportion of total plan expenditure, came down from 4.98 per cent in the First Five-Year Plan to 2.60 per cent in the Third. Furthermore, the medical curriculum in the MBBS programmes mainly primed students for specialization at MD or MS levels rather than making them well-rounded primary physicians.

Physical infrastructure

The story of neglect of physical infrastructure in the first two decades after Independence is very similar to that of primary education and health. Installed capacity for electricity production, which was mostly in the public sector, went up from 1362 MW at end–1947 to 1713 MW at end–1950, and further to 2886 MW, 4653 MW and 9027 MW at the end of the First (1951–56), Second (1956–61), and Third Five-Year Plans (1961–66). The increase in per capita consumption in kWh was from 16 at end–1947 to only 18 at end–1950, and 31, 46 and 74 at the end of March 1956, 1961 and 1966, respectively. The inadequate increase in generation and inefficient transmission and distribution (T&D) led to power cuts affecting economic activity and resulting in many sweating in the dark and sultry summer nights.

Similarly, an efficient transportation network is essential for regional commerce and human mobility. In 1949, China had only 22,000 km of poorly maintained and war-damaged railway line, compared to India's 53,596 km in April 1950. China's railway route km went up to 33,900 in 1960 and almost doubled to 41,000 in 1970, while India's rose to only 56,247 in 1960 and 59,790 in 1970. With faster growth, by 2000, China, with 68,700 km, overtook India with 63,028 km. Similarly, China increased the length of its highways, by thousands of kilometres, from 152 in 1952 to 515 in 1965 and 637 in 1970, while in India, the increase was from around 20 in 1951 to 81 in 1970. Even after taking into account the differences in classification of roads in the two countries and almost three times larger territory of China (9.6 million sq. km) relative to India (3.3 million sq. km), India performed poorly in road development.

IX.2 Resource Constraint and Fiscal Deficit

A part of the reason for neglect of primary education and healthcare and physical infrastructure in the Nehru era was resource constraint. The government focused on investments with quick returns. Returns from education, health and infrastructure would come only after long gestation, while planning with the public sector at the commanding heights was expected to generate high growth and employment, and provide income to the people as well as the government to get on with the job of universal primary education and healthcare and adequate physical infrastructure after a decade or two. Fiscal resources were vigorously channelled into capital expenditure, including CPSEs (Figure IX.1). Some even believed that in a decade and a half, surpluses of the public sector would render taxation superfluous. But, alas, their expectations were not fulfilled and the current revenues of the Union government fell short of its current non-plan expenditure.

The share of the Union government's capital expenditure in its total expenditure, after declining from 13.8 per cent in 1950–51 to 3.9 per cent in 1953–54, went up sharply to 26.9 per cent in 1954–55, and after some ups and downs until 1959–60, remained steady around 43.5 per cent until the end of the Nehru era. Few anticipated the problems of managing CPSEs. To paraphrase Gary Becker, CPSEs *could* improve matters, but that did not imply that CPSEs *actually would improve* them. The issues of whether government running businesses was government business, and

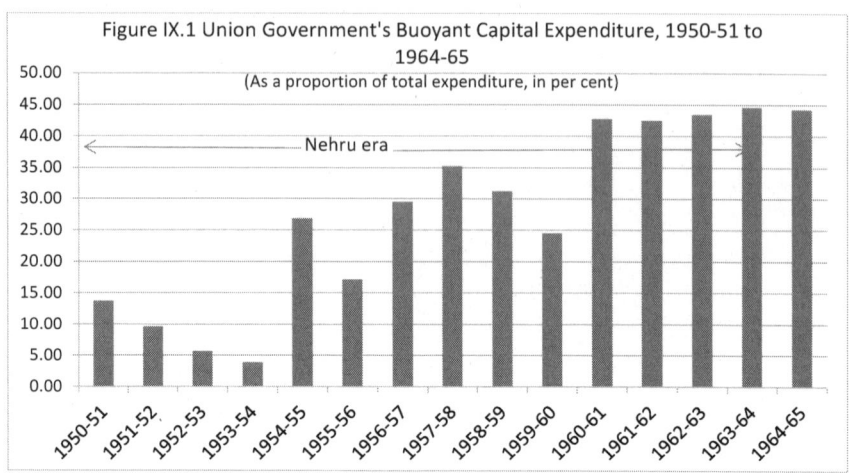

Figure IX.1 Union Government's Buoyant Capital Expenditure, 1950-51 to 1964-65
(As a proportion of total expenditure, in per cent)

Source: Compiled from various issues of Indian Public Finance Statistics and Budget documents of Government of India.

whether many CPSEs would lock up scarce public resources and generate losses, were hardly discussed. The returns from CPSEs in non-tax revenues were insufficient and delayed.

The increase in the Central government's capital expenditure was not simply from a shift from revenue to capital within its total expenditure but also from an increase in its total expenditure, which as a proportion of GDP, went up more than three-fold from 4.2 per cent in 1950–51 to 7.3 per cent in 1957–58, 9.3 per cent in 1960–61 and further to 12.8 per cent in 1963–64 (Figure IX.2). A part of the reason for the increase beyond 1961–62 was the need for enhanced defence expenditure with Chinese aggression in 1962. As we shall see, increasing subsidies, particularly on food, fertilizer and petroleum, as pressure points on outlays came only after the Nehru era.

Fiscal deficit is the difference between total expenditure and total revenue. What is important to note is that it is the difference between total expenditure and total payments, and between total revenues and total receipts. For example, total expenditure includes loan repayments which increases your net worth and hence is not an expenditure. Just as total payments are much more than total expenditure, total receipts, which includes receipts from borrowings, are much more than total revenue. A *revenue receipt*, for example, from income tax or stamp duty, is income for

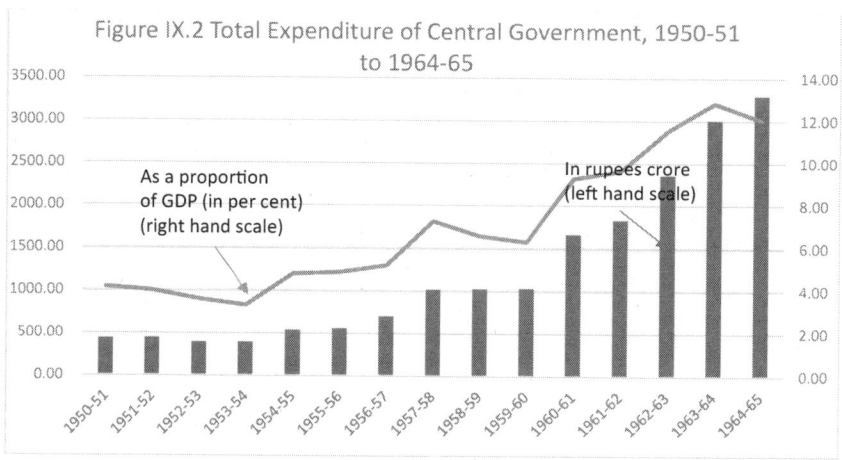

Figure IX.2 Total Expenditure of Central Government, 1950-51 to 1964-65

Source: Compiled from various issues of Indian Public Finance Statistics and Budget documents of Government of India.

the government. But a *receipt* may also be from borrowings, which creates a liability to repay. The fiscal deficit considers only revenue receipts and excludes debt capital receipts, but it treats revenue expenditure and capital expenditure equivalently and sums the two up to get total expenditure. Unlike debt capital receipts which are excluded from the calculation of fiscal deficit, all capital expenditure is factored in because while capital expenditure can create assets of a material and permanent character and generate an income stream for the government in the future, it is critically dependent on how efficiently it is used. The fiscal deficit for the years 1950–51 to 2019–20 are discussed in Box IX.1.

Box IX.1 Derivation of Fiscal Deficit

Prior to 1990–91, what the government reported was the budgetary deficit, which was very different from the fiscal deficit used by economists and analysts as one of the important measures for examining fiscal policy. Way back in 1981, in the Ministry of Finance's Economic Survey 1980-81 (p. 33), the government had noted: 'Deficit financing differs conceptually from the budgetary deficit as defined in budget documents and is a more appropriate measure of the net impact of budget operations upon domestic demand. The budgetary deficit as defined in budget documents covers net sale of treasury bills by the Central Government excluding net purchases by the State Governments, net increase in Ways and Means advances to the State Governments by the Reserve Bank of India and variations in cash balances of the Central and State Governments. Deficit financing refers to the net increase in long- and short-term borrowings of the Centre and States from the RBI plus variations in cash balances during the fiscal year.'

The fiscal deficit of the Central government, which is not readily available in the budget documents prior to 1991–92, have been derived from the financing side and the data is from RBI's Handbook of Statistics on the Indian Economy, Table 95.

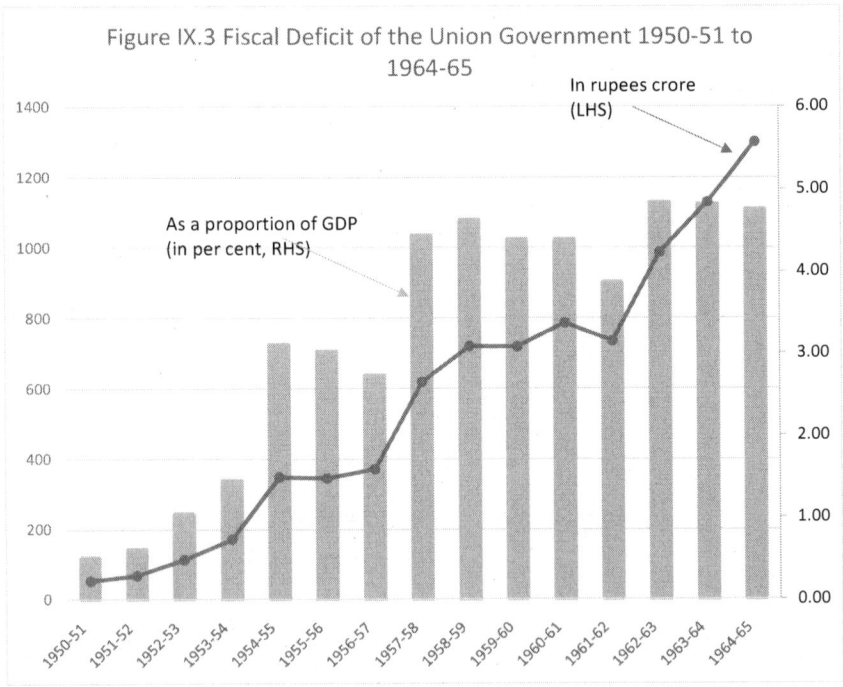

Figure IX.3 Fiscal Deficit of the Union Government 1950-51 to 1964-65

+ indicates fiscal deficit

Source: The fiscal deficit of the Central Government, which is not readily available in the budget documents prior to 1991-92, has been derived from the financing side and the data is from RBI's Handbook of Statistics on the Indian Economy, Table 95. GDP figures (2004-05) series from Ministry of Statistics and Programme Implementation.

In 1950–51, the Government of India had a fiscal deficit of ₹53 crore equivalent to 0.5 per cent of GDP, which increased to ₹68 crore or 0.7 per cent of GDP in the following year. The deficit increased more than tenfold by 1958–59 and remained elevated until the end of the Nehru era (Figure IX.3). The era ended with the fiscal deficit at ₹1299 crore in 1964–65. As a proportion of GDP, it reached a peak of 4.8 per cent in 1963–64 and ended at 4.7 per cent in 1964–65. By feeding into debt, a higher fiscal deficit in a year leaves its imprint on not only the debt at the end of the year but also higher interest payments in the future because of higher debt, and this higher outlay on interest can lead to higher fiscal deficit itself in the future.

From 1954–55, the government, even before servicing its debt and interest obligations, was borrowing to meet its other expenditure obligations. This was reflected in its primary balance, which is the fiscal balance without considering interest payments, turning into a deficit. This primary deficit implied that even with all the loans from the past written off, the government could not meet its expenditure needs from its revenues and would be piling up debt going forward.

Apart from fiscal and primary deficits, there is the concept of revenue deficit, which is the difference between revenue expenditure and revenue receipts. The golden rule of public finance or the principle of 'sound finance' states that, on average, the revenue deficit should be zero, or negative, i.e., there should be a revenue surplus. The government can borrow, not to fund current spending, but only to invest in projects that benefit the future generations. Day-to-day spending that benefits today's taxpayers should be paid for with today's taxes, not with borrowed funds that create a liability for future generations. Economic activity undergoes cyclical ups and downs. Even over the economic cycle, the government can borrow, but only to invest and not to fund current spending. The redeeming feature of the first period under Nehru was the generation of revenue surplus in every year except 1958–59, when a decline of ₹42 crore in customs revenue because of import restrictions resulted in a marginal revenue deficit of about ₹2 crore. But between 1964 and 1991, after Nehru, the problem of revenue deficit would plague the economy every year after 1978–79. Deficit financing would be used not only for public investment but also as a method of pain deferral, financing subsidies and interest payments.

The problem of mounting fiscal deficits did not come to the fore because of the peculiar concept of 'deficit' used in the budgets. The concept was the 'budget deficit' or 'uncovered deficit', equivalent to the gap between expenditure and receipts, including loans, and this 'deficit' would equal the decline in the government's cash balances between the end of the year and the beginning of the year. With large enough borrowings, cash balances at the end of the year could be higher than that at the beginning of the year and 'budget deficit' could be negative! The budget deficits reported until 1990–91 had little to do with the fiscal deficit and had scarce analytical meaning and significance. They meant little except that the government had not been able to balance its receipts and payments by planning to adjust its cash balances and proposing to raise loans in adequate amounts. Budget deficits were financed by expansion of Treasury Bills, which are debt instruments of the government with maturity of less than a year and sold at a discount from the par value of the bills.

From colonial times, India had inherited a 'small' government focused primarily on security and law and order. Thus, in the first budget for independent India presented on 26 November 1947 in very troubled times with large-scale communal disturbances and Partition-related dislocation, the first finance minister, R.K. Shanmukham Chetty, budgeted for a revenue of only ₹171.15 crore for seven and a half months, or less than 5 per cent of GDP on an annualized basis. Revenues did go up after Independence, but not enough for the country to make the necessary outlays on public investment and outlays on physical and social infrastructure. With limited revenues, the problem was in finding the resources (Figure IX.4) for the government to deploy for economic development. While expenditure went up four-fold from around ₹450 crore in the early 1950s to well over ₹1800 crore in 1961–62, the corresponding increase in revenues was from around ₹450 crore to less than ₹1200 crore. The Union government had limited success in mobilizing revenues. As a proportion of GDP, such revenues during the decade of the 1950s remained below 5 per cent except in 1957–58, when they touched 5 per cent. Total revenue of the government included both tax revenues and non-tax revenues. While non-tax revenues might have faltered because of misplaced expectations, the issue of insufficient tax revenues merits closer scrutiny.

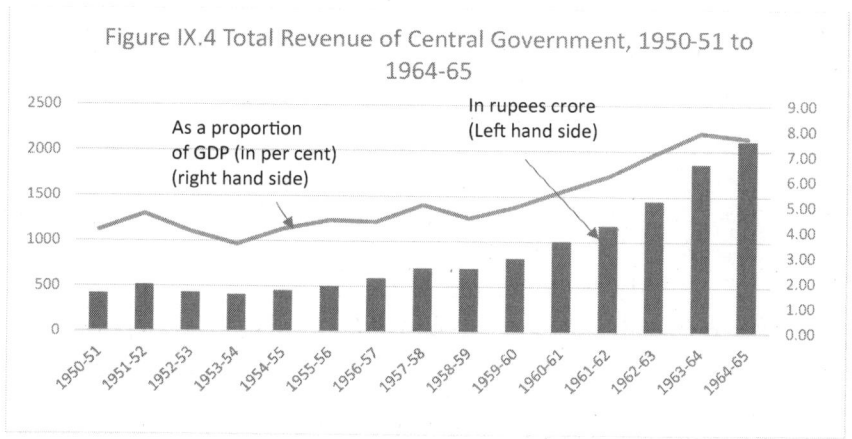

Figure IX.4 Total Revenue of Central Government, 1950-51 to 1964-65

Source: Compiled from various issues of Indian Public Finance Statistics and Budget documents of Government of India. GDP figures (2004-05) series from Ministry of Statistics and Programme Implementation.

IX.3 Insufficient Taxation

In many developed countries, Union government expenditure as a proportion of GDP was in single digit until the Great Recession in 1929, and expanded rapidly only thereafter. Expansion of government expenditure in developing countries, however, was a later, post-Second World War phenomenon, particularly after decolonization. India was no exception. The answer to the question of whether independent India was spending too much or mobilizing too few revenues is best answered by comparing such revenues and expenditures with not only what they were during their own colonial past, but also with what other developing countries were doing.

Total Union government expenditure in India rose from ₹433 crore or only 4.2 per cent of GDP at current market prices in 1950–51 to ₹1664 crore or 9.3 per cent of GDP in 1960–61 and further to ₹3294 crore or 12 per cent of GDP in 1964–65, the year Pandit Nehru passed away. Despite this expansion, in India, the Union government's expenditure as a proportion of GNP, even in 1986, was 16.4 per cent compared with 26.9 per cent in Indonesia, 21.7 per cent in Thailand, 36.6 per cent in Malaysia and 17.8 per cent in the Republic of Korea, and developing countries' average of 26.3 per cent. It is difficult to argue that the Union government was spending too much during the Nehru era.

The problem in India was on the tax revenue front. Total tax revenue of the Union rose from ₹357 crore or 3.4.per cent of GDP in 1950–51 to ₹730 crore or 4.1 per cent of GDP in 1960–61 and further to ₹3294 crore or 5.7 per cent of GDP in 1964–65. While the expected returns from investments in CPSEs did not come, tax revenues of the Central government did not expand fast enough to meet the needs of burgeoning expenditure.

While the optimal investment in CPSEs could have been a matter of debate, there was a consensus on the need for more revenues for the government to accelerate social and economic development. In 1971, Raja C. Chelliah, the doyen of Indian public economics, compared the international experience in tax mobilization across twenty-seven developing countries between 1953–55 and 1966–68. He estimated the income elasticity of tax revenue of the general government (of the Union together with that of the states) for India as the highest at 2.4, and its tax-to-GNP ratio rose from 6.3 per cent to 11.6 per cent. Yet, in 1966–68, seventeen of these twenty-seven developing countries had a tax-to-GNP ratio higher than that of India. So, although the tax-to-GNP ratio was increasing in India, it was not increasing fast enough with the right intensity of tax effort.

Chelliah found that the proportion of total tax revenue of the general government coming from direct taxes, namely on income and property, declined from 41.2 per cent in 1953–55 to 29.1 per cent in 1966–68. Much of the corresponding increase in indirect taxes came from taxes on production and internal transactions, whose share rose from 58.8 per cent to 70.7 per cent. He found the income elasticity of direct taxes in India at 1.7 to be lower than that of nine other countries, including the Republic of Korea and Thailand. The share of income tax in total tax revenue increased in 53 per cent of the sample countries but declined in India from 25.1 per cent in 1953–55 to 19.8 per cent in 1963–66. Like in the other countries, the share of taxes on international trade also declined in India from 25 per cent in 1953–55 to 17.8 per cent in 1963–66, with much of this low realization because of the country's reliance on QRs on imports rather than tariffs.

Evidently, the tax-to-GDP or GNP ratio in a country as well as the composition of its revenue in terms of alternate taxes depend on its capacity to pay taxes and the willingness of its government to levy and collect them. In a ranking of income elasticities of total tax revenues, which he called tax effort, Chelliah found India ranking twenty-first, with the index of tax effort at 1.031 indicating effort just above the average. Chelliah found India, with taxes as a proportion of GNP at 11.6 per cent, ranking thirty-third among forty-nine developing countries, with such proportions varying between 3.2 per cent in Nepal and 28.6 per cent in Zambia. Excluding social security taxes, tax to GNP ratio was 14 per cent in developing countries compared to 25 per cent in developed countries

India's average or above-average tax effort did not indicate that more could not be done. One source of worry was the declining share of income tax in its total tax revenue. Chelliah had concluded that countries wishing to increase their tax revenue at a faster rate than GNP would have to make more intensive use of their income taxation and various forms of sales tax. Furthermore, income tax is universally recognized as one of the most effective ways of achieving equity and distributive justice. Hence, the Indian personal income tax regime merits scrutiny.

The structure of income tax is primarily dependent on the exemption limit and the marginal tax rates at different slabs of income. An exemption limit, a lower limit on income below which no income tax is payable, can be devised to exempt the 'poor' and/or exclude the initial slice of income required for subsistence. It could also be motivated by the idea of avoiding the administrative problem of collecting marginal amounts from too many people. It is widely known that as per capita income rises, in most countries, the exemption limit increases slower than per capita income and an increasing proportion of the population gets covered under income tax. The Indian tax exemption limits only partially conformed to these principles—the limit was too high relative to per capita income, or to the poverty line defined at the subsistence level, and, in a stepwise fashion, rose slower than per capita income, but not slow enough to make the exemption threshold appropriate for the country. In the initial years after Independence, the insufficient attention to revenue mobilization in general and income taxation in particular indicates the capture of democratic politics by the relatively affluent and the middle classes.

IX.4 Tax Exemption on Personal Income

It is always tempting to levy high taxes on a few, buy popularity from a large number by exempting them from tax and also reduce administrative costs and problems. But in practice, most countries have found 'small'—in absolute terms, not necessarily as a proportion of their respective incomes— amounts of taxes paid by all rather than high taxes paid by a few the safer route to pursue. Even the ancient Indian economist Chanakya preferred emphasis on many small tax-payers rather than a few big ones. Before Independence, both land taxation and tax on salt, the two major sources of revenue, conformed to the principle of taxing many small rather than the big few. After Independence, in personal income tax, the government strategy of granting exemptions to many while trying to tax only the few rich was a violation of this principle. There were and are many exemptions on personal income tax, but we will focus only on exemptions in terms of a minimum level of income below which no income tax was and is payable. The Pigouvian criterion—named after economist A.C. Pigou—that the tax on nil income should be nil is well accepted, but what the minimum level of income should be where income tax is payable is a matter of judgement.

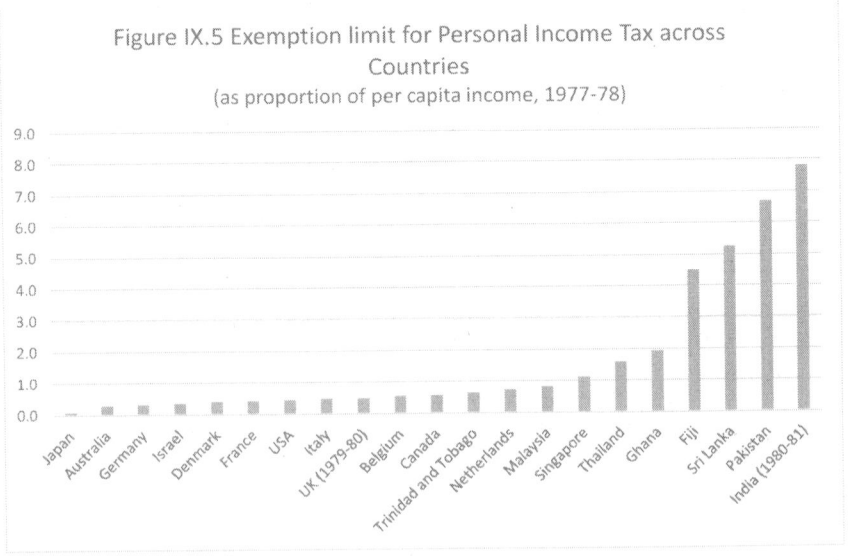

Figure IX.5 Exemption limit for Personal Income Tax across Countries
(as proportion of per capita income, 1977-78)

Source: Amaresh Bagchi: 'Inflation and Personal Income Tax: A Note,' Economic and Political Weekly, 24 April – 1 May 1982, Vol. 17, No. 17/18, pp. 733-735+737-738.

After Independence, the exemption limit for income tax was raised from ₹2000 the year before to ₹2500 in 1947–48, and further to ₹3000 in 1948–50. The limit was raised to ₹3600 in 1951–53 and ₹4200 in 1954–56. From the financial year 1955–56, the exemption limit was reduced to ₹1000 for unmarried individuals and a system of 'family allowances', computed in accordance with the personal circumstances of an individual, with higher concession was made available to married individuals with two or more children. In computation of the exemption threshold, we focus on unmarried individuals and ignore the special allowances that were there for married individuals with or without children. By 1950–51, the exemption limit for personal income tax at ₹3000 was 11.4 times the per capita Net National Product (NNP). Compared with high-income developed countries, such exemption limits relative to per capita income are known to be high in poor, developing countries. A part of the reason is the low per capita income itself in developing countries and administrative problems in mobilizing taxes from the relatively poor, many of whom operate in non-monetized segments. But even in comparison with poor

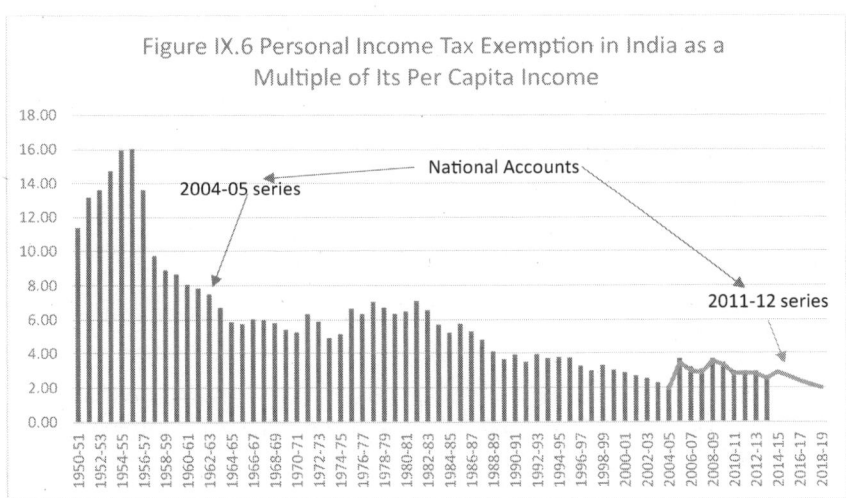

Figure IX.6 Personal Income Tax Exemption in India as a Multiple of Its Per Capita Income

Source: For 1960-61 to 1986-87: Pulin B. Nayak and Pawan K. Aggarwal: "Exemption Limit and Personal Income Tax: An International Comparison," Economic and Political Weekly, 8 July 1989, Vol. 24, No. 27, pp. 1535-1537+1539-1542. P. 1541.Amaresh Bagchi: "Inflation and Personal Income Tax: A Note," Economic and Political Weekly, 24 April – 1 May 1982, Vol. 17, No. 17/18, pp. 733-735+737-738, p. 734. Arindam Dasgupta: "Recent Individual Income Tax Reform," Economic and Political Weekly, 2-8 April, 2005, Vol. 40, No. 14, pp. 1397-1405. Per capita income from Ministry of Statistics and Programme Implementation.

developing countries, India stood out with its very high ratio of personal income exemption limit to per capita income (Figure IX.5).

Beyond the principle of zero tax at zero income, there is wide agreement that a minimum level of income necessary for bare existence should be left untaxed. But, with the poverty line for a household defined at ₹1200 per year in July 1962, and later the threshold for daily income for individuals to qualify for food subsidies defined as ₹12 for rural and ₹17 for urban areas (that is, per family of five members, per year of ₹21,900 and ₹31,025 respectively) at 2004–05 prices, the exemption limits were many times the poverty line. Indeed, the exemption limit as a proportion of per capita income came down around a fluctuating trend from a high of 16 in the mid-1950s to 5.9 in 1964–65 at the end of the Nehru era and further to 2 in 2018–19 (Figure IX.6). But the nagging question that remains is whether it was necessary to increase the exemption limit from ₹1500 to ₹3000 in 1950–51, to ₹3600 in 1951–52 and further to ₹4200 in 1953–54, when the per capita income in the country was between ₹264 and ₹285?

With progressive taxation, tax rates are higher at higher levels of income. When there is inflation, taxpayers with higher nominal income but real income unchanged or even lower than before move on to higher tax brackets and pay tax at higher rates. This is called 'fiscal drag' because this increase in taxes reduces aggregate demand and hence consumer spending, and dampens inflation. As can be seen from Figure IX.7, some of this fiscal drag was neutralized by moving the exemption threshold in line with inflation.

In June 2004, the Task Force Report on Implementation of the Fiscal Responsibility and Budget Management Act, 2003, headed by Vijay Kelkar, provided an analytical framework for analysing and determining the exemption limit of personal income tax. It did so by looking at the social benefit from collecting taxes from the marginal taxpayer in relation to the costs of administration and compliance. It considered raising the threshold level of income, denoted E, by ₹1. With the tax rate applicable at the threshold level of income, the government's revenue loss as well as the tax saving of the individual was tE. The administrative cost of collecting taxes for the government (A) and the cost of complying with the tax laws for the taxpayer (C) also had to be factored in. Furthermore, the

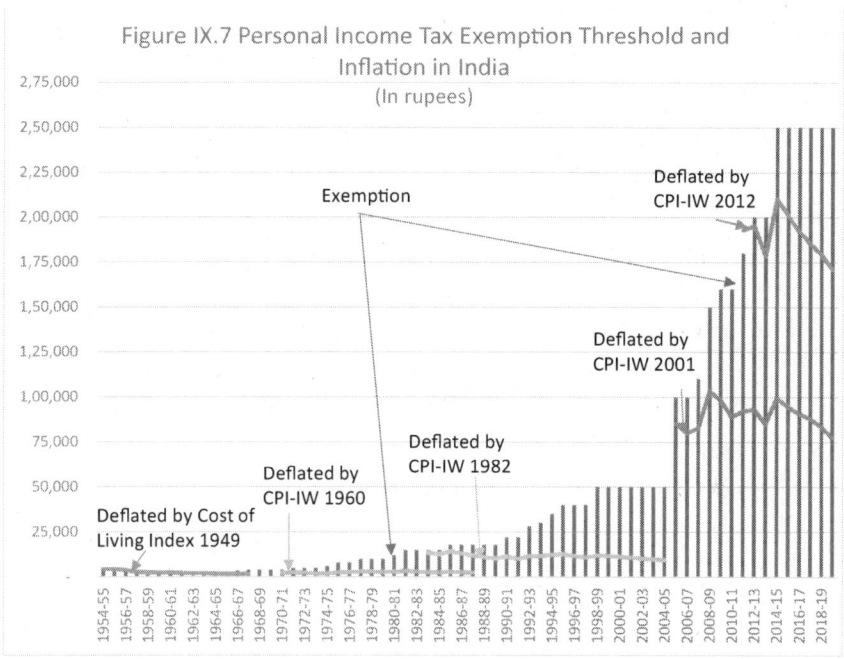

Figure IX.7 Personal Income Tax Exemption Threshold and Inflation in India
(In rupees)

Source: For 1960-61 to 1986-87: Pulin B. Nayak and Pawan K. Aggarwal: 'Exemption Limit and Personal Income Tax: An International Comparison,' Economic and Political Weekly, 8 July 1989, Vol. 24, No. 27, pp. 1535-1537+1539-1542. P. 1541. Amaresh Bagchi: 'Inflation and Personal Income Tax: A Note,' Economic and Political Weekly, 24 April – 1 May 1982, Vol. 17, No. 17/18, pp. 733-735+737-738, p. 734. Bagchi took CPI-AW. Anupam Gupta: 'A Study of Personal Income Taxation in India,' Calcutta Progressive Publishers, 1975, p. 21 (for 3,000 during 1957-65). Indian Public Finance Statistics 2010-11, Ministry of Finance. Table 7.13, p. 110. https://dea. gov.in/sites/default/files/IPFStat201011.pdf. Cost of living index 1955-1967 from 'Compendium on Consumer Price Index for Industrial Workers', Labour Bureau, Ministry of Labour and Employment, Government of India, 2021, p.61. https://labour.gov.in/ebook/Vol-I/index.html. Cost of living index for 1955-56 relates to that in 1955, and so on. Various CPI from RBI Handbook of Statistics on the Indian Economy.

social value of ₹1 in the hands of the government is taken as ₹d, d>1. The optimal exemption limit E was such that the marginal cost to the taxpayer was neutralized by the marginal gain to the government, or

$$tE + C = d(tE - A) \qquad (9.1)$$

Or,

$$E = \frac{dA + C}{t(d-1)} \qquad (9.2)$$

By taking d=1.2, A=100, t=0.1 and C=2,500 for salaried taxpayers, for example, the optimal threshold limit for the salaried employees was derived as ₹1,31,000. The importance of a few parameters, namely d and C, in determining E in (9.2) is worth noting. Furthermore, the average taxpayer impacted by the change in the exemption limit is not only those whose incomes fell from above to below the exemption limit, but, because of the slab system, extends to all with income above the exemption limit, including the rich.

For example, consider a population with 100 people having income of ₹1, ₹2, . . ., ₹100. Let income below ₹10 be exempt from tax, and the tax rate 10 per cent for income between ₹10 and ₹20, 20 per cent for income between ₹20 and ₹30, 30 per cent for income between ₹30 and ₹40, . . . and 90 per cent between ₹90 and ₹100. Increasing the exemption limit from ₹10 to ₹11 will result in tax saving not only of the individual who earns ₹11 and was paying ₹0.1 as tax, but tax of ₹0.1 for each of the ninety taxpayers with an income above ₹10, that is, a total gain of ₹9. At the margin, increasing the exemption limit by ₹1 from ₹11 to ₹12, ₹13, ₹14 . . . and so on would involve tax saving of ₹8.9, ₹8.8, ₹8.7 . . . for the taxpayer. There is some saving in costs of complying with the tax laws, especially for those who become exempt after the increase in the exemption limit, but this saving is likely to be negligible for taxpayers at higher income levels. Given that the 'average' taxpayer in the analysis involves not only the marginal taxpayer who falls out of the tax net after the increase in the exemption limit but also the rich, d can be considerably higher than 1.2 and C can be considerably less than 2500. Taking d as 1.3 and C as 2000 results in optimal exemption level of ₹71,000.

A ready quantification of the revenue losses from the hike in exemption is not available. It seems that there was a tendency to raise the exemption limit in the years of election to the Lok Sabha. The exemption limit was raised before nine of the seventeen Lok Sabha elections held so far until 2019. Was it a deliberate attempt by the ruling party of that time to curry favour with the electorate? Did the gambit pay off in terms of electoral dividends? Or, was it a misperception of what the electorate wanted? Did the electorate want additional and effective outlays on physical and social infrastructure and were willing to finance it by paying income tax with an unchanged exemption threshold? A rigorous answer to the questions requires careful research and is beyond the scope of this book.

Paying taxes increases the sense of ownership of the government among the people and improves public accountability. As we will note later, in the late 1960s, differences arose within the coalition government in UP about the abolition of the land tax on peasants with less than six acres proposed by the communists and socialists. Chief Minister Charan Singh of the Jana Congress was against the abolition; he thought the tax strengthened the peasants' commitment to land ownership. Communist Party of India (ComPI) and Samyukta Socialist Party (SSP) quit the coalition and Charan Singh resigned on 25 February 1968. In not granting exemptions from taxes, Charan Singh was an exception among politicians.

IX.5 Politics Behind Neglect of Education, Health and Physical Infrastructure

The non-democratic regimes of East Asia were more successful than democratic India in the field of primary education and primary healthcare (PHC). Like in the case of insufficient taxation, in India, the root of the neglect of both primary education and PHC, and of physical infrastructure, lay in the democratic politics of the time. First, the public in general, with widespread illiteracy, was not very concerned about either primary education or public health problems. On health matters, for example, they took notice of the problem only when a major epidemic, such as cholera, broke out. For getting votes and winning elections, prevention of a disease by building up a network of PHCs had much less appeal than, say, the promise of setting up a CPSE in the neighbourhood and possible employment, or the supply of highly subsidized food and fertilizer. Furthermore, compared to providing relief once the epidemic starts causing large-scale misery, preventing an epidemic before it breaks out is much less rewarding politically. The promise of turning a poor and illiterate woman's child turn into an educated youth in ten years might not have been considered very effective for political mobilization in the near term. Poverty leads to myopia and for the purpose of getting votes, even large benefits in the future after discounting to the present may have been inferior to small gains in the more immediate future. Education would give returns only after a few years.

Second, there was the capture by the elite. In education, for example, relative to primary and adult education, there was emphasis on expansion of engineering, medical and agricultural colleges, building Indian Institutes of Management (IIMs) and IITs, and setting up of English-medium public schools, for which there was a political demand from the elite. These institutions would primarily benefit children from the upper socio-economic strata. The proponents of the strategy argued that the emphasis should be on those who want to learn rather than those who do not.

The neglect of basic education and PHC was clearly because of political reasons. Jean Dreze and Amartya Sen sum it up succinctly when they say: 'Had the government shown similar apathy and inconsistency while dealing with, say, the demands of the urban population for basic amenities, or of farmers' organisations for adequately high crop prices or of the military establishment for modern hardware . . . it is safe to predict that a major political battle would have followed. The fact that the government was able to get away with so much neglect of primary education (and health, added by the author) relates to the lack of political clout of the illiterate masses. It also reflects the fact that the social value of basic education (and health, added by the author) has been neglected not only by government authorities but also in social and political movements.'4

Compulsory primary education never figured in the election manifesto of any political party in the first few elections and this absence in the political discourse points to the elite's capture of policymaking. India made progress towards making elementary education a right only when the Supreme Court intervened in 1993 in a landmark judgment in the case of Unni Krishnan J.P. versus the state of Andhra Pradesh. The elite bias of political agenda continues, and the absence of the supply of safe drinking water as an electoral promise provides another good example. In most places in the country, the tap water supplied is not safe for drinking. While the elite has come to terms with the problem by installing water purifiers at home, the problem could have been solved at the water supply level itself at a fraction of the cost of installing tens of thousands of expensive water purifiers, and also helping the poor.

Pranab Bardhan succinctly summarizes the problems relating to the inadequate supply of infrastructure, education, public health and sanitation as a shortcoming of governance effectiveness in the delivery of these services as follows. Comparing the extraordinary state capacity displayed in some 'episodic matters, for example, in organising the complex logistics of the world's largest elections', he identifies a 'systemic impasse' behind this governance failure. He imputes it to 'complicity in sinister political nexus, populist pressures and', in the case of inadequate electricity, 'outright theft'.[5] He sums it up: 'The apparent lack of state capacity may be more a symptom of the underlying difficulty of organising collective action (or collectively working out a "social pact"), a problem exacerbated by large heterogeneous population, fragmented polity and extreme social and economic inequality. In such a context, commitments on the part of the state are often not credible and anticipating that different interest and identity groups settle for short-run patronage and subsidies.'

Balance of Payments Crisis, the Ensuing Debate and Policy Hysteresis

In 1994, with the benefit of hindsight, economists Amaresh Bagchi and Nicholas Stern summed it up well when they said: 'The early results of Indian planning were quite impressive. Breaking out of the stagnation of the preceding fifty years, the Indian economy grew at about 4 per cent per annum in the first two plan periods. Per capita income grew at 1.8 to 2 per cent. But this momentum was not maintained. What was more, financing the public sector proved increasingly difficult, leading to larger and larger recourse to "deficit financing" (borrowing from the central bank) with all their attendant consequences.'[1]

In the mid-nineteenth century, the German economist Adolph Wagner propounded the 'law of increasing expansion of public, and particularly state, activities'. Wagner wrote that this law '. . . becomes for the fiscal economy the law of the increasing expansion of fiscal requirements . . . That law is the result of empirical observation in progressive countries, at least in our Western European civilisation; its explanation, justification and cause is the pressure for social progress, and the resulting changes in the relative spheres of private and public economy.'[2] Post-Independence India conformed to the famous Wagner's law. Initially, it was a side effect of planning, and deploying state resources to boost production. But the returns, which came after the gestation period, also fell short of what was required to service the debt that financed it. Although Wagner's Law hit independent India as it became a 'progressive country', during the first seventeen years under Nehru, the deficit was incurred not for distributing subsidies to secure the support of sections of the electorate but for promoting capital formation and hence growth.

The underlying belief was that deficit financing could be legitimately used towards capital formation and hence growth, provided its inflationary impact could be contained. The problem was that the 'attendant consequences' of deficit financing in balance of payments and inflation could not be contained. Over time, the poor performance of CPSEs also dampened the faith in the efficacy of public investment in the productive sectors. Looking back, in 1987, a prominent economist, Amiya Kumar Dasgupta, rued: 'Frankly I did not envisage, while advocating a policy of deficit financing in the early stages of planning, the excesses that our prescription would lead to. If I now say "we have had enough of deficit financing", it is because of our experience over the years, which is not at all edifying.'[3]

X.1 The Journey from a Poor Country but Not So Poor a Government

During the Second World War, the Government of India incurred expenditure on behalf of the British government, which the latter paid in blocked sterling. Under the crown, the government had come a long way from the East India Company days. In 1857, the Company had bequeathed a large debt of ₹558 million, which had increased further to ₹1014 million by 1861. In 1947, the situation was drastically different— the colonial masters left the Government of India with 'sterling balances' of some ₹17.4 billion, which were also India's foreign currency reserves.

In 1948–49, the outstanding debt of the central government, at ₹2412.96 crore, was equivalent to 25.4 per cent of GDP. For 1950, the central government's debt-to-GDP ratio is available for thirty countries, including India, in the data maintained by the IMF. India, with a debt-to-GDP ratio of 26.1 per cent, was in the middle of the ranking, with fourteen countries (nine in Europe, plus the US, Australia, New Zealand, South Africa—all relatively high-income countries active in World War II—and Costa Rica) with a higher debt-to-GDP ratio averaging 51.6 per cent, and fifteen countries (eight in South America, four in Europe—

Austria, Finland, Greece and Portugal—and three in Asia—Malaysia, Thailand and Turkey) with a lower debt-to-GDP ratio averaging 10.3 per cent. If a lower debt-to-GDP ratio is taken as a measure of the higher financial strength of a government, then at Independence, UK left India poor as a country but with not so poor a government.

With limited revenues, the British colonial government had been spending less than 10 per cent of GNP in India—with defence claiming a quarter or a third of that, and a large part leaking out to the UK in the form of 'home charges'. Many countries had similar levels of public expenditure in the third quarter of the nineteenth century, but some, like the UK and Japan, had started increasing such expenditure from the late nineteenth century. As a proportion of GNP, it rose to 30 per cent in 1938 and 39 per cent in 1950 in the UK, and in Japan, from 10 per cent in 1879–83 to 25 per cent in 1905–12. In India, it did not increase under the colonial government, which scrupulously followed the canons of 'sound finance' with current revenues covering current expenditure, and public savings financing capital expenditure. Whenever possible, it used surpluses on current account to amortize public debt. Before Independence, the principle of soundness was sacrificed with relatively large deficits only in seven budgets around the Second World War when there were relatively large deficits in the seven budgets preceding Independence.

After Independence, with the consensus on a planned strategy for economic development, the government's financial support to the plans followed as a corollary. Such expenditure would create assets and enhance the productive capacity of the economy, and hence supplies. Public sector investments were expected to start paying rich dividends and more than make up for future amortization, including interest payments. This expectation was sadly belied.

Even the budget deficit or uncovered deficit became increasingly difficult to finance. This deficit had risen to ₹250 crore in the budget presented for 1954–55. By an exchange of letters, in January 1955, the RBI and the government decided that the government shall maintain with the RBI a cash balance of not less than ₹50 crore on Fridays and ₹4 crore on other days; whenever the balance in the government account fell below the minimum agreed to, the account would be replenished by the creation of ad hoc Treasury Bills in favour of the RBI. Ad hoc Treasury Bills were

IOUs that the government could draw up whenever it wanted, give to the RBI and get cash in exchange. In due course, the instrument to finance short-term cash deficit turned into a means of building up debt, with continuous rollover and piling up of these Treasury Bills.

Budgetary procedures and checks were relaxed in the mid-1950s to accommodate the burgeoning deficits. Loans should primarily be raised for productive and self-liquidating capital expenditure, that is, to create capital assets that produce revenue streams for its repayments and interest servicing. If raised for creating assets such as flood protection works and school buildings, or to meet current expenditures, adequate provisions should be made for their debt servicing out of the revenue account. 'In 1955 the government of India advised the state governments that all expenditure on capital assets, that is durable or fixed though not necessarily productive or self-liquidating assets, should be held eligible for being serviced out of loans, and the amortisation of such loans need not be treated as a charge on the revenue except to the extent that the state governments were bound to provide in accordance with any law or any specific undertaking given in the case of any loan.'[4]

X.2 Debate on Deficit Finance

With the balance of current revenues to support the plans turning negative from the Second Plan (1956–61), there was an intense debate on the role of deficit finance. The joint memorandum entitled 'The Second Five Year Plan: Basic Considerations Relating to the Plan Frame' of a Planning Commission-appointed panel of twenty-one economists, chaired by C.D. Deshmukh, had produced some differing positions. B.R. Shenoy, in his note of dissent, opposed resorting to deficit financing because of its inflationary impact. He was a prophet before his time. He was not against deficit financing per se, but against the level of deficit, which was too high to maintain price stability. A.K. Dasgupta differed with Shenoy, and continued the debate by joining issues with V.K.R.V. Rao in 1987 about the whole question of the relevance of Keynesian economics in an underdeveloped country. This debate, in its wider context, even raised issues about the relevance of the multiplier in an underdeveloped country. As early as 1952, V.K.R.V. Rao had pointed out the problems posed by supply constraints in limiting the role of government expenditure in boosting GDP or national income.

Shenoy's lone voice of dissent was drowned by the clamour for an activist state borrowing and spending on projects that the planners felt the country needed. In the quest for rapid industrialization through the state's interventionist investment, concerns about deficit and debt became of secondary importance. With a consensus on developing rapidly by increasing capital expenditure and putting the state at the commanding heights of the economy, arguing against the state spending more for 'development' was anathema. Even businessmen seemed to be in favour of deficit financing and money creation for increasing productive capacity. They had endorsed the deficit financing strategy for growth in their celebrated Bombay Plan drawn up before Independence. The enthusiasm for public spending to promote growth and development continued, and with it, fiscal deterioration.

Critics such as Shenoy could be dismissed as orthodox or, according to more modern terminology, neo-liberals. But the impact of the rising deficit and, therefore, of mounting debt, kicked in with full fury for everyone to see. Interest payments on government debt, which were only 8.9 per cent of total government expenditure in 1950–51, were pre-empting 10.7 per cent of such expenditure by 1963–64 and went on to increase to 13.9 per cent of such expenditure by 1969–70. As a proportion of GDP, the corresponding increase was from 0.4 per cent to 1.3 per cent.

Inflation as measured by the WPI, which was in single digit or even negative during the 1950s, except for in 1956–57, when it reached 14 per cent, started rising in the following decade. In 1964–65, it reached 11 per cent, and after declining to 7.6 per cent in the succeeding year, rose back to 13.9 per cent in 1966–67 and 11.6 per cent in 1967–68. From 1.7 per cent in the 1950s, annual average inflation during the decade of the 1960s (1960–61 to 1969–70) went up about four times to 6.3 per cent. The high inflation of almost 14 per cent in 1956–57 was 'mainly due to demand pressures, particularly investment demand in the light of the thrust on industrialisation in the second five-year plan'.[5] There was no drought or war around 1956–57, and the inflation was in spite of PL480 import of food grains from 1956 onwards.

Right from the outset, the Indian government accepted only official external loans and no external commercial loans. Until the 1960s, such external debt constituted no more than 10 per cent of its total public debt. Internal debt could always be serviced by taking more credit, if necessary, from the RBI. Whether such action led to crowding out of private investment or inflation could always be debated with alternate arguments. But problems cropped up on the external front. The Suez crisis in 1957 rang the warning bells.

X.3 1957: Suez Crisis—Reality Strikes on the Foreign Exchange Front

Panic struck the Indian government in the early part of 1957 with a crisis in the external sector. The external value of the rupee was tied to the pound sterling, and a balance of payments crisis in the UK did not take long to trigger a similar crisis in India. It all arose from a crisis in 1956 around the Suez Canal, the one-hundred-mile-long canal through Egypt, cutting across the only land bridge joining Africa and Asia, and connecting the Red Sea and the Mediterranean Sea. During the colonial times, the Suez Canal was the UK's 'highway to India'. By 1956, with India no longer a colony, it was critical, not as the British highway to India, but as the highway for oil from the Persian Gulf to Europe. .

In Egypt, then a semi-autonomous province of the Ottoman empire, the French engineer Ferdinand de Lesseps had obtained a ninety-nine-year concession from Khedive or Viceroy Said Pasha to construct the canal. Lesseps founded the Suez Canal Company, completed the canal in 1869, went on to marry at the age of sixty-four a young lady of twenty to father a dozen children, and try unsuccessfully to also construct the Panama Canal joining the Atlantic and the Pacific Ocean. The concession would run out and the canal would have to be reverted to the Egyptian government on 16 November 1968.

From 1936 onwards, Egypt was nominally ruled by King Farouk. On 26 July 1952, military officers under General Mohammed Naguib overthrew the glamorous Farouk and sent him on exile to the French Riviera to acquire further infamy for his numerous girlfriends and corpulence. Egypt became a republic. The tall and handsome Colonel Gamal Abdel

Nasser toppled Gen. Naguib in 1954, and with his pan-Arabist policies, went on to become one of the most charismatic leaders of the Arab world. On 26 July 1956, Nasser nationalized the Suez Canal Company, owned by French shareholders and the British government, by promising to pay the day's closing price on the Paris Stock Exchange. His audacity outraged the French and the British.

On 29 October 1956, following an Anglo-French plan, Israel invaded Egypt's Sinai desert. On the pretext of separating the two sides and preserving the canal for international commerce, the British and French issued an ultimatum to Egypt and Israel to withdraw 10 miles to the west and east of the canal to create a neutral zone for the Anglo-French forces to occupy. Israel was in any case further than 10 miles from the canal, and Egypt refused. On 31 October, when the Egyptian air force was decimated by the British and French bombers, Nasser sank a ship loaded with rocks and concrete to render the canal inoperable. A vast Anglo-French armada started travelling from Malta to reach Port Said at the northern gateway to the canal in six days.

The US under President Eisenhower was not consulted before the Anglo-French-Israeli attack, and refused to support the invasion. On 2 November, the US moved a resolution in the UN General Assembly calling for a ceasefire and withdrawal of forces. The resolution was passed with overwhelming support. Though the former Soviet Union was embroiled in fighting an anti-communist national movement in Hungary, on 5 November 1956, Khrushchev threatened London and Paris with missile attacks if they did not withdraw their forces from Egypt. He sent a similar note to the Israeli government. On 6 November, the UK decided to end the Suez operation, and France followed suit.

With the canal closed, merchandise had to be rerouted around the Cape of Good Hope. Shipping rates to Europe from the East went up sharply. Even the British tea habit became costly, the *New York Times* of 1 January 1957 reported. In the UK, there was not only a shortage of petrol, leading to lay-offs and factory closures, but also its rationing. The price of crude (West Texas Intermediate) went up by more than 10 per cent, from US$2.8 to US$3.10 per barrel. The UK faced an external crisis. There was speculation that the UK would have to abandon the sterling parity of US$2.80. Devaluation would exacerbate the impact of an already high dollar price of oil, hence the UK authorities defended the parity by selling dollars at the rate of US$2.80 for a pound. With losses in November 1956, the British reserves fell below the US$2 billion official floor maintained since 1940. The British government needed foreign assistance to defend the pound, but nothing was forthcoming unless it fully accepted 2 November's UN resolution calling not only for a ceasefire but also withdrawal of forces. The British Cabinet accepted the UN resolution in full and set a deadline of 22 December for full troop withdrawal from Egypt. On 6 December, the IMF approved a package of US$1.3 billion, including its first ever stand-by arrangement (US$739 million) to finance a capital account problem. The pound was saved for the time being.

Just as the UK was suffering from a balance of payments problem, for India, especially with a food grain shortage, the rise in the price of oil following the Suez crisis and the rupee tied to the pound, how to pay for imports became a critical question. The stock of foreign exchange reserves had come down during the First Plan from US$2.161 billion in 1950–51 (end of period) to US$1.895 billion in 1955–56. In a little less than nine months of the Second Plan, that is, by December 1956, there was panic and India went for a stand-by arrangement with the IMF. After some tortuous negotiations, in February 1957 the IMF agreed to lend $200 million, of which $72.5 million were in the nature of a stand-by facility. The Suez Canal was reopened to international traffic on 8 March 1957, after Israel's withdrawal from occupied Egyptian territory, but it took weeks to clean up the wreckage before larger ships could navigate. All this happened almost at the same time (1 April 1957) as India was introducing the *naye paise*—or new coins based on the decimalized system—to replace annas, paisas and pies. The naya paisa was born in such times of tumultuous balance of payments.

X.4 Acrimony About the Balance of Payments Crisis

Average annual growth of GDP was 4.1 per cent under Nehru, between 1951–52 and 1964–65, a great improvement over the pre-Independence decades. What came to the fore during the Nehru era was not the performance of the economy relative to its own potential and to that of the other countries to the east, or questions on 'government failure', but the compatibility of socialist planning with the Constitution, and the associated problems of growing fiscal deficit, inflationary pressures and vulnerability of the external balance of payments. The debates were confined to policymakers and the elite, and their impact on electoral politics was at best indirect.

The acrimony following the balance of payments crisis of 1956–57 provides a good example. The balance of payments crisis led to the departure of Penderel Moon, a former British civil servant serving at the Planning Commission as adviser. A brilliant Oxford scholar and Fellow of All Souls, Moon had joined the Punjab cadre of the ICS in 1928. His book *Divide and Quit*, published later in 1961, is considered a valuable contribution to Indian historical studies. He was friendly with many Indians, including the freedom fighter Rajkumari Amrit Kaur. His correspondence with Amrit Kaur when she was in prison during the Quit India movement attracted the ire of his superiors and led him to resign from the ICS in 1943. He joined the princely state of Bahawalpur (now in Pakistan) as an administrator. After Independence, Nehru invited Moon to join the Planning Commission. Moon stayed back.

Moon, in a broadcast on All India Radio, argued that the steep decline in foreign exchange reserves was due to the increase in import of capital goods. He saw the Second Plan as a product of excessive exuberance and suggested the need for cutting down its ambitious investment targets. K.N. Raj, the noted Indian economist, was unhappy about Moon, a Planning Commission official, misleading the people in a broadcast. Raj saw the decline in foreign exchange reserves as the consequence of excessive domestic demand for consumer goods. The rate of investment was already low at only 8 per cent of GDP, and to argue for even lower investment was not the right recipe for the plan. Raj argued for stricter controls on imports of consumer goods and inessentials. Moon was perhaps right about the infirmities of the Second Plan, but he did not win the battle. In the milieu of the mid-1950s, Moon's chances of success were slim. Moon left India and joined the World Bank.

The acrimonious debate over the foreign exchange crisis was not restricted to economists and planners. Even Finance Minister T.T. Krishnamachari and his predecessor Deshmukh got embroiled in it. Deshmukh had served as the first Indian Governor (1943–1949) of the

RBI, and as the finance minister from 1950 to 1956. After resigning as finance minister, Deshmukh was serving as the chairman of the University Grants Commission (UGC). Prime Minister Nehru had functioned as finance minister for a month before T.T. Krishnamachari took over. There were two important Krishnamacharis in the 1950s—V.T. Krishnamachari as the deputy chairman of the Planning Commission and T.T. Krishnamachari as the finance minister. To avoid confusion, the latter will be referred to henceforth as TTK, as he was popularly known.

Part of the reason for the import boom in 1956–57 was the lagged effect of liberal import licensing, particularly of consumer goods, in 1955–56. In a letter to Prime Minister Nehru, Deshmukh claimed '. . . to have been kept in the dark by the other wings of the government, in particular the Commerce and Industry Ministry, about the liberal import policy. Finance Minister TTK, who was earlier in Commerce and Industry, saw Deshmukh's letter as a personal attack and argued to Jawaharlal Nehru that the crisis was a result of the Planning Commission's sloppy resources arithmetic, about which the Finance Ministry was not consulted, and the former Finance Minister's failure to spot or correct it. The Planning Commission for its part blamed it on adverse changes in India's external environment caused by heavy demands for defence, larger food imports, and the impact of the Suez crisis on prices and freight rates.'[6]

The roots of the foreign exchange problem lay fundamentally in the excess demand that was generated by a shortfall of domestic savings relative to investment. And this excess had a lot to do with the government's expansionary fiscal stance coupled with industrial licensing and large investments in CPSEs. Industrial licensing held back industrial growth, and thereby retarded industrialization, growth and generation of additional income and savings. The deficit had worried the government initially. But such worries disappeared over time. C.D. Deshmukh, in his budget speech for 1954–55, had said: 'There will be some—not many, I expect, in this House and outside who will have doubts as to the wisdom of launching upon deficit financing on this scale. I have given the most careful thought to this question, and, on a balance of considerations, I am convinced that in the conditions as they now are and are likely to be in the near future, we are, not taking any undue risks in going forward in the manner I have indicated. In fact, deficit financing to a moderate extent is necessary under present conditions. The period of inflationary stresses is now well behind us and there are signs that the high levels of production we have attained in various lines, and which we would like to improve upon cannot be sustained without some increase in money supply in the hands of the public.'

Indeed, inflation had come down from the very high levels, prevalent with shortages, during the Second World War. In his budget speech for 1954–55, Deshmukh had also pointed out that the economic effects of the budgetary deficit would be neutralized by a balance of payments deficit. So it did. After all, with the private and public sectors in the country spending in excess of what it produced, the shortfall had to be met through an excess of imports over exports. The excess of government spending over revenue was spilling over to the external balance of payments. The net saving of the private sector was smaller than the government's net dissaving. Merchandise imports started to outstrip such exports by a large margin, and after 1955–56, the current account turned into a sizeable deficit.

By the early 1960s, various reports had pointed out the problems with the socialist planning and industrial licensing regime. The regime had also witnessed high inflation and a balance of payments crisis. The puzzling question is: why did the policy framework continue unchanged? Why was the emphasis only on 'more of the same' with better monitoring and implementation, and not a change in the system itself? We now turn to this critical question of policy hysteresis.

X.5 Policy Hysteresis—Why No Action?

Accepting responsibility for a policy failure is difficult for a politician, for several reasons. First, there is what is called 'cognitive dissonance', the psychological discomfort that a person feels when faced with a lack of congruence between what they believe and what reality turns out to be. This dissonance, which is at the root of people not admitting of having been 'wrong', takes a particularly intense form among politicians. Politicians, like spiritual gurus, project an image of infallibility. Nobel laureate Paul Krugman has written about how American politics in 2017 '. . . at least on one side of the aisle—is suffering from an epidemic of infallibility, of powerful people who never, ever admit to making a mistake'.[7]

The projection of infallibility also stems partly from the challenge of managing the political party. The cadre of the political party 'to spread information, persuade undecided voters, and activate preferences. In their drive to win elections, parties educate voters and mediate the political experience'.[8] An admission of error by the leadership would shake up the loyalty of the party cadre without winning over any from the opposition. Furthermore, there were vested interest groups benefitting from the large network of public sector enterprises and the permit-quota-licence raj. These included the employees of CPSEs, the politicians and bureaucrats, and somewhat counterintuitively, the business magnates.

Vested interests—CPSE employees

First, the number of CPSEs had jumped up from five on 1 April 1951 to seventy-three on 31 March 1966. The corresponding increase in total investment was from ₹29 crore to ₹2410 crore. Though employment in CPSEs was less than 50,000 until the mid-1960s, the CPSE employees provided the trade unions with not only a secure base to operate from but also as a way to rally direct employees of the government, such as in posts and telegraphs, railways, civil aviation and the central public works department. The expectation that, unlike in the private sector, there would be no class conflict between the state as an employer and the workers was proved wrong fairly soon after Independence, when municipal workers in Mumbai were on the brink of a strike in mid-1957.

The wage distribution in CPSEs had a clear pattern—employees at the top end of the wage distribution in CPSEs received less than their private sector counterparts, while those at the lower end received the largest wage premia. Paying less at the higher end and more at the lower end conformed to 'socialist thinking' and helped bolster the government's political image to the people. Those at the lower end of the wage structure were also more numerous and more unionized. The CPSE employees constituted a large part of the then relatively small Indian middle class. They received many in-kind benefits and perquisites, which included not only statutory ones such as medical facilities and lunchrooms, but also non-statutory ones such as educational facilities for children and recreational facilities such as gymnasiums and sports complexes. These perquisites were rare in the private sector.

Until 1957, wages in CPSEs were set through collective bargaining between workers and management, and often by industrial tribunals and judiciary. This system led to 'imitation effects', with concessions granted by management in one unit tending to get extended to others under union pressure. The wage board awards did not have any legal backing, and while CPSEs implemented such awards, they were flouted by the private sector. Average wages in public sector undertakings could be as much as twice that in the private organized sector.

The employees of CPSEs, in sharp contrast to their private industry counterparts, also enjoyed life-long job security. Article 12 of the Indian Constitution defines the State to include the government and Parliament of India, the government and the legislature of each of the states, and all local or other authorities within the territory of India or under the control of the Government of India. The CPSEs fell within the inclusive definition of 'State' under Article 12, and the courts and statutory authorities had powers of judicial review on the matters pertaining to CPSEs in relation to service matters. With so many advantages, the CPSE employees had a vested interest in perpetuating the system with the public sector at the 'commanding heights'. Through their trade unions affiliated to major political parties, they also had the political muscle.

Vested interests—Political leaders and bureaucrats

Apart from the employees of CPSEs, the bureaucrats and political leaders also had a major stake in the perpetuation of the system. The extant permit-quota-licence system had been converted into an exchange system with a 'price' for all the privileges. The bureaucracy dispensing licences liked it because it provided payoffs, power, prestige, patronage and employment for their relatives or even themselves post-retirement. Political leaders had the same incentives, together with campaign contributions and donations from businesspersons.

Who will get the licence for what, how much and where to produce were among the most critical factors in determining business growth and profitability. Established business houses had learnt how to work the system. It was common knowledge that every industrialist had a 'Delhi embassy' to liaise with the government, push files, communicate with the government and lobby, and act as listening posts and collect information. Retired bureaucrats and relatives of political leaders and government officials were employed by industrialists to enhance their lobbying power. Providing financial support and hospitality to political leaders was a common way of currying favour. With high entry barriers to potential domestic competitors through licensing and competition from abroad prevented by QRs on imports, the permit-quota-licence raj allowed established businesses to prosper if they kept the politicians and bureaucrats 'happy'. After the launch of 'socialist planning', industrialists learnt how to do so with alacrity.

Indian business and 'democratic socialism'

Somewhat counterintuitively, vested interests included not only the employees of CPSEs, bureaucrats and politicians, but established businesses as well. Since the Karachi session of the Congress in 1931, planned development and regulation of industry on socialist principles had been an accepted tenet of Indian economic policy. In 1938, under the chairmanship of Netaji Subhash Chandra Bose, a conference of provincial ministers of industries passed a resolution stating that not only was industrialization essential for addressing the problems of poverty, unemployment, national defence and economic regeneration, but also that comprehensive planning was needed for such industrialization. The Congress in 1938, under Netaji's presidency, appointed a National Planning Commission under the chairmanship of Nehru; this commission suggested that basic industries should be largely developed by the public sector and development of large-scale industries should be regulated and guided by the government.

Even the country's leading industrialists were in favour of a planned approach to industrialization. This is clear from 'A Plan for Economic Development of India', popularly known as the Bombay Plan, formulated by Indian industrialists in January 1944. The plan's name came from the Bombay House of the Tatas, which provided the secretariat. The Bombay Plan was signed by J.R.D. Tata, G.D. Birla, Sir Ardeshir Dalal, Lala Shri

Ram, Kasturbhai Lalbhai, A.D. Shroff, John Mathai and Purushotamdas Thakurdas. With an ambitious target of doubling per capita income in fifteen years, it came out before the National Planning Commission had published any documents. In its blueprint for post-war reconstruction and development after Independence, it was not simply reacting to any alternative strategy. However, the minutes of its authors clarify that the apprehension that post-Independence, the government might initiate populist economic measures, especially in the face of organized political demands for redistribution of income and wealth, did play a role in the development of a blueprint for an orderly and more caring path of development before such a contingency arose.

There was remarkable agreement between the political leaders and the leading industrialists about the active role of the government and regulation in the development process after Independence. Business in general may not have been happy with the government playing such an activist role in the economy. But, the Bombay Plan clearly stated '. . . we think that no development of the kind we have proposed will be feasible except on the basis of a central directing authority which . . . possesses the requisite powers and jurisdiction'. It went on to add '. . . in order to prevent the inequitable distribution of the burden between different classes which this method of financing will involve, practically every aspect of economic life will have to be so rigorously controlled by government that individual liberty and freedom of enterprise will suffer a temporary eclipse'. Agreement about this appropriate strategy for industrialization extended even to the colonial government, as attested by its adoption of the Industrial Policy Statement of 1945.

All industrialists, however, were not comfortable with planning and government control. Badridas Goenka, president of the Federation of Indian Chambers of Commerce and Industry (FICCI), in a press statement on 28 April 1945, had said the '. . . fundamental issue for India today is not that of State-versus-private enterprise but of paramountcy of national interest'. He also added a criticism of the 'system of controls and restrictions which only tend to hamper industrial progress and dampen initiative and enterprise'.

The comfort of the industrialists with planning and the government playing a leading role in industrialization was badly shaken soon after

Independence by the report of the Economic Programme Committee, chaired by Nehru, to the CWC on 25 January 1948. According to the report, for attaining the objectives of a national minimum standard, full employment and the establishment of a just social order, it was considered necessary to demarcate industries which should be developed in the decentralized sector, those in large-scale industries, and those which through an integration of the two. New undertakings in defence, key industries and public utilities, as also those which were in the nature of monopolies, or because of scale of operation which could serve large parts of the country, were to be started under public ownership, and existing undertakings in these fields were to be nationalized gradually after a gap of five years. For effective coordination and harmonious development of different types of industries, control of investment and licensing of new undertakings were envisaged. Furthermore, all resources available for investment were to be subject to the control and direction of the state.

When the Economic Programme Committee's report came out in 1948, it was strongly refuted by Homi Mody and G.D. Birla on behalf of FICCI. Because of these controversies, an Industries Conference was convened to consider various problems relating to the future policy for industrial development. Based on these deliberations, the government formulated its own Industrial Policy Resolution (IPR) and announced it in April 1948. It was a much-watered-down version of the Economic Programme Committee's recommendations, confining public ownership to only three industries—munitions, atomic energy and railways. In six others—coal, iron and steel, aircraft manufacturing, shipbuilding, telegraphic and telephonic materials and minerals—while only the government could start new ventures, existing private enterprises were to remain free from government control and not be nationalized for at least ten years. Nehru, to boost business confidence in the government, may have diluted his Economic Programme Committee's recommendations in formulating IPR of April 1948. He was severely criticized for going against an accepted stand of the Congress. The dilution helped to some extent but did not dispel the business perception of a hostile political environment. Birla lamented to Home Minister Govind Ballabh Pant, 'The British have gone and the princes and the zamindars are in the background. The

Congress, accustomed to a target for its hatred, is now finding only one target, the capitalist.'[9]

IDRA in 1951 declared certain industries of all-India importance and advocated a mechanism for their development and regulation. For planned industrial development, there would be an industrial licensing system to bring 'under Central control the development and regulation of a number of important industries, the activities of which affect the country as a whole and the development of which must be governed by economic factors of all India import'. It was expected that it would secure 'planning of future development on sound and balanced lines'.[10] Of course, with imports under QRs, authorization for capital goods import could also be used to channel industrial development to the right course.

A big jolt to Indian business came from the nationalization of the airline and life insurance industries. Air transportation was a relatively new industry. Although a licence was required from the Air Transport Licensing Board from 1946 onwards and only four airline companies were considered optimal, many more were operating in the country. Excessive price competition and low traffic volume had led to losses. Jupiter Airlines had gone into liquidation in 1948 and Ambica Airlines in 1949. Many of the twenty-nine airline operators were in financial distress. One of the successful companies was Air India, owned by Tata Sons, led by J.R.D. Tata, who, in 1929, was the first to obtain a pilot's licence issued in India.

In 1948, Tata had gone into a public-private partnership with the government, with 49 per cent ownership, to set up Air India International to service international flights. The following year, on 30 January 1949, the government inaugurated the Indian Night Air Mail Service, the world's first overnight airmail service. J.R.D. Tata had an acrimonious exchange with Rafi Ahmed Kidwai, minister for communication in Nehru's cabinet, on introduction of this Night Air Mail. Tata felt that it would increase the cost of operations of an already beleaguered airline industry. There are speculations about the impact of the Kidwai-Tata exchange on the government's subsequent decisions regarding the airline industry.

The Air Transport Enquiry Commission under the chairmanship of G.S. Rajadhyaksha was set up in February 1950. It recommended restricting the number of airline companies to no more than four and initiating other revenue-augmenting and cost-cutting measures. Nationalization was not one of the suggested steps. Furthermore, even according to IPR 1948, air transport was to be left to private enterprise subject to the government's supervisory and regulatory control. By 1952, however, the financial position of most airline companies in India was under severe strain, and only two options were left open for the government—heavy subsidization or nationalization. Jagjivan Ram, minister for communication, moved the Air Corporations Bill in the Lok Sabha on 21 March 1953 to nationalize the airline industry. If the industry, particularly given its public utility nature, could survive only with government subsidy, then there was merit in taking it under government ownership, the minister argued.

The Air Corporations Act came into effect from 1 August 1953. All airlines were consolidated under Air India International (for international services) and Indian Airlines (for domestic services). J.R.D. Tata, who was successfully running Air India International, was taken by surprise and greatly offended by the decision. However, the nature of the times and the confidence that the government had in Tata were demonstrated by the fact that the management of Air India, including the chairmanship of J.R.D. Tata, was left undisturbed even after nationalization.

The long history of the life insurance business in India, run by the private sector, tells a similar story. National poet Rabindranath Tagore's grandfather Prince Dwarkanath was a partner in the privately-owned Oriental Life Insurance Society, which had been set up in 1818. But the sector, in spite of some regulatory enactments, had been bedevilled by problems such as unhealthy competition, leading to bankruptcies of many life insurance companies, mis-selling and difficulties in claim settlement. Only about a half per cent of the population had some life insurance cover. For establishing 'a just social order', nationalization of insurance had been strongly recommended by the Economic Programme Committee of the All-India Congress Committee (AICC) in 1948.

Attempts at regulation had not produced the desired results, and the nationalization of the life insurance business in the early part of 1956 appears to have been without 'any doctrinaire bias against the private sector'. It appears to have been based on the inefficient functioning of private insurers, failure of indirect regulation through legislation to deliver the desired results, and the potential of insurance business to provide the financial resources needed for planned investment both in the public and private sectors.

As J.R.D. Tata, one of the authors of the Bombay Plan, was to reminisce later in 1971: 'In the past twenty years, the freedom of action and the scope of operation of the private sector have been subjected to a gradual but continuous process of erosion in the course of which the government has achieved a measure of control and ownership of the means of production and distribution, which would have been inconceivable to any of us if introduced all at once at the start and which is unprecedented in any country other than those under totalitarian rule . . .'[11]

The socialist motive may not have been the dominant one behind the nationalization of the airline or the life insurance business, but Nehru, in May 1956, had stated in Parliament that under the Second Plan, though the private sector will play an important role, 'gradually and ultimately it will fade away'.[12] In 1952, he had stated: 'We are not willing to give private enterprise the high place which some countries have given it', and went on to add 'we are ready to view it with suspicion . . . if you imagine that we should keep private enterprise before us as an axiom or presumption you are mistaken.'[13] Indian businessmen were worried, but many of them believed that 'a businessman is not a businessman unless he can adjust himself to changing conditions'.[14] Furthermore, many businessmen also saw the Congress as the best insurance against the communist alternative.

A large section of the Indian business community followed the strategy favoured by G.D. Birla: '. . . one should never confront or challenge the government directly or openly. One should play along with the government, step on their toes but not too hard, and try to work out agreements with government officials in private'.[15] With the existence of private enterprise itself under uncertainty, a businessman summed up the strategy favoured by Birlas and their sympathizers as '. . . if the life of the private sector in India is to be twenty years then by a process of pressure on government one would at least extend the life of the private sector to thirty years'.[16] In the event, in about four decades, G.D. Birla's strategy proved to be farsighted. Air India, nationalized in 1953, came back to Tata through privatization in 2021!

Congress Party and 'democratic socialism'

Right from before its birth, the vocal majority in the Congress, under the leadership of Nehru, had more or less made up its mind to follow socialism. It was far from a consensus, though. There were misgivings about such a pursuit in the minds of some leaders such as Sardar Patel, Rajendra Prasad and Rajaji. But such misgivings were aired in a rather muted way and not persistently.

In his address to the Congress session in Lucknow in 1928, held under the presidency of his father Motilal, the young Nehru had announced that 'the only solution of the world's problems and of India's problems lies in socialism'.[17] What that 'socialism' precisely meant or how far the party was committed to such socialism was far from clear. So, when Sardar Patel expressed his ideological differences with Nehru on the nature of capitalism and threatened to contest Nehru for the post of Congress president the next year in Faizpur, Nehru clarified that socialism was not his plank for the presidency and Sardar withdrew from the contest. Yet, the opinion of the majority within the party evolved towards the view that economic policy had to be socialist with a pronounced emphasis on a centrally planned strategy.

Congress under Nehru won the first three elections and ruled India. The lasting camaraderie developed during the freedom struggle and the loyalty that Nehru commanded contained dissensions to a minimum. However, in recent times, the extent of disagreement between Nehru and Sardar Patel and their relationship have become matters of some controversy. Some claim that there were irreconcilable differences between the two in terms of not only foreign policy and communal issues but also economic policies, and it was only the older Patel's knowledge that 'the destruction of their party might very well mean the destruction of India that a rupture did not happen during the formative critical years of the Indian republic'.[18] In a letter to Mahatma Gandhi towards the end of the Mahatma's life, Nehru wrote that it was 'true that there are not only temperamental differences between Sardar and me but also are differences in approach with regard to economic and communal matters'.[19] Yet others dismiss such differences as minor and describe it as 'a divide that never was'.[20]

Irrespective of whether Sardar Patel agreed or disagreed with Nehru about planning and 'socialistic pattern of society', he passed away two and a half years after independence on 15 December 1950. Two other sources of potential opposition were Rajendra Prasad and Rajaji. In 1950, on 26 January, Rajendra Prasad became the first President of India, a largely ceremonial post. On 25 October 1951, Rajaji, after serving as the Union home minister from 26 December 1950 onwards, resigned on 'grounds of ill health' and left for Chennai. After serving as the chief minister of Madras from 1952 to 1954, Rajaji resigned from the Congress in January 1957. With Sardar Patel, Rajendra Prasad and Rajaji not there, there was little effective opposition to Nehru's policies of planned development and 'socialistic pattern of society' within the party after the early 1950s.

There was one sector, though, where Nehru and his socialist followers faced stubborn opposition, and that was agriculture. The fascination with what was happening in the Soviet Union around the 1940s was also manifest from the attitude towards agriculture. At the fiftieth session of the Congress Party in 1936, cooperative farming was mentioned as a plank of agrarian reform. The mention of cooperative farming was also there in the party's election manifesto of 1946. The Agrarian Reforms Committee in 1949 had resolved that cooperative farming was the way ahead. The Chinese experiment of forming farmers' cooperatives and benefitting from land consolidation and pooling agricultural machinery inspired Indian leadership, although not so far as to abolish private ownership of land. Even an official delegation was sent to study the Chinese agricultural policy. However, Indian farmers, including those newly enfranchised by the land reforms, under the guidance of new leaders, most notably Chaudhury Charan Singh, the Jat leader from UP and future prime minister for over five months, opposed such a move. Their opposition was reinforced by evidence from the farm management surveys of the Indian Planning Commission that large farms were not more productive than small farms.

The targets for cooperative farming had come down from 5000 as set by the state ministers for cooperation in 1956 and 10,000 set by the Patil Report on Agrarian Cooperatives in China in 1957 to 3000 set by the National Development Council in September 1957 for the Second Plan period. Nevertheless, in January 1959, at its Sixty-Fourth Plenary Session at

Nagpur, the Congress declared that India's future agrarian pattern should be 'cooperative joint farming'. But it stipulated a transition period of three years when 'service cooperatives' would be organized on a large scale. As a reaction, the Swatantra Party, a rightist party focused on efficiency and productivity as keys for economic progress, and emphasizing freedom from state controls, was born in June 1959! It seems that Nehru finally lost his abiding commitment to cooperative farming as the way ahead. The Nagpur resolution did not have any specific targets for cooperative farming at all! If fundamental right to property was a casualty of socialism, cooperative farming was a casualty of liberal, pluralist politics.

Despite the setback to the pursuit of cooperative farming, socialism was formally accepted in a Lok Sabha resolution in December 1954 which stated that the objective of economic policy should be a socialist pattern of society. In January 1955, at its annual session at Avadi, near Chennai, the Congress adopted a resolution on the 'socialistic pattern of society' moved by Nehru. The 'socialistic pattern of development', which would be the model for India's future government, included land reforms and regulations of industries. The Avadi Resolution stated that the private sector was to remain 'only for the present' and Nehru as Congress president said that the private sector was being tolerated 'as something which we want to push out'.

Socialism, a technical term, signifies state ownership of the means of production other than labour. This was not what 'socialistic pattern of society' signified. Socialism in the Avadi Congress session was a loosely used term and this was confirmed by no less than Nehru. As the economist A.K. Dasgupta has noted, 'Nobody knew what precisely was the connotation of the doctrine. The framers of the doctrine had apparently a vague feeling in their minds that they were out to secure a better standard of living for the masses by providing more employment, wider social service schemes and so on. Indeed, when pressed for a precise definition, our Prime Minister, than whom nobody could be supposed to know better, disposed it of by just equating it with welfare state.'[21] The Indore session of the Congress, on the eve of the second general election in 1957, saw the first article of the Congress constitution amended to incorporate the words '. . . the establishment in India by peaceful and legitimate means of a Socialist Cooperative Commonwealth . . .' The '. . . sort of socialism that the

Congress has in mind is more akin to Sarvodaya'[22] and not of the Western variety. The achievement of the socialist cooperative commonwealth by peaceful and legitimate means was basically a gradual transition to socialism by rapid expansion of the public sector.

By the Second-Five Year Plan, a 'socialist pattern of society' was firmly entrenched in the planning approach. According to the 'Approach Paper' of the second plan, 'The task before an underdeveloped country is not merely to get better results within the existing framework of economic and social institutions but to mould and refashion these so that they contribute effectively to the realisation of wider and deeper social values. These values or basic objectives have recently been summed up in the phrase "socialist pattern of society".'

India operated with a touching faith in the CPSEs. Prasanta Chandra Mahalanobis, firmly in the saddle at the Planning Commission by the Second Five-Year Plan, was a firm believer in the public sector. He anticipated that, in fifteen years' time, surpluses of the CPSEs would render the need for extra taxation superfluous in the Indian economy. Alas, the experience was to be quite to the contrary. But the same policies continued as a triumph of hope over experience.

The electorate and 'democratic socialism'

In a democracy, development policy is an interactive process. With the compulsion of winning elections, it is reasonable to expect that what the electorate wants would get reflected in what the political leaders give in terms of policy response. So what role did the principals, namely the electorate, play in the adoption of democratic socialism? In adopting it as the guiding principle of the state, was the leadership reflecting the people's will?

The mass movements leading to Independence had laid the foundation for popular participation in the political process and there was widespread popular support for the 'democratic' part of 'democratic socialism'. The people's view on socialism was quite different. The state of the electorate at the time of adoption of democracy in 1950 can be gauged by the reasons which led to the introduction of symbols in ballot boxes/papers. The overwhelming majority were illiterates. It was realized that it might not be possible for the illiterate voters to cast their votes in favour of the candidate of their choice unless there was some pictorial representation of the candidates on the ballot box/paper. Thus, separate symbols or pictorial representation for each candidate were brought into use. Given this background, the direct role of the electorate in the adoption of the 'socialism' part of democratic socialism was minimal.

The colonial rule and its educational policy left independent India with a strong central authority and a strong grip of the educated political elite upon the masses, which were segmented by religion, language, caste and endogamous kinship groups called jatis. The dominant method of reaching out to the masses in the initial years was mobilization of the persuasive powers of local notables and caste leaders, and by relying on traditional loyalties and dependencies. Prominent leaders enjoyed the delegated authority of the people, and the adoption of socialism in democratic socialism as the guiding principle of the state was an exercise of this authority.

In the first decade after Independence, the Indian state had, just as in the case of socialism, considerable 'autonomy' in policy matters. The system has even been described as one-party democracy. The government consisted of leaders of the freedom movement who had the rare ability in those times to lead the masses as well as to 'speak the language' of the alien ruling class. Having wrested freedom from an imperial power, the Congress party and its leaders had a different sort of acceptability. They knew what the people 'needed'. The collective views of leaders such as Nehru, Sardar Patel or Maulana Abul Kalam Azad were unassailable. With them towering over the political scene, policy had enough scope to be 'top down'. The adoption of a planned approach itself signified the autonomy of the state as an active agent that plans for what the passive society should do. The ruling party could galvanize the people into appropriate responses as desired by the planners. With literacy at only 18.3 per cent (1951) and a large section of the populace steeped in feudal culture, the views of the small political and intellectual elite found natural acceptance.

In economic policy, there was an emphasis on the 'right' ideology, and 'right' was leftist economics with the long shadow of Marx on it. Lack of its precise definition may have led to the embedding of 'socialism' in many Indian minds as a nebulous combination of 'good' pro-people economic policies, akin to *sarvodaya* (or universal uplift). Indians might have been particularly susceptible to the loosely defined ideology of socialism because of two additional innate factors. First, in the traditional chaturvarna or four varna system of Brahmin, Kshatriya, Vaishya and Shudra, the Vaishyas conducting trade and commerce came in the lower half of the stratification. Some Indians might have secretly pined to become rich, but publicly, 'making money' was not a vocation that was extolled for its virtues. Second, Indians have a high tolerance for ambiguity, a trait that facilitated the absorption and synthesis of diverse and even contradictory ideas.

There was a lot of stress on planning, public sector and redistributive policies. Development experts in the 1940s looked at markets with scepticism and had a lot of fascination for public sector-led Soviet-style planned development. The domestic industrialist capitalist class was still in its formative stages. With unhappy memories of what had happened under the East India Company, there was fear of and suspicion about foreign capitalists. Thus, the pursuit of socialist policies with the public

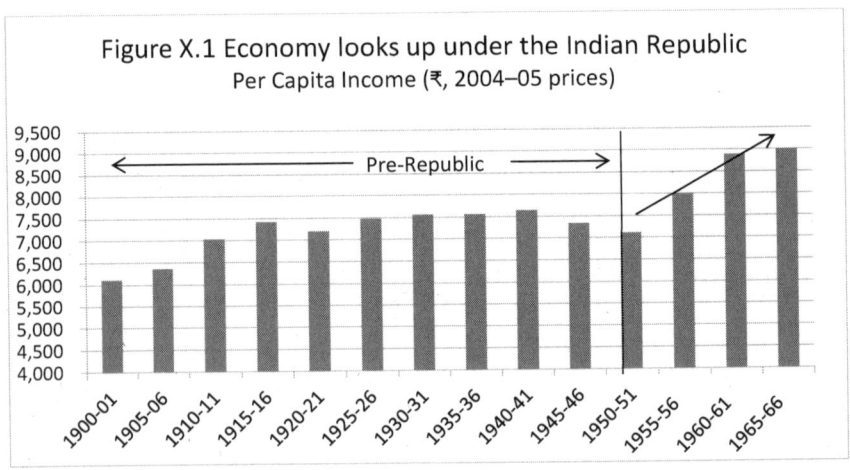

Figure X.1 Economy looks up under the Indian Republic
Per Capita Income (₹, 2004–05 prices)

Source: K. Mukerji: "A Note on the Long Term Growth of National Income in India-1900-1901 to 1952-1953," Papers on National Income and Allied Topics, Vol. I1 (Indian Conference on Research in National Income), ed. V. K. R. V. Rao, A. K. Ghosh, M. V. Divatia, and Uma Datta (Bombay: Asia Publishing House, 1962), quoted in Krishan G. Saini: "The Growth of the Indian Economy: 1860-1960", The University of Texas. http://www.roiw.org/1969/247.pdf. Data for 1950-51 to 1965-66, at 2004-05 prices, are from Table 1 of RBI's Handbook of Statistics on the Indian Economy. Data up to 1945-46 in Mukherjee, which is at 1948-49 prices, have been spliced by using the ratio of per capita income for 1950-51 for the two series.

sector at the forefront during Nehru's time does not come as a surprise. It was the ruling paradigm of economic development practically all over the world. For example, even in Brazil, on 3 October 1953, the staunch anti-communist and dictatorial president Getúlio Vargas established Petrobras to undertake oil sector activities on behalf of the state.

In any case, the performance of the economy looked good when compared to the experience during the British rule (Figure X.1). According to Mukerji's estimates, national income of the Indian Union—that is, the geographical composition of India after the Partition of 1947—at constant 1948–49 prices increased by 80 per cent under British rule in the first half of the twentieth century. The Indian republic, in its first fifteen years, almost matched this performance over half a century. The increase in net national product at constant 2004–05 prices between 1950–51 and 1965–66 was 71 per cent. The difference after Independence was stark in terms of increase in per capita income. Used to economic stagnation, the people had nothing to complain about. These were days well before the explosion of radio and television, and most of the illiterate electorate had hardly any knowledge how the rest of the world lived or how India's neighbours to the east were silently marching ahead of the country. The appeal of socialism as a professed goal for political parties would become an effective tool for electoral mobilization and continue to hold sway for decades, even beyond Nehru's tenure. But India was transforming, and in the process, Indians were changing. As a result, the grip of Congress and its socialist philosophy over the people was loosening as well, and this was evident in the pursuit of Nehruvian policies with a populist twist after Nehru's demise in 1964.

Part III

1964–1991—More Politics Than Economics

Nehruvian Policies with a Populist Twist

XI

Passing of an Era and Interregnum of Hope

In the last years of Pandit Nehru's rule, with the problems of socialist economic planning coming to the fore, continuing challenges of integrating Jammu and Kashmir, Mizoram and Nagaland in the national mainstream, and pending reorganization of Punjab on linguistic lines, his unquestioned leadership of the country was slipping.

In Jammu and Kashmir, Wazir-e-Azam Sheikh Abdullah had arrested Shyama Prasad Mookerjee, the founder of Jana Sangh, for defying the permit system and entering the state on 11 May 1953. There was public outcry when Mookerjee died in prison on 23 June. With doubts about his loyalty to India, on 8 August, the Sheikh was dismissed as Wazir-e-Azam by the Sadr-i-Riyasat, and put under custody. The Sheikh's successor, Bakshi Ghulam Mohammad, reversed his policy of *mujawaza* or compulsory grain procurement and started supplying the people of the state with highly subsidized rice provided by the Union government. It was a costly but popular move. The Constituent Assembly of Jammu and Kashmir ratified the accession to India in 1954 and adopted a constitution declaring it a part of India on 30 October 1956. Elections to the state's legislative assembly in March-May 1957 were marred by complaints of electoral irregularities. The Sheikh was released from prison on 8 January 1958, only to be charged with the 'Kashmir conspiracy' case, which involved establishing contact with Pakistan to procure money and arms to start a bloody revolution, and imprisoned again on 29 April 1958. There were protests in Jammu and Kashmir against the Sheikh's detention and demands for a plebiscite for determining its status and on the issue of independence.

Mautam—the *tam* (famine) associated with the flowering of the *mau* (bamboo)—struck the Mizo Hill District in 1959; Mizos died in large numbers and there was widespread discontent. Phizo, on 22 March 1956, had formed the 'Naga Central Government' and renamed it the 'Federal Government of Nagaland' in 1959. In July 1960, the Government of India had agreed to convert Nagaland from a UT to a state, but in August 1961, Phizo's men killed Dr Imkongliba Ao, the man who had negotiated much of the deal on behalf of the Nagas. In Punjab, by the early 1960s, the SAD was back in electoral politics and intensifying their Punjabi Suba agitation.

In 1957, in the south, Kerala had elected a communist party government. Following agitations against its educational and land reform policies, somewhat controversially, under Article 356 of the Constitution, the communist government was dismissed on 31 July 1959. Furthermore, in the face of severe opposition in south India to Hindi as the sole official language, in September 1959, Nehru had to provide assurance that neither would there be any hindrance on using English as an associate language, nor would there be any fixed time limit for it.

Assembly elections under the Election Commission of India were held in Jammu and Kashmir for the first time in February 1962. Prior to the election, the Jammu and Kashmir National Conference under Bakshi Ghulam Mohammad, in 1960, had reconciled with the left-inclined breakaway Democratic National Conference led by Ghulam Mohammad Sadiq, and unitedly, won seventy of the seventy-five seats. Bakshi continued as Wazir-e-Azam. Then came the Chinese aggression in 1962, blowing away Nehru's dream of '*Hindi Chini bhai-bhai*' or Sino-Indian brotherhood.

XI.1 The Sino-Indian Conflict

Chairman Mao's ultra-radical Great Leap Forward, launched in 1958, instead of making China industrialize and grow rapidly, had resulted in chaos and tens of millions of starvation deaths. Amidst the turbulent Chinese politics, Mao followed the age-old recipe of fomenting external conflict for diverting attention from internal problems and consolidating his position.

China never recognised Taiwan as an independent country under its 'one-China' policy. It massed forces opposite the two islands of Quemoy and Matsu—two groups of Taiwanese islands within tens of kilometres of the mainland—in July 1958, and China began bombardment on 23 August. The crisis abated only when the US stepped in with its defence umbrella over Taiwan. Sino-Soviet relations had become conflicted with the de-Stalinization of the former Soviet Union under Khrushchev and Khrushchev's denouncement of the secret agreement which bound the Soviet Union to provide China with the means necessary for the manufacture of nuclear weapons, and of the Great Leap Forward. From the late 1950s onwards, conflict blew up into open military confrontation around Damansky island on the Ussuri river.

Then came trouble on the Indo-Tibetan border. Since the collapse of the Qing dynasty in China in 1912, Tibet had been a de facto independent country with its own currency, flag, stamps, army and diplomatic relations with a few countries. Theocratic Tibet was ruled by the God-King Dalai Lama, the spiritual leader of Tibetan Buddhism. India borders Tibet in two disjointed parts, on the western side in Aksai Chin in Jammu and Kashmir and on the east in Arunachal Pradesh. The McMahon Line, a part of the 1914 Simla Convention between British India and Tibet, defined the border in Arunachal Pradesh. Barely a month before coming to power on 1 October, in September 1949, the Chinese Communist Party had declared the 'liberation' of Tibet, Taiwan and Hainan Island as top priorities. China had sent its troops into Qamdo in Tibet on 19 October 1950, and after negotiation of a treaty, announced the 'peaceful liberation of Tibet' on 23 May 1951.

India had reacted sharply to the prospect of Chinese military action in Tibet and protested when China decided to intervene militarily. It had called it an invasion. But once the Chinese occupied Tibet militarily, India, in the interest of friendly relations with China, had tacitly accepted Chinese suzerainty over Tibet. Prime Minister Nehru was also the minister for external affairs throughout his tenure. 'Friendship with China had always been central to Nehru's thinking about India's foreign policy.'[1] The slogan was 'Hindi Chini bhai-bhai'. There was also the hope that

China's relations with Tibet would be like India's relations with Bhutan, and China would leave Tibetans to run their domestic affairs.

China disputed the Indo-Tibetan border. After occupying Tibet, China built a 2,086-km road, National Highway 219, from Yecheng (Karghilik) in Xinjiang to Lhatse in Tibet. One of the highest motorable roads in the world, it passed through parts of Aksai Chin belonging to India. Aksai Chin means a desert of white stones, and true to its name, there was hardly any habitation on this desolate territory perched on top of high mountains, with the Karakoram Pass at a height of 18,000 feet. The Indian government learnt about this transgression only in 1957 from Chinese press reports about the road-building feat. One of two Indian reconnaissance patrols sent in July 1958 was detained by the Chinese and deported to India. There was a public uproar and Nehru was determined not to make the border with Tibet a negotiable matter.

In Tibet, internal developments added to the Chinese problem. The Chinese had occupied Tibet when the Dalai Lama was only sixteen years old. Gathering discontent with Chinese domination had led to the start of a revolt in 1956, and by the first week of March 1959, there were reports that the Dalai Lama would be abducted to Beijing to attend the Chinese National Assembly. To prevent abduction, 30,000 Tibetans had formed a thick human shield around Norbulinka Palace, the Dalai Lama's summer residence in Lhasa. On 17 March, in a cloak-and-dagger operation, the Dalai Lama, wearing a soldier's uniform with a gun slung over his shoulder, had quietly slipped out of Norbulinka for his arduous, fourteen-day-long trek across mountains to reach Khenzimane Pass on the Indian border on 31 March 1959. In India, there were angry protests against China. India's grant of asylum to Dalai Lama and his government in exile was regarded by China as an 'unfriendly act'.

Skirmishes had taken place at places such as Longju in Arunachal and Kongka Pass in Ladakh in 1959. With these skirmishes reported in the media, the border dispute was no longer just diplomatic exchanges. Both Parliament and the public were exercised. The Chinese occupation of Aksai Chin and its refusal to vacate was considered a national humiliation not only by the opposition, but also by many members of the Congress. Any negotiations and compromises with China on the border issue were considered a policy of China appeasement. After the failed talks between

Nehru and Chinese Premier Zhou Enlai during April 1960, India decided 'to go and stand on as many parts of Aksai Chin'—called the 'forward policy'—without attacking the Chinese positions. As the operation was on Indian territory, it was not an act of war.

Unfortunately, India was no match for China's military might. Keeping economic development as its top priority, India had neglected the development of its armed forces and spent too little on defence. Also, by early 1961, the defence minister, V. Krishna Menon, a sharp-tongued man and a Nehru favourite, was being described by army officers as an 'evil genius' who was manipulating army promotions to create a clique personally loyal to himself. Furthermore, friendly relations with China were taken as a given—India was second only to Burma in recognizing Mao's People's Republic on 1 January 1950.

The liberation of Goa on the west coast from Portuguese colonial rule in December 1961 might have also added a bit of concern among the Chinese leadership about growing Indian military ascendancy. The polarized world following the Marxist revolutionaries led by Fidel Castro capturing power in Cuba on 1 January 1959 may have also emboldened China to teach a lesson to 'bourgeoise' India. China started a war on India in the early morning of 20 October 1962 with assaults around the Thag La Ridge near Tawang in Arunachal. In the face of cold-blooded Chinese aggression, Nehru accepted the US offer of military aid on 29 October.

There were demands for Defence Minister Krishna Menon's ouster, not only from the members of the Opposition but even from the Congress. The decline in Nehru's standing within the Congress party became manifest when he failed to protect Menon by suggesting that 'if resignations were wanted he might have to proffer his own'. A leading member of the Congress Parliamentary Party reportedly retorted, 'Yes, if you continue to follow Menon's policies we may have to live without you too.'[2] The next day, on 8 November, Menon resigned from the Cabinet.

While US supplies took time to reach India and become effective, with continued aggression, by 18 November, the Chinese had de facto military control of Arunachal Pradesh and dominated the western sector around Aksai Chin. After routing the unprepared Indian army under an incompetent command at Walong, Se La and Bomdi La, China appeared to be all set to enter Assam by running over Tezpur on the northern bank of the Brahmaputra River. On this day of national shame, convicts and inmates of asylums were released in Tezpur. After warning the people about their inability to ensure their safety, the civil administration had ceased to operate in the town. An unscheduled radio broadcast to the nation by Prime Minister Nehru on 19 November sounded almost like a farewell speech to the people of Assam. With his back against the wall, on 20 November 1962, Nehru made an urgent, open appeal for US intervention with bomber and fighter squadrons against the Chinese. But just before midnight of 20 November, China announced a unilateral ceasefire from midnight of 21 November, and beginning 1 December, withdrawal to the line of control that existed on 7 November 1959. It is a matter of speculation whether the Chinese decided to cease fire and withdraw because it was just a punitive expedition or to avoid an Indian counterattack when the snow in winter renders the Himalayan passes inaccessible, their supply lines were disrupted and they were trapped.

XI.2 National Integration of Jammu and Kashmir

Bakshi Ghulam Mohammad continued as Wazir-e-Azam until 12 October 1963, when, amid widespread allegations of corruption against him, he was succeeded by a relatively unknown Khwaja Shamsuddin. Within three months of the takeover, on 26 December 1963, the sacred heir of the Prophet, the symbol of faith and instruction to all Muslims in the Kashmir valley kept at Asaar Sharif at Hazratbal, went missing.

In Sheikh Abdullah's words, 'News of the loss spread like wildfire. Despite the harsh winter, thousands of people congregated around the mosque. Protest demonstrations paralysed the government . . . the frenzied mob burnt down a cinema hall and a hotel owned by the Bakshi brothers. They also burnt down the radio station which had been transmitting disinformation about Kashmir to the Indian public for the last ten years, In Delhi this ominous situation created panic. Nehru was distraught. He sent Bakshi to take control of the situation, but when the people found out that he had reached Srinagar they attacked his residence. The Indian Army rushed to his rescue. Several people were killed in the fray.'[3] Communal riots erupted even in faraway erstwhile East Pakistan and in West Bengal, Madhya Pradesh and Odisha. Fortunately, the relic was recovered on

4 January 1964. Two days later, Nehru suffered a paralytic stroke in Bhubaneshwar, where he had gone to attend a Congress session. He never recovered fully.

On 29 January 1964, Khwaja Shamsuddin was replaced by G.M. Sadiq of the Congress as Wazir-e-Azam. On 6 April 1964, Zulfiqar Ali Bhutto, Pakistan's foreign minister, invited Sheikh Abdullah to visit Pakistan. On 8 April 1964, the government dropped all charges against the Sheikh in the Kashmir Conspiracy case, and released him from prison. On 29 April, he visited Delhi as Nehru's personal guest. Because of his failing health, Nehru could not visit Pakistan himself and asked the Sheikh to do so and encourage President Ayub Khan to start negotiations with India to resolve the Kashmir issue. While the Sheikh was visiting Pakistan, Nehru passed away on 27 May 1964. The integration of Jammu and Kashmir remained a work in progress.

XI.3 The Economy Suffers

The Chinese aggression came at a time when the economy was already in a vulnerable spot. The severe foreign exchange problem after the Suez crisis was continuing. Despite a stand-by arrangement with the IMF, foreign currency reserves were down from $1,648 million at end-March 1956 to only $390 at end-March 1961 and further to $377 million at end-March 1962. Scarcity of foreign exchange led to lack of imported inputs, slowed the implementation of projects and programmes, and resulted in shortages of power, transport, coal and steel in 1961–62, the first year of the Third Five-Year Plan. After Independence, every war invariably complicated economic management, and the problems of 1961–62 were magnified by the Chinese war in 1962.

After a year of bumper crops, 1961–62 turned out to be a year of agricultural disappointment partly because of adverse weather conditions. In 1961–62, at constant prices, crop agriculture suffered a decline of 0.3 per cent, and brought down the overall GDP growth rate from 7.1 per cent in 1960–61 to 3.1 per cent. The year 1962–63 proved to be the second successive year of adverse weather conditions. Rainfall in June 1962 was deficient in most parts of the country and there were floods in Assam, Bihar, Punjab and UP in September and October. Parts of the country in the north also suffered from a locust invasion. To counter the problem of decelerating growth, in 1962–63, the Union and state governments together stepped up their plan budgeted outlay, particularly in agriculture, power, transport and industry, by almost a third over the previous year to ₹1465 crore. To mobilize the necessary resources, the government also hiked railway fares and freights, and imposed higher customs duties on imports. With foreign exchange reserves providing cover for only three and a half months of imports, India also went for its second IMF stand-by for SDR 100 million in July 1962. Soon, with the Chinese aggression looming over the economy, the President of India promulgated emergency and the Defence of India Ordinance on 26 October 1962.

Defence outlays jumped up from ₹290 crore in 1961–62 to ₹425 crore in 1962–63 and further to ₹704 crore in 1963–64. In 1963–64, it was almost 90 per cent higher than the original budgeted amount of ₹376 crore in 1962–63! As a proportion of GDP at current market prices, the jump in defence expenditure was from 1.6 per cent in 1961–62 to 2.3 per cent in 1962–63 and further to 3.5 per cent in 1963–64 and would remain—except for the one year of 1977–78—well above 2.5 per cent until 1990–91. The Chinese aggression changed India's security perspective and increased its defence outlay by almost one per cent of GDP for a long time to come. There were fewer resources left for development.

A Unit Trust is an open-ended (i.e., where money can be invested at any time without any terminal date) mutual fund offering access to a wide range of investments, for example, in shares, bonds and government securities, and even in real estate. Investors in a Unit Trust own 'units' whose price is the net asset value (NAV) of the investment. If you have only ₹1000 to invest, you cannot buy a share of a company (for example, Larsen and Toubro) selling for, say, ₹1100, but through a Unit Trust you can own a part of one share. In its last year in office, the Nehru government set up the Unit Trust of India (UTI) by the UTI Act on 30 December 1963. It was for 'encouraging saving and investment and participation in the income, profits and gains accruing to the Corporation from the acquisition, holding, management and disposal of securities'.[4] Another objective perhaps was to simultaneously revive the capital market languishing in the aftermath of the Chinese war. It was the only mutual fund at that time and was jointly owned by the RBI, LIC, SBI and its associated banks. In 1964, UTI launched its and the country's first mutual fund scheme Unit Scheme-64 (US-64). As we shall see, after a long and successful period of operations, it would get into trouble in the late 1990s.

XI.4 The Story of Gold Control and Peoples' Taste and Culture

Gold, like other convertible hard currency, was a part of foreign exchange reserves. In November 1962, it was considered desirable to mobilize the gold lying with private individuals by the introduction of fifteen-year gold bonds at 6.5 per cent simple interest. The gold, which had to be physically deposited for these bonds, could be used for procuring arms and equipment for the armed forces fighting the Chinese. It mobilized only 16.3 tonnes of gold.

The 'Gold Control Rules, 1963' were notified to conserve foreign exchange and restrict its use for importing gold to meet popular demand. All gold loans given by banks were recalled, private ownership of gold bullion forbidden, and forward trading in gold as well as the production of gold jewellery above 14-carat fineness banned. The rules allowed individuals and families to hold only up to 2 and 4 kg of gold, respectively, and only in the form of jewellery. A licence was required to open a jewellery shop or to make jewellery. Every person, other than a dealer, was required to make a declaration to the Gold Control Administrator within thirty days of the commencement of the rules or within a period specified by a central government notification of the quantity, description or other particulars of the gold owned.

Anecdotal evidence suggests that the success of the Gold Control Rules was rather limited and smuggling of gold and proliferation of illegal purchase, hoarding and selling of gold were rampant. A comparison of the Indian experience with Gold Control Rules in the early 1960s with the US experience with stringent restrictions on private holding of gold in the 1930s is instructive in this context. In the middle of the Great Depression, on 4 March 1933, Franklin Roosevelt became the US President. Two days later, at 1 a.m., with Proclamation 48, he announced a national emergency, a three-day bank holiday, and forbade all banking institutions to 'pay out, export, earmark, or permit the withdrawal or transfer in any manner or device whatsoever of gold or silver coin, or bullion or currency' and 'any other action which might facilitate the hoarding thereof'.[5] Within three months, the right of private property in gold coin or bullion, with some exceptions, was in effect annulled. The US had a fair degree of success in bringing out the private stock of gold and preventing its hoarding. Perhaps differences in cultural, religious and social traditions played a major role in determining the different outcomes in the two countries, albeit in two different periods.

Historically, India has led the countries of the world in terms of its love for gold. To Afghan and other adventurers who invaded it in the past, India was known as *'sone ki chidiya'* or bird of gold and the supreme reward of success was looting the masses of gold. One conservative estimate puts India's private gold ownership at about 18,000 tonnes, a little less than 10 per cent of all the gold mined in history and almost 2.5 times the US official gold reserves. Pliny the Elder, in 77 CE, called India 'the sink of the world's gold'! Francois Bernier, the French doctor in the Mughal court in the seventeenth century, observed, 'It should not escape notice that gold and silver, after circulating in every other quarter of the globe, come to be absorbed in Hindostan.'[6] With the rest of the world wanting to import goods from India, and limited Indian demand for their goods, traders from abroad carried bullion to settle the trade. In other words, countries importing from India financed the external trade surplus of India by gold and silver specie flow for centuries. But even after the external trade surplus in other goods and services had disappeared, the import of gold continued. Gold, by absorbing a good part of private savings, continued, and continues, to divert it away from more productive investments.

XI.5 A Debilitating Blow to a Leader on the World Stage and the Passing of an Era

Prime Minister Nehru had ruled as the undisputed leader of not only the Congress but also the country. His word was the final word in policymaking, and he was the helmsman steering the reconciliation of political democracy with socialist transformation of the economy. But after the Chinese war, his leadership was no longer unassailable or unquestioned. Even President Radhakrishnan described the debacle with China a result of 'credulity and negligence'. Disillusioned by open defiance within the Congress, Nehru was a broken man.

Beyond his grip on domestic affairs, Nehru had built up a formidable reputation as a leader of the recently liberated colonial countries across the globe. In negotiations with India in Beijing on 31 December 1953, Chinese Premier Zhou Enlai had put forward Five Principles of Peaceful Co-Existence, namely, (i) mutual respect for each other's territorial integrity and sovereignty, (ii) mutual non-aggression, (iii) non-interference in each other's internal affairs, (iv) equality and mutual benefit, and (v) peaceful co-existence. At the Bandung Conference of Asian and African states in 1955, hosted by Indonesian President Sukarno and attended by Zhou Enlai, Vietnam's leader Ho Chi Minh, Yugoslav President Josip Broz Tito, Egyptian President Gamal Abdel Nasser, Burmese Prime Minister U Nu, and Prime Minister Kwame Nkrumah of the Gold Coast (renamed Ghana after independence in 1961), Nehru had propounded these five principles as the 'panchsheel' or five restraints. He believed Zhou Enlai and had wanted to build up Sino-Indian friendship based on the panchsheel. In 1962, China violated the panchsheel on the Sino-Indian border.

The Bandung Conference also made the collective pledge to remain neutral in the Cold War. On 19 June 1956, at the height of the Cold War, at the Adriatic Island of Brijuni off the Croatian coast, Nehru, Tito and Nasser had signed an important declaration that laid the foundation of the Non-Aligned Movement (NAM). It advocated a middle path between the western bloc led by the US and the eastern bloc led by the Soviet Union. Nehru was one of the—if not the primary—leading figures of the movement. After the Chinese invasion, Nehru's dream of leading the NAM and securing Sino-Indian friendship were in tatters. China had committed a breach of trust and those countries that Nehru had treated as supporters and friends in the NAM did not support India during its conflict with China. This, together with the lack of support from Moscow, must have come as a blow to Nehru.

The NAM in the 1950s may have cost India possible friends in the east as well as future economic cooperation with them in the short term. As Shashi Tharoor observes, 'Indian sanctimony also periodically antagonized would-be friends among smaller states: in 1957, Thailand cancelled a royal visit to New Delhi after Jawaharlal made scathing references to its "Coca-Cola economy," and the Japanese Ambassador to the UN reported to Tokyo that his attempts to work with India had been rebuffed on the grounds that its policies were not sufficiently independent to make collaboration worthwhile. Such positions may have satisfied the *amour propre* of a self-regarding elite, but to others they were both short-sighted and insufferable, and would not be forgotten when, for years to come, India needed friends amongst those it had spurned.'[7] While the moral content of Nehru's foreign policy could be laudable, in terms of realpolitik, it may have entailed considerable cost to India in terms of political and economic cooperation with possible benefactors.

The last year and a half of Pandit Nehru's life was quite traumatic. His youthfulness disappeared; he stooped and appeared unsteady. On Gandhi Jayanti 1963, K. Kamaraj, the chief minister of erstwhile Madras state since 1954, offered to resign and proposed that all senior Congress leaders should resign from their ministerial posts and devote all their energy to the revitalization of the Congress. Under this plan, which came to be known as the Kamaraj Plan, Nehru also offered to resign but was prevailed upon to continue. Under the plan, all Congress chief ministers of states and central ministers also offered to resign. All could not be relieved, and Nehru accepted the resignation of six chief ministers, including that of Kamaraj of Madras, Biju Patnaik of Odisha and Bakshi Ghulam Mohammad of Jammu and Kashmir, besides that of six Union ministers. Nehru passed away within eight months of the launch of the Kamaraj Plan.

XI.6 Change of Guard in Troubled Times

On 19 January 1964, the New York Times had published an article with the title 'India's big question: who after Nehru?' Within a week of Nehru's demise, Congress president Kamaraj, by implementing the 'consensus' method, produced the answer: Lal Bahadur Shastri. Shastri became Prime Minister on 2 June 1964 and inherited a difficult economic situation in terms of balance of payments and inflation. In his first broadcast as prime minister, Shastri described the way as 'straight and clear . . . to the building up of a socialist democracy . . .'

In 1965, the monsoon failed and food grain production came down from 89 to 72 million tonnes between 1964 and 1965. It was against this backdrop that the Food Corporation of India (FCI) was set up in January 1965, with its headquarters in Delhi, as the Central government's wholly-owned corporate body 'for the purpose of trading in food grains and other foodstuffs and for matters connected therewith and incidental thereto'.[8] In response to the grim food situation, Prime Minister Shastri also coined the slogan '*Jai Kisan, Jai Jawan*' (hail the farmer, hail the soldier), asked the people to participate in the campaign to save food, the farmers to grow more than one crop a year, and people to clean up their backyard and start growing crops and vegetables. He even launched the 'miss a meal' campaign!

Improved agricultural implements and application of chemical fertilizers under IAAP from 1964 onwards had improved yields. In most countries, the 'revolutionary' change in productivity, however, had come from application of hybrid and High Yielding Variety (HYV) seeds. HYVs are early maturing semi-dwarf types that, with appropriate use of chemical fertilizers, irrigation and pesticides, provide much higher yields than traditional varieties. A few Mexican dwarf wheat varieties and exotic varieties of rice, IR-8 and Taichung Native or TN-1, were tried out on selected basis in the mid-1960s, and the results were very encouraging. The draft outline of the Fourth Five-Year Plan, therefore, stressed the need for evolving a new approach for boosting agricultural production over a short span. Two programmes, namely the HYV Programme (HYVP) and the Multiple Cropping Programme (MCP), were launched in 1966–67 under the Fourth Five-Year Plan. Food grain production increased from 95 million tonnes in 1967–68 to 108.4 million tonnes in 1970–71 and further to 121 million tonnes in 1975–76. The period 1965–66 to 1975–76 saw the ushering in of the 'Green Revolution' in India. However, the supply side benefits of the revolution accrued mostly to the rich and middle-income farmers, and the problems of small and marginal farmers, landless labourers and rural artisans remained.

The farmers' integrated dairy cooperative established in Anand town of Kaira district of Gujarat (in erstwhile Bombay State) in 1946, to fight the exploitation of farmers by private traders, popularly known as AMUL (Anand Milk Union Limited), was already looking like a great success story. 'In October 1964, on the occasion of the inauguration of AMUL's cattle feed plant, Prime Minister Lal Bahadur Shastri spent a night as the guest of a village milk cooperative society near Anand. Impressed by the socio-economic changes brought about by the milk cooperatives, he expressed the desire for a national organization to replicate the Anand

Pattern dairy cooperative throughout the country. As a result, in 1965, the National Dairy Development Board (NDDB) was established with headquarters at Anand.'[9] NDDB under Verghese Kurien went on to play a pivotal role in the White Revolution (involving milk) in the years to come, and Kurien came to be known as the Father of the White Revolution.

Foreign currency reserves, up marginally from $377 million at end-March 1962 to $395 million at end-March 1964, declined drastically to $243 million at end-March 1965. Such reserves, inclusive of gold, which had been declining in each of the nine years since 1955–56 except for a minor increase of $23 million in 1963–64, were only $524 million at end-March 1965. At end-March 1965, such reserves, equivalent to ₹250 crore after accounting for ₹200 crore statutory assets of the RBI for its currency liabilities, could finance only half a month of the country's imports. Large repayments of official foreign loans were also due in the next few years.

India went for a stand-by arrangement with the IMF for SDR 200 million in March 1965. It also compressed imports, which resulted in shortages of raw materials and capital goods for industry. Inflation, as measured by the WPI in the last week, which had gone up to 9 per cent in 1963–64, came down only mildly to 8.7 per cent in 1964–65. In 1963–64, the fiscal deficit of the Union government was ₹1151 crore, equivalent to 4.9 per cent of GDP. Much of it was financed by the RBI, and RBI's credit to the Union government had gone up from ₹104 crore in 1960–61 to ₹125 crore in 1961–62 and more than doubled to ₹213 crore in 1963–64. A grim situation on the food grains front, generalized scarcity of goods and the need for RBI financing an increasing fiscal deficit resulted in a crisis in terms of the balance of payments and inflation (Box XI.1).

Box XI.1 RBI Credit to Government, Inflation and Balance of Payments

You cannot sell a house in weeks or months and realize its full value. But you can pay ₹5 in cash or by a bank cheque and get full ₹5 worth of goods or services almost anytime and anywhere in India. Money, both cash and bank deposits, is a medium of exchange and a store of value and is also called 'liquidity'. Liquidity is the property of an asset or commodity (for example, gold or even a piece of paper, like a currency note) which, unlike a house, can be readily exchanged for its 'full value'. Because of the inconvenience of holding cash, its risk of being stolen or lost, and some deposits earning interest, people hold money in a combination of cash and bank deposits.

To get to the crux of the issue of reserve money, consider a simple world where businesses and people hold 40 per cent of their 'liquidity' in cash, and the balance 60 per cent in deposits. RBI commands the confidence of the people and claims on the RBI serve as a medium of exchange and a store of value. You take it because you know I will take it when you offer it to me as payment for some good or service, and I take it because I know my local grocer will accept it as payment for my supplies and so on. Let us start by considering the RBI setting up its business by creating 'reserve money' worth ₹2500 as claims upon itself. Soon, it will be clear why it is called reserve money. So RBI gives loans of ₹1000 to the government and banks each and buys ₹500 worth of foreign exchange, say, US dollars. After receiving the loan of ₹1000 from the RBI, to earn interest income, banks on-lend their ₹1,000 to businesses and people, and the government spends its ₹1000 on salaries for its employees and for building, say, a school or a road. Only 40 per cent of this combined sum of ₹2000, that is, ₹800, will be held in cash and the balance of ₹1200 will be deposited in banks. Even ₹500 that the RBI has spent on buying dollars will not be fully retained as cash. Of this ₹500, 60 per cent, that is, ₹300, will come to the banks as deposits. Thus, of the ₹2500 that the RBI has created as 'reserve money', businesses and people will hold only ₹1000 in the form of cash and deposit ₹1500 in banks.

Banks, when they get ₹1500 as deposits, know that only 40 per cent, that is, ₹600, will be withdrawn in the form of cash. So they lend the balance ₹900 to businesses and people. Again, the borrowers who get ₹900 withdraw only ₹360 in the form of cash and the banks find ₹540 idle cash lying with them. They lends this sum, a part of which again stays back with them. This process will go on and on until 'money' in the economy is equal to

$$2500 + 1500 + 900 + \cdots = 2500\{1 + 0.6 + 0.6^2 + 0.6^3 + \cdots\}$$

$$= \frac{2500}{1 - 0.6} = 6250$$

Note that 'money' in the economy is ₹6250, 40 per cent of it, that is, ₹2500, is cash created by the RBI and ₹3750 is deposit. Banks have created money! Note that given the people's preference between cash and deposit, how much money will be created depends critically on how much the RBI creates as claims upon itself, which in our example is ₹2500. Money is a multiple of how much claims the RBI creates upon itself, and that is why the claims that RBI creates upon itself is called *base money* or *high-powered money*. Nothing in our example would have changed if, instead of assuming that people like to hold 40 per cent of their money in the form of cash, we had assumed that they like to hold all of it in the form of deposits, but the RBI required the banks to hold 40 per cent of their deposits in the form of cash reserves. With this changed assumption, the money creation by banks would continue until they create ₹6250 worth of deposits, the people hold no cash, and the whole of the ₹2500 created by the RBI is held by the banks in the form of reserves. This explains why the claims the RBI creates upon itself are also known as reserve money.

Now, suppose the RBI decides to give an extra ₹500 credit to the government over and above the ₹1000 it has already given. It can do that by giving less credit to banks or buying less foreign exchange or expanding high-powered money or a combination of the three. Suppose the RBI decides to reduce credit to banks and purchase of foreign exchange by ₹100 each and increase high-powered money by ₹300. So credit to government is ₹1500, to banks, ₹900, purchase of foreign exchange ₹400, and high-powered money is higher at ₹2800. It is easy to work out how, because of the banks creating multiple rounds of credit, money supply will be ₹7000, up 12 per cent from the previous situation. Suppose people's income does not go up proportionately with this increase in money supply. Then people would like to get rid of this money by spending on goods and services. This is what many economists describe as too much money chasing too few goods. The result would be higher inflation and/or higher imports of foreign goods and services and/or, in extreme cases, even a switch from rupees to stabler foreign currencies.

What was tried for some time, for example in the Budget presented by Finance Minister TTK on 27 February 1965, were the old medicines of some streamlining and reduction of personal income tax, import compression through increasing tariffs, increasing some excise duties and decreasing others selectively to provide 'relief' to the common man, higher wealth tax and revenue mobilization by unearthing 'unaccounted' money, which in popular parlance is known as black money. Finance Minister TTK also referred to the difficulties in proper monetary management and inflation control because of the existence of unaccounted income and wealth. Such unaccounted income and wealth, which are derived mainly from tax evasion and from violations of price control measures, encourage speculative activities and raise the prices of goods and property in general. Apart from conducting more searches, and strictly enforcing more severe penalties, to encourage voluntary disclosures, he also introduced a Voluntary Disclosure Scheme. Amounts so disclosed were exempted from penalty, and he offered '. . . an opportunity to those who wish to turn a new leaf to do so without undue harassment'. With reduction in tax rates, he hoped, '. . . the scope and incentive for tax evasion in future would be reduced'.

It came to be known as the Sixty-Forty Scheme, as it allowed disclosure of unaccounted incomes by paying tax at the rate of 60 per cent and retaining 40 per cent, with immunity from penalties and prosecution. Apparently, the tax rate of 60 per cent was considered too high by the tax evaders and the scheme could bring out black money of only ₹52.11 crore with a tax yield of ₹29 crore. Disappointed by the results, in September 1965, in Finance (No.2) Act, 1965, TTK allowed the evaders to disclose their unaccounted incomes of any year up to 31 March 1966. It came to be known as the 'Black Scheme' because under it, tax was payable on the disclosed incomes for various years taken as a single block, at slab rates applicable for 1965–66 and not at a flat rate of 60 per cent, and in instalments extending over four years. This led to disclosures of ₹145 crore of 'black money' but the tax yield was only ₹20 crore as most disclosures were made in the names of spouses, children etc. to take the benefit of the lowest slab rate.

In less than two decades after Independence, TTK's was the second tax amnesty scheme after Mahavir Tyagi's first in 1951. In general, like in many other parts of the world, tax amnesty schemes have been found to be problematic. The additional revenues they mobilize often fall short of expectations, and despite the promise of 'never again', create complications for future tax administration by setting off expectations of more amnesty schemes in the future and generating a feeling of inequity among honest taxpayers. As we find, in 1965, fourteen years after the first tax amnesty scheme, India resorted to it again in the false hope that this time it would be different. We shall find that it would do it again in the future.

The Gold Control Rules, 1963 was replaced by Gold (Control) Act, 1968 of Parliament. In the initial years of the act, only 14-carat gold jewellery could be sold. Furthermore, two gold bond schemes, both maturing after fifteen years in 1980, were issued in March and December 1965. The first paid interest at the rate of 7 per cent, while the second— the National Defence Gold Bonds—paid a reduced rate of 6.5 per cent. However, the distinguishing feature of the December 1965 scheme was that it provided an avenue for declaring and legalizing unaccounted income with immunity for the investor from income tax, estate duty, wealth tax and gift tax. Compared to 6.1 tons mobilized by the first scheme, the mobilization of 13.7 tons by the second one despite the lower interest rate was more than twice as much.

Acquiring foreign exchange was a critical mission for the government. To attract such remittances in foreign exchange from abroad, the government instituted a National Defence Remittance Scheme on 26 October 1965 and extended it to 31 May 1966. Under the scheme, receivers of such remittances were entitled to receive certificates from authorized dealers. These certificates were valuable as they entitled the holders to exchange them for precious import licences and were also freely transferable. To encourage such remittances, the Finance Act 1966 amended the definition of 'short-term capital asset' to exclude such certificates, even when they were held for a period of not more than twelve months before the date of its transfer.

XI.7 A Short Interregnum of Hope

In the early 1960s, in economic policy, there was a whiff of change in the air. In 1963, even under Nehru, price controls on sixteen items had been lifted. It appears that, after becoming Prime Minister, Shastri might have been considering economic liberalization as a policy option.

Controls on imports, imposed for conserving foreign exchange as well as protecting domestic industry, had led to a shrinking of India's openness vis-à-vis the rest of the world. Merchandise imports plus exports, as a proportion of GDP, had come down from 15.8 per cent in 1951–52 to 7.7 per cent by 1965–66. Yet, the current account problems had continued. It is in this context that, in 1964, the government had agreed to a detailed multi-volume study of the Indian economy and its policy challenges by a World Bank team led by Bernard Bell.

All-India variable-dividend industrial securities index had declined steadily from 183.7 in 1961–62 to 167.1 in 1963–64 and further to 163.9 in 1964–65. Investor sentiments were down. Relations between the government and the business community had reached a low by the time Shastri came to power. The inauguration of the Thirty-Eighth Annual Session of FICCI in New Delhi was held on 20 March 1965. Prime Minister Nehru used to address these FICCI sessions. Shastri continued with the tradition, and tension between the business community and the government clearly came to the fore with FICCI president K.P. Goenka launching a vehement attack on the government. He raised doubts about the national income growth estimate of 4.5 per cent in 1963–64 and cited cumbersome and dilatory licensing and foreign exchange allocation procedures, and shortage of power, as some of the reasons for the economy not growing fast enough. He pointed out how transfer of ownership of industries or trade would not serve public interest, and how tax rates should be maintained at reasonable levels and exemptions reduced to a minimum. He also ruefully lamented the confused and erroneous notions of the workings of private enterprise, and how, whenever temporary scarcities arose, the private sector was blamed. Prime Minister Shastri responded by recounting how, in the crisis period, with food grains prices soaring, the government did not get any cooperation from the food grains traders. Sensing the rising anti-government feeling of the business community, he sent Home Minister Gulzarilal Nanda to major business centres to assure the business community of the government's bona fide intentions.

Soon after becoming Prime Minister, Shastri also decided to review all controls and eliminate those that had stopped serving any useful purpose.

In May 1965, through Home Minister Nanda, he asked FICCI to provide its recommendations on which controls should be abolished. FICCI's inability, even after multiple meetings, to come up with a list exposed the vested interests of many established industries in continuing the controls. For example, textiles, coal and sugar opposed decontrol. Shastri acted on the Raj Committee report on steel and coal. For rationalizing the controls over prices and distribution of intermediates and manufactured goods, such controls on pig iron were removed in August 1965 and on cement in January 1966.

In December 1964, a constitutional order from Delhi brought Jammu and Kashmir under the purview of Articles 356 and 357, and these empowered the Union government to dismiss elected state governments in the event of a breakdown of law and order. It also allowed striking down tariff barriers with India, opening the state's bureaucracy to non-Kashmiri Indians and also allowing India's Supreme Court to arbitrate on civil and criminal matters. There were violence and arson followed by large-scale arrest of leaders of the Plebiscite Front in Jammu and Kashmir. In March 1965, the Jammu and Kashmir legislative assembly amended the state's constitution, abolished the posts of Sadr-i-Riyasat and Wazir-e-Azam and replaced them with governor and chief minister, like in other Indian states.

In February 1965, Sheikh Abdullah had gone on a Haj pilgrimage, followed by visits to Algeria, Egypt, Jordan, Iraq, Iran, Afghanistan and the UK. In Algeria, he had also met the Chinese premier, Zhou Enlai. In London, he was accused of carrying on a vilification campaign and asked by High Commissioner Dr Jivraj Narayan Mehta to return to India. Sheikh Abdullah returned to India on 7 May 1965, was arrested upon arrival, moved to a bungalow in Kodaikanal, the southern hill resort in Tamil Nadu and kept under detention.

On 5 August 1965, under the codename 'Operation Gibraltar', Pakistan infiltrated India's Jammu and Kashmir with around 30,000 army guerrillas to foment insurgency. Hostilities continued along the ceasefire line in Jammu and Kashmir. India retaliated by crossing the international border into West Pakistan on 6 September 1965. The war witnessed the largest tank battle since the Second World War and continued for seventeen days. There was a UN-mandated ceasefire following diplomatic intervention from the US and the Soviet Union. In January 1966, in response to the Soviet offer to mediate between India and Pakistan, Shastri travelled to Tashkent, capital of the Soviet province of Uzbekistan, to hold talks with Pakistan's President Field Marshall Ayub Khan. On 10 January 1966, Shastri signed the Tashkent Declaration with Ayub Khan. Alexei Kosygin, chairman of the Soviet Council of Ministers, was the witness. A few hours after signing the accord, Shastri died on 11 January 1966.

Prime Minister Shastri had consolidated his position by his bold leadership of the country after the 1965 war with Pakistan and had resolved that a devaluation of the rupee was necessary to salvage the situation. Finance Minister TTK, who did not share his views, was relieved and replaced by Sachin Chaudhuri, a prominent lawyer from Kolkata whom very few people outside Kolkata knew. Shortly after joining as finance minister, Chaudhuri dispatched I.G. Patel from his ministry, along with the RBI governor, to inform the IMF that India was prepared to devalue the rupee after discussion about possible IMF assistance and the extent of devaluation. According to Patel, the decision to devalue in exchange for IMF support was taken '. . . in Shastriji's life and with his full knowledge and support. I have no doubt that if he had lived longer, devaluation would have come earlier, and been managed more smoothly, accompanied or followed by far-reaching reforms. It would also have been politically less divisive given his enormous prestige after the victory in the Pakistan War.'[10] But, before he could pursue further reforms, he passed away on 11 January 1966. What he would have done had he lived longer as Prime Minister is a matter of speculation. An interregnum of hope was over.

Former Chief Economic Adviser Arvind Virmani divides the first thirty years of the Indian republic after Independence under the pursuit of socialism with an Indian face into two sub-periods—the first fifteen years, from 1950–51 to 1964–,65 a period in the 'quest of the commanding heights' of the economy for the state, and the 'socialist' second from 1965–66 to 1979–80. The first sub-period was characterized by an attempt to translate Fabian socialist philosophy into practical policy. The second phase was driven more by political expediency, populism and using economic policy for besting political rivals. So after the interregnum of hope was over, let us get on with the story of the second phase.

XII

Indira Gandhi Becomes Prime Minister
with Economy in Turmoil

Shastri's death, nineteen months after becoming Prime Minister, was a bolt from the blue. No one had speculated about 'after Shastri, who'. For a fortnight, Gulzarilal Nanda was the 'acting prime minister'. The veteran leader Morarji Desai put in his claim to the post. Election in the Congress Parliamentary Party (CPP) followed. Senior Congress leaders, the so-called 'syndicate', were against Morarji because of his strong views and independent nature. Indira Gandhi won over Morarji by 355 to 169 votes and took over as the Prime Minister on 24 January 1966.

Indira inherited an economy in shambles. It was shrinking by 3.7 per cent in 1965–66, and barely grew by 1 per cent in 1966–67. Monsoon, and consequently crops, after failing in 1965–66, were deficient again in 1966. Food grain production crashed by a fifth in two successive years. For the country, already dependent on food even in bumper harvest years, the twin droughts proved disastrous. The WPI for food grains and pulses at end-January 1966 was 35 per cent higher than what it was at end-January 1964. Starvation threatened the poor.

Overall WPI inflation had been in double digits in each of the seven months between August 1964 and February 1965. After remaining in single digits for thirteen months, it climbed back to double digits for each of the twenty-one months between March 1966 and November 1967. The balance of payments had improved marginally, with foreign exchange reserves rallying from the all-time low of $524 million at end-March 1965 to $626 million at end-March 1966. But it still was far from enough to provide the minimum cover of three months of imports considered essential for economic security. As her government started grappling with the economic crisis, she was baptized by fire in less than five weeks. On the last day of February, a violent insurgency rocked Mizoram.

XII.1 Mautam and the Mizo Revolt

The trigger for the violent insurgency in the district of Mizoram in the erstwhile undivided Assam was connected to bamboo, which covered almost half the area of the district. Bamboos, the fifth largest flowering plant family, are monocarpic, that is, they flower and set seeds only once and then die. Mizos categorize two dominant species of bamboo in their area as *mau* and *thing*. All species of a variety, even when separated by hundreds of kilometres, tend to burst into bloom with mauve, yellow and crimson flowers at the same time. The flowering is accompanied by a large-scale increase in the population of bamboo or jungle rats, who consume the bamboo seeds and, with the exhaustion of its bountiful supply, attack standing crops and storehouses of grains, causing devastations ending in famines. Tam means famine, and famines connected with the flowering of the mau and thing bamboos are called *mautam* and *thingtam* by the Mizos.

After mautam in Mizoram in 1861–62 and 1911–12, conventional wisdom predicted its recurrence in 1959–60. For fighting the menace, the rat population had to be controlled, food grains stored and a robust distribution network kept ready. The mau had already flowered in 1959, and the Mizo Hills District Council had sought ₹15 lakh from the government of Assam to prepare for the disaster. The chief minister of Assam, Bimala Prasad Chaliha, had rejected the petition as unscientific. To the Mizos, it betrayed a lack of knowledge about ground realities and even a lack of empathy. In 1959, when Mizos died in large numbers, the government was ill-prepared to deal with the situation. The solitary highway linking Silchar in Assam to the Mizo Hills could handle only jeeps, and not trucks carrying food grains. For famine relief, the Mizos organized themselves under Laldenga, a young Mizo in his early thirties.

Laldenga had retired early as a havildar in the Indian Army to join the civil service and work as an accounts clerk in the district council office.

He had formed the voluntary Mizo Cultural Society in 1955 and was its secretary. This society became the Mautam Front in March 1960 and renamed itself as the Mizo National Famine Front (MNNF) in September 1960. With complaints of indifference and callousness towards the suffering of the Mizos against the Government of Assam, after the famine was over, the MNNF became a separatist political movement and renamed itself the Mizo National Front (MNF) in October 1961. In 1960, the declaration of Assamese as the official language of Assam, of which Mizoram was a district, was another point of grievance. Strong feelings on the language issue led the political parties in the different hill districts to close ranks and form the All-Party Hill Leaders Conference (APHLC) to demand a separate Eastern Frontier State within the Indian Union. After the third general election in 1962, when the APHLC observed 24 October 1962 as the Demand Day, it asked all its members of the legislative assembly (MLAs) in Assam to resign. At that time, two Mizo Union MLAs from Mizoram also resigned. In the by-election in 1963, the MNF won both the seats.

Laldenga, along with some other MNF leaders, visited erstwhile East Pakistan, and Pakistan offered support in the form of military hardware and training. Laldenga and his colleague were arrested for conspiracy against the nation but released on their promise of good conduct. Upon their release, they continued with their secessionist activities, including collection of 'donations' by force, recruitment of MNF members and training them in insurgency operations.

On 30 October 1965, it submitted a memorandum to the Government of India, stating: 'During the fifteen years (1947–1962) of close contact and association with India the Mizo people had not been able to feel at home with India or in India, nor they have been (sic) shared by India. They do not therefore, feel, Indians. Being created a separate nation, they cannot go against the nature to cross the barriers of nationality (to become Indians). They (therefore) refuse to occupy a place with India as they consider it to be unworthy of their national dignity and harmful to the interest of their prosperity. The only aspiration and political cry is (sic) the creation of Mizoram a free and sovereign state to govern itself, to work out her own destiny and to formulate her own foreign policy . . .' The MNF wanted a sovereign Christian state for the Mizos. While the Mizo

Union was critical, MNF had the support of the United Mizo Freedom Organization (UMFO), which was pro-feudal lords.

On the last day of February 1966, in the evening in the Mizo Hills, the MNF, with its armed wing, the Mizo National Army (MNA), launched a large-scale insurgency operation, codenamed Jericho. The MNA or the MNF insurgents cut off telephone lines and managed to neutralize the police and paramilitary forces all over Mizoram except the 1 Assam Rifles Headquarters in Aizawl. The insurgents overran Aizawl treasury and armoury and captured the SBI. Civil administration in Mizoram was paralysed, and the Deputy Commissioner of Mizoram District took shelter in the 1 Assam Rifles Headquarters in Aizawl. On 1 March 1966, Laldenga and sixty other MNF leaders issued a two-page declaration of independence. With telephone lines between Mizoram and Silchar cut, the Indian authorities in Silchar got to know of the insurrection only through a wireless message from the commanding officer of the Border Roads Organization.

Laldenga and the MNF had hoped that if they could keep their flag flying in Aizawl for forty-eight hours, some states like Pakistan would accord them recognition and take up their case at the UN. But that was not to be. On 2 March 1966, the Government of Assam proclaimed the entire Mizoram district to be 'disturbed' by invocation of the Assam Disturbed Areas Act, 1955 and Armed Forces (Special Powers) Act, 1958. The Indian government reacted with overwhelming force. It took recourse to even air strikes—the only instance so far in India of its use against its own people. The MNA was in retreat; it shifted its headquarters from Aizawl to South Hlimen (3 March), then to Reiek (8 March) and finally to the Chittagong Hill Tracts in East Pakistan. In a major operation, people from existing villages were regrouped in what was called the 'Protected and Progressive Villages' along the highways. With constant surveillance of such villages, this regrouping denied the insurgents the opportunity to launch attacks from tiny and scattered villages, and after the attack, to merge with the villagers.

Reconciliation started after MNF was outlawed in 1967. More than 1500 of the 2000 reported insurgents surrendered under an amnesty offer in August 1968. The Mizo Union had criticized the MNF for causing undue loss of life and property, but it also wanted more autonomy and UT status for Mizoram. Mizoram became a UT in 1972 and a state in 1987.

XII.2 Devaluation of June 1966

The Third Five-Year Plan was coming to an end on 31 March 1966. Planning for a fixed five-year period required a fair degree of certainty regarding exogenous factors such as commodity (particularly oil) prices in the world market, weather conditions and war and peace. The uncertain economic situation of the mid-1960s forced the government to postpone the launch of the Fourth Five-Year Plan and substitute it with three Annual Plans in the three subsequent years. The period from 1 April 1966 to 31 March 1969 euphemistically came to be known as the period of Plan Holiday.

One new category introduced in the Fourth Plan was 'special category states'. In 1969, the Fifth Finance Commission had made a case for preferential treatment of certain states, because of their special situation, in terms of central assistance. The National Development Council granted special category status to certain states based on an integrated consideration of their infirmities relating to: (i) hilly and difficult terrain (ii) low population density and/or sizeable share of tribal population (iii) strategic location along borders with neighbouring countries (iv) economic and infrastructural backwardness and (v) non-viable nature of state finances. Special Category Status was granted based on an integrated consideration of these criteria. Initially, three states—Assam, Nagaland and Jammu and Kashmir—were granted this special category status; five more—Himachal Pradesh, Manipur, Meghalaya, Sikkim and Tripura—were added between 1974 and 1979; two more—Arunachal Pradesh and Mizoram—were added in 1990; and finally, Uttarakhand was added in 2001. The distribution of plan assistance was according to the Gadgil-Mukherjee formula, named after two deputy chairmen of the Planning Commission. Following the recommendations of Fourteenth Finance Commission, the Special Category States ceased to exist from 2014.

Two wars in quick succession—the Sino-Indian conflict in 1962 and the Indo-Pakistani war of 1965—and two successive severe droughts in 1965 and 1966 had triggered a major balance of payments crisis. Furthermore, after the 1965 war, foreign aid had been cut off from October 1965 to March 1966. Bernard Bell of the World Bank had submitted his final report on 1 October 1965. It argued that devaluation was necessary to correct the overvaluation of the rupee and restore Indian competitiveness in the global markets. The decision to devalue the rupee had already been taken under Shastri. In April-May 1966, Asoka Mehta, the deputy chairman of the Planning Commission, with deep socialist roots, went to Washington and negotiated an elaborate agreement directly with George Woods, president of the World Bank. 'The Woods/Mehta agreement committed India to major structural reforms: substantial decontrol of imports, reductions in industrial licensing, increases in private foreign investment, decontrol of fertilizer production and distribution, and reductions in state-owned industries.'[1] Finally, the rupee was devalued by 36.5 per cent on 6 June 1966. It happened in less than six months after Indira Gandhi assumed office. Given the balance of payments situation, it is doubtful that there was any other alternative.

The US dollar, which was equivalent to ₹4.75, became worth ₹7.50. There was also an attempt at loosening the rigours of QRs on imports for exporters by introducing licences under the Import Replenishment Scheme in August 1966. An import percentage was allowed for each item of export, subject to the payment of customs duty.

Devaluation in 1966 in India was seen as a debasement of the currency. In the olden days, a currency could be debased in many ways, most notably by clipping off a little from a gold coin. Debasement was a serious crime. In 1124, in England, a disgusted King Henry I had ninety-four mint workers castrated for producing bad coins. After seventeen years of fixed exchange rate of the rupee, the external value of the rupee had somehow acquired a symbolic significance and, as the Indian ambassador to the US B.K. Nehru said, 'It is as if devaluation had castrated India.'[2] There was stringent criticism in Parliament and in the media, and the act was described as the ultimate 'sell-out to America and the World Bank'. Not confined to opposition parties, critics included even Congress president Kamaraj and other leaders such as Morarji Desai, TTK, Jagjivan Ram, Neelam Sanjiva Reddy, Krishna Menon and Manubhai Shah. There was the emotional issue of 'national honour' associated with the devaluation— post-devaluation, foreigners would be paying fewer dollars for the same commodity that they were buying before the devaluation!

The wave of anti-devaluation sentiments was quite contrary to what Merwanji Rustomji, representing the Exchange Brokers' Association of

Bombay, and Romesh Chunder Dutt, representing Bengal, had demanded before the Indian Currency Committee headed by Sir Henry Fowler in 1898. Until 1892, India was effectively on a silver standard. In 1893, in a major move, the Government of India closed Indian mints to silver. The Fowler Committee recommended that India move to the gold standard, as the pound sterling already was, and peg the official rate of the rupee to the pound at 1 shilling 4 pence or 16 pence per rupee. Before the mint was closed in 1893, the rupee had commanded a value of 14 pence. Rustomji and Dutt had argued vigorously before the committee that the rupee be pegged not at 16 pence but at a more devalued level of 14 pence per rupee. Dutt had mentioned the global competitiveness of Indian products as one of his considerations. The hostile popular reaction to the 1966 devaluation was diametrically opposite to what Rustomji and Dutt most likely would have had to say on the issue.

Earlier, soon after Independence, the rupee had been devalued once on 19 September 1949, but under vastly different circumstances. India had joined the IMF on 27 December 1945 as one of its original members. Under the Bretton Woods fixed exchange rate regime, like many former or existing members of the British empire, India operated in the so-called sterling area with its exchange rate fixed vis-à-vis the pound sterling at the rate of 1 shilling and 6 pence per rupee, or ₹13.33 per pound sterling. Because of the dollar shortage in the sterling area, the pound was devalued by 30.5 per cent from $4.03 per pound to $2.80 per pound on 18 September 1949. India did not change its rupee rate vis-à-vis the pound sterling, but, because of the pound devaluation, the rupee also got devalued against the US dollar from 30.2250 cents per rupee to 21 cents per rupee or ₹3.31 per dollar to ₹4.76 per dollar. The 1966 devaluation was different—it was not triggered by any change in the valuation of the pound sterling relative to the US dollar.

XII.3 Food Shortage

The food situation had turned grim by the late 1950s, and from 1956, been managed with supplies under US PL480. The PL480 agreement of 1960 and 1964 for 17 and 4.5 million tonnes of food grains had ensured adequate supplies to urban areas. Two successive droughts in 1965 and

1966 resulted in a dramatic worsening of the food situation. But with relatively low US stock position and a change in policy under President Lyndon Johnson, the supply of US surplus agricultural commodities, chiefly wheat, under PL480 looked increasingly uncertain.

Within two months of becoming prime minister, Indira had visited the US from 27 March to 2 April 1966. By all accounts, her visit and meetings with President Johnson went well. Yet, the package from the Aid India Consortium and the World Bank were disappointing. The 'promised' foreign aid did not come through. The US was also unhappy about India's criticism of its Vietnam war. It amended its PL480 in 1966 to make it contribute to its balance of payments. Further, the amendment required the US President to take steps to assure a progressive transition from sales for foreign currencies to dollar credit sales. India had to entreat the US to supply grains. The US was following a 'ship to mouth' policy regarding food aid and President Johnson was authorizing shipments on a month-to-month basis. At the peak of the shortage, US supply was almost 50,000 tons of grains daily. Ships were arriving at the Indian ports once every 5 minutes and there were even 'ship traffic jams' because of several ships coming so frequently.

WPI inflation, already high at 11 per cent in 1964–65, after declining to 7.6 per cent in 1965–66, shot up to 13.9 per cent in 1966–67 and 11.6 per cent in 1967–68. With the groundswell of opposition and the conservative faction of the Congress led by Morarji Desai contesting her leadership, for Indira, these became politically troubled times.

XII.4 The Popular Upsurge and the Congress Regional Breakaways

Given its nature as an umbrella party, splits within the Congress were inevitable, particularly after Independence. On 1 March 1948, after the Mahatma's assassination, the socialist caucus of the Congress Party—the CSP—under the leadership of Jayaprakash Narayan and Acharya Narendra Dev, had broken away to form the Socialist Party (SP). Similarly, with his belief in the Gandhian ideal of countless village republics, Jivatram Bhagwandas Kripalani, popularly known as Acharya Kripalani, the president of the Congress in 1947, left in 1948 and formed the Kisan

Mazdoor Praja Party (KMPP) in 1951. Rajaji, a stalwart from Madras Presidency, left the Congress in 1957 and formed the Swatantra Party in 1959. After Independence, the Congress provided not only stable governments but also leaders to the opposition parties. The opposition parties in the 1950s, such as the Swatantra, Socialists and Communists, were all-India parties, not regional ones. What was new in the 1960s was the rise of regional parties under leaders who cut their political teeth in the Congress. They manifested a societal upsurge and increasing popular participation nurtured by Indian democracy. On economic policies, the regional parties differed from the Congress more on implementation aspects. They also differed from the Congress in their assertion of identity of groups based on language, religion and caste.

The breakaways from the Congress party gathered momentum after Pandit Nehru's demise in 1964. Kerala Congress under the leadership of K.M. George broke away in October 1964. The splits became most pronounced after Prime Minister Shastri's untimely death in 1966. By splitting from the Congress, Harekrushna Mahatab set up his Orissa Jana Congress, Ajoy Mukherjee formed the Bangla Congress in West Bengal, Chaudhary Charan Singh the Bharatiya Kranti Dal in UP, and Mahamaya Prasad Sinha the Jana Kranti Dal in Bihar. A brief discussion of how they went on to dislodge the Congress and capture power in their respective states follows.

Kerala

The four major communities of Ezhavas, Nairs, Muslims and Christians together comprised about 80 per cent of the population of Kerala. Because of their concentration in different geographic pockets, they also commanded considerable leverage in electoral politics of different parties. Broadly, the Ezhavas supported the communists, the Nairs the Praja Socialist Party (PSP), the Muslims the Muslim League and the Christians the Congress.

A coalition of the Nairs, Muslims and Christians had launched agitations under the banner of the *Vimochana Samara Samiti* or Liberation Struggle Front and brought about the dismissal of the communist government in Kerala in 1959. After the controversial dismissal, elections followed in February 1960 and the Front fought it with seat adjustments. As a result, in the 126-seat Vidhan Sabha, the ComPI's score came down from sixty in 1957 to only twenty-nine in 1960. The large decline in ComPI's seats despite an increase in its vote share from 40.6 per cent to 43.8 per cent reflected the consolidation of votes of the opposition parties under a United Front. In 1960, Congress won sixty-three seats, PSP twenty, and Muslim League eleven. The Congress would not have anything directly to do with the communal Muslim League and the Muslim League's alliance partner PSP. Thus, a government was formed under PSP's Pattom Thanu Pillai, with Congress' support. It proved to be short-lived.

There were communal dissensions within the Congress crystalizing around the Christian Home Minister, P.T. Chacko, and the Ezhava deputy chief minister, R. Sankar. When Pattom Thanu Pillai was elevated to the post of Governor of Punjab, Sankar became the chief minister on 26 September 1962. The Muslims, the Nairs and the Christians were not happy about this ascendancy of the Ezhavas. The break would have come sooner or later, and it came when P.T. Chacko, at the relatively young age of 49, died on 1 August 1964, and the leadership of the Christians in Congress in Kerala went to K.M. George. George and fifteen other Congress MLAs walked out of the government as well as the Congress party and formed his Kerala Congress. The Sankar government collapsed. The vote base of the Congress was badly divided. After R. Sankar, the Congress had a chief minister in Kerala only in March 1977.

Uttar Pradesh

Chaudhary Charan Singh, a Congress activist and freedom fighter from western UP, had become an elected member of the United Provinces' Legislative Assembly in 1937. He was known as the 'champion of Indian peasants' and was instrumental in scuttling the plan of the Congress to introduce cooperative joint farming in the 1950s. He was also a follower of the anti-caste Hindu reform movement Arya Samaj. He took a deep interest in the laws that were detrimental to the village economy and the peasants, and like the Socialist leader Ram Manohar Lohia, was a protagonist of affirmative action.

Charan Singh's views of the ideal economy, in contrast to that of Nehru, were strikingly close to the Mahatma's views of small-scale industry, limiting wants and having idyllic villages. Singh wanted agriculture to be prioritized over industry. In 1939, Charan Singh had proposed a 50 per cent quota in public administration in favour of the sons of the farmers because only an official who understood and thought like a peasant could effectively solve his problems. The All India Jat Mahasabha, or general assembly of the Jats, supported his proposal. He himself was a Jat, the dominant caste in western UP. Given the share of Jats in UP's population at less than 1.5 per cent, there were tactical advantages in trying to forge 'a kisan identity'. But it is more than likely that, like Sir Chhotu Ram, a Jat lawyer and social reformer from Rohtak in undivided Punjab in the 1920s, he genuinely wanted to subsume caste into a new peasant identity. Sir Chhotu Ram had played an important role in the rise of backward castes in north Indian politics by propagating AJGAR (literally python), a *biradari* or peasant brotherhood of the Ahirs, Jats, Gujars and Rajputs.

Charan Singh had a long ministerial career in a series of Congress governments in UP. In 1946, he became parliamentary secretary to Prime Minister Pandit Govind Ballabh Pant in the erstwhile United Provinces. With the Indian Constitution in January 1950, the United Provinces became Uttar Pradesh (UP), and he held ministerial portfolios in successive Congress governments in UP, starting with the portfolio of justice and information in Govind Ballabh Pant's government in 1951. He was a minister under Chief Ministers Sucheta Kripalani and C.B. Gupta. He was aggrieved that his recommended land consolidation policy, prevention of illegal practices of merchants in dealing with the farmers and measures to improve the terms of trade—that is, the price that they get for their produce relative to the price they paid to buy non-agricultural goods—had either not been accepted or accepted with a delay. Perhaps, more importantly, he had been bypassed by his own party, the Congress, for the chief minister's post. From 1962 to 1967, C.B. Gupta, a Baniya or merchant by caste, despite losing the assembly election twice between 1957 and 1962, and not even a member of the Vidhan Sabha, and Sucheta Kripalani, who was not even from UP, had been preferred to him for chief ministership.

In the February 1967 UP Vidhan Sabha election, Congress won only 199 out of 425 seats, down from 249 out of 430 in 1962. Though short of an absolute majority, on 14 March 1967, Congress as the largest single party, with support from independents, formed the government with C.B. Gupta as chief minister. In less than three weeks, on 1 April 1967, Charan Singh crossed the floor with sixteen of his mostly non-upper caste supporters and formed the Jana Congress, or People's Congress. The C.B. Gupta ministry collapsed when he and his associates voted with the Opposition to reject the motion of thanks to the Governor's address. The one-party dominance of the Congress in UP was over. Charan Singh, heading a government of the coalition Samyukta Vidhayak Dal (SVD), or the United Front of Legislators, on 3 April 1967, became its chief minister. He was the first chief minister of UP who was not a *dvija* or an upper caste.

Dissensions were bound to arise in this coalition of parties with deep ideological differences. Swatantra left the coalition in July 1967. Differences arose in the context of the abolition of the land tax on peasants, with less than six acres proposed by the communists and socialists. Charan Singh thought the tax strengthened the peasants' commitment to land ownership and was against the abolition. ComPI and SSP quit the SVD, and Charan Singh resigned on 25 February 1968. Charan Singh's non-Congress coalition government's life in UP may have been limited to only 328 days, but it reflected a pattern in a host of other states—Bihar, Kerala, Odisha, Punjab, Rajasthan and West Bengal. The pattern was: a breakaway faction of the Congress forms a new party and captures power through alliances with other non-Congress parties, like in Bihar.

Bihar

Bihar politics was dominated by the three upper castes of Kayasthas, Bhumihars and Rajputs, who competed as well coalesced to capture power. In Bihar, the charismatic Mahamaya Prasad Sinha, a Bhumihar, had qualified for the prestigious ICS. To participate in the freedom movement, he did not join the service. He had left the Congress, joined Acharya Kripalani's KMPP and got elected from Maharajganj to the Bihar Vidhan Sabha in 1952. After KMPP's merger with the Socialist Party (SP) and subsequent formation of the PSP, Mahamaya joined the PSP and in 1957, represented Muzaffarpur in the Vidhan Sabha. He was one of the many PSP leaders who joined the Congress after Asoka Mehta from the PSP became the deputy chairman of the Planning Commission in 1963.

The raja of Ramgarh, Kamakhya Narain Singh, a Rajput who had battled the government in courts against zamindari abolition, was a force to reckon with in the Chota Nagpur and tribal areas of Bihar, and a fierce opponent of the Congress. By donating land to the *'bhoodan'* (or voluntary land reform) leader Vinoba Bhave, he became a popular leader and a 'would-be' Tory democrat among the tribal people. He had set up the Chota Nagpur and Santhal Parganas Janata Party (CNSJP), and as a contestant himself, won in as many as four Vidhan Sabha constituencies in 1952. In 1957, the raja's wife, mother, brother, sister-in-law and business manager were members of the Lok Sabha. The raja had merged his Janata Party with the Swatantra Party right at its outset and had been its vice president since 1959. He left Swatantra to join the Congress in 1964, only to leave it in 1965 and form his Jana Kranti Dal, or the People's Revolutionary Party. Mahamaya Prasad Sinha became the raja's political disciple.

Bihar suffered a severe drought and devastating floods in its western parts in 1966. *Ravi* or winter food grains production also suffered. In 1967, adverse weather conditions led to a second successive year of output shortfall and resulted in the declaration of famine conditions in 32 per cent of the areas in Bihar. The handling of the crisis was far better than that under the British imperial administration. Yet, there were political fallouts.

Mahamaya left the Congress, and a little before the elections, on 31 December 1966, joined raja of Ramgarh's Jana Kranti Dal. In the 1967 election, with the mystical slogan of 'Rice sale at ₹10 per maund', he led the Jana Kranti Dal to win twenty-six seats in the Bihar Vidhan Sabha election. With the support of 190 others of the 318 members of the Vidhan Sabha, on 5 March 1967, he formed the first non-Congress United Front government in Bihar. After about eleven months, ideological differences, factionalism and floor crossings led to the collapse of the United Front government, and a period of political turmoil and frequent changes of government followed. However, like in UP, the days of Congress dominance in Bihar were over.

Odisha

Under British rule, in 1936, Orissa—now Odisha—had been carved out of the Bihar and Orissa Province on a linguistic basis. Under direct British rule, it was in the eastern part of modern Odisha in the Utkal plains and included the delta of the three rivers, Mahanadi, Brahmani and Baitarani. The Garhjat hills—deriving its name from the Persian word *garh* or fort—is a mountain range formed by a series of low-lying hills. There were Garhjat princely states in the Orissa highlands with Praja Mandals as counterparts to the Congress in British India.

The Garhjat states had acceded to India but wanted to be separate states within it. The king of Patna (a Garhjat state, not to be confused with the capital of Bihar) Rajendra Narayan Singh Deo, Singh Deo henceforth, had even formed the Eastern Zone Native States Association comprising the Garhjat regions of Chhattisgarh and Orissa on 1 August 1947. Intervention by Sardar Patel, V.P. Menon and the Congress leader and first chief minister of Orissa, Harekrushna Mahatab, resulted in the merger of twenty-three Garhjat States with Orissa. In Orissa, under direct British rule, even before Independence, the Congress had internal dissensions between the 'Satyavadi' and 'Alaka' groups, between the young and the old, and those based on caste and local considerations. Competition against it intensified after Independence with the integration of the Garhjat princely states. Before the first general election in 1952, the former rulers of the Garhjat states formed a new party, the Ganatantra Parishad or Democratic Party.

In the 1952 election, the Congress was in for a rude shock. It secured only 37.9 per cent of the votes, and with sixty-seven victories, failed to secure an absolute majority in the Vidhan Sabha with 140 seats. The Ganatantra Parishad won in thirty-one seats and the SP in ten. The Congress formed a government by cobbling together independents as well as members of other parties. However, with devastating floods in 1955, and violent demonstrations against the non-inclusion of Oriya-speaking areas in neighbouring states in the state of Orissa, the going was not easy. The veteran leader Dr Harekrushna Mahatab, who had been appointed as Governor of the state of Bombay in March 1955, was brought back and installed as chief minister in mid-October 1956.

In the second general election in 1957, though the Congress marginally increased its vote share from 37.9 per cent to 38.3 per cent, its seats in the Vidhan Sabha came down from sixty-seven to fifty-six. The Ganatantra Parishad increased its vote share from 20.5 per cent in 1952 to 28.7 per cent and seats from thirty-one to fifty-one. Though Harekrushna Mahatab managed to form a Congress government with the support of five Jharkhand Adivasi Party and nine Communist Vidhan Sabha members, the Ganatantra Parishad was on its way to capturing power in Orissa. With both the Congress and Ganatantra Parishad encouraging floor crossings, there were violent exchanges among members of the two parties in the Vidhan Sabha, including the dismissal of a deputy minister and arrest without warrant of a few ex-rulers of Ganatantra Parishad. Congress finally had to enlist the Ganatantra Parishad as a coalition partner to continue in power.

Leadership of the Congress passed on from Harekrushna Mahatab to a relatively young forty-year-old and charismatic Bijoyananda Patnaik, popularly known as Biju Patnaik. The Congress demanded the resignation of the coalition government. The government resigned and mid-term elections were called for in February 1961. The Congress regained its pre-eminence by securing 43.3 per cent of the votes and winning eighty-two of the 140 seats. Biju became the chief minister. In 1962, Ganatantra Parishad merged with the Swatantra Party and Singh Deo became the president of the Orissa unit of the Swatantra Party. Under the Kamaraj Plan, in 1963, Biju relinquished his chief ministership and was succeeded by his close associate Biren Mitra, a forty-five-year-old Oriya of Bengali origin.

In August 1964, Singh Deo of Swatantra, at the head of thirty-four Vidhan Sabha and Parliament members of Orissa, submitted a memorandum to the President of India listing several charges against Congress ministers, including Biju Patnaik and Biren Mitra. The Central Bureau of Investigation (CBI) was asked to look into the allegations. CBI found some of the allegations to be true and a leaked copy of its report was placed in both houses of Parliament. A sub-committee of the Union Cabinet, which included the renowned lawyer M.C. Chagla, found both Patnaik and Mitra unworthy of holding public office. Biren Mitra resigned as chief minister on 21 February 1965 and was succeeded by Sadashiva

Tripathy until the fourth general election of 1967. In the interim, in 1966, the Jan Congress under Harekrushna Mahatab split from the Congress.

The 1967 election was a disaster for the Congress in Orissa, with its vote share down from 43.3 per cent to 30.7 per cent and its seats from eighty-two to thirty-one only. Even Biju Patnaik lost to a little-known PSP candidate, Chakradhara Satapathy from the Patkura assembly constituency, by over 15,000 votes. While Swatantra's vote share increased only marginally from erstwhile Ganatantra Parishad's 22.3 per cent to 22.6 per cent, its seats jumped from thirty-seven to forty-nine, and it emerged as the single largest party. The newly formed Jan Congress of Harekrushna Mahatab, with only 13.5 per cent vote share, bagged as many as twenty-six seats. Swatantra and Jan Congress together commanded an absolute majority in the Vidhan Sabha and formed the government under Singh Deo as the chief minister. Interestingly, after the 1971 polls, Congress would regain Odisha and rule it until 2000, except in 1977 and 1990, when it would lose to the Janata Party and the Janata Dal, respectively. Biju Patnaik, who led the Janata Dal to victory in Odisha in 1990 and become the chief minister, would pass away in April 1997. His son Naveen Patnaik would go on to set up the Biju Janata Dal (BJD) in December 1997, win every election from 2000 onwards and make Congress appear like a spent force.

West Bengal

With Partition, the Muslim-majority parts of eastern Bengal had formed erstwhile East Pakistan (now Bangladesh). Punjab had also suffered the pangs of Partition-related migration, but the refugee problem in West Bengal was much more severe and protracted than in Punjab. By 1951, with about 2 million Hindus migrating from East Pakistan to West Bengal, and the reverse migration of Muslims from West Bengal to East Pakistan closer to half a million, the demographic change was cataclysmic. In the first three post-Partition decades, an already densely populated West Bengal suffered a further wave of 4.5 million Hindu immigrants from East Pakistan. It was the greatest exodus of human population in world history.

With its Kolkata port, natural endowment of coal, iron ore and other resources, and for historic reasons, West Bengal had a vibrant industrial base. The Partition, by fracturing the single economic zone that was

Bengal, created enormous problems for industry. Rail, road and water transportation were severely disrupted not only between East and the West Bengal, but with parts of a road or rail line connecting the south and the north of West Bengal falling in East Pakistan, even within West Bengal! The west producing industrial goods was left without the fertile east providing it with the raw materials as inputs as well as an outlet for its finished goods. West Bengal, already overwhelmed by the colossal influx of refugees, started off with not only an acute shortage of food but also industrial decline. The ComPI shifted its focus from the *tebhaga* movement, which was in support of the tebhaga (sharing by thirds) demand—two-thirds of the crop for the sharecropper—and chose agitations over food, industrial labour and urban issues.

Right from day one, food was the foremost problem in post-Partition West Bengal. With the famine of 1942 still fresh in people's minds, it was easy to ignite passions. The leftists ascribed the food shortage and high prices to the greedy rice mill owners and hoarders, and a clandestine collaboration between the Congress government and these capitalists. From the late 1950s, city life was disrupted by massive political unrest, strikes and violence. Then, on 1 July 1962, the charismatic Dr Bidhan Chandra Roy, the reputed physician and Congress chief minister, passed away to be succeeded by Prafulla Chandra Sen, a freedom fighter and a Gandhian. Soon thereafter came the Chinese invasion. Two years later, the pro-Chinese faction split from the communist party to become Communist Party of India (Marxist) (CPI(M)), the dominant faction. It launched agitations against the prevailing food crisis.

Chief Minister Sen introduced statutory rationing. The limited rations did not satisfy the consumer. In 1965, he also proposed compulsory levy of food grains with cordoning, rationing and procurement of food grains, which did not go down well with the rural gentry, particularly the relatively backward castes of Mahishyas, Sadgops and Kurmis, who were engaged in farming, in the rice-producing districts. Sen tried to ameliorate the scarcity of milk in West Bengal by banning sweets made of milk by the West Bengal Channa (or cottage cheese) Sweets Control Order on 23 August 1965. Bengalis did not take the ban on their emblematic *sandesh* and *rassogolla* kindly or even rationally. In protest, state-wide general strikes and hartals were observed on 5 August 1965, 10-11 March 1966 and 6 April 1966. The March 1966 general strike resulted in several deaths in confrontations with police forces.

In the election to the Fourth Vidhan Sabha in West Bengal in early-1967, while the split in the communist party after the 1962 Sino-Indian conflict favoured the prospects of the Congress, factionalism within the Congress itself was highly troubling. Ajoy Mukherjee, one of the founders of the Tamralipta Jatiya (national) Sarkar (government) in Tamluk in the western district of Midnapore in Bengal during the Quit India Movement, was a minister under Dr Roy until he was axed under the Kamaraj plan. In 1964, he was the president of West Bengal Congress. On 1 May 1966, Mukherjee decided to dissociate with Atulya Ghosh, the undisputed boss of the Congress party in West Bengal, and form his new party—Bangla (or Bengal) Congress. It did not bode well for the electoral outcome for the Congress in 1967.

The CPI(M)'s main objective in 1967 was to displace the ComPI and emerge as the largest opposition party. It formed the United Left Front with the SSP, the Socialist Unity Centre of India (SUCI) and some other leftist parties. The ComPI, on the other hand, combined with Bangla Congress, the All-India Forward Bloc and the Bolshevik Party of India to form the People's United Left Front. Between the Third and Fourth Vidhan Sabha, with a decline in its vote share from 47.3 per cent to 41.1 per cent, with a split opposition, Congress's seats came down from 157 out of 252 seats to 127 out of 280 seats. The CPI(M), with forty-three seats and a vote share of 18.1 per cent, emerged as the second largest party after the Congress. With a large vote swing from the Congress, the Bangla Congress secured as much as 10.2 per cent of the votes by contesting only in eighty out of 280 constituencies. It defeated the outgoing Chief Minister Sen in Arambagh, and Atulya Ghosh in the Lok Sabha constituency of Bankura.

In the Vidhan Sabha, the Congress with 127 seats had more strength than the United Left Front and People's United Left Front together, with sixty-three seats each. But, with the public euphoria about its defeat, the Congress made no attempt to form the government. The two fronts came together and with the support of PSP, Gorkha League, the Lok Sevak Sangha and some independents, formed a United Front (UF) government. Ajoy Mukherjee was the chief minister and Jyoti Basu his deputy. The precarious food situation continued, and Congress launched vigorous agitations against the government's management of food. On the issue of cooperation with the communists, the Bangla Congress soon disintegrated into six or seven parts.

Prafulla Chandra Ghosh, the first chief minister of the state, had won as an independent candidate in 1967 and become the minister of food and agriculture in the UF government. He resigned as minister in November 1967 and formed the Progressive Democratic Front. Thirteen Bangla Congress MLAs joined him. Sordid cases of defections from political parties followed. Chief Minister Ajoy Mukherjee's government refused to call the legislative assembly and was dismissed by Governor Dharma Vira under Article 164(I). With Congress' support, Prafulla Chandra Ghosh became the chief minister for the second time. The Vidhan Sabha was summoned by the Governor on 29 November, only to be adjourned sine die by its Speaker, Bijoy Banerjee, on the pretext that it was illegally summoned. A constitutional crisis developed, and pro- and anti-government protests continued. With continuing infighting and defections, on 19 February 1968, Chief Minister Prafulla Chandra Ghosh resigned, and advised the Governor to recommend imposition of President's rule under Article 356. In the elections in February 1969, the Congress performed worse than in 1967, bad enough to face an existential question. Between 1967 and 2022, the Congress managed to come back to power in West Bengal only for one five-year stint, during 1972–77. With such developments in some major states, in 1967, Prime Minister Indira Gandhi faced a very hostile political situation.

XIII

The Rise of the Opposition

The 'underdevelopment' of a country and the 'backwardness' of its people—terms used by the famous Myanmarese economist Hla Myint in the 1950s—though often related, are different from each other. A country with a prosperous plantation or mining sector, such as an oil-rich Gulf sheikhdom, may be developed, yet the people may be backward, with much of the income accruing to non-residents or a handful of owners and migrant labour. At Independence, India was 'underdeveloped' and the Indians were 'backward'. India was underdeveloped because its resources—land, water, mineral resources, manufacturing potential—were not developed appropriately. The country lacked infrastructure—roads, bridges, ports and airports, irrigation and power supply. In their economic struggle to align their wants, activities and environment, the Indians, without education and good health, manifested their backwardness in their failure to earn a livelihood.

Progressive socio-economic policies after Independence started changing both India and Indians. Indians became less 'backward' as India 'developed', and political leaders started responding to the demands of the less backward Indians for empowerment, accelerated economic growth and development. This feedback loop between development of the country and the advancement of the people started working. After the Nehru era, there was a period of upsurge in popular participation, with historically disadvantaged groups mobilizing and the rise of regional parties. India moved from a Congress-dominated polity to a multi-party system.

After Independence, until 1964, with a 'national consensus' behind it, the Congress was practically the only party with an effective presence. For much of this period, Prime Minister Nehru 'had no peers in India, and . . . he bestrode the political scene.'[1] With a fine democratic temper, Nehru played a critical role in promoting democratic practice during his seventeen-year-rule. Despite the absence of a robust opposition, he showed utmost respect to those of its members who were present, listened to and argued with them, and tried to accommodate their views. He scrupulously observed good parliamentary etiquette and discipline, and '. . . used to attend Question Hour regularly even on days when his Ministry was not involved in the day's interpellations.'[2] He did not live long enough to see anything but a nascent opposition, but his daughter Indira, soon after coming to power, faced a boisterous one.

By the time Indira came to power, the electoral system had transformed from a dominant one-party system to a multi-party system through societal mobilization. Apart from the Congress breakaways, what emerged were parties of three varieties—(i) with rightist ideology; (ii) regional ones based on identity such as language, religion and caste; and (iii) those with leftist ideology.

XIII.1 From the Right—Swatantra Party

On the ideological front, right after Independence, Congress had faced contests from the right but only in isolated pockets. For example, in the first general election in 1952, Hanwant Singh, the former maharaja of Jodhpur, had formed his union of independent candidates and put them up in thirty-five state assembly constituencies and four Parliamentary seats that made up his former state of Marwar. His candidates won thirty-one out of these thirty-five assembly seats and all the four Lok Sabha seats. After a tumultuous accession to India, it was like Hanwant Singh's last stand. But the threat was short-lived. Tragically, the maharaja died in a plane crash on 26 January, the day of counting of votes. Similarly, in Odisha, PEPSU, Rajasthan and Saurashtra, right after Independence, Congress faced threats from former princes, ruling elites and landed interests. But again, it was a challenge that it successfully managed to meet.

In the first Lok Sabha, Shyama Prasad Mookerjee of Jana Sangh had tried to unite the parties that did not owe their allegiance to the Congress, Socialists or Communists. Thirty members—from Hindu Mahasabha, RRP, SAD, Ganatantra Parishad, Commonweal Party, Tamilnad Toiler's Party and some independents—had joined his 'National Democratic Group'. But Mookerjee's tragic death on 23 June 1953 brought an end to this endeavour. The initial threat to the Congress from the right was not sustained. The Swatantra Party came into the picture only on 4 June 1959, more than five months after the Congress passed its famous Nagpur Resolution at its Sixty-Fourth Plenary Session declaring agriculture's future as 'cooperative joint farming'. The Swatantra Party—or literally, the party with a difference—was born in Chennai at a meeting of the All-India Agriculturists' Federation. Its first president was N.G. Ranga, a leader of the Agriculturists' Federation. Interestingly, V.P. Menon, Sardar Patel's right-hand man in integrating the princely states, was one of the two joint secretaries of the party.

Some other distinguished members of the Swatantra Party were K.M. Munshi, the freedom fighter from Gujarat, Sir Homi Mody, the Parsi businessman associated with the Tata Group, Minocher Rustom Masani, better known as Minoo Masani, and Ardeshir Darabshaw Shroff. Masani, an ardent admirer of the Soviet Union in his student days and a founder of the CSP in May 1934, had become disillusioned by communism in the Soviet Union under Stalin, and become a middle-of-the-road believer in a mixed economy in a free and open society. With Sardar Patel's encouragement, he had set up the Democratic Research Service to educate the public on the dangers to India's freedom from communists who, under instructions from the Comintern in Moscow, were carrying on an insurrection in the early fifties in Telangana. A.D. Shroff was an eminent industrialist, banker and economist, who had served as a non-official delegate from India at the UN 'Bretton Woods Conference'. Shroff was one of the architects of the Bombay Plan in 1944. In 1956, Shroff and Murarji Jadhavji Vaidya, another Mumbai-based industrialist, along with some others, had set up the Forum for Free Enterprise. In its own words, the forum was 'a non-political and non-partisan organisation . . . to educate public opinion in India on free enterprise and its close relationship with the democratic way of life'.[3] After observing the First Five-Year Plan, it believed that Nehru's brand of socialism and comprehensive planning stifled individual initiative and enterprise and was turning the country into a totalitarian state. The government disapproved of the forum, and according to the forum, businesspersons, taking their cue from the government, kept their distance.

Swatantra believed in efficiency and productivity as keys to economic progress and emphasized freedom from state controls. Its focus was not on religious and cultural issues. Its paramount leader Rajaji was universally acclaimed as a brilliant thinker, but he was already over eighty years of age of failing health. Its 'inner circle', consisting of Rajaji, Ranga, Munshi, Masani and Homi Mody, had some differences in their views as well. For example, Rajaji believed in the three 'great' pillars of Indian society—joint family, jati and village. But Munshi was against the caste system, and Masani was a 'modernist' who stood against joint family and the caste system. All the leaders except Mody were former Congressmen who had been marginalized within the Congress. They were brilliant minds and distinguished citizens but could not succeed in 'sinking and/or sustaining roots in Indian political life.'[4]

The Swatantra Party contested in 173 seats in the 1962 election and won eighteen seats by securing 7.9 per cent of votes. This was a good start, and there were substantial electoral gains for the party in the 1967 Lok Sabha election. It contested in almost the same number of seats (178) and managed to increase its vote share to 8.7 per cent and win forty-four seats! But, as we shall see, the party fizzled out by the 1971 election to the Lok Sabha.

XIII.2 Dravida Munnetra Kazhagam

Apart from the Swatantra Party, which was formed on an ideological basis, Chennai—the erstwhile city of Madras—also gave birth to the Dravida Kazhagam or Dravida Federation on linguistic, cultural and other identity issues. In the then Madras State (Tamil Nadu from 1969), Dravidian leaders E.V. Ramaswamy Naicker aka Periyar, and C.N. Annadurai aka Anna, had some early successes in coalescing the anti-Brahmin forces into a robust political party. Political division between Brahmins and non-Brahmins in the Madras presidency had started during the late-nineteenth and early-twentieth centuries, mainly due to caste prejudices and disproportionate Brahminical representation in government jobs. The Justice Party had been formed in 1916 to fight this division. Periyar, an iconoclast, had formed the Self-Respect Movement in the Madras Presidency in the 1920s for the non-Brahmin to respect himself by learning to hate the Brahmins, who had deprived him of self-respect. His movement, however, was more against religion itself and involved mostly the Backward Castes such as Gounders, Mudaliyars, Nadars, Thevars and Vanniyars rather than SCs such as Pallan or Pallar. Under Periyar, the Justice Party and Self-Respect Movement merged in 1938 to become Dravida Kazhagam in 1944.

Periyar preferred British rule to Independence, wanted an independent Dravida Nadu for Dravidians and did not favour the party's participation in elections after Independence to dilute its ideology. Periyar's protege Anna preferred participation in elections. Finally, coinciding with Periyar's marriage to Maniammai, who was forty years younger than him, Anna broke away to form the Dravida Munnetra Kazhagam (DMK) in 1949.

Anti-Hindi agitations from even before Independence provided a fillip to the party. The Justice Party had launched three-year-long spirited agitations against the introduction of compulsory teaching of Hindi in schools in 1937 by the first Congress government led by Rajaji. After the resignation of the Congress government in 1939, the British government had abolished the compulsory teaching of Hindi in schools. Independent India had adopted Hindi as the official language of India, with English continuing as an associate official language for a period of fifteen years, after which Hindi would become the sole official language. Hindi as the sole official language even after the lapse of fifteen years was not acceptable to the DMK.

As a result of agitations by the DMK, Nehru enacted the Official Languages Act in 1963 to ensure the continued use of English beyond 1965. Even that did not satisfy the DMK. They feared that the assurance may not be honoured by governments in the future. Protests intensified as the deadline of fifteen years on 26 January 1965 approached. Riots broke out in Madurai on 25 January 1965 and continued for two months all over the state, with acts of violence, arson, looting, police firing and lathi charges. Paramilitary forces had to be called in to quell the agitation. The agitations ended only when Prime Minister Shastri gave assurances that English would continue to be used as the official language as long as the non-Hindi speaking states wanted. The grounds had been laid for a victory of the DMK in the Madras state in the upcoming elections. After the elections in 1967, Anna, at the helm of the DMK, went on to form the first non-Congress government. The Madras state was renamed Tamil Nadu on 14 January 1969. Until 2022, when this book was written, the Congress had not come back to power in Tamil Nadu.

XIII.3 The Akalis or SAD in Punjab

In Punjab and PEPSU, the Congress faced political challenges right from the first general election in 1951–52. In PEPSU, in the first general election, it did not win an absolute majority, and Gian Singh Rarewala formed a United Democratic Front government with the SAD, the Communists, Lal Communist Party, KMPP, Jana Sangh and independents. PEPSU became the first state to have a non-Congress government. Congress had dismissed its own faction-ridden government in Punjab and imposed President's rule in mid-1951. On 5 March 1953, PEPSU became the second state next to Punjab to come under President's rule.

Politics in Punjab, which had been under British rule, was considerably different from that in PEPSU, an amalgam of eight formerly princely states. Undivided Punjab had been ruled by the Unionist Party, which represented landed interests, included Muslims, Hindus and Sikhs, and was against the division of the country. Its famous leaders, like Sir Sikandar Hayat Khan and Sir Chhotu Ram, however, had passed away by 1945. A coalition of Congress, Unionist and SAD formed the government in 1946 under Prime Minister Malik Khizar Hayat Tiwana of the Unionist Party. It resigned on 2 March 1947 against the decision of the partition of the country. After Independence, East Punjab in India (Punjab henceforth) had started off with a coalition government consisting of the Congress and the SAD. The SAD in the Punjab legislative assembly merged with the Congress on 23 February 1948.

The language issue was a major irritant in Punjab. There were also minority grievances as well as factionalism, both within the Congress and the SAD. Pratap Singh Kairon had steered the Congress to a spectacular victory in Punjab in the Second General Election in 1957. But there were factions within the Congress led by people like Giani Kartar Singh, Gian Singh Rarewala, Prabodh Chandra and Devi Lal (the future chief minister of Haryana and deputy prime minister of India). In the third general election in 1962, because of factionalism, the Congress vote share came down from 47.5 per cent to 43.7 per cent and seats drastically from 120 to ninety. Kairon became the chief minister again, but his victory from Sarhali over the Punjabi Suba activist Mohan Singh of SAD by only thirty-four votes was a body blow to the chief minister. In 1957, he had won from the same constituency by defeating his rival from ComPI by over 20,000 votes.

There was factionalism within the SAD also, and it came to the fore when leaders like Udham Singh Nagoke, Giani Kartar Singh, Baldev Singh and Swaran Singh decided to merge the SAD into the legislative assembly with the Congress, and Master Tara Singh, along with leaders like Pritam Singh Gojran and Harcharan Singh Beg, decided to continue with the SAD. The SAD would disintegrate further in 1963, when Sant Fateh Singh broke up with his mentor Sant Tara Singh.

With corruption charges against him, Kairon resigned as chief minister of Punjab a month after his mentor, Prime Minister Nehru, passed away in May 1964. Intense factional feuds broke out in the Congress after Kairon's resignation. The state was divided into Punjab and Haryana on 1 November 1966 (Section II.5), and Giani Gurmukh Singh Mussafir, from SAD, became the new Punjab's first chief minister. His rule ended with the fourth general election in February 1967. In the reorganized Punjab Vidhan Sabha with 104 seats, Congress managed to win only forty-eight seats, five short of a majority. Akali Dal (Sant Fateh Singh faction, twenty-four seats), Jana Sangh (nine seats), and ComPI (five seats), with support from other non-Congress parties, formed the government on 8 March 1967, and Gurnam Singh, a former judge of the Punjab and PEPSU High Court, became the chief minister. The era of Congress monopoly of power in Punjab was over. In the years to come, Congress would face serious competition from the SAD in winning elections and forming the government in Punjab.

In Punjab's newly created sister state of Haryana, Bhagwat Dayal Sharma of the Congress became the first chief minister on 1 November 1966. There were eighty-one seats in Haryana's Vidhan Sabha. In the fourth general election held in February 1967, by securing forty-eight seats, the Congress won a comfortable majority. But even in Haryana, the Congress was rocked by factionalism. Rao Birendra Singh, a scion of the titular royalty of Rewari and a descendant of freedom fighter Rao Tula Ram, defected from the Congress with many MLAs, formed the Vishal Haryana Party, and became the first non-Congress chief minister of Haryana for 224 days starting 24 March 1967.

XIII.4 Socialist Parties

Acharya Narendra Dev, JP and Ram Manohar Lohia, among others, developed the socialist parties in India. While JP was from Bihar, the other two were from UP. Narendra Dev was a lawyer and an educationist, became the acharya or principal of Kashi Vidyapeeth and acquired the prefix to his name. He was an active Congress satyagrahi and had presided over the Congress conference in Patna in 1934 to establish the CSP and become its first president. JP was the general secretary. He believed in democracy, non-violence, abolition of poverty and end of exploitation for moral and humanist grounds, and the need to propagate Hindi.

After spending seven years studying sociology at US universities, including at Berkeley, JP had come back a Marxist. He advocated the abolition of zamindari and nationalization of heavy industries. At Nehru's invitation, he joined the Congress party at its Lahore session in 1929 and started looking after the labour cell. JP and many others in CSP believed that the Second World War provided an opportunity to press on the British and consolidate the freedom struggle.

In 1942, after the Mahatma launched his Quit India movement in August, on Diwali night, in a daring move, JP and five others escaped from their imprisonment in Hazaribagh Jail. JP became a popular hero. Soon, JP was caught and incarcerated in Hanumantnagar Jail. Underground CSP activists broke into the prison and rescued him again in May 1943. JP, along with Lohia, organized and trained the Azad Dasta or Freedom Brigade to paralyze the government, mainly in Bihar, by raiding ammunition depots, treasuries and government offices. Both he and Lohia were arrested and put in prison. The Mahatma made their release a precondition for negotiations to start with the Cabinet Mission. They were released in August 1946.

Lohia was a fiery speaker, often vitriolic, an iconoclast, and a maverick according to some. He had got a PhD degree from Frederick William University (today's Humboldt University) in Berlin, Germany. Hailing from the trader Agarwal community, he was a Marwari Vaishya by caste. He became the father of OBC reservation by first incorporating caste in the socialist ideology and bringing it into focus in the politics of northern India, particularly UP.

Before Independence, the CSP was worried that, with the formation of the Interim government, the Congress would be totally 'centred on government' and be riven by intense inner-party struggles for power. The CSP leadership had demanded that none of the CWC members would be ministers and members would be allowed enlightened criticism of the government. The demands were not accepted. 'On 28th February 1947, the Working Committee of the CSP decided to drop the prefix "Congress" and opened its door for non-Congress members.'[5] The Congress, in March 1948, amended its constitution to stipulate that no member of any other party could be a member of the Congress. The Socialist Party (SP) was born in the same month. A real challenge for the socialists outside the Congress was of distinguishing their ideologies and demands from that of the Congress as well as of the communists by a mixture of ideological and identity issues and the speed of progress of the country towards socialism.

In the first general election in 1951–52, SP put up candidates in 254 of 489 seats, and secured 10.6 per cent of the votes—second only to the Congress. Victory in only twelve seats with the position of the third largest party after Congress and the Communists was a bit of a shock to the SP leadership. They started looking for allies to increase their electoral strength. On 17 May 1951, J.B. Kripalani resigned from the Congress, and formed the KMPP in the following month. In 1951–52, KMPP contested in 145 seats, and won nine by securing 5.79 per cent of the votes. The SCF formed by B.R. Ambedkar contested in thirty-five seats, secured 2.38 per cent of the votes and won two seats. In 1952, the Socialists were preparing a merger with KMPP and trying for an election pact, or even a political federation, with the SCF. But Ambedkar rejected the proposal as he considered the KMPP as a reactionary party. In 1953, the SP merged with KMPP to form the PSP.

The PSP leadership was an inchoate group. 'Narayan and Acharya Narendra Dev were Marxists, Minoo R. Masani, a former member of the British Labour Party, and Asoka Mehta were democratic socialists. Achyut Patwardhan and Ram Manohar Lohia shared Gandhi's faith in governmental and economic decentralisation and non-violent revolution . . .'[6] SP and PSP were like groups of illustrious leaders in search of parties. Controversies and dissensions started right from the outset. At the Betul Conference of the PSP in 1953, a heated controversy arose over general secretary Asoka Mehta's proposal of collaborating with the Congress based on his thesis 'Political compulsion of backward economy'. There were allegations that JP and Acharya Narendra Dev were behind the proposal. Hurt by the allegations, JP slowly retired from active politics and joined Vinoba Bhave's bhoodan movement. Soon, pre-emption of the socialist ideology by the Congress at its annual session at Avadi in January 1955 created turmoil within the PSP. Over time, T. Prakasam in Andhra Pradesh, Pattom Thanu Pillai in Kerala, Prafulla Chandra Ghosh in West Bengal, Mahamaya Prasad Sinha in Bihar and Triloki Singh in UP defected to the Congress.

Lohia was the general secretary of the PSP. He disagreed with most PSP leaders, who were inclined to collaborate with the Congress. In 1956, Lohia launched his own party by the same name as one of the two parents of PSP—the Socialist Party (SP). The PSP split into PSP and SP partly on the issue of reservation for the OBCs. Soon, a new line of socialist non-Congress leaders, including Karpoori Thakur, Ramanand Tiwari and Basawon Singh, emerged in the SP to charge up backward caste consciousness.

The central leadership of the Congress envisaged development by state-sponsored social change, and in this, did not regard caste as a relevant category. It relied on conservative notables at the local level for popular mobilization. This created a vacuum for direct mobilization of the so-called backward castes, and this vacuum in the northern states of Bihar and UP was captured by socialist leaders Lohia and Karpoori Thakur, who played catalytic roles in mobilizing sections of the OBCs in their fight against the Congress. Lohia, belonging to the Bania caste himself, had stated in 1956:

'I am also fed up with Bania-Brahmin politics . . . Bania-Brahmin alliance is one of the prime movers of Indian history. The Bania lords the nation's belly. The Brahmin lords the nation's mind.'[7] Significantly, this caste-wise mobilization was restricted more to the OBCs than the SCs. Perhaps, the OBCs were most ready for such mobilization, and such mobilization would soon threaten the Congress monopoly of power in Bihar and UP.

The split within the socialist camp was short-lived because of the upward pressure from the bottom. Jana Sangh had improved its position in the Lok Sabha by winning fourteen seats in 1962 compared to only four in 1957. In the 1962 Lok Sabha, PSP and SP, by contrast, by winning twelve and six seats, respectively, fell one short of the united PSP's score of nineteen in 1957. The impact of the division in the socialist ranks was clearly visible from the relativities of the votes and seats. SP and PSP together had secured 30.1 per cent of the votes relative to Jana Sangh's 18.7 per cent but failed to convert the votes into any more than sixty-two seats compared to Jana Sangh's forty-nine. For every percentage point of votes secured, SP and PSP together got 2.1 seats while the Jana Sangh got 2.6 seats. With their split electorally proving to be very costly, there was a de facto merger of PSP and the SP in UP into a United or Samyukta Socialist Group on 13 December 1962. It was an action at the grassroots level, without involving the party leaderships.

There were important policy differences between the SP and the PSP, particularly with regard to the status of English, policy toward the SCs, Chinese aggression in 1962, and the right of public employees other than those in the armed forces to participate in politics. Also at stake was the issue of Lohia's 'equi-distance theory' of opposing the communists as well as the Congress, Swatantra and the Jana Sangh, versus Asoka Mehta's prescription of issue-based support to the Congress.

Another important development in the Congress that affected the PSP in 1962 was the setting up of the Congress Forum for Socialist Action (CFSA) by Gulzarilal Nanda, L.N. Mishra and Mohan Dharia, again with Nehru's approval, to fight both 'right reaction' and 'left adventurism'. The CFSA was almost like a second edition of the CSF. It was in favour of an alliance with the PSP. On 26 September 1963, Asoka Mehta accepted his appointment as the deputy chairman of the Planning Commission. Mehta, who had been in favour of collaboration with the Congress from at least 1953, left the PSP to re-join the Congress. Many PSP members and legislators also defected to the Congress. In its Bhubaneswar session in January 1964, Congress, under President K. Kamaraj, invited all socialists in the country to join and strengthen the organization to achieve its socialist goal. By the mid-1960s, Congress had several former members of the PSP, such as Chandra Shekhar from UP, Mohan Dharia from Maharashtra and Krishan Kant from Punjab, in its fold.

Adoption of social control of banking and a de facto ceiling on income and private property by the Congress Steering Committee increased the appeal of the Congress among the socialists. A worried Lohia offered the recipe of unconditional merger of SP and PSP. In mid-February 1964, PSP accepted the offer and also expelled Mehta from the PSP. The unification of SP and PSP led to the foundation of the Samyukta Socialist Party (SSP) in May 1964. But it was short-lived.

Lohia, the supreme leader of the SP faction, believed that 'the Congress was a coiled cobra sitting tight on all that was essential to national progress'.[8] An uncompromising critic of the Nehru-Gandhi dynasty, he was willing to make common cause with the Communists, Swatantra and the Jana Sangh to bring down the Congress. Such collaboration with anti-socialist and reactionary parties was not acceptable to the former members of the PSP, now in SSP. The merger was effectively over in early 1965 and the PSP was reborn. Lohia remained at the helm of the SSP until his untimely death at 57 on 12 October 1967.

SSP's slogan—coined by Karpoori Thakur—was 'Sansapa ne bandhi gaanth, pichda pave sau me saath' or SSP has taken a vow, backwards should get sixty out of 100. Congress dominance across castes started to decline from the late-1960s in northern India, particularly UP and Bihar, but not as much as in Tamil Nadu, at least in the initial stages. But the strength of the PSP and SSP also came down from thirteen and twenty-three, in 1967 to two and three, respectively, in 1971. Both were practically wiped out, at least for the time being. After negotiations between May and August 1971, they merged on 9 August 1971 to become the new-old Socialist Party with Karpoori Thakur as chairman and Madhu Dandavate as its general secretary. Significantly, Lohia's proteges Mulayam Singh Yadav and Lalu Prasad Yadav would go on to dethrone the Congress from UP in 1991 and Bihar in 1990, but not in Lohia's lifetime.

XIV

Troubled Politics and Rapid Left-Turn

With the food shortage, high inflation, and balance of payments problems, right from the word go, the going was tough for Prime Minister Indira Gandhi. She had to contend with the Opposition and also establish her leadership within the Congress. While Morarji Desai had openly contested her prime ministership, the other established leaders in the Congress, the so-called syndicate, had supported her only because they expected her to carry the halo of her departed father and be pliable at the same time. Parallelly, there were ominous signs of troubled politics in India's two neighbours, namely Pakistan and China, which Indira could not have missed.

In Pakistan, with martial law imposed, General Ayub Khan had introduced 'basic democracy' in 1962. In 1965, to legitimize his presidency, Ayub called for an 'indirect' election for the presidency and put himself up as a candidate. Fatima Jinnah, the sister of Quaid-e-Azam Muhammad Ali Jinnah and Māder-e-Millat ('Mother of the Nation'), was the candidate of the united opposition. Ayub defeated Fatima Jinnah in a controversial indirect election.

Food shortage of 1.5–2.5 million tons in 1965 and 1966 contributed to the unpopularity of the Ayub regime in Pakistan. Moreover, many in Pakistan saw the Tashkent Declaration in January 1966 as a humiliation. Even his foreign minister Zulfikar Ali Bhutto criticized the declaration on public television and lost his job. Fatima Jinnah was found dead on 9 July 1967. 'During her funeral, no common man was allowed to go near her dead body. No one was allowed to see her face for the last time before she was buried.'[1] Speculations continue that she had been murdered. Popular dissatisfaction, including with rising prices of essential food items, led to violent demonstrations. Ayub resigned and Gen. Yahya Khan, commander-in-chief of the army, took over as President on 25 March 1969.

In China, after the failed 'Great Leap Forward' during 1958–61, Mao launched the Cultural Revolution in 1966 to preserve 'true' communist ideology by purging the remnants of capitalist and traditional elements. Millions were persecuted by the young 'revolutionary red guards'. Abuses included public humiliation, arbitrary imprisonment, torture and sustained harassment. Cultural and religious sites were ransacked; historical relics and artefacts destroyed. Millions of urban youths were forcibly displaced to rural regions, disrupting their studies.

In the mid-1960s, what Indira faced in terms of political trouble may have been 'mild' in comparison with that in Pakistan and China. But it was bad enough relative to what her father had to contend with during his seventeen-year rule. Within almost thirteen months of assuming charge, while the devaluation and food shortage attracted vehement criticism, she also had to face the election to the Fourth Lok Sabha during 17-21 February 1967.

XIV.1 Congress System on Trial—Electoral Debacle of 1967

Under Nehru, such was the electoral dominance of the Congress that even Ambedkar, one main framer of the Constitution, lost in not only the first Lok Sabha elections to his Congress rival in the Bombay City North reserved constituency, but also in the by-election from Bhandara in 1954 to a relatively unknown Congress candidate, Bhaurao Borkar. After Nehru's death, this dominance was at risk. The bandwagon effect—voting for the Congress in the belief that others were voting for it—was petering out. In an electoral debacle, the strength of the Congress came down dramatically from 361 in a house of 494 in the 1962 election to the Third Lok Sabha to only 283 in a house of 520 in February 1967 (Figure XIV.1).

After Indira Gandhi took over, there had been food riots in the country. Food shortage was a major contributory factor to the Congress debacle in the fourth general elections in 1967. There was also a generational shift in the electorate. Half the electorate was under thirty-five years of age

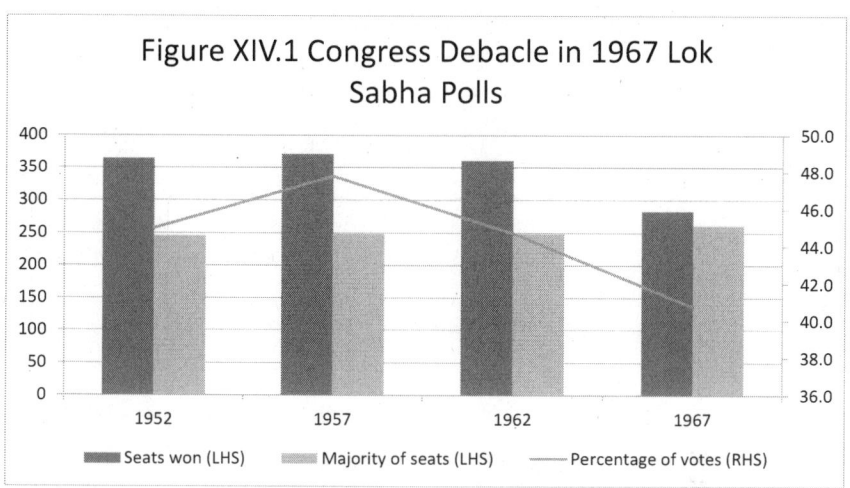

Figure XIV.1 Congress Debacle in 1967 Lok Sabha Polls

Seats won (LHS) Majority of seats (LHS) Percentage of votes (RHS)

Source: Election Commission of India.

and included 35 million who had not been old enough to exercise their franchise in 1962 election. Political loyalties were not guaranteed to survive across generations. Furthermore, the Congress was severely affected by the internecine conflict that had ensued in the selection of Indira as Prime Minister in January 1966. In several states, the Congress breakaways and their pre-poll alliances with opposition parties looked threatening. The proportion of votes polled by the Congress in the Lok Sabha elections, after declining from a high of 47.8 per cent in 1957 to 44.7 per cent in 1962, reached a low of 40.8 per cent in 1967 (Figure XIV.1). The veteran political scientist Rajni Kothari described the period as 'India: Congress System on Trial'. [2]

In 1967, along with the Lok Sabha polls, elections to the Vidhan Sabhas were also held in twenty states. Until 1967, except in Kerala, the Congress had won a majority both in Lok Sabha and Vidhan Sabha elections in each of these twenty. In 1967, in the state-level legislative elections, Congress lost in nine states—Bihar, Haryana, Kerala, Madhya Pradesh, Madras (what became Tamil Nadu from 1969), Odisha, Punjab, UP and West Bengal—where non-Congress governments were formed. The Congress debacle in these nine went beyond their change in government. For example, in Madras, where C.N. Annadurai, the DMK leader, went on to form the first non-Congress government, K. Kamaraj, the Congress president and the former chief minister, had fought from Virudnagar Vidhan Sabha constituency. Injured in an accident, Kamaraj could not campaign and ironically had said, '*Naan paduthu konde jaipen* (I can win in my sleep).' He lost by 1.285 votes to a young DMK student leader, P. Seenivasan. In West Bengal, the Congress-stalwart Atulya Ghosh had been elected to the Lok Sabha twice before and been the treasurer of AICC. In Bankura constituency in West Bengal, Ghosh lost to a relatively unknown ComPI trade union leader, J.M. Biswas, by about 30,000 votes.

Election in 1967 saw a fragmentation of the national party system. In 1967, based on the preceding electoral results, the number of national parties was seven, and state parties fourteen. In 1971, the number of national and state parties increased only marginally to eight and seventeen, respectively. But it was no longer a situation of a few large national parties garnering most of the votes or seats, but the votes and seats getting scattered among many medium- and relatively small-sized parties. Political scientists distinguish between the number of parties and the 'effective' number of parties. This intuition behind this distinction can be illustrated by considering an election with three parties commanding almost equal support of a third of the voters and another election with six parties in the fray but only the two largest parties commanding 50 per cent and 30 per cent of the votes, the other four trailing with only 5 per cent each. Though the number of parties is larger in the second case, the effective number of parties is larger in the first. The Laakso-Taagepera index of effective number of parties (Box XIV.1) in the Lok Sabha exceeded three in terms of seats and exceeded five in terms of votes for the first time in 1967.

Box XIV.1 The Laakso-Taagepera Index of Effective Number of Parties

In April 1979, in the *Journal of Comparative Political Studies*, the Finnish social scientist Markku Laakso, who later turned into a leading expert in the genetics of type 2 diabetes, and Estonian political scientist Rein Taagepera, jointly proposed an index to measure the *effective number of parties* either in terms of votes or seats. It is known as the Laakso-Taagepera index of effective number of parties and is widely used.

We will recall (Section V.6) that a measure of fractionalization is

$$F = \sum_{j=1}^{m} p_j(1 - p_j) = 1 - \sum_{j=1}^{m} p_j^2 \qquad \text{(BXIV.1.1)}$$

where m is the number of parties and with at least one vote or seat and $0 < p_j \leq 1$ is the share of votes or seats for the j-th party. Note that p_j can differ widely among the parties, with some parties commanding little support. Suppose we ask the question: what is the number of parties with equal support that would result in the same measure of fractionalization? Let us call it N. Since all of them enjoy equal support, then $p_j = \frac{1}{N}$ and the measure of fractionalization is

$$\ddot{F} = 1 - \sum_{i=1}^{N} \frac{1}{N^2} = 1 - \frac{1}{N} \qquad \text{(BXIV.1.2)}$$

Since we want $F = \ddot{F}$, we get

$$N = \frac{1}{\sum_{j=1}^{n} p_j^2} \qquad \text{(BXIV.1.3)}$$

as the effective number of parties.

It is easy to check that for the example of with three parties commanding equal support of a third of the votes, the effective number of parties is

$$\frac{1}{\sum_{i=1}^{3}\left(\frac{1}{3}\right)^2} = 3 \qquad \text{(BXIV.1.4)}$$

and is the same as the actual number of parties. In the other case of six parties in the fray but only the two largest parties commanding 50 per cent and 30 per cent of the votes and the other four trailing with only 5 per cent each, the effective number of parties is

$$\frac{1}{(0.5^2+0.3^2+0.05^2+0.05^2+0.05^2+0.05^2)} = \frac{1}{0.35} = 2.86 \qquad \text{(BXIV.1.5)}$$

which is much less than the actual number of parties. Though the actual number of parties in the second case is twice the actual in the first case, the effective number of parties is lower!

What was striking was the consolidation of non-Congress opposition state-by-state, particularly in the Vidhan Sabha elections. It resulted in a fragmentation of the party system at the national level and an end to the uniform Congress party dominance at the Union and state levels, for which the portents had been strong in the run-up to the polls. First, a weak economy with food shortages and high inflation had promoted widespread popular protests in the form of bandhs or general strikes organized by opposition parties. It was not so much a vote in favour of the Opposition's well-thought-out alternative economic policy agenda, but a negative vote against the outcome of Congress's economic policies. Second, demanding a ban on slaughter of cows as enshrined in the Directive Principles of State Policy in the Constitution, on 7 November 1966, which was the auspicious Gopa Ashtami for the Hindus, sadhus or Hindu monks led violent protests, ending in police firing around Parliament and multiple deaths and several injuries.

XIV.2 Last or First True Election?

Looking at the grim situation, the India watcher Neville Maxwell predicted that the fourth general election of 1967 would be the 'last' election in India. Maxwell was wrong. Dr P.B. Gajendragadkar, the vice chancellor of Bombay University and the former Chief Justice of India, was more to the point when he said that future historians would describe the fourth general election as not the last but as 'the first true General Elections that India witnessed.'[3] The increase in the effective number of parties validated Gajendragadkar's prediction.

Before Independence, the Congress had been like a coalition, and its constituents, despite their ideological differences, had stuck together to fight against the common British imperialist enemy. After Independence, this monolithic national movement began to break down into political parties and interest groups, or what we called Congress breakaways. The development was severe enough during 1950–51 for some commentators to describe it as *annus horibilis* of the Congress'.[4] 'Time, and to be fair, the achievements of Nehru . . . pushed India across that stage.'[5] For the first two decades after Independence, India grappled with its problems and lived in the mood of its colonial past. Once this first stage was over, with colonial rule a fading memory and the demise of the charismatic Nehru, the diversity that is India was reflected in the emergence of regional parties. The Planning Commission started driving the economic agenda of not only the Union government but also the states. The roles of the Provincial Congress Committees in drawing up their own provincial development plans became severely circumscribed. The centralization of economic decisions at the Planning Commission by undermining the democratic functioning of the Congress party at the grassroots level might have also contributed to fissiparous tendencies in the party at the state level.

The spread of literacy and information created aspirations, and unfulfilled aspirations created resentment against the ruling party. For example, land reforms promised but not completed led to grievances among small, marginal and landless farmers. And wherever aspirations were fulfilled, it led to even higher aspirations and the government's inability to measure up to these expectations led to disenchantment. Voters looked for political alternatives to the Congress. The multiple crosscutting axes, for example, left-right, secular-communal, centralist-regional autonomist, and a variety of caste-bloc-based axes, which characterized India's polity, started coming to the fore with regional variations. Development itself widened the horizon of possibilities regarding attainment of 'identity' goals or assertion of identities. The OBCs, not so much the SCs and the STs, started their mobilization around specific political parties. Caste became an important and explicit factor in Indian politics from the 1960s onwards.

XIV.3 Meghalaya

For the new Prime Minister, the problem of identity politics in the North-East did not end with the Mizo revolt in early 1966. The demand for a hill state was particularly strong among three matrilineal tribes, the Khasis, the Jayantias and the Garos, living in three adjacent districts of the same names as the tribes.

Language was an explosive and divisive issue in the state of Assam. The 1971 Census classified Assam's population into speakers of seventy-six languages and dialects, with a residual category consisting of forty-eight other languages and dialects. The tribal people in the hill districts wanted only Hindi as the official language. They did not want Assamese even as one of the official languages, as they feared that it would be the beginning of their disintegration and assimilation into the Assamese community. The declaration of Assamese, and for an interim period English, as its official language by the Assamese Official Language Act on 24 October 1960 had triggered the demand for a separate hill state carved out of Assam. The political parties in the Khasi, Jayantia and Garo hill districts as parts of APHLC had met Prime Minister Nehru in November 1960. Nehru had rejected their demand for a separate Eastern Frontier State but agreed to their greater autonomy within the Assam state, like Scotland had in the UK at that time. Soon after this agreement in principle, which came to be known as the Nehru Plan, Nehru died and was succeeded by Lal Bahadur Shastri.

The recommendations in the Nehru Plan of a three-member commission headed by H.V. Pataskar appointed by Prime Minister Shastri came after Shastri's demise. Its recommendations were not acceptable to the hill districts. It fell on Indira Gandhi, the new Prime Minister, to resolve the impasse. A Cabinet Committee appointed in June 1966 to resolve the problem came up with the idea of a sub-state—a Constitutional improvisation—'comprising units of equal status not subordinate to each other'. A communique issued in January 1967 committed the Government of India to (i) reorganize Assam, (ii) have a federal structure after reorganization, (iii) have the details worked out by a committee in six months, and (iv) invite other administrative units to join the sub-federation at a later stage. The APHLC was happy with the sub-federation proposal, but violent protests broke out in the Brahmaputra valley, including by the Assam Congress. The Assamese feared Balkanization and dismemberment of their state. Republic Day 1968 saw the national flag being burnt, and 'Assam for Assamese' slogan being raised in the plains. There were dissensions even within the Congress Party's all-India leadership and Indira Gandhi's cabinet, for example, from Morarji Desai. A thirteen-member committee headed by Asoka Mehta, the union minister for planning, was set up to go into the reorganization of Assam in detail. The Mehta Committee recommended that law and order (except the village and town police already under the control of District Councils), education beyond the middle-school level, and all industries except cottage and small-scale industries be retained at the state level.

Ultimately, after some deft political manoeuvring, a broad consensus was arrived at the sub-state of Khasi and Jayantia Hills, and the Garo Hills having the same paraphernalia of administration—such as chief minister, and secretariat—as any other state, but the subjects of law and order, state highways, major industries, major irrigation, drainage, power and navigation projects, and control over the municipality and cantonment of Shillong, which was the capital of Assam but located in the Khasi and Jayantia Hills, retained by Assam. After the necessary Constitutional Amendment, came the Assam Reorganization (Meghalaya) Act of 1969. On 2 April 1970, an autonomous state of Meghalaya, meaning 'abode of the clouds', was born out of the two districts of Khasi and Jayantia Hills, and the Garo Hills in Assam.

XIV.4 1967 Election in Jammu and Kashmir

In February 1967, legislative assembly elections were held together with Lok Sabha elections in Jammu and Kashmir. The Plebiscite Front officially boycotted the election and was declared unlawful. But several of their members contested as independent candidates. Many nominations were rejected because the candidates failed to take the obligatory oath of allegiance to the Constitution. In twenty-two of the seventy-five constituencies, candidates were returned unopposed. Congress won sixty-one seats, with the Jammu and Kashmir National Conference trailing at eight, and BJP and independents at three each. After his rapprochement with Sheikh Abdullah, even Bakshi Ghulam Mohammad, who had become hugely unpopular during his ten-year rule of 1953–1963, had been rehabilitated as a leader in people's minds and won from the Lok Sabha constituency of Srinagar. After the election, Ghulam Mohammad Sadiq continued as chief minister.

Sheikh Abdullah had called the 1967 election a farce. The victories of Arif Mohammad Naik, the general secretary of the Plebiscite Front, who stood as an independent candidate from the assembly constituency of Tral, and of the former Wazir-e-Azam Bakshi Ghulam from the Lok Sabha constituency of Srinagar, raised doubts about the true popular support of the Congress. Sheikh Abdullah, who had been under detention since May 1965, was released on 2 January 1968. On his return, huge crowds welcomed him in Srinagar. He devoted himself to strengthening the Plebiscite Front. The secessionist threat in Jammu and Kashmir remained.

XIV.5 Communists

On the eve of Bhopal's integration into India, the fear that its nawab had expressed to his friend Viceroy Mountbatten about India, without the princely states, being overrun by the communists had, as Mountbatten had rightly predicted, turned out to be unfounded. Yet, by the mid-1960s, communists were playing a large role in Indian politics. The relation between the communists and the Congress in India had a long history,

Many of the prominent communist leaders—for example, A.K. Gopalan, Hiren Mukherjee, P. Sundaryya and E.M.S. Namboodiripad— were former Congressmen and important Congress officeholders in their early days. In any case, soon after the textile workers' strike organized by the communists, the colonial government had imposed a ban on the ComPI on 23 July 1934 and no one could publicly be active as a member of the ComPI. The caucus in the Congress, namely the CSP, provided a suitable alternative for the communists and membership of the Congress was a necessary condition for joining the caucus. Furthermore, in July 1935, the Communist International, popularly known as Comintern, at its seventh and last congress, formally abandoned its militant sectarian strategy in favour of pursuing the establishment of popular fronts of all progressive forces against fascism. Many underground communists started following what could be called the political strategy of *entryism* and joining the CSP.

By the time of the Lahore Conference of the CSP in 1938, the issue of the war against Fascist Germany came to the fore. Following the Soviet line, the ComPI was supporting Germany, which the CSP found unacceptable, and in 1940, at Ramgarh, its national executive took the decision to expel all communist members from the party. This hiatus, however, lasted only about two years. After the Soviet Union declared war against Germany and became an ally, the colonial government lifted the ban on the party in July 1942 and the ComPI could again carry out overt activities.

Until its break-up in 1964, in terms of seats in the Lok Sabha, the undivided ComPI was the single largest party, next only to Congress in the first three general elections. Two years after the 1962 Chinese aggression, the pro-Chinese faction of the ComPI had split from it to become CPI(M). There was intense hostility between the ComPI and CPI(M). In the 1967 election to the Fourth Lok Sabha, though the division of the pro-Communist votes between ComPI and CPI(M) worked against their successful conversion to seats in favour of the communists, the factions managed to win twenty-three and nineteen seats, respectively, better than the twenty-nine seats the united ComPI had bagged in 1962. In the 1967 Lok Sabha elections—the first one after the split—the ComPI managed to win more seats than the CPI(M), but from 1971 onwards, and in all the subsequent Lok Sabha elections, CPI(M) dominated the ComPI in terms of seats won. The electoral performance of the ComPI, however, did not adequately reflect the intellectual and ideological heft of its galaxy of leaders, which included Hiren Mukherjee, Mohit Sen, C. Rajeswar Rao and Bhupesh Gupta.

'The ComPI's attitude towards the Congress Party fluctuated between contemptuous hostility, regarding the Congress as a "class organisation of the capitalists, and eagerness for cooperation, perceiving in it a progressive element opposed to imperialism and appreciative of socialism".'[6] There had always been a strong lobby within the ComPI that advocated close cooperation with the Congress. For example, many early communist leaders, such as P.C. Joshi, were impressed with Nehru's leadership and thought that collaboration would serve their cause more than fighting the Congress. The party's split in 1964 strengthened those voices in the new ComPI that viewed the Congress favourably.

The ComPI started reviving the strategy of working on the Congress from within and of having an alliance with it with three objectives: to act as a catalyst to transform the Congress into a truly radical party, destroying the rightists and the ultra-left parties including the CPI(M), and strengthening Indo-Soviet relations. There were signals of improving Indo-Soviet relations when, on 21 August 1968, Soviet tanks rolled into Prague, the capital of erstwhile Czechoslovakia, and the Government of India declined to condemn the aggression. What came in handy for the communists was the CFSA. The former communists and ex-socialists took over the CFSA. The CFSA insisted that the election debacles were due to a failure of the party's economic policy. Indira decided to go along with the CFSA.

In 1967, Mohan Kumaramangalam, a prominent ComPI leader, joined the Congress. Kumaramangalam believed that the ComPI cadre, 'instead of attacking the Congress for not being socialists . . . should either work, or work within, the Congress to hold the organisation to its socialist word.'[7] Later, as minister of steel and mines in the Indira Gandhi government during 1971–73, he was instrumental in nationalizing the coal industry. When Indira Gandhi turned left, many communists revived their strategy of working for their ideology inside the ruling Congress rather than from outside, and thereby reinforced Indira's turn to the left.

XIV.6 Indira Gandhi's Turn to the Left

Aggravated by the severe attacks on her for the June 1966 devaluation, Indira had started turning left. The Lok Sabha elections were in February 1967. The changed and hostile political milieu called for a change in policies, and a left turn might have appeared the most expedient. She gave lukewarm support to the liberalization effort and denied that the devaluation was a measure taken under donor pressure. After her official trip to the US, she had stopped at Moscow on her way back in April 1966. Continuing cooperation with Moscow included the setting up of the public sector Bokaro steel plant, for which the US had denied support on the grounds that it was a public sector project competing with the private sector. Indira had followed it up with a state visit to Moscow from 12 to 16 July 1966. The communiqué, signed by her and Alexei Kosygin, criticized the US for its bombing of Vietnam and held imperialist and other reactionary forces responsible for the deterioration in world affairs. India started getting identified with the Soviet bloc.

She and her Congress won the fourth Lok Sabha election in 1967, but with a considerably reduced majority. To salvage the situation, she followed a very diluted version of what Mao did in China—nothing as severe as the 'cultural revolution', but a turn left in both rhetoric and policy. In less than a week of the electoral debacle for the Congress in

February 1967 came the Supreme Court judgment in the celebrated Golak Nath case, wherein it ruled that the Parliament was not competent to amend the Fundamental Rights enshrined in the Constitution. The judgment posed a serious threat to the pursuit of socialism in the country. Indira acted fast. In May 1967, the CWC adopted a radical Ten-Point Programme of: (i) social control of banks, (ii) nationalization of general insurance, (iii) state trading in import and export, (iv) state trading in food grains, (v) expansion of cooperatives, (vi) curb on business monopolies, (vii) provision of minimum needs to the community, (viii) curbing unearned increment in urban land values, (ix) rural works programme and land reforms, and (x) abolition of princely privileges. It was a clear shift to the left with an emphasis more on equitable distribution than on growth.

XIV.7 The Politics behind the Policy Shift

After the 1967 election, the two most populous states in the Hindi heartland, namely UP and Bihar, saw the arrival of former Congressmen Charan Singh and Mahamaya Prasad Sinha as 'formateurs', politicians appointed to lead the formation of post-poll coalition governments. Even Haryana, Madhya Pradesh and West Bengal saw the installation of non-Congress governments headed by former Congressmen Rao Birendra Singh, Govind Narayan Singh and Ajoy Mukherjee, respectively.

What looked very ominous for Indira and her Congress were attempts by the various opposition parties to come together and form an all-India anti-Congress coalition. At the invitation of the chief minister of Bihar, Mahamaya Prasad Sinha, ministers of non-Congress governments and some veteran non-party leaders met in Patna in mid-May 1967. There were delegates from Andhra, Haryana, Madhya Pradesh, Maharashtra, Odisha, Punjab, Tripura, UP and West Bengal representing nine regional non-Congress parties. A steering committee was set up to draw up the preamble and suggest a suitable name for the party. At a meeting in Lucknow in October 1967, many ex-Congress parties—Bangla Congress of West Bengal, Jana Kranti Dal of Bihar, Jana Congress of Madhya Pradesh, Odisha and UP—agreed to create the Bharatiya Kranti Dal (BKD) or Indian Revolutionary Party. They resolved to work 'for the creation of a democratic society free from economic and political exploitation'.

In the late 1960s, the success of the Socialists in Bihar and Charan Singh in UP reflected the growing mobilization of the middle peasantry from the intermediate and low castes. But, thankfully for the Congress, the Socialists and Charan Singh represented two different political traditions. The Socialists' strategy for social emancipation, first articulated by Lohia, emphasized caste. Charan Singh's emphasis, on the other hand, was on kisan identity to promote a new rural solidarity subsuming caste and class divisions. His strategy was to crystallize a cleavage between urban and rural India and thereby mobilize a social majority behind him. Such differing strategies were not conducive to building a coalition.

Independent India was transiting from its first phase of policy autonomy under Nehru to the second phase, where there was a greater need to take the people along on policies. The people had changed. The literacy rate almost doubled from 18.3 per cent in 1951 to 34.5 per cent in 1971. People's faith in the infallibility of the government had been shaken by the humiliating defeat in the 1962 war with China. What excited the people in terms of political stimulus also changed with time. Increasingly, economic policy turned to the reactive mode of responding to what electorally important sections of the population wanted.

In the second phase, political empowerment of the historically exploited and neglected gained in salience and politics and policies became increasingly focused on empowerment. Loyalties to the Congress, which for many was unquestioned, disappeared with Nehru's demise and got divided based on language groups, castes or religions. But narrow identity-based parties could not guarantee electoral success. Fortunately for Indira Gandhi and her Congress, narrow identity-based parties were not willing to broaden their focus beyond a single identity and form alliances with parties based on different identities or non-identity-based parties. India, with its plurality and its first-past-the-post system—wherein voters cast their vote for a candidate of their choice, and the candidate who receives the most votes wins—gave rise to not only small and medium-sized parties in localized pockets, but also ad hoc, temporary and shifting alliances to capture power in the states. Two examples were the KHAM (Kshatriya, Harijan, Adivasi, Muslim) combination in Gujarat and AJGAR in UP.

In the first-past-the-post system of election that India follows, the winner needs to secure more votes than any of the others. The winner thus has a distinct advantage if the competitors are highly divided. During the first phase, social cleavages of religion, caste and language at the all-India level had militated against any organized opposition to arise against the Congress party. The same cleavages progressively became the basis of political mobilization at the state level by various parties during the second phase. With the growing salience of identity politics, during the second phase, neither the communists nor the conservative right managed to garner much broad-based electoral support on a sustained basis. Except for the communists in Kerala and West Bengal, the ones who did were regional or state-based parties associated strongly with identity politics.

In 1966, the Congress, dominating a virtual one-party system, was a loose organization, with groups stretched across the ideological spectrum from extreme right to mild radicalism. Missing only was the colossal and charismatic Nehru who held it together. 'Nothing was less inevitable in modern Indian politics than Indira Gandhi's rise to power,' some argue.[8] She was elevated to prime ministership because of her weakness and indistinctness about diverse policy lines within the party and her ability 'to metonymically extend the charisma of Jawaharlal Nehru'. But 'once it happened nothing was more decisive.' India was facing a serious economic crisis after two wars in succession, two consecutive severe droughts and balance of payments difficulties. There were troubling questions about the validity of the Nehruvian development strategy, but more immediate was the balance of payments crisis. Indira got over the immediate balance of payments crisis by a devaluation and the support of the IMF and the World Bank. But the Aid India Consortium and the World Bank failed to deliver the aid that India was given to understand it would receive after the devaluation.

Critics described the devaluation as 'a shameful act', 'the blackest act of national betrayal since independence' and 'greatest blunder of the day', and a sell-out to foreign capital. Indira, the astute politician, quickly distanced herself from the devaluation and liberal economic policy. She also managed to neutralize the adverse impact of identity politics by spectacular policies such as bank nationalization, abolition of privy purse for the princes, strident slogans like 'Garibi Hatao' and realpolitik. But the problem of fiscal deficit that her father had faced continued; however, unlike in the first phase under Nehru, the deficit was progressively not for

public investment but for subsidies and so-called 'welfare' measures. A turn
to the left promised Indira the twin advantages of distancing herself from
the liberal policies in the immediate past, and of providing her a single
ideological platform for fighting the myriad regional parties or coalitions
that had cropped up in the different states. Indira's fundamental policy
initiatives after the 1967 electoral debacle and the intense factional fights
in the Congress follow in Chapter XV.

XV

More of Command and Control

Indira moved fast to get the CWC-adopted Ten-Point Programme endorsed by the AICC in New Delhi on 23 June 1967 through the High Command's official resolution on 'Implementation of Congress Programmes'. The resolution went beyond the CWC declaration about the privileges of former rulers, which were incongruous with democratic practice, and social control of banks issued in May. The AICC resolved to end not only the privileges of ex-rulers other than privy purses but their privy purses as well. Privy purses had been fixed in nominal terms and were not revised in line with inflation. Thus, the government's financial savings from their abolition were limited. Its salience lay in its symbolism. In terms of spectacular impact on the people's minds, it was like the nationalisation of fourteen major banks, which went beyond the social control of banks espoused in the Ten-Point Programme. Of course, unlike the purely symbolic abolition of privy purses, bank nationalization had significance in terms of making banking services available in smaller cities, towns and rural areas, and making credit available to businesses not related to the owners of banks.

Despite solid evidence that command-and-control system was not delivering the promised goals, Indira also started strengthening it through reservation of items for production exclusively by the small-scale sector, industrial licensing, restrictions on business investments and expansion by large business houses, and an elaborate permit-quota-licence raj in imports. She also started to increase the breadth and depth of the CPSEs and employment therein.

XV.1 Small-Scale Reservation

IPR 1948 had emphasized the role of cottage, village and small-scale industries (SSI) in the development of the national economy and enjoined the government to support them by restricting production in the large-scale sector, by differential taxation or by direct subsidies. SSI was defined under IDRA 1951 in terms of original value of investment up to a limit. Until 1967, the policy for SSI promotion was not protective but mainly developmental in areas such as upgrading their technologies, improving their productivity and remaining competitive through organizations such as the Small-scale Industries Board, training and industrial centres, and provision of easy credit. Protective policy with reservation of items exclusively for SSI and restrictions on large-scale units competing with SSI were proposed as interim arrangements by the Planning Commission's Village and Small-scale Industries Committee under the chairmanship of D.G. Karve in 1955 and then notably by Mahalanobis in 1963. It was a transitory arrangement. 'Until unemployment is brought under control, there should not be . . . any fresh investments to expand factories that compete with the small and household units of production . . .'[1] Mahalanobis argued. He also saw a gradual and steady change-over to more mechanized and efficient forms of production.

To begin with, only forty-seven items were reserved for SSI in 1967. SSI reservation was not a part of the Ten-Point Programme, but done for generating employment and dispersing industry in backward areas and creating self-venture activities. SSI reservation was done in almost complete disregard for what famous economists, such as K.N. Raj and Amartya Sen, had discussed in terms of economic logic. Raj had argued forcefully that economic progress had been historically associated with improved technology, and any policy which retards the pace of technological change—for example, handloom to power loom—is detrimental to development. He had pointed out, though, the need for some protection, 'whether it involves direct subsidization or not', to those displaced by technological change.[2] Amartya Sen had shown how a strategy for maximizing output or employment today may differ from a strategy of maximizing growth, and hence output and employment, over the medium to long run.

In an interesting exercise, Amartya Sen had also examined the much-favoured Ambar Charkha—an improved version of the hand spinning wheel consisting of a carding unit, a *belni* and a spinning frame—as a technique of cotton spinning. The All-India Khadi and Village Industries Board had championed the case for its use, and it had won the government's favour. Assuming the daily output per Ambar Charkha per worker to be 6 hanks, or 1/3 lb of yarn, value added per lb of yarn to be 6 annas and 6 pies, two workers using the charkha simultaneously for 300 days in a year, and maintenance and depreciation cost of the charkha at ₹20 per year, Sen calculated the value added per charkha to be ₹61 and 4 annas. With the Ambar Charkha costing ₹100, the put-to-capital ratio turned out to be a very favourable 0.61. However, Sen also calculated that there was a recurring deficit of ₹276 and 4 annas per charkha, when the value added per year was adjusted for the wage cost of two workers at 9 annas per day. He further calculated that there was a deficit if the daily wage per worker was more than 1 anna and 8 pies! Government policy favoured more labour-intensive processes, but the implication in terms of growth and economic sustainability were very adverse.

XV.2 In the Face of Evidence—Industrial Licensing Continues

Prof. R.K. Hazari, a consultant to the Planning Commission, produced the Report on Industrial Planning and Licensing Policy in September 1967. One of its findings was that industrial licensing had assisted the growth of some large business houses, and even helped them in pre-empting capacities to thwart competition. With concerns about distributive justice, the report created a furore about how the licensing system was functioning in practice. It led to the appointment of the Industrial Licensing Enquiry Committee on 22 July 1967. The findings of its report—aka the Dutt Committee Report—in July 1969 were deeply disturbing.

The Dutt Committee pointed out how the government often decided whom to give the licence to and then referred them to the Licensing Committee for post facto approval. Licensing not only did not prevent 'the further growth of the Larger Industrial Houses, but the process actually worked in their favour'. There was no properly worked out industrial plan to guide the case-by-case decisions, and licensing could not even ensure industrial development according to plan priorities. Industrial development took place in segments which were anyway profitable. The objective of import substitution and hence self-reliance was also not served well. Licences were subject to political pressure. Furthermore, it pointed out that licensing '. . . can prevent wrong locations, but it cannot necessarily further right locations . . . even if . . . licences are given for locations in hitherto less industrialised regions, these might not be implemented'.

The Dutt Committee recommended selective application of licensing and more effective use of financial institutions to channel industry in the right direction. It advocated widespread use of the 'joint sector' concept of public-private collaboration in industry, and noting the difficulties of preparing detailed and fully coordinated plans for every industry, with a focus on planning 'the basic, strategic and critical sectors of economic development'. At the other end of the spectrum, it suggested 'the use of a system of reservations and bans for the purpose of preventing undesirable developments'. Between the two ends, it recommended that 'development of industries in this middle area should be left free, subject to market forces and fiscal and financial devices'.

The Dutt Committee also observed that '. . . licensing has only a small role to play in respect of this objective of preventing concentration of economic power . . . The major instrument for the attainment of this objective is the proposed Monopolies Commission'. Despite this clear and unambiguous diagnosis, the policy hysteresis continued. Admission of a mistaken policy pursued since Independence and that too under the iconic Pandit Jawaharlal Nehru, Indira's father, was not easy. Instead of liberalization, the permit-quota-licence raj was further strengthened and the public sector was emphasized. It was more of the same. Within four days of issuing the ordinance on taking over the management of fourteen banks with retrospective effect, the government also came out with the Industrial Licensing Policy on 18 February 1970 and placed certain restrictions on undertakings belonging to the large industrial houses with assets over ₹35 crore. Furthermore, the number of items reserved for SSI went up from forty-seven on 1 April 1967 to 128 on 24 February 1970 (Table XV.1).

Table XV.1 Reservation for Exclusive Manufacture in Small-Scale Sector

Date of Notification	Number of Items Reserved	Items De-reserved		Resultant Reserved Items
		Number	of which Subitems	[5 (previous row) + 2- {3-4}]
(1)	(2)	(3)	(4)	(5)
Phase 1				
1 April 1967	47	0		47
19 February 1970	8	0		55
24 February 1971	73	0		128
11 November 1971	0	4		124
26 February 1974	53	0		177
5 June 1976	3	0		180
26 April 1978	324	0		504
Phase 2				
26 April 1978[1]	807	0		807
30 December 1978	0	1		806
12 May 1980	27	0		833
19 February 1981	1	1		833
3 August 1981	9	0		842
23 December 1981	2	13		831
14 October 1982	0	3		828
19 October 1982	9	0		837
3 September 1983	35	0		872
18 October 1984	1	0		873
30 May 1986	7	14	3	869
30 October 1986	1	7		863
13 February 1987	0	13		850
20 July 1987	0	3		847
18 March 1988	0	1		846
3 March 1989	3	14		835
31 July 1989	1	0		836
3 April 1997	0	15		821
3 February 1999	0	9		812

1 January 2001	0	1		*811*
29 June 2001	0	14	2	*799*
20 May 2002	0	51	1	*749*
3 June 2003	0	75	1	*675*
20 October 2004	0	85	15	*605*
28 March 2005[2]	0	109	10	*506*
16 May 2006[3]	0	180		*326*
22 January 2007[4]		87		*239*
13 March 2007[5]		125		*114*
8 February 2008[5]		79		*35*
10 October 2008[6]		14		*21*
30 July 2010[7]		1		*20*

[1] In 1978 it was decided to recast the reserved list by following codes adopted by NIC and hence the list increased to 807 items.

[2] As per the Ministry of Small Scale Industries (Annual Report 2005-06), 506 items in the Reserved List. This is consistent if the number of items dereserved is taken as 109 (by including Art Silk/Man-made Fibre Hosiery as a separate item) and not 108 as per Notification S.O. 420(E) dated 28 March 2005.

[3] As per the Ministry of Small Scale Industries (Annual Report 2006-07), 326 items in the Reserved List and not 327 as shown above.

[4] Notification S.O., 62 (E) dated 22 January 2007.

[5] Source: https://msme.gov.in/sites/default/files/MSME%20ANNUAL%20REPORT%202007-08_English.pdf Chapter 2.

[6] Source: https://msme.gov.in/sites/default/files/MSME%20ANNUAL%20REPORT%202008-09_English.pdf Chapter 2.

[7] Notification S.O., 1881 (E) dated 30 July 2010.

XVI.3 Monopolies and Restrictive Trade Practices Act, 1969

The Monopolies Enquiry Commission, in its report in October 1965, had proposed a Monopolies and Restrictive Trade Practices (MRTP) Bill, 1965, to provide that the operation of the economic system does not result in the concentration of economic power to the common detriment for the control of monopolies and the prohibition of monopolistic and restrictive trade practices when found contrary to the public interest and for matters connected therewith or incidental thereto. In line with the sixth of the Ten-Point Programme, namely curb on business monopolies, the MRTP Act (MRTPA) was passed by Parliament in December 1969 and came into force from 1 June 1970. An MRTP Commission was established under the Act. 'Putting fetters on private monopolies' resulted in public acclaim.

In the prevention of the growth of large-scale manufacturing in India, licensing and SSI reservation were ably assisted by the MRTPA of 1969. All 'big' enterprises—single large undertakings or groups of interconnected undertakings—with assets over ₹20 crore were declared national monopolies, required to be registered under the act and seek the MRTP Commission's permission for expansion, establishment of new undertakings, and mergers and acquisitions. The same was the case with enterprises with a market share above 25 per cent in any product. MRTP effectively prevented firms from growing bigger. For example, with MRTP, the annual output of Tata Iron and Steel Company, the pioneer of steel production in India and the largest private enterprise in 1969, remained stuck at 1.5 million tonnes between 1969 and 1981.

XVI.4 Nationalization of Banks in the Run-Up to the Presidential Election

Traditional leaders such as Morarji Desai, Atulya Ghosh, Kamaraj, S. Nijalingappa, S.K. Patil and Sanjiva Reddy of the Syndicate were of a conservative orientation and resisted Indira's drastic moves to the left. In April 1969, at the Congress annual session in Faridabad, Nijalingappa, its president, vehemently criticized Indira's economic policies.

The party, under the leadership of the Syndicate and nominating Congress candidates mostly of their choice, went to the Vidhan Sabha polls in Bihar, Punjab, UP and West Bengal in February 1969. Except in UP, in the three others, Congress suffered losses. The losses weakened the Syndicate's hold on the party, and Indira decided to chart a path independent of the Syndicate. The opportunity arrived when Dr Zakir Hussain, the third President, died in office on 3 May 1969, and Vice President Varahagiri Venkata Giri started to act as President. The presidential election was notified on 14 July, and polling was scheduled for 16 August. The politics of the times called for drastic action for consolidating Indira's leadership of the Congress. Bank nationalization, far beyond the social control of banks of the Ten-Point Programme of 1967, fitted the bill in terms of dramatic effect and popular appeal. It would be the defining milestone in Indira's turn to the left. In it, Indira saw an advantage in showing her socialist and 'progressive' credentials and quickly regaining the initiative within the party.

Social control of banks, which came about in 1967, was intended to bring structural changes in the management of banks by delinking the nexus between big business houses and big commercial banks, ensuring that persons with specialized knowledge and experience could join the board of directors of a bank, and improve the distribution of credit towards agricultural and developmental sectors. The RBI was to get new powers to appoint or sack senior management in a bank. The task of the social control of banks from mid-December 1967 was given to the National Credit Council (NCC), which was constituted on 1 February 1968 along the lines of an institution in France. With eminent members like economist D.R. Gadgil, the NCC was described as the Planning Commission for finance. The NCC complained about the pronounced urban orientation of banks, highlighted the need for greater credit to the rural areas, and advocated the allocation of 15 per cent of banks' deposits to agriculture and 31 per cent to SSI.

Bank nationalization, which had a long history in independent India, finally came about in 1969 to supersede the newly born social control of banks. Barely four months after the third meeting of the NCC, on 9 July, Prime Minister Indira sent a note, through Minister for Industrial Development Fakhruddin Ali Ahmed, to the CWC suggesting the nationalization of fourteen major domestic banks. Finance Minister Morarji Desai refused to go along with the decision. Leaving his status as Deputy Prime Minister unchanged, Indira divested him of his finance portfolio. Morarji resigned from the cabinet on 16 July. Three days later, the Banking Companies (Acquisition and Transfer of Undertakings) Ordinance was signed by acting President V.V. Giri and came into effect to transfer the ownership and management of fourteen major domestic banks to the government. Soon thereafter, Parliament passed the necessary bill. In the Opposition, except for the Swatantra and Jana Sangh, all the other parties—socialists, ComPI, CPI(M), Akalis, BKD and DMK—supported bank nationalisation. After receiving presidential approval on 9 August 1969, came the Banking Companies (Acquisition and Transfer of Undertaking) Act. JP, the veteran freedom fighter, described the step as a 'masterstroke of political sagacity'.

According to the bank nationalization act of 1969, some limited compensation was to be paid to the shareholders and owners of banks through bonds maturing after ten years. On 10 February 1970, a special bench of the Supreme Court ruled 10-1 that the Banking Companies (Acquisition and Transfer of Undertakings) Act, 1969 was unconstitutional, because although Parliament was competent to legislate the nationalization of banks, the act, by giving certain amounts determined according to principles which were not relevant to determine such compensation, violated the Constitutional guarantee of compensation.

With the Supreme Court invalidating the nationalization act, a determined government issued a fresh ordinance on 14 February 1970 taking over the management of the fourteen banks retrospectively from 19 July 1969, without touching their ownership. The move received widespread popular support. As Inder Malhotra reported: '. . . in Delhi, crowds of workers, rickshaw drivers and others danced with joy on hearing the news. Almost none of them had ever darkened the door of a bank or was likely to do so in future.' Indira, with her turn to the left, would go on to nationalize not only general insurance (the second of the Ten-Point Programme), but also coal mining and the petroleum industry. But these came in the early 1970s after the liberation of Bangladesh, the break-up of the Congress and her sweeping victory in the 1971 Lok Sabha election.

XV.5 Priority Sector Lending

'The term 'priority sector' was first used in the context of policy measures when the then Deputy Prime Minister and minister of finance, Morarji Desai, stated in the Lok Sabha on 14 December 1967 that there were persistent complaints that several 'priority sectors' such as agriculture, small-scale industries and exports were not been receiving their due share of bank credit.'[3] While the definition of 'priority sector' and what it includes have varied over time, agricultural credit has always been a part of it. With Prime Minister Indira Gandhi announcing the provision of adequate credit for agriculture, small industry and exports as one of the five objectives of nationalization, priority sector lending got added importance.

There was a major expansion of bank branches in rural and other unbanked areas after the nationalization of banks. To coordinate banks and credit institutions by districts, following the October 1969 report of the Study Group on Organizational Framework for the Implementation of the Social Objectives under Prof. D.R. Gadgil, the Lead Bank Scheme was introduced by the RBI in December 1969.

An Informal Study Group on Statistics relating to advances to the priority sector was set up by the RBI in May 1971. Based on the report of this group, the definition of the priority sector was formalized in 1972. The priority sector consisted of agriculture, small-scale industries, small businesses, exports, professional and self-employed persons, and education.[4] Initially, there were no specific targets in priority sector lending. The targets for priority sector lending and what the sector included would expand in the future to include, for example, export credit to agriculture and micro, medium and small enterprises, housing, social infrastructure, renewable energy and weaker sections. For providing guarantees against the risk of default in payment, the RBI promoted the establishment of the Credit Guarantee Corporation of India Ltd in 1971. It also provided liberal refinance facilities to the banks for priority sector loans. The Rural Electrification Corporation (REC) was set up in July 1969 to facilitate availability of electricity for accelerated growth and for enrichment of the quality of life of the rural and semi-urban population. It started lending to SEBs in 1970.

XVI.6 Administered Interest Rates

As we have already noted, the interest rate on advances granted by banks were subject to floor or minimum from October 1960, and their deposit rates were regulated from September 1964. The deposit rates of cooperative banks were brought under similar regulatory measures in 1974. From 2 March 1968, in place of a minimum came the maximum lending rate to be charged by banks, only to be rescinded and replaced by a minimum from 21 January 1970. Such drastic changes in less than two years raised uncomfortable questions regarding the stability and predictability of policies. In any case, as we will see, inflationary pressures stemming from the first oil shock would soon necessitate tweaking the interest rates in

1973. Interestingly, to attract foreign funds, NRI (non-resident Indians or aliens of Indian origin) deposits were first introduced in February 1970. The initial scheme was a Non-resident (External) Rupee Account (NR(E) RA), with both principal and interest repatriable but maintained in Indian rupees.

XV.7 Operation Flood and the White Revolution

The success of Amul in Gujarat needed replication and the catalytic role of NDDB was scaled up across the country. With this objective, Operation Flood, with NDDB responsible for running it, was launched on 1 July 1970. Under the UN Food and Agricultural Organization's World Food Programme, aid in the form of milk powder and butter oil was obtained from the European Economic Community. These were reconstituted to supply liquid milk and establish liquid milk schemes in major cities. The proceeds from the sale of liquid milk, milk powder and butter oil were used to resettle city-kept milk cattle and boost organized milk production, procurement and processing. The aim was to stabilize the position of major liquid milk schemes. 'It was the first time in the history of economic development that food aid had been used as a buffer stock to stabilise market fluctuations as well as to "prime the pump" of markets that would later be supplied by domestic production. The overriding objective of this was the elimination of the need for aid. The project came to be referred to as the "billion-litre idea" and was formally named Operation Flood.'[5] The NDDB under Verghese Kurien converted what could have been a crippling blow into an instrument for transforming the domestic dairy sector.

During its first phase from 1970 to 1979, '. . . the main thrust was to set up dairy cooperatives in India's 18 best milksheds, linking them with the four main cities of Bombay, Calcutta, Delhi and Madras, in which a commanding share of the milk market was to be captured. It involved organizing dairy cooperatives at the village level; creating the physical and institutional infrastructure for milk procurement, processing, marketing and production enhancement services at the union level; and establishing dairies in India's major metropolitan centres.' Operation Flood would prove to be a grand success, transforming India into the largest producer of milk in the world by 1998.[6]

XV.8 The Patents Act, 1970

The Indian Patents and Design Act, 1911, recognized both product and process patents. Until 1970, under the patent regime, foreign companies dominated the market for products such as drugs and pharmaceuticals, and consumer durables. There were only a limited number of domestic companies in these segments. Under Indira Gandhi came the new Patents Act, 1970. It amended the 1911 Act and recognized only process patents, and not product patents. This new patenting regime was focused solely on manufacturing and opened up the scope for reverse engineering, which is essentially deconstruction of finished products to gain insights into compositions and designs. Such reverse engineering was particularly useful for building up the domestic drugs and pharmaceutical industry, where companies could manufacture without paying royalty to the original patent holders. '. . . the number of patents granted between 1970–1971 and 1980–1981, fell by three-quarters. Furthermore, the 1979 Drug Price Control Order, set a ceiling on the overall profits of pharma companies. This period saw a huge jump in the number of domestic pharma companies (from 2,000 in 1970 to 24,000 in 1995), creating a booming generic drugs industry. It also led to a large-scale exodus of foreign pharma companies.'[7]

XV.9 Abolition of Privy Purse

The erstwhile rulers had enraged the Congress leadership by joining the newly set up Swatantra Party and contributing to the Congress's poor performance in the 1967 election. Abolition of princely privileges had been a long-standing demand of a section of the Congress as well as the socialists and communists, but it involved the breach of a covenant with the former rulers. On the promulgation of the Indian Independence Act, 1947, the princely states merged with the Dominion of India by instruments of merger which guaranteed to the rulers the privy purse, succession according to law and custom to the *gaddi* of the state and personal rights, privileges, dignities and titles.

Sardar Patel had told the Constituent Assembly on 12 October 1949 how the privy purses were a 'small price' to pay given that the rulers had a lot of capacity for mischief and had surrendered all their ruling powers and dissolved their states as separate units. Referring to the agreements reached with the rulers, he had said: 'The rulers have now discharged their part of the obligations by transferring all ruling powers by agreeing to the integration of their States. The main part of our obligation under these agreements is to ensure that the guarantee given by us in respect of privy purses are fully implemented. Our failure to do so would be a breach of faith and seriously prejudice the stabilisation of the new order.'[8] The privileges which formed a part of the merger agreements were guaranteed by the Constitution.

The sum at stake in privy purses was only ₹4 crore, yet their potential abolition held enormous symbolic value and implications in terms of the sanctity of contracts and reneging on a solemn promise by the republic. After the Ten-Point Programme was adopted by the CWC in May 1967, when a privy purse abolition bill introduced in the Lok Sabha by Socialist member Rabi Ray got defeated, it was partly because the Prime Minister promised the government's own bill would be forthcoming soon. Indira introduced the privy purse abolition legislation in the Lok Sabha on 1 September 1970 in the form of a constitutional amendment which required a two-thirds vote in both houses of Parliament. In Parliament, she pointed out the incompatibility of the concept of privy purses and special privileges with an 'egalitarian social order'. While the bill secured the required two-thirds majority in the Lok Sabha (332:154), in the Rajya Sabha vote on 5 September 1970, it fell short by one (149:75). On 7 September, Finance Minister Y.B. Chavan read a Presidential Order in Parliament de-recognizing all the princes. 'When a Planning Commission member asked Indira Gandhi why was she making so much song and dance about such a paltry gain? (sic). With an iconic smile, Indira Gandhi explained what the state gained in material terms was secondary to the political gains that would accrue from the abolition of privy purses.'[9]

Eight of the 'de-recognised' princes challenged the Presidential Order in the Supreme Court. The doyen of Indian lawyers, Nani Palkhivala, argued the case, and the court, by a majority decision on 15 December, ruled that the President had exceeded his authority and the princes were still entitled to all the privileges and privy purses they had enjoyed prior to the Presidential Order. Prime Minister Indira Gandhi sensed a 'moral victory' in this defeat and as we shall see, went on to advise the President to dissolve the Lok Sabha and call for mid-term polls.

XV.10 Presidential Election and the Congress Split

Factional fighting within the Congress party intensified and came to a head after the demise of Zakir Hussain on 3 May 1969. Two days before the notification of the presidential election, at the meeting of the Congress Parliamentary Board in Bengaluru on 12 July 1969, the Syndicate had managed to get Sanjiva Reddy, the Speaker of the Lok Sabha, nominated as the official Congress nominee for President by 6-4 votes, against Indira Gandhi's objection.

The last date for filing nominations was 24 July. After issuing the bank nationalization ordinance the previous day, on 20 July, V.V. Giri laid down office to offer himself as an independent candidate for the presidency. For a few hours, in an unprecedented manner, both the offices of the President and the Vice President were vacant until Chief Justice Hidayatullah was sworn in as the Acting President. Indira had filed the nomination for Sanjiva Reddy but did not issue a whip to the Congress MPs to vote for Reddy. She gave implicit support to V.V. Giri by asking party legislators to 'vote according to their conscience'.

In the election on 16 August, the leftists under the lead of the ComPI and regional parties like the Akalis, BKD and DMK supported Giri, a former labour leader. For the first time, no candidate secured the required majority of votes in the first round. The voting is by a single transferable vote. The candidates from the bottom of the list in terms of first preference votes had to be dropped one by one and their second preference votes transferred to those that remained until a majority emerged. Finally, V.V. Giri did win but by a slender majority of about 1.5 per cent. The Syndicate was astounded that the *gungi gudiya* (dumb doll)—their snide reference to Indira—had a mind of her own. They struck back. On 12 November 1969, Congress president Nijalingappa expelled Prime Minister Indira Gandhi from the party for 'fostering a cult of personality'.

Indira's supporters in the Congress party had been going around since October 1969 collecting signatures of AICC members on a requisition demanding the election of a new Congress president. After her expulsion from the Congress, she formed the Congress (R) (R for requisitionist), officially known as Congress (J) (J for its president Jagjivan Ram). The traditional Congress became Congress (O), O for Organization. Congress (R) had the support of a majority of the Congress legislators in the Lok Sabha as well as the sum total of Congress legislators in Vidhan Sabhas. But Congress (O) had the support of the majority of not only the AICC members but also of the Congress legislators in Gujarat and Karnataka (erstwhile Mysore). The factions went to the Election Commission to get a verdict on who was the Indian National Congress, and who would get the old symbol of a pair of bullocks carrying a yoke. Though Indira Gandhi and her Congress (R) retained the support of most of the Congress parliamentarians and was the single largest party, it did not command a majority in the Lok Sabha. Indira survived with support from some regional parties such as DMK and ComPI. There were—and there continue to be—doubts whether Indira was a socialist on principle or out of political expediency.

The Election Commission decided to recognize Congress (R) as the Indian National Congress. Congress (O) went to the Supreme Court, which decreed that, pending its final ruling, neither party could use the symbol of a pair of bullocks with yoke on and had to choose new symbols. While Congress (R) continued as Indian National Congress in 1971 and 1977 elections, it got a cow nursing a calf as its symbol in the ballot paper. The Congress (O) got a woman turning a charkha, the spinning wheel popularized by Mahatma Gandhi. The pair of bullocks with the yoke on, the enduring election symbol of the Congress, died with the split. Henceforth, following the Election Commission, we shall denote Indira's Congress (R) as the Indian National Congress or Congress in short, and the Indian National Congress (Organization) as Congress (O).

The coalition politics that emerged in the late 1960s, particularly around the time of the Congress split in 1969, was a relegation of ideological positions of political parties to a secondary position. The claim that it was an ideological split is difficult to support. If indeed it was ideological, then why should the former socialist leader Asoka Mehta, who had been with Indira Gandhi since 1963, have sided with the Syndicate? Perhaps the split was more a demonstration of Indira Gandhi's attempt at reducing her dependence on a Congress party that defied close control. It was the result of a careful balancing of 'regional demands and national obligations, sectional interests and national requirements, immediate necessities and long-term strategy'.[10] In the Lok Sabha with 520 seats, after the split of the party, Indira had the support of only 220 MPs, well short of the majority mark by forty-one. She managed to continue in office only by taking the support of ComPI, CPI(M), DMK, some socialists, the Akalis and some independents. After the Congress split, there was no stopping of the leftward turn of Indira Gandhi.

XV.11 Confiscatory Personal Income Taxes

After the Nehru era, there were three major moves to simplify the income tax system. First, super tax was integrated with income tax by the Finance Act, 1965. Second, the distinction between earned and unearned incomes, introduced in 1945, was abolished from 1 April 1968. Third, there was a move to simplify the system of exemption under personal income tax. Under the Finance Act 1965, every individual got relief on account of personal allowance in terms of the amount of tax otherwise payable depending upon the marital status. This was in addition to a minimum exemption limit. This scheme of personal allowance was discontinued by the Finance Act, 1970 and 'first tax free slab' was prescribed for the first time for the assessment year 1971–72 for individuals whose income up to ₹5000 was fully exempt from tax—whatever their marital status may be. This step further simplified the system.

However, there was no respite to the extremely high rates at the higher income brackets. In his Budget for 1968–69, Deputy Prime Minister and finance minister Morarji Desai had increased the basic rates of income tax from 65 per cent to 70 per cent on income between ₹1 lakh and ₹2.5 lakh, and to 75 per cent on income above ₹2.5 lakh. A surcharge of 10 per cent was also applicable and with this surcharge, the highest marginal tax rate was 82.5 per cent. He had also stepped up the rates of ordinary wealth tax from 2 per cent to 2.5 per cent on wealth between ₹10 lakh and ₹20 lakh, and from 2.5 per cent to 3 per cent for wealth above ₹20 lakh.

After the Congress split, in 1970–71, Prime Minister Indira Gandhi assumed charge of the ministry of finance. In her Budget for 1970–71, she reduced the exemption limit from ₹6000 to ₹5000, and for greater progressivity, increased the number of slabs (excluding the slab below exemption limit) from ten to eleven, and increased the highest marginal rate of basic income tax applicable to income above ₹2 lakh from 75 per cent to 85 per cent. With the surcharge of 10 per cent, the highest marginal rate was 93.5 per cent. In her Budget for 1970–71, she clubbed the income of husband and wife, about which I.G. Patel, who was the Finance Secretary at that time, later commented: '. . . a strange and unusual innovation from a woman Prime Minister, but characteristic of Mrs. Gandhi. Needless to say, the provision did not survive for long on the statute book.'[11]

After Indira, Y.B. Chavan became finance minister in June 1970. After the Lok Sabha elections, in his Budget for 1971–72 on 24 March 1971, he left the basic rates unchanged but increased the surcharge for income above ₹15,000 from 10 per cent to 15 per cent. With this increase, at the pinnacle of Indira's socialism, the highest marginal rate of personal income tax became 97.75 per cent! He also increased the wealth tax on net wealth above ₹15 lakh uniformly to 8 per cent. Thus, for a person with income above ₹2 lakh, who was likely to have wealth over ₹20 lakh, out of additional income of ₹100, not only was ₹97.75 taken away as income tax, but the after-tax income of ₹2.25 when added to their wealth would attract, at the rate of 8 per cent, wealth tax of another ₹0.18 in every subsequent year. Experts pointed out that 'For an individual deriving his income from urban wealth, the combined effect of income and wealth taxes imposed an effective ceiling on income after tax when such income reached rupees 50,000'.[12]

This confiscatory level of taxation is likely to have seriously eroded incentives for the highest income earners to venture into more economic activities, especially those involving risks. The loss of even 10 per cent in an investment of ₹100 would have required—even while disregarding the implication of the wealth tax—a pre-tax gross profit of 444.44 per cent to make up for the loss of 10 per cent on the investment of ₹100 with post-tax profit! The exorbitantly high marginal tax rate is likely to have reinforced the proclivity to evade taxes.

In March 1970, the government had appointed former Chief Justice of India K.N. Wanchoo as head of the Direct Taxes Enquiry Committee to suggest concrete measures to unearth black money, to prevent its proliferation and recommend steps to improve tax compliance. The Wanchoo Committee submitted its interim report in December 1970 and the final report in December 1971. Both reports argued for a reduction in the highest marginal rate and had been available for at least two months when Finance Minister Chavan increased the highest marginal income tax rate with surcharge of 97.75 per cent. The only explanation for still increasing the rates could have been that either the government did not have enough time to process the report or the political compulsions on the optical plane were overwhelmingly strong.

XV.12 Corporate Tax, Excise Duties and CST

With the removal of surcharge, the highest corporate tax rate-cum-surcharge for widely held domestic companies came down from 81 per cent in 1964–65 to 80 per cent in 1965–66. In 1966–67, a graded system for companies was introduced with the rate of 45 per cent for total income up to ₹25,000, and 55 per cent for others. After keeping it unchanged in 1967–68, during 1968–70, companies with a total income up to ₹25,000 were exempted from tax and others subjected to a rate of 45 per cent. During 1970–74, the exemption was withdrawn and companies with income up to ₹50,000 subjected to a rate of 45 per cent and the rest to a rate of 55 per cent. During 1974–76, the concessional rate of 45 per cent was extended to companies with income up to ₹1,00,000, and the other rate was left unchanged at 55 per cent.

Apart from the Wanchoo Committee's report, reports of other committees appointed during this period included: (i) Bhoothalingam Committee's Report on Rationalization and Simplification of Tax Structure submitted in two parts, one on 5 April 1967 and the other on 26 December 1967, (ii) the Report of the Working Group of Administrative Reforms Commission on Central Direct Taxes Administration, headed by Mahavir Tyagi (1969), and (iii) the Committee on Taxation of Agricultural Wealth and Income (1972) under K.N. Raj. The Income Tax Act 1961 was amended considering some of these recommendations.

In excise duty, a major improvement after 1969 was the replacement of the physical control system and clearance of manufactured goods from the factory under a Central Excise officer's supervision by self-removal procedure. The trend of widening the coverage of excise duties continued during this period. The number of commodities under excise grew from thirty-three after the first decade of Independence to eighty in the next decade and reached 130 by 1975.

In the case of sales tax, the CST rate on inter-state sales was raised from 2 per cent in 1963 to 3 per cent from 1966. State excise revenues in the aggregate doubled between 1970–71 and 1974–75, but there were some changes in policy towards prohibition in one of the major states, namely Tamil Nadu. In Tamil Nadu, total prohibition, in vogue since 1937, was suspended by Chief Minister M. Karunanidhi of the DMK after he came to power in 1971. Karunanidhi allowed the sale of arrack, toddy and IMFL to stop the inflow of liquor from neighbouring states that did not have prohibition, and the consequent loss of revenue. But with the danger of it becoming an electoral issue in the run-up to the election, total prohibition was brought back in 1974.

XV.13 Gadgil Formula for Plan Assistance

The Union government provided financial assistance to state governments to implement their plans. Until the three Annual Plans (1966–69), such assistance across states was scheme-based and could lead to complaints about subjectivity and inter-state inequity. From the Fourth Five-Year Plan came the Gadgil Formula for distributing central plan assistance to the states. The weightage in the formula was: (i) 60 per cent on population, (ii) 10 per cent on per capita income, (iii) 10 per cent on tax effort, (iv) 10 per cent on ongoing irrigation and power projects, and (v) 10 per cent on special problems. The Gadgil Formula, named after Dr D.R. Gadgil, Deputy Chairman Planning Commission during 1967–71, would be used during the Fourth and Fifth Plans. It was applied, with some modifications, until 1991. From the Seventh Five-Year Plan (1992–97), the modified Gadgil-Mukherjee formula, named after Gadgil and Pranab Mukherjee, Deputy Chairman Planning Commission during 1991–96, would be used for plan assistance. The Gadgil-Mukherjee formula assigned weights of: (i) 60 per cent on population, (ii) 25 per cent on per capita income (20 per cent on deviation method and 5 per cent on distance method), (iii) 7.5 per cent on tax effort, fiscal management and progress in attaining national objectives, and (iv) 7.5 per cent on special problems.

XV.14 Pakistan Threatened with Disintegration

In the meantime, Pakistan started facing serious threats of disintegration. It had been carved out of undivided India in two disjointed parts separated by over 2000 km of Indian territory, and language and culture. Ever since its creation, Bangladeshis, the people of erstwhile East Pakistan, were aggrieved by the adoption of Urdu as the sole official language. Bengali speakers constituted the majority in Pakistan, yet Bengali was missing from Pakistan's currency, coinage and postage stamps. After prolonged agitations, which included the death of several student demonstrators on 21 February 1952—a day commemorated ever since as Shohid Diwas or Martyr's Day—Bengali was recognized as an official language of Pakistan only on 29 February 1956, The fear of cultural domination remained deep-rooted in East Pakistan in the context of Pakistan's language policy and was compounded by its economic exploitation through lopsided allocation of public funds and recruitment to the army—a major source of employment in a heavily militarized country—primarily from the western wing.

General Ayub Khan had been Pakistan's military dictator from October 1958 onwards. In the face of widespread protests, particularly in East Pakistan, he resigned on 25 March 1969 and handed over power to General Yahya Khan. Yahya Khan reversed the 'one unit' policy of President Iskander Mirza and reorganized West Pakistan into four provinces of Balochistan, Punjab, Sind and Khyber Pakhtunkhwa. He also announced elections in October 1970. A devastating cyclone called Bhola hit Bangladesh in October and the elections had to be postponed until 7 December 1970. Elections threw up a clearly polarized verdict and revealed a country deeply divided between the east and the west. The Awami League led by Mujibur Rehman won 160 of the 162 National Assembly seats in East Pakistan, and none from the western part of the country. Zulfikar Ali Bhutto's Pakistan People's Party won eighty-one of the 138 seats in the western part and none from the eastern part of the country. Smaller parties with less than ten seats each divided the rest of the seats among themselves.

With a clear majority in the 300-seat National Assembly, Awami League's Mujibur Rehman, in normal course, should have been called to form the government. But Bhutto threatened to boycott the National

Assembly if Mujibur, because of Awami League's demand for greater autonomy, was called in to form the government. The army and Islamic parties were also opposed to Mujibur, also known as Sheikh Mujib, and his Awami League. Mujibur never received the call, and Yahya Khan announced that the National Assembly would meet in session in Dhaka on 3 March. But Yahya announced the postponement of the National Assembly sine die on 1 March. A constitutional deadlock with widespread agitations in East Pakistan followed. On 3 March, there was a failed meeting in Dhaka between Sheikh Mujib, Bhutto and Yahya Khan. On 7 March 1971, at a meeting at the famous Racecourse Maidan (ground), Dhaka, Sheikh Mujib called for the independence of Bangladesh from Pakistan and also launched a major campaign of civil disobedience and organized armed resistance.

XV.15 From 'Gungi Gudiya' to 'National Hero'

The Fourth Lok Sabha's scheduled term was to end in March 1972. Indira, heading a minority government, advised the president on its early dissolution to seek a fresh people's mandate to implement her policies and programmes. President Giri dissolved the Lok Sabha on 27 December 1970. The polls were to be held during 1-10 March 1971. Indira went to the polls with the populist slogan 'Garibi Hatao'. Before the elections, the liberation of Bangladesh was in progress. With the need to support the Mukti Bahini (Liberation Army) of Bangladesh against the Pakistani oppressors, the country was already 'rallying round the flag' behind Indira. She had sensed the mood of the nation right in going for early polls.

On 30 January 1971, a Fokker Friendship plane named 'Ganga', of the state-owned Indian Airlines, flying from Srinagar to Jammu, was highjacked to Lahore by Al Fatah or Jammu and Kashmir National Liberation Front (JKNLF). The hijackers demanded the release of thirty-six JKNLF members detained in India in exchange for releasing the plane and its twenty-six passengers. The airport authorities managed to get the passengers released. On 2 February, the hijackers burnt the plane down. In retaliation, India suspended overflights of its territory by Pakistan's aircraft, impacting Pakistan's troop movements to its turbulent eastern wing.

On 7 May 1971, the government promulgated the Maintenance of Internal Security Ordinance, which was replaced by the Maintenance of Internal Security Act (MISA) on 2 July 1971. MISA was styled on the Preventive Detention Act of 1950. Its widespread use during the Emergency led to its large-scale notoriety. So much so that Lalu Prasad Yadav, the colourful Janata Party leader, named his eldest daughter, born during the Emergency, Misa!

The 1971 Lok Sabha election was the first mid-term Lok Sabha election. Apart from two Congresses—Congress and Congress (O)—in the fray, it had four major non-communist opposition parties—the Congress (O), Swatantra, Jana Sangh and SSP—fighting the Congress together as the 'Grand Alliance'. Their rallying cry was 'Indira Hatao' or 'Remove Indira'; the Congress responded with the slogan 'Garibi hatao.'

There had been an underlying change in the electorate in almost a quarter century after Independence, and most poll forecasters got the results of the 1971 Lok Sabha elections wrong. A survey by the Centre for the Study of Developing Societies carried out in 1967 had revealed these fundamental changes in voters' attitudes, and its founder Rajni Kothari noted how '. . . a shift from the politics of manipulation of the voters by the party organisational machines to a type of politics in which direct appeal of parties and personalities, the election campaign, and the issues at stake will play a major role.'[13] Another keen observer of Indian politics, Myron Weiner had noted that Indian political parties had operated on the basis of four basic assumptions: (i) voters were less concerned about policies as such than with the way in which concrete benefits were distributed; (ii) patronage powers, e.g. through village panchayats or cooperatives, were most important for electoral success; (iii) success depended on the skills of distribution of favours to the relevant leaders of ascriptive and factional groups; and (iv) voters' loyalties to local leaders were stable, so the securing of these leaders determined the electoral outcome. The continuing validity of these assumptions was in question. Indira challenged these assumptions, bypassed the intermediary structure, and appealed directly to the electorate. The voters responded positively.

The Grand Alliance was trounced by Congress. The outcome clearly demonstrated that the '. . . 1969 Congress split was . . . an uneven race between Mrs Gandhi with her Santa Claus bagful of populist promises—

from abolition of privy purses to nationalization of sugar . . .—and the Syndicate which had long lost the capacity of mass mobilization but had acquired instead the art of fund raising through business contacts'.[14] The scent of an external crisis, with a possible need for India to intervene, is likely to have also contributed to the favourable electoral outcome for Indira and her ruling Congress. Riding on 'Garibi Hatao', it secured 43.7 per cent of the votes and won a two-thirds majority of 352 out of 518 seats in the Fifth Lok Sabha, significantly higher than the 40.8 per cent of the votes and 283 of the 520 seats in the 1967 election. In terms of electoral strength, Congress under Indira in 1971 had gone back to the Congress under Nehru in 1962. The 1971 Lok Sabha election also brought the curtain down on Swatantra, the only political party so far with an openly pro-market and anti-statist ideology.

The outcome of the 1971 Lok Sabha elections transformed Indira's political stature. It also rose with her ability to bring into force, from 5 November 1971, the Twenty-Fourth Amendment to the Constitution, overriding the adverse Supreme Court judgement in the Golak Nath case by enabling Parliament to dilute Fundamental Rights through Amendments to the Constitution.

In the meantime, in East Pakistan, already under martial law, people observed Pakistan's Republic Day on 23 March 1971 as Resistance Day. General Yahya Khan went to Dhaka and departed on 25 March after ordering the launch of Operation Searchlight, an armed forces' offensive to restore order. In the army's rampage, thousands were killed, women were raped, and Sheikh Mujib arrested and taken to West Pakistan. The next day, 26 March, Major Ziaur Rahman, formerly of the Pakistan Army, declared the independence of Bangladesh.

The Pakistani army, with the help of local pro-Pakistan militia consisting of Mohajirs (Muslims whose families had migrated from Bihar and UP) and fundamentalist Muslims of Jamat-e-Islam, were particularly ruthless with the intellectuals and the minority community of Hindus in Bangladesh. Refugees, an estimated 10 million, mostly but not only Hindus, started pouring into India. The influx into the neighbouring Indian north-eastern hill states of Tripura and Meghalaya started to pose serious instability problems by distorting the tribal-non-tribal population balance. The refugee burden was becoming unbearable and

Prime Minister Indira Gandhi described how what Pakistan claimed to be its internal problem had turned into an internal problem for India. It was a humanitarian crisis as well as demographic aggression. In May, Indira Gandhi wrote to US President Nixon about the 'carnage in East Bengal' and the flood of refugees burdening India. On 13 June 1971, the *Sunday Times* in the UK carried an article titled 'Genocide', written by a Pakistani journalist, Anthony Mascarenhas, revealing to the world what was happening in East Pakistan.

India started supporting the Bangladeshi resistance movement. In an Indian cabinet meeting on 28 April 1971, General Sam Manekshaw, chairman of the Chief of Staff Committee, was instructed to go into East Pakistan. Action, however, had to wait for several months because of a host of reasons. With the threat of Pakistan on the western front, harvesting of the winter crop had to be finished in Punjab to avoid ruining the crop by troop movements across cultivated lands. The monsoon, which makes many parts of Bangladesh inaccessible, had to be waited out as well. Winter had to set in to make the Himalayan passes inoperable and stop the Chinese from launching an attack from the north. Furthermore, some lead time was needed for securing spare parts for armoured vehicles and getting the troops into operational readiness.

On 9 August 1971, External Affairs Minister Swaran Singh signed the Indo-Soviet Treaty of Peace, Friendship and Co-operation with his Soviet counterpart A.A. Gromyko. Almost as if in line with the spirit of cooperation with the Soviets, with the ministry of steel and mines under Mohan Kumaramangalam, a former communist, 214 coking coal mines were taken over on 16 October 1971. Indira went on a six-nation tour of Europe and North America—Austria, Belgium, France, the UK, the US and West Germany—between 23 October and 13 November 1971 to clarify that what India desired was only an early return of the refugees under conditions acceptable to them.

Indian Army Eastern Command had been imparting training to Bangladesh's Mukti Bahini from 15 August 1971 onwards. From October, the Mukti Bahini had started liberating small chunks of Bangladeshi territory from the Pakistani army. Pakistan complained that such operations were backed by Indian troops and artillery. There were skirmishes between the Pakistani and Indian army as well. On 24 November, Prime Minister

Gandhi informed the Lok Sabha that 'Indian forces had been instructed to enter East Bengal territory in self-defence'.[15]

On 3 December, Pakistan launched Operation Chengiz Khan, involving airstrikes on Indian air force bases and radar stations. India struck back, and a de facto war started. The next day, a US ceasefire resolution in the UN Security Council did not pass because of a veto from the Soviet Union. The Indian navy blockaded Bangladesh on 5 December. And by 6 December, the Indian air force had practically destroyed Pakistani air power in Bangladesh. On 10 December, a US Task Force, spearheaded by the aircraft carrier USS Enterprise, started for the Bay of Bengal, and the Soviet Union also deployed its own navy as a counterbalance.

In the UN Security Council debate on the call for a ceasefire, Indian Minister of External Affairs Sardar Swaran Singh spoke for two full days, on 12 and 13 December, insisting on consecutive rather than simultaneous translation into the four official UN languages. In the meantime, the Indian army had launched a multi-pronged attack on East Pakistan from the west, north and east, bypassed pockets of Pakistani military strongholds and entered the capital city of Dhaka. Lt Gen. Amir Abdullah Khan Niazi, heading the Eastern Command of the Pakistani army, decided to surrender. The public surrender took place at 4.30 p.m. on 16 December 1971 at the Racecourse Maidan. When informed by Gen. Sam Manekshaw, Indira went to the Lok Sabha and announced, 'Dhaka is now the free capital of a free country . . .' The humiliation of the 1962 debacle with China had been partly repaired and Pakistan, a constant source of trouble, had been cut down to size. Whether the refugee problem caused the Indo-Pakistan war over Bangladesh or was only the occasion for it will continue to be debated. But Indira Gandhi had transformed herself from a 'gungi gudiya' to a national hero.

XVI

Boiling in Oil: The Turbulent Seventies

After the liberation of Bangladesh, *The Economist* described Indira Gandhi as 'Empress of India'. But soon, the sheen of the empress started to fade. To resolve the problem of 93,000 Pakistani prisoners of war (POWs), and to have a blueprint for good neighbourly Indo-Pak relations by abjuring conflict and confrontation, Indira signed the Simla Accord with Pakistan's President Zulfikar Ali Bhutto on 2 July 1972. The Simla Accord came in for some criticism, and the rapid improvement in Bangladesh's relations with Pakistan created consternation. Furthermore, there were dark clouds over the Indian economy and separatist trouble in Punjab.

Wars, for example, the one with China in 1962, invariably led to trouble for the Indian economy. Growth had declined from 3.1 per cent in 1961–62 to 2.1 per cent in 1963–64. In 1965–66, with a war with Pakistan, and of course also a severe drought, the corresponding decline was from 7.6 per cent in the previous year to -3.7 per cent, that is, a contraction in GDP. The liberation of Bangladesh was no exception. Growth declined from 5 per cent in 1970–71 to 1.0 per cent in 1971–72 and further to -0.3 per cent in 1972–73. This was in sharp contrast to the wartime boom experienced by many countries, for example, the US during the Second World War. The difference may be explained by the short durations of the conflicts involving India, and, in the absence of a vibrant indigenous defence industry, India's large-scale reliance on the rest of the world for its supplies of arms, ammunition and other defence equipment.

The Indian economy was also hurt by two external factors of grave concern. First, the unravelling of Bretton Woods I and the US default on the fixed exchange value of its dollar into gold at US$35 per troy ounce. Second, the Yom Kippur War in 1973 and the first oil price shock. Inflation shot up. With fiscal profligacy, conditions in India were ripe for a balance of payments crisis.

XVI.1 Unravelling of Bretton Woods I and the US Default

It was a troubled world in the late 1960s with increased deployment of regular US combat units in Vietnam in 1965, the Arab-Israeli War for six days in June 1967 and the formation of the Organization of Arab Petroleum Exporting Countries (OAPEC), and the Tet Offensive by the North Vietnamese in 1968. The Bretton Woods I system of international transactions became a casualty.

Under the historic Bretton Woods Agreement of 1944, from December 1946, the US dollar had had a fixed exchange rate of US$35 per troy ounce of gold and thirty-two countries had declared the par values of their currencies in terms of the currencies of the others. Nations other than the US were obliged to settle their trade deficits in a currency other than their own, while the US could settle its trade deficit in dollars. It was an enormous and unique US privilege, also described as an 'exorbitant privilege'. In Barry Eichengreen's words, 'It costs only a few cents for the Bureau of Engraving and Printing to produce a $100 bill, but other countries had to pony up $100 of actual goods in order to obtain one.'[1]

The US ran persistent balance of payments deficits from the 1950s. Initially, such deficits were financed by the willingness of both private creditors and foreign monetary authorities to hold dollars. Things changed during 1958–60, when, on average, annually, US$1.5 billion of US gold reserves was transferred to foreign ownership. Such deficits and gold outflows evoked concerns. The promise of a troy ounce of gold for every $35 looked less and less reliable. The system looked unsustainable and the 'exorbitant privilege' of the US under the system started to come under attack.

In 1960, Robert Triffin, the Belgium-born professor of economics at Yale University, had predicted a 'gold and dollar crisis' irrespective of whether or not the US ran balance of payments deficits. If it did not, then the growth of world reserves needed could not be fed adequately by gold production at $35 an ounce, and if it did, its foreign liabilities would exceed the ability of the US to convert dollars into gold upon demand. In a decade, he proved prescient. Policymakers in France also had their discomfort about the gold exchange standard at US$35 per troy ounce of gold.

In 1967, the British pound sterling came under attack. Despite a persistent balance of payments deficit since the mid-1950s, the UK had not devalued the pound sterling, and had defended the fixed rate by depleting its liquid assets and reserves. Bad news from foreign trade data intensified and finally, the pound was devalued by 14.3 per cent from US$2.80 per pound to US$2.40 per pound on 18 November 1967. The devaluation dealt a body blow to the 'prestige' of the pound sterling, and its role as reserves of other countries was on a path of perennial decline. Next, it was the US, which had to face the heat.

Demand for gold in exchange for US dollars increased, particularly with the war escalating in Vietnam from 1968. On Friday, 8 March 1968, 100 tons of gold were sold, twenty times what was sold on a normal day. In the ensuing week, there were several planeloads of gold airlifted from the US for sale in London on Wednesday and Thursday. On Thursday evening, after an emergency meeting at Buckingham Palace, the Queen declared Friday, 15 March, a 'bank holiday'. On Monday, 18 March 1968, there were two significant developments. First, the US Senate repealed the 25 per cent gold cover for the supply of US dollar currency. Second, the seven members (after France's departure) of the London gold pool agreed to a two-tier system for gold. Monetary gold used as reserves and transferred among countries in settling international debts would sell at a fixed price of US$35 per troy ounce, and gold used as an ordinary commodity would sell at a freely fluctuating market-determined price.

Dual pricing involves multiple problems, particularly arbitrage between the two markets. Furthermore, with accelerating inflation, the fixed price of gold was not sustainable and even the two-tier gold market did not survive for long. In the last two weeks of March 1971, when the London gold market remained closed, gold traded at more than US$44 per troy ounce in Zurich and Paris. As the US unemployment rate inched up to 4.9 per cent by 1970, reducing unemployment became the foremost goal of US policy. President Richard Nixon met his fifteen advisers at the presidential retreat at Camp David during 13-15 August 1971, and in his address to the nation on 15 August 1971, announced the closing of the gold window. It came to be known as the 'Nixon Shock'. With it came down the edifice built in 1944 at Bretton Woods. It was a US default, the biggest default in a few hundred years, and it all happened on the twenty-fourth anniversary of Indian Independence.

XVI.2 Constructively Ambiguous Indian Exchange Rate Management, 1971–73

The Indian rupee had remained pegged to the pound sterling since 1931. Even after Independence, India had continued as one of the thirty-eight members of the overseas sterling area. After the devaluation of 1966, the rupee's link to fine gold had been changed from 0.186621 grams to 0.118489 grams, and by implication to a US dollar from ₹4.76 to ₹7.50 and to a pound sterling from ₹13.33 to ₹21. When the UK devalued the pound sterling in November 1967, several countries, such as Ceylon (now Sri Lanka), Hong Kong, Israel, New Zealand and Spain, followed suit. But India did not. What it did was to adjust, in line with the new parity of pound sterling to gold and to the US dollar, from ₹21 to ₹18 per pound sterling.

After the Nixon shock in August 1971, currencies started floating and members of the IMF were required to decide on the choice of the reserve currency. With the UK declaring its dealings not subject to any ceiling linked to the parity of the sterling at US$2.40 a pound, it was effectively a float of the pound sterling. To avoid the bitter political fallout of a devaluation, like in 1966, as well as any overvaluation of the rupee reducing external competitiveness and creating a balance of payments problems, the Indian authorities started following a policy of pegging the rupee to the potentially weaker of the two currencies, namely the US dollar and the pound sterling. With the pound sterling the intervention currency, the RBI bought and sold pound sterling against the rupee. A week later, without changing the gold parity and consequently the rupee–dollar parity of ₹7.50 to the US dollar, the RBI announced that it would buy and sell pound sterling for ready delivery at rates determined daily with reference to the par value of the rupee in terms of US dollars. Consequently, the exchange value of the pound sterling daily in the London foreign exchange market started floating freely upward against the dollar. By shifting the peg from the pound sterling to the weaker US dollar, what India did in effect was to devalue the rupee 'surreptitiously'. The rupee's peg of ₹7.50 to the US dollar from late August, however, did not last for more than three months.

Intense negotiations were on for four months among the finance ministers and Central Bank Governors of the Group of Ten (G-10), the club of developed countries consisting of Belgium, Canada, France, Germany, Italy, Japan, the Netherlands, Sweden, the UK and the US. Finally, on 18 December 1971, came the Smithsonian Agreement with a proposed 7.89 per cent devaluation of the US dollar against gold to US$38, and continued suspension of the convertibility of the US dollar into gold. The new US dollar rate of the pound sterling was up from US$2.4 to US$2.6. After the Smithsonian Agreement, the IMF permitted member countries to adopt central rates, which were temporary fixed rates for exchange transactions and such rates could be different from those based on their par values. The buying and selling rates could vary from the central rate by ±2.25 per cent.

The massive outflows of funds from the US prior to the 7.9 per cent devaluation of the US dollar under the Smithsonian Agreement were expected to partly reverse themselves, and to strengthen the US dollar vis-à-vis the pound sterling. There were advantages to changing the peg for the Indian rupee from the dollar to the pound sterling. The rupee was back to its peg to the pound sterling. From Monday, 20 December 1971, the new rupee-sterling central rate was taken as ₹18.9677 per pound, down 5.1 per cent from ₹18 per pound. However, with the US dollar-pound sterling central rate at US$2.6 per pound sterling, the rupee-dollar rate worked out to ₹7.28, a 3 per cent revaluation of the rupee vis-à-vis the US dollar.

Following the coalminers' seven-week strike in the UK in January–February 1972, the UK's economy was threatened with the risk of a dock strike and high inflation. Its balance of payments prospects looked dim. Its trade balance had moved to a deficit by February, and March saw a growth-promoting expansionary budget. The UK's balance of payments continued to be in the red. On 1 May, the UK joined the 'EEC currency snake', wherein the members committed to maintain stable exchange rates by preventing exchange rate fluctuations of more than 2.25 per cent. Speculators expected the pound sterling to devalue and the other European currencies, particularly the deutsche mark, to appreciate vis-à-vis the dollar. They started to short the pound sterling while going long on the deutsche mark and other EEC currencies. The pound sterling was at the bottom of the band, and its exchange rate needed support by concerted intervention by the Bank of England and other allied European Central Banks. On Friday, 23 June, in its bulletin of 8 a.m., the BBC carried the news about a temporary float of the sterling and its withdrawal from the snake. The Smithsonian Agreement started to crumble with the British float and gold price went on to rise to US$60 per ounce by mid-1972. On the same day, the UK also dismantled the sterling area.

With so much turmoil in world currency markets, a huge refugee problem from the Pakistani genocide in Bangladesh, and indifferent harvests, India faced a very tough period of economic management. Hamstrung by the strident criticism after the 1966 devaluation, the Indian exchange rate policy displayed a preference for holding down the external value of the rupee to maintain external competitiveness, but only in what can be described as a constructively ambiguous way. Arguably, with the par value of the rupee in terms of the gold constant, and the central rate of the rupee unchanged at ₹18.9677 per pound sterling since end-1971, technically, the Indian government could claim that there was no depreciation of the rupee. But there was some force in the argument of hidden devaluation, and that was precisely what was pointed out by critics of the government in Parliament. In the third quarter of 1973, at the Joint Select Committee on the Foreign Exchange Regulation Bill, Jyotirmoy Bosu, the outspoken CPI(M) MP, claimed that the RBI and the government had devalued the rupee thrice without saying so. Coming from Bosu, the allegation carried some extra weight; he had the distinction of having exposed some sensational scandals, like the one involving Rustom Sohrab Nagarwala, which we will be discussing.

XVI.3 Boiling in Oil

After the Smithsonian Agreement of 1971 started to crumble after the British float in June 1972, gold price per ounce rose from US$60 to as much as US$90 by early 1973. On 12 February 1973, the US devalued the dollar by an additional 10 per cent from US$38 to US$42 per ounce of gold. Still, speculation against it continued. Within a month, nearly all major currencies were floating. And then came the first oil price shock after the Yom Kippur War in October 1973.

To punish the western countries' 'flagrantly hostile attitude, and its support for the Zionist enemy', on 7 October 1973, Iraq nationalized Exxon and Mobil, two American companies, as well as the Dutch affiliate of British Petroleum Company.[2] Soon thereafter, the Organization of Arab Petroleum Exporting Countries (OAPEC) decided on an oil embargo and cut production incrementally by 5 per cent per month until Israel withdrew from occupied Arab lands and Palestinians' rights were restored. By the end of the embargo in March 1974, the price of oil per barrel had skyrocketed from US$3 to nearly US$12. India was badly hit. Despite exploration and drilling for over a hundred years, not much oil had been found in India (Box XVI.1). In the early 1970s, India was importing almost two-thirds of its hydrocarbon energy needs.

It may be recalled that during the Suez Crisis in 1956, the British and the French had expected their long-standing ally, the US, to release emergency oil supplies as a part of the US support to their invasion of Egypt. But US President Eisenhower was pitted against Democratic aspirant Adlai Stevenson in an electoral battle, and the last thing he wanted was an international crisis undermining his electoral appeal. He had also not been consulted before the Anglo-French invasion. When told that the British and French expected the US to release emergency oil supplies, the furious President reportedly said, let the British and French 'Boil in their own Oil'.[3] In the mid-1970s, India boiled not in its own oil, but in oil imported from abroad.

With India's heavy dependence on imported petroleum, the fourfold increase in international crude oil prices raised the Indian petroleum import bill from US$265.9 million in 1972–73 to US$.1457 million in 1974–75 (Figure XVI.1). Reeling under a foreign exchange crisis, in 1973, through an amendment, it strengthened FERA of 1947 into FERA 1973. To curtail outflows in the form of fees, royalties and profits, the amendment required foreign equity in the consumer goods sector to be no more than 40 per cent.

Box XVI.1 A Brief History of Oil Exploration in India

Hydrocarbon exploration began in India around Digboi shortly after Col Drake had successfully drilled the first oil in Titusville, Pennsylvania, US, in 1859. In 1866, a British gentleman by the name 'Goodenough' of Kolkata-based McKillop Stewart Co. drilled a well near Jaypore in upper Assam and struck oil. In 1867, he also discovered oil at Makum, about 26 km from the present oil town of Digboi in Assam. Production from these two were, however, unsatisfactory. Drilling at Digboi Well No-1, the first well with satisfactory output, was started in September 1889 and completed in November 1890. It initially produced 200 gallons per day at a total depth of 662 ft. It was drilled under the direction of Mr W.L. Lake, a Canadian engineer of the Assam Railways and Trading Company (AR&TC). In fact, legend has it that Digboi got its name from 'Dig Boy, Dig', which Mr Lake shouted at his men as they watched elephants emerging out of the dense forest with oil stains on their feet. The oil interests of AR&TC were taken over by the Assam Oil Company in 1899. But, beyond Digboi, not much oil was discovered in India, and production peaked at 435 barrels per day in 1917. With the growth of the economy, increasing demand led to increasing import dependency on petroleum.

Post-Independence, the Assam Oil Company discovered the Nahorkatiya oilfield in 1953, and in 1956, with insufficient evidence, announced an annual production target of 2.5 million tons. Oil was also discovered in 1956 in Assam at Hugrijan and Moran. With insufficient progress in achieving the target, Oil India Limited (OIL) was formed as a joint venture between the government and Burmah Oil in 1959 to take over the management of the discovered oil fields of Nahorkatiya and Moran. State-owned ONGC started exploring and drilling for oil in the country. IPR in April 1956 placed the mineral oil industry among the schedule 'A' industries, the future development of which was to be the sole and exclusive responsibility of the state. ONGC had struck oil in Cambay in 1958, in Assam in 1960, and discovered oil in the structures of Bombay High off the coast of Mumbai in 1963. Minister Malaviya had declared that India would be self-sufficient in oil by 1965–67. But that was not to be. It was only in 1974 that ONGC sunk a significant oil well in Bombay High, and domestic oil production started to increase only thereafter to peak at around 33 million tonnes in the 1990s and 2000s. Before Bombay High was discovered, India was hit by the first oil price shock in October 1973.

It is instructive to compare China with India in terms of vulnerability to the international oil price. In oil production, relative to India, China made much better progress, albeit with better luck. Prior to 1949, it used to import all its petroleum needs. In 1959, it discovered large reserves in Songhua Jiang-Liao basin in the northeast, and Daqing in Heilongjiang Province started producing in 1960. In 1965, oil was found in Shengli, Shandong, Dagang and Tianjin. By 1973, China was not only meeting its entire petroleum needs from domestic production but was also exporting crude to Japan. With rapid economic growth, China started importing oil only in 1993. Unlike India, China's balance of payments was not affected by the first oil shock.

Surprisingly, in all the time since 1955–56, for the first time, the current account produced a surplus in the balance of payments in 1973–74 (Figure XVI.2). Net invisible receipts increased with an inflow of ₹1654 crore of PL480 funds, and the current account surplus was primarily because of a quantum leap in 'net invisibles' receipts from a *negative* US$186 million in 1972–73 to US$2093 million in 1973–74, more than wiping out the trade deficit. In 1973–74, not only was the current account in surplus after a gap of eighteen years, but that too by almost US$1.5 billion. After meeting the debt servicing and other capital account liabilities, reserves grew by US$107 million. Reserves had grown in earlier years as well, but mainly through loans showing up as surpluses in the capital account. The surfeit of 1973–74 was different. But it was a one-off event, and the surplus turned into a deficit the following year. The trade deficit jumped to US$1,498.5 million in 1974–75 and there was serious trouble on the inflation front (Section XVI.3).

The early 1970s was a period of heightened instability in foreign exchange markets, with an underlying trend for the US dollar to depreciate vis-à-vis other hard currencies. Such volatility elevated the risks in international settlements, that is, in 'A' making a payment (in favour

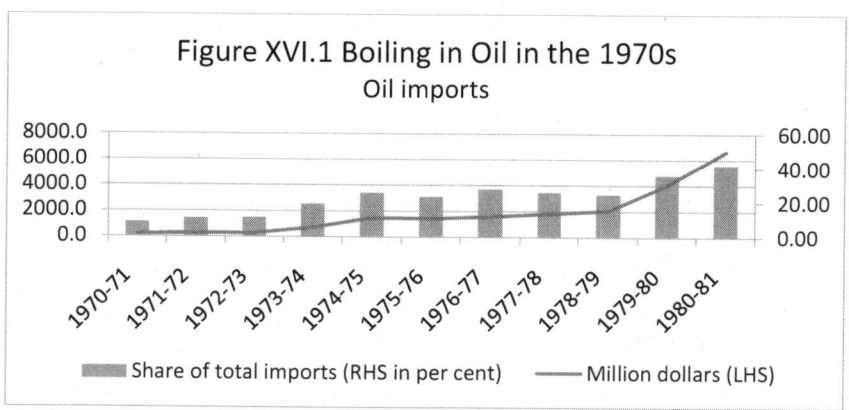

Source: RBI's Handbook of Statistics on the Indian Economy, Table 127 – India's Foreign Trade in US dollars

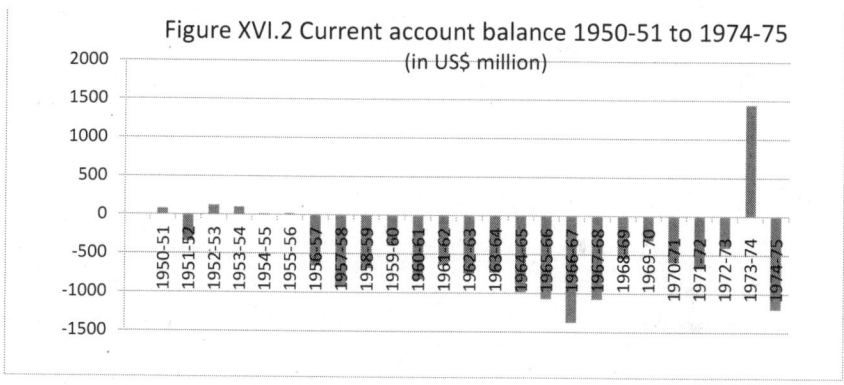

Source: RBI's Handbook of Statistics on the Indian Economy, Table 142 – Key Components of India's Balance of Payments in US dollars

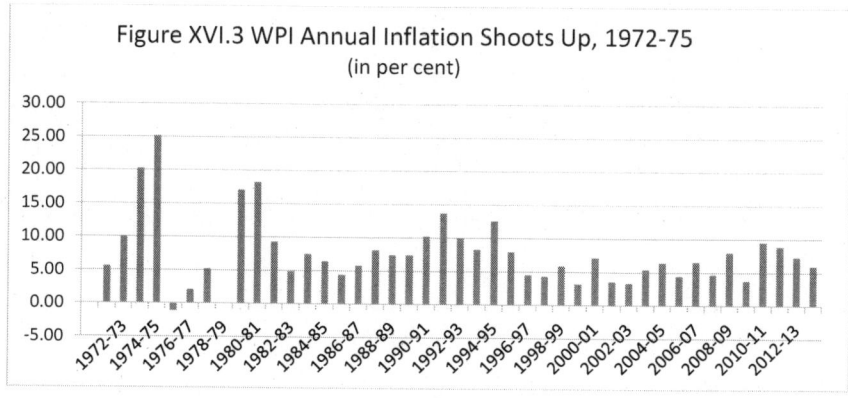

Source: RBI's Handbook of Statistics on the Indian Economy

of 'B' in country 2) in their bank in country 1 in the domestic currency and 'B' receiving the funds in country 2 in their domestic currency. There was also the additional problem of A's bank going bankrupt after they had paid the money for transfer to B but before B received the money. This settlement risk in an interconnected world came to the fore in the West German city of Cologne on 26 June 1974. That is the day when the privately-owned bank Bankhaus I.D. Herstatt K.G.a.A., popularly known as Herstatt Bank, went bankrupt and the counterparties in New York never received the funds.

To respond to the cross-jurisdictional implications of the Herstatt debacle, the advanced countries of the world—G-10 countries plus Switzerland, Luxembourg, and Spain—formed the Basel Committee on Banking Supervision (BCBS), a standing committee of representatives from central banks and regulatory authorities, under the auspices of the Bank for International Settlements (BIS). BCBS recommended Basel Norms in 1988 would be implemented in India from 1992. Meanwhile, nationalization of general insurance companies and coal mines followed.

XVI.4 Nationalization of General Insurance and Coal Mining

Nationalization of general insurance, the second of the Ten-Point Programme from 1967, was still pending. The General Insurance Business (Nationalisation) Act, 1972 delivered on this promise by nationalizing the general insurance business in India with effect from 1 January 1973. General Insurance Corporation of India (GIC) was formed on 22 November 1972 to become the holding company for the government's shares in all general insurance companies.

Next in line was coal mining. Coal mining in India went back a long way to the last quarter of the eighteenth century. Indian entrepreneurs started coming into the sector from the mid-nineteenth century. Yet, at Independence, the coal industry was dominated by a few European managing agency houses. While its nationalization was not a part of the Ten-Point Programme, it was a part of the First Schedule, IDRA 1951 under industries which '. . . in the public interest . . . the Union should take under its control.'[4]

There was a Director General of Mines Safety with the responsibility of enforcing the safety norms in the industry. But clear laxity in enforcement was evident, for example, in the 182 deaths in the Chinakuri Colliery explosion in 1958 and the 268 deaths in the Dhori Colliery disaster in Dhanbad in 1965. In 1971, coal mining was scattered over 797 mines, with as many as 586 small ones each producing less than 120,000 tons annually and accounting for 22.7 per cent of the country's total output. With primitive technology, these mines could use only shallow mining, resulting in the loss of underlying reserves forever through waterlogging, subsidence and even underground fire. Between 1966 and 1969, the country faced a serious scarcity of coal not because of inadequate production, but because of transportation bottlenecks. Pit-head stocks rose while user industries cut down on production because of want for coal. Smaller mines involved greater transportation problems, but they also produced most of the high-quality coking coal, which was in short supply.

Coal came under the Essential Commodities Act, 1955 and was under price control until 1967. The problem of coking coal being used inefficiently in industries other than steel and the shortage of coking coal for metallurgical purposes was due to the inadequate price premium attached to coking coal. There was not enough investment forthcoming in the coal mining industry and coal supply was falling short of demand, particularly metallurgical demand. Furthermore, malpractices in wages and other statutory dues to workers and violation of safety norms for workers were rampant in the industry. These were the primary reasons given for nationalization. What was ignored, however, were the root causes of the sorry state of coal and the limits of government capacity to run a large sector such as coal.

Coal mines were nationalized in stages between 1971 and 1973. First, as we know, shortly after the Indo-Soviet Treaty of Peace, Friendship and Co-operation was signed in August 1971, under Mohan Kumaramangalam, the former ComPI leader as the minister of steel and mines, 214 coking coal mines were taken over on 16 October 1971. On 1 May 1972, under the Coking Coal Mines (Nationalization) Act, 1972, all the coking coal mines, and the coke oven plants other than those with the Tata Iron and Steel Company Limited and Indian Iron and Steel Company Limited, were nationalized and brought under the Bharat Coking Coal Limited

(BCCL), a new CPSE. The rest were taken over on 30 January 1973 under the Coal Mines (Taking Over of Management) Act, 1973, and nationalized on May Day 1973 under the Coal Mines (Nationalization) Act, 1973.

Railways, power, and steel were dominated by government ownership, and together accounted for about 65 per cent of coal demand. After 1967, with railways, a government-run industry, as the major consumer as well as its transporter, playing a prominent role, the government set the price as a monopsonist. The Government had set up the National Coal Development Corporation (NCDC) as an undertaking in 1956 with the collieries owned by the railways as its nucleus. Limited government capacity in running businesses was apparent in NCDC failing to meet its production target. Nationalization of coal was yet another demonstration of victory of faith and hope over experience. But it was valuable to the government because it sent out a strong message about its socialist credentials. Coal would continue to be a problem area for the Indian economy for decades to come. The main challenge in the immediate aftermath of the 1973 oil shock as well as the coal shortage, however, was not so much the balance of payments or lack of availability of coal, but the price rise. High inflation was notorious for its negative impact on the popularity and electoral fortune of ruling parties in almost all countries.

XVI.5 High Inflation, State Trading in Food Grains and Nationalization of Petroleum

WPI inflation roughly doubled in each of the two years, 1971–72 and 1972–73, from 5.6 per cent in 1970–71 to 10.04 per cent in 1971–72 to 20.22 per cent in 1972–73. With the impact of high fuel prices in the world market, it went to a record high of 25.20 per cent in 1973–74.

Food was scarce, with the output of wheat declining from 26.4 million tonnes in 1971–72 to 24.7 million tonnes in 1972–73 and further to 21.8 million tonnes in 1973–74. State trading in food grains was number four in the Ten-Point Programme. In April 1973, the government nationalized the wholesale trade in wheat to stop profiteering and hoarding by private traders and procure more food grains for PDS. It proved counterproductive, added to inflationary expectations, and strengthened hoarding. Against a target of 8 million tons, procurement in 1973–74 was even less than what was procured in 1972–73. Nationalization was reversed in April 1974, with traders permitted to operate by handing over a half of their purchases to the government at the procurement price, a stipulation that came to be known as 'levy'.

Farmers constituted a major segment of the electorate, and the government faced a serious challenge in terms of the economics of fertilizer. With low feedstock (naphtha) price before the oil price shock, the maximum retail price (MRP) of urea, under control since 1957, had been higher than the cost of production and distribution. With the oil price shock, feedstock prices went up and MRP of urea per tonne had to be almost doubled from ₹1050 to ₹2000 on 1 June 1974.

In its quest for the commanding heights, the government responded to the burgeoning inflation by nationalizing the foreign oil companies and introducing a complex administered pricing mechanism (APM). It acquired 74 per cent of shares in Esso in March 1974, and in 1976, fully took over Caltex and Burmah Shell, and the remaining 26 per cent shares in Esso. Hindustan Petroleum Corporation Limited (HPCL) represented erstwhile Esso in India, and Bharat Petroleum Corporation Limited (BPCL) Caltex and Burmah Shell. By 1968, the government already had four public sector and two joint sector refineries. With Indian Oil Corporation (IOC), Oil and Natural Gas Corporation (Commission rather than Corporation until 1994) (ONGC) and OIL under its full ownership, government control over the petroleum sector was complete.

Initially, the entire blame for the high inflation was laid on the rise in the price of oil and the two bad harvests since 1971–72. While nothing was attributed explicitly to fiscal profligacy, there were attempts to tighten macroeconomic policies. On 31 July 1974, outside his regular budget, for 1974–75, Finance Minister Y.B. Chavan introduced new taxation proposals, restrictions on declaration of dividends, impounding of a half of the additional dearness allowance (for cost-of-living adjustment) and wages, and compulsory deposit by income taxpayers in higher income brackets. The government also applied price controls and monetary brakes.

XVI.6 Welfare Schemes

The first employment guarantee scheme (EGS) in the country was perhaps the one launched in parts of Tasgaon Block of Sangli district in Maharashtra in 1964–65. It was an experiment under the Integrated Area Development Scheme by V.S. Page, a well-known Congressman with socialist leanings and the then chairman of the Maharashtra Legislative Council. Following an enthusiastic public response, the pilot project had been expanded to cover first the entire Tasgaon block, and then in a modified form in November 1970 to all eleven districts of the state. During the elections in 1971, the Congress in Maharashtra had committed itself to EGS as a part of its fifteen-point program to tackle the problems of poverty and unemployment. In fulfilment of its election promise, EGS was extended to all rural areas in the state in May 1972. Designed primarily as a safety net to provide employment to the vulnerable in rural areas in need of employment and income, EGS concentrated on providing unskilled manual work and took up labour-intensive projects with ratio of wages to a total cost at 60 per cent or more.

Soon after its state-wide adoption, EGS was suspended during the peak drought period of late 1972 to early 1974 and superseded by Union government programmes with Crash Scheme for Rural Employment (CSRE) as a component of Indira's 1971 'Garibi Hatao' program. In Maharashtra, in 1974–75, unhappy with the state's dependence on the Union government for drought relief, Congress Chief Minister V.P. Naik, with the support of opposition parties, set up a permanent EGS funded entirely by the state government. Two years later, the Maharashtra Employment Guarantee Act, 1977 provided the legal basis for the EGS scheme.

In the mid-1970s, Indira Gandhi was trying to centralize power within the Congress in her hands. In Maharashtra, in the Congress, one faction owed its allegiance to Y.B. Chavan and the other to Indira Gandhi. Three successive droughts during 1970–73 had led to acute shortage of food grains and drinking water, rural-urban migration and even alleged starvation deaths. Opposition parties were trying to mobilize the rural masses against the government. A non-party political formation was spearheading the agitation and it had the tacit or moral support of the

Congress faction pitted against the Chavan faction to question the latter's legitimacy to rule. Some scholars claim that the ruling Maratha elite, with Y.B. Chavan, Vasantdada Patel and Chief Minister V.P. Naik at the helm, took a leaf out of Indira Gandhi's populist 'Garibi Hatao' strategy to launch EGS in the rural areas of Maharashtra in 1972 and regain the initiative.

In its evaluation, EGS proved problematic vis-à-vis its second aim of financing only productive works. Given the inequities in the distribution of assets, EGS projects either benefitted rich farmers who owned the land and other productive resources or resulted in building roads and other facilities that would soon get washed away by the rains. In the event, because of the technical and organizational gaps and the large number of incomplete projects under the scarcity relief programme of the early 1970s, EGS turned out to be the completion of these incomplete projects. There was also a diversion of normal plan work to the EGS. Moreover, Taluka (or a small part of a district serving as an administrative unit) Committees found it difficult not to activate EGS where employment was otherwise available.

The most difficult problem was the insufficiency of financial resources. Resources for the EGS were to come from special taxation in urban and rural areas and a matching grant from the state's general revenues in its annual budget. The special taxation covered six major heads: taxes on professions, trades, callings and employments; additional tax on motor vehicles; additional sales tax; special assessment of irrigated agricultural lands, surcharge on land revenue; and tax on non-residential urban lands and buildings. But the additional revenue was insignificant. Although the beneficiaries of assets created under EGS were the landed affluent gentry, there was an unwillingness to levy and collect money from such beneficiaries.

Experience with CSRE from 1971–72 indicated the need for a more concentrated effort in solving the problem of rural unemployment, and hence the Pilot Intensive Rural Employment Project (PIREP) was launched for a period of three years as an action-cum-research project in fifteen blocks of the country, spread across agro-climatic zones, in November 1972. Unlike CSRE, which was spread thinly over the entire district and covered about 100 persons in a block on a selective basis at the rate of one per family, PIREP was concentrated over the smaller area of a block to cover all who wanted employment to study in depth the problem underlying the full utilization of rural manual labour for development.

Drought Prone Areas Programme (DPAP), the earliest area development programme, was launched by the Central government in 1973–74 to tackle the special problems faced by those fragile areas which were constantly affected by severe drought conditions. Furthermore, the draft Fifth Five-Year Plan provided for a National Programme of Minimum Needs. In his Budget Speech for 1974–75, Finance Minister Y.B. Chavan reiterated how this programme aimed to achieve a certain minimum level of social consumption in the form of elementary education, rural health, drinking water, provision for slum clearance, rural roads and rural electrification.

The Differential Rate of Interest (DRI) Scheme was instituted in 1972 to cater to the needs of the weaker sections—landless labourers, physically handicapped persons, orphanages, women's homes, and SCs and STs who had little income and no tangible security to offer as collateral. DRI loans were given in rural areas and at a very concessional rate of 4 per cent. The minimum quantum of lending under this scheme for each bank was one per cent of its total advances of the previous year. The major problem in banks administering this scheme was the identification of the weakest among the many eligible borrowers. Furthermore, as an evaluation of the scheme in 1980 by Prof. M.A. Oommen revealed, the loans did not go to the poor and the needy and a part of the loans were used for non-productive purposes, creating problems for loan recovery.

XVI.7 Constitutional Changes

The Indian Constitution, during the first fifteen years of its life before Indira Gandhi's rule, had undergone seventeen amendments. In the eleven years of Indira's rule—between 1966, when she assumed power, and 1977, when she demitted office after losing the election—she brought about twenty-five amendments. These included the Twenty-Fourth Amendment to the Constitution in 1971 to dilute fundamental rights, the Twenty-Fifth Amendment taking away the jurisdiction of courts to determine the adequacy of compensation on the government's acquisition of private property, the Twenty-Sixth Amendment to abolish the privy purses of rulers of erstwhile princely states, and the Thirty-Fourth Amendment to place land reform acts and their amendments in Schedule 9 of the Constitution, which parks laws that are beyond judicial reviews. Furthermore, there were reported attempts at having not only a committed bureaucracy but also a committed judiciary. Justice A.N. Ray was known to be sympathetic to the government's economic viewpoint and had delivered dissenting opinions in both the bank nationalization and Kesavananda Bharati cases. His appointment as Chief Justice of India in April 1973, superseding three senior judges, created considerable controversy.

XVI.8 Cobweb of Controls—Cotton Textiles, an Example

In India, controls interacted, reinforced each other, became entrenched in the system, and had large unintended consequences such as stifling an industry, or build-up of huge stocks of food grains with mounting subsidies while the challenge of starvation and malnutrition continued. Controls were nothing new, but what evolved under Indira was an intricate cobweb of controls. Cotton textiles, an ancient industry in India, provides a good example of its deadly impact.

Under colonial rule, the cotton textiles industry had suffered from deliberate attempts to harm it to benefit the UK. It should have revived after Independence. In fact, during the Second World War, with the disruption of imports of cotton textile from Japan and the UK along with the increase in demand, particularly from the military, there were signs of a resurgence. But after Independence, any such resurgence was nipped in the bud by the licensing system and other misguided policies.

Industrial 'sickness', defined as chronic losses and the need for regular infusion of external funds to stay afloat and produce, had become a major problem by the late 1960s in cotton textiles and many other sectors. The controlled cloth scheme in 1964, whereby 45 per cent of the total textile mill production had to be of the controlled variety and sold at 60 per cent of cost through co-operative marketing channels to subsidize cloth purchase by the masses, along with variations in the price of raw cotton and cotton yarn, preferential treatment of handloom and power loom over mills, and restrictions on the expansion of productive capacity, were major sources of the sickness in the textile industry. The government passed the Cotton Textiles Companies (Management of Undertaking and Liquidations or Reconstructions) Act in December 1967, and by 1972–73, took over management of 103 mills, roughly a third in western India and the south each. In 1968, both the statutory price control scheme and, under it, the quota system of controlled cloth was reduced from 45 per cent to 25 per cent. But the sickness continued.

In 1968, the government set up the National Textile Corporation (NTC) and entrusted it with the running of sixteen sick textile mills in the private sector taken over by the government. The number of such sick textile mills rose to 103 by 1972–73. Sick Textile Undertakings (Nationalization) Act came in December 1974 to acquire sick textile units, reorganize and rehabilitate them to 'subserve the interests of the general public by the augmentation of the production and distribution, at fair prices, of different varieties of cloth and yarn'. The 103 mills taken over managerially were nationalized and handed over to the NTC. Controlled cloth production was partially shifted to the nationalized mills, while the others were required to fulfil a portion of controlled cloth quota. Down the line, NTC reported operating losses right from its inception, and liquidated seventy-eight unviable mills under the Industrial Dispute (ID) Act during 2002-2011. Hope of a resurgence of the textile sector was buried deep during Indira's rule by MRTPA, high duty and QRs on import of synthetic fibre preventing production of blended fabric, controlled cloth scheme, preference for handloom and power looms and SSI reservation.

XVI.9 Administered Pricing Mechanism (APM) and Mounting Subsidies

Increase in the prices of items such as rice, wheat, sugar, fertilizer and kerosene, which were important to the common people, was politically sensitive. So what was devised was an APM for each to keep their prices, particularly under PDS, not only at levels affordable for the common man but uniform throughout the country. Doing that, while ensuring that producers got remunerative prices overall, was a formidable, if not practically impossible, challenge. To facilitate APM, the relevant sectors were protected from foreign competition and from competing abroad by high tariffs and/or QRs and canalized foreign trade.

Specialized agencies were set up for determining the appropriate 'producer price' of various products of interest to the government. For agricultural goods, the Agricultural Prices Commission was instituted in 1965. For industrial products, there was the Tariff Commission from 1951 and the Bureau of Industrial Costs and Prices (BICP) from 1960. On the advice of two Oil Price Committees in 1968 and 1974, an Oil Coordination Committee (OCC) under the ministry of petroleum and chemicals was established in 1975 for the petroleum sector. For the fertilizer industry, the Fertilizer Industry Coordination Committee was set up in December 1977. For rice and wheat, the FCI would do most of the job, with subsidies from the central government reimbursing it for the difference between its 'economic cost' of food grains and the CIP. For other items, such as sugar, petroleum and fertilizer, what the government devised were ingenious coordination committees and 'self-balancing' funds.

The most complex was the 'Oil Pool Account' for petroleum to allow not only the sale of products of different refineries at the same price to the consumers but also the sale of items such as high-speed diesel, used for mass and goods transportation, cheap by selling motor spirit at high prices' as 'to permit the sale of items of mass consumption and goods transportation, such as kerosene and high-speed diesel, cheap by selling motor spirit at high prices. There was also a Crude Oil Price Equalization Account from 1974 to deal with the problem of the difference between the price of imported crude and administered price of indigenous crude that different refineries used. The APMs had complex cost-plus pricing systems for producers, and equally complicated and elaborate cross-subsidization schemes for end users through the various self-balancing funds.

APM was meant to reconcile the interests of the producers with those of the consumers, particularly the vulnerable ones. The reconciliation looked fine on paper, but foundered on the rocks of practical applicability and political reality. With exogenous shocks, such as an increase in the price of an imported input, prices to be paid to the producers had to be increased to maintain their viability. But prices to the consumers could not be increased because of the political backlash. Over time, the funds became extra-budgetary operations with sizeable fiscal implications.

According to one estimate, total subsidies, after steadily declining from ₹2 billion in 1966–67 to ₹0.5 billion in 1968–69, went up to ₹9.5 billion in 1976–77. Subsidies went up in the 1970s, mainly on account of food, fuel and fertilizer. Subsidy is an implicit transfer linked to the production or consumption of a specific commodity or service. Transfers without such linkages would come much later when the Union government would launch the National Social Assistance Programme (NSAP).

Food grains

Food subsidy consisted of two parts—on food grains, which was the dominant component, and on sugar. To distribute food grains to the consumers, there was a need to redress the perennial shortage of food grains by paying farmers a remunerative price and boosting production. The Foodgrains Prices Committee under the chairmanship of L.K. Jha, in August 1964, had recommended a minimum price which would be assured to farmers through support operations as well as a procurement price for wholesalers and retailers such that producers were able to secure 'a rupee or two' more than the minimum price. The procurement price was also the 'maximum price'. By 1967, the FCI, established in 1965 to 'discipline the chaotic tendencies of private trade', covered the whole of the country. The food policy of the government had multiple objectives: promoting production and self-reliance, reducing undue fluctuations in food grain prices, and protecting the vulnerable sections of the people. They were not easy to reconcile.

The Commission for Agricultural Costs and Prices (CACP)—renamed Agricultural Prices Commission in 1985—came into existence in January 1965 to recommend the MSPs. It started announcing a procurement price and an MSP, which from 1968–69 became the MSP-cum-procurement price. Procurement was through the parastatal FCI. With remunerative MSP and free supply of electricity to farmers, water-scarce Haryana, Punjab and western UP became the vanguard states in the Green Revolution and the granaries of India only through the unsustainable practice of seriously depleting their sub-soil water.

Committees were appointed to go into the cost of cultivation and decide the procurement price, but the procurement price was often more than what they recommended. MSP determined without reference to demand conditions led to enormous surplus stocks of food grains, particularly wheat, which could be exported only with more subsidies. Furthermore, given that farmers often had to sell their food grains to traders at prices lower than the MSP, even the decision as to where the FCI would carry out its procurement was politically determined.

The central government started making food grains available to the states at the central depots at a uniform central issue price (CIP). The central government also reimbursed the difference between the economic cost of the FCI—the price paid to farmers together with other incidental operating and storage costs including mandi fees, handling, transportation and wastage—and the CIP in the form of subsidies. Dharm Narain, chairman of the Agricultural Prices Commission during 1970–1975, described it well by saying 'the procurement price is more politics than economics'.[5] Dharm Narain's observation proved uncannily prescient.

Under industrial licensing, Indians had become used to 'shortages' of items such as Ambassador cars, scooters and telephones, and waiting periods of four–five years for an 'allotment'. But the shortage of basic food grains had high political sensitivity. The only way consumers could be provided with food grains at a reasonable price while farmers received a 'remunerative price' was through subsidies. Food subsidies mounted as the overall cost of procuring the grains—known as economic cost—went up much faster than the price collected from the states for distribution to the consumers through PDS, with or without further subsidies from such governments (Figure XVI.4). With offtake already falling short of allocation of food grains, an enduring solution to the problem did not lie in increasing the CIP collected from the states/consumers. The S.R. Sen Committee had clearly pointed out that a mechanical fixation of price on the basis of the cost of cultivation would 'freeze the price relationships to the demand-supply situation prevailing in the past and thereby obstruct allocation of resources as per changing economic situation'.[6]

By the early 1970s, economists had pointed out how the artificially high price for food grains and the availability of new HYV seeds, particularly wheat, was leading to a shift of acreage from other food and cash crops, and was likely to result either in a progressively increasing stockpile of wheat or the search for an export outlet. Dharm Narain had warned: 'Since, given the

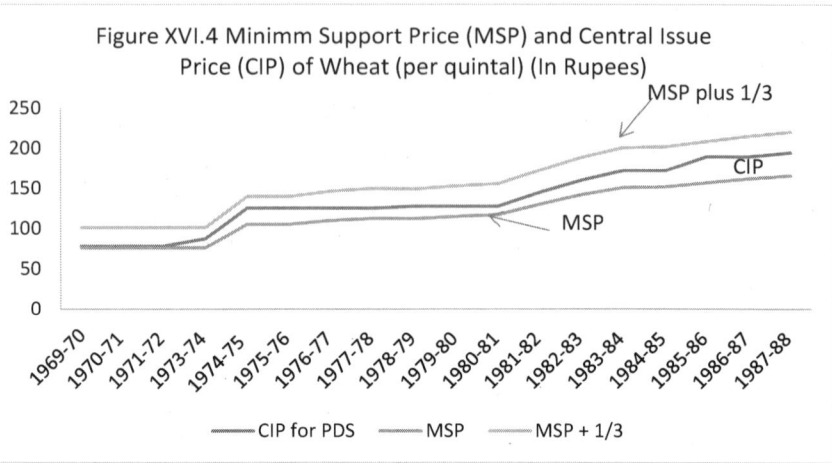

Figure XVI.4 Minimm Support Price (MSP) and Central Issue Price (CIP) of Wheat (per quintal) (In Rupees)

Source: R.S. Deshpande: 'Impact of Minimum Support Prices on Agricultural Economy (Consolidated Report)', Agricultural Development and Rural Transformation Unit, Institute for Social and Economic Change, Nagarbhavi, Bangalore-560 072, p. 31, December 2003

ruling international prices for this cereal, domestic wheat cannot be exported without a sizeable subsidy, the feasibility as well as the desirability of this course of action will have to be properly assessed. The building and carrying of a progressively rising stock of wheat is, likewise, a costly operation and it would be neither desirable nor possible to undertake it on a continuing basis.'[7] Alas, that is precisely what happened over time: stocks piled up and grains were exported with large subsidies to cover the difference between the world price and the economic cost of procuring grains.

Sugar

The regime of MSP proliferated in the 1970s. MSPs for coarse cereals (*jowar* or pearl millet, *bajra* or sorghum, maize and *ragi* or finger millet) and gram were announced from 1968–69, for oilseeds from 1972–73, and for pulses (*arhar* or red gram or pigeon peas, *moong* or green gram and *urad* or black gram) and cotton from the mid-1970s. Without any procurement operations for most of these agricultural items, however, MSP remained only a signalling device.

The case of sugarcane was different. India is the second largest producer of sugar in the world, next only to Brazil. During much of British rule,

India remained an importer of sugar. The sugar industry—the industry producing sugar by the vacuum pan process as opposed to *khandsari* or *bura* sugar—started to come up only with the Sugar Industry (Protection) Act, 1932. Given its perishable nature, there is a critical interdependence between a sugar mill and the sugarcane producers in the adjoining area. A sugar mill can do little business without the sugarcane supplied by the farmers and the farmers can do little with their sugarcane without the sugar mill nearby purchasing their cane. The sugar industry was included in the First Schedule of IDRA 1951 and required a licence for setting up a new unit or substantial expansion of capacity. Sugar Cane (Regulation of Supply & Purchase) Act to regulate the supply and purchase of sugarcane required for the use in a sugar factory, khandsari unit and for manufacture of *gur* or jaggery, followed in 1953, and the necessary rules in 1954.

The cost of producing sugar was and is considerably higher in India than in competitor countries, e.g., Brazil and Thailand, and, for its survival, in normal times, the Indian sugar industry required protection from international competition. In 1957, with the Suez crisis and poor beet crop in Europe, however, the price of sugar in the world market went up over its cost price in India, and India made an entry into the world sugar market, especially in Asia and East Africa. The price advantage was short-lived, but the incentives for earning foreign exchange remained with the Sugar Export Promotion Act of 1958. It specified the Indian Sugar Mills Association as the export agency and authorized the central government to specify the quantity to be exported in the aggregate as well as the export quotas of the individual factories. Failure to deliver on the export quota attracted, on the relevant amount, an additional excise duty of ₹17 per maund (37.3242 kg) over and above the regular excise duty. This additional duty of excise leviable on failure to deliver on the export quota drove a wedge between export and the domestic price and constituted an implicit subsidy to sugar exports. Apart from this implicit subsidy, there was an explicit subsidy as well. With the cost price well above the export price, the industry demanded and got a subsidy from the central government. Such subsidies went up from ₹5.5 crore in 1961–62 to ₹8.60 crore in 1970–71.

Within six months of coming to power, Indira Gandhi, under the Essential Commodities Act, 1955, got the Sugar (Control) Order 1966 passed. It provided wide-ranging powers to the central government to regulate the production, sale, movement and quality of sugar, to call for information, and to inspect, search and seize stocks in case of violation. Its statutory provisions governed the pricing of sugarcane as well, and the central government started fixing, not the MSP or minimum support price, but the Statutory Minimum Price (SMP) of sugarcane. It was illegal for sugar mills to purchase sugarcane at a price below the SMP. Over time, for political reasons, the states started jacking up this SMP by as much as 20–50 per cent and announce State Advised Price (SAP). The government could procure sugar from producers at declared prices, decide on free sale open market quotas for producers, and give them monthly release orders. The extent of control and decontrol kept changing over time.

In sugar, levy sugar prices were worked out for different areas and factories keeping in view the cost of sugar cane, manufacturing cost, duties paid and reasonable return on capital employed. In October 1972, a detailed scheme of pooling the ex-factory prices of sugar was worked out to equalize the price of levy sugar to the consumers across the country. FCI was to operate a 'Sugar Price Equalization Fund', into which the price differential of low-cost zones would be credited, and the extra payments involved in distributing levy sugar in high-cost areas would be debited. The fund would always be balanced and never be allowed to become negative, through a mechanism of reviewing the retail issue price of levy sugar to the consumers from time to time. The fund was given legal backing through the Levy Sugar Price Equalization Fund Act of 1976. Even after considerable liberalization, in 1998, a High-Powered Committee on Sugar Industry, after surveying the major sugar-producing countries of the world, observed 'The Indian sugar system ranks among one of the most complex systems in the world . . .'

Fuel

Until the oil price shock, the pricing of petroleum products was on import parity principles. Petroleum being a transportation fuel and a universal intermediate, an increase in its price tended to rapidly feed into overall inflation. It touched everyone's pocket, had high political visibility, and any increase in its domestic price was unwelcome. Thus, in July 1975, such pricing was shifted to cost plus principles under APM. Various oil pool accounts were maintained with the objective of i) ensuring stability in selling price; ii) insulating consumers against international price fluctuations; and iii) cross-subsidization of the consumer prices of certain products like kerosene for public distribution and domestic LPG from other products like petrol, Aviation Turbine Fuel etc. and indigenous crude oil. The pool accounts started accumulating deficits, and until its dismantling in 2002, introduced inefficiencies through distorted relative prices. For example, kerosene was used for the adulteration of petrol and diesel, which in turn aggravated the problem of environmental pollution in metropolitan cities. Similarly, subsidies on naphtha and fuel oil used by the fertilizer industry resulted in a sub-optimal inter-fuel substitution. A low price of diesel relative to petrol, which was maintained to keep freight costs low, inadvertently subsidized luxury cars and generator sets running on diesel and used by the rich.

Fertilizer

Fertilizers are critical for soil fertility and crop productivity, and India is highly import-dependent in fertilizer. 'Between 1944 and 1966, the Ministry of Agriculture operated a central fertilizer pool which pooled imported as well as indigenously produced fertilizers and arranged for equitable distribution materials at fair prices to the States. Under the Essential Commodities Act, Government passed the Fertilizer Control Order in 1957 to regulate the sale, price, and quality of fertilizer. In 1966, the Government enunciated a new fertilizer policy under which freedom was given to the industry to price and market half of their production.'[8] It was part of the structural reform agenda negotiated between Asoka Mehta, the deputy chairman of the Planning Commission, and George Woods, president of the World Bank, around the time of the 1966 devaluation. But this freedom was short-lived due to the oil price shock.

In 1973, fertilizer distribution and inter-state movement were regulated by bringing in the Fertiliser Movement Control Order. We know how the feedstock (naphtha) prices for producing urea went up with the oil price shock and the MRP of urea almost doubled in 1974. In 1975, under the Essential Commodities Act, the government fixed the maximum selling prices for fertilizers containing nitrogen only. 'Single super phosphate was taken out of the purview of such price fixation and responsibility for fixing the price of this was given to the Fertilizer Association of India. In March 1976, maximum selling prices were fixed along with a flat subsidy of ₹1250 per ton of phosphoric acid produced and sold in the form of fertilizer.'[9] With India's entire requirements of potassic fertilizers met through imports, and such imports and distribution handled by the government-owned Indian Potash Limited, the pricing of such fertilizer was with the government.

A committee under the chairmanship of Dr S.S. Marathe was set up in January 1976 to study the problem of reconciling the challenge of ensuring a reasonable rate of return on investment in the fertilizer industry while providing fertilizer at reasonable and uniform prices to the farmers. On the committee's recommendation, the government of India, in November 1977, introduced the Retention Price Cum Subsidy Scheme (RPS) for indigenous nitrogenous fertilizer units. RPS was later extended to phosphatic and other complex fertilizers in February 1979 and Single Super Phosphate in 1982.

Increasing the use of fertilizer, which was facilitated by policies to enhance production and availability of fertilizers at reasonable prices

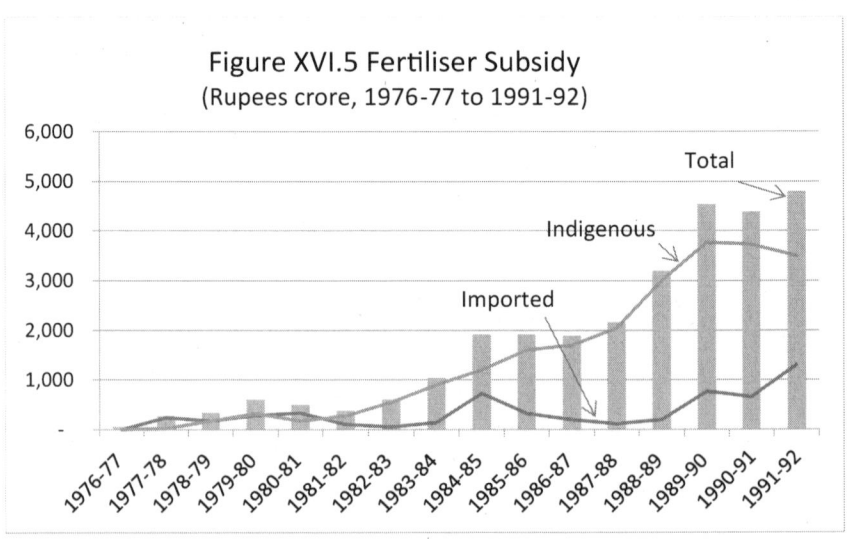

Figure XVI.5 Fertiliser Subsidy
(Rupees crore, 1976-77 to 1991-92)

Source: Annual Reports, Deptt. of Fertilizers. Consolidated figures available at https://www.faidelhi. org/general/Central%20subsidy%20on%20fertilisers.pdf

in the country, without a doubt, played a large role in the success of India's Green Revolution and self-reliance in food grain production. However, an important side-effect was the growing burden of fertilizer subsidies. No subsidy was paid on fertilizers till 1977 except on potash only for a year in 1977. The burden of fertilizer subsidies quickly started to mount, from ₹60 crore in 1976–77 to ₹604 crore in 1979–80, and became an entrenched fiscal problem for the central government (Figure XVI.5).

Mounting subsidies

Explicit central government subsidies, for example on kerosene for residential consumers under PDS, had been continuing in India at least from the Second World War. What was new under Indira Gandhi was the rapid increase in their scale of operations and significance for the central government's budget. The explicit central government subsidies exploded from ₹0.94 billion in 1970–71 to ₹18.21 billion in 1979–80 (Figure XVI.6). The corresponding increase in terms of the share of subsidies in total central government expenditure was from 1.67 per cent to 4.22 per cent and further to 9.60 per cent.

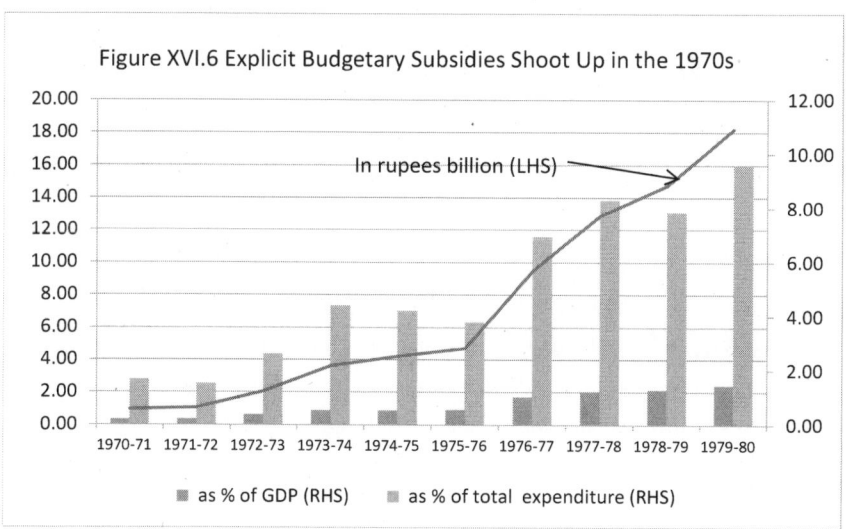

Figure XVI.6 Explicit Budgetary Subsidies Shoot Up in the 1970s

Source: RBI Handbook of Statistics of the Indian Economy, Table No. 103. . Total expenditure refers to total Central Government expenditure.

Subsidies became a major drain on the budget and left reduced scope for other developmental interventions, including in primary education and health. Furthermore, even these large increases in explicit budgetary subsidies grossly underestimated the true extent of the subsidies. The underestimation stemmed from the debate about what constituted a 'subsidy'. First, there are mundane issues, such as the losses of government departmental enterprises engaged in the provision of goods and services covered under subsidies. For example, what if FCI incurred losses of, say, ₹X crore beyond what it received for incidental costs? Similarly, what about the cost of unrecovered loans to and investments in such enterprises?

Second is the crucial issue of which goods and services should be covered under the purview of subsidies. Clearly, there is a difference between such a provision in the case of defence and law and order on the one hand and distribution of food grains at affordable prices on the other. Government expenditure on public goods—goods or services characterised by non-excludability and non-rivalry in consumption, e.g. law and order or roads—are not considered to be subsidies. For a public good or service, such as a good law and order system, only Rahim cannot be included, and Ram excluded from enjoying its benefits. Ram and Rahim are not rivalling in the 'consumption' of law-and-order facilities. On the other hand, there are private goods and services, for example, potato chips, which are characterized by excludability, rivalry and no externalities. Rahim cannot consume the potato chips that Ram is eating and vice versa. Government expenditure on a purely private good is a subsidy.

There are certain goods and services, such as education, which are called merit goods and services, which an individual or even society should have on the basis of some concept of benefit, rather than ability and willingness to pay. Problems arise with such merit goods or services which, though characterized by excludability and rivalry, also have some externalities. Providing free education to Ram's young daughter is good not only for Ram, but also for Rahim and Mathew. But again, the externality to Rahim and Mathew is different when the education involved is primary and when it is higher-level education such as a PhD or engineering. Subsidies can be considered unrecovered costs of governmental provision of goods/services that are not classified as public goods or at least merit goods. A subsidy is a negative indirect tax—a reverse flow or transfer from the government to the public—or an income/consumption supplement for individuals.

A finer analysis of government expenditure in 1987–88 subsequently published in 1991 by two professors of NIPFP revealed how explicit subsidies seriously underestimated the true volume of subsidies in government operations. Sudipto Mundle and Govinda Rao estimated that, in 1987–88, central government subsidies were ₹160.65 billion compared to such explicit subsidies of only ₹59.80 billion. Subsidies which might have been unexceptionable by themselves or were supportive of higher-level goals, were easy to grant, but once granted, gave rise to vested interest groups and an overly complex system that became exceedingly difficult to disband politically. The 1970s can be seen as the decade that laid the foundation of the widespread subsidy regime encompassing mainly fuel, food and fertilizer which, because of the unsustainability of the associated public expenditure, the Central government has been trying to rationalize ever since.

XVI.10 Monetary Brakes

Greatly worried by the ratcheting up of WPI inflation from 5.6 per cent in 1970–71 to 25.20 per cent in 1974–75, the government and the RBI applied the monetary brakes with full force. In 1973, the CRR, which had remained unchanged at 3 per cent since 16 October 1962, was raised in quick succession to 5 per cent on 29 June, 6 per cent on 8 September and 7 per cent on 22 September. The SLR, which had been 25 per cent between 16 September 1964 and 5 February 1970, saw a more gradual increase in five steps of 1 percentage point each to reach 30 per cent on 17 November 1972. But then it was hiked from 30 per cent to 32 per cent on 8 December 1973 and further to 33 per cent on 1 July 1974.

The administered interest rates were also used for containing demand and tackling the high inflation and balance of payments problems. From 1 June 1973, the RBI imposed a minimum lending rate of 10 per cent on all loans, except for the priority sector. However, to boost exports, export credit was moved into the priority list (outside the purview of QRs on credit). Term deposit rates of longer maturities were adjusted upwards between 1973 and 1974. Minimum rate chargeable under selective credit controls was also raised in July 1974.

The rate of growth of (annual average) high-powered money declined sharply from 22.5 per cent in 1973–74 to only 7.1 per cent in 1974–75. The government also cut down on its ever-increasing demand for credit from the banking sector and the rate of growth of such credit fell from 19–20 per cent in the previous three years to less than 10 per cent in 1974–75. Net foreign exchange assets of the banking sector fell from around ₹600 crore in each of the previous three years to ₹516 crore in 1974–75. With moderation of expansion on the asset side of the banking sector's balance sheet, the rate of growth of its monetary liabilities or broad money (M2) declined from 19.8 per cent in 1973–74 to 13.6 per cent in 1974–75 and further to 12.5 per cent in 1975–76. The world price of oil remained relatively stable from mid-February 1974 until the end of 1978, and with the monetary brakes, the rate of increase of annual average WPI (1970–71 series) was reversed from a high of 25.2 per cent in 1974–75 to a *decline* of 1.2 per cent in 1975–76 and an increase of only 2.1 per cent in 1976–77. Between 1974–75 and 1976–77, the corresponding movement in consumer price index (CPI, average of months, base 1960–61) was even more precipitous, from 34.6 per cent to -4.0 per cent and further to -13.8 per cent for agricultural workers and, for industrial workers, from 26.8 per cent to -1.3 per cent and further to -7.3 per cent.

In November 1974, public sector banks were advised that their priority sector lending should reach a level of not less than one-third of the outstanding credit by March 1979. Apart from the overall target, sub-targets for weaker sections of society were also laid down. The proliferation of directed credit arrangements, multiple interest rate prescriptions based on a variety of criteria (such as economic activity, commodity and location) and the resultant cross-subsidisation created an overly complex administered interest rate structure with a very limited role for market forces to play in the pricing and allocation of credit.

Even with the success in taming inflation, the concern for the government was the decline in the rate of growth of the economy. Growth of GDP, which in 1972–73, after being -0.3 per cent, or a marginal decline, had revived to 4.6 per cent in 1973–74, again declined to 1.2 per cent in 1973–74. While the government indeed brought inflation down by demand management, whether such management through excesses contributed to a recessionary condition in 1974–75 became a matter of debate.

XVI.11 Taxation Policy—Some Reprieve from Confiscatory Levels

In his budget for 1974–75, Finance Minister Y.B. Chavan started making amends to the confiscatory 97.75 per cent marginal rate of personal income tax-cum-surcharge rate, the highest ever in India, that he had imposed three years ago. In line with the Direct Taxes Enquiry Committee's recommendations, Chavan increased the exemption limit from ₹5000 to ₹6000, reduced the rate of taxation for all income slabs, and fixed the marginal rate for the highest income slab of ₹70,001 and above at 70 per cent. With a unified surcharge of 10 per cent at all levels, the highest marginal rate came down from 97.75 per cent to 77.0 per cent. To balance the distributive impact of the reduction in the highest marginal rate, he increased the rates of wealth tax by 1 percentage point. By contemporary standards, the highest marginal rate of personal income tax of 77 per cent, particularly with the wealth tax, continued to look confiscatory.

An important reform in Budget 1974–75 was, without subjecting agricultural income to income tax, taking such income into account for calculating the applicable rate and tax liability. A new Foreign Travel Tax was introduced from 15 October 1971. Two cesses introduced in this period were (i) the cess of up to ₹1 per metric tonne on limestone and dolomite for labour welfare under the Limestone and Dolomite Mines Labour Welfare Fund Act, 1972, and (ii) a cess on indigenously produced crude under the Oil Industry (Development) Act, 1974. In 1974, ONGC had drilled a significant oil well in Bombay High. Under the Oil Industry (Development) Act, the Oil Industry Development Board (OIDB) was established on 13 January 1975. With the cess, the OIDB could mop up the difference between the cost of production of indigenous crude and international price and provide financial assistance for the development of the oil industry. The cess was ₹60 per tonne between 23 July 1974 and 12 July 1981. The OIDB cess was used for various purposes, including for subsidizing petroleum products and fertilizer; and many of these raised questions about whether they served the purpose of developing the oil industry.

In the Budget for 1973–74, Finance Minister Chavan introduced auxiliary customs duty of 20 per cent, 10 per cent and 5 per cent on imported goods. In customs duty, a major step was the Customs Tariff Act 1975, and under it, the introduction of Additional Customs Duties. These duties, equivalent to the excise duty on similar goods manufactured in India, were also referred to as countervailing duties. This removed a long-standing bias against domestic industry vis-à-vis imports. There was some liberalization of QRs in 1975–76, for example, with the grant of automatic licence to 'actual users' to import raw materials equal to the quantity used or the quantity of import licences in the previous year, and six items added to the OGL list.

Camouflaging inter-state sale of goods as transfer on consignment, or depot or branch transfer, provided an avenue for avoiding the CST levy. The CST Act, 1956 was amended in 1972 to put the burden of proving that the transfer of goods was 'otherwise than by way of sale' on the dealer who claimed exemption from tax on the grounds that there was, in fact, no sale. Sales tax revenues of states in the aggregate more than doubled every five years from ₹365 crore in 1965–66 to ₹755 crore in 1970–71 and further to ₹1550 crore in 1974–75. The corresponding increase as a proportion of GDP was from 1.27 per cent to 1.58 per cent and further to 1.92 per cent. Sales tax was the fastest growing tax source of the states and its share in states' total tax revenue increased from 33.1 per cent in 1970–71 to 37.7 per cent in 1974–75.

XVI.12 Jammu and Kashmir and 'Delhi Accord'

In the meantime, in Jammu and Kashmir, G.M. Sadiq had passed away on 12 December 1971, and been replaced by Syed Mir Qasim as chief minister. The enthusiasm of the secessionists waned in the wake of the break-up of Pakistan and the creation of an independent Bangladesh. Except for some short breaks, Sheikh Abdullah had been mostly in prison since 1953. He was turning 70 in December 1975. In return for Sheikh Abdullah's release and appointment as Jammu and Kashmir's chief minister, on 24 February 1975, his associate, Mirza Afzal Beg, signed the 'Delhi accord' with the diplomat G. Parthasarathy, Indira Gandhi's emissary. It more or less reaffirmed the terms of Jammu and Kashmir's incorporation into India since 1953. Sheikh Abdullah replaced Mir Qasim as the chief minister on 25 February 1975. Sheikh Abdullah and Mirza

Afzal Beg converted the Plebiscite Front into the National Conference. In a reversal of Bakshi Ghulam Mohammad's policy of subsidized rations, the Sheikh announced a phased withdrawal of subsidy for rations. The Congress in Jammu and Kashmir, which had installed the Sheikh as the chief minister, started protesting the policy.

Among the people of Jammu and Kashmir, there was resentment against the Delhi Accord. There was a dent in Sheikh Abdullah's popular appeal. The Jammu and Kashmir Agrarian Reforms Act of 21 August 1976 which, apart from providing transfer of land in ownership rights to tillers, reducing the ceiling on land from 186 (22 acres) to 100 kanals (12.5 acres) and abolishing absentee landlordism, allowing non-Kashmiris to buy estates on lease, added to the resentment. The act was considered an infringement on the state's subject laws.

Relations between Sheikh Abdullah's National Conference and Congress deteriorated further with problems in seat-sharing in the Srinagar Municipal election, but the arrangement continued almost until the next assembly election in 1977.

XVII

Mid-Seventies Nightmare and Its End

This post-Nehru period of popular upsurge from 1964 to 1991, what we call the period of Nehruvian policies with a popular twist, also saw a worsening of the fiscal crisis, with the state spending far more than its revenues, and repeated crises on the external balance of payments front.

Despite populist moves such as bank nationalization and abolition of privy purses, the catchy slogan 'Garibi Hatao', widespread subsidies, and her successes on the external relations front such as the liberation of Bangladesh, Prime Minister Indira Gandhi found it difficult to tame the upsurge in popular participation in the early 1970s. The demands were also for empowerment and governance reforms, particularly the removal of corruption. Social mobilization almost overwhelmed the capacity of the state and the state had to suspend fundamental rights and democracy by promulgating an internal emergency for nineteen months. With the refugee problem after the Pakistani genocide in its erstwhile East Pakistan and the oil price shock, the situation was so bad that, in the mid-1960s, to some western observers, India, with its poverty, scarcity, regional conflicts and corruption, appeared like the Weimer Republic or Kuomintang China.[1]

Neville Maxwell's projection that the 1967 election in India would be the last general election was wrong, but not completely off the mark. After 1967, the next general election in 1971, for some time in the mid-1970s, looked like the last general election in India. Indira Gandhi's younger son, and heir apparent according to many, had told the veteran journalist Kuldip Nayar that 'he had assumed his mother would not call elections for three to four decades'. On 16 July 1947, in the House of Lords, Roundell Palmer, Third Earl of Selmore, had said, 'One thing we can be sure of, and that is that there cannot be democracy in India. There never was any hope of democracy in India in the Anglo-Saxon and Scandinavian sense of the term, because the conditions which make democracy possible do not exist.'[2]

A nightmare in the mid-1970s threatened to validate the dismal prediction about the future of Indian democracy by the third Earl of Selmore in 1947 and Neville Maxwell in 1967.

XVII.1 India—An Island of Democracy Among Authoritarian Regimes

A democracy is characterized by regularly held and meaningful elections, the peoples' right to organize freely to contest those elections, and a broadly enfranchised population of voters. In 1974, looking for a democracy in Africa, the Middle East, Latin America and Asia was like looking for a needle in a haystack.

In 1974, Africa was still full of colonial vestiges. Angola, Cape Verde, Djibouti, Madagascar, Mozambique and Seychelles, for all effective purposes, were under colonial powers. Southwest Africa was formally recognized as Namibia by the UN in 1968, but still under South African rule, apartheid was on in South Africa and Nelson Mandela still in jail in Robben Island, and Zimbabwe was still Rhodesia under Ian Smith. Except for Botswana, Mauritius and the Gambia, there was hardly any other country which could be described as a democracy in Africa. The continent was more well-known for dictators such as Félix Houphouët-Boigny of Côte d'Ivoire, Idi Amin of Uganda, Col Gaddafi of Libya, Joseph-Désiré Mobutu of Zaire (erstwhile Congo) and Emperor Jean-Bédel Bokassa of the Central African Republic. Each of these distinguished leaders had their own notoriety. For example, after the UK broke off diplomatic relations with Uganda in 1977, Idi Amin conferred upon himself the title of Conqueror of the British Empire (CBE). He killed 3,00,000 Ugandans and threw several of his own ministers to the crocodiles of Lake Victoria. On his cannibalism, he said, 'I don't like human flesh. It's too salty for me.'[3]

Except in Turkey, there was no democracy in the Middle East in 1974. Bahrain, Iran, Jordan, the Sultanate of Oman, Qatar and Saudi Arabia were monarchies. Cyprus was in the middle of a civil war. In Egypt, after Nasser's death, in an election in October 1970, Anwar El Sadet was the sole candidate. Voters only had a chance to say yes or no. Sadet secured 90 per cent of the votes and became President. Iraq, since July 1968 bloodless coup d'état, had been under the Arab Socialist Ba'ath Party, with General Ahmed Hassan al-Bakr as President and Saddam Hussein as Vice President. Kuwait was a monarchy, and at best, semi-democratic. Palestine was only a de jure state until 1988. The West Bank (of the Jordan River) was occupied by Jordan, and Sinai and Gaza by Egypt. From 1970 onwards, Lebanon had been under Suleiman Kabalan Frangieh, a controversial Maronite warlord. Syria, after a coup d'état, was under Hafez al-Assad. There were two Yemens in 1974—Yemen Arab Republic or North Yemen, and People's Democratic Republic of Yemen or South Yemen. South Yemen was a one-party state and while North Yemen was a multi-party democracy on paper, de facto it was a one-party state.

Latin America in 1974 still had two remnants of imperialism, namely Belize (erstwhile British Honduras) as a British colony and Surinam as a Dutch colony. It also had a few 'banana republics', such as Honduras and Haiti. Cuba was a communist country under Fidel Castro. Quite a few countries, e.g., El Salvador and Guatemala, were undergoing civil war. Bolivia, Brazil, Chile, Dominican Republic, Ecuador, Guyana, Mexico, Nicaragua, Panama, Paraguay, Peru and Uruguay were under dictatorships. Sadly, apart from Argentina, Colombia, Costa Rica and Venezuela, there was no other democratic country in Latin America.

In 1974, even in Asia, except for India and Japan, democracies were difficult to find. Hong Kong was a British colony, Macao and Timor Leste belonged to Portugal, and Armenia, Azerbaijan, Georgia, Kazakhstan, Kyrgyzstan, Tajikistan, Turkmenistan and Uzbekistan were parts of the Soviet Union, while Bhutan, Brunei and Nepal were monarchies. China was communist under Mao, and in the throes of the Cultural Revolution. In communist North Korea, the Supreme Leader Kim Il-Sung, while preparing his country for a continued fight against imperialism, was also paving the way for peaceful succession by his son Kim Jong-il and eventually grandson Kim Jong-un. South Korea was continuing with its Miracle on the Han River, but since 1961, under the continued iron rule of Park Chung-hee. Taiwan was a one-party state under Generalissimo

Chiang Kai-shek, and Mongolia a communist state aligned with the Soviet Union and under the leadership of Yumjaagiin Tsedenbal. Burma (now Myanmar) was ruled by Gen Ne Win, who had seized power in 1962 in a coup d'état and declared parliamentary democracy unsuitable for Burma. Thailand was a monarchy in turmoil in 1974, and Chief Justice Sanya Dharmasakti had been appointed Prime Minister not by election, but by royal command. Though US troops had been withdrawn by March 1973, Vietnam, along with Lao and Cambodia, were deeply mired in civil war.

In Indonesia, President Sukarno, the hero of the freedom struggle against the Dutch, considered democracy unsuitable for the country and had replaced western-style democracy with 'guided democracy' in 1957. In 1974, Gen Suharto, after replacing Sukarno in March 1967, was ruling Indonesia. Malaysia, after racial riots in Kuala Lumpur in May 1969, had declared a state of emergency and suspended Parliament. In 1974, Malaysia was a semi-democracy; it followed the democratic procedure of holding regular elections but also checked electoral competitiveness 'through severe malapportionment of districts, hurried campaign periods, bans on open-air opposition rallies, and the government's uninhibited use of media outlets, state facilities, and on-the-spot development grant'.[4] Singapore was a de facto one-party state with regular elections but severe restrictions on freedom of speech and assembly. In the Philippines, Ferdinand Marcos, after having won the presidential election for the second consecutive time in 1969, had declared martial law on 21 September 1972 and extended his rule beyond the constitutional two-term limit by highlighting the threats of Communist and Muslim insurgencies.

In South Asia, Afghanistan, after a coup d'état in 1973, had descended into violent factional fights and civil war. In 1974, Pakistan under Prime Minister Bhutto was still a democracy, but dissensions within his party were growing and the country was moving towards military rule in July 1977; Bhutto died by hanging on 4 April 1979. Recently liberated Bangladesh, with excessive rainfall and devastating floods, was ravaged by a famine and widespread corruption. On 28 December 1974, Prime Minister Mujibur Rahman declared a national state of emergency to deal with widespread lawlessness, corruption and economic chaos. On 25 January 1975, by a Constitutional amendment, Bangladesh came under a presidential form of government. The president was authorized to form one national party and suspend all political groups that refused to join the national party. Sheikh Mujib went on to float the Bangladesh Krishak Sramik Awami League (BaKSAL) or 'Bangladesh Worker-Peasants' Awami League' as a political front comprising Bangladesh Awami League, Communist Party of Bangladesh, National Awami Party (Mozaffar) and Jatiyo League, making it a national party. Already under emergency from 16 March 1971, Sri Lanka was rocked by the communist Janatha Vimukthi Peramuna insurrection revolt during April-June 1971, and the root causes of the civil war—discrimination against the Tamils—that was to ravage it for over a quarter of a century until 2009 were already taking shape in the country. On 4 May 1972, the Tamil United Front, the precursor of Tamil United Liberation Front, had been formed. Velupillai Prabhakaran had formed the militant organization Tamil New Tigers on 22 May 1972. Several explosions during Prime Minister Sirimavo Bandaranaike's visit to Jaffna in 1974 gave an early indication of the civil war and disruption of democracy in Sri Lanka in the years to come. Maldives was under the tight, authoritarian rule of President Ibrahim Nasir.

In 1974, even in the relatively advanced continent of Europe, only less than half of today's states were democracies. In Eastern Europe, Albania, Bulgaria, Czechoslovakia (not yet Czech Republic and Slovakia), Hungary, Poland, Romania and Yugoslavia (not yet Bosnia and Herzegovina, Croatia, Macedonia, Montenegro, Serbia, Slovenia and Kosovo) were communist states. Belarus, Moldova, Russia, Ukraine and the three Baltic states of Estonia, Latvia and Lithuania were parts of the communist Soviet Union.

Western Europe, consisting of Austria, Belgium, Denmark, Finland, France, Germany, Greece, Iceland, Ireland, Italy, Luxemburg, Malta, Monaco, the Netherlands, Portugal, Spain, Sweden and Switzerland, was democratic except for Portugal and Spain. Spain was under the dictatorship of General Francisco Franco until his death on 25 November 1975. In Portugal, the dictator António de Oliveira Salazar, in power since 5 July 1932, had fallen sick and been replaced by Salazar's own party Estado Novos's leader Marcelo Caetanoan on 25 September 1968. Estado Novo's rule came to an end only on 25 April 1974, amid the Carnation Revolution and widespread popular democratic unrest.

Thus, India was an island of democracy in a sea of authoritarian countries, particularly developing ones. Furthermore, democracy appeared to some as a 'western institution'. It is no surprise therefore that quite a few external observers doubted how long democracy would last in India. The build-up to the demise—fortunately, temporary—was already there in the early 1970s.

XVII.2 Prelude to the Nightmare

Chimanbhai Patel, the two-time chief minister (1973–74 and 1990–1994) of Gujarat on the western coast, was a master politician. In his 1990 poll speeches, BJP leader Atal Bihari Vajpayee described him as Duryodhana, the antagonist in the epic Mahabharata, famous for plotting against his adversarial cousins, the Pandavas, in a variety of ways. But this astute Chimanbhai could not have chosen a worse time than mid-July 1973 to topple his own Congress party's Ghanshyam Oza to become chief minister. After the oil price shock, prices rose almost every month in 1973, but the largest increases were in the period May-July, just as Chimanbhai was taking office. Food price inflation was higher than overall inflation. Edible oil prices skyrocketed by almost 50 per cent in 1973. There were allegations of malpractice against Chimanbhai Patel, including that his men had been bought over by oil mill owners.

Withdrawal of subsidized rations led to an increase in the mess bill in student hostels. In December 1973, five months after Chimanbhai became chief minister, there were student protests and vandalism against a 20 per cent rise in the mess bill at Morbi Engineering College. Forty students were suspended, and the college closed for an indefinite period. More student unrest, for example, at L.D. Engineering College, Ahmedabad, and stern government action, including arrests of hundreds of students, followed. What started as student unrest in isolated colleges, with the participation of workers' unions, teachers' unions and opposition parties, soon snowballed into a mass movement against price rise and corruption. They demanded not only Chimanbhai's resignation but the dissolution of the legislative assembly. Different groups merged to form the Nav Nirman Samiti or Constructive Reforms Society and launched a movement. With protests, and curfew for sixty-three days in twenty-three towns, under pressure from Delhi, Chimanbhai resigned on 9 February 1974 and Gujarat was put under President's rule. JP, who had retired from active politics in 1954, was impressed by the political change that the students were achieving in Gujarat.

In Gujarat, students demanded the resignation of members of the legislative assembly and, if they did not resign, threatened Chinese 'cultural revolution style' humiliation of painting their faces black, shaving their head, and parading them on donkeys. Ninety-five members of the 168-strong legislative assembly resigned. On 11 March, veteran leader Morarji Desai started an indefinite fast demanding the dissolution of the state assembly and broke his fast only when the central government dissolved the Gujarat assembly on 15 March 1974.

Just as Nav Nirman was exercising its de facto 'right to recall' and ousting an elected government in Gujarat, on 18 February, the Bihar Chhatra Sangharsh Samiti (BCSS or Bihar Student's Struggle Forum) had been formed to press their demands related to education and food bills. In early April, JP was asked to lead the movement; he agreed. By May 1974, there were demands for the Bihar government's resignation and dissolution of the assembly, but unlike in Gujarat, Indira Gandhi was not prepared to concede to this demand.

Soon, on 5 June, JP was calling for Sampoorna Kranti, or total revolution. He asked students to boycott examinations, people not to pay taxes, set up Janata Sarkar or people's government and Janata Adalat or people's courts in villages, parallel to that of the government, and hold elections for a 'people's assembly' in Bihar. A three-day-long Bihar Bandh from 2 to 4 October was followed by rival Republic Day celebrations in January 1975. JP joined forces with opposition parties to launch Gujarat- and Bihar-style agitations in other states. Leading the struggle against Indira Gandhi's Emergency in the mid-1970s, JP would go on to become the 'Lok Nayak' or people's leader.

In the meantime, there were problems on the industrial front. With high inflation, sluggish growth and allegations of corruption at high places, the time was ripe for industrial unrest. In July 1974, to restrain high inflation, the government had introduced Compulsory Deposit Scheme (Income Tax Act), 1974, impounding all wage increases and half of dearness allowance (paid to compensate for price increases). It proved unpopular. The number of workdays lost owing to all industrial disputes in India touched 40 million in 1974, not only more than double that recorded in any single year during the preceding decade but also the highest for any country in the world. A defining moment of all this unrest was a strike by railwaymen on 8 May 1974.

In the mid-1970s, Indian Railways, owned by the government, employed close to 1.5 million workers and was critical for the supplies of essential items such as food grains, coal and cement all over the country. Railwaymen demanded better pay and better working conditions. Under George Fernandez, the fiery socialist leader and president of the All-India Railwaymen's Federation, they struck work on 8 May 1974. The strike threatened to paralyse the country, was forcefully suppressed by the government, and called off on 27 May 1974. Later, in Indira Gandhi's handling of the railway strike, scholars would read a change in her orientation from socialism to a more pragmatic and business-friendly approach. In the middle of all this, India carried out its first nuclear bomb test on 18 May 1974 at Pokhran in Rajasthan. It created some 'rally round the flag' effect, but not enough to quell the unrest. In November 1974, Indira stated that elections were due in 1976 and polls would decide who was more popular. JP accepted the challenge and launched his protests all over India.

The economy was in bad shape in 1974–75, with growth negligible at 1.2 per cent, inflation at a record high, food shortage and unemployment. There was hardly any good news on the economic front except for the sign of a surge in private transfers in the balance of payments. Such transfers steadily increased from $143 million in 1972–73 to $295 million in 1974–75 and further to $524 million in 1975–76, a trend that would continue for decades, well into the new millennium.

The political situation was complicated further by widespread allegations of corruption at high places. There was the Nagarwala case from four years ago. Just before the liberation of Bangladesh, on 24 May 1971, Ved Prakash Malhotra, the chief cashier of the SBI, had handed over ₹6 million to Rustom Sohrab Nagarwala, whom he did not know. Malhotra had heard the 'voice of Prime Minister Indira Gandhi' instructing him to withdraw ₹6 million and hand it over to a 'Bangladeshi'. Malhotra learnt about the impersonation when he went to collect the receipt at the Prime Minister's residence. Nagarwala was caught on the same day and the money was recovered. The Opposition alleged corruption. While the case was being investigated, the investigating officer, D.K. Kashyap, died in a car accident, and in the same year, Nagarwala died of a heart attack in prison.

The popular assumption was that almost all contracts between government and business involved bribery and corruption. Under a control regime, import licences, which could also be obtained as entitlements against exports or from exporters who already had such licences, were precious and commanded considerable premia. In late 1974, the Pondicherry (now Puducherry) scandal, in which L.N. Mishra, the railway minister, was allegedly involved, caused an uproar in Parliament. It was alleged that in 1971, Mishra, who was then in the ministry of foreign trade, had issued import licences to several firms in Puducherry based on forged letters of recommendation from twenty-one MPs. The licences for the import of liquor, electronic goods and other luxury items were sold by these firms to businesspersons in Mumbai at a huge profit. On 2 January 1975, Mishra died in a suspicious bomb blast at the Samastipur railway station in his home state of Bihar. Rumours about Mishra, the fundraiser for the ruling party, knowing 'too much' and being 'removed' by people in power, which still have not died out, created more problems for the government's reputation.

On 12 January 1946, shortly before Independence, with the post-war inflation raging, the colonial government had demonetized high value notes over ₹100 with the express objective of containing black marketing. It did not meet its declared objective, and the Direct Taxes Enquiry Committee, headed by Justice Wanchoo, in its interim report, observed, 'Demonetization was not successful then, because only a very small proportion of total notes in circulation were demonetized in 1946 . . .' 'Black money' had become a big problem at least in public perception in the early 1970s. Describing black money as a 'cancerous growth in the country's economy', among other things, the Wanchoo Committee had recommended demonetization of high-value currency notes. Y.B. Chavan, the finance minister, after detailed deliberations, accepted demonetization along with some other reforms suggested by the committee. Given the sensitivity of the subject, Chavan went to meet Prime Minister Indira Gandhi and seek her approval. 'When Y.B. Chavan told Indira Gandhi about the proposal for demonetization and his view that it should be accepted and implemented forthwith, she asked Chavan only one question: "Chavanji, are no more elections to be fought by the Congress Party?" Chavan got the message, and the recommendation was shelved.'5

Simultaneously, there were ominous developments in neighbouring Bangladesh. Factionalism within the Awami League had started to affect Sheikh Mujib's political credibility. On 24 February 1975, Mujib had made his new party BaKSAL the only political party in Bangladesh by outlawing other parties. On 6 March 1975, in a rally at the Boat Club grounds in Delhi, JP called upon the armed forces to defend democracy and stand up against authoritarianism. He repeated this advice on several other occasions. This was worrying for the government, especially in view of the revolt by the Provincial Armed Constabulary (PAC) in UP in May 1973 to press their demands for better pay and work conditions, which had to be put down with the help of the army. On 20 March 1975, there was an attempt by two Anand Margis on the life of A.N. Ray, the controversial Chief Justice of the Supreme Court, who JP had called Indira's stooge.

On the international front, Indira Gandhi continued to make solid progress. Kazi Lhendup Dorji, the elected prime minister of Sikkim, had appealed to the Parliament of India for representation and a change of status to statehood, and in a referendum on 14 April 1975, 97.5 per cent voted in favour of accession into India. On 16 May 1975, Sikkim became the twenty-second state of India. But domestic politics continued to remain highly threatening for Indira.

Two important developments took place on the same day of 12 June 1975. First, after its dissolution on 15 March 1974, on 2 April 1975, Morarji had started a second hunger strike demanding immediate election to the Gujarat Vidhan Sabha. 'A week later, the Central government gave into his demand and Indira Gandhi wrote to Desai, indicating that the Centre would like to have the polls in June.'6 JP and Morarji Desai formed the Janata Morcha, or People's Forum, as an alliance of political parties opposed to the Congress and Indira Gandhi. The constituents included the Congress (O), Jana Sangh, SP and the BLD. The Janata Morcha won the Gujarat elections in the first half of June 1975. Congress seats came down from 140 to seventy-five. The Congress (O) with fifty-six seats formed a government with the support of Jana Sangh (eighteen), BLD (two), SP (two) and some independents.

Second, Raj Narain of the SSP, who had lost to Indira Gandhi the Lok Sabha election from Rae Bareli in 1971 by a huge margin of 1,11,810 votes, had filed a case in the Allahabad High Court that Indira, by employing Yashpal Kapoor as her election agent on 7 January 1971, had violated the Representation of the People's Act, 1951, and ought to be disqualified. Kapoor, an officer on special duty (OSD), was in government employment until 13 January 1971. On 12 June 1975, Justice Jagmohanlal Sinha found Indira guilty of misusing government machinery for election campaign, unseated her from Lok Sabha and banned her from contesting elections for six years. Indira Gandhi appealed to the Supreme Court against the Allahabad High Court verdict. The vacation judge, Justice Krishna Iyer, granted an interim stay, allowing her to continue as Prime Minister and speak as Prime Minister in both houses of Parliament, but neither take part in the proceedings nor vote, and not draw any salary. Indira Gandhi continued as Prime Minister. Congress, under the leadership of Sanjay Gandhi, arranged for crowds in support of Indira Gandhi to pour into Delhi between 12 June and 20 June.

On 18 June, the Congress Parliamentary Party passed a resolution affirming Indira Gandhi's indispensability not only to the party but also to the nation. In this meeting, Congress president Dev Kant Barooah, for the first time, made his oft-quoted remark: 'Indira is India and India is Indira'. A rally at the Boat Club grounds in Delhi on 20 June in support of Indira Gandhi was described as the greatest event in history, with one estimate claiming that 1.5 million people were in attendance.

The ball started rolling fast thereafter. On 25 June 1975, in a mammoth rally at Delhi's Ramlila Grounds, JP announced the launch of a satyagraha from 29 June 1975. A Lok Sangharsh Samiti, with Morarji Desai as the chairman and Jana Sangh's Nanaji Deshmukh as convenor, was formed to gherao the Prime Minister at her official residence. While the Ramlila Grounds meeting was on, Indira Gandhi, with her adviser Siddhartha Shankar Ray, went to the Rashtrapati Bhavan and convinced President Fakhruddin Ali Ahmed about the need to declare an internal emergency, even without Cabinet approval. Sanjay Gandhi, the anointed heir, reportedly told his mother that the Emergency was necessary, and Siddhartha Shankar Ray, a lawyer by training, confirmed that the Constitution provided for it.

On 26 June 1975, President Fakhruddin Ali Ahmed, under Article 352(1) of the Constitution on the grounds of 'internal disturbance', declared a state of Emergency and authorized the Prime Minister to rule by decree. Elections were suspended and civil liberties curbed. Clearly, the Indian state had been overwhelmed by Indian society, and was trying to get the balance back. In the sea of dictatorship, until 1974, the stellar exception of India with its democracy was about to disappear at least for a while. Neville Maxwell's prediction of the 1967 general election being the 'last' had been proved wrong, but by the end of June 1975, Maxwell seemed to have missed only the year of his prediction by about eight.

XVII.3 The Emergency

Within a week of declaring Emergency, on 1 July 1975, in a radio broadcast to the nation, Prime Minister Indira Gandhi warned about punitive fines for destruction of state property and gave a call to the nation to 'shake off any sense of helplessness' and 'make a difference to the country's economic outlook'. Simultaneously, she announced measures to help the people and revive the economy. These measures, which came to be known as the famous twenty-point programme, were: (i) measures to check the price rise, (ii) implementation of land ceilings and distribution of land among rural landless, (iii) provision of house sites for the landless in rural areas, (iv) abolition of bonded labour, (v) liquidation of rural indebtedness to non-institutional sources, (vi) review of minimum wage for agricultural labour, (vii) programme of increasing the area under irrigation, (viii) accelerated power development programme, (ix) development of the handloom sector, (x) improvement of the controlled cloth scheme, (xi) laws to impose ceilings on ownership and possession of vacant urban land, (xii) special squads for valuation of urban property and prevention of tax evasion, (xiii) confiscation of smugglers' properties, (xiv) simplification of procedures and liberalization of industrial licensing, and check on the misuse of import licences, (xv) schemes for workers' participation in industries, (xvi) national permit scheme for road transport, (xvii) income tax relief to fixed income groups by raising the minimum exemption relief from ₹6000 to ₹8000, (xviii) provision of essential commodities at controlled prices to students residing in hostels, (xix) provision of books and stationery at controlled prices to all students, and (xx) amendment to the apprenticeship act for the organized sector to take a larger number of apprentices and promote employment opportunities for educated young people. It was a heady mix of populist welfare schemes which were beyond the state's financial and implementation capacity.

Even the reform measures gave mixed signals of both tightening and liberalizing the command-and-control regime, with a tilt towards further tightening. For example, the measures for checking price rise relied heavily on price controls, the Essential Commodities Act and selective credit policy. Promotion of the handloom sector and improvement in the quality of control cloth relied on a more rigorous implementation of SSI reservation and restrictions on the cotton textile industry. On the other hand, in October 1975, in thirty important industries, foreign companies and monopoly houses could extend their capacity beyond the licensed limit provided they sold the additional output according to the government's direction or in export markets. Furthermore, enterprises not covered by MRTP were freed from licensing requirements if their investment did not exceed ₹1 crore in a new unit, and ₹5 crore in expanding a heavy industry. Provision was also made for regularizing unauthorized capacity. However, licensing was reintroduced in twenty-one industries, which had been delicensed in 1973. Similarly, the Urban Land (Ceiling and Regulation) Act, which was implemented in 1976, aimed at using surplus lands in urban areas for the common good. However, as Rajiv Gandhi noted in his budget speech in 1987–88, 'the results achieved have been disappointing. Although 10 years have passed, less than one half of one per cent of the land declared surplus has actually been used for construction.'

On Gandhi Jayanti 1975, the government launched the Integrated Child Development Services (ICDS) to: (i) improve the nutritional and health status of children in the age group to six years, (ii) lay the foundation for the child's proper psychological, physical and social development; (iii) reduce the incidence of children's mortality, morbidity, malnutrition and school dropout; (iv) effectively coordinate policy and implementation of child development programmes across various departments; and (v) enhance the capability of the mother to look after the normal health and needs of the child through proper nutrition and health education. In the years to come, ICDS, after expansion and suitable modification, despite various shortcomings, particularly with regard to quality, would go on to make a considerable difference in child development. Basic ICDS services would include supplementary nutrition (in many places through hot, prepared meals), growth monitoring, nutrition counselling, health education, immunization, healthcare, referral services and pre-school education.

To meet the growing electricity needs in the country, in November 1975, the Union government established the National Thermal Power Corporation (NTPC) and the National Hydroelectric Power Corporation (NHPC). The Fifth Five-Year Plan (1974–78) had identified rural electrification as a basic need of the people and launched the Minimum Needs Programme in 1974 to enhance, among other things, access to electricity in rural areas. Universal access was its guiding philosophy. In 1976, the Conference of Chairmen of SEBs announced that 100 per cent of villages would be electrified by 1995. However, given the difference between connecting a village to electricity supply and providing electricity connection to every household, the goal was less than satisfactory.

Labour market rigidities were an impediment to employment creation in the organized sector. Chapter V-B of the Industrial Disputes Act, 1947 required all industrial units employing more than 100 workmen to seek the government's permission to retrench a worker or close a unit down resulting in such retrenchment. There was an attempt to relax these inflexibilities during the Emergency. An amendment in 1976 raised the employment requirement from 100 or more workers to 300 or more workers for requiring government permission for layoffs, retrenchments and closures. In 1975, the Working Group on Rural Banks headed by M. Narasimham conceptualized the creation of Regional Rural Banks (RRBs) as a new set of regionally oriented rural banks, 'which would combine the local feel and familiarity of rural problems characteristic of cooperatives with the professionalism and large resource base of commercial banks'. RRBs were established under the Regional Rural Banks Act, 1976. The government also tried to emphasize the importance it attached to rural areas by launching the Integrated Rural Development Programme (IRDP) in March 1976 in twenty selected districts. It was a continuation of the Community Development Project that Nehru had introduced in 1952 to bring about a social and economic transformation of village life through the efforts of the people themselves.

Table XVII.1 Foreign Currency Deposits in India

Month and Year		Name of scheme	Repatriability		
Beginning	End		Principal	Interest	Held in
Feb-70	NA	Non-Resident (External) Rupee Account (**NR(E) RA**)	Yes	Yes	Rupees
Nov-75	Aug-94	Foreign Currency Non-Resident Account (**FCNR(A)**)	Yes	Yes	Foreign currency
Aug-90	Mar-91[1]	Foreign Currency Non-Resident Account for NRIs in the Gulf region	Yes	Yes	US dollars
Nov-90	Jul-93	Foreign Currency (Bank & Others) Deposits (**FC(B&O)D**)[2]	No	No	Foreign currency
Jun-91	Aug-94	Foreign Currency Ordinary Non-repatriable (**FCON**)	No	No	US dollars
Oct-91	Nov-91	India Development Bonds for NRIs and Overseas Corporate Bodies	Yes	Yes	Foreign currency
Oct-91	Nov-91	Remittance of Foreign Exchange and investment in Foreign Exchange Bonds (Immunities and Exemptions)[3]			
Jun-92	Apr-02	Non-Resident (Non-Repatriable) Rupee Deposits (**NR(NR)RD**)	No	Yes	Rupees
May-93	NA	Foreign Currency Non-Resident (Banks) (**FCNR(B)**)	Yes	Yes	Foreign currency
Aug-98	Sep-98	Resurgent India Bonds (**RIB**) for NRIs and Overseas Corporate Bodies	Yes	Yes	Foreign currency
May-00	NA	Non-Resident Ordinary (**NRO**) Rupee Accounts	Up to $1 million a year	Yes	Rupees

| Oct-00 | Nov-00 | India Millennium Deposits (**IMD**) | | | Foreign currency |
| Jan-16 | NA | Special Non-Resident Rupee Account (**SNRR**) | | | Rupees |

[1] Economic Survey 1990-91. p. 167. https://www.indiabudget.gov.in/budget_archive/es1990-91/9%20The%20External%20Sector.pdf Circular No. 590, dated 30-01-1991 - Income Tax Department
[2] Other corporate bodies owned by NRIs.
[3] Anil Nauriya. 'Foreign Exchange Flux: A King's Ransom.' *Economic and Political Weekly*, vol. 26, no. 44, Economic and Political Weekly, 1991, pp. 2501–05.

To attract foreign funds from abroad, from 1 November 1975, the government also introduced the FCNR(A)—Foreign Currency Non-Resident (Account)—for non-resident Indians (NRIs) and aliens of Indian origin (Table XVII.1). FCNR(A) ensured convertibility and provided protection from exchange rate risk by permitting the holders to maintain the deposits in specified foreign currencies such as the US dollar and claim interest and repayments in the same currencies. With the RBI taking on the exchange rate risk, arguably FCNR(A) was quasi-fiscal debt.

The incentives offered to banks for mobilizing non-resident deposits included, apart from lower CRR and SLR requirements for such deposits, such deposits not being subject to interest rate regulations and lending out of such deposits not being considered as part of net bank credit for the purpose of priority sector lending. For such FC deposits, there was a 2 per cent premium over and above the rates applicable on domestic deposits of comparable maturities. While the FCNR(A) would be discontinued from August 1994, special deposits for NRIs would proliferate for more than two decades.

In mid-December 1974, to prevent smuggling of foreign goods, particularly gold, and stop outflow of precious foreign exchange, the government had brought into force the Conservation of Foreign Exchange and Prevention of Smuggling Activities Act (COFEPOSA). In January 1976, another legislation passed by Parliament was the Smugglers and Foreign Exchange Manipulators (Forfeiture of Property) Act. The Emergency, during its initial days, saw attempts at curbing economic offences. However, in a court of law, proving the offences within the permitted period proved to be a challenge. Also, confiscation of the smugglers' properties turned out to be difficult with many of them *benami* (transferred to one person for consideration paid by another person, in this case, the smuggler) or unaccounted for in terms of title.

With the Emergency came the Taxation Amendment Act of 1975, giving more powers to the Income Tax authorities to conduct income tax raids and seizures. It was believed that with the people psychologically terrified by income tax raids and searches, given an opportunity, those who had concealed their income for tax purposes would like to come clean. Thus, by an Ordinance on 8 October 1975, the government announced a scheme effective from that very date till December 1975. So, after the Tyagi scheme in 1951 and TTK's scheme in 1965, this was the third tax amnesty scheme in less than three decades of Independence! The additional revenue mobilized was again disappointing.

In 1976, after a decade of its working, the ownership of the IDBI was transferred to the Government of India to enable the RBI to concentrate on its central banking function. Under the Coal Mines (Nationalization) Act, 1973 coal mining was exclusively reserved for the public sector. By an amendment to the Act in 1976, two exceptions introduced to this policy were (i) captive mining by private companies engaged in production of iron and steel, and (ii) sub-lease for coal mining to private parties in isolated small pockets not amenable to economic development and not requiring rail transport. The Urban Land (Ceiling and Regulation) Act, 1976 came in February 1976 to provide for the imposition of a ceiling on vacant land in urban agglomerations, for the acquisition of such land in excess of the ceiling limit, and to regulate the construction of buildings on such land.

The Emergency provided the government the freedom from political compulsions to undo some of the excesses of the past in income taxation. C. Subramaniam, one of the chief architects of the Green Revolution in the mid-1960s, succeeded Y.B. Chavan as the finance minister in October 1974. After bringing down the personal income tax rate (with surcharge) for the highest income slab from 97.75 per cent to 77 per cent in the Budget for 1974–75, in the Budget for 1976–77, the wealth tax rates too were reduced (minimum rate from 1 per cent to 0.5 per cent and the maximum rate from 8 per cent to 2.5 percent). In the interim budget for 1977–78, before the elections, he would go on to reduce the highest marginal rate with a surcharge of 66 per cent and make it applicable to income above ₹1 lakh.

While Subramaniam left the customs duties almost unchanged, with improvement in the foreign exchange front, the import policy for 1976–77 eased the QRs on imports to some extent by placing many capital goods, spare parts and raw materials on the OGL list, and liberalized the free licensing system. The Import Replenishment Scheme from 1966 was also liberalized and expanded to a considerable extent, with new items allowed to be imported under the scheme and an increase in import entitlements.

Like his predecessors and successors, Subramaniam continued the policy of expanding the coverage of specific commodities under excise duties and adjusting rates upwards and downwards. One of his major contributions in 1975–76 was the introduction of a new item, Tariff Item 68, in the Central Excise Tariff Schedule to cover all goods produced for sale or other commercial purposes not elsewhere specified in the Schedule with a few exceptions and subjecting them to a 1 per cent ad valorem duty. It covered the production of all units under the Factories Act, 1948, except those which employed not more than forty-nine workers while using electric power, and not more than ninety-nine workers in the case of non-power operated factories. There was no change in customs duties in 1975–76. One retrograde step in 1975–76 was the increase in the rate of CST, which had been 3 per cent since 1966, to 4 per cent from July 1975.

An extra cess introduced during the Emergency was the Beedi Workers Welfare Cess Act, 1976. 'Bidis' or 'beedis' are about 0.2 g of sun-dried and processed tobacco flakes, rolled in a tendu leaf (diospyros melanoxylon) or *temburni* leaf and held together by a cotton thread. Associated with the beedi industry were also the people, mainly tribal, who collected the tendu or other leaves for rolling the beedis. The estimated number of people employed in the beedi industry was 6.4 million in 2013. The Beedi Workers Welfare Cess Act, 1976 provided for the levy as a duty of excise by way of a cess at ₹0.25 per kg of tobacco, issued from a warehouse for any purpose in connection with the manufacture of beedi. The Beedi Workers Welfare Fund was constituted out of the cess.

There is some evidence that tax compliance improved during the Emergency, perhaps partly due to the fear of detection and punitive action. As a proportion of GDP at current market prices, total tax revenue of the general government increased from 11.42 per cent in 1974–75 to 12.90 per cent in 1975–76 and further to 13.20 per cent in 1976–77. In July 1976, the government set up the Indirect Taxation Enquiry Committee headed by L.K. Jha and with distinguished members such as the economist Raja Chelliah. It had a broad mandate, including levels of indirect taxes such as customs and excise, and feasibility of introducing VAT. The report, however, came in 1978, well after Indira Gandhi demitted office.

With inflation coming down, while the SLR was left unchanged, in 1974, the CRR was brought down in three steps from 7 per cent on 30 June to 4 per cent on 28 December. As interest rates charged by banks had become extremely high, with particularly adverse impact on small borrowers, on 15 March 1976, the RBI prescribed, in addition to the minimum lending rates, the maximum rates for bank loans. The banks, for the first time, were also advised to charge interest at quarterly rests. The rate of growth of reserve money was revived from 7.1 per cent in 1975–76 to 14.9 per cent in 1976–77 and further to 18.9 per cent in 1977–78. The corresponding increase in the growth of broad money (M2) was from 12.5 per cent in 1975–76 to 19.9 per cent in each of the two subsequent years. Despite the revival of monetary growth, inflation remained subdued, partly because of a benign world oil market with stable oil prices.

The economy did relatively well during the emergency. Growth was 8.50 per cent in 1975–76, partly a bounce-back after the sluggish performance of the economy for four years in a row since 1970–71 and the result of 'exceptionally good weather'. Index of agricultural production at constant 1960–61 prices, which had declined by 3.5 per cent in the previous year, jumped up by 15.6 per cent in 1975–76. With bumper agricultural output, WPI inflation was down from 25.2 per cent in the previous year to a negative 1.1 per cent, that is, deflation, in 1975–76! But fortunes turned adverse in 1976–77. With unfavourable rainfall, agricultural output declined by 6.7 per cent and although growth of industrial output accelerated from 6.1 per cent in 1975–76 to 10.4 per cent, overall economic growth was a paltry 1.6 per cent. WPI inflation remained low at 2.1 per cent even in 1976–77. And, with the end of the oil price shock and growth in private transfers, the external balance of payments was secure with an overall surplus of $707 million and $1905 million in 1975–76 and 1976–77, respectively. However, with signs of a resurgence in inflation, the 3-percentage point decline in CRR in 1973 was largely reversed in two steps of 1 percentage point each on 4 September and 13 November 1976.

The Prime Minister's son, and 'successor' according to many, Sanjay Gandhi, at a meeting of the Delhi Pradesh Congress Committee in March 1976, initially spelled out a four-point programme 'in which Congressmen could play a vital role'[7]. 'A fifth point—the abolition of the dowry—was subsequently added. Sanjay Gandhi particularly emphasized the importance of the program for the Youth Congress workers. Variously worded, the Five-Point Program appeared on calendars, posters, and leaflets. (1) Each one teach one. (2) Plant a tree. (3) Eliminate dowry. (4) Plan your family. (5) Remove caste.' Progress on the twenty-plus-five points of Indira and Sanjay Gandhi's programmes was slow and not spectacular. What created turmoil was the implementation of policies on family planning, especially with the suspension of the right to freedom of citizens under Article 19 of the Constitution from January 1976, and removal of slums, particularly near Delhi's Turkman Gate.

XVII.4 Sterilization and Slum Removal

India was a pioneer among developing countries in launching a programme for population control in 1951. Yet, the rate of growth of population had accelerated from 1.96 per cent during 1951–1961 to 2.20 per cent during 1961-1971. This was primarily because while the death rate had declined from 22.8 (per thousand) to 19 during the reference period, the birth rate had remained practically unchanged from 41.7 to 41.2. Following Sanjay Gandhi's proclamation of the Five-Point Programme, there was added emphasis on 'family planning'. The National Population Policy, issued on 16 April 1976 by Dr Karan Singh, the minister of health and family planning, stated: 'Indisputably we are facing a population explosion of crisis dimensions which has largely diluted the fruits of the remarkable economic progress that we have made over the last two decades. If the future of the nation is to be secured, and the goal of removing poverty to be attained, the population problem will have to be treated as a top national priority and commitment.'[8]

In Sanjay's Five Point Programme, what got emphasized was a sterilization programme. Before launching the programme nationwide, it was piloted in Delhi. 'Voluntary' on paper, the sterilization process was turned into a threatening one, with 'quotas' allocated to government servants, including teachers and doctors. Failure to fulfil the quota meant ineligibility for promotion. Desperation to fulfil the quotas led to draconian measures, such as forced sterilization, and then protests, riots and police firings. The number of sterilizations almost doubled from 1354 thousand in 1974–75 to 2669 thousand in 1975–76. *Nasbandi* in Hindi (or vasectomy) became a dreaded word during the Emergency, and Emergency itself was succinctly described by Morarji Desai as the period when democracy was vasectomized. Mostly the poor, the minorities and the Dalits were at the receiving end of this compulsory sterilization policy. According to some Muslims, family planning was haram (proscribed) in Islam. Stories of brutalities associated with forced sterilization would contribute to the defeat of the Congress in the 1977 elections. Furthermore, with sterilization getting a bad name, there would be a sharp drop in sterilization once normalcy was restored.

The Emergency also became notorious for the forcible and brutal eviction of slum dwellers in Delhi's Turkman Gate area. Slums had been an almost perpetual problem in Delhi, particularly in the twentieth century. From 1912 onwards, the construction of New Delhi as the capital of British India had seen a large expansion of the population of old Delhi or Shahjahanabad, leading to even more congestion in an already crowded city. The Delhi Development Authority (DDA) was set up in 1957, and a Master Plan for Delhi introduced in 1962. It contained a land management plan designating areas for conservation, rehabilitation and clearance on the basis of the proportion of households with monthly income less than ₹100, living in temporary structures, average number of persons living in a room, and availability of water supply, latrines, electricity and kitchen.

During the Emergency, demolitions were carried out in the Jama Masjid, Turkman Gate and Karol Bagh areas of Delhi for slum clearance. What became most notorious and attracted the most attention was Turkman Gate. Apart from Sanjay Gandhi, who had become the de facto authority during the Emergency, the other main persons involved in the Turkman Gate affair were DDA Vice Chairman Jagmohan, Delhi Lt Governor Krishan Chand and his private secretary Navin Chawla, DIG Police P.S. Bhinder, and socialite Rukhsana Sultana. In Turkman Gate, the slum clearance and resettlement drive, which was expected to make an unhindered view of Jama Masjid from Connaught Place a reality, began on 18 April 1976. The area was packed with police and by 10.30 a.m., more than fifteen bulldozers ringed the area. Following pitched battles between the residents and the police and demolition squads, and police firing, a month-long curfew followed. Within a mere twenty-one months, an estimated 70,000 people were displaced from slums and commercial properties in old Delhi. The Turkman Gate demolition and firing became the symbolic and infamous case of political oppression and police brutality during the Emergency. Jagmohan got the Padma Bhushan award in 1977.

XVII.5 End of the Nightmare

In normal course, the life of the Fifth Lok Sabha was to end in March 1976. On 16 February 1976, under the Emergency, the House of The People (Extension of Duration) Act, 1976 extended its life by one year. On 2 November 1976, a few months before the Lok Sabha's life was to end, the Forty-Second Constitution Amendment Bill was passed, making India a socialist, secular, republic and laying down the fundamental duties of citizens. By amending Article 83 of the Constitution, it also changed the life of the Lok Sabha from five to six years. Together with the House of The People (Extension of Duration) Act, 1976, it effectively extended the term of the Fifth Lok Sabha from March 1976 to March 1978.

At 8 p.m. on the night of 18 January 1977, a little over two months after extending the life of the Fifth Lok Sabha until March 1978, Indira Gandhi, in a broadcast over All India Radio, announced that the Lok Sabha had been dissolved and fresh elections would be held in March. After the President dissolved the Fifth Lok Sabha on 18 January, before its expiry date, to everybody's surprise, on 23 January 1977, she called for elections on 16-19 March 1977. Emergency regulations were relaxed, all political prisoners were released and the process of restoration of parliamentary democracy began.

Fali Nariman, the noted lawyer, has described it as 'the unsolved problem of our times: Why did Indira Gandhi call off the Emergency and decide to hold elections in March 1977?'[9] Some argue that it was her commitment to democracy and the Constitution. Others suggest that it was her omnipotent son Sanjay's plot of quickly shifting India from a parliamentary system to a presidential system, perhaps with Indira as President for Life, that got her worried. Without informing or consulting Sanjay Gandhi, she decided to call for elections. Did she worry about destroying the Indian democratic dream that her father Pandit Nehru assiduously tried to nurture throughout his life? Did she believe that she would win an election and become legitimate? Or did she realize that India could not be held together without democracy? No one can vouch for the answer.

The Opposition parties were taken by surprise and sought JP's support to fight the Congress. JP insisted on a united opposition as the price of his support. On 23 January 1977, BLD, Congress (O), the Jana Sangh and the Socialist Party managed to get united under the Janata Party umbrella, a repeat of the pre-emergency Janata Morcha experiment in Gujarat. The major issue of the 1977 election was more political than economic, namely, how to reverse the authoritarian usurpation of democratic power. All the alliance partners, despite their diverse and conflicting ideologies, considered the restoration of the pre-emergency Constitutional regime to be the paramount mandate. A formal merger would take time, so they decided to postpone it until the elections were over and agreed to fight under the BLD symbol of a farmer carrying a plough on his shoulder. A week later, the CPI (M) announced that, to avoid a splintering in the opposition vote, they would not run candidates against the Janata party.

On 2 February, Jagjivan Ram, the towering leader of the SCs, resigned from both the Cabinet and the Congress and formed Congress for Democracy (CFD). Jagjivan Ram's CFD was not willing to merge but was committed to contesting the election in alliance with the Janata Party. It would contest the election with the same manifesto as the Janata Party and would join it in Parliament but would otherwise retain a separate identity.

The Janata Party's manifesto was released on 10 February 1977. It emphasized how the choice before the electorate was '. . . a choice between freedom and slavery; between democracy and dictatorship; between abdicating the power of the people or asserting it; between the Gandhian path and the way that has led many nations down the precipice of dictatorship, instability, military adventure; and national ruin . . .'

Election results started coming in on 20 March. Within hours, it was clear that Congress has been practically wiped out in the northern parts of the country, or what is called the Hindi belt. Congress's tally in the Sixth Lok Sabha came down to 154 out of 542, less than half of 352 (out of 518) in the previous Lok Sabha. There was a serious dent in the Congress's popularity. Its vote share came down by over 9 percentage points from 43.7 per cent to 34.5 per cent, and with the opposition united, its previous advantage as the single largest party fighting a multi-cornered contest also disappeared. Vote-to-seat conversion depends on how united the opposition is. With the opposition united as one party, more than 50 per cent votes are required to win a seat. If the opposition is split into three parties getting 25 per cent, 23 per cent and 22 per cent of votes, you can win the seat by getting 26 per cent or more. The more splintered the opposition, the less votes are required to win a seat. The Janata experiment of a pre-poll alliance of non-Congress parties reaped rich electoral dividends and resulted in victories in 330 of the 542 seats. The Lok Sabha election in 1977 saw the largest shift, not only in voters' choice vis-à-vis the Congress, but also a major change in the vote-to-seat conversion. The vote share of the Congress came down by 9.2 percentage points to 34.5 per cent. The number of seats won for every 1 per cent of votes came down from 8.1 in 1971 to 4.5 in 1977.

In UP, the Congress failed to win even a single out of the eighty-five Lok Sabha seats. Indira herself lost from the Lok Sabha constituency of Raebareli, a traditional Congress stronghold in UP. She had won the constituency in 1967 and 1971, and her husband Feroze Gandhi had won it in 1952 and 1957. In 1977, the winner was Raj Narain, the colourful Janata leader.

The Congress managed to secure seats mostly in the southern states of Andhra Pradesh, Karnataka, Kerala and Tamil Nadu. The results demonstrated the diversity that is India by the success of the Congress in garnering more than 50 per cent of the votes and winning forty-one out of forty-two Lok Sabha seats in Andhra Pradesh, ten out of fourteen Lok Sabha seats in Assam, and twenty-six out of twenty-eight Lok Sabha seats in Karnataka. Apart from these three, the Congress also managed to get more than 40 per cent of the votes in Arunachal Pradesh, Gujarat, Maharashtra, Manipur and Nagaland. The excesses of Emergency, like forcible sterilization, had not affected the states outside the Hindi belt. Thus, among the southern states, even in Kerala and Tamil Nadu, Congress performed well in the 1977 Lok Sabha elections.

Indira Gandhi declared an end to the Emergency on 21 March 1977 and resigned from the Prime Ministership the following day. The selection of the leader of the Janata Parliamentary Party, and hence prime minister, proved to be highly divisive. There was a keen contest among Morarji Desai, Charan Singh and Jagjivan Ram. A potentially divisive contest was avoided by asking JP and Acharya Kripalani to select the party's leader. They chose Morarji Desai, and a Janata government headed by Morarji Desai assumed office from 24 March 1977. The merger of the different parties was completed on 1 May 1977, a day after the National Conventions of BLD, Congress (O), the Jana Sangh and the Socialist Party. The CFD merged with the Janata on 5 May 1977. Chandra Shekhar became the first president of the Janata Party, Ramakrishna Hegde from Karnataka its general secretary, and Jana Sangh's Lal Krishna Advani the spokesperson. In the absence of Indira, Y.B. Chavan of the Congress became the leader of the Opposition.

Although the Janata government came to power with a resounding victory in the 1977 Lok Sabha polls, the Congress was still far from a spent force because of its strength in the Rajya Sabha and its continued electoral dominance in several states, particularly in the south. Simultaneously with the Lok Sabha polls, Vidhan Sabha polls were held only in Kerala. In Kerala, Congress did well both in the Lok Sabha and Vidhan Sabha polls, and along with its alliance partners, formed the government. Elections to the Lok Sabha and Vidhan Sabhas in most states had fallen out of step with each other with dismissals of non-Congress governments at the state level over the years by Congress governments at the Centre, as well as the ending of the term of the Fourth Lok Sabha a year in advance of the scheduled March 1972 and calling for the first mid-term Lok Sabha election in Indian history in 1971.

At a practical level, the continued strength of the Congress created three problems for the Janata government at the Centre. First, the many states under Congress rule could jeopardize the pursuit of cooperative federalism, for example, by giving indiscriminate tax concessions and reliefs, and higher dearness allowance to its state government employees. Second, the Presidential election was due in August 1977, and the Electoral College for this purpose included the elected members of state assemblies. Third, in the bicameral Indian Parliament, the Rajya Sabha or Council of the States had the power to upturn legislations approved by the lower house or Lok Sabha, or at least create major difficulties in their passing.

In the past, even with simultaneous Lok Sabha and Vidhan Sabha elections in a state, there were occasions when Congress won at the all-India level to form the Union government, but a non-Congress party won the Vidhan Sabha polls and formed the government in the state. But, generally, in the past, the Congress would do badly in the state both in the Lok Sabha and Vidhan Sabha elections. Because of the asynchronous elections, in 1977, what arose is an anomalous situation, with Congress having won in the Vidhan Sabha election a few years before 1977 and ruling at the state level but losing badly in the Lok Sabha seats in the state in 1977. This was particularly true of the states in northern India. In states where the Congress was 'totally rejected' in the 1977 Lok Sabha polls, while constitutionally there was nothing wrong in the continuation of its rule in these states, questions could be raised about the moral legitimacy of their continuation. JP raised this moral question after the 1977 election: were such Congress governments truly representative of the changed popular will and should they resign? The Congress chief ministers did not oblige and in the last two days of April, the Janata government dismissed a total of eight Congress governments in Bihar, Haryana, Himachal Pradesh, Madhya Pradesh, Odisha, Punjab, Rajasthan and UP. General elections to the Vidhan Sabhas in these eight states, together with the three states of Jammu and Kashmir, Tamil Nadu and West Bengal, and the three UTs of Delhi (Metropolitan Council), Goa and Puducherry, where such elections were due in 1977, were scheduled for June.

Sheikh Abdullah, the chief minister of Jammu and Kashmir, had supported the Forty-Second Amendment to the Constitution during the Emergency. The state, because of its special status under Article 370, had not been affected by the Emergency. It had been nearly five years since the previous Vidhan Sabha was constituted in Jammu and Kashmir in 1972, and Vidhan Sabha elections were called. The 1977 Vidhan Sabha elections in Jammu and Kashmir, held in June, by some accounts were the freest and fairest since 1951. The Jammu and Kashmir National Conference won forty-seven of the seventy-six seats, with Janata Party at thirteen and Congress a poor third at eleven. Sheikh Abdullah became the chief minister again on 9 July 1977. He promulgated the Public Safety

Ordinance in October 1977, which was like the MISA that Indira Gandhi had introduced on 2 July 1971. A few months later, it was replaced by the Public Safety Act of 1978. It provided for administrative detention without trial for a maximum of two years for acting against the security of the state and a maximum of one year for acting in any manner prejudicial to the maintenance of public order. The Janata government in Delhi was outraged, and the outrage only increased when the act was selectively used against supporters of the Janata Party.

The nightmare of the Emergency was over. Peaceful elections to the Sixth Lok Sabha with a turnout of 60.5 per cent—higher than the turnout of 1971 by almost 5 percentage points—proved the rumours and fears about the imminent demise of Indian democracy to be downright wrong. The heightened conflict between the state and society had been resolved, and the balance restored not by a revolution but a peaceful election. The Congress and Indira Gandhi that brought in the 'dictatorship' got punished at the polls, but the punishment was temporary. The united opposition could win the election but lacked the cohesion to stick together and provide an effective government. India was still not ready to do without the Congress for long.

XVIII

The Second Oil Shock and the Demise of the Janata Government

Between 1967 and the mid-1970s, alliances of non-Congress parties had formed governments in many states. But these were post-poll alliances which did not yield the high electoral dividends that pre-poll alliances could. At the all-India level, the Janata Party in 1977 was a unique experiment of a pre-poll alliance and reaped handsome electoral dividends. But it was an uneasy marriage of convenience. With the only common agenda of getting rid of Indira Gandhi amid the vestiges of the Emergency, it proved to be highly unstable. Soon, contradictions among the alliance partners came to the fore and serious doubts developed about how long it would last. The economic developments in 1977–78 were satisfactory, but the subsequent slowdown and the second oil price shock added to its woes and soon brought the curtains down on the Janata government.

XVIII.1 The Janata Rule

The purely political nature of the Janata Party formation showed up in its economic and social policies, which were not only delayed but also even more socialist, command and control-oriented and populist than what they were under Indira. There were taxes on the rich, greater protection for SSI, limitations on industries where foreign direct investment (FDI) was allowed (but with greater freedom of operations wherever they were allowed), attempts to disburse industries for balanced regional development and subsidies for agriculture. The Food for Work Programme (FWP) for providing direct employment to the unemployed in rural areas, which had been drawn up during 1976–77 under Indira Gandhi, was launched by the Morarji government on 1 April 1977. It would be restructured and relaunched as National Rural Employment Programme (NREP) by Indira again on 2 October 1980. The Janata Party's announcement of eradicating unemployment in ten years had the same bravado as Indira Gandhi's 'Garibi Hatao.'

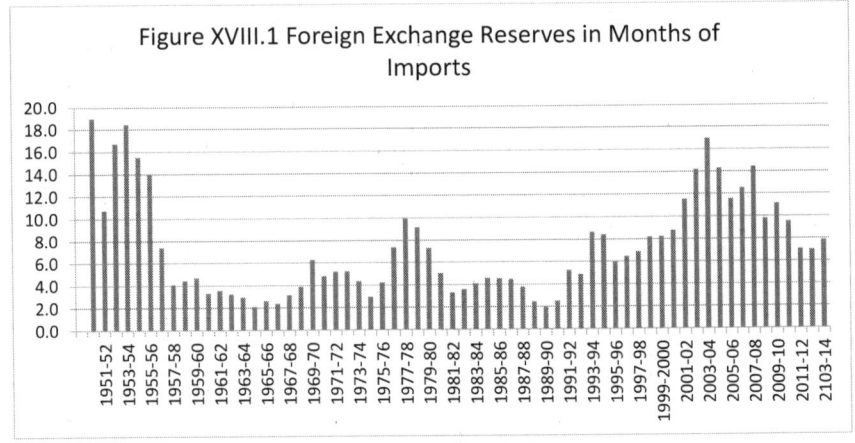

GDP at current market prices refer to 2004-05 series until 2003-04 and 2011-12 series thereafter.
Source: RBI's Handbook of Statistics on the Indian Economy.

The economy performed well, though, in the first year of the Janata government. Growth of GDP jumped from 1.2 per cent in 1976–77 to 7.5 per cent in 1977–78 (Figure I.1). Annual average WPI inflation crept up from 2.1 to 5.2 per cent in 1977–78 but was still not too high. With buoyant private transfers, the striking development was on the balance of payments and foreign exchange reserves fronts (Figure XVIII.1). Foreign exchange reserves by end-March 1978 crossed US$5.8 billion, equivalent to 9.9 months of import cover, a level not seen since 1955–56. Policymakers, with some euphoria, started to worry about what to do with the reserves. Import Policy for 1978–79 established OGL on a more comprehensive scale by introducing a negative list. Conceptually, the items in the OGL list were either not made in the country or were not likely to be made for the subsequent three years.

Phase II of Operation Flood, announced in Budget 1977–78 and implemented during 1979–85, would go on to cover some 136 milksheds linked to over 290 urban markets. By 1985, a self-sustaining system of 43,000 village cooperatives would cover 4.25 million milk producers and production of milk powder would go up from 22,000 tonnes to 1,40,000 tonnes in 1989.

Health sector

Immunization, a critical ingredient of preventive healthcare, was introduced as 'Extended Programme for Immunization' in 1978. Following the Hathi Committee's recommendations in 1975, the government declared a Drug Policy in 1978 and the Drug Price Control Order (DPCO) in 1979. DPCO 1979 brought 347 drugs under price control. Drugs were divided into four categories depending on the nature of their essentiality. DPCO allowed maximum profit margin on the least essential ones (Categories I and II), with the expectation that such high-profit margins would compensate for low margins on life-saving and essential formulations. But pharma companies stopped producing life-saving and essential drugs.

Rolling plans

The Fifth Five-Year Plan, launched in 1974–75, was coming to an end in 1978–79. The Janata government terminated the Fifth Plan at end-March 1978, a year ahead of schedule. Rumours of the Planning Commission being wound up, with its functions transferred to the ministry of finance, proved false. Only the Planning Commission was reconstituted, and a rolling plan to substitute the plan for a fixed period of five years proposed. Under rolling plans, every year, planning would be done for a rolling or sliding five-year horizon by considering the most recent developments. The plan horizon would continue to be five years, but the 'shift' in priorities, strategies and allocation would take place every year. One of the decisions of the Janata government was to appoint the committee on Panchayati Raj under Asoka Mehta in December 1977. This committee's report in August 1978 would play a major role in the attempts to strengthen the Panchayati Raj in the country in the years ahead.

The increase in human and livestock population, depletion of vegetative cover, increase in soil erosion and fall in groundwater table had led to great stress on the natural resources of drought-prone and desert areas. On the recommendations of the National Commission on Agriculture, the Desert Development Programme (DDP) was started in 1977–78.

Taxation

H.M. Patel, a distinguished former civil servant and Finance Secretary, became the finance minister on 24 March 1977 and continued in this post for the first twenty-two months of the Janata rule. In 1977–78, in the interim budget, the highest marginal personal income tax rate after surcharge had been brought down to 66 per cent; in the regular budget, it went up to 69 per cent with an increase in the rate of surcharge from 10 per cent to 15 per cent. The exemption limit, slabs and basic rates remained almost the same throughout the Janata rule; only the rate of surcharge was higher by these extra 5 percentage points. Patel left the surcharge for income tax of companies unchanged at 5 per cent. In the 1977–78 Budget, the graduated wealth tax rates for slabs between ₹2.5 and ₹15 lakh of net wealth were increased by a uniform half a per cent, and for the highest slab over ₹15 lakh, by 1 percentage point to 3.5 per cent. In 1978–79, the exemption for estate duty was raised from ₹50,000 to ₹1 lakh.

Under item 68 (the not elsewhere specified category) of central excise tariff, H.M. Patel raised the ad valorem duty from 1 per cent to 2 per cent in 1977–78 and further to 5 per cent in 1978–79. In 1978–79, on coal, he imposed a levy of ₹5 to ₹10 per ton to meet the expenses on fresh investment in the coal sector after its nationalization. There were three other important changes in indirect taxation during Patel's tenure. First, as per Section 37 of the Finance Act, 1978, a special excise duty of 5 per cent was imposed under the Central Excise Act, 1944. Second, an auxiliary duty of customs was levied in an amount equal to 20 per cent of the value of the goods. Third, halfway through the year, with effect from 4 October 1978, there was a levy of an additional duty equivalent to 10 per cent of the excise duty on textiles under the Additional Duties of Excise (Textiles and Textile Articles) Act, 1978 to finance the controlled cloth scheme.

Succeeding H.M. Patel, Charan Singh became the finance minister on 24 January 1979. On 30 March 1979, the RBI appointed a committee to suggest improvements in the existing arrangements for institutional credit for agriculture and rural development. The committee noted that problems of agricultural credit had not only grown in complexity and size but had also merged with the larger tasks of rural development. It recommended the setting up of a new apex bank—the National Bank for Agriculture and Rural Development (NABARD). NABARD, however, could be set up only in 1982, well after the tenure of the Janata government.

In his Budget for 1979–80, Charan Singh, while keeping the income tax rates unchanged, raised the surcharge on income tax for companies from 5 per cent to 7.5 per cent. The wealth tax, which had been slashed from 8 per cent to 2.5 per cent during the Emergency, was enhanced to 5 per cent. The farmers' leader, in his explicitly pro-agriculture budget, slashed excise duties on all chemical fertilizers and on light diesel oil used for energizing pump-sets by about a half. This was compensated to some extent by increased duties on luxury items such as air-conditioners and not-so-luxury items like soaps and toothpaste. Charan Singh also increased the rate of duty on the residuary heading Item 68 of the Central Excise Tariff from 5 per cent to 8 per cent ad valorem. One of the casualties of Charan Singh's solo budget was the Beedi Workers' Welfare Fund, financed from the levy as a duty of excise on unmanufactured tobacco by way of a cess. The Budget for 1979–80 exempted unmanufactured tobacco from the levy of central excise duty, including additional excise duties. As a result, the cess for the Beedi Workers Welfare Fund could no longer be collected from 1 March 1979. To restore funding, the Beedi Workers' Welfare Act 1976 was amended in 1981 to levy a cess on manufactured beedis.

The Union government's tax revenues as a proportion of GDP declined from 8.85 per cent in the last year of the emergency to 8.37 per cent in 1977–78, the first year of Janata rule, but climbed back to 9.18 per cent in 1978–79 and 9.52 per cent in 1979–80. It declined thereafter to 8.81 per cent in 1980–81 before stabilizing around 9 per cent in the next three years. So, the gains in compliance during the Emergency, if any, might have been short-lived at best. The corresponding change in the combined tax revenues of the Union and the state governments as a proportion of GDP was from 13.2 per cent in 1976–77 down to 12.51

per cent in 1977–78, and then back up to 13.54 per cent in 1978–79 and further to 14.06 per cent in 1979–80. Prima facie, the buoyancy of combined tax revenues of the Union and the states during the Janata rule casts doubts about the tangible gains achieved in the field of tax compliance during the Emergency.

States' sales tax revenues, as a proportion of GDP, after declining from 2.43 per cent in 1976–77 to 2.28 per cent in 1977–78, rose to 2.42 per cent in 1978–79 and further to 2.55 per cent in 1979–80. Gujarat and Tamil Nadu continued with their policy of total prohibition; the UT of Lakshadweep introduced it in 1979. State excise revenue fluctuated between 0.51 and 0.56 per cent of GDP.

The Indirect Taxation Enquiry Committee headed by L.K. Jha appointed during the Indira regime in 1976 had submitted its report in 1978. Finance Minister Patel in his 1978–79 Budget speech referred to the desirability of introducing VAT to avoid the cascading effect of taxes on raw materials and components of finished products recommended by the Jha committee. 'I have had a series of discussions with the Chief Ministers and Finance Ministers of the States to achieve this desirable objective. The total revenue from sales tax is of the order of Rs. 2500 crores and it is growing steadily. It constitutes the main source of revenue of the States. The Chief Ministers of the States have generally showed a lack of enthusiasm for the abolition of the sales tax. In view of the attitude of the States and since sales tax is a State subject, the task of persuading the States to give up sales tax calls for persistence and patience. It certainly cannot be regarded as something which can be accomplished in the immediate future,' he added. Next year, his successor Charan Singh pointed out how extending proforma credit facilities in respect of input duty paid in the manufacture of finished products would have major revenue implications, apart from being an additional administrative burden. India had to wait for another decade and a half for CENVAT.

Subsidies

Under Indira Gandhi's government, the MRP of urea had been reduced from ₹2000 per ton to ₹1850 from 18 July 1975, ₹1750 from 16 March 1976, and further to ₹1650 from 8 February 1977. Not to be outdone by her in popularity with farmers, the Janata government reduced the MRP of urea from ₹1650 per ton to ₹1550 per ton from 12 October 1977. Furthermore, to 'benefit the farmers', the procurement prices of wheat and paddy were increased by ₹2.50 per ton in 1977–78 and by ₹3 in 1978–79 over the CACP recommended prices, without increasing the issue prices. Explicit budgetary subsidies almost doubled from ₹947 crore in 1976–77 to ₹1821 crore in 1979–80.

Import policy

Within nine months of coming to power, the Janata government, in November 1977, appointed the Committee on Import-Export Policies and Procedures headed by P.C. Alexander. In January 1978, in its first report, the committee recommended liberalizing import licensing, expanding the OGL scheme, relaxing the actual user condition, recognizing the developmental role of imports and to emphasize this recognition, changing the name of the Chief Controller of Imports and Exports to Director General of Foreign Trade (DGFT). The import policy for 1978–79 raised foreign investment limits and liberalized imports as per the committee's recommendations, which was also consistent with the government's objective of utilizing the foreign exchange reserves for useful and productive purposes. A major change was the shift from positive lists of permitted imports to a negative list system: whatever was not specifically restricted or licensed was freely allowable and was under OGL. The value of restricted items that could be imported under automatic licence was increased by 10 per cent. Simultaneously, however, capital inflows were discouraged under FERA 1973.

Foreign investment

The Janata government drew up a list of twenty-two product groups in which foreign investment was no longer considered necessary. FERA 1973, under Article 29, required companies where the foreign equity exceeded 40 per cent to obtain RBI's permission to continue to hold or acquire equity in any commercial or industrial enterprise in India. Companies such as Coca-Cola and IBM, which were unwilling to dilute their equity, had to leave. The Policy Statement of 1977 issued a list of industries where indigenous technology was already available and foreign collaboration of a financial or technical nature was banned. Fully owned foreign companies were allowed only in highly export-oriented sectors or sophisticated technology areas. Later in the early 1990s, this approach was memorably summarized by the irrepressible BJP president Dr Murli Manohar Joshi as 'Computer chips YES, potato chips NO'.[1]

While restrictions were put on the role of foreign investment in industries, for all such approved investments, complete freedom was provided for remittance of profits, royalties, dividends and repatriation of capital. Furthermore, for balanced regional development, licences would not be issued to new industrial units for location within certain limits of large metropolitan cities and urban centres with population exceeding 10 and 5 lakh, respectively. In a regressive step, on 23 December 1977, under industrial policy, the list of industries reserved for SSI was expanded from 180 to more than 500 items.

Administered interest rates

There was some progress in rationalizing the administered interest rate structure in June 1977, when the spreads between short- and long-term rates were widened. From July 1977, savings accounts which were functionally savings-oriented and without cheque facilities were paid 5 per cent interest, while those which were transactions-oriented and with cheque facilities earned a lower rate of 3 per cent. In March 1978, these two accounts were merged into a single saving deposit account with limited cheque facilities and interest of 4.5 per cent. In 1978, commercial banks and RRBs were directed to charge a flat rate of 9 per cent on all priority sector loans, irrespective of size. The authorities believed that cost of credit, rather than access, was the key constraint facing the rural poor. In November 1978, private sector banks were also advised to maintain one-third of their total advances to the priority sectors by the end of March 1980.

Demonetization

The Congress government under Indira had not implemented the demonetization of high-value currency notes as an antidote to the menace of black money recommended by the Wanchoo Committee. On 16 January 1978, the Janata government under Morarji went ahead with its High Denomination Bank Notes (Demonetization) Ordinance. Notes of denominations ₹1000, ₹5000, and ₹10,000 ceased to be legal tender. An act by the same name as the ordinance stated that the action was needed as high denomination bank notes facilitate '. . . the illicit transfer of money for financing transactions which are harmful to the national economy or which are for illegal purposes'.[2]

On 16 January 1978, the total amount of currency notes of denominations ₹1000, ₹5000, and ₹10,000 in circulation was ₹145.42 crore. Of this, 89.0 per cent or ₹129.4 crore came back for exchange. It is reasonable to assume that, for fear of detection, 'black money' circulating in the form of currency has a tendency not to come back for exchange. Much larger sums than the ₹16 crore that did not come back were suspected to be 'black' wealth acquired by illegal means. Prima facie, the outcome was disappointing. Despite the previous failures, demonetization would be tried again in end-2016, with disheartening results.

Limited success

The short-lived Janata Party could not pursue economic reforms because of the nature of its coalition character. It consisted of veteran socialists, trade unionists and pro-business leaders. Any major economic reform would trigger a public divide. Furthermore, as is to be expected, there were various demands for additional outlays of a current nature, and such demands were met by enhancing the central government's revenue expenditure, which jumped by 17.3 per cent from ₹91.1 billion in 1977–78 to ₹106.8 billion in 1978–79, the first year of Janata rule. As a proportion of GDP, the increase was 1.72 percentage points, from 14.65 per cent to 16.37 per cent. Revenue increased by 15 per cent too, but from a smaller base, resulting in a widening of the fiscal deficit. As a proportion of GDP, the fiscal deficit increased from 3.48 per cent in 1977–78 to 4.98 per cent in 1978–79 (Figure XVIII.2).

Despite the expansionary fiscal and monetary policy, the WPI remained unchanged in 1978–79. With two successive good harvests,

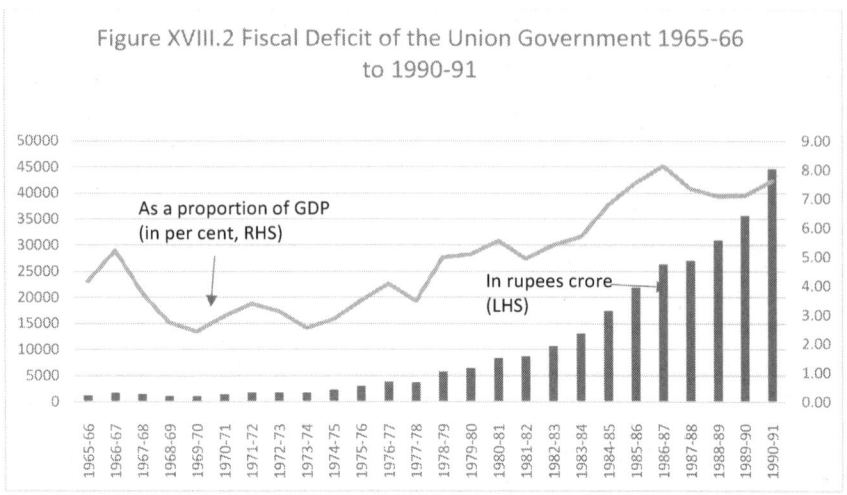

Figure XVIII.2 Fiscal Deficit of the Union Government 1965-66 to 1990-91

Source: RBI Handbook of Economic Statistics Table No. 103 Major Heads of Expenditure of the Central Government

prices of agricultural and agriculture-based commodities, particularly fruits and vegetables, raw cotton and oil seeds, declined and neutralized the price increase in industrial goods to result in zero inflation.

With its partial liberalization, imports soared by US$2.5 billion to US$9.5 billion in 1978–79 and the trade account deteriorated from a small deficit of US$698 million in 1977–78 to a large deficit of US$2,696 million in 1978–79. This, in turn, led to the current account turning around from a surplus of US$1313 million to a small deficit of US$290 million. Yet, with capital inflows continuing, foreign exchange reserves grew by US$1.2 billion in 1978–79, but not enough to maintain the reserve cover of imports in a number of months at the same level as in 1977–78. But this was just the lull before the storm. With the Iranian Revolution, the second oil shock was waiting to hit the country with its full fury. It was almost a repeat of 1973–75. There was turmoil in Iran, a major oil supplier, and Mohammad Reza Pahlavi, the Shah of Iran, left his country in January 1979, never to return. By the end of 1979, crude oil prices had more than doubled from their levels a year ago. The Indian balance of payments was in jeopardy.

XVIII.2 Second Oil Shock

During 12-16 October 1971, the Shah of Iran had celebrated the 2,500[th] anniversary of the Persian Empire set up by Cyrus the Great. At the Golden City recreated for the occasion in the ancient city of Persepolis near Shiraz, the Shah had wined and dined heads of states and other dignitaries in a style unparalleled in history. Iran was a country of Shia Muslims. Shah claimed to be a modernizer, but his opponents, mainly fundamentalist Shias, looked upon him as a corrupt western stooge. Ayatollah Khomeini was not only the undisputed leader—spiritual if not also political—but also vehemently opposed to the Shah. He had been exiled in 1964 for opposing the Shah and his modernizing white revolution (not to be confused with the one in India under Kurien).

Religious leaders and the ulema (Islamic scholars) were upset with the Shah for introducing a secular calendar in place of the old Islamic one in 1976. There was labour unrest from early 1977. To quell violent demonstrations in cities across the country, martial law was declared. Demonstrations intensified and so did the repression by SAVAK, Shah's secret police. By August 1977, the demand turned to 'Shah must go' and to bring back Ayatollah Khomeini.

Iran supplied about 9 per cent of the world's total oil. On 13 October 1978, workers in Abadan refinery, the world's largest at that time, went on strike. By November, the strike had the participation of 37,000 workers at all of Iran's nationalized oil refineries and reduced output by three-fourths to about 1.5 million barrels per day. Saudi Arabia made up for the shortfall, yet the strike unnerved the oil markets. The prospects for India, a major oil importer, did not look promising.

In September 1978, the Camp David Accords were signed by Egyptian President Sadat and Israeli Prime Minister Menachem Begin, with US President Jimmy Carter as witness. Ayatollah Khomeini's son died in Najaf in October 1978, with suspicion about the Shah's hand in this death; in Iran, demonstrations against the Shah intensified. The Shah's repression and attempts at reconciliation failed. On 16 January 1979, the Shah, with his family, left for a vacation in Egypt, never to return. Ayatollah Khomeini made his triumphant return to Teheran on 1 February 1979 and became

Iran's supreme leader on 12 February. On 26 March 1979, Sadat and Begin signed the Egypt-Israel Peace Treaty. Soon, in the Organization of the Petroleum Exporting Countries (OPEC) at Geneva, all Gulf states, except Saudi Arabia, agreed to add a surcharge premium of US$1.20 per barrel, irrespective of quality. Five days later, Arab League leaders expelled Egypt from the league. After a controversial referendum, the Islamic Republic of Iran was born on 1 April 1979, and the Iranian revolution was complete.

During the Iranian revolution, damage to oil supplies went beyond the disruption of Iranian output. The fall of the Shah, a staunch US ally, raised questions about the dependability of the US. The US was seen to be keener in securing its oil supplies than in supporting friendly regimes. With the historic hostility between Shias and Sunnis, Sunni-run Arab neighbours Iraq, Saudi Arabia, Kuwait and other Persian Gulf states, most of them monarchies and all with sizeable Shia populations, felt insecure. Saudi Arabia, a US ally and the key oil producer, on 20 January, expressed its displeasure by announcing a drastic cut in first-quarter production, and spot prices of Middle East light crude jumped up by 36 per cent. Speculation, together with Iraq's invasion of Iran in September 1980, led to the second oil price shock, with the nominal price of crude oil going up from $14 in 1978 to $35 per barrel in 1981.

XVIII.3 Indian Economy after the Second Oil Shock

By the end of 1979, crude oil prices more than doubled from their levels a year ago and so did Indian oil imports, from $2 billion in 1978–79 to $4 billion in 1979–80 and further to $6.7 billion in 1980–81 (Figure XVIII.3). With this tripling of the net oil import bill in two years, the first oil price shock looked mild in comparison. Correspondingly, the current account deteriorated, and the surplus observed in 1976–77 and 1977–78 not only vanished in 1978–79, but rapidly became deficits of $685 million, $2.8 billion, $3.2 billion and $3.4 billion in the three subsequent years (Figure XVIII.4). India was again heading for a balance of payments crisis.

The oil price shock was compounded in many parts of the country by devastating floods in 1978 and a severe drought in 1979, which depleted the reservoirs and affected hydroelectric power generation. The complicated management of the economy added to the woes of the ill-fated and fractured Janata coalition. Growth in GDP declined from

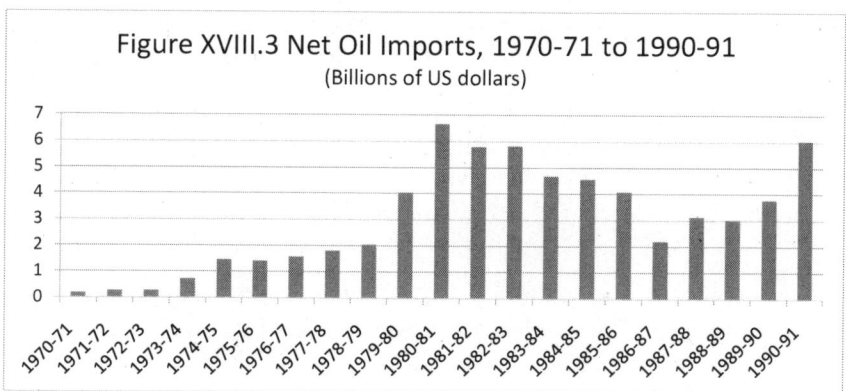

Source: RBI's Handbook of Statistics on the Indian Economy, Table No 127 India's Foreign Trade

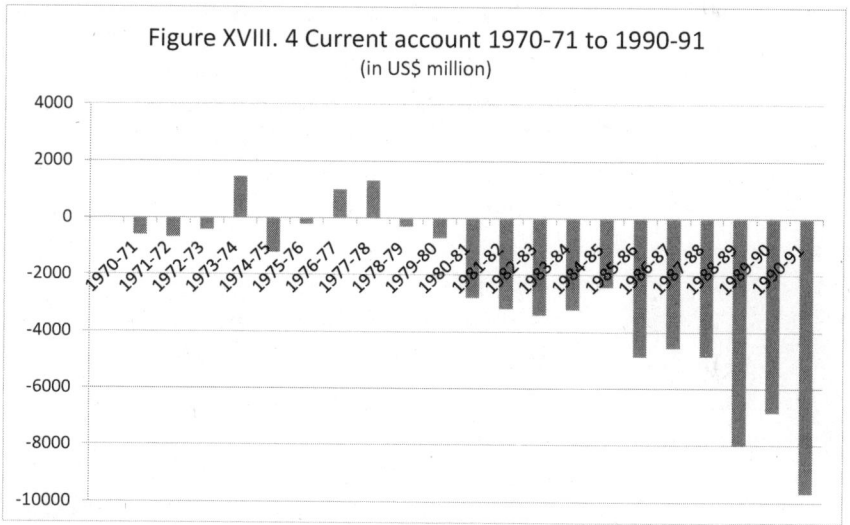

Source: RBI's Handbook of Statistics on the Indian Economy, Table 143

7.5 per cent in 1977–78 to 5.5 per cent in 1978–79 and turned negative (-5.2 per cent) in 1979–80. WPI inflation jumped up from almost zero in 1978–79 to 17.1 and 18.2 per cent in the two subsequent years.

XVIII.4 Janata Government Disintegrates

Prime ministerial aspirants had been fighting each other from even before the Janata government was formed. On 26 March 1977, at the swearing-in of Morarji Desai and nineteen members of his Cabinet, five, including notables such as Jagjivan Ram, Nanaji Deshmukh and Raj Narain, did not turn up because of grievances. Cracks had appeared in the coalition on other issues as well.

On October 1977, Home Minister Charan Singh, against the wishes of Prime Minister Desai, got Indira Gandhi arrested by the CBI. The courts released her the following day on insufficient grounds for arrest. Embarrassed by this mishandling, Janata Party president Chandra Shekhar conveyed his anguish to Charan Singh. Charan Singh put in his resignation but was persuaded to take it back. Factional fights intensified in UP. Health Minister Raj Narain, a hardcore Charan Singh loyalist, criticized the party president and the members of the erstwhile Jana Sangh. In June 1978, in Shimla, capital of the Janata-ruled Himachal Pradesh, Raj Narain led an agitation defying prohibitory orders. The party served him a show cause notice, and he, his mentor Charan Singh and some of his other followers resigned from the Cabinet on 30 June 1978.

Within a week of his resignation, Charan Singh struck back at Prime Minister Morarji Desai with allegations about his son Kantilal Desai misusing his office for making ill-gotten money. With Sanjay Gandhi's deals during his mother's rule still fresh in public memory, the allegations tainted Kanti with shades of Sanjay. By late January 1979, Singh was persuaded to rejoin the cabinet again as Deputy Prime Minister, but this time in charge of the ministry of finance and not the ministry of home affairs. With no rehabilitation, Raj Narain remained free to conspire with the Congress, bring down Morarji and install Charan Singh as Prime Minister in six months' time.

Tension between Janata constituents of the erstwhile Jana Sangh and others flared up after communal riots in Bihar and UP in early 1979. Differences among the constituents came to a breaking point on the issue of dual membership—whether any member of the Janata Party could simultaneously be a member of an alternate political or social organization such as the RSS, the Jana Sangh's ideological parent. Deputy Prime Minister Charan Singh along with leaders such as Raj Narain, Madhu Limaye and George Fernandes raised the issue of dual membership of some of the senior ministers, erstwhile Jana Sangh members, who continued to be members of the RSS. The charge was that of having a party within a party. Raj Narain had been confabulating with Sanjay Gandhi, Indira

Gandhi's son, in March-April 1979. On 9 July 1979, he led a group of nine MPs to declare that they were quitting the Janata Party and would sit in Lok Sabha as a separate group. That was the beginning of the Janata Party (Secular) or Janata (S).

The next day, Y.B. Chavan of the Congress moved a motion of no-confidence in the Lok Sabha. The motion carried, and the Janata government under Morarji Desai resigned. When called upon by the President, Chavan, the Leader of the Opposition, declined the offer to form the government. Then the President called Charan Singh, the leader of the Janata(S)-Congress coalition, to form the government, with the proviso that it must face Parliament and establish its confidence before the third week of August. Charan Singh was sworn in as Prime Minister on 16 July 1979. On 27 July, Morarji Desai stepped down as head of the Janata Party. That was the end of the Janata coalition, which had started off with many more seats than what was needed to form a government. After Morarji Desai, Charan Singh headed a minority coalition precariously dependent on outside support for survival. In 1979, Raj Narain became notorious for being Charan Singh's Hanuman by self-declaration and his Mephistopheles—the devil in medieval German legend to whom the erudite Faust sells his soul to acquire power, knowledge and material gain—according to some others.

Charan Singh's government launched the 'Training Rural Youth for Self-Employment' (TRYSEM) on 15 August 1979 to provide technical skills to the rural youth to enable them to seek employment in fields of agriculture, industry, services and business activities. Eligibility under TRYSEM was restricted to only youth in the age group of 18-35 belonging to BPL families, with priority accorded to those belonging to SC and ST, ex-servicemen and those who were ninth pass. But, as we will see, the life of this Charan Singh government was too short to leave its imprint on economic policies or the fiscal affairs of the country.

XVIII.5 Indira Splits Congress Again and Bounces Back

Ever since the Congress split in 1969, Indira Gandhi had enjoyed tight control of the Congress party. She preferred 'leaders' without mass following. As president of her party, at the end of Shankar Dayal Sharma's two-year tenure in 1975, she had chosen the relatively unknown Dev Kant Barooah from Assam, who did not lose much time in acquiring fame and immortality with his quote 'Indira is India and India is Indira'. Taking responsibility for the defeat in the Lok Sabha polls, Barooah resigned on 2 April 1977, and Indira chose Swaran Singh, another leader without mass following, as his successor interim president. But in the meantime, after her defeat in the Lok Sabha polls, Indira had been losing her grip over the party. Within the Congress, there were strong feelings both in favour of and against Indira Gandhi.

At the AICC meeting on 4-5 May in Delhi, Brahmananda Reddi, by defeating Siddhartha Shankar Ray, Dr Karan Singh and Neki Ram Sharma, became the president of the Congress. Reddi had been the home minister under whose charge the Emergency had been declared but he knew little about its planned imposition. He had Indira's support and even said that he would vacate the presidency if she wanted it. Ray, one of the prime advisers of Indira in imposing the Emergency, had switched sides after her defeat.

On 28 May 1977, the Janata government appointed a judicial Commission under Jayantilal Chhotalal Shah, former Chief Justice of India, to investigate the excesses under the Emergency. Indira refused to testify before the Shah Commission; the refusal carried a potential penalty of six months' imprisonment and/or fine. There was also the potential danger of prosecution of Sanjay Gandhi for excesses during the Emergency, including the destruction of all the copies of *Kissa Kursi Ka* or the story of the fight for the throne, a satirical film on political personalities produced by a Congress MP, Amrit Nahata, in May 1975.

After her defeat in the Lok Sabha elections in March 1977, for almost three months, Indira did not go anywhere outside the national capital. In the June 1977 Vidhan Sabha elections, Congress governments were unseated in nine states. While her political prospects looked threatened, she could not be kept down for long. On 24 July, she flew to Nagpur to go to Panaur and visit Acharya Vinoba Bhave, famous as the Mahatma's spiritual successor as well as the leader of the Bhoodan movement. The Acharya blessed her with the cryptic remark '*Chalte raho*', or keep going forward. Enthused, her supporters rallied with the slogan '*Indira Gandhi aage badho, hum tumhare saath hain*', or Indira, march ahead, we are with you. Her next visit was to Belchi in western Bihar in mid-August.

On 16 May 1977, in Belchi, eleven SCs had been burnt to death and several SC thatched homes destroyed by arson by the Kurmis, an intermediate caste group which had supported the Janata Party in the recent Lok Sabha elections. Indira flew to Patna on the morning of 13 August. On her way from Patna, about 15 km from Belchi, the roads had been cut-off by incessant rains. Perched on an elephant, an undaunted Indira arrived at Belchi. She was back in the news on the national and international media. This visit helped her Congress reinvent itself among the SCs, who in 1977, for the first time, had voted against the party. On the following day, she made a courtesy call on JP at his residence in Patna. It lasted 50 minutes. JP wished Mrs Gandhi 'a brighter future than the bright past she has already had'.[3] On the same day Indira Gandhi was on her way to Belchi, four of her close aides—P.C. Sethi, former minister for petroleum, Yashpal Kapoor, an MP, R.K. Dhawan, who was additional private secretary to Indira Gandhi, and N.K. Singh, a civil service officer deputed to the minister's office—had been arrested by the CBI following searches conducted at various office and residential premises in Delhi and Patna. Indira was arrested on 3 October 1977 on corruption charges in the 'jeep scandal' case and released the following day when the government did not demand a police remand. The arrest was full of drama, with Indira demanding to be taken away in handcuffs and the police refusing.

Many Congress leaders were smarting under the humiliation of total servility to her during the Emergency and were reluctant to bear the onus of the Emergency misdeeds. She was out of power, and there was no more fear of being hounded by her. Those against Indira included Y.B. Chavan, the Maharashtra mass leader and leader of the Congress parliamentary party. Indira was not pleased that her party was not doing enough to mobilize public support for her cause.

There was an AICC session in October 1977. With no sign of reconciliation in sight, the pro-Indira group decided to follow the same strategy as in 1969, that of going around collecting signatures of AICC members on a requisition demanding the election of a new Congress president. After some failed attempts at reconciliation, the requisition move was dropped because of inadequate support among the CWC members.

What was planned instead was a National Convention of Congressmen in New Delhi on 1-2 January 1978.

On 1 January 1978, Brahmananda Reddi expelled Indira from the Congress party. On the following day, thirteen of the twenty-one CWC members met and re-elected Reddi as Congress president. On the other hand, in a convention of what they claimed 'the real Congress' on 1-2 January, dissidents led by Indira elected her as the president. By a resolution in the same convention, she was 'authorised to take appropriate steps to organise the party at all levels'.[4] So the Congress was split again and Indira got back a part that was under her direct control.

A fierce struggle raged between the two groups of the party for the office premises, funds and election symbol of a cow nursing a calf. The moral authority of the Congress led by Reddi was questioned by some on the ground that it consisted of 'sycophants of yesterday turned rebels of today'.[5] The faction led by Indira Gandhi came to be known as Indian National Congress (I) or Congress (I). The 'I', 'which obviously stood for Indira',[6] dispelled all doubts as to whose party it was! The Election Commission could not decide the issue of the symbol in time for the elections in 1978, for example, to the Vidhan Sabha in Andhra Pradesh, Assam, Karnataka, Maharashtra and Meghalaya in February. So it recognized the Congress led by Reddi as the Indian National Congress and allowed it to retain the symbol of a cow nursing a calf for the time being. For Congress (I), Indira reportedly chose the hand symbol after hearing about a Parvathy temple on the outskirts of Palakkad, where the idol is a figure of two hands. The hands symbolized the goddess, fearing attack from demons, seeking help after jumping into a local river. Lord Shiva rescued her after seeing her hands. Soon, the Election Commission froze the symbol of a cow nursing a calf, and the Congress led by Brahmananda Reddi got the charkha (or spinning wheel) as its symbol.

In early 1978, in both Andhra Pradesh and Karnataka, Congress (I) defeated the Reddi faction hands down and formed the government with Marri Chenna Reddy and Devaraj Urs, respectively, as chief ministers. Indira's political fortunes showed signs of revival in her victory in Andhra and Karnataka. Brahmananda Reddi accepted responsibility for the defeat and resigned from the presidency of the Congress on 27 February 1978.

Swaran Singh took over as president and the Congress party came to be known as Congress (S). By November 1978, Devaraj Urs of Karnataka also managed to bring Indira Gandhi back into the Lok Sabha. Urs offered the Chikmagalur Lok Sabha constituency in his state for Indira to contest in a by-election. Urs was Indira Gandhi's election manager. The slogan was *'Ek (one) sherni (lioness), sau (hundred) langur, Chikmagalur, Chikmagalur'*. Indira won the seat and was back in the Lok Sabha as a member. On 21 November 1978, Indira was found guilty of the breach of privilege and contempt by the Parliamentary Privilege Committee. She allegedly prevented officials from collecting information needed to reply to a Lok Sabha question on the affairs of Maruti Limited, a company connected with Sanjay Gandhi. On 20 December, she was not only expelled from Parliament but also sent to jail for seven days.

In the meantime, the constitution of the Congress party was suitably amended to allow Indira, even though no longer an MP, to be a member of the CPP. Once a member, she also became the chairperson of the CPP, and being the party president, her grip on Congress (I) was complete. In December 1978, Indira issued a statement calling upon all Congressmen to 'close ranks'. This opened an avenue for the merger of the two Congress factions. But the talks broke down on Indira's insistence on her son Sanjay Gandhi having a place in the united Congress party and the united party immediately launching struggles to defeat the designs of the Janata government to put her and her son Sanjay in prison. Indira's insistence on a suitable place for her son Sanjay was clearly demonstrated by the switching of Devaraj Urs, a long-term Indira loyalist, from the Congress (I) to Congress (S).

Indira was on the comeback trail. Her desire to come back to power might have been reinforced by the Shah of Iran leaving Teheran on 16 January 1979, never to return, and former Prime Minister of Pakistan Zulfikar Ali Bhutto being condemned for alleged murder and hanged on 4 April 1979. After Charan Singh's ambition of being the Prime Minister had been fulfilled only on 28 July 1979, Indira withdrew Congress (I) support to his government on 20 August 1979, ostensibly for his refusal to scrap the special courts set up for her prosecution. On the morning of the day when the Lok Sabha was to meet to show its confidence in him as the Prime Minister, Charan Singh resigned without facing the Lok Sabha. He became the only one to serve as Prime Minister without facing Parliament for a single day. On his advice, by a Presidential proclamation, the life of the Sixth Lok Sabha was cut short by two and a half years by dissolving it on 29 August 1979, and elections were called. He continued as the caretaker Prime Minister.

In the elections on 3 and 6 January 1980, Indira swept the polls by winning 354 of the 529 Lok Sabha seats and was back as the Prime Minister on 14 January 1980. Factional squabbles of the Janata Party, the mishandling of her arrest by the CBI and her elevation to the status of a victim of political vendetta, plus Charan Singh's backroom negotiations with Congress (I) to fulfil his ambition of being the Prime Minister, played an important role in her coming back to power. But in Indian politics of the time, both within and outside the Congress, her bounce-back through deft political manoeuvres also demonstrated that, politically, she had hardly any peers.

XIX

Beyond 'Hindu' Rate of Growth with Ideology in the Backseat

After three tumultuous years, Indira was back as Prime Minister on 14 January 1980. In 1981, the Election Commission recognized Congress (I) as the Indian National Congress. We shall call Congress (I) the Congress from now on.

Indira inherited a country besieged by a contracting economy, high inflation and balance of payments problems. One of her important decisions was to drop the scheme of rolling plans of the Janata regime, reconstitute the Planning Commission, launch the Sixth Five-Year Plan for 1980–1985 and dovetail the annual plan for 1980–81 into the Sixth Plan. In 1979–80, with large parts of the country in the grip of a drought and rainfall erratic in others, GDP from agriculture and allied activities declined by 13 per cent. Poor performance of power, coal and railways resulted in infrastructural bottlenecks, and even the GDP from manufacturing declined by over 3 per cent. With growth plummeting from 5.5 per cent in 1978–79 to -5.2 per cent in 1979–80, the economy was contracting.

Tight supply conditions in agricultural markets compounded the inflationary pressure already operating after the second oil price shock. WPI inflation, which had been in two-digit levels every month from June 1979, not only crossed 25 per cent by February 1980 but remained in two-digit levels every month until July 1981 (Figure XIX.1).

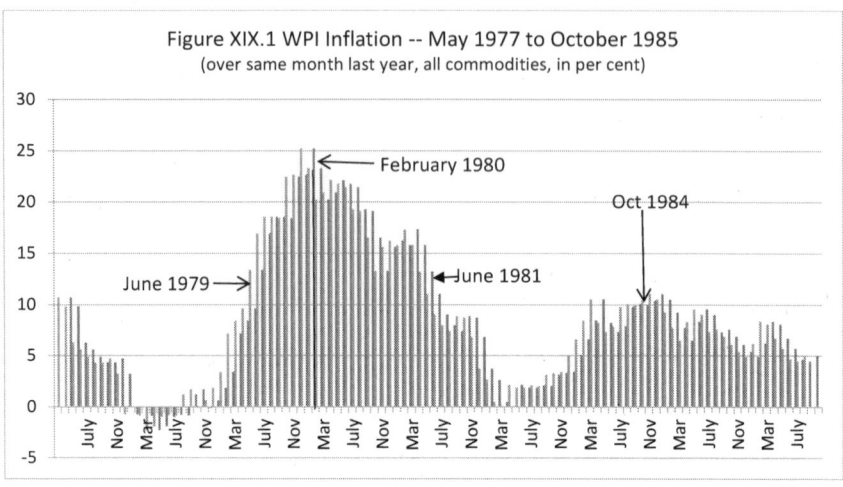

Source: Office of the Economic Adviser, Department for Promotion of Industry and Internal Trade, Government of India

The critical problem was the balance of payments. The second oil shock had come just after the government, with its import policy for 1978–79, had liberalized imports as per the Alexander Committee recommendations. It had considerably simplified procedures and rationale of licensing, combined it with reduction in the degree of import control, especially with respect to imported intermediate inputs into industry, and moved from a positive list of permitted imports to a negative list system of what could not be imported freely under OGL. Together with the second oil price shock, it resulted in a sharp deterioration of the balance of payments.

The balance of payments came under severe strain from 1979 to 1980, with the import bill going up from $9,512 million in the previous year to $12,076 million and further to $16,314 million in 1980–81 (Figure XIX.2). A large contributor was the oil import bill, which more than tripled from $2038 million in 1978–79 to US$4035 million in 1979–80 and further to US$6655 million in 1980–81 (Figure XIX.3). Exports were relatively sluggish, and both the trade and current account deficits started to deteriorate. By 1981–82, foreign exchange reserves, which were equivalent to a comfortable 9.9 months of imports in 1978–79, had also been drawn down and, with imports soaring, covered only 3.3 months of such imports. The government went to the IMF for balance of payments support.

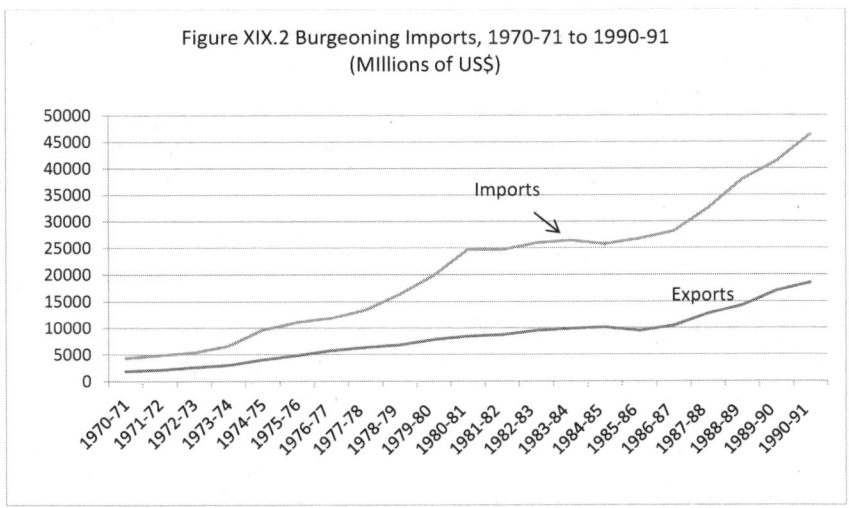

Figure XIX.2 Burgeoning Imports, 1970-71 to 1990-91
(MIllions of US$)

Source: RBI's Handbook of Statistics on the Indian Economy, Table 132.

XIX.1 IMF Programme

Apart from the second oil shock and import liberalization, insufficient adjustment of the external value of the Indian rupee was a contributory cause to the balance of payments crisis. After the demise of the Bretton Woods agreement, the pound sterling had weakened considerably against other currencies, and with its peg to the pound sterling, the rupee had depreciated with the pound. But it was not enough.

From 24 September 1975, the rupee was pegged to a basket of currencies and its exchange rate was determined with reference to the daily movements of currencies of a selected number of major trading partners. Initially, it was a five-currency basket, of which one was variable and depended on the pattern of payments falling due. The currencies included in the basket and the weights assigned to them were not disclosed. The pound sterling, however, continued as the intervention currency. The IMF classified India's exchange rate arrangements as 'managed float'. The multi-currency peg was operated with many discretionary elements. In the event, although the rupee depreciated in real effective terms, it was again not enough to prevent the balance of payments crisis. By 1980, India needed IMF support.

The IMF's official history reports: 'The decision to request the use of Fund resources was controversial and highly political in India. The prime minister, Indira Gandhi, was personally active in (and would later become the chairperson of) the Non-Aligned Movement, which was officially opposed to IMF conditionality. Drawing on the Fund would subject her government to criticism from leftist parties in parliament . . . The key for overcoming the opposition would be to ensure that the government was not required to alter the economic policies already envisaged under the Five-Year Plan.'[1] Because of news leaks, negotiations were carried out outside India in Libreville (Gabon), Paris, London and Washington. In spite of all the confidentiality, much of what was negotiated and how was exposed between 16 and 20 October 1981 by N. Ram, a young journalist who later went on to become the leading light of the respected The Hindu Group of publications.

On the policy front, the approach was what Vijay Joshi and I. M. D. Little (1994) have called one of 'expansionary adjustment' by enhancing investment, particularly in infrastructure, and promoting public savings and exports.[2] However, the government also raised interest rates, and indirect taxes through an increase in the auxiliary duty of customs across the board by 5 percentage points. The government also raised the administered prices of kerosene and fertilizer to reduce the subsidies.

There was some opposition within the IMF, particularly from the largest shareholder, namely the US, against India obtaining IMF funds for structural adjustment which was, in a way, a matter for the World Bank to deal with. Some US legislators insisted that the program should be rejected because of India's commitment to spend $3 billion buying Mirage fighter jets from France. Nevertheless, in November 1981, India entered an Extended Fund Facility (EFF) arrangement of SDR 5 billion over three years.

XIX.2 Indira Gandhi After 1980—'Grin without a Cat'

After suffering a defeat, a less ideological Indira Gandhi, not a firebrand socialist anymore, came to power in 1980. Perhaps she had read or heard about the on-going reforms in post-Maoist China under Deng Xiaoping and how the leader had said that 'I don't care if it's a white cat or a black cat. It's a good cat so long as it catches mice'.[3] She may have also realized that her anti-market, anti-big capital, and small-is-beautiful populism pursued earlier was not delivering the expected results in terms of economic development. In any case, there is little evidence of any ideological dogmatism in Indira Gandhi. She became the Prime Minister after Shastri's death not because of her ideology, but because of her lack of it. She was 'weak' and non-controversial relative to her adversary Morarji Desai, who was known for his decisiveness and dogmatism, and hence acceptable to all sections of the Congress party, including the Syndicate.

Her ideological flexibility was manifest in the chequered history of her attitude to the communists. As president of the ruling Congress party in 1959, she got the first communist party government in Kerala dismissed on 31 July 1959, in spite of resistance from both her father Nehru and husband Feroze Gandhi. A decade later, after the Congress split, she turned left and sustained her minority government during 1969–1971 with support from the ComPI and pushed through a radical economic programme. The Soviet Union and by implication, the ComPI, lent her support during the critical years of the Emergency. In June 1975, however, she said that 'I do not believe that a democratic society has the obligation to acquiesce in its own dissolution'.[4] Then she also declared that Marxism had no place in Indian democracy. Similarly, we will recall how, during the setting up of the public sector steel plant at Bokaro and the Bangladesh liberation struggle, Indo-US relations had nosedived and India had been closely identified as a member of the Soviet gang. After the Soviet invasion of Afghanistan on Christmas Eve 1979, the Janata government had condemned the act. After Indira's re-election in 1980, relative to her predecessor's, her reaction was somewhat muted. Her changed approach to world politics was also evident in her rapprochement with the United States and her highly cordial meetings with US President Ronald Reagan at Cancun in October 1981 and in the US in July 1982.

Simultaneously with her flexibility, one of her prime strengths was '. . . her symbolism of Nehru' which '. . . was in a sense false; . . . but she could benefit . . . from her connection with Nehru without any inheritance of his reformism'[5] Her policies were primarily designed for furthering political ends, and the expansion of CPSEs provide a good example. Rapid expansion of employment and public investments in the

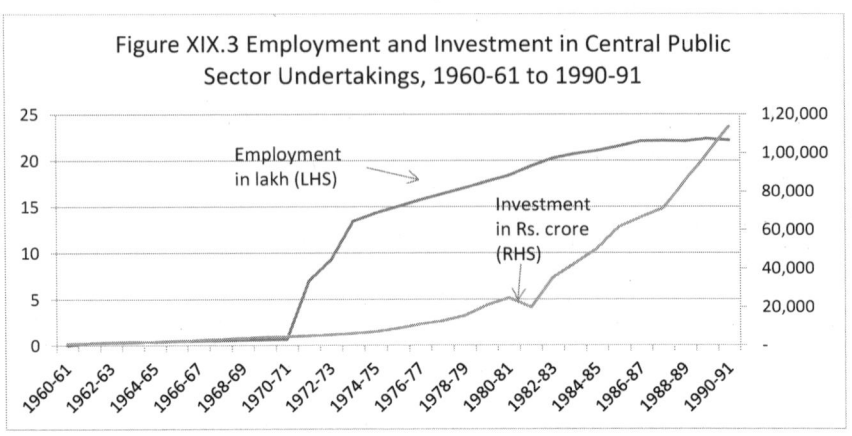

Figure XIX.3 Employment and Investment in Central Public Sector Undertakings, 1960-61 to 1990-91

Source: Public Enterprise Survey, various issues

CPSEs happened in the 1970s under Indira Gandhi, well after the Nehru era (Figure XIX.3). Employment in CPSEs went up from about 66,000 in 1970–71 to over 15 lakh in the mid-1970s with the nationalization of coal and hydrocarbon industries. And so did investments. In 1984, near the end of Indira Gandhi's rule, a news magazine observed: 'The public sector is in sheer variety and size, a marvel of industrial development. It makes everything from bread and shoes to ships to satellites. But it does so in a most inefficient way. In 1982–83, its Rs 30,000 crore investment yielded a wispy profit of 2 per cent—a level at which no private investor could survive.'[6] CPSE expansion under Indira had little to do with the commanding heights of the economy.

Indira Gandhi's changed pragmatic outlook on the economic front was reflected in the approach to the Sixth Five-Year Plan which she launched in 1980. After the First Five-Year Plan, the subsequent three five-year plans had fallen short of their growth targets and only the Fifth had met the target. Buoyant growth was crucial for the realization of socio-economic objectives such as removal of poverty, generation of gainful employment and technological and economic self-reliance. The Sixth Five Year Plan categorically acknowledged this. Furthermore, it paid attention to capacity constraints, especially in sectors with relatively long gestation such as major irrigation, power, transport and steel, and eschewed the path of favouring quick maturing and directly productive projects for accelerating growth in the short run at the cost of growth in the medium- to long-run. In the event, partly because of buoyant agriculture, the Sixth Plan met its growth target. Venkataraman was the finance minister under Indira Gandhi from 14 January 1980 onwards. He was succeeded by Pranab Mukherjee on 15 January 1982. They both operated under a 'different Indira Gandhi' after 1980.

Two examples—telecom and cement

The telecom and cement industries provide good examples of the 'different Indira Gandhi' after 1980. IPR 1956 had put the manufacture of most telecommunication equipment—telephones and telephone cables, telegraph, and wireless apparatus (excluding radio receiving sets)—under Schedule-A containing industries whose future development were to be the exclusive responsibility of the state. The Indian Telephone Industries (ITI) was established as the first CPSE in 1948. It had a manufacturing plant in Bengaluru. Almost the whole output was sold to a single customer, the Department of Posts and Telegraphs (P&T). The inefficiency of the choice of technology, plant locations, fragmentation of capacity as well as too much emphasis on employment generation had led to congestion of telephone lines as well as long waiting times for a new connection. There was a waiting time of over two years to get a landline telephone connection. India's telephone density, or the number of telephone connections per 100 people, at 0.4 in 1981, was well below not only that in developing countries as a block (2.8), or Asia (2.0), or Latin America (5.5) but even Africa (0.8). The number of telephone connections in the whole country was slightly over only 1,00,000 telephones.

In a move away from the import substitution strategy, an electronic switching technology transfer was concluded with Alcatel in 1982. In August 1984, the Centre for Development of Telematics (C-DOT), under the autonomous Telecom Technology Development Centre of the Government of India, was set up to develop state-of-the-art telecommunication technology to meet the country's telecommunication needs. In 1983, the government moved telecommunications from the list of 'luxury' industries to 'core' industries and increased the scope for plan finance.

The cement industry's path from February 1982 onwards provides another illustration of the difference between Indira Gandhi in the 1980s and Indira of the earlier period. From the Second World War, stringent controls on the cement industry across distribution channels, purchase prices and quotas for open market sales had continued. Imports of cement were canalized through the STC ever since it was set up in 1956. STC also had the distribution monopoly. Purchase prices, based on plant age, technology and incentives for capacity addition, were of three kinds in 1958. Because of a lack of incentive, capacity in the cement industry had expanded from around 3 million tonnes in 1950–51 to only 22.8 million tonnes in 1978–79. There was a severe shortage of cement and a great deal of so-called 'black marketing'. The shortage, we will see, would even lead to scandals embarrassing the government. In February 1982, the government introduced partial decontrol through a dual price policy for cement—a levy price for government supplies and an open market price. The levy quota was roughly two-thirds of installed capacity. The balance could be disposed of in the free market. The states could work out their own distribution machinery for quota cement. The levy price was raised, first in February 1982 and again in July 1984, to allow for cost escalations. Capacity expanded and cement output, which was 21.1 million tonnes in 1981–82, went up to 30.2 million tonnes in 1984–85. Now let us turn to taxation.

Taxation

In the area of personal income taxation, under the different Indira Gandhi, the top marginal rate declined from 69 in 1979–80 under Janata rule to 61.875 per cent in 1984–85. Finance Minister Venkataraman also raised the exemption limit, which had been ₹10,000 since 1977–78, to ₹12,000 in 1980–81, and further to ₹15,000 from 1981–82. With some broad banding of slabs, the number of personal income tax slabs (including the slab exempt from taxation) came down from 9 under Charan Singh in 1979–80 to 8 under Venkataraman's last Budget of 1981–82. The surcharge on corporate tax was down from 7.5 per cent to 2.5 per cent in 1981–82.

Venkataraman also launched the fourth tax amnesty scheme of independent India. What the Special Bearer Bonds (Immunities) Act 1981 offered to tax evaders was, according to the tax expert S.S. Khan, 'the best in a long time'. Black money that had evaded tax, when invested in these bonds, became white in ten years with a free premium of 20 per cent. Yet, like for the three previous tax amnesty schemes, the outcome was again disappointing, and the amount declared no more than an estimated 5 per cent of the black economy. Furthermore, closer to maturity, these bonds, which were freely transferable, became alternate currency commanding a market premium. The holders of these bonds, who had converted their black money into white through these bonds, could reconvert these white funds into black again at a premium. In 1981, while introducing the Special Bearer Bonds, Finance Minister Venkataraman had described the scheme as 'a major initiative to direct some of the resources circulating in the black economy into the exchequer'.[7] In 1985, Bhabatosh Datta, a respected economist, commented: 'He did not continue as Finance Minister to be able to see that by spreading a red carpet for the black market overlords, he had only created an additional instrument for holding black money, commanding a high premium in the market.'[8] In 1990-91, their year of maturity, in his Budget Speech, Madhu Dandavate rued '. . . the instrument to render black money white was itself used with vengeance to reconvert white money into black!'

Under Pranab Mukherjee, the income tax slabs underwent some bifurcations and consolidations in both 1983–84 and 1984–85, but the number of slabs (excluding the exempt slab) remained unchanged at eight. While Mukherjee, from 1983–84, increased the rate of surcharge from 10 per cent to 12.5 per cent, in 1984–85, he reduced the applicable basic rates in many of the slabs by up to 7.5 percentage points. At the end of Mukherjee's term in 1984–85, the effective highest rate of marginal tax was 61.875 per cent. Revenue mobilization under personal income tax under Indira Gandhi from 1980 was disappointing. As a proportion of GDP, such revenues declined from 0.38 per cent in 1979–80 to a low of 0.22 per cent in 1982–83 before reviving to 0.27 per cent in 1984–85. Even revenues from corporation tax as a proportion of GDP declined along a fluctuating trend from 1.11 per cent in 1979–80 to 1.00 per cent in 1984–85.

On the indirect taxes front, the auxiliary duty of customs almost across the board, already up by 5 percentage points in 1981 after the EFF arrangement with the IMF, was increased by another 5 percentage points each in 1982–83 and 1983–84 for balance of payments reasons. The basic customs duty rates were also increased on many items. The exchange rate of the rupee per US dollar had depreciated by 14.1 per cent from ₹8.19 at end-March 1981 to ₹9.35 at end-March 1982. As a result of the enhanced duties and depreciation of the rupee, revenues from customs increased by over 26 per cent in 1982–83 and a further 19 per cent in 1983–84. Mukherjee increased the rate of duty on the residuary heading Item 68 of the Central Excise Tariff, which was 8 per cent since 1979, to 10 per cent in 1983–84. With this as well as increases in rates on several items such as cement, high-value electronic goods and toilet preparations, revenues from excise duties went up from ₹3409 crore in 1980–81 to ₹5583 crore in 1983–84. An important development in the ambit of indirect taxes was the Forty-Sixth Amendment to the Constitution in 1982. It inserted entry 92B in the List I (Union List) to the Seventh Schedule of the Constitution, empowering Parliament to levy taxes on consignment of goods in the course of inter-state trade.

The states' own tax revenues as a proportion of GDP increased only mildly from 4.51 per cent in 1979–80 to 4.70 per cent in 1983–84. Odisha and Bihar repealed their agricultural income tax in October 1979 and January 1981 with retrospective effect from early 1979. In 1981–82, after seven years of complete prohibition, Tamil Nadu again went back to limited prohibition with liquor permits. The state-owned Tamil Nadu State Marketing Corporation took over wholesale liquor trade from June 1983, and the entire retail segment as well from 1985–86.

Reform and other measures

On 23 July 1980, hardly six months after coming to power, Indira Gandhi's government came out with a Statement of Industrial Policy. Its avowed aim was promotion of competition in the domestic market, technological upgradation and modernization. To promote a stronger nexus between large-scale and small-scale manufacturing, it envisaged allowing the setting up of a few nucleus plants. But, in a harking back to the logic of licensing, it would allow such nucleus plants only in identified industrially backward districts. For the fullest utilization of existing industrial capacities, particularly in core industries and in industries with a long-term export potential, it allowed automatic expansion of capacity of 5 per cent per annum or 25 per cent in a five-year plan period to be taken in one or more stages in all Appendix I industries. It also promised to consider requests for setting up 100 per cent export-oriented units and for expansion of existing units for purposes of export sympathetically.

Under Janata rule, IRDP's coverage was about 2300 blocks by 1979–80. After coming back to power, from 2 October 1980, Indira extended IRDP to all the blocks in the country with a total of 600 families in each to be covered under the programme—400 through agriculture and related activities, and 100 families each through rural industries, and through rural services and business enterprises. All BPL persons came under IRDP, and this target group consisted of small and marginal farmers, tenants and sharecroppers, landless labourers and rural artisans.

Indira also launched the National Rural Employment Programme (NREP) on 2 October 1980. It was an anti-poverty programme through generation of employment opportunities in rural areas, especially for the landless labourers, and within landless labourers to those belonging to the SCs and STs. Wages were paid partly in cash and partly in subsidized food grains. It was a restructured FWP from 1 April 1977 under the Janata government. Indira Gandhi formulated a fifteen-point programme for the welfare of minorities in May 1983 and followed it up with a new programme, Rural Landless Employment Guarantee Programme (RLEGP), on 15 August 1983.

Following the Sivaraman Committee's Report, Indira Gandhi's government, with Pranab Mukherjee as the finance minister, set up NABARD on 12 July 1982 under the NABARD Act of 30 December 1981. With the agricultural credit functions of the RBI and the refinance functions of the ARDC transferred to it, NABARD became the apex of the institutional network concerned with rural credit. One significant, and according to many scholars retrograde, step during Indira Gandhi's rule from 1980 onwards was the farm loan waiver granted to the Maharashtra farmers by newly elected Congress Chief Minister B.R. Antulay.

I.G. Patel, who was the Governor of RBI at that time, recounts: 'His (Antulay's) first step as Chief Minister was to announce that he would write off certain debts of farmers. In fact, this promise was first made by

Sharad Pawar during the elections and I had opposed the idea publicly. For this, I was gheraoed by Pawar's supporters at the Aurangabad airport. I had no choice but to repeat my opposition when an incumbent Chief Minister made a similar announcement. Antulay reacted publicly in style—so much so that R.K. Laxman was inspired to sketch a cartoon showing Antulay running away with, I think, Rs 40 crores and myself trying to catch him while remaining half behind a screen . . . (In a face-to-face meeting) Antulay asked me very politely how I could have any authority over an elected leader—a very legitimate question. I clarified that my opposition was to the proposal to use RBI money through NABARD to write off the loans. He was sharp enough to reply that in that case, he would use the state exchequer to fulfil his electoral promise. I said that while I could not prevent him from doing so, I was bound to advise him and the Union Finance Minister that this would set a very bad precedent and would not contribute to financial discipline.'[9]

Indira Gandhi's ideological flexibility was also evident in the reversal of the amendment of Chapter V-B introduced in 1976, raising the threshold from 100 or more workers to 300 or more workers for requiring government permission for layoffs, retrenchments and closures. By an amendment in 1982, which took effect in 1984, the threshold was again restored to 100 workers.

To tap the resources of NRIs, Pranab Mukherjee, Venkataraman's successor from 15 January 1982 onwards, in his Budget for 1982–83, allowed NRIs and their overseas corporate bodies (OCB) to purchase shares of up to a total of 40 per cent in existing Indian companies listed in the Indian stock exchanges. While there was a limit of 1 per cent of the shares in any company being bought by an NRI individual or an OCB, there was no embargo on an individual acquiring additional shares operating through different companies. With Indian business families controlling companies with small proportions of equity, this soon led to trouble.

DCM and Escorts were two well-known Indian companies set up by Lala Sriram and the Nanda family in 1889 and 1944, respectively. 'The Shriram family controlled DCM with only 10 per cent of the equity and the Nandas controlled Escorts with only 5 per cent.'[10] Swaraj Paul, a London-based NRI, acquired 13 per cent of the total equity in DCM and 7.5 per cent in Escorts. Paul wanted to improve the management of these companies and hoped the financial institutions that were large shareholders in these companies would help in the process. Families 'controlling large private sector groups argued that public financial institutions had acquired large shareholdings in their companies because of the convertibility clause that was compulsorily included in loans when these companies borrowed from these institutions . . . they had no option but to accept this option because the financial system was dominated by public sector institutions . . . The Government quickly modified the policy to limit the total direct and indirect acquisition by an NRI to no more than 5 per cent of total equity.' These provisions did not apply to Swaraj Paul's acquisitions of shares of DCM and Escorts retrospectively. 'The managements fought back by refusing to register the change in ownership of the shares in his favour! In the end, the Government buckled and brokered an agreement under which Paul sold his shares back to the Nandas and the Shrirams at "agreed prices," at which he would not incur a loss.'

The remarkable development under the different Indira Gandhi was '. . . the state's changing role since 1980, especially the abandonment of left-leaning, anti-capitalist rhetoric and policies, prioritising of economic growth, and a slow but steady embrace of Indian capital as the main ruling ally.'[11] Three important committees were set up to examine economic administration reforms, trade reforms and financial sector reforms with L.K. Jha, Abid Hussain and M. Narasimham, respectively, as chairmen. The three respected economic administrators, in their reports, gave important recommendations to free up business and promote growth. The government started implementing many of these recommended reforms.

The government's shift from its former leftist stance was also evident in amendment of MRTPA 1969 in 1981 and 1982. The amendments gave considerable flexibility to monopoly houses to expand the installed capacity of their companies beyond their licensed limit and, for companies engaged in output of high national priority products or exclusively for exports, to expand capacity without becoming a 'dominant' undertaking and falling foul of the MRTPA.

One perceptive commentator observed that Indira as a representative of the radical forces, in 1970, had claimed credit for enacting the MRTPA with provisions regarding the definition of 'concentration' more stringent than what had been recommended by the Monopolies Enquiry Commission. In Alice in Wonderland: '. . . the cat vanished quite slowly, beginning with the end of the tail and ending with the grin, which remained sometime after the rest of it had gone. "Well, I have often seen a cat without a grin," thought Alice, "but a grin without a cat! It is the most curious thing I ever saw in my whole life."'[12] 'The Vanishing MRTP Act: Will Only the Grin Remain?' was the title of an interesting article on how the same Indira in her pro-growth re-incarnation was amending the MRTP Act that she adopted in her leftist incarnation.

In March 1980, the target for priority sector lending was raised to 40 per cent of their total advances by March 1985. Subsequently, on the recommendations of the Working Group on the Modalities of Implementation of Priority Sector Lending and the Twenty Point Economic Programme by Banks, all commercial banks, including private and foreign banks (with twenty or more branches), were advised to achieve this target of priority sector lending at 40 per cent of aggregate bank advances by 1985. Sub-targets were also specified for lending to agriculture and the weaker sections within the priority sector. Controls on interest rates were tightened on 2 March 1981. In December 1982, Dr Manmohan Singh, Governor of RBI set up a committee under the chairmanship of Prof. Sukhamoy Chakravarty to review the functioning of the Indian monetary system. The report had far-reaching recommendations but became available only in April 1985, when Indira Gandhi was no more.

Indira Gandhi, according to some, had moved away from socialism to a more pragmatic and business-friendly approach even before the Emergency, with her brutal crackdown on the railway strike in May 1974. The move was accompanied by welfarism through programmes such as NREP and IRDP. Furthermore, on 14 January 1982, Indira also announced a restructured twenty-point programme:

1. Increase the irrigation potential to develop and disseminate technologies and inputs for dry land agriculture.
2. Make special efforts to increase production of pulses and vegetable oil seeds.
3. Strengthen and expand coverage of IRDP and NREP.

4. Implement agricultural land ceilings, distribute surplus land and compile completed land records by removing all administrative and legal obstacles.
5. Review and effectively enforce minimum wages for agricultural labour.
6. Rehabilitation of bonded labour.
7. Accelerate programmes for the development of SCs and STs.
8. Supply drinking water to all problem villages.
9. Allot house sites to rural families who are without them and expand programme for construction assistance to them.
10. Improve the environment of slums, implement programmes of house building for the economically weaker sections, and take measures to arrest the unwarranted increase in land prices.
11. Maximize power generation, improve functioning of electricity authorities and electrify all villages.
12. Pursue vigorously a programme of afforestation, social and farm forestry and development of biogas and other alternative energy sources.
13. Promote family planning on a voluntary basis as a people's movement.
14. Augmentation of universal PHC facilities and control of leprosy, tuberculosis and blindness.
15. Accelerated programmes for the welfare of women and children and nutrition programmes for pregnant women, nursing mothers and children, especially in the tribal, hill and backward areas.
16. Spread of universal elementary education for the age group 6-14 with special emphasis on girls, and simultaneously involve students and voluntary agencies in programmes for the removal of adult illiteracy.
17. Expand PDS through more FPS, including mobile shops in far-flung areas and shops to cater to industrial workers, students' hostels; make available to students' textbooks and exercise books on a priority basis and promote a strong consumer protection movement.
18. Liberalize investment procedures and streamline industrial policies to ensure timely completion of projects; give assistance to handcrafts, handlooms small and village industries to develop and update their technology.
19. Continue strict action against smugglers, hoarders and tax evaders and check black money.

20. Improve the working of public enterprises by increasing efficiency, capacity utilization and generation of internal resources.

This restructured twenty-point programme differed starkly from the original one announced during the Emergency in 1975. Except for minimum wage for agricultural labour, land reforms and improved facilities for students, there was hardly any overlap. The 'populist' elements of the original programme of 1975 were missing from the restructured one in 1982. Education and health figured in the restructured programme. The emphasis was on growth. According to political scientist Atul Kohli '. . . the post-Emergency Indira Gandhi was a different Indira Gandhi: she downplayed redistributive concerns and prioritised economic growth; sought an alliance with big business; adopted an anti-labour stance; put brakes on the growth of public sector industries; and demoted the significance of economic planning and of the Planning Commission. As suits a complex democracy, these changes emerged in fits and starts; they were also often camouflaged, helping maintain some of Indira Gandhi's credentials as the leader of the masses.'[13]

In 1950, India had hosted the first Asian Games, a mini-Olympics with athletes from Asia held every five years. The IX Asian Games were held in Delhi from 19 November to 4 December 1982. Jagmohan, the DDA vice chairman during the turbulent Emergency with Sanjay Gandhi at the helm, was the Lt Governor of Delhi from 17 February 1980 to 25 April 1984, except for the period from April 1981 to 1 September 1982. The success of the Asian Games not only boosted Indira's image but also added to the reputation of Jagmohan as a successful administrator. He had already got the Padma Shri in 1971 and Padma Bhushan in 1977.

XIX.3 Growth Spurts with Ideology in the Back Seat

Even after a rough start following the disastrous economic performance in 1979–80, and facing the second oil price shock thereafter, the Indian economy did reasonably well in terms of growth and inflation during the 1980s. Throughout the decade of the 1980s, except for the year 1982–83, the proverbial 'Hindu rate of growth' of around an annual 3.5 per cent had been consistently surpassed. Average annual growth between 1979–80 and 1989–90 was 5.6 per cent.

In 1988, Nobel Laureate Robert E. Lucas Jr, in his paper on the mechanics of economic development, asked: 'Is there some action a government of India could take that would lead the Indian economy to grow like Indonesia or Egypt's? If so, what exactly?'[14] Fortunately, there had been signs of improvement in growth performance since the early 1990s or late 1980s. Commenting on Lucas's famous statement, Robert J. Barro, another Nobel Laureate, in his celebrated macroeconomic textbook a few years later, wrote: 'When Lucas wrote these words in the mid-1980s, India had been growing more slowly than Egypt and Indonesia for some time. The growth rates of real GDP per person from 1960 to 1980 were 2.5% per year in Egypt, 3.5% in Indonesia, and 1.6% in India. However, India did manage to surpass the other two countries in terms of growth rates from 1980 to 2000: the growth rates of real GDP per person were 2.7% per year for Egypt, 3.5% for Indonesia, and 3.8% for India. Thus, the Indian government may have met Lucas's challenge by the 1980s.'[15] Scholars have done detailed econometric analysis of the trend in GDP data, including removing the effect of rainfall, to conclude that the new phase of accelerated growth started from 1980–81 and not 1979–80.

After Nehru, during the period 1965–66 to 1979–80, the average annual growth at 3.2 per cent had been lacklustre with the limits of import-substitution reached, public sector management problems magnified in poor returns, and the capacity of the state in implementing socialist policies severely tested with firms evading the control regime. With India doing badly relative to many developing countries, especially in the east, there was a change in the orientation of the government from socialism to the market. There was a realization of the importance of 'utpadan badhao' or increase output relative to and even for 'Garibi Hatao.' As Virmani reports, '. . . there was a change in the rhetoric of the government and of intellectuals . . . This change in orientation started in the late seventies when the still "socialist" oriented Mrs Gandhi broke the railway strike in 1976. The change continued with the coming to power of so called "right-wing" political parties such as the Congress (O) and the BJP (though some of the coalition partners were Indian socialists).'[16]

On her return to power in 1980, reversing the earlier policies was relatively easy for Indira Gandhi because of two reasons. The return of Congress could be credited mainly to Indira Gandhi's own electoral appeal and hardly anyone could oppose her within the party. Second, as Virmani reports, 'In any case many in the opposition had been critics of her earlier policies and could not reverse their position without losing their own credibility. Whatever reforms were introduced were seen as examples of the new direction she was setting.'[17]

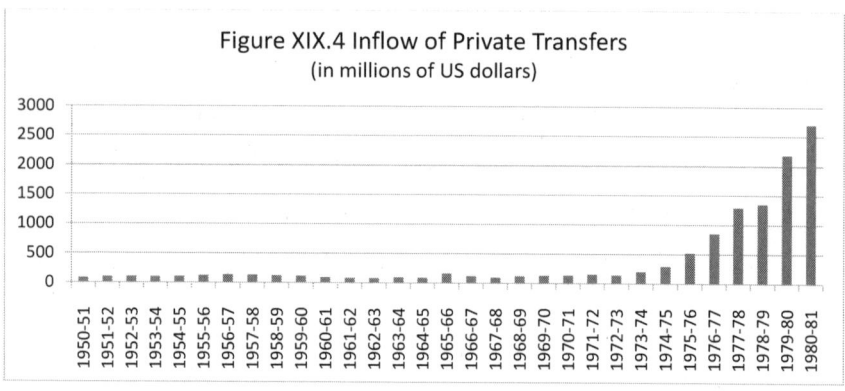

Figure XIX.4 Inflow of Private Transfers
(in millions of US dollars)

Source: RBI's Handbook of Statistics of the Indian Economy, Table 132.

Fortunately for Indira Gandhi, the second oil shock started to peter out by mid-1981 and crude oil prices in world markets started to soften. Furthermore, Bombay High off-shore production of oil, which had started in 1976, increased every year from 1980 to 1985 and reduced the country's import-dependence for petroleum. With their newfound affluence after the oil price shocks, the nearby oil-exporting countries of the Middle East were embarking on a host of economic and investment activities, and needed a large pool of workers, both skilled and semi-skilled. They attracted millions of Indian workers, who started sending money to their near and dear ones back home. Indian workers' remittances from the Middle East, which had started increasing after the first oil shock, boomed after the second oil shock (Figure XIX.4). On 15 January 1984, Prime Minister Indira Gandhi, in a nationwide radio broadcast, informed the country that India's balance of payments was strong enough for the government to forgo the final year's drawings from the IMF. The EFF was cancelled effective 1 May 1984.

Lingering doubts remain about the sources of accelerated growth during the 1980s. Was it a change towards more business-friendly policies, or simply expansionary fiscal policy? There was no doubt that total factor productivity increased, but what is not clear is whether it was due to value-added growth and higher learning-by-doing and scale economies with faster growth, or to some factor other than growth acceleration itself, such as liberalization. Some scholars suggest that it could have been the expansionary fiscal policy that led to a growth spurt and growth of productivity, and liberalization may have played only a minor role.

The main source of growth appears to have been expansionary fiscal policy. According to economist Amitava Krishna Dutt, 'Regression analysis suggests that cross-industry differences in total factor productivity growth can be largely attributed to value-added growth. This implies that faster growth leads to higher productivity growth due to learning-by-doing and scale economies. Thus, higher growth may have led to higher productivity growth rather than the other way around. This explanation suggests that expansionary fiscal policy is the main factor explaining the growth spurt of the 1980s, with liberalization playing a smaller role than usually suggested.'[18]

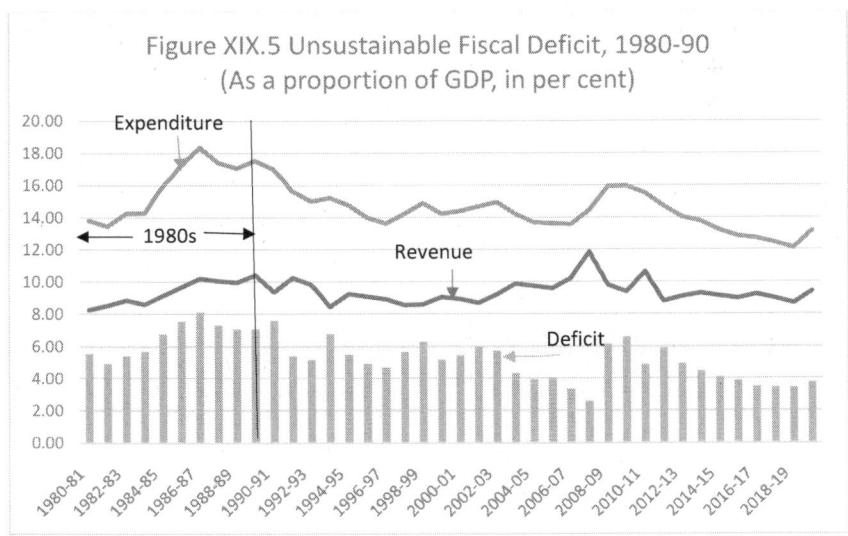

Figure XIX.5 Unsustainable Fiscal Deficit, 1980-90
(As a proportion of GDP, in per cent)

Source: The fiscal deficit of the Central Government, which is not readily available in the budget documents prior to 1991-92, has been derived from the financing side and the data is from RBI's Handbook of Statistics on the Indian Economy, Table 95.

While growth indeed sped up from 1980–81, the difficulty in marking 1980–81 as the beginning of the new era of higher growth arises from the unsustainability of the expansionary fiscal policy of the Union government that drove this acceleration. Expenditure growth outpaced revenue mobilization to result in unsustainable fiscal deficits (Figure XIX.5). Anything that is unsustainable, by definition, must come to an end. The unsustainability of the strategy that unleashed higher growth in the 1980s makes it difficult to mark 1980–81 as the beginning of the new Indian high growth era.

There was some remarkable regularity about the Indian experience with high fiscal deficit, oil price shock, balance of payments difficulties and seeking IMF support. In 1972–73, when the Union government's expenditure and fiscal deficit reached a temporary peak with the first oil price shock, India went to the IMF for the Compensatory Financing Facility in 1973–74. With the build-up in expenditure and deficit at the end of the seventies and the second oil price shock, in November 1981, India entered an EFF arrangement of SDR 5 billion with the IMF over three years. By the end of the 1980s, with the build-up in fiscal deficit, India was ripe for another IMF programme. All it needed was another oil crisis, and, as we will see, when it occurred due to the Gulf War in 1991, India was back to the IMF for another programme. The policies India pursued in the 1980s resulted in considerable vulnerabilities in its macroeconomic situation; its fragile economy was easily destabilized by an external shock.

XIX.4 After Sheikh Abdullah, His Son, Farooq, Takes Over in Jammu and Kashmir

On 8 March 1980, a controversial bill, named 'The Jammu & Kashmir Grant of Permit for Resettlement in (or Permanent Return to) the State', was moved in the Assembly by Abdul Rahim Rather of the ruling National Conference party. It proposed that 'any person who was a state subject before 14 May, 1954 and has migrated to Pakistan after 1947 could be recommended for resettlement in the state on scrutiny by the state authorities'.[19] From the bordering areas of Jammu, a considerable number of Muslims had gone to Pakistan as refugees around Independence. With

3 lakh non-Muslim refugees who migrated from West Pakistan in 1965 and 1971 occupying huge chunks of such evacuees' land in the Jammu border areas, the bill posed considerable practical complications as well as potential law and order problems. Furthermore, by eroding the sole competence of the Union government to grant citizenship of India, it proved to be highly controversial. Both houses of the state legislature passed the bill in April 1982, but Governor B.K. Nehru returned it for reconsideration.

On 21 August 1981, in a massive public rally, following the practice of primogeniture, Sheikh Abdullah announced his eldest son Farooq Abdullah as the president of the National Conference, and by implication, after his demise, his heir apparent as chief minister. A medical doctor by training, Farooq had been practising in the UK. He had campaigned for his father in the 1977 election and become a member of the Lok Sabha in 1980 from the Srinagar constituency, unopposed. When his father died on 7 September 1982, Farooq, who had already been the health minister for two months, became the chief minister. His succession triggered a family feud. Sheikh Abdullah's eldest child Khalida was married to Ghulam Mohammad Shah. Khalida was extremely close to her father and G.M. Shah, a comrade-in-arms of the Sheikh from 1944, had spent a long time in prison along with the Sheikh in 1959 and 1969–70. Older than Farooq by sixteen years, he had been the general secretary of the Plebiscite Front founded by Sheikh Abdullah, a minister of state in the 1975 Sheikh ministry and a cabinet minister under the Sheikh since 1977.

Within a week of assuming office, Farooq sacked all the cabinet ministers, which included many old guards and associates of Sheikh Abdullah, and inducted a new team. Within a few months, he also dissolved the thirty-one-member executive committee of the National Conference. There were also complaints against Farooq's cavalier attitude towards his chief ministerial responsibilities, both within and outside the National Conference. He was attending office infrequently and making too many trips outside the state. There were growing dissensions within the National Conference party.

The six-year term of the Jammu and Kashmir legislative assembly was ending in 1983. Indira Gandhi and her Congress, back in power at the Union level, wanted to have a pre-poll alliance with Farooq Abdullah and his National Conference for the assembly polls. Farooq and his National Conference refused. In the elections, in June 1983, the National Conference won forty-six of the seventy-five seats and Congress twenty-six. Farooq returned as chief minister. In October 1983, Farooq expelled G.M. Shah and seven other leaders from the party for anti-party activities. In the same month, he also organized a large conclave of fifty-nine leaders from seventeen non-Congress parties in Srinagar to discuss Centre-state relations. It was attended by veteran leaders such as Jyoti Basu, N.T. Rama Rao, I.K. Gujral, Chandra Shekhar, Jagjivan Ram, Sharad Pawar, H.N. Bahuguna, Parkash Singh Badal and S.S. Barnala. G.M. Shah and his wife Begum Khalida went on to form a new party, the Awami National Conference.

In April 1984, in a major reshuffle of several Governors in different states, B.K. Nehru was shifted to Gujarat and replaced by Jagmohan, the Lt Governor of Delhi. On 2 July 1984, G.M. Shah and a dozen leading members of the legislative assembly defected from the National Conference. Shah had the support of the twenty-six Congress members of the legislative assembly. Jagmohan, the newly appointed Governor of Jammu and Kashmir from late April 1984, sacked Farooq Abdullah as the chief minister and dissolved the council of ministers headed by him for having 'lost the confidence of the majority in the legislative assembly'. Without a floor test, he installed Farooq's brother-in-law G.M. Shah as the chief minister.

There was unrest in Jammu and Kashmir following the appointment of G.M. Shah as CM. According to the political scientist Sumantra Bose, he earned '. . . the sobriquet "curfew chief minister"—for seventy-two of the first ninety days of his administration the Valley was under curfew orders to prevent protest demonstrations.'[20]

XIX.5 National Health Policy 1983

At the end of an international conference on PHC organized by the World Health Organization (WHO) and United Nations Children's Emergency Fund (UNICEF) from 6 to 12 September 1978 in Alma Ata, Kazakhstan (former USSR), came the Alma Ata declaration. It promoted a rights-based approach to health with a viable strategy for its achievement. It gave a call for Health for All by the year 2000—a level of health that would not only be disease-free but permit them to lead a socially and economically productive life. Representatives of 134 countries and sixty-seven international organizations identified PHC as the key to the attainment of the goal of health for all. Indira Gandhi's restructured twenty-point programme of January 1982 contained augmentation of universal PHC facilities and control of leprosy, tuberculosis and blindness.

After the Alma Ata declaration, the Indian Council of Medical Research and Indian Council of Social Science Research (ICMR-ICSSR) Joint Panel, in 1980, stressed the need for a more integrated and comprehensive health system and called on the government to formulate a national health policy. Five years after the Alma Ata declaration, India came out with National Health Policy 1983 duly approved by Parliament. Prior to 1983, the successive five-year plans had been providing the framework for the states to develop their health services infrastructure and facilities for medical education and research. With National Health Policy 1983, India moved to an integrated, comprehensive approach towards the future development of medical education, research and health services.

With the National Health Policy 1983, there was a move from the high emphasis on the curative to the more balanced approach on the preventive, promotive, public health and rehabilitative aspects of healthcare. It advocated decentralized provision of health services through PHCs and emphasized the importance of immunization against preventable diseases, small family norms, safe drinking water, adequate nutrition, proper housing and environment for the weaker sections. The National Health Policy 1983 pointed out how a large majority of health functions could be effectively handled and resolved by the people themselves, with the organized support of volunteers, auxiliaries, paramedics and adequately trained multi-purpose workers of various grades of skill and competence, of both sexes. Universal education could play a major role in the promotion of health. It recommended a referral system for specialized treatment at a well-dispersed network of centres equipped to provide speciality and super-speciality services. To contain the fiscal stress because of the high cost of providing such services, it advocated encouraging private investments in specialised fields so that while most of such centres within the governmental set-up would provide adequate care and treatment to those entitled to free care, the affluent sectors could be looked after by the paying clinics. It set up goals for improvements by 1985, 1990 and 2000 in health indicators such as infant, prenatal and pre-school, and maternal mortality rates, babies with a weight of more than 2.5 kg, crude birth and death, net reproduction rates, life expectancy, immunization of children and the proportion of arrested cases out of those detected with leprosy and tuberculosis.

XIX.6 Troubles Galore and Tragic End to the Indira Era

The early 1980s was a troubled period for Indira Gandhi. She was bereaved by the tragic death of her younger son and political successor Sanjay in June 1980. And she was besieged by not only the Antulay cement scandal but also discontent in Assam in the east and insurgency led by the Sikh godman Jarnail Singh Bhindranwale in Punjab in the west. Nation-building was still an ongoing project.

If, in life, Sanjay Gandhi was famous for his imperious ways, he remained true to his style even in his tragic death at the young age of 33. On the morning of 23 June 1980, he was flying a red and white aerobatic single-engine biplane owned by the Delhi Flying Club. The plane was doing aerobatics, including loops, when it went into a dive and crashed. Sanjay died instantly. Indira was devastated by the loss of her younger son and political successor.

Then, in October 1981, broke the scandal involving Indira Pratisthan set up by Maharashtra Chief Minister Abdul Rehman Antulay. Antulay, a barrister close to Sanjay Gandhi, had become the chief minister of his state Maharashtra on 9 January 1980. Antulay was a diehard Gandhi-family loyalist—Congress (I) was born at Antulay's residence. Antulay set up a financial aid scheme for the poor and the destitute called the Sanjay Gandhi Niradhar Yojana, and the Indira Gandhi Pratibha Pratisthan (or Talent Establishment) Trust to encourage talent and artists. This trust proved to be his undoing. With acute scarcity, cement was under a rationed regime, and allocated by the government. Antulay was reported to have collected money for Indira Pratisthan by out-of-turn allotment of cement. Veteran journalist Arun Shourie wrote about this irregular practice in the daily *Indian Express*. As members of the Opposition voiced vociferous protests in Parliament, several writ petitions were filed in the Mumbai High Court to maintain the status quo and prevent further excesses. After the Mumbai High Court admitted a writ petition on 12 January 1982, Antulay resigned.

There was trouble for Indira even in the Congress's bastion of Andhra Pradesh, where her party had won forty-one out of forty-two Lok Sabha seats both in 1977 and 1980. She had changed the chief minister from her party five times between 1978 and 1983. In March 1982, the celebrated actor N.T. Rama Rao, popularly known as NTR, had formed the Telugu Desam Party (TDP) to get rid of the corruption and ineptitude under the Congress and redeem the Telugu pride. In 1983, in Andhra Pradesh, NTR's newly founded TDP went on to sweep the Vidhan Sabha polls and form the government. Congress dominance in Andhra Pradesh was over for some time to come.

Starting with the bifurcation of Punjab into Punjab and Haryana in 1966, Indira had achieved considerable success in reorganizing states. But there was great turmoil involving insurgencies and terrorism in the two strategic states of Assam and Punjab.

In Assam, in 1978, following the death of Janata Party Member of Parliament (MP) Hiralal Patowary, a by-election was scheduled in the Mangoldoi constituency. 'The All Assam Students' Union (AASU) demanded that the election be postponed, alleging that the electoral rolls, which were being revised, contained the names of "lakhs" of illegal Bangladeshi immigrants. Launching an agitation, it wanted an intensive revision of the electoral rolls in the entire State to detect foreigners, delete their names from the list and deport them. In no time the agitation led by AASU president Prafulla Kumar Mahanta and general secretary Bhrigu Kumar Phukan assumed the form of a mass movement popularly known as the 'Assam Movement' or the "anti-foreigner movement."[21] The movement transformed the perceived fear of the 'Assamese people'— about losing their identity and being reduced to a minority by the influx of foreigners through the porous India-Bangladesh border—into a strong identity-based movement clamouring for constitutional, legislative and administrative safeguards. The six-year-long agitation witnessed violence and, at its peak, led to the infamous Nellie massacre in 1983.

Then there was the violent Sikh separatist movement in Punjab culminating in Operation Blue Star in June 1984. After the creation of the Punjabi Suba in 1966, the Akalis wanted to have Chandigarh—the former capital of Punjab which had been converted into a UT to serve as the capital of both Haryana and Punjab—and the Punjabi-speaking areas left in Haryana transferred to Punjab, and sought the control of Bhakra Dam and other hydro power projects and headworks.

Dr Jagjit Singh Chauhan, a dentist, was Deputy Speaker under the Akali-Jana Sangh-ComPI coalition government in 1967 and finance minister in the succeeding Congress-supported government under Lachhman Singh Gill. In 1969, he stood as a candidate of the Punjab Janta Party in Tanda Vidhan Sabha constituency and lost to the Congress candidate. In 1971, he led a Sikh delegation on a tour of Europe and US to present the 'true picture' of the Sikhs in India, visited Nankana Sahib in Pakistan to set up a Sikh government, and on 13 October 1971, placed an advertisement in *The New York Times* proclaiming an Independent Sikh State. It was titled 'Sat Siri (sic) Akal. The Sikhs demand an independent state in India . . . (sic) the only guarantee for peace in the sub-continent.'

Punjab was in political turmoil. It saw four chief ministers in the four years between 1967 and 1971. After a period of President's rule, Punjab Vidhan Sabha elections were held in 1972, after the liberation of Bangladesh. Congress, with 42.8 per cent of the votes and sixty-six out of the 104 seats in the Vidhan Sabha, was securely back in power under Chief Minister Giani Zail Singh, a Ramgarhia Sikh as opposed to the Jat-Sikh leadership of the Akalis. Ramgarhias are a caste composed of artisans such as carpenters, stonemasons and blacksmiths. Zail Singh, who later went on to become the President of India, was described by some in the media as 'The President who reveled in playing politics'.[22] For the time being, Punjab looked quiet and peaceful under Congress rule. But a storm was brewing.

After the Emergency was lifted, there were three governments under the Akalis, then the Congress and then the Akalis again. The Akalis had fought in alliance with the Janata Dal and CPI(M) in 1977 elections and won in Punjab. Under the Akali government headed by Prakash Singh Badal, tensions mounted with the Sikh-Nirankari clash in early 1978. Nirankari is a reformist movement within Sikhism from the nineteenth century that believes in a living guru as opposed to the scriptural guru

Guru Granth Sahib. Traditional Sikhs consider that heresy. The day of 13 April 1978 was Vaisakhi—the day to celebrate the birth of the Khalsa. A peaceful Sant Nirankari convention headed by their leader Gurbachan Singh was organized in Amritsar. After delivering angry sermons from Golden Temple premises, Jarnail Singh Bhindranwale had threatened not to allow this convention and to go there and cut them to pieces. Bhindranwale with his followers and Fauja Singh of the Akhand Kirtani Jatha attacked the convention and in the ensuing conflict, two of Bhindranwale's followers, eleven members of the Akhand Kirtani Jatha and three Nirankaris were killed. With factionalism rampant in the party, the Akali government was on the back foot as Bhindranwale considered the killing of Sikhs with an Akali as chief minister to be outrageous. The Sikh-Nirankari clash brought Bhindranwale into limelight. He was the leader or *jathedar* of the Damdami Taksal, also known as Bhindran Taksal, a Sikh educational organization headquartered in the town of Chowk Mehta, near the holy city of Amritsar.

There are reports that, after the Emergency, at the behest of Sanjay Gandhi and with the active participation of Giani Zail Singh of the Congress, Bhindranwale was put up as a 'Sant' to challenge the Akali government. Violence escalated in Punjab, with Bhindranwale increasing his rhetoric against the perceived enemies of Sikhs and developing a sentiment justifying extra-judicial killings of the perceived enemies of Sikhism. With the emigration of Sikhs to Europe, North America and the Middle East, the influx of poor Hindu agricultural workers from UP and Bihar in response to a labour shortage further threatened the religious composition of the population. In the meantime, the Anandpur Sahib resolution was presented at the eighteenth session of the All-India Akali Conference at Ludhiana on 28 and 29 October 1978 and endorsed without any dissent. The resolution emphasized the separate identity of Sikhs and demanded greater decentralization of power from the Union to the states, which the government thought to be secessionist. Sant Harchand Singh Longowal took over the reins of the Akali Dal in 1980 and launched his civil disobedience movement to press their demands under the Anandpur Sahib Resolution.

Indira Gandhi sacked the Badal government on 17 February 1980 after returning to power and imposed President's rule. Nirankari Guru

Gurbachan Singh was murdered on 24 April 1980 by a member of the Akhand Kirtani Jatha posing as a carpenter. In the elections to the Punjab legislative assembly on 30 May 1980, the Congress won sixty-three of the 117 seats and formed the government on 6 June 1980 with Darbara Singh as CM. Senior journalist Lala Jagat Narain was murdered on 9 September 1981 and Bhindranwale was accused of the murder and arrested. An Indian Airlines Boeing 737 was hijacked to Lahore on 29 September 1981 in protest against Bhindranwale's arrest. The plane was rescued with the collaboration of Pakistani commandos and Bhindranwale released in early October. He became a 'saint', according to his ardent followers, and an 'ayatollah' and a terrorist according to others. In July 1982, Sant Longowal invited him to take up residence in the Golden Temple Complex and later in a building adjacent to the Akal Takht. On 19 July 1982, Bhindranwale, anticipating his imminent arrest, with a large group of armed followers, moved into the sanctuary of Guru Nanak Niwas, a hostel in the precincts of the Golden Temple. In August 1982, the Akali Dal launched the Dharam Yudh Morcha—Rallies for the Religious Struggle—in collaboration with Bhindranwale to win more autonomy for Punjab. In November 1982, Sant Longowal threatened that the Akali Dal would disrupt the Asian Games to be held in Delhi soon.

The demand for a separate Sikh nation, Khalistan, grew shriller and Bhindranwale's notorious hit-squads mounted on motorcycles spread terror on the non-Sikhs. Between 4 August 1982 and 3 June 1984, there were 1200 violent incidents in which 410 persons were killed and more than 1180 injured. Bhindranwale's followers fortified the Golden Temple complex with machine guns and anti-tank launchers using the services of a disaffected former Indian army official, 'General' Shahbeg Singh, to train his supporters. With increasing incidents of violence, the Darbara Singh ministry was dismissed, and President's rule imposed in Punjab in October 1983. The state was also declared a disturbed area.

Between 3 and 8 June 1984, the Indian army launched Operation Bluestar to remove Bhindranwale from the complex. Bhindranwale's men, who were well-armed and well-trained, put-up fierce resistance. Bhindranwale was killed and the terrorists were flushed out of the complex only after more than 500 fatalities and some damage to the temple complex. With simmering discontent against Operation Bluestar among a section of the Sikhs, Prime Minister Indira Gandhi was brutally assassinated at her residential compound by two of her own Sikh bodyguards on the morning of 30 October 1984. In a macabre twist to the story, what followed was gruesome rioting against innocent Sikhs all over the country. Reportedly, some 20,000 lives were lost.

XX

The Camelot Days

Rajiv Gandhi, the elder of Indira Gandhi's two sons, was an airline pilot. After his younger brother Sanjay's tragic death in 1980, Rajiv, at the behest of his mother, had entered politics reluctantly. The Amethi Lok Sabha seat in UP had fallen vacant with Sanjay's death. Rajiv won it in a by-election in August 1981. Prime Minister Indira Gandhi, who was simultaneously the president of the Congress Party, elevated him as one of the several general secretaries of the party. On 30 October 1984, after Indira's assassination, Rajiv, with less than five years' experience in politics, became the prime minister. Only 40, he became the youngest PM of India.

Soon, elections to the Eighth Lok Sabha were announced for 24-28 December 1984. Riding on a sympathy wave for Indira Gandhi and her bereaved son, the Congress under Rajiv garnered 49.1 per cent of the votes polled and secured a two-thirds majority of 404 out of 514 seats. This was better than what the Congress had ever done before under Rajiv's grandfather and mother!

XX.1 A Period of Elevated Hope and Optimism

Expectations were high with the coming of Rajiv. His mother had promised 'a government that works' he promised 'a government that works faster'. He wanted to take India to the twenty-first century and declared that his task was to bring India to the threshold of the twenty-first century free of the burden of poverty, and capable of meeting the rising aspirations of the people. The people were enthused.

With Indira's last few years mired in corruption scandals, at the centenary session of the Congress in Mumbai on 28 December 1985, Rajiv said, 'The war on corruption will go on without let or hindrance. The country needs a clean social and political environment, the Congress is determined to give it.'[1] He also denounced the self-perpetuating clique of power brokers within the party who had converted a mass movement into a feudal oligarchy and how corruption was not only tolerated but regarded as the hallmark of leadership. During a visit to drought-affected Kalahandi in Odisha in 1985, the Prime Minister lamented, 'Of every rupee spent by the government, only 17 paise reached the intended beneficiary.'[2] Described as 'a reluctant politician', Rajiv Gandhi, unlike his younger brother, acquired a reputation that led to him being called 'Mr Clean'.

Some held that 'Unlike his grandfather, Jawaharlal Nehru, or even his mother, Indira Gandhi, Rajiv appears to have been singularly lacking in intellectual attainments, and his interventions in Parliamentary debates were notoriously prosaic and dull.'[3] About Rajiv's mission of taking India to the twenty-first century, some observed that 'He did not want to discover India's past, but was eager to script India's future.'[4] Yet, according to a distinguished former colleague, 'Charismatic, amiable and full of new ideas, he endeared himself to those he came in contact with. His support base was truly pan-Indian.'[5] Like the US did with President John F. Kennedy, India dreamt of a Camelot in the young Rajiv Gandhi.

One source of corruption in Indian politics was the 'Aya Ram Gaya Ram' (return of the Ram who had gone) phenomenon, another name for floor crossings, sometimes for monetary incentives or ministerial appointments. Governments operating on thin majorities were vulnerable to such changes in party loyalties in Parliament or state legislatures. For example, in the troubled period of 1967–71, there were 142 defections in Parliament and 1969 defections in state assemblies across the country. Thirty-two governments collapsed and 212 defectors were rewarded with ministerial positions. In Haryana, in 1967, Gaya Lal, the MLA representing Hassanpur, created history by changing parties three times in a fortnight—after changing from Congress to the United Front, he had gone back to the Congress, only to come back to the United Front. During one such change, the CM of the United Front Government, Rao Birendra Singh, took him to the state capital Chandigarh and famously remarked that 'Gaya Ram was now Aya Ram', giving rise to the phrase 'Aya Ram Gaya Ram'.

One of the earliest legislative moves by Rajiv was an Anti-Defection Law. The bill was moved on 24 January 1985 and the relevant Constitution (Fifty-Second Amendment) was unanimously passed by Parliament six days later.

Interestingly, the Anti-Defection Law would go on to play an important role in curbing the misuse by the Union government of Article 356 to dismiss governments in states ruled by other parties. The President of India could use Article 356 to dismiss a state government if they were 'satisfied' with the Governor's report that the administration of the state could not be carried on in accordance with the Constitution and/or that the government no longer enjoyed the support of the Vidhan Sabha. While the President's 'satisfaction' was beyond the purview of the court, the question of majority support in the Vidhan Sabha became a different matter with the Anti-Defection Law. Article 356 had been used generously during Prime Minister Indira Gandhi's two stints (1966–77, 1980–84) a total of fifty times, and during Morarji Desai and Charan Singh's rule (1977–1980) twenty times. Rajiv used it only six times during his five years as Prime Minister. But one of these six dismissals in April 1989—that of Chief Minister S.R. Bommai of the Janata Dal in Karnataka—because of the Anti-Defection Law, would result in a landmark judgment by the Supreme Court in 1994 and curb the potential 'abuse' of Article 356.

A source of worry on the external front was the civil war in Sri Lanka. Tamils, who constituted about 10 per cent of the population in Sri Lanka, were concentrated in its northern and eastern provinces, and had deep cultural, religious and linguistic links with the people in the southern Indian state of Tamil Nadu, about 55 km away from the island state. Tamils—mostly Hindus and Muslims—in Sri Lanka differed from the Buddhist Sinhala majority both in religion and language. The majoritarian policies of the Sri Lankan government had led to a separatist movement by the Tamils from the early 1970s onwards and by 1976, to the formation of

Liberation Tigers for Tamil *Eelam* (LTTE) under Velupillai Prabhakaran. *Eelam* is the old Tamil name for Sri Lanka. The Tamil Eelam problem in Sri Lanka had major security and other implications for India. 'In July 1983, after a series of ethnic riots left thousands of ethnic Tamils dead, Indira Gandhi decided that a settlement to the conflict could only be brought about through Indian intervention. New Delhi adopted a policy of strategic coercion against Sri Lanka Government, involving support for Tamil insurgents, threats of invasion, as well as the positioning of India as a mediator.'[6] On assuming power, Rajiv inherited this ominous Sri Lanka problem.

XX.2 Finance Minister V.P. Singh and Long-Term Fiscal Policy

After becoming Prime Minister, Rajiv Gandhi had inducted V.P. Singh as his minister of finance, and after the election, Singh continued in his assignment. As finance minister, Singh, in his first Union Budget for 1985–86, announced the need for putting the annual Budget exercise in a longer time frame and promised the introduction of a long-term fiscal policy. The Seventh Five-Year Plan was starting, and he promised to make it coterminous with the plan.

The Long-Term Fiscal Policy came into effect in December 1985. It aimed at imparting 'a definite direction and coherence to the sequence of annual budgets' and 'a greater role for rule-based fiscal and financial policies and less reliance on discretionary case-by-case administration of physical controls.'[7] It announced that the 'major contribution of fiscal policy to poverty alleviation has to come through an effective programme for mobilization of additional resources, which can be used for financing the anti-poverty programmes.' It targeted non-inflationary financing of plans by greater reliance on budget surpluses and CPSE profits, and progressively increasing the share of direct taxes in total tax revenue. For stability of direct taxes, it promised to keep the tax rate schedule on personal income and wealth unchanged for a minimum period of five years, with surcharges on such taxes imposed as a temporary measure to respond to 'compelling circumstances'. It said that the rates of corporate taxation would not be reduced further; however, the surcharge and surtax along with investment allowance would be abolished with effect from 1 April 1987 and depreciation allowance streamlined.

Long-Term Fiscal Policy proposed to consolidate all duties related to excise, except additional excise in lieu of sales tax and cesses for specific purposes, and remove numerous exemptions granted 'through over 500 notifications'. Exemptions, when granted under compelling circumstances, would be subject to a 'sunset rule' of automatically lapsing after three years. A major reform proposed was a phased move to a modified system of VAT or MODVAT, wherein proforma credit would be provided as set-off for excise and countervailing duties paid on most inputs, except on a few items like petroleum, tobacco and textile products. The proposed MODVAT reform was a giant step towards partly removing the problem of 'tax-on-tax'. The policy said that the harmonized system of nomenclature (HSN), which was under implementation in customs tariff, would also be extended to excise duties.

In the area of customs tariff, Long-Term Fiscal Policy proposed to classify goods into five broad categories: (i) essential consumer goods, (ii) raw materials, (iii) intermediate goods and components, (iv) capital goods, and (v) non-essential consumer goods. While the long-term goal would be to have a single rate for all, in the interim, the rates would be restructured, with the rate generally rising from one category to the next with a ban on the imports of the last category.

A critical innovation under Rajiv's rule was the introduction of a computerized allotment of Permanent Account Number (PAN) to income tax assessees. Before 1972, the assessees were identified by their General Index Register (GIR) number under a manual system. The GIR number was unique only within an Assessing Officer's ward or circle and not throughout the country. To overcome these shortcomings, PAN (old series) was first introduced in 1972 and made statutory under Section 139A of the Income Tax Act from 1 April 1976. Blocks of PANs were allotted to each Commissioner's Charge by the CBDT. The Commissioners made the allotment of PANs to assessees under various Assessing Officers in their charge from within the blocks allotted to them. The old series did not fully insure against an assessee evading taxes by having more than one PAN. To solve this problem, computerized allotment was introduced through thirty-six computer centres covering the entire country in 1985.

Income tax

In 1985–86, Singh started the reform of personal income tax by raising the exemption limit from ₹15,000 to ₹18,000, broadbanding the slabs and cutting down their number (excluding the exempt slab) from eight to four, reducing the applicable basic rates by up to 16.25 percentage points and abolishing the surcharge. As a result, the highest marginal rate, inclusive of surcharge if any, came down from 61.875 per cent in 1984–85 to 50 per cent from 1985–86. The eminent lawyer Nani Palkhivala in 1965 had famously written how, with the marginal rate as high as 80 per cent, it may be 'more profitable to evade tax on Rs. 20 than to earn Rs. 100'.[8] A study on black money published in March 1985 by the NIPFP had revealed how widespread the problem of tax evasion could be. Thus, there was not much opposition to the reduction of direct tax rates. After the presentation of Long-Term Fiscal Policy in 1985, the rates of personal income tax with no surcharge were maintained for the next six years until 1990-91. The surcharge on the corporate tax of 5 per cent was abolished from 1986–87.

Singh also reduced the corporation tax rate by 5-10 percentage points and reduced various concessions such as depreciation allowance. He reduced the rates of wealth tax and raised the exemption limit. He said that 'a tax, however laudable in intent, should have no place in the statute book if it has outlived its utility'.[9] The estate duty was not proving to be a cost-effective method for revenue generation, and Singh abolished it in his Budget for 1985–86.

There was what some experts describe as a tax amnesty scheme, not with Parliamentary approval but by 'stealth', through seven CBDT circulars between 26 June 1985 and 17 February 1986. These allowed tax evaders to disclose their unaccounted incomes and wealth of any year before end-March 1986, and pay due tax on it, on the assurance that penal interest would be waived and immunity from penalties would be granted. There was no immunity in respect of excise duty, sales tax etc. The scheme extended up to end-March 1987 and mopped up black money of about ₹700 crore. Two more amnesties introduced through the back door were Indira Vikas Patra (Development Bonds) in 1986 and Kisan (Framer) Vikas Patra in 1988.

Customs duty

In 1985–86, Singh reduced the basic customs duty on many items such as project imports, machinery, computer parts and zip fasteners, but increased the duty on a few others, and most notably, increased the auxiliary customs duty on petroleum and petroleum products. He abolished export duty on a host of items and retained it only in the cases of coffee, unmanufactured tobacco, mica other than bridge mica, and hides and skins.

Excise duty

In Union excise duties, Singh increased the Central Excise Tariff Item 68, the residual category, which had been raised to 10 per cent in 1983–84, to 12 per cent in 1985–86. He also increased the rate on a few items such as vegetable products, aerated waters and cement and introduced four new line items, including what is ubiquitous in India today as 'pan masala'—'a preparation containing betel nuts and any one or more of other ingredients such as lime, catechu, cardamom, copra and menthol, put up for sale in unit containers'.[10] Singh maintained the special excise duty levied at 10 per cent of the basic excise duty only on thirty-two products and abolished or integrated it with the basic excise duty on others. To promote their growth, he liberalized the excise duty concession to small-scale industrial units. In 1985–86, Singh abolished the annual license fee on radio and video cassette recorder (VCR) and replaced the annual license fee on TV with a one-time levy at the time of its purchase. Following the recommendation of the Eighth Finance Commission, he also raised the rates of stamp duty on bills of lading and letters of credit.

The MODVAT scheme was introduced in 1986–87 for all goods covered by thirty-seven specified chapters of the Central Excise Tariff Act, 1985. Both excise and customs saw the selective adjustment of rates both ways. There were signs of rescinding from the position espoused in favour of rules against discretion in the Long-Term Fiscal Policy. Politics was staging a tactical come back.

XX.3 Change of Guard at the Finance Ministry

After businesses' and business associations' complaints of a 'raid raj' by V.P. Singh, he was shifted from the ministry of finance to the ministry of defence on 24 January 1987. For a few months, Prime Minister Rajiv Gandhi, like his mother and grandfather, was the finance minister as well, and presented the Budget for 1987–88. Rajiv Gandhi demitted the post of FM in July 1987, and two ministers, Narain Dutt Tiwari and Shankarrao Bhavrao Chavan, followed in quick succession to present the budgets for 1988–89 and 1989–90.

Income tax

The rates of income tax and the exemption limit remained unchanged, but exemptions—for example, on amortization payments for housing loans and liberalized depreciation allowances for corporates—were back under Rajiv Gandhi as FM. One prominent exemption was with respect to the Constituency Allowance of Hon'ble MPs, without any monetary ceiling! Exemptions in the past for corporates had led to the problem of highly profitable companies paying 'zero tax', and V.P. Singh, in 1983, had introduced a new Section 80VVA in the Income Tax Act restricting allowable deductions to 70 per cent of income before deductions. In his 1987–88 Budget, Rajiv noted that it had not produced the desired results. So he withdrew this provision and introduced what came to be known as the 'Minimum Alternate Tax' (MAT), which was a tax on 30 per cent of book profit. The holding period for qualifying for concessional tax treatment under capital gains was reduced from three years to one year.

Tiwari inherited an economy troubled by two successive bad monsoons followed by droughts and floods in 1987–88 in different parts of the country. In December 1987, to meet the exigencies of the situation, Tiwari amended the Finance Act of 1987 to introduce a surcharge of 5 per cent for income above ₹50,000. But, under personal income tax, he also raised the rate of standard deduction from 30 per cent to 33.33 per cent and the ceiling from ₹10,000 to ₹12,000. He also gave concessions under corporate income tax. Next year, in 1988–89, in personal income tax, in a breach of the Long-Term Fiscal Policy propounded less than four years ago, Finance Minister S.B. Chavan lowered the tax rate for the first slab of ₹18,000 to ₹25,000 from 25 per cent to 20 per cent and raised the surcharge for income above ₹50,000 from 5 per cent to 8 per cent. Furthermore, there were a plethora of exemptions and concessions on repayment of housing loans, income from poultry farms and investments by retiring government employees. By a notification of the President on 7 November 1988, the Income Tax Act was extended to the state of Sikkim from the assessment year 1989–90. One important change was in the recasting of the assessment system from 1989–90. For example, before the assessment year 1989–90, the 'previous' year could be the previous year ending on a date even before 31 March. From the assessment year 1989–90, the previous year had to end on 31 March.

One significant reform was the change in the provision of professional tax. The Indian Constitution, under entry 60 of List II relating to powers of the states, specifies 'Taxes on professions, trades, callings and employments'. However, Article 276 (ii) of the Constitution also stipulated that 'The total amount payable in respect of any one person to the State or to any one municipality, district board, local board or other local authority in the State by way of taxes on professions, trades, callings and employments shall not exceed two hundred and fifty rupees per annum.' By the Constitution (Sixtieth Amendment) Act, 1988, this limit was raised to ₹2500. Yet, there were many states—for example, Haryana, Rajasthan and Uttarakhand—which did not levy a professional tax even in 2020-21!

Customs duty

With Rajiv Gandhi as FM, while there were some selective increases and decreases for specified products under customs duty, one welcome change was the reduction in import duty on computers, computer parts and peripherals and data communication equipment. Several stalwarts from the halcyon days of the IT boom in India, like Nandan Nilekani, a cofounder of Infosys, have acknowledged the role that this policy of Rajiv played in promoting the nascent industry.

In December 1987, to meet the budgetary needs created by inclement agricultural weather conditions, Finance Minister Tiwari imposed, as he had done for income tax, a surcharge of 5 per cent by way of auxiliary duty of customs on imported goods other than essential commodities.

Excise duty

In the area of indirect taxes, a significant move under Rajiv was the extension of MODVAT to most of the remaining areas except textiles, tobacco and the petroleum sector. To avoid valuation problems in levying excise on cigarettes, he moved to a system of levy based on their length.

In the Budget for 1988–89, Tiwari imposed a surcharge by way of a special excise duty of 5 per cent—already applicable to income tax and customs duty from December 1987—on the basic duty of excise. In terms of concessions to the agricultural sector, Tiwari's budget for 1988–89 had strong similarities with Charan Singh's budget for 1979–80. In 1988–89, excise duty was reduced on several agricultural, including agro-processing equipment, and machinery. Furthermore, there were a host of concessions and exemptions granted together with some increases in excise duty to provide relief to the consumer and people building homes. The principle of few concessions and exemptions enunciated by the Long-Term Fiscal Policy in December 1985 virtually unravelled under Tiwari in 1988 and Chavan in 1989.

In excise duties, Finance Minister S.B. Chavan pointed out how 70 per cent of excise revenues were derived from commodities carrying duties at specific rates which had not been revised for many years. In 1989–90, he revised these specific duty rates upward on items other than those for mass consumption, most notably iron and steel, cigarettes and molasses. Chavan increased the rate of Foreign Travel Tax per ticket from ₹50, where it had remained unchanged since its introduction in 1979, to ₹100 for travel to neighbouring countries, and from ₹100 to ₹300 for travel to other countries. In 1989, after a gap of sixteen years, the Inland Air Travel Tax, which had been abolished in 1973, came back as a 10 per cent tax on the basic fare to pay for the expenses incurred in developing airports and maintaining them.

Other measures

Finance Minister Narain Dutt Tiwari, an old-world politician from the command-and-control days, in his Budget for 1988–89, announced a series of steps such as reducing the interest on farm loans, raising the sub-target for agricultural lending under the directed credit programme, and special price discount for fertilizer to the farmer. His successor S.B. Chavan, in 1989–90, raised the target for direct finance to agriculture by public sector banks, as a proportion of their total outstanding advances, already up from 16 per cent to 17 per cent in the previous year further to

18 per cent. He also proposed to modify the Gold (Control) Act of 1968 to help the jewellery industry.

Under Rajiv Gandhi, during 1984–89, as a proportion of GDP, tax revenues of the Union government increased from 6.75 per cent in 1983–84 to a peak of 7.73 per cent in 1988-89 before declining marginally to 7.64 per cent in 1989–90. During this six-year period, despite a fall in direct tax revenue—again as a proportion of GDP—from 1.37 per cent to 1.20 per cent, the overall tax revenue increased because of revenues from indirect taxes going up from 5.38 per cent to 6.44 per cent, mainly on account of customs duties.

During the Rajiv Gandhi era, as a proportion of GDP, the aggregate taxes of the states increased from 4.70 per cent in 1983–84 to a peak of 5.25 per cent in 1987–88 before declining marginally to 5.18 per cent in 1989–90. The corresponding increase in sales tax revenue was from 2.73 per cent in 1983–84 to 3.00 per cent in 1989–90. With no addition to the ranks of states imposing prohibition, state excise revenues increased from 0.69 per cent to 0.77 per cent.

XX.4 Reforms under Rajiv Gandhi

Rajiv Gandhi, right after coming to power, launched what came to be described as his 'New Economic Policy'. To free up business and promote growth, he acted on many of what three important committees under L.K. Jha, Abid Hussain and M. Narasimham had already recommended. In the area of foreign trade, for example, to bring about continuity and stability in line with the recommendations of the Abid Hussain Committee of 1984, import-export policy was announced for a period of three years from 1985 to 1988.

Industrial licensing

Broadbanding of industrial licences was introduced for the manufacture of two-wheelers below 350 cc capacity from 11 January 1985, extended to the paper industry a month later, and further to twenty-four other industries such as four-wheelers and chemicals. This was to enable manufacturers to change their product mix to respond to changing demand without getting their licence changed. In the 1985–86 Budget, to reduce rigidities, improve the environment for industrial growth and reflect the considerable increase in costs, the asset limit for MRTP companies, fixed in 1969, was revised to ₹100 crore. For SSI, the ceiling on investment in plant and machinery, fixed in 1980 at ₹20 lakh, was revised up to ₹35 lakh, and for ancillaries from ₹25 lakh to ₹45 lakh. In March 1985, twenty-five broad categories of industries—such as steel structural, automotive ancillaries and electrical tools—were delicensed subject to the units not being under MRTPA 1969 or FERA, or not producing items reserved for the SSI, or being located in specified urban areas. In June 1985, the New Textile Policy announced by the government removed curbs on the expansion or creation of new capacity in the mill sector and gave full flexibility in the use of cotton and man-made fibres and yarns in the industry. Licensing policy for synthetic yarn and fibres was liberalized. To promote the sugar industry, a levy proportion for sugar mills was reduced from 65 to 55 per cent.

A policy of capacity re-endorsement for all units that had achieved 80 per cent of their licensed capacity in any of the previous five years preceding end-March 1985 was introduced in late 1985. In some industries, to prevent fragmentation of capacity at uneconomic levels and improving cost efficiency, the government specified minimum capacity rather than putting ceilings on capacity, for example, in toilet sops and milk products in 1987–88. By 1989–90, there were 108 industries with specified minimum economic capacity.

MRTP and foreign companies had been allowed to participate in industries that were of 'basic, critical and strategic' importance for the growth of the economy and had long-term export potential from 1980. In December 1985, the Appendix I list of such specified industries was expanded to thirty broad groups. Also, the export obligation of MRTP and FERA companies setting up non-Appendix I industries was brought down from 50 per cent to 25 per cent in backward districts of category B and C, and from 30 per cent to zero for category A.

In July 1986, roller flour milling was exempted from licensing requirements. Certain chemical industries were freed from licensing in September 1986. The facility of broadbanding of production, introduced in the previous year, was extended during 1986–87 to industries such as glass, steel pipes and tubes and textile machinery. In 1987–88, the computer software industry was exempted from licensing requirement. In 1988–89, all units, except those with investment in fixed assets of more than ₹50 crore in centrally declared backward areas and of more than ₹15 crore in non-backward areas, were exempted from licensing requirement. The negative list of industries requiring a licence, regardless of investment size, was brought down from seventy-seven to twenty-six. In 1989–90, automobile tyres and tubes were freed from licensing requirement. From 1988–89, the limit on imported inputs was increased from 15 per cent of ex-factory value of annual production subject to a ceiling of ₹75 lakh to 30 per cent of ex-factory value of production. Controls on the price and distribution of cement were removed from 1 March 1989.

Foreign trade

Most items on the list of automatic items, which were not indigenously available, were shifted to the OGL list. All items belonged to one of the four categories: OGL, licensable, canalized and banned.

Labour market

The requirement under Chapter V-B of the Industrial Disputes Act, 1947 for all industrial units employing more than 100 personnel to seek the appropriate government's permission to retrench a worker or close a unit down resulting in worker retrenchment affected both the private and public sector, but perhaps the latter in a more acute fashion. The Bureau of Public Enterprise, in October 1988, introduced the Voluntary Retirement Scheme (VRS) as a win-win solution for both the enterprise and the workers. For employees who were at least forty years old with ten years of service, VRS promised ex gratia payment of forty-five days' emoluments (salary plus daily allowance) for each year of service completed. The package was much more lucrative than the retrenchment compensation of only fifteen days' wages for each completed year of service available under the IDRA.

Public health

In 1985, the Union government modified the Expanded Programme of Immunization introduced in 1978 as 'Universal Immunization

Programme' (UIP) to be implemented in phases to cover all the districts in the country by 1989–90. Through UIP, the government would provide free vaccination against preventable diseases. In 1986, the Urban Basic Services Programme (UBSP) was launched in some of the slums in the major Indian cities to improve and upgrade the quality of life of the urban poor, particularly women and children. The major thrust areas were child survival and development, learning opportunities for women and children, water and sanitation, and community organization. In 1986, the government launched Mediclaim, an insurance product offering a minimum and maximum health coverage of ₹15,000 and ₹5 lakh, respectively.

A centrally-sponsored Rural Sanitation Programme (CRSP) was launched in October 1986 with the objective of improving the quality of life of the rural people and to provide privacy and dignity to the women. To supplement the efforts of the states, the programme provided 100 per cent subsidy for the construction of sanitary latrines for SCs, STs and landless labourers, and subsidy as per the rate prevailing in the states for the general public.

Drugs and pharmaceuticals

After the Janata Government's Drug Policy 1978 and DPCO 1979, in 1986, Rajiv government announced a new drug policy and came out with DPCO 1987, which reduced the number of drugs with price control from 347 to 142 to allow greater profitability. The new policy introduced only two categories subject to any price control: Category I, including 'drugs, required for the National Health Programme' for which the maximum allowable post-manufacturing expense (MAPE) was 75 per cent, and Category II, with 'drugs other than those in Category I which are also considered essential for the health needs'[11] with an allowable MAPE of 100 per cent.

One of the controversial decisions of the Rajiv Gandhi government was the promulgation of the Narcotic Drugs and Psychotropic Substances Act, 1985 banning charas (separated resin, crude or refined), hashish (a purified form of charas), ganja (flowering or fruiting top of the cannabis plant) and any mixture with or without any neutral mixture. Cannabis is a drug derived from Indian hemp plants such as cannabis sativa and cannabis indica. Its use in India went back thousands of years. The rationale for banning, whether the ban could be effectively enforced and whether it was done under immense pressure from the US, continues to be debated.

Telecommunications and information technology

In the field of telecommunication, to break up the monopoly of the telephone department and introduce some elements of competition, Mahanagar Telephone Nigam Limited (MTNL) was set up on 1 April 1986. The objective was to upgrade the quality of telecom services, expand the telecom network, introduce new services and raise revenue for telecom development needs of India's key metro cities of Delhi and Mumbai. Videsh Sanchar Nigam Limited (VSNL) was incorporated in 1986 as a public sector enterprise to cater to overseas communication services. Coin-dropping public call offices were set up all over the country. In 1987, to counter the problems of exorbitant and complex pricing of Subscriber Trunk Dialled (STD) and International Subscriber Dialled (ISD) calls, and to assure that calls would be metered and priced correctly, the equipment at every STD/ISD booth was standardized.

Now it is widely recognized that India achieved a revolution in the field of telecommunication in the last few decades, with teledensity going up from less than 1 per cent even in the early 1990s to 81.8 per cent by end-November 2015. Some claim that Rajiv Gandhi, assisted by Sam Pitroda, was the father of the telecom revolution in India. Others point out that the revolution was basically a private sector telecommunication companies' mobile-driven revolution and it came after the telecommunication sector was opened for private participation in 1993 and the New Telecom Policy announced in 1999. Rajiv Gandhi's endeavour was a change led by the public sector and this did not produce the requisite results.

In November 1984, the government announced a package of measures for computers, including a drastic reduction in duties on imported components and raw materials and liberalization of import policy for computers. Rajiv encouraged Texas Instruments, one of the largest manufacturers of semiconductors in the world, to set up a satellite facility in Bengaluru, which it did in 1985.

Financial sector

Ever since it was set up in 1963, the UTI had been the only mutual fund in the country. It had proved to be a popular investment vehicle and ever since setting up in 1963, its assets under management (AUM) had grown to ₹6700 crore in 1987–88. Permission was granted to many public sector banks and insurance companies to enter the mutual funds industry.

From 1988–89 onwards, there were significant changes in the system of administered interest rates. The deposit rates continued to be controlled, but the ceiling rate of 16.5 per cent on bank loans was replaced by a floor rate of 16 per cent from October 1988. In 1988, the first credit rating agency in India, the Credit Rating Information Services of India Limited (CRISIL), was set up by ICICI, UTI, SBI, LIC and the Housing Development Finance Corporation (HDFC). Under the National Housing Bank (NHB) Act, 1987, the NHB was set up on 9 July 1988 as an apex-level autonomous housing finance institution. RBI, together with some financial institutions, set up the Discount and Finance House of India (DFHI) in March 1988. Call money refers to the unsecured segment of the money market that is designed for short-term management of liquidity, mostly overnight. To avoid excessive fluctuations in call money rates, in 1973, Indian Banks' Association (IBA) had introduced a formal system of self-discipline by recommending a ceiling on such rates. After freeing the operations of DFHI from the interest rate ceilings, the ceilings on money market rates were removed on 1 May 1989. The first issue of NRI bonds was launched in 1988 and it netted $92 million.

The liberalization of the financial sector included raising the ceiling on the interest rate on convertible debentures of non-MRTP and non-FERA companies, free transfer of securities of public limited companies, liberalization of rules regarding listing requirements of closely held companies and allowing the introduction of convertible cumulative preference shares. Rajiv Gandhi also legalized companies contributing to political parties out of their profits.

The government was worried about agricultural credit. The central cooperative banks financed their lending partly by refinance credit lines from NABARD, but with mounting overdues, partly because of the drought, these central cooperative banks could not utilize these credit lines. In 1988–90, the government introduced a scheme of central assistance for these cooperative banks. With effect from 1 March 1988, it also reduced the rate of interest on agricultural loans by 1.5–2 per cent to provide relief to farmers. Starting from August 1987, the overdue agricultural loans from farmers were also rescheduled. It is important to note, however, that Rajiv Gandhi did not give any loan waivers to farmers and eroded the credit culture. Such waivers were promised by the Janata government in its 1989 electoral campaign and delivered, after Rajiv Gandhi's defeat, by the Janata government's Deputy Prime Minister Devi Lal. The target for priority sector lending of 40 per cent of the banks' total advances by March 1985, set in March 1980, was achieved. But the problem that continued was in loan recovery.

Capital markets and industrial sickness

Many industrial units were troubled by 'sickness'. Such units were incurring chronic losses and relying on regular infusion of external funds to stay afloat and produce. The inability to either close them down or rehabilitate them was resulting in value destruction by obsolescence of machinery and equipment, industrial land lying unutilized and idle workers facing huge uncertainties. To address the problem of industrial sickness, the Sick Industrial Companies Act (SICA) was passed in 1985. The Act defined a sick industrial unit as one that had been in existence for at least five years and had incurred accumulated losses equal to or exceeding its entire net worth at the end of any financial year. Under SICA 1985, two quasi-judicial bodies, namely the Board for Industrial and Financial Reconstruction (BIFR) and Appellate Authority for Industrial and Financial Reconstruction (AAIFR), were set up in January 1987 and 1989, respectively. BIFR would determine the sickness of industrial companies, assist and revive those that may be viable and shut down the rest. The government also made the workers' dues rank pari passu with secured creditors in the case of liquidation of a sick company. Soon, the problem discovered was that of companies resorting to a declaration of sickness merely to escape their legal obligations and gain concessional access to financial institutions. Rajiv had announced the formation of the

Securities and Exchange Board of India (SEBl) in 1987, but nothing much happened until the Securities and Exchange Board of India Act, 1992.

GAIL, Power Finance Corporation, National Highways Authority and Ganga Action Plan

In August 1985, the Gas Authority of India Limited (GAIL, renamed just GAIL in 2002) was established as a CPSE to promote natural gas in the country. For financing power projects and renovation and modernization of existing facilities, the Power Finance Company (PFC) was established as a CPSE on 16 July 1986. Over time, the PFC would become one of the most important players in the Indian power sector. The National Highways Authority of India (NHAI) Act was issued in December 1988 for 'the development, maintenance, and management of national highways (NH) and for matters connected therewith or incidental thereto'. The NHAI became operational in mid-June 1989 and in the years ahead, would go on to improve the highway infrastructure in the country in a significant way. In 1985–86, the Ganga Action Plan for the prevention of pollution of river Ganga was launched under the Central Ganga Authority. In 1989, Integrated Watershed Development Programme (IWDP) was launched under the aegis of the National Wasteland Development Board for the development of wastelands on a watershed basis.

Panchayati Raj institutions

Since Independence, various committees headed by Balwantrai Mehta (1957), Asoka Mehta (1977), G.V.K. Rao (1985) and L.M. Singhvi (1986), P.K. Thungon (1988) and V.N. Gadgil (1988) had considered the issues of devolution of powers to local bodies. After becoming Prime Minister, Rajiv had been talking about the need to devolve power to the Panchayati Raj institutions and urban local bodies to plan as well as implement projects at the grassroots level. Deliberations were held with officers and elected representatives of local bodies in different parts of the country. To revitalise Panchayati Raj institutions, his government introduced the Constitution (Sixty-Fourth Amendment) Bill in the Lok Sabha on 15 May 1989. A similar bill relating to urban local bodies, the

Constitution (Sixty-Fifth Amendment) Bill was introduced in the Lok Sabha on 7 August 1989. Before the two Constitution Amendment bills relating to local bodies could be passed by the Rajya Sabha, the term of the Eighth Lok Sabha ended on 27 November 1989.

Slowing down of reforms

While there was no bonfire of all licensing, as I.G. Patel had wanted, there was substantial progress under Rajiv Gandhi in dismantling at least a large part of the permit-quota-licence raj. Rajiv slashed tax rates, abolished estate duty, cut import duties and eliminated licensing restrictions in many industries in the first two years of his government. The speed of reforms slowed down thereafter, with trouble brewing on the social and political fronts, together with allegations of corruption. To add to its woes, a drought of an intensity unseen for decades, and the third worst in a century, struck the country in 1987.

Growth indeed had picked up from 3.96 per cent in 1984–85 to 4.16 per cent and 4.31 per cent in 1985–86 and 1986–87, respectively. Despite the drought and a fall in agricultural GDP, overall growth was 3.5 per cent in 1987–88. After that, it was a slow pick-up, as if the fruits of efficiency gains were accruing slowly over time. The underlying reasons for the growth pick-up have been a matter of some debate. Economists Dani Rodrik and Arvind Subramanian, for example, argued that the standard explanations in terms of trade liberalization, expansionary demand, a favourable external environment and improved agricultural performance were not the factors at play. The trigger may have been an 'attitudinal shift by the government in the early 1980s that, unlike the reforms of the 1990s, was probusiness rather than pro-market in character, favouring the interests of existing businesses rather than new entrants or consumers. A relatively small shift elicited a large productivity response, because India was far away from its income possibility frontier.'[12] Economist T. N. Srinivasan, however, is unconvinced by this explanation of the 'mysterious growth transition.'[13] Srinivasan argues that though the relaxation of controls in the 1980s stimulated growth, it was not extensive and not systematic in a sustained way. The increase in productivity in the organized manufacturing sector in the 1980s, he claimed, was purely the result of better capacity utilization with lower employment.

Between 1984–85 and 1987–88, while inflation remained in single digits, it showed some signs of accelerating towards 10 per cent and beyond. Fiscal deficit of the Union government, as a proportion of GDP, annually was between 6.8 per cent and 8.1 per cent during 1984–89, and 7.4 per cent on average. During 1984–1988, in each of the four years, with pressures on government expenditure and limited revenues, net bank credit to government increased by 19-20.6 per cent, and of broad money (M2) between 16.6 per cent and 18.3 per cent.

With fiscal policy on the side of expansionary, financial repression continued and monetary policy was contractionary. In five steps of 0.5 percentage points each, RBI increased the CRR from 9 per cent on 4 February 1984 to 11 per cent on 30 July 1988. By a mega jump of 4 percentage points on 1 July 1989, it took the CRR to its statutory ceiling of 15.0 per cent. The overuse of CRR led to the loss of its manoeuvrability. With multiple steps of 0.5 percentage point each, the SLR was up from 35 per cent on 30 October 1981 to 38 per cent by the beginning of 1988 and quite close to its statutory ceiling of 40 per cent in the Banking Regulation Act, 1949.

Rajiv Gandhi introduced welfare schemes to buy popular support for the reforms. In 1985–86, he proposed to introduce subsidized crop insurance for cover against crop loans, and insurance of ₹3000 against accidental deaths of earning members of the rural poor households. To mobilize popular support, he also followed in his mother's footsteps in strengthening, or at least repackaging, rural employment generation programmes. Indira Gandhi had introduced IRDP in 1976, NREP in 1980 and RLEGP in 1983. For the poor, particularly SCs and STs, Rajiv launched the Indira Awaas Yojana (IAY) (or housing programme) in May 1985 as a sub-scheme of RLEGP. By merging NREP and RLEGP, on 1 April 1989, he launched the Jawahar Rozgar Yojana (JRY) (or Employment Programme) as the largest employment programme to date. The objective was to provide 90-100 days' employment per person, particularly in the rural areas of backward districts. The BPL people were the main targets. JRY was implemented through Panchayati Raj institutions with aid and support from District Rural Development Authority (DRDA). It was a Centrally

Sponsored Scheme (CSS), with expenditures shared by the central and state governments in the ratio 80:20. On the same lines as JRY, Nehru Rozgar Yojana was introduced from 1989–90 in the urban areas.

Rajiv also launched the Kutir (cottage or hutment) Jyoti (lighting) Programme in the Nehru Centenary Year 1988–89 to provide single-point light connection (60w) to all BPL households in the country. To benefit workers and employees, he raised the rate of interest on the General Provident Fund, Public Provident Fund, Employees Provident Fund, Coal Mines Provident Fund and such others to 12 per cent. Furthermore, on 15 December 1988, the Lok Sabha also unanimously adopted the Constitution (Sixty First Amendment) Bill and changed Article 326 to lower the voting age from twenty-one to eighteen years. Rajiv described it as 'an expression of our full faith in the youth of the country'.

But mired in scandals, the Rajiv regime was on the back foot, and reforms stalled after the first two years. Liberalization is expected to reduce the scope for discretion and hence corruption, but Rajiv Gandhi was a Prime Minister besieged by allegations of corruption. Why did reforms slow down so soon? Perhaps because Rajiv Gandhi represented a classic case of what Atul Kohli has described as 'centralisation and powerlessness'.[14] Rajiv, riding a sympathy wave, won the 1984 election on his personal appeal. He emerged as the unquestioned national leader who won on the basis of general, non-programmatic promises. His mandate did not contain many specific policies. Pursuit of democracy had led to the erosion of traditional authority in the social structure. The patronage links forged and utilized by his party, the Congress, with local influential people had weakened over the three and a half decades after Independence. The organizational strength of the party had been worn out by factional fights, e.g., between Congress and Congress (O). India underwent substantial socio-political change, but Congress failed to develop and mobilize new groups into its politics.

As a party, in processing the demands of various groups, Congress failed to provide the necessary support to Rajiv Gandhi, a novice in politics when he became Prime Minister. Without a systemic link of authority with the social periphery, his policy initiatives evoked opposition even from former supporters. Rajiv was in backtracking mode by 1987. The immediate provocation may have been the 1987 Vidhan Sabha election in

Haryana—the first state in the Hindi heartland to go to the polls after the 1984 Lok Sabha elections. The Congress' vote share declined from 37.6 per cent in 1982 to 29.2 per cent in 1987. The corresponding decline in the number of seats won out of a total of ninety seats was from thirty-six to five. Rajiv did not reverse his policies, but the emphasis from 1987 was no more on economic liberalization but more on political mobilization through populist agendas pursued in the past by his mother Indira Gandhi. According to Kohli: '. . . the more torn he became by the conflicting pulls of economic and political rationality, the less he used economic policies as tools of electoral mobilisation.'[15]

XX.5 Growing Problems in the Electricity Sector

Electricity is a concurrent subject, under the jurisdiction of both the Union and the states, and the SEBs, set up in the 1950s, were to supply electricity in their respective states by the establishment of the 'grid system'. They were bundled utilities dealing with the generation of electricity, developing the T&D network as well as engaging in distribution and servicing the retail consumers.

Until the mid-1970s, India made reasonable progress in augmenting power supply, and total installed capacity increased more than ten-fold from 1,362 MW in December 1947 to 16,664 MW in March 1974. But as the electricity needs of the economy increased, and generation capacity needed expansion, the SEBs did not have the financial strength to enhance their capacities. Many of them were not even capable of covering their variable costs. At the root of it all was the problem of subsidies and inefficiencies. From the mid-1970s, there had been a proliferation of subsidies to agriculture for mobilizing electoral support from backward rural communities and middle farmers who were growing politically powerful. Reportedly, Jalagam Vengala Rao, the Congress CM of Andhra Pradesh, was the pioneer in using electricity subsidy as a political tool by promising flat-rate tariff—tariffs based on the capacity of the pump rather than metered consumption—during the 1977 elections after the Emergency. Soon, neighbouring Tamil Nadu, Maharashtra, Karnataka and other states would follow suit, with Punjab joining in the fray in 1996. In some states, existing electricity meters were no longer monitored or simply removed and returned to the SEBs. By the end of the 1990s, a preponderant section of electricity consumers was being subsidized by a small proportion of commercial and High Tension (HT) bulk industrial consumers of electricity. The average tariff realizations for commercial and HT were ₹4.48 and ₹3.99 per unit, respectively, while the average domestic and agricultural tariff realisations were ₹1.80 and ₹0.46 per unit, respectively.

The state governments were not compensating the SEBs for the electricity subsidy to agriculture. The SEBs were trying to make up for it through a policy of cross-subsidy from industry and keeping industrial tariffs high relative to the average or even marginal cost of supply. Industry started to migrate to their own captive generation sets and their share of total SEB sales dwindled from nearly two-thirds in 1960 to about two-fifth in 1991. The policy of cross-subsidy was killing the goose that laid the golden eggs and could no longer bridge the revenue gap.

XX.6 End of the Camelot Days

In the US, the days under the young, handsome and charismatic President John F. Kennedy are often referred to as the 'Camelot Days'. Camelot was the castle where the legendary King Arthur used to live with his beautiful wife Guinevere. King Arthur's rule is idealized as one built on lofty principles, a western version of Indian 'Ram *rajya*'. As is well-known, Kennedy's Camelot ended in little less than three years through his presidency, when he was assassinated on 22 November 1963. Tragically, Rajiv Gandhi, like Kennedy, was also assassinated, but his rule ended a year and a half before his unfortunate death. The trouble had built up rapidly right from the time Rajiv Gandhi assumed power.

The riots following Indira Gandhi's assassination claimed over 2,733 Sikh lives. In less than five weeks of becoming Prime Minister, Rajiv faced the Bhopal Gas Tragedy. A gas leak at the Union Carbide pesticide plant in Bhopal, the capital of Madhya Pradesh, on 2-3 December 1984 led to 3787 deaths and 5,58,125 injuries. Four days later, on 7 December 1984, Union Carbide Chief Executive Officer (CEO) Warren Anderson arrived in Bhopal. He was arrested on arrival but was granted bail and allowed to fly back to the USA. Rumours that he was allowed to escape for a quid pro quo for the US Presidential pardon for Adil Shahriyar was a damaging one. Shahriyar, the son of Mohammad Yunus, a former Indian ambassador and a close associate of Jawaharlal Nehru and Indira Gandhi, was serving a thirty-five-year prison sentence in the US for charges including felony and fraud. In 1985, on the first anniversary of Indira Gandhi's assassination, Rajiv's statement '*Bada ped girta hai, toh dharti toh hilegi hi*' (when a big tree falls, the earth will shake) was taken as an indirect justification of the riots and became extremely controversial.

Rajiv had departed from the old style of government and dispensed with some of the old politicians and old timers. For example, Pranab Mukherjee, a veteran senior minister in Indira's cabinet, not only did not find a berth in the government, but was even expelled from the Congress on 26 April 1986, without even being informed. Kamalapati Tripathi and R.K. Dhawan were some of the other old-timers who were eased out from the charmed circle. There was a new and considerably younger 'inner group' advising the Prime Minister. Two important members of his inner group were the two Aruns—Arun Nehru and Arun Singh. Arun Nehru and Rajiv shared the same great-great-grandfather. Arun Singh, from the princely family of Kapurthala, was a close friend of Rajiv. They had attended Doon School and University of Cambridge together. He was working at Reckitt and Coleman, a multinational dealing in health, hygiene and home products, when he was recruited by Rajiv in 1984 as minister of state in the Prime Minister's Office. Apart from the two Aruns, there was Vijay Dhar, the son of D.P. Dhar, former Indian ambassador to the Soviet Union; Amitabh Bachchan, a film actor and family friend; and Mani Shankar Aiyar, an Indian Foreign Service officer. The veteran journalist Romesh Thapar called Rajiv's ménage of advisers a 'Baba-Log Government'. 'YES, a baba-log government—that's how it is seen in the bazaars these days. It's the ayahs' expression for the molly-coddled kids of the upper classes. They are seen as playing games, playing government, and for the fun of it.'[16] Ira Pandey described them as those 'who had grown up in an atmosphere so rarefied that their only brush with poverty was what they saw in their servants' lives.[17]' The political management of problems by Rajiv Gandhi's new team appears to have been quite poor.

For example, to Rajiv Gandhi's credit is the Punjab or Rajiv-Longowal Accord, which he had signed on 24 July 1985 with Harcharan Singh

Longowal, the President of the Akali Dal. But soon, the poor management of political problems became evident in the Shah Bano controversy, which came to a head in 1985, and the Babri Masjid-Ramjanmabhumi (or birthplace) dispute around the same time. On 25 April 1985, a five-judge bench of the Supreme Court upheld the 1980 Madhya Pradesh High Court judgment granting sixty-three-year-old Shah Bano, a divorced mother of five, monthly maintenance alimony of ₹179.20 from her former husband Mohammed Ahmad Khan. Khan had claimed that, beyond the one-time alimony of ₹5400 granted under Islamic law that he had already paid, he had no further obligation to Shah Bano. Some sections of the Muslims, with AIMPLB in the lead, saw the judgment as interference in Islamic personal law. There were demonstrations, and in what some claimed to be a policy of 'minority appeasement', on 23 February 1986, the Rajiv government introduced the Muslim Women (Protection of Rights on Divorce) Bill to nullify the Supreme Court's judgment. The Bill, duly passed by Parliament, became an act after receiving Presidential assent on 19 May 1986.

The simmering Babri Mosque–Ramjanmabhumi dispute in Ayodhya in UP had been gathering steam for some time. The mosque had been locked ever since an idol of Ram and Sita 'miraculously' appeared inside on 23 December 1949. Under Section 145 of the Criminal Procedure Code, to avoid a breach of peace, the property was attached by the government on 29 December 1949. The structure was under lock and key with restrictions on visits, except for some limited worship by priests, since then. There were demands for removal of the mosque at Ayodhya and the construction of a mandir (temple) for Rama by the Vishwa (world) Hindu Parishad (council) (VHP). On 25 January 1986, a twenty-eight-year-old lawyer, Umesh Chandra Pandey, petitioned the munsif court for the removal of restrictions on worship. The munsif declined. An appeal was filed on 31 January 1986 before the District Judge of Faizabad, K.M. Pandey. On 1 February 1986, the District Judge ordered the opening of the locks on the disputed structure since the locks at the gates were not necessary to maintain law and order.[18] The opening of the locks was seen as a move by Rajiv to placate Hindu sentiments after bowing down to fundamentalist Muslim demands in the Shah Bano case. The opening of the locks on the disputed Babri Mosque-Ramjanmabhumi structure in

Ayodhya in UP led to violent protests in Srinagar and other parts of the Kashmir valley with the slogan 'Islam in danger'.[19]

By end-1986, there was tension between Rajiv Gandhi and President Zail Singh, who, after Indira Gandhi's death, had sworn in Rajiv as Prime Minister even before his formal election as the leader of the Congress legislative party. With corruption charges circulating, there were rumours that the President might dismiss the Prime Minister. This was the same Zail Singh '. . . who was acknowledged as the best-known loyalist of the Gandhi family, who once accepted Sanjay Gandhi as his *rehnuma* (patron) and publicly stated that he was willing to sweep the floor if so directed by Indira Gandhi, had become anathema to the surviving son - Rajiv Gandhi'.[20]

In the middle of all this, fresh allegations of corruption cropped up, and V.P. Singh became active. By mid-1986, there were newspaper articles about Rajiv Gandhi's administration with captions such as 'Trouble in Camelot'. The trouble from V.P. Singh was somewhat unexpected because he had been a Gandhi family loyalist for over a decade. As Rajiv's finance minister, V.P. Singh, besides introducing tax reforms, including the Long-Term Fiscal Policy and MODVAT, had also started a series of tax raids or questioning of practically every leading business house. Some well-known industrialists, such as Lalit Thapar and S.L. Kirloskar, were arrested as well. Chambers of Commerce, such as FICCI, accused Singh of launching a 'raid raj'. In many cases, though, businesspersons apologized and paid up the taxes due. Singh, critics argued, was spoiling the business and investment environment. But he was also usurping a part of the image of 'Mr Clean'. V.P. Singh was shifted from finance to defence in January 1987, barely a month before presenting the budget in parliament. There was widespread suspicion that Singh was shifted not because he was needed in the defence ministry but because of pressure from lobbyists. Trouble multiplied after his shift to defence.

First, there was the Fairfax controversy, which started with the surfacing of a brief letter, alleged to be a forgery by some, written by an official of the private US investigative agency Fairfax to a newspaper columnist, S. Gurumurthy, which mentioned investigating Swiss properties of the actor Amitabh Bachchan, a close friend of Rajiv Gandhi. The Opposition alleged that Prime Minister Rajiv Gandhi was shielding his close friends, and V.P.

Singh was shifted from finance to defence to facilitate this protection. Later, it transpired that the ED, the agency under the ministry of finance that investigated foreign exchange violations, had engaged Fairfax under Michael Herschman to look into any possible FERA violations by the famous industrialist Dhirubhai Ambani, who was allegedly close to Rajiv Gandhi. When this Fairfax appointment came to light, questions were raised about procedures followed in making payments to a foreign agency. There were allegations as well that the payments were made by Ambani's rival industrialist Nusli Wadia of Bombay Dyeing. Opposition parties wanted to know whether the government had followed the due processes in the appointment of a foreign agency.

Second, there was the HDW submarine contract dating back to December 1981 under Prime Minister Indira Gandhi. Of the four submarines to be obtained from the West German firm HDW, only two had been procured until 1987. V.P. Singh, after becoming defence minister, upon hearing that the Germans might have overcharged, tried to renegotiate the price. The Indian ambassador from Bonn, in a secret telegram in late February 1987, informed that Germans were not inclined to renegotiate the price as securing the contract had involved paying a 7 per cent commission. Singh ordered an enquiry and the HDW scandal was on.

Third, the Government of India had signed a deal for $285 million with AB Bofors of Sweden in March 1986 to secure 410 Haubits FH-77 guns, which are 155 mm howitzers, and replace the old field guns and artillery of the Army. Bofors, a renowned company, was once owned by the famous Alfred Nobel. In April 1987, Swedish Radio, a private media company, reported that Bofors had paid a commission to Indian politicians and bureaucrats for securing the contract. The chief of the Swedish police, Sten Lindstorm, acted as a whistleblower and leaked hundreds of documents. The revelation that Ottavio Quattrocchi acted as a middleman for the Bofors deal made matters worse for Rajiv. The Italian businessman was close to Rajiv's family. There was a furore in Parliament, and under immense pressure, a Joint Parliamentary Committee was set up on 6 August 1987 to investigate the deal. The report came out two years later.

V.P. Singh, as minister of defence, ordered an investigation of possible payoffs in the HDW submarine deal. There were rumours that the inquiry was to embarrass or topple Rajiv. To nail the lie that he was overambitious, he resigned as minister of defence on 12 April 1987. Three months later, on 15 July, Rajiv sacked three former cabinet ministers—his cousin Arun Nehru, the conscientious objector in the Shah Bano case Arif Mohammed Khan, and V.C. Shukla. Soon, Rajiv's government got 'bogged down in limiting the damages of scandals and political embarrassments' that were 'popping up like wild mushrooms after a rainstorm'.[21] The business of government, including implementation of time-bound decisions, suffered. V.P. Singh launched the Jan Morcha or People's Front as a non-political organization on 2 October 1987, and it became a major rallying point for all anti-Congress forces.

On 17 October 1989, elections to the Ninth Lok Sabha were announced for 22 and 26 November 1989, and the Eighth Lok Sabha was dissolved on 27 November 1989. Allegations of corruption haunted the Rajiv government in the run-up to the elections. Rajiv's 'Mr Clean' reputation had been seriously tarnished. Opposition parties campaigned with slogans such as '*Gali gali mein shor hai, Rajiv Gandhi chor hai*' or every lane and alley is abuzz with the news that Rajiv Gandhi is a thief, and 'Mr Clean, Mr Clean, *gandi kyon hai tope machine?*' or Mr Clean, Mr Clean, why does the cannon stink? Congress under Rajiv lost the election, and the Camelot days came to an end.

XX.7 The Messy End to the Decade and a Half of Political Churning

To fight the Congress, V.P. Singh and some others such as Arun Nehru, Arif Mohammed Khan and V.C. Shukla formed the Jan Morcha or People's Front in 1987. 'V. P. Singh played a major role in uniting opposition parties to fight the Congress. He first persuaded, the Janata Party, Lok Dal (A), Lok Dal (B), the Indian National Congress (Jagjivan) and others to merge under the label Janata Dal on 11 October 1988, the birth anniversary of JP. The next step was the formation of a National Front against the Congress. In the National Front, the Janata Party, DMK, ComPI, CPI(M), Congress (S), AGP (*Asom Gana Parishad*) and others retained their identity but agreed on a common platform to defeat the Congress.'[22]

Congress vote share came down from 49.1 per cent in 1984 to 39.5 per cent in 1989. The decline in seats was even more precipitous, from 404 to 197. The Congress debacle was like what Indira had suffered between 1971 and 1977, when the party's vote share after the Emergency had come down from 43.7 per cent to 34.5 per cent and seats from 352 out of 518 to 154 out of 542. The National Front managed to win 275 out of the 529 seats and went on to form the government under V.P. Singh as the Prime Minister on 2 December 1989.

Riven by factionalism, the National Front Government under V.P. Singh was unstable almost right from the beginning. Devi Lal, after resigning from the chief ministership of Haryana on 2 December to become the Deputy Prime Minister, had installed his eldest son, Om Prakash Chautala, as the CM of Haryana. It all started in February 1990 in Meham, a Vidhan Sabha constituency in Haryana, where Chief Minister Chautala was contesting in a by-election. On 27 February, 'polling in a charged atmosphere witnessed widespread rigging and assaults on journalists'. In a repoll in eight booths the next day, 'police opened fire on villagers— who're protesting alleged rigging by Chautala's son Abhay Singh— killing six persons and injuring 25 others in Bainsi'.[23] There was a public outcry, the election was countermanded by the Election Commission, but Chautala continued and resigned only on 22 May when he was unable to get elected to the state legislative assembly within the required six months. He was replaced by B.D. Gupta as CM Chautala was elected to the Vidhan Sabha in a by-election held in the Darba Kalan constituency and was re-inducted as CM on 12 July 1990 after B.D. Gupta resigned. This led to what came to be known as the 'five-day' crisis. Thirteen Union ministers, including Arun Nehru and Arif Mohammed Khan, resigned to protest the reinduction. Even Prime Minister V.P. Singh offered to resign. The crisis blew over when Chautala 'resigned' from the chief minister's post in Haryana, but the unity of the National Front was badly fractured. Insurgency in Jammu and Kashmir and in Punjab also complicated the National Front Government under V.P. Singh.

It may be recalled that Morarji Desai had set up the Mandal Commission in January 1979. The report became available at end-December 1980 under Indira Gandhi as Prime Minister. Neither Indira, nor her successor Rajiv had acted on the Mandal Commission report.

Reportedly also to gain some political mileage, on 7 August 1990, in the Lok Sabha, Prime Minister V.P. Singh announced the acceptance of the report and its recommendations. The Mandal Commission had provided for 27 per cent reservation in government jobs for the backward classes, which was in addition to the reservation of 22 per cent jobs for the SCs and STs already in force. It immediately started the virulent caste polarization with widespread violent protests, particularly by students. Buses and trains were burnt, traffic was disrupted. There were police firings and lathi charges. Simultaneously, the Babri Masjid dispute also started to agitate the nation leading some commentators to describe the period as that of Mandal-Kamandal politics—*kamandal* being an oblong waterpot carried by Hindu ascetics in India.

As the agitation against the proposed implementation of the Mandal Commission recommendations gathered pace, BJP launched a Ram Rath Yatra or Ram Chariot Pilgrimage from the Hindu holy city of Somnath in Gujarat to Ayodhya on 25 September 1990. It was to lend support to the agitation by VHP and other Sangh (RSS) Parivar or family affiliates for a Ram temple in Ayodhya. In sharp contrast to the Mandal Commission recommendations, the Yatra presumably could 'produce a relative and temporal obliteration of social cleavages—particularly caste divisions' in Hindu society.[24] The Yatra, led by Lal Krishna Advani, the BJP president, 'could shift the terms of the political debate away from Mandal and caste and back towards religion and the mandir/mosque question'.[25] The threat of communal provocation led Lalu Prasad Yadav, the Janata Dal chief minister of Bihar, to take Advani under preventive custody at Samastipur on 23 October 1990 under the National Security Act. In the few minutes after being served the warrant of arrest but before being taken into custody, Advani, as BJP president, wrote a letter to the President of India 'informing him that the BJP had withdrawn its support to the National Front government headed by V.P. Singh'.[26] Singh did not last a year as Prime Minister. He laid down office on 10 November 1990.

Chandra Shekhar defected with sixty-four MPs and on 5 November, formed his Samajwadi (Socialist) Janata Party. He went on to form a government on 10 November 1990 with external Congress support. Even Chandra Shekhar's government did not last beyond four months. It lost the tactical Congress support, ostensibly for two Haryana policemen's suspicious activities near Rajiv's residence on 2 March 1991. Chandra Shekhar resigned on 6 March 1991. Elections followed.

By the mid-1980s, when Rajiv was in power, the LTTE's movement had resulted in a virtual civil war in Sri Lanka. It had major security and related implications for India in general and the state of Tamil Nadu in particular. In the middle of his term, Rajiv Gandhi had travelled to Colombo to sign the Indo-Sri Lanka Peace Accord on 29 July 1987 with Sri Lankan President J.R. Jayewardene. The accord was expected to end the civil war by implementing federal devolution principles through the Thirteenth Amendment to the Constitution of Sri Lanka and the Provincial Councils Act of 1987, the Sri Lankan Government withdrawing the troops from the Tamil areas and Tamil rebels surrendering their arms. The LTTE was not a party to the talks and agreed to surrender their arms only to the Indian Peace Keeping Force (IPKF). At the request of President Jayewardene, the IPKF was inducted into Sri Lanka in late 1987. But the LTTE put up a strong fight and refused to surrender arms. They were disarmed by the IPKF, with casualties on both sides, and the IPKF came back to India only under Prime Minister V.P. Singh in March 1990. In the middle of the three-phase election, Rajiv Gandhi was assassinated on 21 May 1991 by a suicide bomber from the LTTE at Sriperumbudur in Tamil Nadu.

XX.8 Instability in Jammu and Kashmir

The relationship between the Abdullahs and Gandhis went back two generations to the time of the Sheikh and Jawaharlal, and the scope for a rapprochement between the National Conference and the Congress slowly opened up after Rajiv's succession as Prime Minister on 30 October 1984. In Jammu and Kashmir, the G.M. Shah government had been ruling since 2 July 1984 (Section XIX.4). After a breakdown of law and order, the G.M. Shah government was dismissed on 6 March 1986. At the end of six months, the state came under President's rule on 6 September 1986. After months of hectic parleys, Rajiv Gandhi and Farooq Abdullah signed an accord that reinstated the latter as chief minister on 6 November 1986 and proposed a roadmap for stabilizing the state. Many of the constituents of the National Conference and the Congress were disgruntled by the accord and denial of berths in the cabinet of ministers. In mid-December

1986, the Jammu and Kashmir assembly was dissolved and elections to the legislative assembly were held on 23 March 1987.

An ad hoc coalition of disparate groups, based mostly in the Kashmir Valley, called the Muslim United Front (MUF), was formed to contest the elections in opposition to an alliance of the National Conference and Congress. One of the constituents of the MUF was Jama'at-i-Islami. In 1987, because of its recent origin, MUF was, however, a party 'unrecognised' by the Election Commission of India, and its candidates had to contest as independent candidates. The National Conference won forty of the seventy-six assembly seats, Congress twenty-six, BJP two, and independents eight. It was a 'sweeping' victory for the National Front-Congress alliance, but a very controversial one. There were allegations of widespread electoral malpractice.

'Chunks of the valley—Anantnag, Sopore, Handwara, Baramulla—were under virtual curfew even as votes were being tabulated at some counting stations five days after they had been cast,' reported a senior journalist.[27] One oft-quoted instance is the Amirakadal constituency in the middle of Srinagar, where G.M. Shah of the National Conference was pitted against Jama'at-i-Islami's Mohammad Yusuf Shah, a candidate from the MUF. According to political scientist Sumantra Bose, 'As counting of ballots begins, it becomes clear that the MUF's Yusuf Shah, a member of a conservative religious party called the *Jama'at-i-Islami,* is winning by a landslide. This is his third attempt to be elected to the IJK (Indian Jammu & Kashmir) assembly, and finally the public seems to be en masse on his side. The other Shah, routed in the contest, leaves the counting center in a visibly dejected mood and goes home. But he is summoned back—to be declared the winner by presiding officials. As the crowd protests, police arrive in strength and summarily arrest the MUF candidate and his supporters, including his election manager, Mohammad Yasin Malik, a twenty-one-year-old resident of the adjoining lower middle-class Maisuma neighbourhood.'[28] Yusuf Shah would become famous under his nom de guerre Syed Salahuddin as the commander in chief of Hizb-ul Mujahideen, the largest guerrilla force fighting India in Jammu and Kashmir. His young campaign manager Yasin Malik would go on to become a core member of the Jammu Kashmir Liberation Front (JKLF) group, which launched an insurrection in the Valley.

Farooq Abdullah was sworn in as chief minister of Jammu and Kashmir on 23 March 1987. The 'Durbar move' was an old tradition from the days of the monarchy to shift the Durbar or royal court every six months from Srinagar to Jammu during winter and back again to Srinagar in summer. Muslim-majority Kashmir was a stronghold of the National Conference and Hindu-majority Jammu was that of the Congress and BJP. On 7 October 1987, Farooq's government suddenly announced that while the capital would shift to Jammu during winter, some twenty departments would remain at Srinagar. From 3 November, for ten days, Jammu remained paralysed. On 14 November, Farooq rescinded the order. But this turnaround aggrieved a section of the people in the Kashmir valley, and the valley was paralysed by protests and bandhs on 14 November 1987.

Many young men from the valley mysteriously went 'missing' after the 1987 election, only to come back after training in Pakistan. Codenamed 'Operation Topac', it was a plan that was to be launched in 1991. It had to be prematurely implemented by the sudden death of Gen. Zia-ul-Haq, the President of Pakistan, in an air crash on 17 August 1988. There was large-scale rioting in Srinagar, Baramulla, Pulwama, Bhaderwah and Anantnag, which eventually became areas of militant strongholds. The detonation of bombs, demonstrations and rioting to whip up the passions of local population continued until the insurrection was ended by the security forces in 1988.

The Lok Sabha elections were scheduled for November 1989. The militants gave a call for poll boycott in Jammu and Kashmir, and turnout in the Lok Sabha election came down from 66.41 per cent in 1984 to 25.68 per cent in 1989. In the Kashmir valley, the drop in turnout was even more precipitous. The National Conference candidate was returned unopposed in the Srinagar constituency, while in the other two constituencies of Baramulla and Anantnag, with the turnout at less than 5.5 per cent. Its candidates were elected virtually unopposed with only 'independent' candidates in the fray polling less than a thousand votes each.

On 8 December 1989, Mufti Mohammad Sayeed's third and youngest daughter Rubaiya, a twenty-three-year-old medical intern, was abducted from Srinagar by the JKLF. Mufti Mohammad Sayeed had become the union home minister in the V.P. Singh government only six days earlier. He was the first Muslim home minister of the country. The JKLF demanded the release of five of their colleagues detained for terrorism in exchange for that of Rubaiya. They were released in exchange for Rubaiya on 13 December 1989. Most experts believe that the exchange of hostages boosted the morale of the terrorists and gave a fillip to the violence and insurgency that followed in the state in the years ahead. Some consider 8 December 1989 as the day the 'conflict phase' of Jammu and Kashmir started.

XX.9 The Deceptive 1980s—Living on Borrowed Money

V.P. Singh, while serving as finance minister under Rajiv Gandhi, had favoured decontrol of the economy. But after becoming Prime Minister at the end of 1989, with growing trouble on the fiscal and balance of payments fronts and his new coalition supporting government intervention, he shelved any liberalization proposals except for some changes in taxation of income. He chose the socialist leader Prof. Madhu Dandavate as finance minister, who in the Budget for 1990-91, raised the exemption limit for personal income tax from ₹18,000 to ₹22,000 per year and reduced the entry rate of tax from 25 per cent to 20 per cent. Similarly, the corporate income tax rate for widely held domestic companies (with surcharge), which had gradually gone up from 52.75 per cent in 1985–86 to 54 per cent in 1989–90, was brought down to 43.2 per cent. SSI exemption, investment allowance and deposits for direct taxes were also abolished, together with MAT, introduced in 1987–88. On the expenditure side, in 1990–91, he became the pioneer in introducing rural debt waiver, a precedent which was to be followed by many of his successors.

The government under V.P. Singh terminated the Import-Export Policy for 1988–91 and introduced a new Policy for 1990–93. It had emphasized the liberalization of imports related to computers and electronic instruments. The OGL list was expanded and the burden of discretionary licensing controls on actual users and exporters eased. By June 1990, the scarcity of foreign exchange was acute, and the government had to control imports by cutting down on import entitlements and restricting the issue of foreign exchange to some importers.

A special FCNR deposit scheme, without any definite term restrictions on withdrawal any time and denominated in US dollars, was introduced from 21 August 1990 to attract deposits from the Gulf region. In

November 1990, a non-repatriable scheme, the Foreign Currency (Bank & Other) Deposits (FC(B&O)D)—O standing for OCB—open to banks as well as both foreigners and NRIs, was also introduced. Dandavate repealed the Gold Control Act of 1968 in June 1990, arguing that it was prudent to allow imports and earn tax revenue than lose it on imports through unofficial channels. Although Dandavate had complained about the misuse of Special Bearer Bonds, which had been introduced in 1981, he proposed to consider yet another tax amnesty scheme. He, however, did not survive long enough as finance minister to bring it out. Chandra Shekhar, after becoming Prime Minister on 10 November 1990, appointed Yashwant Sinha, a bureaucrat-turned-politician, as finance minister.

By November, when Chandra Shekhar came to power, severe strain on foreign exchange had forced the government to stop issuing fresh import licences and subject past licences to fresh scrutiny. The second issue of NRI bonds with a validity of seven years from the date of opening and carrying 1 per cent more interest than FCNR deposit on the date of opening was launched by the SBI in November 1990. The issue closed in January 1991 and netted $215 million. By December, foreign exchange outflow was virtually stopped, and, by notification, basic and auxiliary duty of customs increased by 5-20 percentage points.

The 1980s was a decade of high fiscal deficits. From 1979–80 to 1986–87, the fiscal deficit of the Union government as a proportion of GDP increased every year except in 1980–81, to reach 8.13 per cent in 1986–87. After coming down marginally in 1987–88, until 1990–91, it fluctuated between 7.08 per cent and 7.61 per cent. By 1989, the Union government in India was running high fiscal deficits by international standards. Internationally, twenty-five countries that had the highest fiscal deficit as a proportion of GDP during 1989–97 included Bahrain, Colombia, Cyprus, France, Greece, Italy, Malta, Pakistan, Romania, South Africa, Sri Lanka, Turkey and Zimbabwe, among others. In 1989, India ranked sixth by registering a deficit lower than only that of Greece, Italy, Sri Lanka, Bahrain and Nepal. By 1990, it had raced ahead and occupied the fourth position, behind only three countries, namely Greece, Italy and Sri Lanka!

The problem of increasing deficit was not restricted to the Union government alone but also applied to the state governments. The state governments used to borrow from the Union government, and under Article 293(3) of the Constitution, the Union government could and can control the fiscal deficit of a state government by denying it the necessary permission to borrow and finance its fiscal deficit. The decade of the 1980s, however, was characterized by an all-pervasive mood for fiscal expansion, where the Union government, by expanding its own fiscal deficit, had also lost its moral authority to restrain the states. The fiscal deficit of the states in the aggregate, as a proportion of GDP, rose from 1.62 per cent in 1976–77 to a high of 3.20 per cent in 1984–85 and 1990–91 before declining to 2.80 per cent in 1991–92 (Table XX.1).

The combined total liabilities of the central and state governments climbed up more than 5.5 fold from ₹717 billion in 1980–81 to ₹4036 billion in 1990–91. As a proportion of GDP, the increase was from 48 per cent to 69 per cent. The weighted average interest rate on dated securities of the central governments had gone up from 9.98 per cent in 1984–85 to 11.41 per cent in 1990–91. The corresponding increase in interest for state governments from 9 per cent to 11.50 per cent was even steeper. Growth in outstanding debt as well as a hardening of the interest rates on such loans resulted in a more than eight-fold growth of interest payments (excluding that from state governments to the Centre) from ₹30 billion in 1980–81 to ₹251 billion in 1990–91. As a proportion of GDP, it was a doubling from 2 per cent to 4.3 per cent. External debt of the government had also increased from ₹135 billion or 9 per cent of GDP in 1980–81 to ₹663 billion or 11 per cent of GDP. In the 1980s, starting with Mexico in 1982, while Latin America suffered from debt crises, India managed avoiding them, but not for long.

Dandavate, in his Budget speech for 1990-91 had said: 'The fiscal imbalance is the root cause of the twin problems of inflation and the difficult balance of payments position.' But he could not stem the rot. Between 1989–90 and 1990–91, as a proportion of GDP, the Union government's revenue receipts went down by more than 1 percentage point from 10.42 per cent to 9.37 per cent. The corresponding decline in total expenditure from 18.51 per cent to 17.96 per cent could not prevent the fiscal deficit from climbing up from 7.10 per cent to 7.61 per cent.

On 4 March 1991, Sinha, in his Interim Budget speech for 1991–92, categorically pointed out a fiscal crisis. He said: 'I need hardly stress that

Table XX.1 Living on Borrowed Money — Exploding Fiscal Deficit and Debt

Year	Prime Minister	Union Government			State Governments	General Government	
		Finance Minister	Fiscal deficit	Outstanding liabilities	Fiscal deficit	Fiscal deficit	Outstanding liabilities
1976-77	Indira Gandhi[1]	C. Subramanian[9]	4.07	35.97	1.62	...	...
1977-78	Morarji Desai[2]	H. M. Patel[10]	3.48	37.95	1.93	...	...
1978-79			4.98	37.93	2.31	...	...
1979-80	Morarji Desai[2] Charan Singh[3] Indira Gandhi[4]	Charan Singh[11] H. N. Bahuguna[12] R. Venkataraman[13]	5.08	39.94	2.29	...	...
1980-81	Indira Gandhi[4]	R. Venkataraman[13]	5.55	41.39	2.48	7.20	47.94
1981-82		Pranab Mukherjee[14]	4.93	41.77	2.31	6.03	48.92
1982-83			5.40	46.48	2.54	5.65	53.29
1983-84			5.69	45.47	2.78	6.97	52.55
1984-85	Rajiv Gandhi[5]	V. P. Singh[15]	6.79	48.10	3.20	8.58	55.95

Year	Prime Minister	Finance Minister					
1985-86	Rajiv Gandhi[5]	V.P. Singh[15]	7.55	52.38	2.60	7.66	60.51
1986-87		Rajiv Gandhi[16]	8.13	56.44	2.86	9.50	64.85
1987-88		N.D. Tiwari[17]	7.34	59.52	3.05	8.81	68.15
1988-89		S. B. Chavan[18]	7.08	59.08	2.67	8.21	67.70
1989-90			7.10	60.94	3.07	8.59	70.06
1990-91	V. P. Singh[6] Chandrasekhar[7]	S.B. Chavan[18] Madhu Dandavate[19] Yashwant Sinha[20]	7.61	59.59	3.20	9.14	68.85
1991-92	Chandrasekhar[7] P. V. Narasimha Rao[8]	Yashwant Sinha[20] Manmohan Singh[21]	5.39	63.42	2.80	6.80	72.89

Sources: For the Union, fiscal deficit and outstanding liabilities are from Tables 93 and 113, respectively, of RBI Handbook of Statistics on the Indian Economy (HBS). Outstanding liabilities of the Union for 1976-77 to 1979-80, which are not available in HBS, are taken from CAG's Report No. 1 of 2003. For States, fiscal deficit is from Tables 102 of HBS. For general government, that is Union and States consolidated, deficit and liabilities are from HBS Tables 107 and 115, respectively. GDP figures used relate to 2004-05 series and are from HBS Table 1.[1] Demitted office on 24 March 1977.[2] Assumed office on 24 March 1977 and demitted office on 28 July 1979.[3] Assumed office on 28 July 1979 and demitted office on 14 January 1980.[4] From 14 January 1980.[5] Rajiv Gandhi from Indira Gandhi's assassination on 31 October 1984 until 2 December 1989.[6] From 2 December 1989 to 10 November 1990.[7] From 10 November 1990 to 21 June 1991.[8] From 21 June 1991.[9] Until 24 March 1977.[10] During 24 March 1977 to 24 January 1979.[11] During 24 January 1979 to 28 July 1979 and 25 October 1979 to 14 January 1980.[12] During 28 July to 25 October 1979.[13] During 14 January 1980 to 15 January 1982.[14] From 15 January 1982 to 31 January 1984.[15] From 31 January 1984 to 24 January 1987.[16] From 24 January 1987 to 25 July 1987.[17] From 25 July 1987 to 25 June 1988.[18] From 25 June 1988 to 2 December 1989.[19] From 2 December 1989 to 10 November 1990.[20] From 10 November 1990 to 21 June 1991.[21] From 21 June 1991.

neither the Government nor the economy can live beyond its means for long. The room for manoeuvre, to live on borrowed money or time, has been used up completely. The soft options have been exhausted.' It was an Interim Budget; Sinha only outlined measures to try and reduce expenditure and left the structure of taxes unchanged. One of his contributions, however, was yet another tax amnesty scheme through the Voluntary Deposits (Immunities and Exemptions) Act, 1991. Though it came out in November 1991, after he had demitted office, Sinha had announced it in his Budget in March. It allowed any person to deposit money with the NHB by end-November 1991 without disclosure of source, be subject to a special levy of 40 per cent for financing slum clearance and low-cost housing for the poor and withdraw the balance without any lock-in period. In the event, the scheme mobilized such deposits of only about ₹60 crore.

Sinha said that the economy was in a crisis and added, 'The Wholesale Price Index registered an increase of 8.5 per cent, while the CPI rose by 11.9 per cent, during the first eight months of the current financial year. The sharp deterioration in the balance of payments situation led to a rapid depletion of foreign exchange reserves, which dropped to Rs. 3142 crores at the end of November 1990 and was not even sufficient to finance imports for one month.'[29]

Two economists—Willem Buiter of Yale University and Urjit Patel, the would-be RBI Governor—in their 1989 original draft of a famous paper in 1992 had warned: 'Unless measures to reduce the primary deficit are taken, a fiscal crisis is bound to come. Where and when it will strike cannot be predicted with certainty. Often a fiscal crisis first manifests itself in the foreign exchanges. Actual or imminent international reserve exhaustion is a common trigger for emergency measures including recourse to IMF standby financing and the conditionality this implies. Such foreign exchange crises can happen even if, as in the case of India, the external debt burden of the country is quite modest.'[30] Indeed, the country had a balance of payments crisis in 1990-91 and had to go the IMF for exceptional support. Apart from the Camelot days, what was coming to an end during the deceptive 1980s was living on more and more borrowed money.

Part IV

1991–2020—Reforms with Its Ups and Downs

XXI

Crisis and the Launch of 1991 Reforms

Pamulaparthy Venkata Narasimha Rao, a veteran Congress freedom fighter, had been a successful chief minister of Andhra Pradesh, and had handled several portfolios, including home, defence and external affairs at the Union level. He was both erudite and a polyglot. In 1991, he was 70. He had decided not to seek re-election to the Lok Sabha and to retire from politics. He had even taken his leave from Congress President Rajiv Gandhi. At his New Delhi residence, he was packing for his trip back to his native state of Andhra Pradesh on the night of 21 May 1991, when he was informed about Rajiv's assassination. Rao stayed back.

The 1991 elections to the Tenth Lok Sabha were in three stages. With the sympathy wave, the Congress did quite well in the two rounds of polling that took place after the assassination, but not well enough to secure an absolute majority in the Lok Sabha with 537 seats. It emerged as the single largest party, but with only 244, it was short of the majority mark. Its ally, the AIADMK, won eleven; but still, with only 255 along with its ally, it did not command a majority. But, as the single largest party, it had the first right of refusal to form a government. The CWC's unanimous choice for the Congress president's and country's prime minister's post was Rajiv's widow, Sonia Gandhi. The grief-stricken Sonia resolutely refused. On her advice, the country's Vice President Shankar Dayal Sharma was offered the post. Sharma declined because of age and ill health, and the choice fell on Narasimha Rao. Congress formed a minority government with Narsimha Rao as Prime Minister on 21 June 1991, exactly a month after Rajiv's assassination. In the forty-four years since Independence, Rao became the second Congress Prime Minister after Lal Bahadur Shastri from outside the Nehru-Gandhi family and the only Prime Minister outside the family to complete the full five-year term. Except for Morarji Desai from Gujarat, every Prime Minister of India before Rao had been from the biggest state of UP in the Hindi heartland. His ascendance attested to the growing Indian integration.

XXI.1 The 1991 Reforms

Rao inherited a macroeconomic crisis manifested starkly in the dwindling foreign exchange reserves and double-digit inflation. Iraq had invaded and occupied Kuwait in August 1990, and to liberate Kuwait, Operation Desert Storm was launched by a US-led coalition force of thirty-four nations on 17 January 1991. The operation, popularly known as the Gulf War, ended on 28 February 1991. It severely impacted India by more than doubling the price of oil, drying up the remittances from the Middle East, and creating the need to repatriate and rehabilitate 1,80,000 Indian workers from the war-affected zones. A crisis was brewing. The Gulf War blew the lid on it.

Inflation (on an end-of-period basis) was already in double digits at 12.1 per cent in 1990–91. Foreign currency assets of the RBI came down to $975 million on 12 July 1991, equivalent to less than a month's import cover. A part of the government's gold had to be transported and pledged to borrow abroad, and foreign loans had to be raised on a continuous—often on an overnight—basis to avert a default on external debt. India had already been in touch with the IMF, the lender of the last resort for member countries, and withdrawn the reserve tranche of SDR 490 million in July-September 1990. In December 1990, it applied for the first credit tranche of SDR 552 million and negotiated withdrawals under the contingency compensatory finance facility totalling SDR 1352 million between January and September 1991. A twenty-month stand-by programme with the IMF with an upper credit tranche facility of SDR 731 million was signed in October 1991. A US$500 million Structural Adjustment loan came from the World Bank in December 1991 for: (i) helping India to cope with a balance of payments crisis of unprecedented severity; and (ii) supporting a broad-based set of policy reforms aimed mainly at liberalizing the Indian economy and opening it up to more competition, both from within and abroad. A blueprint for reforms was already available from the time of the Chandra Shekhar government and Rao had no time to lose.

The country was close to a default on its external debt. First, Rao had to choose his finance minister and he chose Dr Manmohan Singh, a former Chief Economic Adviser and RBI Governor. While previous governments had shied away from reforms, in 1991, Rao, with Manmohan Singh as the finance minister, responded immediately with demand compression and followed it up with a major shift in India's development strategy, or 'reforms', including internal and external liberalizations. The rupee was under 'managed float' and tied to a basket of currencies since September 1975. The external balance of payments was precarious and the spot rate of the rupee at ₹21.14 per US dollar on 30 June 1991 was clearly unsustainable. Within almost a fortnight of assuming office, this overvaluation was corrected by a two-step 18 per cent devaluation on 1 and 3 July 1991. NRIs were exempt from Indian taxes. In October 1991, with the Remittances of Foreign Exchange and Investment in Foreign Exchange Bonds (Immunities & Exemptions) Act, the government launched a bond that, subscribed to by the NRIs, when gifted, would also be exempt from taxes in the hands of the recipient. Also, NRIs and their overseas corporate bodies could invest in five-year tax-free India Development Bonds denominated in US dollars issued by SBI and gift them to residents.

A day after the second devaluation, Chidambaram, the minister of state (independent charge) in the ministry of commerce, announced a new foreign trade policy and substantially relaxed the system of import controls. It was a new scheme—a liberalized system of the erstwhile Import Replenishment Scheme from August 1966. A new and transferable instrument called 'Exim Scrip' calculated at the rate of 30 per cent of the foreign exchange earned by exporters was issued to enable them to get incentives faster and easier.

In support of his measures, Rao invoked the work that had already been done by the predecessor Chandra Shekhar government. President Venkataraman had sworn him as Prime Minister on 21 June on the condition that he won a vote of confidence in the Lok Sabha within four weeks. Rao moved a motion of confidence on 12 July and three days later, on the day of the vote, said: 'So, it is not as if the measures which we have taken just dropped from the heaven overnight. We were not even three-four days old, how could we prepare all those papers? The papers were ready . . . Chandra Shekharji's Government was not in a position to take those decisions and it is as well that they did not take those decisions. The result was that the accumulated decision making fell on our head and we had no time to lose and, therefore, we had to take all these decisions.'[1] BJP voted against the motion. The members of the Lok Sabha wanted to avoid another election, and there were many abstentions. The Rao government survived.

XXI.2 Macroeconomic Policy Reforms

Under the 1991 reforms, the dismantling of the industrial licensing regime, reduction in import tariffs and removal of QRs on imports have attracted considerable attention and applause. What is perhaps not emphasized as much is the ingenuity of the government in using the crisis as an opportunity to push through structural reforms that had little to do with the immediate crisis itself but were critical in the transformation of the functioning of the Indian economy in the medium to long term in fundamental ways. The crisis was first and foremost a macroeconomic one and required a resolution at the macroeconomic level. About a month after assuming office, on 24 July 1991, Finance Minister Manmohan Singh, in his Budget speech for 1991–92, said as much: 'For improving the management of the economy, the starting point, and indeed the centre-piece of our strategy, should be a credible fiscal adjustment and macro-economic stabilisation during the current financial year, to be followed by continued fiscal consolidation thereafter.' While no discussion of macroeconomic policy can be complete without an analysis of structural reform measures, before turning to these microeconomic reforms, the macroeconomic policies pursued to bring the situation under control merit attention.

The three salient features of the shift in fiscal and monetary policies were—building an institutional structure for fiscal consolidation, tax reform and a market-friendly monetary and exchange rate policy. These features constituted an interrelated and mutually reinforcing trio. For example, apart from expenditure compression, fiscal consolidation required revenue-enhancing tax reforms. Greater macroeconomic stability and higher investment from fiscal consolidation led to an acceleration of growth and contributed to higher tax revenues, a greater scope for tax reforms and further efficiency enhancement. Fiscal consolidation also facilitated the pursuit of a prudent and market-friendly monetary and exchange rate policy.

Fiscal consolidation

For fiscal consolidation, one significant change in the institutional structure was the switchover from a somewhat hollow concept of a budgeted or uncovered deficit in the central government's annual financial planning to a more meaningful 'fiscal deficit' concept. The switch had been recommended in 1985 by the Committee to Review the Working of the Monetary System—more popularly known as the Chakravarty Committee. The Chakravarty Committee had pointed out how prudent monetary policy was a necessary condition for price stability, and how such a policy required avoidance of excessive reliance on RBI credit for financing the fiscal deficit. These recommendations were made operational only after the crisis of 1990–91. Finance Minister Manmohan Singh, in his Budget Speech for 1991–92, even defined the fiscal deficit for the benefit of the MPs and said '. . . fiscal deficit of the Central Government, which measures the difference between revenue receipts and total expenditure, is estimated at more than 8 per cent of GDP in 1990–91, as compared with 6 per cent at the beginning of the 1980s and 4 per cent in the mid-1970s.' In 1991–92, to mobilize 'black money' into the government's coffers, he confirmed the amnesty scheme through NHB deposits which his predecessor Sinha had already announced.

A major institutional change for better fiscal discipline was the announcement to limit the automatic monetization of the fiscal deficit. The automatic replenishment of the government's cash balances with the RBI, whenever such balances fell below a specified minimum, by the government creating an equivalent amount of ad hoc Treasury Bills in favour of the RBI, in vogue since 1955, had degenerated into automatic monetization of government debt. In his Budget for 1994–95, Manmohan Singh announced a phasing out of the government's access to ad hoc Treasury Bills over a period of three years. He described it as '. . . a historic step which will in due course contribute to a significant improvement in fiscal and monetary discipline and give the Reserve Bank greater scope for effective monetary management.'

Manmohan Singh, in his first Budget speech, describing the crisis as 'deep', said, 'The increasing difference between the income and expenditure of the Government has led to a widening of the gap between the income and expenditure of the economy . . . This is reflected in growing current account deficits in the balance of payments. The crisis of the fiscal system is a cause for serious concern.' The new government 'moved urgently to implement a programme of macroeconomic stabilisation through fiscal correction'.

Right in his first Budget in July 1991, Manmohan Singh had pointed out how interest payments during 1991–92, estimated at ₹27,450 crore, constituted 42 per cent of the Union government's net revenue receipts and could be brought down only through strict discipline on government borrowing, that is fiscal deficit, for a period of three years. India had sought exceptional balance of payment support from the IMF, and fiscal consolidation was a standard ingredient of IMF-assisted reform-cum-stabilization programmes. The fiscal deficit as a proportion of GDP was reduced from 7.6 per cent in 1990–91 to 5.4 per cent and 5.2 per cent in 1991–92 and 1992–93, respectively, but it went up to 6.8 per cent in 1993–94 before declining to 5.5 per cent and 4.9 per cent in the two subsequent years (Figure XXI.1). Much of the heavy lifting was done by expenditure compression. Tax revenue as a proportion of GDP went down from 7.4 per cent in the first year of 1991–92 to 6.7 per cent in the last year of 1995–96. Manmohan Singh in his Budget Speech for 1995–96 admitted, 'After the initial successes in fiscal consolidation, further progress has proved much more difficult.'

Measures to rein in expenditure included raising the price of motor spirit, LPG and aviation turbine fuel for domestic use by 20 per cent to reduce petroleum subsidies, abolishing sugar subsidy, and raising the price of high analysis (i.e., with at least 30 per cent nutrient) fertilizers by 40

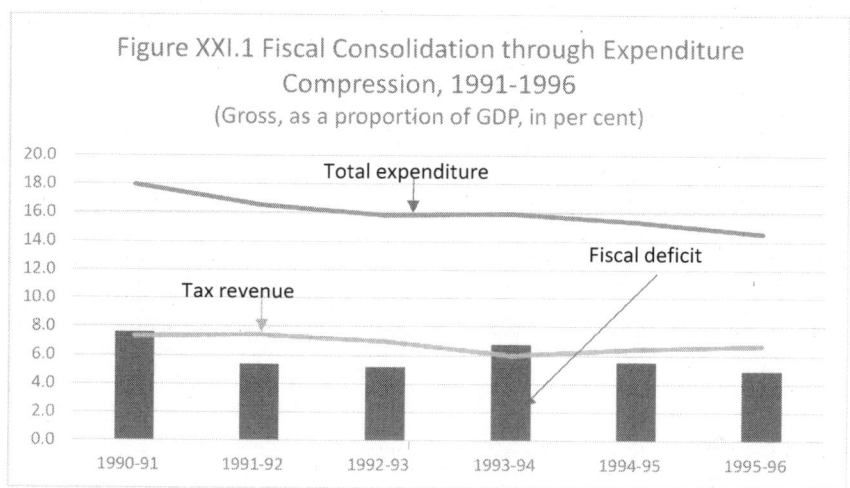

Figure XXI.1 Fiscal Consolidation through Expenditure
Compression, 1991-1996
(Gross, as a proportion of GDP, in per cent)

Source: RBI Handbook of Statistics on the Indian Economy

per cent, plus removing price and movement control on others to reduce fertilizer subsidy.

The universal PDS, available to all, had failed to deliver the benefits to the poor in the backward regions, yet the food subsidy bill associated with it had been mounting. Inefficiencies and corruption had cast serious doubts about its usefulness. The benefits did not reach the poor adequately. On 1 January 1992, Prime Minister Rao announced the launching of the Revamped PDS (RPDS) in the most backward blocks of the country to supplant the essential supplies programme (ESP) of 1982. Essential commodities—not only wheat and rice, but also levy sugar, imported edible oil, kerosene and soft coke—were to be supplied in the RPDS blocks at subsidized prices. Twenty kilos of food grains per month per family were to be supplied at ₹5 per kg. RPDS was a location-targeted scheme, and available to all in the selected areas.

One controversial announcement from the Prime Minister on 23 December 1993 was regarding Members of Parliament Local Area Development Scheme (MPLADS) under the ministry of rural development. It was controversial for three reasons. First, the Constitution clearly assigns expenditure responsibilities among the three tiers of government, namely Union, state and local bodies (panchayats and municipalities). MPLAD brought in an additional tier. Second, by assigning a semi-executive function to the legislators, it diluted the almost sacred principle of the separation of legislature, executive and judiciary. The fiscal outgo could be considerable.

Tax reform

The government started tax reforms in a cautious way to avoid undue revenue risks. After the correction of the rupee's overvaluation and the introduction of the Exim Scrip, in his Budget for 1991–92, Manmohan Singh abolished the export subsidy. Furthermore, for greater competitiveness, he reduced the ad valorem rates of basic plus auxiliary duties of customs to a maximum of 150 per cent in general and of 80 per cent for capital goods. He postponed the major decisions and only reduced the customs duty on a few items such as machinery and parts thereof, and newsprint. Next year, the maximum ad valorem rate of basic plus auxiliary duties of customs was reduced from 150 per cent to 110 per cent in general and from 80 per cent to 60 per cent for capital goods. There was a selective reduction in customs duty on some items such as seeds and pesticides, and feedstock for petrochemical industries.

Just over two months after assuming office, the Rao government had appointed the Tax Reforms Committee under the chairmanship of Raja Chelliah of the NIPFP. In Budget 1993–94, Manmohan Singh focused mainly on reform of customs duty, in which the Chelliah Committee had recommended tariff rates of 5, 10, 15, 20, 25, 30 and 50 per cent to be achieved by 1997–98. He merged the separate auxiliary duty, which had been in vogue since 1973, with basic customs duty. He also broadbanded the customs duty rates and reduced such duties on machinery and components, ferrous metals, chemicals and electronic goods. The peak customs duty rate was cut from 85 per cent to 65 per cent, except on items like baggage and liquor, in 1994–95, and further to 50 per cent in 1995–96 (Table XXI.1). He unified duty rates for many similar classes of goods, such as raw materials and capital goods, removed anomalies of raw materials and components having higher customs duty rates than finished products and pruned the notifications, including end use exemptions, by about a half.

Table XXI.1. Evolution of Customs Duty Structure for Non-Agricultural Goods

Year Rates (ad valorem)	No. of Major Basic Duty (ad valorem)	Peak Basic Rate (Special Customs Duty(SCD))	Basic Surcharge	SAD
	(in per cent)	(in per cent)		(in per cent)
1990-91	22	More than 300	-	-
1991-92	20	150	-	-
1992-93	16	110	-	-
1993-94	16	85	-	-
1994-95	12	65	-	-
1995-96	9	50	-	-
1996-97	8	50	2% SCD	-
1997-98	7	40	5% SCD	-
1998-99	7	40	5% SCD	4
1999-00	5	40	10% surcharge	4
2000-01	4	35	10% surcharge	4
2001-02	4	35	-	4
2002-03	4	30	-	4
2003-04	5	25	-	4
2004-05	4	20	-	-

Source: 'Report on Task Force on Implementation of the Fiscal Responsibility and Budget Management Act', Ministry of Finance, Government of India, New Delhi, July 2004. p. 76.

In excise duty, rates were reduced and broadbanded, MODVAT was extended to more commodities and the coverage of service tax was extended to more services. The special excise duty was raised from 5 per cent to 10 per cent. A major change in excise administration in 1992–93 was the abolition of licensing controls on production and manufacture under the Central Excises and Salt Act, 1944. The need for five-yearly renewal of the licence was dispensed with by making the licence valid if production continued. In 1993–94, in excise duties, Manmohan Singh merged the special excise duty, which had been levied since 1988, with basic excise duty, and the rate was reduced on many items of mass consumption. In 1994–95, he extended MODVAT to capital goods and petroleum products, shifted the bulk of excise taxation from specific to ad valorem rates, reduced the total number of ad valorem tax rates to about half the existing number, unified many rates for similar commodities, and reduced the number of special exemption notifications by about a half. In 1995–96, he reduced excise duty on plastics, and aluminium, and unified the rate on parts of capital goods at 15 per cent. He proposed to broadly align the Central Excise Tariff on textiles along HSN lines.

With the increasing share of the services sector in GDP, its exclusion from the domain of indirect taxation was having an adverse effect on the tax-to-GDP ratio. Halfway through the Rao government's tenure, service tax was introduced in a limited way from 1 July 1994. The jurisdiction entitled to levy a tax on services was not explicitly mentioned in the Constitution. Under the residuary entry No.97, List I in the Seventh Schedule of the Constitution, three services—telephone services, stockbroking and general insurance—were brought under a new tax, called service tax, in 1994–95.

There was considerable progress in income taxation. In personal income tax, the Chelliah Committee had recommended an exemption limit of ₹28,000 and marginal rates of tax (inclusive of surcharge, if any) of 20 per cent for total income in the range of ₹28,000 to ₹50,000; 27.5 per cent for total income in the range of ₹50,000 to ₹1,00,000; and 40 per cent for total income exceeding ₹1,00,000. Manmohan Singh reduced the personal income tax slabs from four to three in 1992–93 and removed the surcharge of 12 per cent on income above ₹1 lakh from financial year 1994–95. But simultaneously, the exemption limit was rapidly raised from ₹22,000 in 1990–91 to ₹28,000, ₹30,000, ₹35,000, and ₹40,000 in the four subsequent years. This increase in exemption limit, together with the raising of the upper limits of the first two tax slabs of 20 per cent and 30 per cent from ₹50,000 to ₹60,000 and from ₹1,00,000 to ₹1,20,000, respectively, in 1995–96 and granting of several concessions to not-so-poor special categories such as women and senior citizens, compromised the revenue potential of the reform. The tax concessions for senior citizens went up rapidly in subsequent years, raising questions about the appropriateness of favouring the rich elderly compared to the poor young. Presumptive taxes for the unorganized sector, originally introduced in 1992–93 for two years, continued.

In the Budget for 1991–92, Manmohan Singh increased the corporate tax rate for widely held companies from 40 to 45 per cent and for closely held companies from 45 to 50 per cent, and, for tax purposes, reduced the general rate of depreciation for plant and machinery from 33.33 per cent to 25 per cent. In 1994–95, he unified the rate on widely held companies (40 per cent) and closely held companies (45 per cent) at 40 per cent. For foreign companies, he reduced the rate from 65 per cent to 55 per cent. The surcharge on corporate tax continued. In 1995–96, tax concessions were extended to companies in infrastructure areas of highways, expressways and new bridges, airports, ports and rapid mass transport systems, new industrial undertakings, hotels and shipping, and to software exporters and venture capital funds. He enlarged the scope of tax deduction at source (TDS).

Overall, particularly given the fact that the Chelliah Committee report was available to the government, the tax reforms were half done. Where the Rao government failed was in the removal of tax concessions on selected categories of taxpayers and goods and broadbanding the indirect taxes into a handful of rates. The reforms fell short on mobilization of revenues.

Market-friendly monetary and exchange rate policies

The essence of the reforms was in moving from a command-and-control regime to a more market-based system, not only in industrial licensing and import controls but also in government intervention in the monetary and exchange rate spheres. From 1 March 1992 came the dual exchange rate—a market-determined rate and an official rate—under the Liberalized Exchange Rate Management System (LERMS). Under LERMS, 60 per cent of all export earnings and foreign exchange receipts could be converted at the market-determined exchange rate and the balance, namely 40 per cent, had to be converted at the official rate. This allowed the abolition of 'Exim Scrip', which had been introduced on 3 July 1991. In June 1992, a new rupee-denominated scheme, the Non-resident Non-repatriable (NRNR) account was introduced, under which only interest income was repatriable.

A unified exchange rate regime was introduced on 1 March 1993. From August 1994, India achieved current account convertibility, which means that there were no restrictions on foreign exchange availability for trade in goods and invisibles (such as tourism or paying educational fees for studies abroad). India embarked on a gradual shift towards capital account convertibility—that is, free availability of foreign exchange for transactions such as buying a house or a company's shares abroad—with the launch of the reforms in the early 1990s.

Deposits under FCNR(A) were denominated in currencies like the US dollar and the pound sterling, offered attractive rates of interest, and carried an underlying guarantee by the RBI to provide for any exchange rate losses. The RBI had to make good the difference between the exchange rate at which the deposits were booked and the rate when they were redeemed, making it a big draw for investors, especially in the Middle East. The losses associated with operating FCNR(A) on account of the depreciation of the rupee were proving to be a worry for the RBI. With effect from 15 May 1993, to replace FCNR(A), the Foreign Currency Non-Resident (Banks) or FCNR(B) scheme was introduced for banks, under which banks accepting such deposits had to bear the associated foreign exchange risk. With this discontinuation, NRI deposits could no longer be described as quasi-public debt. The experimentation with various types of deposits denominated in foreign currency to attract inflow of funds from foreigners, particularly NRIs, continued. Apart from special bonds issued for NRIs and others, there would be basically three types of deposits—NRE accounts for saving or depositing earnings from abroad in India in rupees, NRO accounts for saving and depositing earnings in India in rupees and FCNR accounts for saving or depositing earnings in foreign currencies. As the pressure on the balance of payments subsided, the terms of the NRI deposits were made less generous.

FDI was liberalized from July 1991. Restrictions related to only a short negative list. Although foreign natural persons, except NRIs, were prohibited from investing in financial assets, such investments were permitted by Foreign Institutional Investors (FIIs) and OCBs with suitable restrictions. From 14 September 1992, FIIs were allowed to invest in all securities traded on the primary and secondary markets, but the holding of a single FII and of all FIIs, NRIs and OCBs in any company were subject to the limit of 5 per cent and 24 per cent of the company's total issued capital, respectively. In equities, FIIs could invest up to the applicable sectoral cap.

In the area of mutual funds, UTI and those owned by government-owned banks and insurance companies were the only ones operating until 1992–93. In 1993, the mutual funds industry (except UTI) was put under the regulatory authority of the SEBI and also opened up for entry by the private sector. From 1992–93, AUM of mutual funds increased over 2.5 times to ₹1,21,000 crore in January 2003.

In line with the recommendations of the Narasimham Committee, there were attempts to reduce financial repression by reducing CRR and SLR, but not with much success. With WPI inflation since 1990–91 in double digits every year except in 1993–94, there was a need to exercise caution on the monetary front. While the CRR, after its gradual reduction from its statutory limit of 15 per cent gradually to 14 per cent on 15 May 1993, was raised in stages back to 15 per cent on 7 August 1994, there was more progress on the SLR front. The SLR was reduced in stages from 38.75 per cent to 31.50 per cent on 29 October 1994.

Selective credit control was not delivering the desired results and might even have been counterproductive. With the existence of non-banking financial channels, its effectiveness in controlling prices was questionable at best. Trade's demand for its abolition was backed by the World Bank and UNCTAD, and such controls were lifted from wheat on 12 October 1993, from paddy and rice on 18 October 1994, and from other food grains (i.e., coarse food grains), oilseeds, oils, sugar, gur and khandsari, and cotton and kapas on 21 October 1996. To replace the extremely complicated interest rate structure of scheduled commercial banks that had resulted from the excessive proliferation of rates, in September 1990, a simplified new structure of lending rates linking them to loan size was prescribed.

An asset becomes a Non-Performing Asset (NPA) when it ceases to generate income. In banks, loans or investment accounts where payment of interest and/or repayment of principal is not forthcoming are called NPAs. Until the mid-1980s, the management of NPAs in India was left to the banks and the auditors. With the need for fine-tuning regulatory structures to deal with the changing risk-profile of banks, the first-ever system of classification of assets for the Indian banking system had been introduced in 1985. This system, called the 'Health Code' system, involved the classification of advances into eight categories ranging from 1 (Satisfactory) to 8 (Bad and Doubtful Debts). But the system continued to suffer from a large dose of subjectivity and was not in line with international standards.

The Narasimham Committee on Financial Sector Reforms had suggested a four-fold classification of banks' assets into: (i) standard (ii) sub-standard, (iii) doubtful, and (iv) loss. An asset was sub-standard if it was NPA for a period not exceeding two years. Doubtful assets were those that remained NPA for more than two years but not yet written off, and loss assets were those that had been written off. An asset that was not sub-standard, doubtful or loss was standard. A significant change came in April 1992 with the introduction of prudential norms on income recognition, asset classification and mathematical methods for the computation of provisioning requirements. A graded norm for NPA recognition was brought in, beginning with four-quarters for the classification of advances as non-performing. An asset was considered an NPA if interest and/or instalment of principal remained 'past due' for a specific period or duration. An amount was considered 'past due' when it remained outstanding for thirty days beyond the due date. This specific period of 'past due' was brought down from four quarters to three quarters on 1 April 1994 and further to two quarters on 1 April 1995. Partly because of the new norms of asset classification, the NPA of public sector banks went up from ₹174 billion or 14.5 per cent of gross advances on 31 March 1992 to 23.2 per cent (₹392.5 billion) and further to 24.8 per cent (₹410.4 billion) at end-March 1993 and 1994, respectively. Introduction of norms for the classification of NPAs in conformity with international standards had to wait until 2004.

For expeditious adjudication and recovery of debts due to banks and financial institutions, insolvency resolution and bankruptcy of individuals and partnership firms, came the Recovery of Debts and Bankruptcy Act, 1993, providing for the setting up of Debts Recovery Tribunals (DRTs) and Debts Recovery Appellate Tribunals (DRATs).

The BCBS's recommendations contained in its document 'International Convergence of Capital Measurement and Capital Standards', popularly known as Basel I, was available from 1998. Also called the Basel Accord, it was an agreement or accord among the G-10 central banks to apply common minimum capital standards to their banking industries by end-

1992. Basel I wanted banks to act as shock absorbers in the face of market volatility and adverse developments. The banks could do so only if they had adequate capital relative to their risky assets or credit risk. Thus, Basel I categorized assets of financial institutions into four risk categories—0 per cent (e.g., cash, home-country government debt), 20 per cent (e.g., mortgage-backed securities with AAA rating), 50 per cent (e.g., municipal bonds residential mortgages) and 100 per cent (e.g., most corporate debt). Under Basel I, banks were required to maintain a Capital to Risk (Weighted) Assets Ratio (CRAR), or Capital Adequacy Ratio, of 8 per cent.

Manmohan Singh, in his Budget speech for 1993–94, clearly recognized the capital adequacy norms, provisioning requirements and the need to recapitalize the public sector banks. The RBI stipulated that all banks must attain a capital adequacy ratio of 8 per cent by 31 March 1996. The government supported the public sector banks by recapitalizing them with ₹14,987 crore in 1993–95. These banks were also allowed to access the capital markets, including by a 1993 amendment to the SBI Act, 1955 to enable the SBI to do so. Interest rates were gradually deregulated. Liberalization of the financial sector promoted competition and efficient intermediation.

Control of capital issues was removed, and SEBI was made functional through statutory provisions to provide the regulatory platform. Holding securities in physical form involved considerable inconvenience, including the well-known 'bad deliveries' in transactions. A 'depository' facilitates holding of securities in the electronic form and enables transactions in securities to be processed by book entry by a Depository Participant (DP), who is an agent of the depository and offers depository services to investors. The Depositories Ordinance promulgated on 7 January 1996, which was subsequently made into a law in August 1996, provided a legal framework for establishment of depositories to record ownership details in book entry form. The National Securities Depository Limited (NSDL) started trading in dematerialized or demat form on the National Stock Exchange (NSE) from December 1996, and on the Bombay Stock Exchange (BSE) a year later. Securities in demat form revolutionized the stock and securities markets in India and put the country ahead of many advanced countries in securities market architecture. The setting up of the Insurance Regulatory

Authority—although on a non-statutory basis—in January 1996 was a milestone in the field of insurance.

XXI.3 The End of Industrial Licensing and Structural Reforms

While macroeconomic policies could stabilize the economy and pull it out of the immediate balance of payments crisis in the short run, a durable solution to the problem of vulnerability required structural reforms. In 1991, the government 'decided to take a series of measures to unshackle the Indian industrial economy from the cobwebs of unnecessary bureaucratic control.'[2] The reforms involved, apart from the end of industrial licensing, new policies for CPSEs and control of monopoly power.

End of industrial licensing

After three and a half decades of industrial licensing, the bonfire of the restrictions finally came with the Statement on Industrial Policy tabled in Parliament on 24 July 1991. The objective of the policy was 'to build on the gains already made, correct the distortions and weakness that might have crept in, maintain sustained growth in productivity and gainful employment, encourage further growth of entrepreneurship and upgrade technology to attain international competitiveness'. It announced 'industrial licensing will henceforth be abolished for all industries, except those specified, irrespective of levels of investment. These specified industries (Annex-II) will continue to be subject to compulsory licensing for reasons related to security and strategic concerns, social reasons, problems related to safety and over-riding environmental issues, manufacture of products of hazardous nature and articles of elitist consumption.' In July 1991, the list of seventeen industries reserved for the public sector was pared down to eight. Only items where security and strategic concerns dominated remained reserved for the public sector.

It was announced that in high-priority industries, requiring large investments and advanced technology, FDI up to 51 per cent would be approved. To avoid 'unnecessary governmental interference on a case-to-case basis involving endemic delays and fostering uncertainty' and for 'injecting the desired level of technological dynamism in Indian industry,' provisions were made for automatic approvals for technology agreements in high priority industries within specified parameters. In October 1991, the government announced the opening up of electricity generation to private participation as well as FDI. The Coca-Cola Company, which had left the country during Janata rule in the late-1970s, was back in India through its wholly owned subsidiary. The inter-ministerial specially empowered Foreign Investment Promotion Board (FIPB) was set up in the Prime Minister's Office to consider and approve FDI that did not come under the automatic approval route.

After liberalization, both the telecommunications and pharmaceutical sectors underwent rapid transformations. There was recognition that telecommunication was not a luxury but a necessity for rapid economic development and, given its technology- and capital-intensive nature, its rapid acceleration required huge resources, which were beyond the reach of the government. Under the National Telecom Policy 1994, it was a phased liberalization, starting with opening up mobile service in four metros to private sector participation in 1994. In early January 1995, tenders were invited for cellular and fixed telecom services in twenty telecom circles or states of India. The selection was through a single-stage bidding process and thirty-four licences in eighteen circles fetched ₹20,038 crore for 10-year licences. As we shall see, in retrospect, the bids would turn out to be exorbitantly high and a new telecom policy would have to be implemented from 1999. Teledensity, that is the number of telephones per 100 people, went up from 0.77 in 1993 to 2.33 in 1999 and further to over 90 by 2017. Growth in teledensity would accelerate after the National Telecom Policy in 1999 and Unified Access Service Licence in 2003.

Liberalization of the pharmaceutical sector in 1994 coincided with the signing of the Trade-Related Aspects of Intellectual Property Rights (TRIPS) agreement by 164 countries, including India. The General Agreement on Tariffs and Trade (GATT), with India as one of the twenty-three original signatories, which came into effect from 1 January 1948, dealt mainly with trade in goods and paid little attention to services and intellectual property rights (IPR). The World Trade Organization (WTO) came into being on 1 January 1995, along with the deadline on TRIPS mandating patent protection on both products and processes for a period of twenty years. Reverse engineering was no longer possible in pharmaceuticals after TRIPS. The sagacity of the 1994 liberalization measure was fully demonstrated in the rapid growth of the pharmaceutical sector and India transforming itself into the pharmacy of the world by the time the COVID-19 epidemic struck in 2020.

The indirect control on industry through restrictions on import was also relaxed by introducing automatic approval for project import of capital goods in cases where foreign exchange was available through foreign equity, or if the cost including insurance and freight (CIF) of imported capital goods was less than a quarter of the total value of plant and equipment, up to a maximum of ₹2 crore. Furthermore, the phased manufacturing programme, under which manufacturers were required to increase the domestic input content of their products, was also abolished for new projects. Registration schemes—Delicenced Registration, Exempted Industries Registration, DGTD registration—were abolished. Entrepreneurs were required to file only an information memorandum on new projects and substantial expansions with the Secretariat of Industrial Approvals (SIA) in the Department of Industrial Development.

After allowing private participation in the electricity sector in 1991, there was a need for a relook at coal, a critical input in power generation. The Coal Mines (Nationalization) Act, 1973 was amended to allow, from 9 June 1993, private sector participation in captive coal mining for generation of power, for washing of coal obtained from a mine or for other end uses to be notified by the government from time to time. Allocations to public sector companies were made directly by the ministry of coal, and those to the private sector, on the recommendations of a Screening Committee. In September 2014, the lack of transparency and competitive bidding would lead the Supreme Court to declare all such allocations since 1993 illegal.

New policy for central public sector enterprises

The Statement on Industrial Policy 1991 recognized 'serious problems' with CPSEs in terms of 'insufficient growth in productivity, poor project management, over-manning, lack of continuous technological upgradation, and inadequate attention to R&D and human resource development.' Further, it noted the 'considerable dilution' of the 'original concept of the public sector' manifest in the 'most striking example' of 'takeover of sick units from the private sector' and 'this category of public sector units accounting for almost one third of the total losses of central public enterprises.' It added that 'another category of public enterprises, which did not fit into the original idea of the public sector being at the commanding heights of the economy, was the plethora of public enterprises which are in the consumer goods and services sectors.'

The policy defined the priority areas for growth of CPSEs in the future to be: (i) essential infrastructure goods and services, (ii) exploration and exploitation of oil and mineral resources, (iii) technology development and building of manufacturing capabilities in areas which are crucial for the long-term development of the economy and where private sector investment is inadequate, and (iv) manufacture of products where strategic considerations predominate, such as in defence equipment. It announced that, in selected enterprises, a part of the government's equity holdings would be disinvested to provide market discipline to their performance. It also proposed to take up disinvestment of chronically sick CPSEs incurring heavy losses, operating in a competitive market, and serving little or no public purpose.

India began disinvestment in the year 1991–92, with thirty-one selected CPSEs disinvested for ₹3038 crore. Through disinvestment, while it mobilized ₹1913 crore in 1992–93 and ₹4843 crore in 1994–95, receipts under this head were nil in 1993–94 and limited to only ₹361 crore and ₹380 crore in 1994–95 and 1995–96, respectively. Apart from disinvestment in CPSEs, there was the policy of restructuring employment in CPSEs affected by technological change and providing a safety net for workers with a National Renewal Fund. The fund came into effect in February 1992 and was used mostly for restructuring employment in CPSEs.

An important reform relating to the public sector launched by the Rao government was the amendment of the National Highway Act, 1956 in June 1995 to allow the private sector to invest in NH projects, levy, collect and retain fees from users, and to regulate the traffic of such highways in terms of the provisions of the Motor Vehicles Act, 1989. In the years ahead, this amendment would provide the basis for public-private partnership in the roads sector.

New policy for control of monopoly power

The MRTPA, which equated size with monopolistic or restrictive trade practice and imposed pre-entry restrictions on large industrial houses, was amended in September 1991 to remove the threshold limits of assets in respect of MRTP companies and dominant undertakings. The concept of an 'MRTP undertaking' was removed and the new emphasis was on unfair trade practices. Entrepreneurs, irrespective of size, were freed from the need to seek government approval for establishing new undertakings or expanding existing capacity. The provisions for mergers and acquisitions were also simplified. The problem of unfair trade practice was addressed by extending the jurisdiction of the Consumer Protection Act, 1986 to all sellers and suppliers of goods and services. Government-owned enterprises were beyond the old MRTPA, but the amended MRTPA in 1991 brought them under its jurisdiction. The MRTP Commission was authorized to enquire into a restrictive trade practice based on a consumer complaint or reference by the central or state government or application by the Director General (Investigation and Registration) or suo moto.

The results of the structural reform-cum-stabilization efforts were gratifying. Prior to the 1980s, India had an annual average growth rate of 3 to 3.5 per cent. During the 1980s, the Indian economy pierced this benchmark and grew at an annual average rate of 5.6 per cent, but it was on borrowed money and accompanied by serious macroeconomic imbalances. Inflation (on an end-of-period basis) was in double digits—12.1 per cent—in 1990–91. In July 1991, foreign currency reserves had declined to less than a billion dollars, enough only for paying a fortnight of imports. What the Rao government achieved was growth with stability. Growth accelerated every year from 1.4 per cent in 1991–92 to peak at 7.3 per cent in 1995–96 (Figure XXI.2). Annual average growth rate during 1992–96, the last four of the five years of the Rao government after the crisis year of 1991–92, was 6.2 per cent, relative to 5.6 per cent during 1981–90.

Furthermore, the Rao government achieved the growth acceleration with a large measure of inflation control (Figure XXI.3). Despite the substantial devaluation that it started with right after coming to power, it managed to contain the wage-price spiral that accompanied a devaluation

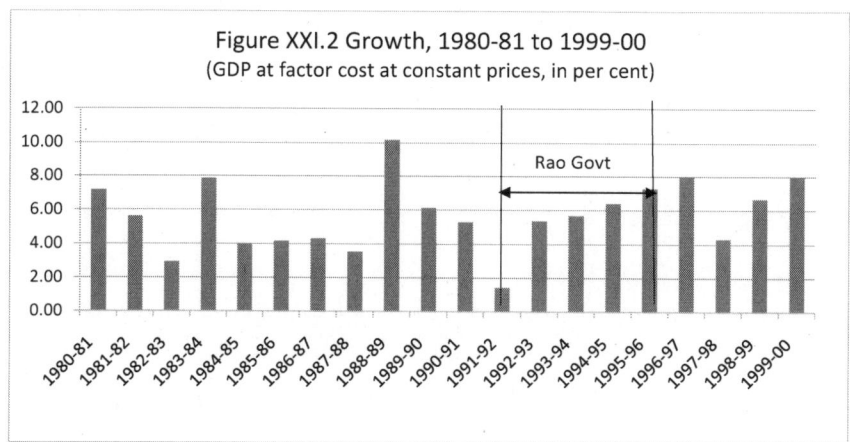

Source: RBI Handbook of Statistics on the Indian Economy

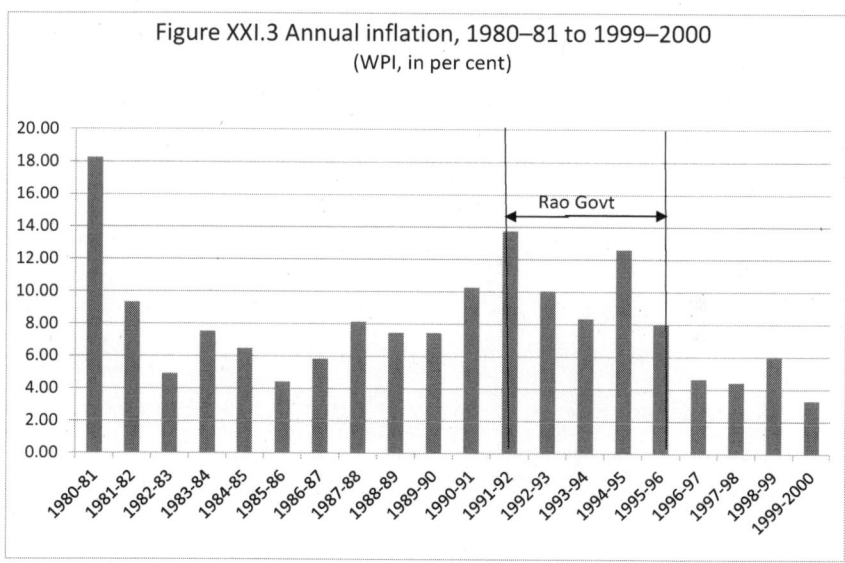

Source: RBI Handbook of Statistics on the Indian Economy

in many countries. All this was primarily due to the modicum of success that it had, despite a stop-go pattern, in containing the fiscal deficit as a proportion of GDP (Figure XXI.4). The annual average gross fiscal deficit of the Union government as a proportion of GDP was 5.6 per cent during 1991–96, relative to 6.7 per cent during 1981–90.

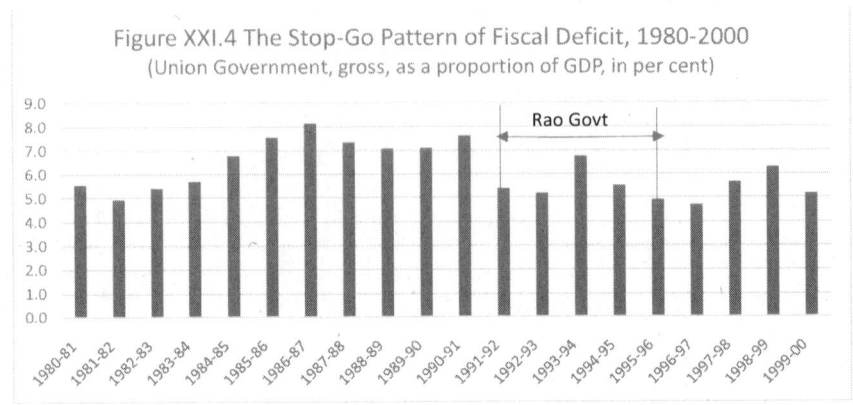

Figure XXI.4 The Stop-Go Pattern of Fiscal Deficit, 1980-2000
(Union Government, gross, as a proportion of GDP, in per cent)

Source: RBI Handbook of Statistics on the Indian Economy

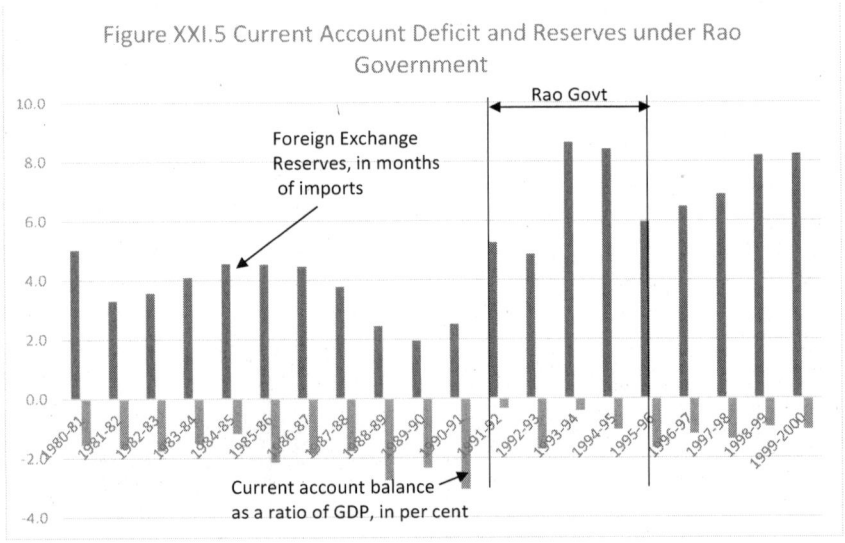

Figure XXI.5 Current Account Deficit and Reserves under Rao Government

Source: RBI Handbook of Statistics on the Indian Economy

Most significantly, there was a sea change in the external balance of payments (Figure XXI.5). The current account balance, which had been in deficit of over 2 per cent of GDP since 1988–89 and at a high of 3.05 per cent in 1990–91, was contained well below 2 per cent of GDP in each of the Rao years. With buoyant capital flows and a limited current account deficit, there was a healthy build-up of foreign exchange reserves. Such reserves reached as much as 8.6 months of imports before declining to a still comfortable half a year of imports in 1995–96. By the time Rao demitted office, he had put India's economic crisis of 1990–91 well behind the country.

There is a debate among economists about whether the Indian reforms started from 1991 or earlier. For example, Arvind Virmani claims that the breaking point came in 1981, after Indira abandoned socialist policies, while Kaushik Basu, another former Chief Economic Adviser, disagrees with Virmani partly because of the unsustainable fiscal policy stance in the 1980s. Some others point to the liberalization attempt by Rajiv Gandhi in 1985. But that process under Rajiv was short-lived and came to a halt in 1987 because of the Bofors scandal. Reforms without macroeconomic stability are unsustainable. Anything unsustainable must stop. The reforms before 1991 did not emphasize fiscal consolidation and macroeconomic stability and were doomed to failure. The 1991 reforms under Narasimha Rao were different.

Many, including Manmohan Singh, consider Narasimha Rao as the father of Indian economic reforms. According to Pranab Mukherjee, the former President, Narasimha Rao '. . . held additional charge of the Industry Ministry himself and therefore, also played a direct role in dismantling the Licence Raj'.[3] Even during his rule, Rao was acclaimed as the chief architect of the Indian economic reforms. Before his US visit in the summer of 1994, the *New York Times* gushed: '. . . the 72-year-old Mr. Rao has become, in effect, the Deng Xiaoping of India—an aging party leader who, in his sunset years, has abandoned many, if not all, of the economic precepts that had guided earlier governments, challenging not only the old orthodoxies but an entrenched network of vested interests that had built up under the old system.'[4]

Welfare schemes

Strictly speaking, whether employment generation through schemes is what the Constitution wanted the central government to do is debatable, but in a democracy, the political dividends from launching such schemes for poverty alleviation were too tempting to forego. The schemes were often modified, renamed and launched as new initiatives for mobilizing popular support. Thus, FWP under Janata from 1977 was restructured and renamed NREP under Indira Gandhi and her Congress in 1980. Indira had also launched RLEGP in 1983. NREP and RLEGP were merged and renamed JRY under Rajiv Gandhi in 1989.

To balance its reform agenda with welfare schemes, the Rao government took a leaf out of past efforts to launch its Employment Assurance Scheme (EAS) from 2 October 1993 in the rural areas of 1778 blocks in drought-prone regions and in desert, tribal and hill areas. Gradually, it was extended to all the rural blocks of the country. Its primary objective was creation of additional employment opportunities during the period of acute shortage of wage employment through manual work for the rural poor, while the secondary objective was the creation of durable community, social and economic assets for sustained employment and development. With minimum wages paid under the scheme, only BPL people were expected to self-select. From 1 April 1999, EAS, a demand-driven scheme, became an allocation-based one.

The Prime Minister's Integrated Urban Poverty Eradication Programme (PMIUPEP) was introduced in November 1995 with ₹800 crore allocated for the period up to 2000. PMIUEP was perhaps the first central sector or CSS welfare scheme with the Prime Minister or Pradhan Mantri mentioned in the name of the scheme. Perhaps the prefix PM was meant to leave no doubts in the minds of the voters that the initiative and the funds were coming from the Union government and not the states. The prefix in the names of various schemes would proliferate under NDA rule in the future.

IAY, introduced under Rajiv Gandhi in May 1985 as a sub-scheme of RLEGP, was made into an independent scheme from 1 January 1996. IAY's aim was to provide grant-in-aid to help rural BPL people, particularly those belonging to SCs/STs and freed bonded labourers, construct dwelling units and upgrade existing unserviceable *kutcha* houses.

The Rao government expressed its disquiet at the inadequacy of public investment in agriculture. States, which by Constitutional assignment are responsible for agriculture, had neglected investment in infrastructure for agriculture. Many rural infrastructure projects were lying incomplete for want of resources. They represented a major loss of potential income and rural employment. To encourage completion of such projects, a new Rural Infrastructural Development Fund (RIDF) within the NABARD was established in April 1995. RIDF would provide project-specific loans to state governments and state-owned corporations for completing ongoing projects relating to medium and minor irrigation, soil conservation, watershed management and other forms of rural infrastructure.

One of the great failings of Indian economic policy, namely the neglect of the education sector, continued under the Rao government. In the Twelfth Lok Sabha, Purno Sangma, the member from Meghalaya, pointed out that '. . . a solution to most of our problems lies in education, whether you talk of population control or anything . . . I have been advocating on the floor of this House that as against 3.9 per cent of the GDP that has been earmarked for education, it should be made a minimum of ten per cent . . . Shri P.V. Narasimha Rao took a decision that from the Ninth Plan onwards at least six per cent of the GDP shall be earmarked for education. I was very happy with that.'[5] Alas, given the pulls and pressures on government's resources, the wait for achieving the goal of ramping up the allocation for education would continue for decades.

With economic reforms, there were tax and other incentives for setting up private hospitals and clinics, and this resulted in rapid growth in private sector participation in the health sector. In 1995, for optimal and focused development of medical systems other than allopathy—Ayurveda, yoga and naturopathy, Unani, Siddha and homoeopathy, which are practised in the country—the Department of Indian Medicine and Homeopathy (ISM&H) was created in the Union ministry of health and family welfare.

Article 41 of the Constitution of India directs the State to provide public assistance to its citizens in case of unemployment, old age, sickness and disablement and in other cases of undeserved want within the limit of its economic capacity and development. In accordance with these principles, the Union government launched the NSAP as a CSS from 15 August 1995. It comprised of National Old Age Pension Scheme (NOAPS) (₹75 per month for destitute over sixty-five years), National Family Benefit Scheme (NFBS) (₹5000 for death of the primary breadwinner due to natural causes and ₹10,000 for accidental death) and National Maternity Benefit Scheme (NMBS) (₹300 per pregnancy up to the first two live births).

End of specialized development finance institutions

The relevance of domestic development finance institutions changed with the end of industrial licensing and widespread controls, and the resulting enhanced credit risk of industrial projects. Furthermore, there was the question of surviving competition in the market for financial intermediation. Compartmentalization of activities lead to greater transaction costs, and no intermediary can survive if it does not allow itself flexibility to change.

In July 1993, IFCI was converted from a statutory corporation to a company under the Indian Companies Act, 1956, to facilitate fundraising directly through capital markets and achieve greater operational flexibility. IFCI broadened its ownership structure through an initial public offering in December 1993 and was listed on the stock exchanges. The government's shareholding even after the public offering remained at 56 per cent and, mainly because of mismanagement, IFCI almost collapsed in less than two decades.

From 1992, IDBI started providing indirect financial assistance by way of refinancing of loans extended by SFCs and banks, and by way of rediscounting of bills of exchange arising out of the sale of indigenous machinery on deferred payment terms. The IDBI Act, 1964 was amended in 1994 to permit the IDBI to raise equity from the public, subject to the government's shareholding not falling below 51 per cent. After the public issue of IDBI in July 1995, the government shareholding in IDBI came down from 100 per cent to 72.14 per cent.

ICICI promoted the ICICI Bank in 1994 as a wholly-owned subsidiary, reduced its shareholding in ICICI Bank to 46 per cent through a public offering of shares in India in 1997–98, and further an equity offering in the form of American Depository Receipt (ADR)—a negotiable certificate issued by a US depository bank representing a specified number of shares—and became the first listed Indian company on the New York Stock Exchange in 1999.

XXI.4 Efforts to Solve the Electricity Problem and Dabhol Controversy

By end-March 1990, the cumulative losses of 17 SEBs had mounted to ₹3265 crore. The commercial losses of SEBs increased from ₹3,083 crore in 1990–91 to ₹26,343 crore in 1999–2000, mainly due to high T&D losses, low recovery (of cost) rate in-built in their tariffs, low plant load factor, high level of receivables, and high establishment and administrative expenses. While the Electricity (Supply) Act, 1948 required them to pay a three per cent return on their fixed assets, the SEBs registered a negative return of 12.7 per cent in 1992–93, which went up to 43.1 per cent in 1999–2000. The SEBs were in financial distress. They were not being able to pay for the power, equipment and raw material supplied by CPSEs and others.

A series of reports, including by Committees of Chief Ministers in the 1990s, urging the reintroduction of agricultural tariffs did not elicit the required response. In the meantime, there were widespread electricity shortages, manifested in not only poor quality and reliability (e.g., large voltage fluctuations) but also long disruptions in electricity supply, popularly known as blackouts. Even in the national capital of Delhi, a UT, there was a shortage of 15.8 per cent at peak time in 1992. In the country, in 1992, the unmet demand for electricity at peak time was around 30 per cent. Apart from widespread disruptions in household activities such as children studying and homemakers cooking, and physical discomfort without fans at the height of very hot summers, many manufacturing units, without electricity for lights, motors and machines, could not produce anything. There was an electricity crisis in India in the early 1990s, and neither the SEBs nor the Union or state governments, nor international financial institutions such as the World Bank and the IMF, had the requisite resources to invest in generation capacity. Thus, India decided to open up generation to private investment, including from foreign sources.

Through a series of notifications from October 1991, the Union ministry of power started encouraging the entry of privately-owned (including those 100 per cent owned by foreign equity holders) generating companies, which later came to be known as Independent Power Producers (IPPs). Some of these notifications were later incorporated into the Electricity Laws (Amendment) Act of 1991. IPPs were expected to establish, operate and maintain generation plants. Generous incentives were granted to the IPPs in the form of long-term power purchase agreements with SEBs, guaranteed minimum return on equity—'. . . the most noteworthy of which was a guaranteed minimum 16 per cent (repatriable) return on equity for plants that operated at their rated capacity for at least 6,000 hours in a year, with additional bonuses for improved capacity utilisation'—'a five-year tax holiday, a two-part tariff (the first part covering fixed costs including the assured return, the second covering variable costs), equity requirements that were as low as 20 per cent of project costs, and selective counter-guarantees from the central government to cover payment default by SEBs.'[6]

'From both domestic and international investors, the response to the incentives offered was overwhelming. By mid-1995, there were about 189 offers to increase capacity by over 75GW, involving a total investment of over US$100 billion. Of these, 95 projects for a total installed capacity of 48,137 MW had reached the stage of Memoranda of Understanding (MoUs) or Letters of Intent (LoIs) with state governments. But meanwhile, since none of the projects had yet reached financial closure, the central government introduced another set of carrots, granting "fast-track" status to eight of the most promising projects and agreeing to offer them counter-guarantees. The results of IPP policy were disappointing.'[7]

The most discussed of the eight fast-track IPP projects was in the Ratnagiri district of Maharashtra at a place called Dabhol, about 180 km south of Mumbai. Promoted by the US power company Enron together with Bechtel and General Electric, the Dabhol Power Company (DPC), also popularly known as Enron, launched a 2184 MW project in two phases of 740 MW and 1444 MW. It constituted the largest single FDI in India at that time.

After being away as defence minister in Narasimha Rao's government in Delhi, Sharad Pawar returned to Maharashtra as its chief minister on 6 March 1993. At the end of 1993, DPC signed a complex power purchase agreement (PPA) with a duration of twenty years with Maharashtra SEB (MSEB). It was in the form of take or pay, that is, MSEB was expected to pay for the power even if there was no demand and hence no off-take. The details of the PPA were kept away from public gaze. With secrecy shrouding the Dabhol deal with Enron, there were allegations of corruption against the Congress government in the state and Chief Minister Sharad Pawar. In the run-up to the Vidhan Sabha election in Maharashtra in 1995, alleged corruption in the Dabhol deal became a major issue drummed up by the BJP-Shiv Sena alliance against Congress. At Dabhol, where the plant was coming up, BJP's Gopinath Munde roared: '(We will) throw the project in the Arabian Sea . . . (I) promise you that I will be fighting along with you till the time Enron is removed from this land.'[8] BJP and Shiv Sena won sixty-five and seventy-three of the 288 seats in the Vidhan Sabha, and with the support of fourteen independents, on 14 March 1995, formed the government under Chief Minister Manohar Joshi of Shiv Sena.

The Maharashtra government constituted a 'Sub-Committee to Review the Dabhol Power Project' chaired by Deputy Chief Minister Gopinath Munde of the BJP on 3 May 1995. The sub-committee submitted its report to the state cabinet on 18 July 1995, and based on this report, in the legislative assembly, on 3 August 1995, Chief Minister Manohar Joshi announced the cancellation of both phases of the project. While it was true that the contract was not awarded through competitive bidding, yet, without concrete proof of charges of corruption, a cancellation entailed the breach of an international business contract. The DPC served a notice of arbitration to the state government on 4 August and asked it to carry out its contractual obligations or pay the damages. The cancellation of the contract could entail payment of damages between $300 million to $500 million, over and above the reputational risks to the country.

'On 3 November 1995, Enron's CEO Rebecca Mark visited the Shiv Sena supremo Bal Thackeray. It must have been an interesting meeting—five days later, the Maharashtra Government constituted a negotiation committee, asked to "revive" the project.'[9] Chief Minister Manohar Joshi received the report of the negotiation committee on 20 November 1995. On 8 January 1996, the Maharashtra government announced its decision to invite Enron back on new terms. Dabhol appeared back on track. According to the agreement, in October 1998, Maharashtra Power Development Corporation Ltd, a fully owned subsidiary of MSEB, acquired 30 per cent of Enron's shares in DPC. As we shall see, the problems with DPC would continue for a long time and raise fundamental questions about the lack of probity in award of government contracts and the roots of the power sector problem.

The ministry of non-conventional energy was created in 1992 and it launched the Integrated Rural Energy Programme (IREP) from 1994–95. The IREP would continue as a plan scheme during the Ninth Five-Year Plan (1997–2002) and as a CSS during the Tenth Plan (2002–2007).

IREP included, apart from supply of improved *chullahs* or stoves and biogas plants, village electrification and energization of pump sets.

XXI.5 Disintegration of the Soviet Union

In the context of the reforms launched in 1991, two questions could be asked: (i) 'why so little?' and/or (ii) 'how so much?' There was something sacred about socialism and planning in India, and all governments in India since Pandit Nehru's demise had been at pains to explain how their proposed steps were in consonance with Nehruvian socialism. So the more interesting question in the context of the reforms launched in India in 1991 is 'how so much?'

What helped were the changes in the world of ideology, and developments in the former communist countries of Eastern Europe and the former Soviet Union itself. Three years after the death of Leonid Brezhnev, Mikhail Gorbachev had become the general secretary of the Communist Party of the Soviet Union in 1985. The Soviet economy was stagnating. At the Twenty-Seventh Congress of the Communist Party of the Soviet Union in February 1986, Gorbachev launched a new policy of *glasnost* or openness, and *perestroika* or restructuring. The underlying idea was to bring in more democratization and acceleration of economic development.

On 12 June 1987, standing in front of the closed Brandenburg Gate on the Berlin Wall, dividing Germany between the communist East and capitalist West, US President Ronald Reagan, in a famous speech, had said, 'Mr. Gorbachev, open this gate! Mr. Gorbachev, tear down this wall!'[10] Few could have imagined that the gate would indeed be opened so soon thereafter, and the Berlin Wall broken down. Communism in Eastern Europe, in the countries belonging to the Soviet Bloc or Warsaw Pact, started to crumble from 1989. Poland was the first to break out of the communist fold. Hungary was the next to follow. East Germans started to vote with their feet and flee via Czechoslovakia to Hungary and then via Austria into West Germany. The Brandenburg Gate was opened on 22 December 1989, two and a half years after Ronald Reagan's speech exhorting Gorbachev to open the gate. Soon, the communist party rule was over in East Germany, and German reunification was well underway.

Communist rule ended in Czechoslovakia with the Velvet Revolution in November-December 1989, and in Bulgaria between January and November 1990. Starting with the provinces of Croatia and Slovenia, communist rule in Yugoslavia started to crumble from 1990 onwards, and the country was in the middle of a violent civil war by mid-1991. Most dramatic was the fall of communism in Romania and the execution of its leader Nicolae Ceausescu and his wife on Christmas Day 1989. With Gorbachev at the helm in Moscow, there was no application of the Brezhnev doctrine and no military intervention to stop a hostile takeover in Warsaw countries.

Ironically, at the same time, far away in communist China, the authorities were planning a massacre in Tiananmen Square in Beijing to put down student unrest and secure Communist Party rule by brute force. Unlike in China, the communist leadership in the former Soviet Union allowed Eastern Europe to break out without any armed resistance. Soon, the Soviet Union's survival itself was in jeopardy. With glasnost, by 1988, Moscow under Gorbachev's leadership was losing control of the republics in the Baltics (Estonia, Latvia and Lithuania), in the Caucasus (Armenia, Azerbaijan and Georgia) and the western region (Belarus, Moldova and Ukraine). One-party rule ended with the general elections in March 1989, which were open to candidates not belonging to the Communist Party. In the first multi-party elections in the fifteen constituent republics in 1990, the Communist Party lost the elections in six republics—Estonia, Latvia, Lithuania, Armenia, Georgia and Moldova. In the important constituent republic of Russia, Boris Yeltsin, the chairman of the Presidium of the Supreme Soviet of the Republic, resigned from the Communist Party in July 1990. In a referendum in March 1991, more than three quarters of the voters endorsed the retention of a reformed Soviet Union, but Estonia, Latvia, Lithuania, Armenia, Georgia and Moldova boycotted the referendum.

By the end of 1991, India's steadfast strategic ally as well as inspiration for its path of socialist planning, the former Soviet Union disappeared through disintegration. Indian foreign minister Madhavsinh Solanki had gone to Moscow in mid-November 1991, when the Soviet Union was de jure still alive. Reportedly, when the Indian delegation asked who India should negotiate with, Gorbachev had claimed that he had salvaged the

Union. Later, on the same day, when asked the same question, the Russian leader Boris Yeltsin got up, made his fists into a pair of binoculars, looked through it and said that he did not see even a spec of the Union! On Christmas eve of 1991, Gorbachev left the Kremlin and the Russian flag started to fly where the Soviet flag had flown for over half a century.

In 1991, the conflict of ideology in the twentieth century among liberal capitalist democracy, fascism and communism was finally coming to an end, at least temporarily, after fascism was defeated jointly by the other two through a world war. In 1991, it looked as if capitalist democracy had won the day over communism. Douglas North blamed the decay and disappearance of the Soviet Union in less than a century to the rigidity of its systems and inflexible institutional framework. The Indian system displayed its flexibility and adaptive efficiency in 1991 by launching comprehensive reforms. The 'magic' that Nehru had seen in Soviet planning in the 1930s had disappeared in half a century and this facilitated the launch of the reforms.

On 15 July 1991, the departure of the reforms from socialism and what Gorbachev was doing in the former Soviet Union came up in the parliamentary debate on the motion of confidence in the council of ministers moved by Narasimha Rao three days earlier. Indrajit Gupta, the veteran parliamentarian from ComPI, said, 'It may be your argument that things have changed so much in the world and India that all that old framework has to be given a go-by now. If so, you have to explain it here to the country and to the House.'[11] Jaswant Singh, from the BJP and the future finance minister, echoed Indrajit Gupta's sentiments and wanted an honest evaluation of what had gone wrong in the past and how it was being corrected. Arjun Singh, from the Congress, in a repartee, said, 'We are not shutting our eyes to the realities of the situation. If Comrade Gorbachev could not shut his eyes, I don't think you can blame our Prime Minister for that.'

Prime Minister Rao, in his reply, said: '. . . we are deregulating the economy, but at our own pace. We welcome foreign investment, but on our terms and in area we deem important and critical. This is the cardinal principle subject to which we are doing this. If we consider that in an area no industrialisation is necessary or if it is injurious from the point of view of a developing country—and we can conceive of many such situations where it may not be injurious from their point of view in their countries, but it is certainly injurious from our point of view in our country—the Government reserves the right to stop that kind of industry from coming here. It is not as though we have opened up to an extent where everybody is welcome to come and do everything here. It is not possible. So, bulk of our controls, we have found have hampered the economic activities in the past. This has been the experience. Time has come according to everyone because this change is sweeping the whole world. I do not want to say anything about Comrade Gorbachev and what is happening in other countries. All this has been said already.'[12]

Nine days later, Manmohan Singh provided more clarity on the issue of what was wrong with the old approach. Referring to the Soviet approach to industrialization, in his Budget speech, he said '. . . recent developments have shown that this approach too suffered from major weaknesses, particularly in its allocative efficiency, in the management of technical change, control of environmental degradation and in harnessing the vast latent energy and talents of individuals.'

XXI.6 The 1991 Reforms and the IMF and World Bank

The Rao government's 1991 reforms were supported by two standby arrangements for SDR 2.2 billion and SDR 1.4 billion Contingency Financing Facility from the IMF, and a structural adjustment loan of $500 million from the World Bank. How many of the reforms reflected a genuine political resolve for change and how many stemmed from the necessity of observing Fund-Bank conditionalities continue to be debated. But, with the dismantling of much of the licence-permit raj, 1991 also saw a change in the institutional design of the Indian state and it endured through changes in governments. While it is of course possible that the conditionalities once observed were found to be beneficial and hence not reversed, if the reforms were only because of the conditionalities, then they were likely to have been reversed once the crisis was over and the conditionalities no longer operated. Such reversals had indeed taken place before, in the mid-1960s after the stand-by arrangement with the IMF in 1965 and in the early 1980s after the EFF arrangement with the IMF in November 1981.

Furthermore, when Narasimha Rao and Manmohan Singh launched the reforms, the Congress party was far from unanimous about the path the policies should follow. 'Congress (I) manifesto had put the rolling back of the prices of essential commodities, in particular of diesel, kerosene, salt, edible oils, cycles and two-wheelers, electric bulbs, cotton sarees and dhotis, stoves including smokeless *chullahs* (stoves), newsprints, postcards, inland letters and envelopes to the July 1990 level. This was to be the first great achievement within a short period of 100 days. Pranab Mukherjee, when he was still hopeful of taking charge of the finance ministry, had declared that rolling back prices with fiscal and administrative measures would be no problem at all. What he had hinted at was that taxes on production, sale and purchase of the selected commodities would be withdrawn to bring down their prices for the consumer and penal action would take care of profiteering by the traders.'[13]

As Fukuyama has observed, institutional reform does not take place in the absence of such demand. In many countries, the absence of such demand led to the failure to comply with conditions for institutional reform attached to structural adjustment, project and programme lending by various foreign lenders, including the IMF and World Bank. While the role of Fund-Bank conditionalities in the 1991 reforms will continue to be debated, the least that Prime Minister Narasimha Rao and Finance Minister Manmohan Singh deserve credit for is to have judged the time ripe for introducing the change. The change endured and did not get reversed, and in Indian democracy, that is an endorsement of the change by the Indian people, who had changed sufficiently since the time such reversals took place in the mid-1960s and early 1980s.

India had to make amends to avert the repeated balance of payments crises, chronic low growth and bouts of high inflation. To come out of the crisis, with changed policies, the government started the third period from 1991 of what we call the period of reforms with its ups and downs. The symbiosis between wholesome policies and the voters' increasing endorsement of and demand for such policies became the critical determinant of India's future. Arun Shourie, former minister in the first NDA government under Vajpayee, summed up the symbiosis well when he said, '. . . Reforms are not the whim or fancy of some individuals. They are dictated by the compulsions that our polity and economy face on the one side, and are propelled by the opportunities that have opened up on the other . . . Each Reform paves the way for the other one. Whoever carries a Reform through at one place—say, in a state—enables someone else to carry it through elsewhere. Indeed, one Reform creates pressures that other Reforms be put through. Import-Export licensing is abolished. Trade increases. Traders and manufacturers demand that the ports be improved so that turn-around times may come down to Singapore levels, that the DGFT accepts electronic filing of forms.'[14]

XXII

End of Narasimha Rao Government

In his five-year rule, Narasimha Rao had become the father of economic reforms. He had steered the economy from a crisis mode, with growth at only 1.4 per cent in 1991–92, to accelerating growth with macroeconomic stability. In his last full year in office, 1995–96, growth was 7.3 per cent, foreign exchange reserves were equivalent to six months of imports, and WPI inflation was down from 12.1 per cent in June 1991 to 5 per cent in April 1996, the last month before the country was going to elect the Eleventh Lok Sabha. But there was trouble brewing for not only Rao's leadership of the Congress but also for his party's electoral prospects.

Heredity for determining accession to power is out of fashion in modern times. But going beyond heredity as the deciding principle makes succession a lot more controversial. Rao's elevation to the Prime Ministership in 1991 was no exception. Narasimha Rao had become Prime Minister only after Rajiv's widow, Sonia Gandhi, resolutely refused to take up the office. Several Congress leaders considered themselves as eminent as Rao and just as qualified to occupy the coveted post. Many senior Congress leaders did not see why Rao, and not them, should be the leader of the party.

Leadership of the Congress in the run-up to the 1996 election became hotly contested. Among the top-ranking leaders contesting, at least indirectly, Rao's leadership were Arjun Singh, Narain Dutt Tiwari and Sharad Pawar. Arjun Singh had been miffed when Rao, the Prime Minister himself, and not he became the Congress president at Tirupati on 27 February 1992. What complicated matters further for Rao was the rise of regional parties in UP based on caste consolidation, the demolition of the sixteenth-century Babri Masjid (or mosque) in Ayodhya in UP on 6 December 1992, and a multitude of scams.

XXII.1 Regional Parties Based on Caste Consolidation

UP, the largest state in India, had been steadily losing its political clout at the all-India level. Traditionally, starting with Nehru, with Lal Bahadur Shastri, Indira Gandhi, Charan Singh, Rajiv Gandhi, V.P. Singh and Chandra Shekhar to follow, the Prime Minister of India had been from UP. But there were already two exceptions—Morarji Desai from Gujarat, and then Narasimha Rao from Andhra. With fractured politics and the end of Congress dominance, between 1967 and 1989, UP saw fourteen chief ministers come and go. While Congress was increasingly incapable of accommodating the conflicting interests of various social groups, particularly castes and religious, there was the rise of regional parties focused on different castes such as Yadavs and the SCs. Prime among them was Mulayam Singh Yadav's SJP, which he had set up on 4 October 1992. Before forming his SJP, Mulayam had been in the Janata Dal, and with the outside support of the BJP, had formed the government in UP in 1989 and become its chief minister.

Most significantly in UP, there was the Bahujan Samaj Party (BSP) or the party of the majority of the people (Bahujan). Set up by Kanshi Ram in 1984, BSP could induct all sections of society except the upper castes. BSP focused on SCs and OBCs. Kanshi Ram's 'Bahujan Samaj' included all the victims of the caste system—intermediate castes, OBCs, SCs and STs, and also the various religious minorities. BSP coined several slogans, of which the most popular and controversial was '*Tilak, tarazu aur talwar, inko maro joote chaar*' (Brahmin, baniya and thakur, thrash them with shoes). Mayawati, the daughter of a minor post and telegraph official, had faced privations in her childhood, including the bias against girls typical in many Indian households, but successfully managed to educate herself and acquire a bachelor's degree in arts and education, and a degree in law. At the age of 24, she, a schoolteacher, was preparing for the Indian Administrative Service (IAS) examination and also working for the Janata

Party, when Kanshi Ram met her and spotted her talent. Kanshi Ram adopted her as a disciple. He persuaded her to join politics and work for the betterment of the lives of the Dalits. Instead of becoming an IAS herself, she could, in the course of time, 'control' hundreds of IAS officers, he assured her. BSP contested the Lok Sabha elections in 1989, won two seats in UP and one in Punjab, and became a recognized state party in UP in 1991.

By following a policy of building alliances with other sections of the Bahujan Samaj, and pursuing non-agitational politics, the crowning glory for Kanshi Ram and BSP—a glory never enjoyed by any Dalit leader or party—came in the December 1993 Vidhan Sabha elections in UP. With a poll alliance with Mulayam Singh Yadav's SP, while its vote share increased only to 11.1 per cent, its number of victories jumped to sixty-seven. By securing 17.9 per cent of the votes, Mulayam's SP won 109. On 3 June 1995, Mayawati—a Jatav, a part of the Chamar caste, one of the erstwhile 'untouchable' communities—was sworn in as chief minister. She became the youngest CM in the state's history, and the first Dalit CM in India. Away in Paris, to the captains of trade and industry, Prime Minister Narasimha Rao described her, a woman hailing from the most neglected section of the society, as a 'miracle of democracy'. The country had come a long way from 1979, when Babu Jagjivan Ram had griped about losing the prime ministership because of his cobbler caste. A member of the cobbler caste, a woman at that, was the CM of India's largest state. Mayawati's mentor Kanshi Ram had told her it would be so fifteen years ago.

In the meantime, in October 1994 came the Supreme Court's landmark judgment in the famous Bommai case. Chief Minister S.R. Bommai and his Janata Dal government in Karnataka had been dismissed on 25 April 1989 because of the alleged defection of twenty MLAs. Chief Minister Bommai wanted the Vidhan Sabha to be called and a floor test to be conducted to establish whether his government had indeed lost its majority. The Governor did not comply. A writ petition filed in the Karnataka High Court on 26 April 1989 was dismissed. Bommai went to the Supreme Court with the plea that although the President's satisfaction with the Governor's report in such cases was beyond judicial purview, matters had changed with the Anti-Defection Act on 1 March 1985. The Supreme Court judgment in the Bommai case in October 1994 made a floor test in the Vidhan Sabha obligatory to prove the majority support of the government and, among other things, declared the competence of the court to examine the material evidence behind the proclamation of President's rule. Imposition of President's rule became much less frequent after this judgement.

XXII.2 Babri Masjid Demolition

The polarization of the electorate along communal lines on the controversial Babri Masjid-Ramjanmabhumi issue in Ayodhya had been underway for quite some time. The VHP, formed in 1964, had been at the forefront of the campaign. In early April 1984, it convened the first meeting of the Dharma Sansad or Religious Council, which issued a call for the removal of the three mosques built by 'Muslim marauders' at Ayodhya, Mathura and Kashi.[1] However, the Lok Sabha elections held shortly thereafter, in December 1984, which followed the assassination of Indira Gandhi, proved disastrous for the BJP, with the party winning only two seats, lower than even what its predecessor Jana Sangh had managed in the 1957 elections. In 1986, the opening of the locks on the disputed Babri Masjid-Ramjanmabhumi structure for performing puja to Ram Lalla or the idol of young Lord Rama had added fuel to the communal polarization. On 9 November 1989, the *shilanyaas* or laying of the foundation ceremony by the VHP for the proposed temple, described as a landmark event in the Ayodhya movement, held with the tacit approval of the Congress government in UP led by Narain Dutt Tiwari, compounded the problem. BJP's strength in the Lok Sabha had jumped from two in 1984 to eighty-five in 1989. UP was at the vortex of the temple-mosque controversy, and communal polarization, together with the consolidation of backward caste votes in the state, proved to be a disastrous combination for the electoral prospects of the Congress.

In the politics of the state, charged with Ramjanmabhumi-Babri Masjid issue, Mulayam Singh Yadav soon turned his anti-Congress plank to an anti-BJP secularist one. When thousands of *kar sevaks* or volunteers from all over the country gathered in Ayodhya to construct the Ram temple on 30 October 1990, Mulayam's security forces fired on the crowd, resulting in fatalities. There were 1.85 lakh arrests all over the state. The BJP withdrew support, Mulayam's government fell, and elections were called for UP Vidhan Sabha simultaneously with the Lok Sabha polls between 20 May and 15 June 1991. The political situation was supercharged on the Ramjanmabhumi issue, particularly the firing on the kar sevaks on 30 October 1990. The BJP's strength in the Lok Sabha jumped further from eighty-five in 1989 to 120 in 1991.

The Rath Yatra in support of Ramjanmabhumi in 1990 contributed significantly to the consolidation of the BJP's vote bank in 1991. The impact was most pronounced in UP, where the BJP won 221 of the 425 seats in the Vidhan Sabha elections in UP in 1991 and went on to form a government under Kalyan Singh, an OBC leader from the Lodh community. Allegedly, BJP had projected Kalyan Singh as chief minister to counter the Mandal agitation.

The masjid was demolished on 6 December 1992 when BJP, VHP and RSS leaders had gathered at the site to offer prayers and perform a symbolic *kar seva* or religious service. A police cordon had been placed around the disputed structure, but the cordon was breached and the police did not act. Forthwith, on the same day, the BJP government in UP under Kalyan Singh was sacked and President's rule imposed. In rapid succession, BJP governments in three other states were also sacked—Rajasthan under Bhairon Singh Shekhawat, Himachal Pradesh under Shanta Kumar on 15 December 1992, and Madhya Pradesh under Chief Minister Sunderlal Patwa on 16 December 1992. On 16 December 1992, the government set up a commission under Justice Liberhan to enquire into the masjid demolition. The following day, the BJP brought a no-confidence motion against the government, which was duly defeated.

On 12 March 1993, there were a series of twelve bomb blasts in Mumbai, killing 257 people and injuring hundreds. The blasts, in retaliation for the killings during the riots following the Babri Masjid demolition in 1991, came to be known as the Mumbai bomb blasts. The Mumbai blasts exposed the blind spots of the intelligence agencies and a probable nexus between criminal gangs and bureaucrats and politicians. Following the Mumbai blasts, in July 1993, the government established a committee headed by N.N. Vohra, the Home Secretary, 'to take stock of all available information about the activities of crime Syndicates/ Mafia organisations which had developed links with and were being protected by Government functionaries and political personalities.'[2] The Vohra Committee concluded that 'The various crime Syndicates/Mafia organisations have developed significant muscle and money power and established linkages with governmental functionaries, political leaders and others to be able to operate with impunity.'[3] It recommended the setting up of a nodal agency for the collection, collation and operationalization of all information relating to crime syndicates.

Criticism of Narasimha Rao's government increased after the demolition of the Babri Masjid. 'It is believed Rao had the option to impose central rule in UP in July and had even sought a contingency plan to protect the mosque.'[4] In written assurances as well as speeches in the UP assembly, Chief Minister Kalyan Singh had insisted that his government would provide security to the disputed structure. He had even submitted 'a four-point affidavit to the Supreme Court promising security of the mosque and assuring that only a symbolic *kar seva* would be allowed.'[5] Rao had agonized over the question of dismissing the state government, but eventually did not. After the Babri Masjid demolition, Rao described the demolition as an 'utter perfidy'.[6] Many, even some inside the government, faulted Rao for taking a legalistic route on the Babri Masjid issue and trusting the assurances of the UP government, the BJP and the RSS.

Criticism of Rao, especially after the demolition, was not limited to people outside the Congress. At the forefront of his critics within the Congress was Arjun Singh, minister of human resource development in the Rao government. 'He was among the first to press for Mrs Sonia Gandhi's election as the Congress President; he persisted in this enterprise even after Mrs Gandhi had firmly rejected the offer more than once, and his endorsement of the new economic policy at cabinet meetings did not dissuade him for quite some time from criticising it not so privately to journalists.'[7] Arjun Singh held anti-BJP rallies in UP. He was against the party's soft stand against the BJP. On top of the list of leaders trying to dislodge Rao from within the Congress was, along with Arjun Singh, another Nehru-Gandhi loyalist, Narain Dutt Tiwari. Also, there was Sharad Pawar, the Congress leader who had been the CM of Maharashtra. Pawar, described as a 'crafty climber' by the media, also had his ambitions.[8] Pawar had made an abortive move to become Prime Minister in 1991 after Rajiv Gandhi's assassination.

Rao's term as president of the Congress party expired on 27 February 1994. Because of the upcoming Vidhan Sabha elections in four states, the term of the Congress president and the Congress Working Committee was extended indefinitely. The defeat of the Congress in the Vidhan Sabha polls in the two large states of Andhra Pradesh and Karnataka in 1994 was a political setback for Rao. On 24 December 1994, Arjun Singh resigned from the Union Cabinet. In an open letter, he demanded that 'justice be done to Indira-Rajiv loyalists in the distribution of tickets' for the upcoming Vidhan Sabha elections in 1995.[9] He was suspended from the Congress party on 25 January 1995. On 19 May 1995, at a Congress Workers' Conference in Delhi, Arjun Singh announced the appointment of Narain Dutt Tiwari as the new president of the party. This resulted in a Congress split, with the breakaway Congress group called Congress (T), named after Narain Dutt Tiwari. Meanwhile, Narasimha Rao faced continuing problems in Jammu and Kashmir and was also plagued by numerous scams.

XXII.3 Continuing Problems in Jammu and Kashmir

In Jammu and Kashmir, the government was following a four-pronged strategy of 'wearing out the militants through a long battle of attrition, restoring local trade and normal life, sealing the border more effectively and isolating Pakistan internationally'.[10] But not-so-infrequent violent incidents continued. The insurgents were divided on the issue of Jammu and Kashmir as an independent country or as a part of Pakistan. For example, the pro-Pak Hizb-ul Mujahideen was dead against pro-independence JKLF. Apart from JKLF and Hizb-ul Mujahideen, there were also other terrorist groups or factions operating in the valley. The All Parties Hurriyat (Freedom) Conference (APHC), an alliance of secessionist parties and leaders, was formed on 9 September 1993 as a political front of the militants to serve as a political interlocutor with Delhi. One of the founders of APHC was Jama'at-i-Islami leader Syed Ali Shah Geelani, who represented the Sopore assembly constituency in 1972, 1977 and 1987.

On 23 April 1993, an Indian Airlines flight from Delhi to Srinagar was hijacked to Amritsar. The Hizb-ul Mujahideen hijacker was killed by the commandos and the plane, crew and the passengers were safe.

Around the same time, Jammu and Kashmir policemen went on strike over the killing of a constable in an army search operation. They held demonstrations raising anti-India/pro-Azadi slogans, and the army had to disarm the striking cops to end the strike.

In 1993, terrorists started using the holy Hazratbal mosque as a hideout. On 14 October 1993, sensing a risk to the holy relic of the Prophet's hair inside the mosque, the security forces surrounded the mosque and decided to lay siege to tire the forty-odd terrorists out. Given the experience of Operation Bluestar in 1984, storming the mosque was not considered an option. Besides the terrorists, there were 170-odd civilian hostages inside the mosque. On 22 October, in Bijbehara, a town in Anantnag district about 45 km from Srinagar, security forces had to fire on demonstrators approaching the road to Srinagar against the siege of Hazratbal. About forty people were killed. The government was divided into two groups about the siege: one favouring supplying food and water to those inside, the other cutting such supplies off. The first group prevailed. Finally, after 32 days, the siege was lifted and terrorists were granted safe passage. One leading magazine reported the siege as 'Operation Blunder'.[11]

Wanting independence, JKLF under Mohammad Yasin Malik, the twenty-one-year-old campaign manager of Hizb-ul Mujahideen's Syed Salahuddin, a.k.a. Yusuf Shah, in the controversial 1987 election in Amarikadal, had been fighting the security forces as well as the pro-Pakistan Hizb-ul Mujahideen. Yasin Malik was captured in a wounded state and arrested in August 1990. He was released from prison on 17 May 1994. Four days later, he announced a unilateral ceasefire with the Indian government.

Charar-e-Sharief in Budgam district in the valley housed a Muslim Sufi shrine and mosque from the fifteenth century by the same name. From December 1994, infiltrators from across the border had started seeking shelter there to escape the winter. By the first week of March 1995, when their numbers grew to about seventy-five, apprehending a repeat of Hazratbal, the army had cordoned off the town. The siege was ineffective, and the terrorists refused to surrender despite the assurance of safe passage. Almost all the residents left town by mid-March. The terrorists, to fortify their positions, built bunkers and mined the area around the shrine with improvised explosive devices and booby traps rigged with LPG cylinders.

On the evening of 8 May, the militants set ablaze a few houses in a deserted residential locality near the shrine, perhaps to escape in the resultant confusion. A strong wind spread the fire to other parts of the town, and on 11 May, the historic shrine—which belonged to a Sufi saint from the Shia community, as opposed to the ruling Sunni community in Pakistan—was on fire. A gunbattle ensued; fire tenders had difficulty fighting the fire amid the battle. The security forces carried out cordon-and-search operations, about twenty-seven militants and four security personnel were killed, and several terrorists arrested. In terms of its fallout in adverse popular sentiment, the Charar-e-Sharief tragedy was even worse than the botched-up Hazratbal incident in 1993. Despite the JKLF ceasefire from 1994, terrorist violence continued in Jammu and Kashmir. The terrorists started abducting foreign tourists in the valley, demanding the release of their peers and leaders held in detention by the government and killing them when their demands were not met.

Since 19 January 1990, Jammu and Kashmir had been first under Governor's rule and then under President's rule. Elections to the Jammu and Kashmir legislative assembly had not been held after March 1987. In late 1995, the Narasimha Rao government was keen to hold elections for the legislative assembly in Jammu and Kashmir. Rao's talks with the National Conference and its leader Farooq Abdullah since 1994 had not satisfied the latter's demands about the state's autonomy. Furthermore, the government's proposal to hold elections was rejected by the Election Commission headed by T.N. Seshan. The commission doubted whether 'free and fair' elections could be held in the state in the prevailing situation.

Elections to the Eleventh Lok Sabha were held during April-May 1996. In Jammu and Kashmir, the turnout was 48.96 per cent, about 10 percentage points less than the all-India average. The National Conference boycotted the polls, and the contest was essentially among Congress, BJP, Janata Dal, and to a limited extent the BSP. Elections to the legislative assembly took place only in September-October 1996, after Deve Gowda became Prime Minister.

XXII.4 Scams Plague the Rao Government

The long shadow of the Bofors scandal eclipsed even the Rao government. On 1 February 1992, Madhavsinh Solanki, as foreign minister in the

Rao government, had given his Swiss counterpart Rene Felber a letter requesting an immediate end to the ongoing investigation into the Bofors deal. The contents of the letter were leaked to the media, and Solanki was forced to quit on 31 March 1992. Even under intense media pressure, Solanki refused to name the person who had given him the letter. The pro-development image of the Rao government was overshadowed as more scams were revealed. Corruption became a major issue in the 1996 Lok Sabha elections.

St Kitts case

St Kitts, officially known as the Federation of Saint Christopher and Nevis, is a Caribbean island state about 100 sq. miles in area and with a population of 50,000. Its popular name derives from Christopher's common nickname Kitt. Allegedly, Ajeya Singh had opened an account in the First Trust Corporation Bank on the island, deposited $21 million, and made his father V.P. Singh its beneficiary. Opening such an account was a crime and punishable under FERA, 1973, and could even come under the Prevention of Corruption Act. The documents claiming that Ajeya Singh had opened such an account were reportedly forged. The St Kitts story first hit the headlines in India in August 1989. The Rajiv government asked the ED to probe.

Under the National Front government that came to power with V.P. Singh as Prime Minister on 2 December 1989, the CBI registered criminal cases against former ED K.L. Verma, the controversial tantric Chandraswami, his secretary K.N. Aggarwal alias Mamaji, his disciple and arms dealer Adnan Kashoggi's son-in-law Larry J. Kolb, and First Trust Corporation's managing director George McLean. Before the cases could proceed, V.P. Singh's government collapsed. There was little progress under Chandra Shekhar's government. Media reports had started to circulate how the St Kitts case was based on forged documents and deliberately planned by the Rajiv Gandhi government, in which Rao was the external affairs minister.[12]

It was rumoured that Rao, and the then Minister of State for Information and Broadcasting K.K. Tewari, Rajiv's friend Satish Sharma and his aide R.K. Dhawan, had stage-managed the entire operation. In a press interview, less than three weeks after becoming Prime Minister, Narasimha Rao, in response to a question about his role in the St Kitts case, said, 'When I was in New York, I got a phone call from quarters from where such a call would mean a direction to me saying that an officer of the ED was in New York. He was investigating a case and had certain documents which were to be authenticated urgently because they were needed for Parliament purposes. I was told to see to it that there was no delay. This was what I told the officer who was leaving the town the next day.'[13] Though Rao along with the other accused were finally acquitted by courts of law, the ghost of St Kitts beleaguered his government during its entire tenure.

Harshad Mehta securities scam

The stock market had soared after the launch of the 1991 reforms. The BSE-100, the index including the top 100 companies listed at the Bombay Stock Exchange (BSE), had rocketed from 506.6 in January 1991 by over 265 per cent to reach 1850.9 in April 1992 (Figure XXII.1).

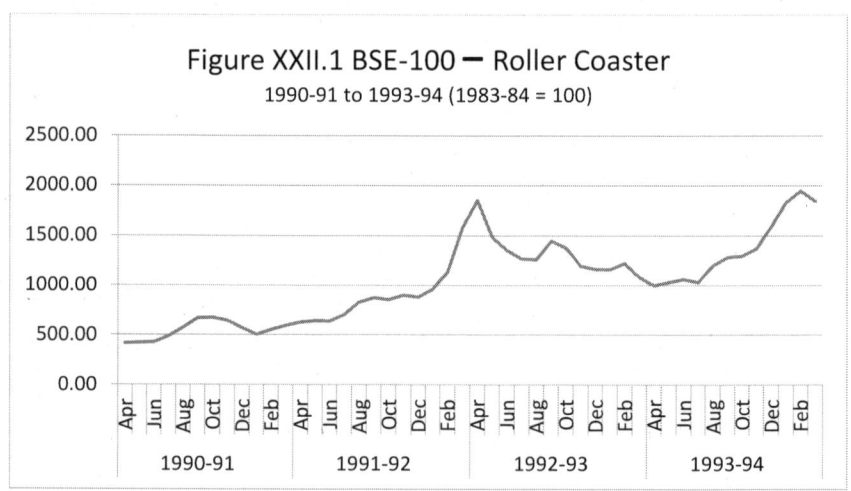

Source: RBI Handbook of Statistics on the Indian Economy. Monthly average of BSE 100

It proved to be more than just irrational exuberance. BSE-100 started to decline from May 1992 and fell by almost a half to reach 993.6 in April

1993. It was clear case of a scam with enough colour to lend itself to a web series Scam 1992 and a Bollywood film, *The Big Bull*, in 2020.

The decline in the stock market from April 1992 onwards coincided with the reported shortfall of government securities held by the SBI, the country's largest bank. The report about the shortfall turned out to be the tip of the iceberg—many in the financial sector were involved. The market had been booming until April 1992 and aggressive stockbrokers were hungry for funds to play the market and make a quick buck. The most obvious source of funds was the banking sector. The ready forward (RF) deals—essentially a short-term loan, say for fifteen days, against government securities—provided a convenient vehicle. But formally, RF was dressed as a repurchase agreement—that is, bank A selling securities to bank B with a contract to buy the securities back from bank B at a slightly higher price. RF provided a convenient route for banks to meet not only their short-term liquidity management needs, but also manage their SLR requirement of holding 38.5 per cent of their liabilities in specified securities.

RBI as the manager of the government's debt, through its Public Debt Office (PDO), acted as the custodian of government securities for its constituents. Transactions were represented, not by physical transfer of securities, but by book entries at the PDO. 'The ledger in which the PDO maintained these accounts was called the Subsidiary General Ledger (SGL).'[14] Brokers found a way of intermediating the settlement of the RF deals among banks, crediting the cheques received from the bank buying the securities into their own accounts rather than that of the selling banks and taking positions on the underlying securities on their own accounts. Furthermore, the deals were often done based on banker's receipts (BR), which were confirmations of the sale of securities, a receipt for the money received and a promise to deliver the underlying securities. With the PDO not functioning efficiently, SGL transfer forms taking long to clear and even bouncing because of insufficient balance of such securities in the seller's account, BRs gained in popularity. There were RF transactions through BRs, even when the bank did not have the underlying securities, because the selling bank needed an unsecured loan and believed that the price of the underlying securities was likely to move down. In such cases, these were fake BRs. The price of the underlying securities indeed fell between September 1991 and June 1992 and made selling a bond to buy it back later a profitable exercise.

The most aggressive of all stock market players was Harshad Shantilal Mehta. In his mid-thirties, he represented a rags-to-riches story and was known as the Amitabh Bachchan—the famous Bollywood star—of the stock market. Some brokers, with Harshad Mehta in the lead, started using fake BRs to receive unsecured loans and speculate in the stock market. Part of the stock market boom reflected this activity. Internal controls in the banks, their auditors and RBI failed in checking the deals, and verifying whether the sum total of specified securities tallied with the total issued by the relevant government.

The scam came to light with the SBI finding a shortfall in its holding of securities in the SGL around April 1992. The NHB had drawn a cheque on 3 January 1992 for ₹95.39 crore on the RBI in favour of the State Bank of Saurashtra, a subsidiary of SBI. Towards the end of April 1992, NHB found the underlying transactions still outstanding, and it did not possess any BRs or supporting documents or securities in respect of such transactions. When NHB asked SBI for the BRs or securities, SBI denied any 'outstanding transaction'. The scam unravelled soon thereafter. Investors panicked, and the stock markets recorded their biggest ever fall on 28 April 1992 when the BSE Sensex lost 570 points. An RBI Committee was set up under Deputy Governor Janakiraman to probe the scam. The accused, including Harshad Mehta, were arrested and their properties and bank accounts seized. The names of some important people, such as a member of the Planning Commission and senior bank officials, were associated with the scam. Manohar Pherwani, chairman of NHB, was found dead on 21 May 1992. Matters appeared even murkier when, on 16 June 1993, Harshad Mehta claimed that he had paid ₹1 crore to Prime Minister Rao himself. By then, the Rao government had become embroiled in the Jharkhand Mukti Morcha (JMM) cash-for-votes scam.

JMM cash for votes scam

In July and December 1992, Rao's government had faced and survived two no-confidence motions in Parliament moved by Jaswant Singh and Atal Bihari Vajpayee, respectively. The first was based on economic policies, corruption management of internal and external matters related to national security, and the system's collapse. The second was based on the murder and mayhem which took place before and after the Babri Masjid demolition on 6 December 1992.

After the Harshad Mehta scam, in the monsoon session of Parliament on 26 July 1993, the Rao government faced a formidable challenge from a no-confidence motion moved by Ajay Mukhopadhyay, a CPI(M) MP. While Mukhopadhyay complained about its economic and industrial policies that had endangered the base of a self-reliant economy, others joined in with allegations of corruption, 'anti-people' economic policies, mismanagement of the Babri Masjid Ramjanmabhumi issue, and insecurity of the minorities. With a broad coalition of the Opposition across BJP, ComPI, CPI (M), Janata Dal and many others arrayed against it, the government was in a tight spot. In the Tenth Lok Sabha of 537 seats, Congress and its ally AIADMK together had only 255. It needed the support of another fourteen members and/or abstentions to survive the no-confidence motion. In the event, seven MPs from Ajit Singh's twenty-member Janata Dal group (JD-A) and four MPs from JMM voted against the no-confidence motion, while three MPs each from Mulayam's group of Janata Party (Socialist) and BSP abstained. The Rao government survived with 266 votes against and only 531 total votes cast. Soon, there was a complaint with the CBI that Narasimha Rao had hatched a criminal conspiracy with V.C. Shukla, R.K. Dhawan, Satish Sharma, Ajit Singh, Bhajan Lal and Lalit Suri to prove the majority of the government on the floor of the House by bribing some of the MPs with over ₹3 crore. Scandals were breaking out like volcanic eruptions. The Jain hawala scandal followed.

Jain hawala scam

The Hindi daily *Jansatta* front-paged the story of the now infamous 'Jain diary' on 24 August 1993, carrying most of the names found in the diary. In the same month, Vineet Narain, a journalist, through his video news cassette *Kalchakra*, publicized the details of the Jain diaries. The gist was as follows: 'On 25th March, 1991, one Ashfak Hussain Lone, alleged to be an official of the terrorist organisation Hizbul Mujahideen, was arrested in Delhi. Consequent upon his interrogation, raids were conducted by the CBI on the premises of Surrender Kumar Jain, his brothers, relations and businesses. Along with Indian and foreign currency, the CBI seized two diaries and two notebooks from the premises. They contained detailed accounts of vast payments made to persons identified only by initials. The initials corresponded to the initials of various high-ranking politicians, in power and out of power, and of high-ranking bureaucrats.'[15] With the money sourced from foreign companies in foreign exchange converted into Indian rupees through the 'hawala' or the system of 'money transfer without money movement' outside the official banking channel, the case was also known as the Jain hawala scam.

Allegations were that the initials indicated the involvement of a former Prime Minister and Cabinet ministers. Leaders from practically all major political parties, except for the left, were implicated. L.K. Advani resigned from his Lok Sabha membership and declared that he would not contest an election until his name was cleared. Madhavrao Scindia, V.C. Shukla and Balram Jakhar resigned from the Cabinet when the CBI sought permission to chargesheet them. There were rumours that Rao himself was involved and was using this case to get rid of people within his party to secure his leadership. '. . . much of the muck that was being raked up splattered all over Rao as well when Atal Behari Vajpayee, leader of the Opposition in the Lok Sabha, released portions of a CBI interrogation report in which businessman S.K. Jain, following the seizure of the diaries, had alleged in March 1995 that he paid over Rs 3 crore to Rao from hawala money. Demanding the prime minister's resignation, Vajpayee said: "I expect the highest executive of the country to emulate the example set by my party president who has quit his parliamentary seat after his name was dragged into the controversy."'[16]

Sugar scam

Then there was the sugar scandal. In the twelve months leading up to February 1994, the wholesale price of sugar went up by 28.6 per cent. A shortfall in production had been anticipated for the 1993–94 sugar season, but the food ministry, headed by Kalpanath Rai, had denied this risk, argued it incorrect to pamper the consumer at the cost of the farmers and relied instead on the sugar industry's optimistic—some even say, deliberately misleading—estimate. While private traders had been allowed to import sugar under OGL, imports by the FCI were not allowed until it was too late, and prices in world markets had gone up. Even STC and Minerals and Metals Trading Corporation (MMTC) imported sugar when the price in the world market had gone up by as much as $27 per ton. There was a political controversy, and it took 'an ugly turn, there was talk of corruption, a scandal, perhaps even a financial scam. The BJP squarely blamed the ruling party for "deliberately creating the sugar muddle to raise massive political funds for the ensuing state elections".'[17] Prime Minister Narasimha Rao set up the Gyan Prakash Committee on 17 July 1994 to investigate the sugar scandal.

Lakhubhai Pathak case

Lakhubhai Pathak, the 'pickle king' of the UK, claimed that he had met Narasimha Rao when the latter was the external affairs minister in Indira Gandhi's government, outside tantrik Chandraswami's room in a New York hotel in 1983. Chandraswami had taken $100,000 from Pathak to secure a contract, and Rao, after coming out of the hotel room, had assured him that Swamiji had told Rao everything, and Pathak's work would be done. Nothing happened for years. When Rao took over as PM, Pathak wrote to Rao on 4 January 1992, to 'force this crooked swami to refund my hard-earned money'.[18] Pathak wrote a series of letters and claimed that the issue involved him, Rao and Chandraswami. Frustrated by the lack of progress in getting his money back, on 15 March 1995, Lakhubhai wrote to Rao: 'You are nothing. You are lower than dirty dust (sic) . . . Mr Rao, your downfall is imminent and absolutely sure; it will be so miserable, humiliating and degrading that no gurus and swamis can save you.'[19]

Sukh Ram telecom scandal

The telecom liberalization happened after Pandit Sukh Ram, an MP from Mandi, Himachal Pradesh, succeeded Rajesh Pilot as minister of state (independent charge) for communication. In December 1995, Parliament was rocked by the allegation that in installing rural telecom services, Sukh

Ram had favoured Himachal Futuristic Communications Ltd with about ₹250 crore. There were allegations against him of favouring another handful of companies in awarding telecom contracts and pocketing hefty bribes. Sukh Ram soon got embroiled in what one media reporter describes as 'mother of all scams'.[20] 'In August 1996, the CBI raided Sukh Ram's official residence and found ₹2.45 crore of unaccounted cash. Another ₹1.16 crore was seized from his ancestral home in Mandi. In September 1996, in a midnight drama, Sukh Ram was arrested on his return to India from London. Two more raids led the CBI to more cash that had been stashed away.'[21] He was expelled from the Congress, convicted in three separate cases and sentenced to two, three and five years of imprisonment, running concurrently. Later, he secured bail on health grounds. The Sukh Ram scandal raised damaging doubts in the public mind about the ability of the government to manage privatization on a large scale.

Urea scam

In September 1995, National Fertilizers Limited (NFL), a CPSU, had floated a global tender for the supply of 2 lakh tonnes of urea. In March 1996, the NFL, bypassing established procedures, advanced the entire amount of ₹133 crore to Karsan Danismanlik Turzim Sanayi Ticaret Ltd or Karsan, a Turkish firm, without any bank guarantee. Karsan took the money but did not deliver the urea. On 24 March 1996, Fertiliser Secretary Indrajit Chaudhari had written to the Prime Minister's Office that 'major deviations' had been made in awarding the contract to a 'relatively unknown and bogus company' called Karsan. On 2 April again, Chaudhari shot off a letter to Cabinet Secretary Surendra Singh, detailing the one-sided agreement. When a large part of the money disappeared and no urea arrived, news of the scam broke.

Narasimha Rao's youngest son, P.V. Prabhakar Rao, and former Union fertilizers minister Ram Lakhan Singh Yadav's son, Prakash Chandra Yadav, were accused of receiving around $4 million (₹14 crore) as kickbacks for arranging the deal between NFL and Karsan, a little-known tourism firm listed in Turkey. The kickbacks charge was made by Karsan's Indian agent, M. Sambasiva Rao, during CBI's interrogation and corroborated by the NFL's former managing director C.K. Ramakrishnan and former executive director (marketing) D.S. Kanwar. There were allegations that the government was deliberately going slow in the investigations to shield the culprits. Just before Narasimha Rao demitted office, the urea scam was the most sensational of all the scams that tainted the legacy of his government.

XXII.5 The Right to Information (RTI) Movement

Governments in India divided documents into two categories: classified and non-classified. The 'classified' category was further subdivided into 'top secret', 'secret', 'confidential' and 'personal—not for publication'. But officials were barred from communicating even non-classified information that came into their possession in the course of their official duties without authorization by general or special orders. Information to the press was to be communicated through the Press Information Bureau.

In the meantime, a small public hearing in a village in the western state of Rajasthan on 2 December 1994 snowballed into a massive movement for RTI. The Bhim Tehsil, on the border of the three districts of Pali, Ajmer and Rajasamand in Rajasthan, was one of the most backward regions of the state. The Mazdoor Kishan Shakti Sangathan (MKSS), an NGO working in the region, had been trying to find out the root problems behind the non-payment of wages for government works under the department of public works and forests. Projects such as schools, dispensaries and water supply schemes were complete on official records, but the school buildings had no roof, dispensaries no walls and dams were incomplete. 'Muster rolls', which were daily attendance registers of employees, were critical for payment of wages in most public works and were allegedly tampered with for siphoning off public funds. For years, MKSS had wanted the government records but could not get them.

When they finally did get some details from a young bureaucrat about the Kot Kirana village, they held a public hearing, a *jan sunwayi*, in the same village. It was a form of social audit. When the details of the bills and invoices and names of people were read out, there were howls and screams. The brazenness of the misappropriation was astounding. The government maintained that all records were available for scrutiny. But in January 1995, the *gram sewaks*, the lowest development officials, decided not to part with documents giving details of government expenditure and declared a strike. The jan sunwayi continued until April 1995, when Chief Minister Bhairon Singh Sekhawat (BJP), in a historic announcement, said that every citizen had the RTI.

Despite the chief minister's assurances, when no records were available, from 6 April 1996, MKSS declared an indefinite strike in Beawar town of Ajmer district. Journalists, lawmakers, artists and many others came to Beawar to express their support. The title of the *Jansatta* editorial on the subject, *'Hum Janenge, Hum Jiyenge'* (We will know, we will live), by senior journalist Prabhash Joshi after his visit, provided the future slogan of the RTI movement in India.[22] The forty-day-long protests gave rise to the National Campaign for People's RTI. Conflict between the democratic requirements of openness and the need to preserve official secrecy came into the open.

XXII.6 End of Narasimha Rao

For the Eleventh Lok Sabha polls in April-May 1996, there were forebodings for the Congress from the Vidhan Sabha elections in 1994 in Andhra Pradesh and Karnataka, and in 1995, in Bihar, Gujarat and Maharashtra. Congress was in power in 1995 only in Haryana, Himachal Pradesh, Kerala, Madhya Pradesh, Orissa and Punjab. Factionalism posed a heavy risk to its Lok Sabha poll prospects. Arjun Singh and Narain Dutt Tiwari had already formed the breakaway Congress (T). After being denied a Congress ticket in the 1996 polls, even Madhav Rao Scindia, the titular maharaja of Gwalior, left the Congress to set up his Madhya Pradesh Vikas Congress.

The southern states of Karnataka and Tamil Nadu had a running dispute on the sharing of water of the Cauvery River. A tribunal was examining the issues. There were anti-Tamil riots in Karnataka in early 1992 when the central government notified the Cauvery tribunal's interim order on sharing of water. It happened under a Congress government led by Chief Minister S. Bangarappa in Karnataka. With charges of corruption against Bangarappa, Rao had replaced him with Veerappa Moily as CM on 19 November 1992. Bangarappa was from the backward Idiga (toddy tapper) caste and had a sizeable following among the backward castes, particularly his own. Upon his removal, he started a tirade against Narasimha Rao, was expelled from the party in early January 1994, and launched a new party, the Karnataka Congress Party, in April 1994.

The AIADMK under Jayalalitha had come to power in Tamil Nadu by fighting the Vidhan Sabha election in 1991 in alliance with the Congress. Relations had soured soon, and she openly claimed that her resounding victory had little to do with the alliance. Jayalalitha was accused of many corruption charges. The celebration of her foster son Sudhakaran's wedding on 7 September 1995 in Chennai had been described as 'mother of all weddings' in terms of ostentation and glamour. For example, the wedding pandal was 70,000 sq. ft, 1000 VIPs were invited, and the invitation included a silver plate with containers, a silk saree and silk dhoti, each costing ₹20,000! Union Minister of State for Commerce P. Chidambaram, who is from Tamil Nadu, led the corruption campaign against her government, and state Congress leaders like G.K. Moopanar resolutely opposed an alliance with the AIADMK. Rao, however, was convinced that an alliance with the pro-LTTE DMK would hurt the Congress' prospects and arouse suspicions that he was siding with the killers of Rajiv. He unilaterally revived the alliance with Jayalalithaa. In response, Moopanar floated the Tamil Maanila Congress (TMC) on 29 March 1996. The Congress in Tamil Nadu was transformed almost in its entirety into the TMC.

Dogged by scams, dissensions within the party and the poor performance of coalition partners, the Congress led by Rao lost the Eleventh Lok Sabha election. Rao, though, won his Lok Sabha seat of Nandyal in Andhra Pradesh. He resigned as the Prime Minister on 10 May 1996, but not only continued as the leader of the Congress Parliamentary Party but also as the Congress president. There were demands, though, for his resignation from the president's post of the party.

The CBI was probing Rao in several cases. Shortly before being summoned in court in the Lakhubhai Pathak case, Rao resigned from the presidency of Congress on 21 September 1996 but continued as the leader of the CPP. But Sitaram Kesri, the Congress president who succeeded him, served him an ultimatum in December to resign his CPP leadership, and Rao laid down his office on 19 December 1996. Dogged by a series of court cases, after being president of the Congress Party, Rao did not get a berth in the AICC or a place in it as a special invitee. Rao was a melancholic, lonely old man suffering legal battles and an unfriendly press.

It is only after his death on 23 December 2004 that tributes started pouring in. The Prime Minister of India, Manmohan Singh, whom Rao had picked as his finance minister, said that Rao would 'forever be remembered as the father of economic reforms in India'.[23] But the father of Indian economic reforms also got the distinction of being the only former prime minister of India whose remains, after his death, were not encased in a memorial in the capital city of Delhi. He was cremated in Hyderabad, ostensibly according to the wishes of his family members. Narasimha Rao had been a staunch Indira-loyalist Congressman throughout his political career; even during the Emergency, he had stuck it out with Indira Gandhi's Congress. But Sonia Gandhi, the Congress president and UPA chairperson, was also 'never fond of' Rao.[24] Sonia was reportedly upset about the slow pace of the trial of her husband Rajiv Gandhi's killers under Rao's government. But there were other reasons too. Narasimha Rao almost succeeded in running the Congress without the Nehru-Gandhi family.

XXIII

Nineteen Months with Three Governments

In the run-up to the elections to the Eleventh Lok Sabha, Lal Krishna Advani was the president of the BJP. Because of Rao's handling of the Babri Masjid demolition, his detractors were calling the Congress under his leadership 'Advani Congress', and desperately trying to get Sonia Gandhi to intervene in the party and the government. But Rao insisted that there could be no intervention on an informal or extra-constitutional basis, and Sonia had 'the option to either plunge into active politics or sit at home'.[1]

XXIII.1 1996—A Triangular Contest

Ever since the Janata electoral sweep in 1977, the opposition's dream had been to close ranks and put up a united front against the Congress. But between 1991 and 1996, the Janata Party and its offshoots had splintered further into several regional parties. For example, Mulayam Singh had left the Janata Dal and founded the SJP in 1992, and a faction led by George Fernandes and Nitish Kumar had split from the Janata Party to become the Samata Party in 1994. Furthermore, the rift between the BJP on the one hand and the left, the Janata Party and many of its splinter groups on the other was too deep for such a united opposition. In terms of pre-poll alliances, the contest in the 1996 Lok Sabha polls turned out to be triangular with (i) Congress and AIADMK, (ii) BJP, Haryana Vikas Party (HVP), Shiv Sena and Samata Party, and (iii) the National Front (Janata Dal, SJP and TDP)—Left Front (CPI (M), ComPI, Revolutionary

Socialist Party (RSP), and All India Forward Block) alliances as the three main contestants. The AGP, DMK, TMC and SAD were some of the important parties that did not join any of the three pre-poll alliances.

In 1996, Congress performance in terms of seats (140) was worse than in 1977 after the Emergency (154). Its ally, the AIADMK, failed to win any. By contrast, BJP bagged 161 seats, the maximum in its history either as BJP or as Jana Sangh. BJP was given the first right to form a government and Atal Bihari Vajpayee became the Prime Minister on 16 May 1996. Along with its pre-poll allies—HVP (three), Shiv Sena (fifteen) and Samata Party (eight)—it commanded the support of only 187 of the 543 MPs in the Eleventh Lok Sabha. Failing to garner the requisite support from other parties, after thirteen days, Vajpayee resigned as Prime Minister before seeking a vote of confidence.

A thirteen-party United Front was formed with the four constituents of the National Front (seventy-nine) and the Left Front (fifty-two) each, and DMK (seventeen), AGP (five), All India Indira Congress (Tiwari) (four), TMC (twenty) and the Maharashtrawadi Gomantak Party (one). With the support of some minor parties, such as JMM, Indian Union of Muslim League and Sikkim Democratic Front, and some independent MPs, it commanded a strength of 192 in the Lok Sabha. Congress offered support from outside. In their search for a Prime Minister, the consensus choice was Jyoti Basu, the CPI(M) veteran and CM of West Bengal since 21 June 1977. But the CPI(M) Central Committee, its highest decision-making body, vetoed the proposal. V.P. Singh declined because of his poor health. Moopanar could not be chosen because of opposition from DMK. Finally, a United Front government headed by the Janata Party's H.D. Deve Gowda, former CM of Karnataka, with outside support from the Congress, came to power on 1 June 1996. He was the second Prime Minister since the 1996 elections.

XXIII.2 The Common Minimum Programme

CPI (M) did not accept any cabinet berths but supported the Deve Gowda government based on a Common Minimum Programme (CMP) that the United Front adopted as its charter. The CMP affirmed the Front's commitment to remain steadfast on the course of reforms and liberalization to accelerate growth, make such growth balanced across sectors and create employment, ensure fiscal prudence, viable balance of payments through buoyant exports and foreign investment flows, and macroeconomic stability, promote human development and infrastructure, and help the poor by providing them with basic minimum services in a time-bound manner. P. Chidambaram of TMC, with reformist antecedents, was the finance minister in Deve Gowda's government. As the minister of state (independent charge) in the ministry of commerce in the Rao government, he had ended the system of import controls.

In Budget 1996–97, his first, on 22 July 1996, Chidambaram did not increase the personal income tax exemption limit but raised the standard deduction for salaried employees from ₹15,000 to ₹18,000 and reduced the rate for the first slab from 20 per cent to 15 per cent. He raised the income limit for the special tax rebate of 40 per cent available for senior citizens from ₹1 lakh to ₹1,20,000 and gave tax exemption to LIC's personal-cum-family pension scheme premium up to ₹10,000.

On corporate income tax, Chidambaram reduced the surcharge from 15 per cent to 7.5 per cent in 1996–97 and promised to abolish it in 1997–98. The chequered career of MAT on companies continued: introduced by Rajiv Gandhi in 1987–88 and abolished by Madhu Dandavate in 1990–91, it was reintroduced by Chidambaram in 1996–97. For companies with assessable taxable income less than 30 per cent of the book profit, the total income of such a company was deemed to be 30 per cent of the book profit and charged to tax accordingly. Companies engaged in power and infrastructure sectors were exempt from MAT.

In the area of customs duty, Chidambaram reduced rates on crude oil and other basic petroleum intermediates, on raw materials, such as chemicals, plastics, natural rubber and metals, on computers and computer components, and machinery to modernize the textiles and garments sector. He also reduced exemptions and unified some rates to reduce classification disputes. In the area of customs duty, in 1996–97, to step up public investment in infrastructure, he introduced a 2 per cent special customs duty on all imports, except those carrying nil rate of duty and gold and silver carried by incoming passengers from abroad.

In the area of Union excise duty, Chidambaram emphasized the need for moving to a VAT, both at the Union and state levels. He noted the need for reducing the diversity of eleven ad-valorem Union excise duty rates ranging from 0 to 50 per cent and of moving to a four-rate structure—zero, a lower rate of excise duty on goods of mass consumption, a single normal rate on all other goods and a higher rate on luxury items. Such a move would 'put an end to wasteful litigation and have a transparent and simple tax structure', he said.[2] While he could not fully make such a move given the paucity of time in preparing the 1996–97 Budget, he made some initial moves and proposed to do so going forward.

In 1996–97, he granted excise duty exemption to some 'widely consumed articles' such as vanaspati and margarine, writing and printing paper supplied to all State Textbook Corporations, and animal fats and oils. With effect from 1 October 1996, the excise procedures were changed from requiring the furnishing of copies of invoices along with the monthly returns to a simple return indicating the duty paid on self-assessment basis. Routine examination and checking of returns and documents furnished by the assessees was replaced by a system of selective audit. Simultaneously, the mandatory penalty for evasion of duty was made equal to the amount of duty evaded. Even without any duty on salt after Independence, the relevant act, called the Central Excise and Salt Act, 1944, had continued with the same name for another half a century! Chidambaram proposed to rename it without any reference to salt.

In 1996–97, about MODVAT credit, Chidambaram proposed to clarify the scope of eligible capital goods by specifying the heading and sub-headings of the tariffs relating to capital goods in the MODVAT Rules and plug loopholes leading to misuse. He widened the service tax by bringing in advertising services, radio paging services and courier services under the tax net.

In Budget 1996–97, he announced a new Accelerated Irrigation Benefit Programme (AIBP) to take up major, medium and extension, renovation and maintenance projects in irrigation that could be completed within four years. He also announced higher subsidies for phosphatic and potassic fertilizers, the setting up of the Infrastructure Development Finance Company (IDFC) to provide long-term finance for projects and speed up the development of infrastructure, shore up the capital base of NHAI by ₹200 crore, and restructure PDS to focus on BPL households. He also announced the government's commitment to bringing the fiscal deficit below 4 per cent of GDP over time by raising more revenues and restructuring expenditure. He proposed to place before Parliament a discussion paper on subsidies to initiate an informed debate on the issue.

Chidambaram announced the launch of two new affordable insurance products, Jeevan Suraksha (Life Protection) and Jan Arogya (People's Well-being) by the government-owned LIC and GIC, respectively, and also enhancement of the ceiling of health insurance claims under Mediclaim. He proposed to give the Insurance Regulatory Authority set up by his predecessor in January 1996 a statutory basis, amend the RBI Act to strengthen its regulatory powers over all kinds of non-banking financial companies, and rewrite the Companies Act, 1956 to incorporate aspects such as debarring defaulting companies from raising deposits, enhancing the limit on claims of arrears of wages and salaries, granting voting rights to mutual funds and venture capital funds, and putting a limit on non-voting shares as a proportion of issued capital.

In his first Budget, Chidambaram provided ₹909 crore for recapitalizing public sector banks and raised the maximum limit of 5 per cent for an individual FII in the stock of a listed company to 10 per cent, subject to the existing aggregate limit of 24 per cent for all FIIs in the stock of a listed company. Since 1991, FDI in the trading sector was allowed only up to 51 per cent in trading companies and that too in those which were engaged primarily in the export business. In 1997, subject to approval from the FIPB, FDI of up to 100 per cent was allowed in trading companies engaged in: (i) exports, (ii) bulk imports with ex-port/ ex-bonded warehouse sales, (iii) cash and carry wholesale trading, and (iv) other import of goods and services provided at least 75 per cent of their procurement and sale was to companies of the same group.

The draft Fifth Five-Year Plan had provided for a National Programme of Minimum Needs, and Finance Minister Y.B. Chavan, in his Budget Speech for 1974–75, had reiterated how this programme aimed to achieve a certain minimum level of social consumption in the form of elementary education, rural health, drinking water, provision for slum clearance, rural roads and rural electrification. In his Budget Speech for 1996–97, Chidambaram drew attention to the decision of the chief ministers' meeting in 1996 on Basic Minimum Services (BMS), which adopted the goals of achieving, by 2000: (i) 100 per cent coverage of provision of safe drinking water; (ii) 100 per cent coverage of primary health centres; (iii) universalization of primary education; (iv) public housing assistance to all shelter-less poor families; (v) extension of the mid-day meal scheme; (vi) road connectivity to all villages and habitations; and (vii) streamlining the public distribution system targeted to families below the poverty line. In 1996–97, a separate budget head was introduced with provision for additional central assistance (ACA) for BMS with flexibility granted to the states to reallocate funds among the sectors according to their needs. In 1996–97, Chidambaram made an allocation of ₹2466 crore of ACA for BMS. Insufficient funds were again a problem—he could neither mobilize extra revenues nor make any major expenditure restructuring to deploy the extra funds necessary for these purposes. But he raised the allocation of ACA for BMS to ₹3100 crore in 1997–98.

In August 1996, the government set up the Disinvestment Commission under the chairmanship of G.V. Ramakrishna to advise, supervise, monitor and publicize the gradual disinvestment of CPSEs. Entry of private telecom service providers led to the need for an independent regulator. The Telecom Regulatory Authority of India (TRAI) was established on 20 February 1997 by an Act of Parliament with the mandate to regulate telecom services, including fixation/revision of tariffs for telecom services, which were earlier vested with the central government.

On the monetary policy front, the RBI reduced the CRR from 13 per cent to 12 per cent on 6 July 1996, and then in four equal reductions of 0.5 per cent each on 26 October and 9 November in 1996, and on 4 and 18 January 1997, to 10 per cent.

XXIII.3 Change of Guard and the Dream Budget

Deve Gowda's United Front government had come to power on 1 June 1996 with outside support from the Congress when Narasimha Rao was its president. Rao resigned in September 1996, to be succeeded by the seventy-six-year-old Sitaram Kesri. Kesri, a veteran freedom fighter from the backward Bania (or business) caste in Bihar, had been the treasurer of the party since 1979. Without much popular appeal, he was more of a backroom man and had been elected only once to the Lok Sabha in 1967.

Reportedly, Kesri had ambitions of becoming the Prime Minister himself, and was 'an old man in a hurry'—a term used in the Lok Sabha by the outgoing Prime Minister Deve Gowda.[3] Changing the Congress support to the United Front ministry from an unconditional one to an issue-based one was a part of this preparation.

Congress support to the United Front government was deemed conditional after 4 November 1996 and became issue-based after 16 February 1997. Furthermore, central agencies had started criminal or revenue-related investigations against several Congress leaders, including Kesri. A high-profile investigation was being conducted into the 1993 murder of Dr Surendra Tanwar, a government physician close to Kesri. On 30 March 1997, Kesri wrote a letter to President Shankar Dayal Sharma withdrawing support to the United Front government. He complained of the government 'marginalising the Congress and allowing urgent national issues to take a back seat', and failing to check communal, divisive and separatist forces in the country.[4] President Sharma set a deadline of 11 April for the Gowda ministry to seek a vote of confidence. A day after delivering the letter of withdrawal of support from the Deve Gowda government, Kesri had also staked a claim to form a government and had hoped that sections from the United Front would ally with him. Congress insisted on Deve Gowda's resignation, but Gowda refused and precipitated a vote of confidence in the Lok Sabha. The United Front declined to dump Gowda and support a Congress-led government. Gowda sought and lost a vote of confidence in Lok Sabha on 11 April, and BJP wanted fresh elections.

To complicate matters, the Finance Bill associated with the Budget for 1997–98, presented on 28 February 1997, had not been passed yet, which created a threat to the financial affairs of the government coming to a standstill. Gowda was requested to continue as the head of a caretaker government. In the end, the United Front leaders such as Mulayam Singh Yadav, Lalu Prasad Yadav, Sharad Yadav, G.K. Moopanar and M. Karunanidhi preferred to change the Prime Minister than to face the electorate. The Congress also agreed to support a United Front government under Inder Kumar Gujral, the external affairs minister under Gowda. Gujral became the Prime Minister on 21 April 1997. He retained all but one of the cabinet ministers of the Deve Gowda government. Even P.

Chidambaram, the finance minister under Gowda, who was initially not in the Gujral cabinet because of his party, the TMC, giving support only from the outside, was reinstated from 1 May 1997. So, almost during the entire period of the United Front's rule, Chidambaram held the finance portfolio and presented the Budget for 1997–98.

In 1997–98, Chidambaram presented what came to be called the Dream Budget, with the rates of personal income tax, across the board, down in a significant manner. The new rates were down from 15 per cent to 10 per cent for the first slab of ₹40,000 to ₹60,000, from 30 per cent to 20 per cent for the second slab of ₹60,000 to ₹1,50,000 (this was a new slab to replace the old slab 60,000 to ₹1,20,000), and from 40 per cent to 30 per cent for the highest slab above ₹1,50,000 (the highest slab was above ₹1,20,000 in the previous year). For all salaried employees, he also increased the limit of standard deduction uniformly from ₹18,000 to ₹20,000. The tax rebate for senior citizens went up from 40 per cent to 100 per cent subject to a limit of ₹10,000, in effect raising the exemption limit to ₹1 lakh for senior citizens.

To widen the personal income tax base, he made the 'voluntary' filing of income tax returns a 'normal' requirement for residents of large metropolitan cities who satisfy any two of the following four economic criteria, namely, (i) ownership of a four-wheel vehicle, (ii) occupation of immovable property meeting certain prescribed criteria, (iii) ownership of a telephone, and (iv) foreign travel in the previous year. He also abolished the presumptive tax scheme for retail traders introduced in 1992–93 by a new Estimated Income Scheme.

He also announced the Voluntary Disclosure of Income Scheme (VDIS) until 31 December 1997. Reportedly, the VDIS became a major avenue for not only declaring black money acquired in the past but also for concealing income in the future. One of the popular ways was to declare tons of silver and gold acquired in the past and suddenly discovered by the owner which could be valued at the prices on 1 April 1987. The 'amnesty' part of the scheme arose from the rate of 30 per cent payable on undisclosed income in the past, when the rate of tax payable was much higher. With 4.75 lakh declarations aggregating ₹33,697 crore of previously undisclosed income and tax revenue of ₹9729 crore under VDIS, the government declared it a great success.

But, as a proportion of GDP, the disclosure was '0.79% of the GDP while the amnesty scheme of 1985 had brought out 4.63% of the GDP'.[5] The Comptroller and Auditor General (C&AG), in his audit of VDIS-1997, severely criticized the scheme for its various lacunae and unfairness towards honest taxpayers. VDIS was challenged in court as being unfair to honest taxpayers. 'The Supreme Court, while dismissing the matter noted Government's commitment that, in future, it would not resort lightly to schemes favouring dishonest taxpayers.'[6]

In corporate taxes, Chidambaram redeemed his pledge to remove the surcharge on corporate tax by reducing the rate of surcharge from 7.5 per cent to nil. He reduced the income tax rate on domestic companies from 40 per cent to 35 per cent and on foreign companies from 55 per cent to 48 per cent. MAT, which had been introduced in the previous year to counter the problem of too many exemptions, itself became subject to exemptions for export profits! Tax credit for MAT also became eligible for carry-forward for five years. Chidambaram abolished the tax on dividends in the hands of the shareholder and replaced it with a dividend distribution tax—a tax on distributed profits—at the rate of 10 per cent for companies. Though it was an efficient revenue-enhancing measure, it was controversial from the equity point of view. Why should rich and not-so-rich shareholders implicitly receive the same tax treatment at the 10 per cent rate, critics asked.

For progressively aligning customs duty rates to the East Asian levels by the turn of the century, he reduced the peak rate of customs duty from 50 per cent to 40 per cent. In excise duties, in line with his avowed objective of reducing the multiplicity of rates and end-use exemptions and gravitating to a mean rate of 18 per cent, he dispensed with the rates of 10 per cent and 20 per cent, and introduced three new rates of 8 per cent, 13 per cent and 18 per cent. However, cotton yarn continued with a rate of 5 per cent and for revenue purposes, metals and a few other commodities with 15 per cent. Effectively dealing with the problem of exemptions from excise duty proved difficult—writing ink continued to be exempt from excise, and so did not only agricultural and horticultural machinery but also milking machines and other dairy machinery and parts which he added. The jute industry was ailing, and he granted full exemption to jute and jute products from excise duty. He promised to take up the issue of exemptions in the next year's budget, a budget that he never got to present due to a change in government. On 1 April 1997, the Duty Entitlement Passbook Scheme (DEPB) was launched as an export incentive scheme to refund customs duties paid on import content of exports in the form of credit. The credit was a varying percentage of the value of specified exports.

In 1997–98, Chidambaram extended the service tax net to: (i) transportation of goods by road, (ii) consulting engineers; (iii) custom house, steamer and clearing and forwarding agents; (iv) air travel agents, tour operators and car rental agencies; (v) out-door caterers, pandal contractors and *mandap* keepers; and (vi) manpower recruitment agencies. The service tax on goods transport operators, however, was withdrawn after a nationwide road transporters' strike.

The difference between the procurement price and issue price of food grains, together with the leakages and inefficiencies, over time, had bloated the food subsidy bill of Government of India from ₹2850 crore in 1991–92 to ₹6066 crore in 1996–97. Resources were being frittered away on unintended beneficiaries while the poor were serviced inadequately. Thus, a targeted PDS (TPDS) scheme was launched in June 1997. It intended to effectively cover the poor in all the areas of the country and supplanted RPDS, launched five years earlier under Narasimha Rao, which covered all in the poor areas of the country. TPDS divided the population into two cardholding categories: above the poverty line (APL) and BPL. APL prices were 80 per cent of the economic cost, whereas BPL prices were half of the economic cost. TPDS also restricted PDS entitlements to 10 kg per month per card for both APL and BPL cardholders. BPL families were estimated at 596.23 lakh. The TPDS was operated jointly by the Union and state governments.

The obvious benefit of TPDS was in delivering support to the poor with the least expenditure. Studies clearly showed that the income transfer required to substantially improve the nutrition levels for the poor made a universal system fiscally unsustainable. However, the debate on the merits and demerits of TPDS relative to a universal PDS continued, especially because of 'errors of exclusion' of BPL families under TPDS, possibility of a non-BPL family identified based on past data slipping into BPL category but being denied benefits, and administrative shortcomings.[7]

Not only some economists, but on 31 July 2002, even a High-Level Committee on Long-term Grain Policy appointed by the government and headed by Abhijit Sen recommended an end to targeting and a return to universal PDS.

As we know, in his Budget for 1994–95, Manmohan Singh had announced phasing out of the government's access to ad hoc Treasury Bills over a period of three years; Chidambaram in his 1996–97 Budget had taken a year's extension for its termination. The termination of the system of ad hoc Treasury Bills became effective on 1 April 1997.

From 1997–98, finally, it was decided to put the reporting of 'budget deficit' to an end. In his Budget Speech for 1997–98, he said, 'Therefore, it is proposed to discontinue the practice of showing the "Budget deficit"; instead, Gross Fiscal Deficit . . . would become the key indicator of deficit. The extent of RBI support to the Central government's borrowing programme will be shown as "Monetised deficit" in the Budget documents.' The Tenth Finance Commission, which had submitted its report to the President on 26 November 1994, had recommended a single pool of all taxes—rather than just personal income tax and excise duties—levied by the Union government for sharing with the states. Prima facie, Chidambaram endorsed the recommendation in the national interest, but given that its implementation required a Constitutional amendment, he proposed to circulate a paper for debating the relevant issues.

In the financial sector, from 22 October 1997, RBI gave banks the freedom to fix their own interest rates on domestic term deposits of various maturities. The interest rate on savings deposits in all banks continued to be administered by the RBI. The SLR at 31.5 per cent since 29 October 1994 was reduced to 25 per cent on 25 October 1997. The RBI increased the CRR from 10 per cent to 10.5 per cent on 17 January 1998. In December 1997, Chidambaram also set up a committee on Banking Sector Reforms under the chairmanship of M. Narasimham to review the implementation of banking reforms since 1992 with the aim of further strengthening the financial institutions of India. But the report of the committee, which came to be known as Narasimham II, was made available only a month after the United Front demitted office.

The Balika Samriddhi Yojana or Girl Upliftment Scheme on 2 October 1997 aimed to raise the status of the girl child and bring about a positive change in family and community attitudes. It covered up to two girl children born on or after 15 August 1997 in a BPL family and gave a one-time grant of ₹500 to a mother giving birth to a girl child in such a family. On the structural front, some other important measures included: (i) repeal of many controls on agricultural processing industries such as rice milling, ginning and pressing and cold storage; (ii) removal of fourteen items from the 836 reserved for small-scale industry; (iii) for petroleum and petroleum products, announcement of a New Exploration Licensing Policy (NELP); (iv) raising the limit of aggregate investment in a company by FIIs, NRIs and NRI-OCBs from the existing 24 per cent in the stock to 30 per cent subject to the approval of the company's Board of Directors and general body; and (v) replacement of the FERA 1973 by a Foreign Exchange Management Act (FEMA), consistent with current account convertibility and progressive move towards capital account convertibility.

The economy did well in 1996–97. Growth in GDP accelerated from 7.3 per cent in the previous year to 8 per cent. But growth declined to 4.3 per cent in the next year, mainly due to a decline in agriculture with inclement weather and a lacklustre industrial performance due to inadequate infrastructure services such as power, railways and roads, both in terms of quantity, quality and price. With moderate growth in money supply, WPI inflation declined from 8 per cent in 1995–96 to 4.6 per cent in 1996–97 and 4.4 per cent in 1997-98. The balance of payments was comfortable, with the current account deficit well below 1.5 per cent of GDP and foreign exchange reserves at well over eight months of imports. The improvement was enough for the US to complain to the WTO against India's notification on 19 May 1997 of its plan to phase out its QR on imports of most of the 2714 HS tariff lines in nine years for balance of payments reasons.

The problem was on the fiscal front—the fiscal deficit as a proportion of GDP, after declining from 4.91 per cent in 1995–96 to 4.70 per cent in 1996–97, climbed back to 5.66 per cent in 1997–98. Nascent pressures were already building up on the fiscal front, and these were compounded by the implementation of the Fifth Central Pay Commission's recommendations regarding salaries and wages (Table XXIII.1).

Table XXIII.1 Union Government's Expenditure on Salaries and Pension

				(Rs crore)
Item	1995-96	1996-97	1997-98	1998-99 (BE)
(A) Salary Bill	14,895	17,013	22,732	26,484
	(18.1)	(14.2)	(33.6)	(16.5)
(B) Pension	4,300	5,108	6,896	7,356
	(17.3)	(18.8)	(35.0)	(6.7)
(C) Total (A+B)	19,195	22,121	29,628	33,840
	(17.9)	(15.2)	(33.9)	(14.2)
	As per cent of Revenue Receipts (net to centre)			
1. Salaries	13.5	13.5	16.4	16.3
2. Pension	3.9	4.0	5.00	4.5

Note: Figures within parenthesis indicate percentage change over the preceding year.
Source: Economic Survey 1998-99, Chapter 2, Box 2.1

Interestingly, the Union government not only implemented the recommendations of the Fifth Pay Commission but added extra benefits beyond what the commission had recommended and did not rationalize employment by reducing its workforce by about 30 per cent. On 1 March, the number of employees in Union government remained more or less unchanged: 37.87 lakh in 1998, 37.46 lakh in 1999 and 37.77 lakh in 2000. The salary and pension bill of the Union government went up by 76.3 per cent between 1995–96 and 1998–99 (BE). Some experts pointed out that Union government employees as per se 1 lakh population, were not excessive but unaffordable. Furthermore, too many employees at the lower levels without the required skill and expertise were not useful for delivering the required public services.

XXIII.4 Continuing Problems in the Electricity Sector

Meanwhile, there were legal challenges to the fast-track IPP Dabhol project. In April 1996, the Centre for Indian Trade Unions (CITU) and an energy analyst, Abhay Mehta, filed a public interest litigation (PIL) against the government and the company. It alleged that the clearances required for the project were not obtained; and the government of Maharashtra, after having charged DPC and Enron with 'fraud, misrepresentation, corruption and bribery' should not have negotiated and drawn up a contract with DPC and Enron.[8] The case, with all its technical complexities, was basically about the high cost of power in the PPA with DPC. The Mumbai High Court ruled that the plaintiff did not produce any evidence of corruption and upheld the PPA. In 1997, the Supreme Court admitted a CITU petition challenging the Mumbai High Court order upholding the PPA and issued notice to MSEB on the role of government and its officials in the signing of the agreement.

There was an urgent need for de-politicizing the determination of electricity tariffs. Odisha became a pioneer in this by enacting the Odisha Electricity Reform Act, 1995 (Odisha Act 2 of 1996) for restructuring the electricity industry and rationalizing generation, transmission and distribution of electricity, for opening up the sector to private sector participation, and, importantly, the establishment of an independent State Electricity Regulatory Commission. The Odisha Electricity Regulatory Commission became functional on 1 August 1996.

Deliberations between the Union and the States led to the 'Common Minimum National Action Plan for Power' (CMNAP) at the Chief Ministers' Conference in December 1997. It recommended: (i) corporatization of SEBs, initially with public ownership followed by gradual privatization; (ii) focus of SEBs on improving efficiency in both generation and distribution via reorganization, efficient metering and energy audits; (iii) creation of independent State Electricity Regulatory Commissions (SERCs), answerable only to the state High Court; (iv) tariffs setting—with immediate effect—to yield a return on capital employed of at least 3 per cent; (v) cross-subsidization subject to no user paying less than 50 per cent of the average cost, including farmers in three years' time and farmers immediately paying at least ₹0.50/kWh; (vi) simplification of procedures, including automatic incorporation of adjustments for changes in fuel charges in the tariff structure as a pass-through cost. The CMNAP formed the basis for the June 1997 guidelines on the generation in power sector, including by the private players.

However, the SERCs failed to revise tariffs regularly—some even failed to do so for a decade. Deepak Parekh, a renowned banker and business leader, summed up the state of affairs in the electricity sector well: 'India's power sector is a leaking bucket; the holes deliberately crafted and the leaks carefully collected as economic rents by various stakeholders that control the system. The logical thing to do would be to fix the bucket rather than to persistently emphasize shortages of power and forever make exaggerated estimates of future demands for power. Most initiatives in the power sector (IPPs and mega power projects) are nothing but ways of pouring more water into the bucket so that the consistency and quantity of leaks are assured . . .'[9]

XXIII.5 The Short-Lived United Front Experiment

Keeping the coalition and the outside support intact was a challenge for Gujral. Controversially, he went slow on investigations by central agencies. Investigations were going on into the fodder scam in Bihar. It involved about ₹1000 crore of fraudulent reimbursement from the treasury for fodder, medicines and animal husbandry equipment for livestock that did not exist. Soon after becoming Prime Minister, Gujral had transferred CBI Director Jogender Singh, who was pursuing these investigations, including Lalu Prasad Yadav's possible involvement. Nevertheless, fissures within the Janata Dal came into the open when the Janata Dal expelled Lalu Yadav and he went on to form the RJD. Furthermore, developments in UP became a major irritant for securing continued Congress support from the outside.

Rifts had developed in the BJP-BSP coalition government in UP, and the Congress feared that BJP would continue to rule by indulging in horse-trading, i.e., by securing the support of defectors from other parties by unfair means. On 21 September 1997, after BSP leader Mayawati, BJP's Kalyan Singh had become the chief minister of UP. Congress President Kesri reportedly had promised BSP supremo Kanshi Ram that when BSP withdrew support to the BSP-BJP government, he would get the Vidhan Sabha dissolved. Some alliance partners in the United Front, e.g., Mulayam Singh of SP, also wanted the government in UP to be dismissed and President's rule imposed. But going by the Supreme Court judgment in the Bommai case, UP Governor Romesh Bhandari asked Chief Minister Kalyan Singh of the BJP to go for a floor test in the Vidhan Sabha on 21 October.

Unprecedented violence took place inside the Vidhan Sabha on the day of the confidence vote. BJP survived with the support of the UP Loktantrik Congress, a last-minute breakaway from the Congress, and three defectors from the Janata Dal. On the same day, late in the night, under intense pressure from Mulayam Singh and the Congress, the Union Cabinet—on the basis of Governor Bhandari's report—sent a recommendation to President K.R. Narayanan for dismissal of the Kalyan Singh ministry and proclamation of President's rule under Article 356. President Narayanan was not satisfied with the Governor's view that the constitutional machinery had broken down in UP and, considering the Supreme Court's judgment in the Bommai case, sent it back to the Cabinet for 'reconsideration'.[10] The Cabinet knew that while a reiteration of the recommendation for President's rule would oblige the President to sign the proclamation, the political fallout could be deeply embarrassing. It never sent the recommendation back, the Kalyan Singh government continued in UP, and Kesri and his Congress were not amused.

The Jain Commission's interim report provided the nail in the coffin of the Gujral government. The Jain Commission under Milap Chand Jain, the retired Chief Justice of the Delhi High Court, had been appointed on 23 August 1991 to make an inquiry into the assassination of the former Prime Minister Rajiv Gandhi at Sriperumbudur on 21 May 1990. The Commission submitted its seventeen-volume interim report to Home Minister Indrajit Gupta on 28 August 1997. On 17 September, Congress Vice President Jitendra Prasada, in a letter to Prime Minister Gujral, demanded that the report be made public to take the people into confidence. Home Minister Gupta, under severe pressure, announced that the report would be tabled on the first day of the coming winter session of Parliament with an action taken report. To Prime Minister Gujral, his advice was 'stall or prepare to depart'.[11]

In the event, the interim report of the Jain Commission was tabled in Parliament on 20 November 1997, but only after the magazine *India Today* had published excerpts from the report almost two weeks earlier on 8 November. The report had hinted at the connivance of M. Karunanidhi and his DMK, one of the alliance partners of the Gujral government. Congress demanded that all DMK ministers be dropped from the Gujral government, until such ministers had been cleared by the Jain Commission.

Unruly scenes started unfolding in Parliament. Without any direct evidence of their involvement, Gujral refused to drop them. On 28 November 1997, Congress withdrew support from the Gujral government, and on the same day, Gujral tendered his and his cabinet of ministers' resignations to the President of India on 'moral grounds'. Gujral did not recommend dissolution of the Parliament. The constituents of the UF informed the President of India that they would not support either the Congress or the BJP in forming a government. President Narayanan held consultations with all the major parties in the Lok Sabha to ascertain the prospect of a government being formed with majority support in the Lok Sabha. 'The President also kept in view the request made to him by a group of first-time MPs from several parties including the Congress, the BJP and the Janata Dal, that the Eleventh Lok Sabha should not be dissolved.'[12]

In the meantime, there was turbulence in the foreign exchange market. The Thai baht, after remaining range-bound between 24.9 baht and 25.6 baht per US dollar from 1990, had collapsed in July 1997. The proximate reason was the burst of a credit bubble that had been fuelled by excessive speculative capital inflows in the absence of strict supervision of the financial sector. With slowdown in the Thai economy and appreciation of the US dollar, there was a reversal of capital flows in Thailand. It switched to a flexible exchange rate policy on 2 June 1997. By the end of 1997, the Thai baht depreciated by more than 50 per cent and reached the bottom at 48.80 baht per US dollar in December 1997. The panic spread from Thailand to Indonesia and South Korea with severe intensity, and also to Hong Kong, Laos, Malaysia, the Philippines and some other countries of East Asia. It came to be known as the East Asian Crisis of 1997.

The relative stability of the Indian rupee vis-à-vis the US dollar from March 1996 came to an end with the East Asian crisis. 'Between August 19 and September 8, the rupee had depreciated against the US dollar by 2.7 per cent from ₹35.71 on August 19 to ₹36.69 on September 8. Thereafter, the rupee-dollar rate showed a tendency to appreciate. In early November 97, the rupee came under renewed downward pressure.'[13] While the contagion from the East Asian Crisis could have triggered the weakening of the rupee, at a fundamental level, there was also the need for a correction to its overvaluation that had taken place with an almost fixed nominal exchange rate and inflation higher than in partner countries.

Political uncertainty associated with rapidly changing governments heightened the need.

The year 1997 was the Golden Jubilee year of Indian Independence. So, on 1 December 1997, during all the political turmoil, the government launched the Swarna Jayanti Shahari Rozgar Yojana (SJSRY), or Golden Jubilee Urban Employment Programme, by subsuming the earlier three schemes for urban poverty alleviation, namely Nehru Rozgar Yojana (NRY), Urban Basic Services for the Poor (UBSP) and Prime Minister's Integrated Urban Poverty Eradication Programme (PMIUPEP). The key objective was to provide gainful self- or wage-employment to the urban unemployed or underemployed poor by various means, including skill development and training programmes.

The president was worried about the impact of the political developments on the stability of the rupee. On 2 December, he asked Prime Minister Gujral and Finance Minister Chidambaram about the steps being taken to safeguard the value of the rupee. They informed him that an early Presidential decision would help in this regard. By the evening of 3 December, it was clear to the President that no political combination in the Lok Sabha could muster the support of the critical minimum number of MPs required to secure a majority in the House. On the same evening, Prime Minister Gujral also wrote a letter recommending dissolution of the Eleventh Lok Sabha. On 4 December, the President dissolved the Eleventh Lok Sabha, and ordered the constitution of the Twelfth Lok Sabha by 15 March 1998. After ruling for only seven months, Gujral's was the fifth government at the Union level—after Charan Singh's, V.P. Singh's, Chandra Shekhar's and Deve Gowda's—that collapsed in less than a year. The Eleventh Lok Sabha, formed on 15 May 1996, lasted only until 4 December 1997. In the intervening nineteen months, India saw three Prime Ministers. Gujral continued to head the caretaker government until 19 March 1998.

XXIII.6 Assembly Elections in Jammu and Kashmir

Elections to the legislative assembly in Jammu and Kashmir had not been held for nine years since 1987. In his negotiations with Prime Minister Narasimha Rao's government, Farooq Abdullah had found the offer of proceeding on the basis of the Sheikh Abdullah-Indira Gandhi accord of 1975 unsatisfactory. Farooq wanted to go back to his people with the Union's offer of greater autonomy. The CMP of the United Front in 1996 provided him that assurance. Furthermore, the people of the state appeared to want an end to the bloodshed and a renewed focus on jobs and development. The Lok Sabha elections in May 1996 also bolstered the confidence that indeed elections could be held in the state. Elections to the legislative assembly were held in four phases on 7, 16, 21 and 30 September, and campaigning was limited to just fourteen days.

In the election, there were '. . . the mainstream parties consisting of the Congress, Janata Dal, CPI(M) and BJP; the pro-India regional parties like the NC, Panthers Party, Awami League . . .; the anti-Indians who challenge the accession, comprising Hurriyat . . . and various militant factions some of which favour a dialogue with India and some of whom see no solution except by the gun.'[14] Turnout was 53.92 per cent. The number of constituencies had gone up from seventy-six to eighty-seven by the twentieth amendment to the Jammu and Kashmir Constitution in 1988. Of these eighty-seven, the National Conference won fifty-seven. On 9 October 1996, Farooq was sworn in as chief minister.

Since 1990, under threat of life from the Islamic militants, the Hindu Kashmiri Pandits have been fleeing from the valley and this had polarized the politics of Kashmir along religious lines. After assuming power in 1996, 'Farooq Abdullah's government was preparing to bring the migrants back. Farooq, in fact, had issued an ultimatum to Pandit employees to return or quit their jobs.'[15] But killings of Kashmiri Pandits by Islamic militants, for example in Sangramora in March 1997, Wandhama in January 1998 and Chapnari in June 1998, continued albeit on an abated scale. The Pandits did not go back.

XXIV

The First NDA Government

The run-up to the Lok Sabha polls in February-March 1998 saw two important developments: a change of leadership of the Congress and the formation of the National Democratic Alliance (NDA), a pre-election coalition of fourteen parties headed by BJP. By end-1997, Kesri had discredited himself as Congress president by unseating two Union governments without being able to capture power. Many leaders had been wanting Sonia Gandhi to lead and rejuvenate the party. She joined the Congress as a primary member in December 1997 and started her election campaign for the party on 11 January 1998 from Sriperumbudur, where her husband had been assassinated in 1991. Many in the Congress wanted Kesri to step down and Sonia to become president. Removing a duly elected president of the party was not an easy affair, but Kesri was replaced by Sonia in what has been described as a coup in a CWC meeting on 14 March 1998.

The second major development was the formation of a pre-poll alliance called the NDA by the BJP. Since 1991, BJP had been described as 'the Government in waiting'.[1] But, in 1996 elections, compared to Congress's 140, though it secured 161 of the 543 Lok Sabha seats, along with its three pre-poll allies, namely HVP, Shiv Sena and Samata Party, BJP could not establish its majority. BJP perceived an urgent need to widen its pre-poll alliance and pursue a carefully orchestrated strategy of expanding its base in states where its footprint was weak. In terms of its support base in the mid-1990s, the seventeen large states could be divided into: (i) primary: Himachal Pradesh, Madhya Pradesh, Rajasthan, UP (and the UT of Delhi), (ii) secondary: Bihar, Gujarat, Haryana, Maharashtra and Punjab, and (iii) tertiary: Andhra Pradesh, Assam, Goa, Karnataka, Kerala, Odisha, Tamil Nadu and West Bengal.

In May 1998, BJP took the initiative of launching the NDA as a pre-poll alliance with two national parties, Janata Dal (in Punjab and Bihar) and Samata Party (in Bihar and UP), eleven state parties—NTR TDP (Lakshmi Parvati) in Andhra Pradesh, HVP in Haryana, Lokshakti in Karnataka, Shiv Sena in Maharashtra, Biju Janata Dal (BJD) in Odisha, SAD in Punjab, Sikkim Democratic Front in Sikkim, Janata Party, AIADMK, Marumalarchi DMK (MDMK) and Pattali Makkal Katchi (PMK) in Tamil Nadu—and the West Bengal Trinamool Congress, which had been established in West Bengal on 1 January 1998. To rally allies that did not subscribe to its Hindutva ideology, the BJP made it amply clear that it would put the contentious triad of issues, namely Ramjanmabhumi temple in Ayodhya, Uniform Civil Code and abrogation of Article 370 of the Constitution, on the backburner and not take them up until the BJP had an absolute majority in Parliament.

Congress managed to win 141 seats, only one more than its worst-ever performance in 1996. The tally for the NDA was 257, requiring fifteen more to reach the majority mark of 272 in the Twelfth Lok Sabha with 543 seats. The NDA could muster the support of twelve MPs from TDP led by Chandrababu Naidu, four MPs from Devi Lal's Haryana Lok Dal (Rashtriya), two MPs from Arunachal Congress (AC), and one MP from Sikkim Democratic Front to establish a majority. Atal Bihari Vajpayee, the chairman of the NDA, became the Prime Minister on 19 March 1998. This was the first NDA government under Vajpayee.

XXIV.1 The National Agenda for Governance

A day before assuming office, NDA released its National Agenda for Governance (NAG).[2] NAG was to the NDA what the CMP was to the UF government under Deve Gowda in 1996. In the NAG, the NDA committed itself to continue with the reform process but to give it a strong 'swadeshi' or indigenous thrust. While it clarified that this was 'to ensure that the national economy grows on the principle that "India shall be built by Indians"', many worried whether it implied a move back to protectionism. The NAG highlighted the aim of achieving GDP growth of 7-8 per cent, controlling fiscal deficit, enhancing national savings to 30 per cent of GDP, promoting infrastructure, agriculture, rural development and irrigation, removing bureaucratic control on industry, encouraging FDI in core areas and discouraging it in others, comprehensively reforming the CPSEs through restructuring, rehabilitation and divestment, and establishing an appropriate legal framework for the protection of the environment and unveiling a National Environment Policy to balance development and ecology. The NAG's catchy slogan 'berozgari hatao' or 'abolish unemployment' reminded some of Indira's 'Garibi Hatao' in 1971.

Reflecting the pre-poll understanding, there was no mention in the NAG of the Ramjanmabhumi in Ayodhya, Uniform Civil Code or abrogation of Article 370. However, the NAG clearly promised to 're-evaluate the nuclear policy and exercise the option to induct nuclear weapons'. Within fifty-two days of coming to power, on 11 May 1998, in the same Pokhran in the deserts of Rajasthan where Indira had carried out the first nuclear test almost twenty-four years ago, under NDA, India detonated one fusion and two fission nuclear devices. Detonation of two more fission devices followed two days later on 13 May. One of the major architects of the nuclear weapons programme was scientist A.P.J. Abdul Kalam, the future president of India. The tests were followed by almost immediate sanctions by many countries, including the US and Japan.

After India's nuclear explosions on 11 and 13 May, Pakistan conducted five underground nuclear tests in Chagai district in Balochistan on 28 May and followed it up with one more two days later. After these tests, Pakistan, like India, also came under international sanctions. With both India and Pakistan as nuclear powers, there were great concerns in the international community about any dispute between the two estranged neighbours escalating to a nuclear war. The two had already fought three wars and there was a need for confidence-building measures. On 19 February 1999, Prime Minister Vajpayee went on a bus *yatra* or trip to Lahore and declared '*Hum jung na hone denge . . . Teen bar lad chuke ladayi, kitna mehnga sauda . . . Hum jung na hone denge . . .*' or 'we will not let a war happen, we have fought three times, very costly affairs, we will not let a war happen'.[3] In Lahore, at Minar-e-Pakistan, built where, in 1940, the Muslim League had passed the resolution asking for a separate and independent homeland for the Muslims, he wrote in the visitors' book: 'A stable, secure and prosperous Pakistan is in India's interest. Let no one in Pakistan be in doubt. India sincerely wishes Pakistan well.'[4]

XXIV.2 Yashwant Sinha and the 1998–99 Budget

As his finance minister, Vajpayee chose Yashwant Sinha, who had been the finance minister for about seven months from November 1990 under Chandra Shekhar. Sinha had left the civil service in 1984 to join the Janata Party, then moved on in November 1990 as a part of Chandra Shekhar's Janata Party (Socialist) and further to the BJP in 1993.

On 25 March 1998, Yashwant Sinha presented the Interim Budget for 1998–99. It was only a vote on account to allow the government's financial business to continue unhindered beyond the end of the financial year on 31 March 1998. In May 1998, the government raised the age of retirement from fifty-eight to sixty as recommended by the Fifth Central Pay Commission. This led to almost 1.5 lakh of its employees not retiring in the following two years, no need for fresh recruitment to fill up their vacancies and consequent annual saving in the pension bill of ₹5200 crore in each of the two subsequent years. In his regular budget that followed on 1 June 1998, Sinha hinted at how 'swadeshi' did not mean autarchic or isolationist, but self-reliant. One leading magazine reported: 'The Union Budget for 1998-99 has stayed squarely within the framework of the post-1991 economic reform process and its tenets of privatisation, liberalization and a significantly reduced economic role for the state.'[5] An early setback for the NDA government was the announcement of a small increase in urea prices to rein in the subsidy as well as remove the imbalance in application of too much of nitrogen (N), and too little of phosphorous (P) and potassium (K) and its almost instantaneous roll-back.

Following the nuclear tests, the sanctions as well as downgrades, actual or potential, by the rating agencies led Sinha to announce the launch of the Resurgent India Bond by the SBI on 5 August 1998, to mobilize foreign exchange resources from NRIs, OCBs and banks acting in fiduciary capacity on behalf of NRIs/OCBs. These bonds were transferable to others, including Indian residents, were exempt from income, wealth and gift tax, and mobilized $4.2 billion. Sinha raised the limit for NRI secondary market investment in Indian companies from 1 per cent to 5 per cent and the limit on aggregate NRI investment from 5 per cent to 10 per cent. He also announced that Persons of Indian Origin (PIO) cards would be issued for NRIs living in specified foreign countries and having foreign passports. Holders of PIO cards would be entitled to visa-free entry into the country and other special economic, educational, financial and cultural benefits.

Finance Minister Sinha reaffirmed the policy of the previous government towards fiscal consolidation, progressive liberalization of FDI, removal of 'inspector raj' or bureaucratic control over industry, employment restructuring and disinvestment in CPSEs, and expressed the government's aim to bring down its shareholding—except where strategic considerations were involved—to 26 per cent. He announced that there would be disinvestment in IOC, GAIL, VSNL and Container Corporation of India Limited, and Indian Airlines would be restructured, with the government's shareholding pared down to 49 per cent over three years. While he expressed the government's commitment to implementing the sharing of a divisible pool of all Union taxes with the states through a Constitutional amendment as recommended by the Tenth Finance Commission, he rejected the Commission's recommendation of freezing the states' share in the divisible pool for fifteen years and preferred to leave it for review by successive Finance Commissions every five years.

The problem of elevated NPAs in the financial system was continuing and Sinha announced that, to resolve the problem, Asset Reconstruction Companies would be allowed. Furthermore, he set a target for capital adequacy of 9 per cent by March 2000. He also proposed to allow FIIs to invest in unlisted securities, open the insurance sector for private sector participation, give statutory basis to Insurance Regulatory Authority, and allow treatment of derivatives as securities through legislative amendments.

Sinha enhanced allocations for education, agriculture, rural development including drinking water supply and irrigation, and announced the introduction of the Kisan (or farmers) Credit Cards by NABARD for meeting the credit needs of the farmers for production, marketing, investment and consumption purposes. He also laid emphasis on rural and urban housing through enhanced budgetary allocations, tax deduction for housing for the first ten years, and for interest on home loans and repairs. He promised to repeal the Urban Land (Ceiling and Regulation) Act 1976 to enhance the supply of land. He also prioritized infrastructure, particularly energy (including production of oil and petroleum refining), transportation and communication, through enhanced budgetary allocations, extension of tax concessions to the sector and financial strengthening of the NHAI. In a significant move, to generate funds for the development of roads, an additional duty at the rate of ₹1 per litre on petrol was introduced to garner an expected ₹790 crore in a year and augment the corpus of NHAI.

The power sector was suffering from financial distress with the loss-making SEBs accumulating arrears in payment to generation and transmission companies and the latter in turn accumulating arrears to the coal companies. To clear the logjam, Sinha promised to provide government guarantees to convert outstanding dues of about ₹10,000 crore from SEBs to NTPC, Coal India, etc. into investible funds for financing projects. Also, in 1998, at the Union level, came the Electricity Regulatory Commission Act and a Central Electricity Regulatory Commission (CERC). We will recall that Odisha had set up its Electricity Regulatory Commission in August 1996. 'The 1998 Act marked, in a sense, the national coming out of the Odisha model.'[6] The 1998 Act allowed the states to set up their own SERCs either based on the Union's Act or through their own legislations. All the States and UTs had set up their own or joint SERCs by 2011. Typically manned by a former bureaucrat as chairperson and two members with technical and financial backgrounds, their performance in terms of independence from the government has been quite diverse, with many being seen as mere extensions of the government.

Sinha raised the excise exemption limit for SSI from ₹30 lakh to ₹50 lakh and promised greater and cheaper availability of credit to SSI. On personal income tax, Sinha left the rates unchanged but increased the exemption limit from ₹40,000 to ₹50,000. A one-page return form called Saral (or simple) was introduced for personal income tax. Gift tax was discontinued, and gifts became taxable in the hands of the recipient. For quick realization of tax arrears and settlement of disputes, the Samadhan (or solution) scheme was introduced which involved payment of the highest rate of tax applicable to personal or corporate income as relevant.

While corporate income tax rates were left unchanged, the film industry was granted relief, and exemptions were granted on grounds such as additional employment generation, promoting women and child welfare, road safety and environmental protection.

In 1997–98, his predecessor Chidambaram had introduced a '2 by 4' scheme to cover twelve important cities under which fulfilment of any two of the four criteria obliged the person to file an income tax return. In 1998–99, Sinha expanded it to a '1 by 6' scheme under which fulfilment of any one of the existing four—possession of a house, subscription to a telephone, spending on foreign travel and possession of a motor vehicle—plus two new ones, namely, holding a credit card and membership of expensive clubs, created an obligation to file an income tax return. He also extended the coverage of the scheme from twelve to thirty-five cities.

In 1998–99, Sinha continued with the past trend of rationalizing excise duties to reduce the wide diversity of rates and reducing customs duties. India was a signatory to the WTO's Information Technology Agreement (ITA) of 13 December 1996. The ITA covers many high-technology products, including computers, telecommunication equipment, semiconductors, semiconductor manufacturing and testing equipment, software, scientific instruments, as well as most of the parts and accessories of these products. By the ITA, signatories were required to bind and eliminate customs duties and other duties and charges of any kind through equal rate reductions of customs duties beginning in 1997 and concluding in 2000. In 1998–99, Sinha started reducing customs duties on high technology items, for example, on floppy, hard disk and CD-ROM drives, from 12 per cent to 5 per cent.

Customs duties were increased in a few cases such as cold rolled coils of iron and steel and wrought copper. While he imposed 8 per cent countervailing duty or additional duty of customs on imports to provide a level playing field to domestic industry, the rate was reduced in mid-June 1998 to 4 per cent. He increased the duty-free allowance for baggage for passengers coming from abroad from ₹6000 to ₹12,000. It may be recalled that the country had a commitment at the WTO to remove QRs on imports in phases by end-March 2001. Accordingly, there was the replacement of QRs by tariffs resulting in an increase in the imports-weighted average tariff rate. Additional duties over and above the basic rates also contributed to the increase.

Following the reports of the R-Group and Expert Technical Group on Petroleum in August 1996 and June 1997, the government had accepted the relevant recommendations for restructuring excise and customs duties on petroleum and petroleum products consistent with a proposed move from APM to a market-determined pricing mechanism in the petroleum sector. Accordingly, in 1998–99, in a calibrated move, Sinha reduced the customs duty on crude from a total of 27 per cent to 22 per cent, increased the excise duty on motor spirit from 20 per cent to 35 per cent, and imposed customs duty on kerosene imported for parallel marketing at 32 per cent, including special duty of 2 per cent. Sinha extended service tax to twelve new services, but also exempted goods transport by road, outdoor catering and pandal contracts. The tradition of granting exemptions under excise and customs continued.

India's NH system in the late 1990s was a major constraint on transportation of goods and passengers, and hence on growth. Two per cent of the country's 58,000-km network carried two-fifths of road traffic. These highways were congested and in poor condition. Vajpayee used to ask '*Humaare desh mein sadko mein gaddhe hain ya gaddoh mein sadak hain?*', or does our country have potholes in roads or roads in potholes.[7] On 24 October 1998, at the FICCI Annual Conference, the Prime Minister announced: 'The government will start within this year and from twenty different places from across the country work on a major 7,000-km road project.'

In a significant move, to garner funds for NHAI, an additional duty at the rate of ₹1 per litre on petrol had already been introduced in the 1998–99 Budget. In 1999, Vajpayee's October 1998 announcement led to the conceptualization of the Golden Quadrilateral, a four- and six-lane 5846 km-long NH network connecting the four major metro cities of India, namely Delhi (north), Kolkata (east), Mumbai (west) and Chennai (south), as well as most of the major industrial, agricultural and cultural centres of India. The main objective of these highways was to reduce the distance and time among India's four megacities.

The Golden Quadrilateral started a road revolution in India, like the railroad revolution in the US in the nineteenth century or the transportation revolution in China after 1990, when China started to make huge amounts of public investment in domestic transportation infrastructure. Building new transportation infrastructure benefits the most when there is already a demand for it, and there appears to be a consensus that India started building the Golden Quadrilateral when there already was a crying need for it. An important point to note in this context is the effect of the highways on places, including rural and semi-urban areas, through which they pass. NHs are likely to contribute to higher GDP overall without necessarily benefitting every locality through which they pass. This is because of factor mobility. Just as economic activity can relocate from congested cities to better-connected rural and semi-urban areas, with better road connectivity, factors of production can also move from the hinterlands to the cities and towns.

In the meantime, Basel I from 1988 had been amended several times to accommodate risks from off-balance-sheet activities. In 1996, trading positions in bonds, equities, foreign exchange and commodities were removed from the credit risk framework and given explicit capital charges related to the bank's open position in each instrument. In its mid-term review of Monetary and Credit Policy in October 1998, the RBI raised the minimum regulatory CRAR from 8 per cent to 9 per cent, and advised banks to attain this level by 31 March 2000. It also prescribed various surrogate capital charges such as a investment fluctuation reserve of 5 per cent of a bank's portfolio and a 2.5 per cent risk weight on the entire portfolio for these risks between 2000 and 2002.

Policymaking was often 'behind the curve', that is, taking policy action when an adverse development, such as a hike in inflation, had already taken place rather than in its anticipation and to prevent it from happening. Monetary policy in 1998 illustrated such an infirmity: on 17 March, two days before the NDA assumed office, the RBI had raised CRR from 10 per cent to 10.5 per cent; soon thereafter, with two reductions of 25 basis points each on 28 March and 11 April, the CRR was back at 10 per cent, only to be hiked again, with signs of inflationary pick-up, to 11 per cent on 29 August!

XXIV.3 1999–2000 Budget

Growth accelerated from 4.3 per cent in 1997–98 to 6.7 per cent in 1998–99, but so did WPI inflation from 4.4 per cent to 6 per cent. There was an improvement in the current account balance with the deficit shrinking from 1.33 per cent to 0.93 per cent. Disinvestment receipts of ₹5371 crore against a budgeted ₹5000 crore was prima facie encouraging but involved receipts from cross-purchases by three public sector companies— GAIL, ONGC and IOC—of each other's shares. Nevertheless, the Union government's fiscal deficit as a proportion of GDP went up from 5.66 per cent in 1997–98 to 6.29 per cent in 1998–99, and the challenge of fiscal consolidation and of ramping up growth to an annual 7-8 per cent remained. Moreover, the East Asian Crisis was not yet over, the bellwether BSE Sensex (monthly average) after declining from a high of 4,276 in August 1997 to a low of 2,865 in August 1998, was still at 3289 in February 1999. The NPAs of public sector banks continued to be high and the UTI was in financial distress.

The distress in UTI was related to Unit Scheme-64, popularly known as US-64, which the UTI had introduced in 1964. It was an open-ended scheme, into which investors could enter by buying units and exit from by selling units at any time of the year. The sale and re-purchase prices of units were announced in July and progressively increased every month to reflect the accumulation of dividends, thus giving a particular return to existing investors and also allowing new investors to enter the scheme. With the sale and re-purchase price of units determined by trend line, US-64 was not driven by NAV. The UTI also distributed dividends regularly on the units of US 64. For close to three decades, with a prudent investment policy and a high debt-equity ratio, US-64 ran without difficulties. Trend pricing and regular dividends had made the US-64 an almost assured scheme and attracted plenty of small investors. Almost assured returns and tax benefits also led to corporates investing in US-64. By 1998, US-64 had over 25 million investors.

Problems arose with a shift to speculative investments in equity. Fluctuations in equity prices led to large departures of trend line pricing from NAV, and problems were compounded by a dividend distribution policy divorced from the income of the scheme. Set up under an Act of Parliament in 1964 before the advent of SEBI, UTI was not under SEBI jurisdiction. From 1994, UTI came under the voluntary compliance of SEBI mutual funds regulations for all its new schemes, but not for US-64 and its assured returns schemes. For four years in a row—1994–95 to 1997–98—especially when reserves were not adequate to cover the value of the units at the administered redemption price, UTI declared dividends more than income. Later, S.S. Tarapore, who headed a High-Level Committee in 2001 to look into the affairs of the UTI, described the UTI as a prisoner of its own pricing policy which was not NAV-driven.

Decline in stock prices during May-June 1998 resulted in significant valuation losses for the investment portfolio of US-64. But UTI decided to maintain its dividend rate of 20 per cent. In UTI's balance sheet, with a change in accounting practices to account for unrealized capital losses, its reserves turned negative at ₹1098 crore in June 1998. October 1998 was a rough month for the stock market and low stock prices added to the nervousness of investors in US-64. In late 1998, there was redemption pressure—that is, more repurchase (or sale of units) than purchase by clients—and for cashflow reasons, UTI had to sell shares. Finance Minister Sinha had to assure the market that UTI 'cannot fail and will not be allowed to fail'.[8] UTI set up the Deepak Parekh Committee to undertake a comprehensive review of the functioning of US-64, and recommend measures for sustaining investor confidence and strengthening the operations of the scheme. The Committee's Report became available in February 1999.

This was the context in which, at 11 a.m. on 28 February 1999, Yashwant Sinha presented his Budget for 1999–2000. The timing was a break with the colonial tradition of presenting the Budget at 5 p.m. in consideration of the time difference between London and Delhi and make it convenient for the secretary of state for India and his colleagues in London. In his Budget for 1999–2000, Sinha reiterated the government's resolve to begin a medium-term process of reducing both the revenue and fiscal deficits to 'free more resources for productive investment and growth and contain inflation'. In the area of food security, he not only continued with TPDS introduced by the predecessor United Front government but proposed to suitably strengthen it in terms of coverage and efficiency by involving the Gram Panchayats. After its announcement in Budget 1999–2000, Annapurna, a new scheme named after the Hindu goddess of food and nutrition, was launched from 1 April 2000. It provided 10 kg of food grains per month free of cost to indigent senior citizens with no income and no one to take care of them.

For rural development, the DRDA scheme was introduced from 1 April 1999, with salary and administrative expenses shared between the Union and the states in the ratio of 75:25. IRDP was to be implemented by DRDA with assistance from block-level machinery. The aim was to raise the income of the BPL families in the rural areas to APL level on a lasting basis by giving them income-generating assets and access to credit and other inputs. For this same purpose, the Swarnajayanti Gram Swarozgar Yojana (SGSY) or Golden Jubilee Village Self-employment Programme, was launched from 1 April 1999. It aimed at promoting micro-enterprises to assist BPL families through the process of social mobilization, training, capacity building and provision of income-generating assets financed jointly by bank loans and government subsidies. The cost-sharing of the governmental part was in the ratio 3:1 between the Union and the states. Furthermore, from 1 April 1999, a credit-cum-subsidy scheme was introduced for rural families having annual income up to ₹32,000.

Sinha continued with his focus on SSI by further increasing the limit on their composite loans from ₹2 lakh to ₹5 lakh, the eligibility for 20 per cent of annual turnover as working capital from ₹4 crore to ₹5 crore and launching a credit insurance programme for SSI. To resolve the NPA problem of banks, he proposed to increase the number of DRTs and DRATs, encourage these banks to set up their settlement advisory committees to have one-time settlements, and provide tax deductibility for provisions made for NPAs. To attract capital flows, he proposed to prepare a list of industries and services for automatic approval of FDI, set up a Foreign Investment Implementation Authority to expedite implementation of FDI, and extend automatic approval for investment by NRIs and OCBs up to 100 per cent for almost all items.

The Budget for 1999–2000 made some attempts at establishing a partnership with states and local bodies in augmenting the availability of public services such as education, health and irrigation. Thus, Sinha proposed to implement an Education Guarantee Scheme and provide an elementary school in every habitation, which did not have one within a radius of 1 km. Similarly, he proposed to provide a one-time management subsidy and annual assistance for an initial period of three years to all registered Water Users Associations which would be linked to incremental collection of water charges. To encourage better management and maintenance of costly irrigation assets, he proposed to provide larger financial assistance from the Union to those states that rationalized their water rates to cover at least operation and maintenance (O&M) costs.

Sinha emphasised infrastructure in his 1999–2000 Budget and proposed a new credit-linked capital subsidy scheme for construction of cold storages and godowns to improve the very weak post-harvest storage and marketing infrastructure. He targeted the creation of additional cold storage capacity of 12 lakh tons and rehabilitation and modernization of 8 lakh tons of existing units. He extended the infrastructure tax holiday to power transmission to improve the efficiency of the transmission infrastructure. NHAI received a boost in the 1999–2000 Budget from an additional duty of ₹1 per litre on imported and domestic high-speed diesel accruing entirely to the Union. He proposed to allocate half of this revenue to support rural development and social sectors. A major building block for Vajpayee's ambitious Golden Quadrilateral project was in place with the extension of the ₹1 per litre cess on petrol to high-speed diesel.

Then there was the announcement of the introduction of a gold deposit scheme without any tax amnesty and a system of zero-based budgeting. Both had been tried in the past without much success. Gold bonds had been tried in November 1962, and in March and December 1965. The Gold bonds issued in December 1965 even had a tax amnesty going with it. Zero-based budgeting had been adopted by the department of science and technology in 1983, and by 1986 it was made compulsory for all ministries to review their activities and programmes and prepare their expenditure estimations based on the concept of zero-based budgeting.

After mobilizing ₹5371 crore in 1998–99 against the budgeted ₹5,000 crore in 1998–99, Yashwant Sinha emphasized disinvestment in his Budget for 1999–2000 by setting up an ambitious target of ₹10,000 crore from disinvestment. Significantly, he included strategic sale as one of the ways for disinvestment and 1999–2000 saw the first strategic sale with the privatization of Modern Food Industries Limited. Yet, the actual realization from disinvestment in 1999–2000 at ₹1860 crore was less than a fifth of the budgeted figure.

In 1999, one major change in the fiscal arrangement was the setting up of the National Small Savings Fund (NSSF) in Public Account. The

Government of India maintains two accounts—Consolidated Fund of India and Public Accounts—but has the treasury single account with the RBI where all cash receipts are deposited and from which all payments are made. The following: (i) small savings, deposits and provident funds, (ii) 'other accounts', and (iii) reserve funds and deposits, which accrue to Public Accounts, are mobilized by the government in its capacity as a banker and are not secured under the Consolidated Fund of India. The cumulative net inflows from these three items are not treated as parts of internal debt, but only added to internal debt to arrive at internal liabilities of the government. There was an urgent need to be clear about the sustainability of the government's operations as a banker. In 1999, the NSSF was set up following the recommendations in the Report of the Committee on Small Savings chaired by R.V. Gupta, submitted in September 1998. The NSSF in Public Account was to be administered by the Union ministry of finance under National Small Savings Fund (Custody and Investment) Rules, 2001, framed by the President under Article 283(1) of the Constitution. The objective of NSSF was to de-link small savings transactions from the Consolidated Fund of India and ensure their operation in a transparent and self-sustaining manner.

In Budget 1999–2000, in income tax, Sinha left the rates unchanged but gave numerous exemptions and rebates, e.g., for mergers, acquisitions and demergers of companies, infrastructure such as cold chains and power transmission, R&D expenses of corporates, for industries in the North-East and medical expenses of senior citizens. He increased the ceiling on exemption of interest on home loans from ₹30,000 to ₹75,000 and reduced the rate of tax on long-term capital gains for residents from 20 per cent to 10 per cent. Simultaneously, he also imposed a surcharge of 10 per cent across all categories of income (except for those with income less than ₹60,000). Encouragingly, he reported good progress in issuing of PAN cards and favourable results from the '1 by 6' scheme introduced in thirty-five cities for identifying potential taxpayers. He proposed to extend the '1 by 6' scheme to nineteen more cities.

To increase the attractiveness of the UTI and other mutual fund schemes, Sinha not only fully exempted income from such schemes from income tax, but for three years also the income distributed by such funds as dividends from the dividend distribution tax, provided more than 50 per cent of the investment of such funds was in equity. The equity component of the troubled US-64 portfolio of UTI was well above 50 per cent.

Sinha compressed excise duties, which were spread across eleven rates, into three rates with a central rate of 16 per cent and merit and demerit rates of 8 per cent and 16 per cent, respectively. However, for revenue considerations, with surcharges (special excise duty) of 6 per cent and 16 per cent on some of the commodities (such as motor spirit) with 16 per cent excise duty, effectively the rates were more than three. Sinha pointed out that machinery and capital goods, for which the excise duty rate was going up from 13 per cent to 16 per cent, were eligible for MODVAT credit and that he was raising the limit of MODVAT adjustment for manufacturing from 95 to 100 per cent.

From 28 February 1999, Sinha removed the special customs duty of 5 per cent imposed in two stages of 2 per cent in 1996–97 and 3 per cent in 1997–98. He also proposed five basic rates of customs duty of 5 per cent, 15 per cent, 25 per cent, 35 per cent and 40 per cent for all goods except those associated with the IT sector. He imposed a 10 per cent surcharge on crude oil and petroleum products, items attracting 40 per cent basic customs duty, certain items where the rates were at the GATT-bound levels, and gold and silver.

Sinha, in his Budget for 1999–2000, also said '. . . conceptually, I am averse to zero custom duty, since our domestic industry generally merits some minimal protection'. Consequently, he proposed the imposition of a duty of 5 per cent rate for some of the commodities previously exempt from duty while exempting this category from the 4 per cent special additional duty. The rate structure became complex with yet another category—project imports for power generation, coal mining, refinery, telecom and fertilizer projects—introduced to attract a nominal basic customs duty of only 5 per cent and also be subject to applicable rates of countervailing duty.

On 13 March 1999, the RBI reduced the CRR from 11 per cent to 10.5 per cent. The first NDA government under Vajpayee did not last beyond a little over a month and a half after the presentation of the budget. It resigned on 17 April 1999, and continued thereafter only in a caretaker capacity until 10 October 1999, when it was voted back to power in the Thirteenth Lok Sabha elections. During this caretaker period, RBI reduced the CRR from 10.5 per cent to 10 per cent on 8 May 1999.

XXIV.4 Fall of the First NDA Government by a Solitary Vote

In the Lok Sabha in 1998, the NDA with 257 seats was fifteen short of an absolute majority and came to power by securing the support of some other parties. One of the constituents of the NDA was the AIADMK headed by Jayalalitha. AIADMK had eighteen members in the Twelfth Lok Sabha. Its rival DMK had been ruling in Tamil Nadu since 1996, and AIADMK, in its 1998 Lok Sabha poll campaign, had assured the people that the DMK government would be dismissed.

In January 1991, the DMK government under M. Karunanidhi, elected with an overwhelming majority in the 1989 Vidhan Sabha polls, was dismissed and President's rule was imposed in Tamil Nadu. The stated reason was deterioration in law and order, while the unstated reason was Karunanidhi's covert support for LTTE. In Tamil Nadu, Vidhan Sabha elections were held in 1991, and Jayalalitha's AIADMK swept the polls to form the government. In the 1996 Vidhan Sabha election, AIADMK won only four seats, and DMK returned to power with an overwhelming mandate (173 of the 234 seats). DMK, after coming to power, had initiated a series of corruption cases against Jayalalitha and she wanted the NDA to dismiss the DMK government and impose President's rule. The NDA was not willing.

In end-December 1998, a controversy broke out about the sacking of Admiral Vishnu Bhagwat, the chief of naval staff. The Admiral had publicly refused to accept the appointment of Vice Admiral Harinder Singh as his deputy and was relieved of his duties on 30 December 1998 under Article 310 of the Constitution. George Fernandes was the defence minister. AIADMK, like ComPI and CPI(M), claimed Bhagwat was sacked because he raised allegations of corruption. DMK had initiated a series of corruption cases against Jayalalitha, and AIADMK upped the ante for the dismissal of the DMK government in Tamil Nadu.

Jayalalitha, along with the opposition, was keen to unseat the NDA government, and that was possible only if both her AIADMK and Sonia Gandhi's Congress joined forces. But relations between the two ladies were strained. In 1998, Jayalalitha had described the possibility of Sonia becoming prime minister as a potential national tragedy. This strained relationship changed when Subramanian Swamy, the Harvard-educated economist-turned-politician, came into the picture in early 1999. Swamy had been the minister of law and justice in January 1991 when the DMK government under M. Karunanidhi was dismissed, and President's rule imposed in Tamil Nadu.

It was the same Swamy who, in April 1995, had filed a petition demanding an investigation into Jayalalitha's assets disproportionate to her income. In 1996, Swamy had also filed cases against the sale of land at throwaway prices by the state-owned Tamil Nadu Small Industries Corporation to enterprises owned by Jayalalitha. Relations between Swamy and Jayalalitha had become strained. Swamy, a brilliant academic, had a chequered political career. In 1969, Swamy, still not 30, had been a pioneer in arguing for India acquiring nuclear strike capability as a strategic deterrent to China. Swamy had joined politics and started off in 1974 as a Jana Sangh MP in the Rajya Sabha from UP. He was a crusader against the Emergency, represented Mumbai North-East in the Sixth (1977–79) and Seventh (1980–84) Lok Sabha as a Janata Party MP, and been a member of the Rajya Sabha from UP during 1988–94. He had not been invited to join the BJP when the party was formed after breaking away from the Janata Party in April 1980. Swamy had been the president of the remnant of the Janata Party from 1990, and minister in the short-lived Chandra Shekhar government from November 1990 to June 1991.

Jayalalitha had mended fences with Swamy by first supporting his Janata Party's candidate Chandralekha against DMK Chief Minister Karunanidhi's son M.K. Stalin, the future CM of Tamil Nadu, in the October 1996 election to the post of Mayor of Chennai Corporation. In 1992, during Jayalalitha's rule, V.S. Chandralekha, a former IAS officer, after protesting against the Jayalalitha government's proposed disinvestment in Southern Petrochemical Industries Corporation (SPIC) at a throwaway price, had been the victim of an acid attack disfiguring her face forever. Fingers were pointed at Jayalalitha for the acid attack. Anyway, Jayalalitha made further concessions to Swamy in the 1998 Lok Sabha election by not putting up any AIADMK candidate against him in Madurai and helping him win the seat.

On 29 March 1999, Swamy organized a tea party at Ashok Hotel in Delhi and invited both Sonia Gandhi and Jayalalitha. There was palpable uncertainty about the future of the Vajpayee government, particularly after the Indian National Lok Dal (INLD)—the new name for the Haryana Lok Dal from 1998 onwards—on the grounds of the government's inability to roll back the prices of items under PDS, particularly of cooking gas and urea, had withdrawn support to the NDA government on 16 February. On 5 April 1999, Jayalalitha announced the resignation of Union Law Minister M. Thambidurai and Minister of State for Finance Kadambur M.R. Janardhanam, and that she would camp in Delhi from 12 April for talks with other parties on formation of an alternative government. On 14 April, she delivered a letter to the President withdrawing support to the Vajpayee government. President Narayanan asked Prime Minister Vajpayee to seek a vote of confidence.

How the Lok Sabha MPs from DMK (six), BSP (five) and INLD (four), and from other smaller parties including independents, would vote was a matter of suspense and the fate of the first NDA government uncertain. There were dramatic developments on 17 April, the day of voting on the motion of confidence. BSP leader Mayawati announced that her party would oppose the government, and Saifuddin Soz defied his party's National Conference and voted against the government. The NDA government under Vajpayee lost the motion by a solitary vote. Vajpayee tendered the resignation of his cabinet to the President. President Narayanan asked him to get the Budget passed when Parliament reconvened on 19 April and continue as head of a caretaker government. Days full of suspense and political back-and-forth activity followed.

XXV

The Second NDA Government

BJP demanded that any alternative government, before being formed, must demonstrate majority support in the Lok Sabha in writing. On 21 April, Congress President Sonia Gandhi met the President, staked her claim to form the government and sought two days' time to produce letters of support. Mulayam Singh Yadav's SJP with twenty seats in the Lok Sabha, RSP with five and Forward Block with two seats clearly stated that they would not be supporting the Congress. Budget 1999–2000 was passed without any discussion by both houses of Parliament on 22 April. The next day, Sonia wanted more time from the President to produce letters of support and form her Congress-led government. On 24 April, Jayalalitha and Mulayam Singh Yadav proposed a third front government led by West Bengal Chief Minister Jyoti Basu of CPI(M). On 25 April, Sonia met the President to express her inability to form the government and to say that Congress would not support a third front government, and the CPI (M) politburo rejected the proposal of a third front government headed by Jyoti Basu as unworkable. On the President's suggestion, the Union Cabinet met on 26 April to recommend dissolution of Lok Sabha and holding of fresh elections. President dissolved the Twelfth Lok Sabha on the same day.

Climatically, the most difficult period in the country is May to end-September, the hot summer months followed by monsoon rains. Elections are thus mostly held between November and April, or at best, in May. The Thirteenth Lok Sabha had to meet by 21 October 1999, before the expiry of six months from the last meeting of the Twelfth Lok Sabha.

After consultations with all recognized parties (six national and forty-eight state parties), the Election Commission announced elections to the Thirteenth Lok Sabha in the month of September and the first week of October 1999. Elections were to be held over five days, one week apart, starting from 5 September and ending on 3 October. Under Vajpayee's caretaker government, in the run-up to the election, two major challenges of governance that cropped up were the Kargil War, and the resolution of the US-64 problem.

XXV.1 Governance Challenges for the Caretaker-Vajpayee Government

The Kargil district of Jammu and Kashmir lies south of the Line of Control (LoC), with Pakistan-occupied Gilgit-Baltistan to the north. NH1, the only road connecting Srinagar and Leh, passes through Kargil. Not even three months had passed since Vajpayee's historic bus trip to Lahore, when on 3 May 1999, local shepherds reported Pakistani intrusion in Kargil. The infiltration had occurred along a 160-km long stretch of difficult-to-reach ridges at heights of 5000 m or more overlooking NH1. In winter, temperature in these places drops well below the freezing level. Pakistani soldiers disguised as Kashmiri militants had carried out a pre-emptive seizure of many of the unoccupied military outposts, for example on Tiger Hill and Tololing, on the Indian side of the LOC. The LOC was inviolable by the Simla Agreement of 1972. Within days of a discovery of the intrusion, India started military operations to flush out the enemy from these areas, and the Kargil war was on. As India made progress in recapturing positions, there was a threat of a nuclear breakout. The US intervened and asked Pakistan to remove troops and irregulars from Kargil. Indian troops recaptured some positions; from others, Pakistan retreated. Officially by end-July, well before the election to the Thirteenth Lok Sabha, the Kargil war was over. The unexpected expenses of the Kargil war led the government to increase the surcharge on personal income above ₹1.5 lakh from 10 per cent to 15 per cent mid-way through 1999–2000.

To manage the US-64 crisis, the government followed the recommendations of the Deepak Parekh Committee to restructure the UTI. It did a debt-for-equity swap with US-64. On 29 June, UTI launched the Special Unit Scheme (SUS) 1999 with US-64 investments in the shares of state-owned companies. The book value of shares of state-owned companies in SUS-99 was ₹3300 crore, but the market value was only ₹1516.74 crore. The Union government invested ₹3300 crore in SUS-99 with government bonds of five-year maturity. Critics described it as a bailout of the holders of US-64 using taxpayers' money. Two separate Asset Management Companies—one for debt and another for equity—were also established for US-64.

The US-64 crisis brought into focus two problems related to mutual funds owned and managed by the government. First, conflicted objectives. Such mutual funds, for example, US-64, runs the risk of intervening in markets not for benefitting the subscribers but for managing volatility and propping up specific stocks, particularly of CPSEs. Thus, UTI was a major participant on the buy side of the government's disinvestment programme. How far such purchases were motivated by a desire to generate value for the investors in US-64 or by the need to make disinvestment a success is a matter of debate. However, it should be noted that when SUS-99 went on to offload these CPSE shares in later years, it made handsome profits.

Second was a whiff of politics and corruption in the dealings of the UTI. Presciently, in December 1963, in the parliamentary discussion on the UTI Bill, Swatantra Party leader Minoo R. Masani had warned Prime Minister Nehru of the pitfalls of the government running an investment fund. 'Think Sir, of the financial power of corruption that will be implicit in such an arrangement . . . The granting of credit (or capital) will be a favour and the denial of credit will be punishment,' he had said.[1] On 8 September 1998, reportedly at the insistence of alliance partner AIADMK leader Jayalalitha, P.S. Subramanyam had been appointed as UTI chairman. There were serious allegations against Subramanyam of malfeasance related to UTI's investment in securities of various companies such as Cyberspace and DSQ Software.

XXV.2 Political Churning in the Run-Up to the 1999 Lok Sabha Elections

In the run-up to the election, the Congress was in turmoil. Three prominent members of the CWC, Sharad Pawar, P.A. Sangma and Tariq

Anwar, in a letter dated 15 May, argued against projecting Sonia Gandhi, born an Italian and an Indian citizen only by naturalization, as the party's candidate for the prime minister's post. Before that, except for 'an odd VHP functionary here and a tempestuous George Fernandes there', even the BJP had not made Sonia's foreign origin an electoral issue. Significantly, the three signatories of the 15 May letter were a Hindu, a Christian and a Muslim. Sonia Gandhi resigned from the post of Congress president. There were 'hunger strikes, protest marches and self-immolation dramas in front of her residence by Congress workers from across the country, pleading and begging her to resume the mantle of leadership'.[2] On 20 May, Pawar, Sangma and Anwar were expelled from the Congress for six years, Sonia took back her resignation as Congress president on 24 May, and the expelled trio went on to form the Nationalist Congress Party (NCP) on 25 May 1999.

In Karnataka, when Deve Gowda moved to Delhi to become Prime Minister in the United Front government, J.H. Patel had become the CM in the Janata Dal government from 31 May 1996. A part of the Janata Dal, with Patel of Karnataka and Sharad Yadav of Bihar in it, wanted to support the NDA before the 1999 election, while the faction headed by Deve Gowda wanted to distance the Janata Dal from both the Congress and the BJP. The faction headed by Sharad Yadav came to be known as Janata Dal (United) (JD(U)) and the one headed by Deve Gowda as Janata Dal (Secular) (JD(S). There was an informal arrangement among Samata Party, Lok Shakti Party and JD(U) to come together before the 1999 Lok Sabha election.

BJP under Vajpayee got busy stitching together a pre-poll alliance to secure a majority in the next Lok Sabha. The party did not have a significant presence in many states, particularly in the eastern and southern parts. Its most important moves were in Andhra Pradesh, Karnataka and Tamil Nadu. In Andhra, in 1993, NTR, at the age of seventy, had gotten married to Lakshmi Parvathi, thirty-eight, and was trying to groom her as his successor. On 1 September 1995, NTR's son-in-law Chandrababu Naidu managed to stage a coup d'etat and dislodge him as the TDP chief as well as the CM. NTR passed away in January 1996 and Lakshmi Parvathi, his widow, went on to found NTR TDP (Lakshmi Parvathi). In 1998, as part of the NDA, the party contested in five constituencies in

Andhra Pradesh and lost all five. Chandrababu had emerged as the real successor to NTR, his charismatic father-in-law. BJP dropped NTR TDP (Lakshmi Parvathi) from the NDA and stitched up an alliance with TDP in Andhra Pradesh.

In Karnataka, after the split in the Janata Dal, JD(U) was the new NDA partner. In Tamil Nadu, after AIADMK's withdrawal of support from the NDA government on 14 April 1999, AIADMK's arch-rival DMK had voted in its favour in the motion of confidence. DMK, together with MDMK, PMK, MGR-ADMK and TRC were the NDA's new alliance partners in Tamil Nadu in the 1999 election. In Haryana, the INLD was back in the NDA. In Odisha and West Bengal, the BJD and AITC continued in the NDA. In the North-East, there were new alliance partners in the Arunachal Congress, Manipur State Congress Party and Sikkim Democratic Front. NDA in 1999 consisted, including affiliates, at least of twenty parties.

Congress was an all-India party with significant footfalls in practically all states, except in Tamil Nadu, Kerala and Bihar. Coalition with other parties may maximize votes but can also create confusion about the party's own ideological position and where it stands differentiated from the positions of its alliance partners. Tamil Nadu was different, though, as the state's politics were centred primarily around the DMK-AIADMK rivalry. Congress had contested in thirty-five of the thirty-nine Lok Sabha seats in 1998, secured only 4.8 per cent of the votes and forfeited its deposit in all thirty-five. Following the withdrawal of AIADMK's support to the Vajpayee government in April 1999, the Congress struck a pre-poll alliance with the AIADMK before the 1999 Lok Sabha election. In Kerala, as a constituent of the United Democratic Front since the late 1970s, it continued its alliance with the Kerala Congress, Kerala Congress (Mani) and Indian Union of Muslim League. Bihar, where the electoral strength of the Congress had eroded over time and Jagannath Mishra was the party's last CM in March 1990, was the other state where the Congress went for a pre-poll alliance with another party. Janata Dal, and after its split, RJD and JD(U) had dominated Bihar's political landscape ever since. In 1999, Congress fought in alliance with Lalu Yadav's RJD.

The electoral strategy of the BJP was richly rewarded. Prime Minister Vajpayee's handling of the Kargil war, low inflation and 6.7 per cent and 8 per cent growth in 1998–99 and 1999–2000 also helped. For the Congress, the controversy regarding Sonia's origin was a political impediment. Its tally came down to 114, the worst ever since Independence. The NDA, with outside support of Chandrababu Naidu's TDP, commanded a majority of 299 in the Lok Sabha with 543 seats.

XXV.3 Jammu and Kashmir

In 1998, in Jammu and Kashmir, Farooq Abdullah, chief minister since October 1996 at the head of the National Conference, had inducted his son Omar Abdullah into the state's electoral politics. Not yet twenty-eight, Omar won the Srinagar constituency in 1998 to become the youngest Lok Sabha MP. Although not a member of the NDA, the National Conference had extended outside support to the first NDA government in Delhi and, in the vote on the motion of confidence on 17 April 1999, sided with the NDA.

Mufti Mohammad Sayeed, the union home minister in the V.P. Singh government in 1989–90, had rejoined the Congress in 1996, and in the 1998 Lok Sabha elections, won from the Anantnag constituency as the party's candidate. In 1998, with his eldest daughter Mehbooba Mufti, he had walked out of the Congress, and, in July 1999, barely three months before the Lok Sabha elections, founded the Jammu and Kashmir People's Democratic Party (PDP) to 'persuade the Government of India to initiate an unconditional dialogue with Kashmiris for a resolution of the Kashmir problem.'[3] Mufti was unanimously elected as the president of the PDP. One of the major aims of PDP was to provide a regional alternative to fight the National Conference in the three seats of Anantnag, Baramulla and Srinagar, and announce its presence as a prospective competitor. Of the six Lok Sabha seats in the State, National Conference won four and the BJP two. Farooq Abdullah and his National Conference did not join the NDA but offered its support to the Vajpayee government after the election. Under Vajpayee, Omar Abdullah would become the minister of state for commerce and industry on 13 October 1999 and the minister of state for foreign affairs from 23 July 2001.

Maulana Masood Azhar of Pakistan, the founder of Lashkar-e-Taiba, while on a secret mission to mediate some factional fight in the terrorist organization Harkat-ul-Mujahideen, had been arrested in February 1994 in the valley's Anantnag district. After several unsuccessful attempts to get Azhar freed, Harkat-ul-Mujahideen, on 24 December 1999, hijacked Indian Airlines flight IC-814 from Kathmandu to Delhi with 180 passengers and crew members and took it to Kandahar, in Taliban-controlled Afghanistan. The hijackers killed one passenger and demanded the release of Azhar and two others in exchange for the rest of the hostages. In India, tremendous public pressure was building up on the government to get the hostages released before the new millennium. The exchange of detained terrorists for the release of Rubaiya Sayeed, the daughter of a union minister in 1989, had created a bad precedent. Like then, in 1999, Farooq Abdullah, the chief minister of Jammu and Kashmir, was against such an exchange, but, on 31 December 1999, the three terrorists were released in exchange for the hostages.

Fidayeens are suicide bombers motivated by fundamentalist Islamic religious zeal. Maulana Masood Azhar's Jaish-e-Mohammad, or army of Mohammad, together with his Lashkar-e-Taiba, or the army of the pure, would become what the media described as the 'fidayeen factories' for brainwashing and training young men from Pakistan's Punjab for terrorist attacks on Jammu and Kashmir.[4] The two would be reportedly involved in the attack on the Indian Parliament on 13 December 2001, and 26/11 or the Mumbai terrorist attack on 26 November 2008, among others. US President Bill Clinton was visiting India for five days from 19 March 2000. On 20 March 2000, in the mainly Sikh village of Chattisinghpura in Anantnag district in the Kashmir valley, Lashkar-e-Taiba gunned down thirty-six Sikh men.

In June 2000, under Farooq Abdullah, the Jammu and Kashmir Legislative Assembly passed the 'Autonomy Resolution', seeking to restore the pre-1953 constitutional position in the state as it felt that 'acceptance of the resolution would set the clock back and reverse the natural process of harmonizing the aspirations of the people of Jammu & Kashmir with the integrity of the nation'.[5] The Union government under Vajpayee rejected the resolution. The National Conference's alliance with the NDA was strained, but it continued.

Reportedly, with the encouragement of Bill Clinton, the Hizb-ul-Mujahideen, through its representative Abdul Majid Dar, declared a unilateral ceasefire on 24 July 2000. The declaration of the ceasefire opened a rift within the APHC between the hardliners under the leadership of Jamaat-e-Islami's Syed Ali Ahmad Shah Geelani, and some others. All terrorist groups did not agree to the ceasefire and violence continued. The ceasefire was followed by talks between the government and Hizb-ul-Mujahideen. Hizb-ul-Mujahideen wanted tripartite talks involving them, India and Pakistan. The Vajpayee government did not want to involve Pakistan at this early stage. On 3 August 2000, the commander in chief of Hizb-ul-Mujahideen issued an ultimatum from Islamabad that India must agree to tripartite negotiations including Pakistan by 8 August 2000. The government wanted to negotiate within the confines of the Indian Constitution and did not agree. The ceasefire collapsed.

In January 2001, George Bush succeeded Bill Clinton as the US President. In Bush's first year in office, on 11 September 2001, terrorists attacked the twin towers of the World Trade Centre in New York as well as the Pentagon using hijacked aircrafts. With the month written before the date in the US, it became notorious as 9/11. Osama bin Laden and his Al Qaeda were operating under the protection of the Taliban in Afghanistan and were responsible for 9/11. In the past, the US had supported the Taliban and provided it with arms and funds to fight the Soviets in Afghanistan. The tragic loss of about 3000 lives and property in 9/11 turned world opinion against terrorism. On 28 September 2001, the UN Security Council, by its unanimous Resolution No. 1373, made it obligatory for all members to end all terrorist activity and to bring the perpetrators to justice.

In a complete turnaround, the US staged a global war on terrorism, particularly against the Taliban. Pakistan, under duress, also had no option but to follow suit and not only join the US in its fight against the Taliban but also scale down its active support to the terrorists operating in Jammu and Kashmir. Organizations such as Jaish-e-Mohammad and Lashkar-e-Taiba were aggrieved and turned against Pakistan itself. Nevertheless, violence continued in Jammu and Kashmir.

Elections to the Jammu and Kashmir legislative assembly, last held in 1996, was due after six years in 2002. Earlier in the year, Omar Abdullah had been anointed as the president of the National Conference and his father Farooq Abdullah intended to continue his political career at the all-India level. The legislative assembly election was a multi-cornered fight, mainly among the National Conference, Mufti Mohammad Sayeed's PDP and the Congress.

The APHC, fractured between the hardliners and moderates, saw further division around the 2002 polls. The issue was popular election to settle the question about its representative character. In late January 2002, APHC chairman Abdul Ghani Bhat announced that it would hold elections with its own election commission. The possibility of holding such elections in phases in the different regions, according to some, had an important signal. Any regional election was likely to result in very different outcomes in the Muslim-majority Kashmir valley, Hindu-majority Jammu region and Buddhist-dominated Ladakh, and pave the way for a final division of Jammu and Kashmir on communal lines as had been suggested by Pakistan's foreign minister Sartaj Aziz before the Lahore summit between Vajpayee and Pakistan's Prime Minister Nawaz Sharif.

The militants called for a poll boycott, and some 580 individuals died in pre-poll violence. Although the turnout was down at 43.7 per cent from 53.9 per cent in 1996, the 2002 Jammu and Kashmir assembly election was 'considered the fairest ever held in the state'.[6] The tally of National Conference came down dramatically from fifty-seven in 1996 to twenty-eight, with the Congress winning twenty (up from seven in 1996), and the PDP sixteen. The defeat of Omar Abdullah by Qazi Mohammad Afzal of the PDP in Ganderbal, a traditional Abdullah stronghold in the valley, came as a shock to the National Conference. With a hung assembly, Jammu and Kashmir was placed under Governor's rule from 18 October to 2 November 2002.

PDP and the Congress agreed to form a coalition government with PDP's Mufti Mohammad Sayeed becoming chief minister for the first three years on 2 November 2002 and a leader of the Congress for the next three. Sporadic violence by terrorists on civilians as well as clashes with the security forces continued. However, there seemed to be an underlying waning tendency for terrorist violence after the election (Table XXV.1).

Table XXV.1 Trends of Violence in Jammu and Kashmir

Year	Incidents	Security men killed	Civilians killed	Terrorists killed
2002-03	3860	994	433	1536
2003-04	3362	753	326	1491
2003	3401	795	314	1494
2004	2565	281	707	976
2005	1990	189	557	917
2006	1667	151	389	591
2007	1092	110	158	472
2008	708	75	91	339
2009	499	78	71	239
2010	488	69	47	232
2011	340	33	31	100
2012	220	15	15	72
2013	170	53	15	67
2014	222	47	28	110
2015	208	39	17	108
2016	322	82	15	150
2017	342	80	40	213
2018	614	91	39	257
2019	594	80	39	157

Source: Ministry of Home Affairs Annual Report 2003-04 (for 2002-03 to 2003-04), 2004-05 (for 2003), 2008-09 (for 2004 to 2008), 2013-14 (for 2009 to 2012), 2017-18 (for 2013 to 2016) and 2019-20 (for 2017 to 2019).

XXV.4 The Second NDA Government

After the elections, Vajpayee was sworn back into office on 13 October 1999, and Yashwant Sinha was again his finance minister. The major reforms that followed included: National Highways Development, introduction of VAT, Fiscal Responsibility and Budget Management Act, a restructured pension scheme for government employees, National Health Policy 2002 and Sarva Shiksha Abhiyan (Education for All) 2003.

National Highway Development Plan

With funds secured by the ₹1 cess per litre of petrol and diesel each
and Prime Minister Vajpayee's October 1998 announcement that road
connectivity would be improved, there was rapid progress in expansion
and improvement of NHs. Apart from the Golden Quadrilateral, there
was also talk of the North-South (NS) and East-West (EW) corridors
connecting Srinagar to Kanyakumari and Silchar to Porbandar. The
National Highway Development Project I (NHDP I), at an estimated
cost of ₹30,300 crore (at 1999 prices), was approved in December 2000
to build the Golden Quadrilateral (5,846 km), 981 km of the NS-EW
corridors, 380 km of port connectivity and 315 km of other NHs: a total
of 7522 km. To facilitate fundraising for NHDP, in his 2000–2001
Budget, Sinha gave tax exemption to capital gains on investment in bonds
of maturity of five years or more to be issued by the NHAI.

The target date for completion of NHDP I was December 2006, but
it got completed only in January 2012, mostly on account of difficulties
in land acquisition, litigation relating to contracts and law and order
problems. Private sector participation was mostly through engineering,
procurement and construction (EPC) contracts. The NHDP I was followed
up in December 2003 by the launch of NHDP II at an estimated cost of
₹34,339 crore (at 2002 prices) comprising 6,161 km of NS-EW corridor
and 486 km of other NHs. The broad range of support for NHDP across
political party lines would be manifest in the launch of NHDP III to
NHDP VII by December 2007, well after the NDA government demitted
office in May 2004.

Liberalization of insurance and Insurance Regulatory and Development Authority (IRDA)

In April 2000, following the recommendations of the Malhotra Committee
the year before, the autonomous Insurance Regulatory and Development
Authority (IRDA) was incorporated as a statutory body. Its mandate
was promoting competition to increase consumer choice and lower
premia, while ensuring the financial security of the insurance market.
Insurance was opened for private sector participation in August 2000 and

foreign companies were allowed ownership of up to 26 per cent. IRDA started framing various regulations to protect policyholders' interests. In December 2000, the subsidiaries of the government-owned GIC were restructured as independent companies and the GIC converted into a national re-insurer. The four subsidiaries were subsequently delinked from GIC in July 2002.

Prior to 1986, health insurance was available only to government employees through the Central Government Health Insurance Scheme (CGHS), and private sector employees through the Employees State Insurance (ESI) Scheme. From 1986, the Union government had been offering to the people Mediclaim, an insurance product. Opening up of the sector saw the entry of private companies into the insurance, including health insurance, market.

Value Added Tax (VAT)

VAT, a method of taxing, by instalments or in stages, final consumer spending in the economy, had become the most favoured form of taxing domestic trade in many parts of the world by the late 1990s. The number of countries with VAT had increased from two in 1965 to 135 in 2000. Introduction of VAT to replace domestic trade taxes was a major reform pending.

We will recall that the Indirect Taxation Enquiry Committee headed by L.K. Jha in its report in 1978 had highlighted the desirability of introducing VAT to avoid the cascading effect of taxes on raw materials and components of finished products, but successive finance ministers had shied away from moving forward because of the major restructuring required and revenue implications involved from input duty rebate. Only the Union government had made progress by introducing input tax credit under Union Excise Duties in the form of MODVAT in stages in 1986–87, 1987–88, 1991–92, and 1996–97. In Budget 2000–2001, Yashwant Sinha announced the introduction of a single-rate Central VAT or CENVAT. The issue of replacing state sales tax on domestic trade with VAT remained an unfinished agenda. Sales tax being a state subject, the central government could only play the role of a facilitator for successful implementation of VAT.

In 1992, the Tax Reform Committee headed by Raja Chelliah had suggested two options for rationalizing the taxes on domestic goods: i) to centralize all indirect taxes on goods into a single retail-stage VAT levied by the Union government, or ii) to rationalize and gradually expand the prevailing MODVAT of the Union government into a wholesale stage VAT, and to transform the states' sales taxes on goods into a VAT up to the retail level.

In 1994 came the seminal Report on Reform of Domestic Trade Taxes in India prepared by the NIPFP under Amaresh Bagchi, who had succeeded Raj Chelliah as its director. The report emphasized how VAT is a multi-stage tax, like the turnover tax, but is levied on the value added at each stage and not on gross turnover. It pointed out how a multi-stage consumption type VAT, with input tax credit available at every level of transaction, by definition, has to be of the 'destination' variety, that is the final tax on consumption would be collected at the destination where such consumption takes place.

The recommended design had three important virtues. First, there was no cascading of taxes, or tax on tax. With credit available for taxes paid at earlier stages, vertical integration of production or lack thereof would yield no gain or loss in terms of taxes. Second, the incidence of the tax would equal the VAT rate, and commodities or transactions, for example, exports, could be completely relieved of all taxes by 'zero rating', that is zero tax at the final stage and reimbursement of all taxes paid at earlier input stages. Third, with its multi-point character, it was self-enforcing in nature. With denial of the corresponding input tax credit to the vendor at the next stage, evasion at an earlier stage would entail no loss to the exchequer. Businesses would demand invoices from their suppliers to avail credit for taxes paid at earlier stages.

The Constitution assigns concurrent jurisdiction in taxation of internal commodity transactions to the Union (in the form of excise duties at the manufacturing stage) and the state governments (beyond the manufacturing stage as sales tax). In introducing a destination-based VAT in the country, how would you treat goods produced in one state sold to another? The 1994 NIPFP-Bagchi Report listed three options, namely a VAT administered by (i) exclusively the Union, (ii) exclusively by the states, and (iii) a dual VAT administered concurrently by the Union and the states. The first two options were ruled out because neither the states nor the Union would be willing to surrender their powers to mobilize the equivalent of a sales tax and Union excise duties. The Union's jurisdiction over VAT was also necessary for harmonization of VAT across the country and implementing a destination-based VAT by reimbursing the destination state for any VAT imposed on an inter-state sale. Thus, the report favoured a dual VAT system: the Union government should levy the tax only on manufacturing as under MODVAT, but covering all commodities, and at least some services, and the states should convert their sales taxes into VAT. Furthermore, VAT should replace all indirect taxes at the state level.

In 1995, at the first preliminary meeting of chief ministers on state-level VAT convened by Union Finance Minister Manmohan Singh, only the basic issues on VAT had been discussed in general terms. Periodic interactions of state finance ministers followed. In preparation for the introduction of VAT, by 1 January 2000, by consensus, the states introduced some floor rates for an agreed set of commodities and withdrew various schemes for tax-based incentives to industry for new investment. These two measures were important to stop a race to the bottom among states and promote their cooperation in the reform of domestic trade taxes. On the recommendation of state chief ministers, an Empowered Committee of State Finance Ministers was constituted on 17 July 2000 to study the different aspects of the proposed VAT system and make recommendations regarding the design and features of VAT. In May 2001, the report on 'Tax policy and tax administration for the Tenth Plan' by Parthasarthi Shome endorsed a transition to a nationally integrated Centre-state VAT in parallel or dual format. In 2002, Jaswant Singh succeeded Yashwant Sinha as the Union finance minister. In an important meeting on state-level VAT convened by Prime Minister Vajpayee on 18 October 2002, he declared 1 April 2003 as the date for VAT's introduction. But only Haryana met the deadline.

There was considerable opposition to the introduction of VAT. It came first from the traders and transport associations because of what they feared in terms of increased compliance costs, the trouble of maintaining detailed accounts and, in some cases, perhaps more difficulties in evading taxes. Second, it came from many states on account of the prospective phasing out of CST on inter-state sales. CST revenues accrued to the states. But, the CST, which was origin-based, was completely antithetical to the rationale of destination-based VAT and needed to be abolished. Third was the opposition from the states because of their general risk-aversion to tinkering with the most important source of their own revenue, namely the sales tax system. Furthermore, VAT became a victim of the isolation paradox, with some states claiming that there was no point of introducing VAT unless all other states also did it. At least on paper, every state was waiting for every other state to introduce VAT!

To secure their revenue interests after introduction of VAT, the states demanded the right to tax services. Taxes on services were not explicitly mentioned in any of the three lists in the Constitutional assignment of expenditure and taxes, and the Union government was levying service tax on an increasing number of items under the Constitution's Entry 97. As a halfway house, the Constitution (Eighty-eighth Amendment) Bill, 2003 was introduced on 7 March 2003 with a new Article 268A allowing the Union government to levy service tax and both the Union and the state governments to collect and appropriate the proceeds 'in accordance with such principles of collection and appropriation as may be formulated by Parliament by law'.[7] Simultaneously, Jaswant Singh, in his 2003–04 Budget, increased the rate of service tax from 5 per cent to 8 per cent, extended the tax to ten more services, and made service tax credit available across all services.

There was the challenge of harmonizing VAT legislation and commodity classification across states and ensuring that a 'dealer' meant the same entity in Arunachal as in Maharashtra, or that 'a pencil in Haryana will not be called a pen in Punjab'.[8] On the issue of implementation, the Union government agreed to help the states with a series of measures. For example, it would draft a VAT model law and secure the President's assent for those states that wished to adopt it. Similarly, it would bear half the cost of setting up a Tax Information Exchange System (TINXSYS) to facilitate inter-state transactions, help the states, particularly those in the North-East, to set up computerized VAT administration, and aid with publicity of VAT.

Some salient features of the design of VAT suggested by the Empowered Committee of State Finance Ministers were: (i) rates on various commodities should be uniform for all the states/ UTs, with two basic rates of 4 per cent and 12.5 per cent, besides an exempt category and a special rate of 1 per cent for a few selected items; (ii) elimination of the multiplicity of taxes; (iii) Input Tax Credit to be available on inter-state purchases; (iv) exports to be zero rated, (v) a business-friendly VAT with self-assessment by the dealers with a threshold limit of annual turnover and provision for composition of tax liability below that annual turnover limit; (vi) no fresh sales tax/VAT-based industrial incentives would be permitted.

The states were wary of potential revenue loss from the introduction of VAT and wanted the Union government to underwrite any revenue losses from the introduction of VAT in the place of sales tax in the first three years. The Union government was reluctant unless the states agreed not to change any rate of tax under VAT for the first three years. Finally, in Budget 2003–04, Finance Minister Jaswant Singh announced '. . . in the initial years of introduction of VAT, the Central Government has agreed to compensate 100 per cent of the loss in the first year, 75 per cent of the loss in second year and 50 per cent of the loss in the third year of the introduction of VAT; this loss being computed on the basis of an agreed formula.'

When the NDA government under Vajpayee was succeeded by the UPA government under Manmohan Singh on 22 May 2004, no state apart from Haryana had introduced VAT. Yet, the critical role the BJP-led NDA played in taking the VAT agenda ahead is widely acknowledged. In India's robust democracy, its successor UPA government with P. Chidambaram as the finance minister would complete the introduction of VAT during its tenure.

Fiscal Responsibility and Budget Management Act

Despite a consensus on fiscal consolidation, and repeated budgetary exhortations about its virtues, the decade of the 1990s had ended with the fiscal deficit of the Union government at 5.2 per cent of GDP in 1999–2000, at the same level as that achieved in the first full year of reform, namely 1992–93. The corresponding rise in the level of total liabilities of the Union government had been three-fold, from ₹3,54,661.93 crore to ₹10,21,029.38 crore. Article 292 of the Constitution stipulates: 'The executive power of the Union extends to borrowing upon the security of the Consolidated Fund of India within such limits, if any, as may from time to time be fixed by Parliament by law and to the giving of guarantees within such limits, if any, as may be so fixed.' But no such legal limits had been fixed by the legislature.

Developments in the 1990s moved in favour of statutory provisions under Article 292. A committee, chaired by Finance Secretary E.A.S. Sarma, was set up on 17 January 2000 to go into various aspects of the matter and recommend draft legislation on fiscal responsibility. In its report submitted on 4 July 2000, the committee recommended the enactment of a Fiscal Responsibility and Budget Management (FRBM) law. The committee defined fiscal responsibility in relation to: (a) revenue deficit, (b) fiscal deficit, (c) borrowing, as well as (d) debt. Under borrowing, it proposed the prohibition of certain types of borrowing from the RBI. The enforcement contemplated was in terms of compliance at stages of both budget approval (ex ante) and budget execution (ex post). Further, the compliance evaluation of actual performance was not only in terms of end of the year but also contemporaneous or intra-year performance. The FRBM Bill was introduced in Lok Sabha on 22 December 2000 and referred to the Parliamentary Standing Committee on Finance. In the public debate that ensued after the introduction of the bill, there were apprehensions about creative accounting, and about yet another law that would be observed more in its breach. Questions were also raised about the appropriateness of the penalty, which was only reputational, for non-compliance. Doubts lingered about the system of name and shame alone in the Indian political context. Would there be sufficient punishment from the political market for a loss of reputation, sceptics asked.

The FRBM Committee had recommended that for a shortfall of revenue or overshooting of expenditure vis-à-vis the intra-year targets, the Budget should pre-announce what adjustment in taxation/pricing and/or expenditure cutback or imposition of a surcharge would be triggered. It should also define the principles to determine differences between permissible deviation and material deviation. This recommendation was not included in the FRBM Act (FRBMA). Instead, a quarterly review was prescribed, and certain mid-year triggers fixed in terms of three indicators, including non-debt capital receipts falling below 40 per cent of BE, and either fiscal or revenue deficit exceeding 45 per cent of BE. The recommended periodical reporting directly to the public, with remarks on the same by a Fiscal Management Review Committee, was not accepted because of prejudice to Parliamentary Estimates Committee and C&AG. Quarterly reporting, without the Fiscal Management Review Committee, was started with effect from April-June 2003, even before the notification of the rules, to demonstrate the government's willingness to assume the obligations it had proposed under the law still under consideration of Parliament.

The FRBM Committee had recommended normative ceilings and timeframes for fiscal indicators. Revenue deficit was to be reduced by half per cent or more of the estimated GDP at the end of each financial year commencing on 1 April 2001 and the within a period of five financial years ending on 31 March 2006. For fiscal deficit, the recommendation was a reduction by an amount equivalent to one-third of one per cent or more of the estimated GDP at the end of each financial year commencing on 1 April 2001, and its reduction to no more than three per cent of the estimated GDP for that year within a period of five financial years ending on 31 March 2006. It had recommended capping guarantees at half per cent of the estimated GDP in any financial year. With the delay in enactment, the end-March deadlines were moved from 2006 to 2008. The second NDA government enacted the FRBMA on 26 August 2003 but could not notify the rules before demitting office on 22 May 2004. Like for VAT, it was again the successor UPA that notified the rules and brought the FRBMA into force from 5 July 2004.

Before demitting office, Finance Minister Jaswant Singh, on 18 February 2004, constituted a task force for implementation of the Fiscal Responsibility and Budget Management Act, 2003, with the economist and veteran policy maker Vijay Kelkar as chairman. The task force report, which would go on to play a major role in fiscal reforms, including the introduction of the GST, however, became available only in mid-July 2004, after the UPA had replaced NDA as the government.

New pension scheme

The old age income security system consisted of: (i) civil services scheme, (ii) employees provident fund organization (EPFO) schemes, (iii) occupational pension schemes such as the Bank Employees' Pension Scheme and Insurance Employees' Pension Scheme, and (iv) public provident fund (PPF) scheme. Furthermore, there was NOAPS, but with very limited benefits for the destitute above the age of sixty-five. With increases in the old-age dependency ratio, there was a need to have a close look at the old-age income security system.

In 2001–02, in his Budget speech, Finance Minister Sinha had noted the unsustainable increase in the Union government's pension liability as a proportion of GDP, from about 0.5 per cent in 1993–94 to 1 per cent in 2000–2001. The civil service pension scheme was an unfunded, pay-as-you-go defined benefit system—that is, it promised specified proportion of last pay drawn as pensions and was supposed to be financed by the pension contributions of serving employees. Problems arose as pension contributions of serving employees fell short of the pension payments to retirees. Sinha proposed to introduce the new, funded, defined contribution scheme for new entrants into the Union government's service after a specified date. Under a defined benefit pension system, the pension amount is predetermined as a lump sum amount or by a predetermined formula. Under a defined contribution system, contributions are defined as a lump sum amount, or a proportion of salary, and benefits depend on the returns on cumulative contributions.

The new restructured pension scheme for the new employees of the Union government was ready by 2003–04. In his Budget for 2003–04, Jaswant Singh announced that it would apply only to new entrants to government service, except to the armed forces, and upon finalization, offer a basket of pension choices. It would also be available, on a voluntary basis, to all employers for their employees, as well as to the self-employed. The new pension system (NPS) would be based on defined contributions, shared equally in the case of government employees between the government and its employees. For non-government employees, the contributions would be from the employer and the employees. It would be portable, allowing transfer of the benefits in case of change of employment, and would go into 'individual pension accounts' with pension funds. The ministry of finance would oversee and supervise the pension funds through a new and independent Pension Fund Regulatory and Development Authority (PFRDA). The NPS became applicable for employees, except for the armed forces, individuals entering Union government service or service in central autonomous bodies on or after 1 January 2004. The new scheme had mandatory employer and employee contributions. An interim PFRDA was set up by an executive order on 10 October 2003, and the need for a statutory one remained.

Opening up defence production to the private sector

In July 1991, even with widespread abolition of industrial licensing, arms and ammunition and allied items of defence equipment, defence aircraft and warships, was one of the eight industries that was retained in the public sector. India had thirty-nine ordnance factories, eight Defence Public Sector Units (DPSUs) and fifty research and development laboratories, yet it continued to be dependent on the rest of the world for its defence requirements. In May 2001, the NDA government allowed 100 per cent private sector participation in defence production, subject to licensing. It also allowed FDI of up to 26 per cent in such companies.

National Health Policy 2002

There had been progress in the health sector after the adoption of National Health Policy 1983. In 2000, life expectancy reached around sixty-five years (64.6 years), surpassing the target of sixty-four years in the National Health Policy 1983. But there were shortfalls in several areas, such as infant mortality and crude birth rates. Similarly, the incidence of malaria had seen a resurgence in the1980s; mortality through 'lifestyle' diseases, namely diabetes, cancer and cardiovascular diseases, had increased; there was a persistent incidence of macro- and micro-nutrient deficiencies, especially among women and children, leading to the birth of underweight babies with the serious risk of mental and physical retarded growth. The circumstances prevailing in the health sector had changed since the announcement of 1983 policy, and most importantly, the 1983 policy had not pointed out the financial resources that needed to be devoted to achieving its lofty objective of health for all by 2000.

Public health expenditure, as a proportion of GDP, had declined from 1.3 per cent in 1990 to 0.9 per cent in 1999. Such expenditure, annually per capita, around 2002 was no more than only ₹200. Of the aggregate health expenditure of 5.2 per cent of GDP, only 17 per cent was public spending, the balance was out-of-pocket expenditure. With this background, National Health Policy 2002 formulated targets consistent with realistic expectations about financial resources, and public health administrative capacity. It drew pointed attention to the differentials in the health status in rural and urban areas and across states. Policy 2002 noted how funding was generally insufficient; the presence of medical and paramedical personnel often much less than that required by prescribed norms; the availability of consumables frequently negligible; the equipment often obsolete and unusable; and the buildings in a dilapidated state. It emphasized that, though under the Constitution, public health was the states' responsibility, and improvements in the decentralized public health services in the country would require an injection of substantial resources from the Union Budget into the health sector.

Policy 2002 drew pointed attention to a critical shortage of expertise in the areas of 'public health' and 'family medicine'. It recommended the use of indigenously manufactured low-cost generic drugs and imparting information relating to the basic principles of preventive healthcare to school and college students, who are the most impressionable targets for imparting such information. It also underscored the need for having a National Population Policy to stop a rapid growth in population neutralizing the impact of National Health Policy. Policy 2002 set up the targets of eliminating polio and yaws, and leprosy by 2005, kala azar by 2010, lymphatic filariasis by 2015, achieving zero-level growth of HIV/AIDS by 2007, reducing mortality on account of TB, malaria and other vector-borne disease by 50 per cent by 2010, and reducing infant mortality rate (per 1000) to 30 and maternal mortality rate (per lakh) to 100 by 2010.

On the financial side, by 2010, it envisaged the country spending 6 per cent of GDP on the health sector, with a third of it coming from the public sector. Thus, it recommended: (i) increasing health expenditure by the government—Centre and states combined—as a proportion of GDP from 0.9 per cent to 2 per cent by 2010, (ii) increasing the share of central grants to constitute at least 25 per cent of total health spending by 2010 from 15 per cent, and (iii) increasing the state governments' health sector spending, as a proportion of their total expenditure, from 5.5 per cent to 7 per cent by 2005 and further to 8 per cent by 2010. It emphasized PHC and recommended the increased allocation of 55 per cent of the total public health investment for the primary health sector; the secondary and tertiary health sectors being targeted for 35 per cent and 10 per cent, respectively. It urged decentralized administration of the health schemes through autonomous bodies at the state and district levels and recognizing the practical need for levying reasonable user charges for certain secondary and tertiary public health care services, for those who can afford to pay.

AYUSH is the acronym for Ayurveda, Yoga and Naturopathy, Unani, Siddha and Homeopathy, the medical systems apart from allopathy that are being practised in India. AYUSH approaches health, disease and treatment in a holistic way. The Department of Indian Medicine and Homeopathy (ISM & H) created in the Union ministry of health and family welfare in 1995, was renamed in 2003 as the Department of AYUSH.

Sarva Shiksha Abhiyan

The founding fathers of the Indian Republic cherished the goal of providing free and compulsory education for all children in the age group six to fourteen years. The Constituent Assembly, after considering putting free and compulsory education for children of six to fourteen years as a fundamental right within ten years, for cost reasons, put it under the non-justiciable fundamental rights, which were later renamed Directive Principles of State Policy. The Indian Constitution puts education in its Concurrent List of the Seventh Schedule, and both the Centre and the States have jurisdiction over education, except for some special institutions such as the central universities. As we have already discussed, ever since the Forster's Education Act, 1870 in the UK, Indian leaders had demanded similar compulsory education acts for India. There were many education acts both before Independence and after it until 1962, but experience showed that just legislation was not good enough. There had been several versions of the National Policy on Education also from 1968 onwards, but with inadequate outlays, progress was tardy at best.

In 1993, in a judgment in the case of Unnikrishnan versus State of Andhra Pradesh, the Supreme Court said that Article 45 in Part IV of the

Constitution must be read in 'harmonious construction' with Article 21 (Right to Life) in Part III since right to life is meaningless if it is without access to knowledge. It said: 'The passage of 44 years—more than four times the period stipulated in Article 45 has converted the obligation created by the Article into an enforceable right. At least now the state must honour the command of Article 45 and make it a right.' In 1994, the District Primary Education Programme (DPEP) was launched to move away from focusing on only enrolment to a more holistic approach to universalize access, improve retention and enhance learning achievement. Furthermore, it was a decentralized approach, with districts given considerable latitude to select their strategy.

The United Front under Prime Minister Deve Gowda, after coming to power in June 1996, appointed a Committee of State Education Ministers under the chairmanship of Muhi Ram Saikia, Union minister of state, ministry of human resource development. The Saikia Committee, in its report submitted in January 1997, recommended amending the Constitution to make the right to free education up to the age of fourteen years a fundamental right. The Constitution (Eighty-Third Amendment) Bill, 1997 was introduced during the second stint of the United Front government under Prime Minister I.K. Gujral. After incorporation of the amendments suggested by the Parliamentary Standing Committee, it was introduced as the Constitution (Ninety-Third Amendment) Bill, 2001 under the NDA government headed by Atal Bihari Vajpayee. The bill was passed as the Eighty-Sixth Constitution Amendment Act on December 12, 2002, with a new Article 21 (A) stating: 'The State shall provide free and compulsory education to all children of the age of six to fourteen years in such manner as the State may, by law, determine,' and amending Article 51A on fundamental duties to include as Clause (k) the duty of '. . . a parent or guardian to provide opportunities for education to his child or, as the case may be, ward between the age of six and fourteen years . . .'

In the meantime, in 2001, the government launched the Sarva Shiksha Abhiyan or education for all campaign, to be jointly funded by the Centre and the states. It aimed to provide eight years of quality elementary education for all children up to the age of fourteen years in a mission mode with a thrust on community ownership, disadvantaged groups and girls' quality education and alternative modes of education. All existing schemes on elementary education would converge with this scheme after the Ninth Plan and cover all the districts in the country by March 2002. The plan allocation to the Department of Elementary Education and Literacy went up from ₹3732 crore in 2001–02 to ₹4454 crore in 2002–03 and further to ₹5403 crore in 2003–04.

Total Sanitation Campaign (TSC)

A Baseline Survey on Knowledge, Attitudes and Practices in rural water supply and sanitation, conducted in 1996–97 by the Indian Institute of Mass Communication, showed that 55 per cent of those with private latrines were self-motivated. Only 2 per cent of the respondents claimed the existence of subsidy as the major motivating factor, while 54 per cent claimed to have gone in for sanitary latrines due to convenience and privacy. The study also showed that 51 per cent of the respondents were willing to spend up to ₹1000 to acquire sanitary toilets. In view of these findings, the CRSP was improved and moved towards a 'demand driven' approach called Total Sanitation Campaign (TSC) in 1999.[9] It emphasized information, education and communication, human resource development, capacity development activities to increase awareness among the rural people and generate demand for sanitary facilities.

In September 2000, after a three-day Millennium Summit of world leaders at the UN, New York, the UN General Assembly adopted, among others, eight Millennium Development Goals (MDGs) with twenty-one targets, with a series of measurable health and economic indicators. Goal 7 on environmental sustainability included the target (7C) of halving by 2015 the proportion of population without access to improved sanitation. Sanitation referred to the management of human faeces at the household level.

In October 2003, the government instituted an award called the Nirmal Gram Puraskar (NGP) or Clean Village Award for districts, blocks and gram panchayats that achieve 100 per cent sanitation coverage of individual households, 100 per cent school sanitation coverage, are free from open defecation and maintain a clean environment. In 2006, not only TSC, but schemes such as Rajiv Gandhi Grameen Vidyutikaran

Yojana for providing rural electrification, National Rural Drinking Water Supply Scheme and others, were dovetailed into IAY, a flagship scheme of the ministry of rural development that addressed rural housing needs by giving grants for the construction of dwelling units for BPL families. This convergence of TSC and other schemes allowed the use of government funds for the construction of sanitary toilets in IAY houses.

Railway fare rationalization

On 13 October 1999, Mamata Banerjee, chairperson of AITC, had become the railway minister in the second NDA government. In the world markets, petroleum prices had skyrocketed from a twenty-five-year low low of $11 per barrel in February 1999 to a peak of close to $35 per barrel in the first week of September 2000. Domestic petroleum prices had been revised upwards, for example, for petrol from ₹26.07 per litre to ₹28.44 per litre and LPG cylinder (14.2 kg) from ₹196.55 to ₹232.25, on 30 September 2000. On the same day, Mamata had resigned along with her AITC colleague Ajit Panja, minister of state for external relations, in protest against the hike in petroleum prices. She took back her resignation without specifying any reasons and continued as the railway minister.

In the meantime, the 'coffingate' scandal broke out in the context of the recently concluded heroic Kargil war. The flag-draped coffins of nearly 500 heroes, who had sacrificed their lives to throw the Pakistani invaders out from the high mountains, were flown to their villages or hometowns, for families, friends, and admirers to pay their last homage before cremation or burial. The hurriedly crafted wooden coffins, reportedly procured from the US at exorbitant costs, were found to be not usable on the occasion. Metallic coffins were hurriedly bought from Israel to allow the funerals to be held on time. The coffingate scandal broke out and Defence Minister George Fernandes could not escape a part of the implicit responsibility. For the NDA government, things took an uglier shape with the news website Tehelka.com releasing video footage of their investigation into the murky world of Indian defence deals in January 2001. Masquerading as defence dealers, Tehelka captured Jaya Jaitley, the president of George Fernandes' Samata Party, a constituent of NDA, accepting a payment of £3000 in the defence minister's living room. 'Sting on a shoestring,' The Guardian, 21 March 2001.

Fernandes offered to resign. On 14 March 2001, Mamata wrote to Prime Minister Vajpayee demanding the acceptance of Fernandes' resignation and a probe. She threatened to resign unless this was done. Mamata resigned as railway minister on 15 March 2001 before Prime Minister Vajpayee accepted Fernandes' resignation as defence minister on 16 March 2001. Nitish Kumar of JD(U), a constituent of NDA, succeeded her as the railway minister on 20 March 2001.

Freight earnings accounted for about two-thirds of the Indian Railway's earnings. Passenger traffic accounted for the rest. Railways had been losing money in the passenger segment of its business, charging freight rates that were uncompetitive and as a result, losing market share to road transport in the freight business. Fare per passenger-kilometre in India was one of the lowest in the world, and its fare per ton-kilometre of freight was one of the highest.

Kumar, in his Railway Budget speech on 26 February 2002, said: 'The Railways have not been passing on fully the cost of running the system on to the users, particularly, the passengers. They themselves have been bearing the financial burden of implementation of the recommendations of the V Pay Commission along with escalation in other inputs. Sir, I feel that the time has now come when the Railways just cannot do without transferring at least some of the increase in the cost of operating the system.' It was a much-needed move that the NDA government with Nitish Kumar as railway minister mustered the courage to do.

Monetary policy

Soon after the second NDA government came to power, it reduced the CRR from 10 per cent to 9.5 per cent on 6 November 1999, and by further reductions of 50 basis points each on 20 November 1999, and on 8 and 22 April 2000, brought it to 8 per cent. In 2000, the CRR was increased to 8.25 per cent and 8.5 per cent on 29 July and 12 August, respectively. After these two increases, the CRR continued to decline through the rest of the NDA regime to 4.5 per cent on 14 June 2003. It remained there until Vajpayee demitted office in May 2004.

From end-March 2000 and 2001, a risk weight of 2.5 per cent for market risk was introduced on investments in government and other approved securities, and on investments in securities outside SLR, respectively. The proportion of banks' portfolio of government and approved securities, which is required to be marked to market, was progressively increased from 75 per cent from the year ending 31 March 2000. Furthermore, from 30 September 2000, the entire investment portfolio of banks was required to be classified under three categories, namely, Held to Maturity, Available for Sale and Held for Trading. As already mentioned, the CRAR was enhanced to 9 per cent from 31 March 2000. Furthermore, to bring the NPA guidelines at par with international standards, on 1 April 2004, the minimum period over which interest and/or principal had to remain overdue for becoming an NPA was brought down from two quarters to ninety days.

On 26 June 2004, the BCBS released 'International Convergence of Capital Measurement and Capital Standards: A revised Framework', commonly known as Basel II. Basel II augmented Basel I, which in its amended form already had credit risk and market risk, by incorporating operation risk. The RBI set up a steering committee comprising representatives of banks and different supervisory and regulatory departments to take stock of all issues relating to its implementation of Basel II.

Facilitation of recovery of debt

The legal framework of commercial transactions had not kept pace with the changing commercial practices and financial sector reforms. There were mounting problems in the recovery of loans and NPAs in financial institutions. Financial institutions had to take recourse to lengthy and time-consuming civil suits in courts to recover their dues. Narasimham Committee II had suggested new legislation for securitization and empowerment of banks and financial institutions to gain possession of the securities and to sell them without any intervention of the courts. An attempted remedy to the problem was the Securitization and Reconstruction of Financial Assets and Enforcement of Securities Interest (SARFAESI) Act, 2002, which came into effect on 17 December 2002.

Under SARFAESI Act, if a borrower defaulted on a loan financed by a bank against collateral, the bank got sweeping powers to recover its dues.

After giving a notice period of sixty days, the lender could take possession of the pledged assets, take over the management of such assets, appoint any person to manage them or ask debtors of the borrower to pay their dues, too, with respect to the asset. This streamlined recovery procedure saved banks and financial institutions a lot of time and problems which, in its absence, would have arisen due to the intervention of courts. Asset Reconstruction Companies (ARCs), which buy out distressed assets and focus on their efficient resolution, provided a useful alternative to banks for settling their NPAs. The first ARC, ARCIL, was set up in 2002.

Petroleum sector reforms

In 2002–03, the NDA government dismantled APM in the petroleum sector and oil pool account. To soften the hit on the consumer, it decided to continue the subsidy on LPG, diesel and kerosene with a commitment to paying the subsidy to state-owned oil companies 'directly' from the Budget.

New telecom policy 1999

The award of telecom licences through a single-stage bidding process in January 1995, in retrospect, turned out to be overly optimistic bids on the part of the telecom companies. 'The environment of liberalization, the attractiveness of the Indian market in terms of low teledensity, long waiting list for telephones (high latent demand) and a burgeoning middle class, etc.,' the Cellular Operators Association of India noted, 'generated a huge hype leading companies with little or no experience to bid exorbitant amounts for the Circle licenses.'[10] The high license fees were reflected in high cellular mobile tariffs of around ₹10 per minute, low affordability for consumers, default in roll-out obligations, and limited coverage. By end-1998, most of the circle cellular licensees were on the brink of bankruptcy. A Group on Telecommunications, under the chairmanship of Jaswant Singh, the then Deputy Chairman, Planning Commission, was set up on 20 November 1998 to investigate the problem and provide a solution. On 6 December 1998, Jagmohan, the former Governor of Jammu and Kashmir as well as vice-chairman of DD, became the minister of communications.

Following the recommendations of the Group of Telecommunication, a New Telecom Policy 1999 became effective from 1 April 1999. New licences would be issued, not on a fixed licence fee, but as a proportion of the revenues generated by the licensee, with the proportion depending on the area where the service was offered. The existing licensees under the old policy could migrate from a fixed licence fee to the revenue-sharing model from August 1999. But the question of arrears of the telecom companies under the old licence regime in licence fee on a pro-rata basis until end-July 1999 remained. Jagmohan, the minister of telecommunications '. . . insisted that moral hazard issues were involved and banks must encash the guarantees from private operators. In his view, any other course would confer a largess with serious public criticism . . . Vajpayee took the audacious step of moving Jagmohan out of the Telecom Ministry of Housing and Urban Affairs. The PM took over the portfolio himself on 8 June 1999. Thereafter, following many rounds of discussion with Soli (Sorabjee, Attorney General) . . . earlier practice of fixed licence fee was replaced effectively by a revenue-sharing agreement.'[11] With the new policy, telecom tariffs fell and telecommunications vastly improved. In August 2003, TRAI submitted its report on a two-phase roadmap for how licences should be allocated to telecom companies under a Unified Access Service Licence (UASL) regime. These recommendations were endorsed by the government as its UASL policy in October 2003.

Disinvestment

Disinvestment, either through strategic sales (involving an effective transfer of control and management to a private entity) or an offer for sale to the public, with the government retaining control of the management, gathered some speed during the second NDA regime. The strategic sales included Bharat Aluminium Co. Ltd, Hindustan Zinc Ltd, twenty-one hotels of Hotel Corporation of India and Indian Tourism Development Corporation, Jessop and Company Ltd and Modern Food Industries (India) Ltd. Valuations realized by strategic sales were found to be higher than by minority stake sale. Disinvestment raised ₹21,163.7 crore in the aggregate against the target of ₹38,500 crore during this period.

Other reforms and measures

In the Interim Budget for 2004–05, to reduce transaction costs, stamp duty on all instruments, where the Union government had the authority to fix rates, was halved. The White Revolution in India was continuing. Production of milk, which was 56 million tons in 1991–92 when milk was delicensed and subjected to the Milk and Milk Product Order (MMPO), had gone up to 81 million tons in 2001–02. Budget 2002–03 announced an amendment of MMPO to remove restrictions on new milk processing industries while continuing to regulate health and safety conditions. With this reform boost to the sector, milk production would go up from 81 million tons in 2001–02 to 128 million tons in 2011–12.

A major finding of researchers was that growth and employment creation was positively related not so much to the size of the firm but to how old it was. Despite the report of various expert committees and research findings regarding the adverse impact of reservation for SSI on employment and growth, the number of items reserved for manufacture by SSI had only gone up during the first seventeen years since its introduction in 1967. It had increased from forty-seven on 1 April 1967, to 807 (according to the newly adopted NIC codes, 504 according to the old classification) on 26 April 1978 and further to a peak of 873 on 18 October 1984. In March 1998, when the first NDA government took office, the number of items reserved for SSI was still high at 821. Before the second NDA government demitted office on 22 May 2004, the number of items reserved for SSI came down, particularly under Jaswant Singh as Finance Minister, to 675. Removing all items from SSI reservation would happen only during the successor UPA government.

The allocation for Additional Central Assistance under BMS was enhanced from ₹3684 crore in 1998–99 to ₹4043 crore in 1999–2000. Pradhan Mantri Gramodya Yojana (PMGY), or Prime Minister's Village Development Plan, was launched in 2000–01 across the country to focus on rural roads for connectivity and on human development in the five basic areas of education, health, housing, drinking water and nutrition. Rural electrification was added as an extra component in the succeeding year. PMGY replaced the BMS programme. Programmes for rural connectivity got a half of the allocation, with the other half going to the other components. The road connectivity component, called Pradhan Mantri Gram (Village) Sadak (Roads) Yojana (PMGSY), was fully funded by the Union government.

In 2000, a drought-like situation arose in large parts of the country, for example in Chhattisgarh, Gujarat, Madhya Pradesh, Odisha and Rajasthan. To meet the resulting high demand for wage employment and food security, the FWP was introduced in January 2001 and continued in 2001–02. JRY, after restructuring, streamlining and making it more comprehensive, was launched on 1 April 1999 as Jawahar Gram Samridhi Yojana (JGSY) or village development programme. An ambitious Sampoorna Grameen Rozgar Yojana (SGRY) or comprehensive rural employment programme to create 100 crore man-days of employment in a year was launched on 25 September 2001. Under SGRY, annually, 50 lakh tonnes of food grains, amounting to ₹5000 crore (at economic cost), were proposed to be provided free of cost to the state governments and UTs, and the remaining ₹5000 crore going to them for meeting the cash component of wages and the material cost. The expenditure of the scheme would be shared by the Centre and states in the ratio of 87.5:12.5. The two programmes—FWP and JGSY—for wage employment in rural areas were consolidated into SGRY from 2002–03.

Antyodaya Anna Yojana, or the food for the upliftment of the poorest of the poor programme, was launched by the Prime Minister on Christmas Day 2001. Under the programme, 25 kg of food grains per month were made available for 1 crore of the poorest among the BPL families at the highly subsidised rates of ₹2 per kg of wheat and ₹3 per kg of wheat. The quantity of food grains was enhanced to 35 kg per month from 2002–03. On 2 December 2001, Prime Minister Vajpayee formally launched the Valmiki Ambedkar Awas Yojana (VAAY), or housing programme, to facilitate the construction and upgradation of dwelling units for the urban slum dwellers living below the poverty line with a subsidy of 50 per cent provided by the Union government and the balance coming from the states. Freedom fighter Jayaprakash Narayan was born on 11 October 1902. To mark his birth centenary, the second NDA government announced the Jaya Prakash Rozgar Guarantee Yojana (JPRGY) in the Budget 2002–03. But, it never gained traction. From 2002–03, the credit-cum-subsidy scheme introduced from 1999–2000 for rural families having annual income up to ₹32,000 would become a part of Indira Awaas Yojana.

With its abundant water resources and favourable soil structure, eastern India has the potential to substantially increase the productivity of different crops. However, its full potential was not being realized due to a lack of any major scheme for utilizing the groundwater in this region. A new scheme 'On Farm Water Management, for Increasing Crop Production in Eastern India', was launched in March 2002 in 171 districts of Arunachal Pradesh, Assam, Bihar, Chhattisgarh, Jharkhand, Manipur, Mizoram, Odisha, Uttar Pradesh and West Bengal.

The Kargil war had led Sinha to raise the surcharge on income above ₹1.5 lakh from 10 per cent to 15 per cent during 1999–2000. On the morning of 26 January 2001, on Republic Day, a severe earthquake hit the region around Kutch in Gujarat, killing over 13,000 people and wreaking heavy damage to homes and other physical infrastructure. In 2000–01, the government imposed a surcharge of 2 per cent on all taxpayers for Gujarat earthquake relief. In 2000–01, the tax rebate for senior citizens under income tax was enhanced from ₹10,000 to ₹15,000, effectively making their income up to ₹1.3 lakh tax-free. In 2003–04, Jaswant Singh increased the rebate further to 20,000, resulting in their income up to ₹1.53 lakh tax-free. In the field of excise duty, in 2003–04, his major achievement was the rationalization of excise duty on textiles by abolishing the system of deemed credit and completing the CENVAT chain to promote compliance, encourage modernization and reduce evasion. In the same year, he also reduced the peak rate of customs duty, except on agricultural and dairy products, from 30 per cent to 25 per cent, and from January 2004, to 20 per cent.

In 2000, as part of the Export-Import Policy, there was some relaxation of FDI beyond trading for exports and imports and wholesale cash and carry, in: (i) companies providing after-sales service, (ii) domestic trading of joint ventures, (iii) trading of hi-tech items, including medical and diagnostic items, (iv) items produced by small-scale industries, and some others. A comprehensive Cabinet paper on FDI in retail prepared by the NDA government in 2002 and considered by a Group of Ministers argued that FDI in retail was essential to improve the supply chain in agriculture and bring benefits to both producers and consumers. However, because of opposition from the traders' lobby, there would be no further progress until 2006.

Prevention of Money Laundering Act (PMLA), 2002

From 1988, the UN had been concerned with the problem of laundering of money derived from illicit trafficking in narcotic drugs and psychotropic substances, as well as from other serious crimes. Such laundering had expanded to become a global threat to the integrity, reliability and stability of financial and trade systems and even government structures. There were calls for countermeasures by the international community to deny safe havens to criminals and their illicit proceeds. A significant international initiative in combating money laundering was the formation of the Financial Action Task Force (FATF) at the G-7 summit in Paris in 1989. The UN General Assembly in June 1998 called upon the member states to adopt national anti-money laundering legislation and programme. India responded with the Prevention of Money Laundering Act (PMLA), 2002. Financial Intelligence Unit—India (FIU-IND) was set up on 18 November 2004 as the central agency responsible for receiving, processing, analysing and disseminating information relating to suspect financial transactions.

The Telgi scam

On 19 August 2000, the arrest in Bengaluru of two men who were transporting fake stamp papers snowballed into the big Telgi scam. Their interrogations led to the recovery of a huge amount of fake stamp papers and other legal documents and revealed a network supplying these fake documents. The kingpin of the network was Abdul Karim Telgi, a school dropout who sold peanuts in railway stations in the 1980s. He was absconding at that time.

Telgi had acquired a stamp paper licence in 1994. Over time, Telgi and his team started printing counterfeit documents such as stamp papers, judicial court fee stamps, revenue stamps, special adhesive stamps, foreign bills, brokers' notes, insurance policies, share transfer certificates, insurance agency stamps—and also creating a scarcity of authentic documents. To print the illegal documents, Telgi bribed the officials of Indian Security

Press at Nashik to obtain printing and perforating machines declared as junk and meant to be destroyed. With the help of some officials of the Indian Security Press, he also managed to dispatch legal papers worth hundreds of crores to addresses that did not exist and created a scarcity. One of the problems with Telgi's stamp papers and other such documents was that they were 'real' and as good as the ones produced by the government, only they were produced in an illegal way.

In November 2001, Telgi was arrested when he was going on a pilgrimage to Ajmer Sharif in Rajasthan. The investigations were progressing slowly, and a Special Investigation Team (SIT) was appointed by the court only in November 2003 after anti-corruption activist Kisan Baburao Hazare from Ralegaon Siddhi in Maharashtra, popularly known as Anna Hazare, filed a public interest petition in the Bombay High Court. During interrogations, Telgi claimed that 'he was only a small part of a massive scam, involving politicians and bureaucrats'.[12] According to him, he also learnt 'that the right sum of money into the right pocket at the right time ensures that an official head will look the wrong way when wanted'.[13] On 29 June 2007, Telgi was sentenced to thirteen years of rigorous imprisonment and a fine of ₹202 crore. While many were dissatisfied with the results of the investigations, the unsubstantiated complaints were mostly about the complicity of politicians, bureaucrats and their henchmen in a few states such as Maharashtra and Andhra Pradesh and of some employees of the India Security Press. Yet, for the NDA government, it was a troubling episode.

The Freedom of Information Act

The RTI movement struck a sympathetic nerve across the nation. Various NGOs started proposing model freedom of information laws. The Consumer Education and Research Council (CERC) proposed a draft RTI Act in 1993. In 1996, Parshuram Babaram Sawant, the former Justice of the Supreme Court and chairman of the Press Council of India, drafted a model RTI Law and sent it to Parliament and chief ministers of states. Some of the state governments responded earlier than the union government. In April 1997, Tamil Nadu became the first Indian state to have an RTI Law. In the same month, Prime Minister Deve Gowda, leading the United Front government, constituted a working group under the chairmanship of consumer activist and retired civil servant H.D. Shourie to draft a Freedom of Information bill. The working group report, submitted on 21 May 1997, was discussed in the Chief Ministers' Conference on 24 May 1997. Goa and Tamil Nadu passed an RTI Act in 1997, Madhya Pradesh followed in 1998, and Karnataka, Maharashtra and Rajasthan in 2000.

The Shourie Task Force's draft bill was revised by the central government and, under the NDA government, passed by Parliament as the Freedom of Information Act in December 2002. Since RTI does not find specific mention in Lists of the Seventh Schedule of the Constitution, it applied to both the Centre and the states except for Jammu and Kashmir. There were murmurs of protests by social activists against the Freedom of Information Act, 2002. They complained about the exclusion of information about some organizations (e.g., security and intelligence agencies) and types of information about others (e.g., relating to sovereignty and security of the nation, and cabinet papers) from the ambit of the act, lack of independence of the organizations adjudicating disputes about the application of the act, and inadequate penal provisions against officials defying the law. The delay in notifying the act even after it received Presidential assent was also not acceptable. Furthermore, there were demands for changing the name from 'Freedom of Information' to 'RTI' to emphasize that information was a right of the people, and for better protection for whistle-blowers.

XXV.5 The Long Shadow of Enron and Power Sector Reforms

Electricity had been a problem sector in the Indian economy at least since the mid-1970s. The initial solution to the problem through more generation in the public sector failed because of inadequate public sector resources. The attempt to enlist the private sector and Independent Power Producers (IPPs) in generation foundered because of the lack of confidence in the ability of the sector to pay for the power it procured from the private generators. Even granting 'fast-track' status, with additional incentives and guaranteed returns with counter-guarantees, to the eight of the most promising IPPs did not prove successful. From the early 1990s, DPC, the fast-track IPP, promoted by Enron, had got embroiled in controversies about lack of probity in award of government contracts. There were issues about the roots of the power sector problem as well. The IPP, including DPC, turned out to be—in Deepak Parekh's words—nothing but ways of pouring more water into a leaking bucket to ensure the consistency and quantity of leaks.[14] Even Vajpayee's second NDA government came under DPC's and Enron's long shadow.

The long shadow of Enron

The DPC had started supplying power from May 1999. From December 1999, the MSEB started falling behind in its payment schedule and from June 2000, it started defaulting on its monthly dues. MSEB, already in financial distress, had three serious problems with the take-or-pay agreement in terms of tariff fixed in dollar terms. First, demand was lower than anticipated, resulting in low dispatch. With capacity charges payable regardless of energy consumed, the tariff was higher at lower levels of dispatch. Second, the rupee had depreciated consistently and stood above ₹46 to the dollar as compared to ₹32 assumed when the contract was signed. Third the price of oil, which determined the price of LPG and naphtha feedstock, had more than doubled from around $13 per barrel during the negotiations.

In the meantime, as we have already noted, Sharad Pawar, after being expelled from the Congress on 20 May 1999, had gone on to form the NCP. The elections to the Lok Sabha and the Maharashtra Vidhan Sabha were held simultaneously in early September 1999. Even though they fought against each other in the polls, after the results were out on 7 October 1999, in the Vidhan Sabha with 288 seats, Congress with seventy-five seats, NCP with fifty-eight, Peasants and Workers Party of India with five seats, SJP and CPI(M) with two each, and ten independents, came together to form a UPA government under Chief Minister Vilasrao Deshmukh on 18 October 1999.

MSEB refused to pay DPC, and in February 2001, DPC invoked the counter-guarantee of the Union government. The matter got embroiled in the courts. An Energy Review Committee under the chairmanship of Madhav Godbole was constituted on 9 February 2001, and on 10 April

2001, in its report it pointed out that, at that time, the average tariff realizations for commercial and HT industrial categories were ₹4.48 and ₹3.99 per unit respectively, while the average domestic and agricultural tariff realisations were ₹1.80 and ₹0.46 per unit, respectively.

Given its tariff structure, MSEB could not afford to buy power from DPC. Effort to find SEBs in other states to purchase DPC base load power met with limited success. In July 2001, Enron CEO Kenneth Lay formally announced Enron's intention to sell its equity stake in DPC. Arbitration proceedings had started in a commercial court in London, and the court, in October 2001, restrained the State government from taking any legal action against arbitration initiated by DPC. On 6 November 2001, Enron announced that it would serve a termination notice to close the power project after 19 November and to transfer the 2184 MW asset to MSEB and demand compensation based on independent valuation. In response to a lawsuit filed by domestic lenders, such as SBI and ICICI, demanding immediate recommencement of the plant to protect their investments, on 9 November 2001, the Mumbai High Court issued a stay order against DPC's final notice of termination.

In the meantime, the US economy was in recession from March 2001. In November 1999, Enron had launched EnronOnline, an electronic trading website for commodities, and before the recession, with high speculation about the bright prospects of almost all internet-related companies—the dot-com bubble—had flourished. The dot-com bubble burst.

'Enron Corporation itself, the main promoter of DPC, was in trouble in the US.' Enron had flourished during the dot-com bubble—a stock market bubble—in the late 1990s, when there was high speculation about the bright prospects of almost all internet-related companies. The US economy, however, was in recession from March 2001.

Intriguingly, Enron's share had peaked at $90.75 on 23 August 2000, and Enron managed to escape a meltdown in stock prices until 2 December 2001. But it transpired that it managed mainly by taking advantage of the minimal regulatory environment. Enron had adopted the marked-to-market accounting method and, by using not actual cost but 'fair value', logged estimated profits for actual profits. By April 2001, analysts had started questioning Enron's accounts and accounting policy.

In mid-August 2001, Enron's broadband division reported losses of $137 million and analysts dropped their ratings of Enron stock. Arthur Andersen LLP was the accounting firm for Enron, and in October 2011, its legal counsel told it to destroy all Enron files except the most basic documents. In October 2001, Enron reported losses of $618 million, and also that it was facing a probe by the US Securities and Exchange Commission. From $84.88 at end-August 2000, Enron's share price declined to $13.90 in end-October 2001. In November 2001, Enron admitted that it had been inflating its income by around $586 million since 1997. Just as the disagreement between DPC and the MSEB, Maharashtra government and Government of India was coming to a head, the main promoter of Dabhol, Enron, filed for bankruptcy under Chapter 11 in the US. Shortly before declaring bankruptcy, Enron walked out of the DPC by selling its 66 per cent shares to Bechtel and General Electric.

Power sector reforms

The 1990s with its IPP policy have been described as 'a wasted decade' in terms of power sector reform by some researchers. Power shortages continued to plague the economy while power utilities did not have enough money to pay their dues. Accelerated Power Development Programme (APDP) was launched in February 2000 to finance specific projects related to renovation and modernization, life extension and up-rating of old thermal and hydel power plants, upgrading and strengthening of sub-T&D network (below 33 KV or 66 KV), including energy accounting and metering in the distribution circles in a phased manner. Yet, progress was very limited. At end-February 2001, the SEBs owed about ₹41,473 crore, including ₹15,746 crore by way of surcharge/interest on delayed payments.

The prevailing conditions threatened to precipitate a collapse in the power situation, cripple the finances of the state governments and jeopardize economic growth of the country. A Chief Ministers' Conference in March 2001 expressed grave concern about the crisis engulfing this sector, and following the conference, an expert group under the chairmanship of Montek Singh Ahluwalia, member, Planning Commission, was appointed to examine the issues. In early May, the group pointed out how the large outstanding dues to CPSEs arose 'not because of any exceptional event, or because of problems that arose in the past and are no longer operative, but because the current operations of SEBs have been and continue to be inherently unviable. Revenue realisation per unit of power produced is much less than the average cost of production and supply, with the result that all SEBs are running large current deficits. Since these deficits are not covered by budgetary subventions from the State Government, they show up in non-payment of CPSE dues as also defaults on other loans.'

The Ahluwalia Expert Group recommended a sharing of the burden of resolution of the arrears among CPSEs, their owner the Union government, and the state governments participating in the scheme, together with some reform conditionalities. For better discipline, it recommended a reduction in power and coal supplies from CPSEs for default in current payments, adjustment of overdues for ninety days or more against releases from the Union government, and reform-based performance milestones such as setting up of SERCs, metering of distribution feeders and improvement in revenue realization in MOUs to be signed with the ministry of power.

After the Ahluwalia Report, the expert group headed by N.K. Singh, member (energy), Planning Commission, suggested a one-time settlement of dues for capital restructuring of the SEBs, including the provision of Structural Adjustment Loans to tide over the financial crisis, make them operationally viable and improve their credit rating. The recommendation was accepted in the Union Budget of 2002–03 as the Accelerated Power Development and Reform Programme (APDRP) with an allocation of ₹3500 crore. States' access to the APDRP funds was based on agreed reform milestones, 'the centre piece of which would be the narrowing and ultimate elimination of the gap between unit cost of supply and revenue realisation within a specified time frame.'[15] APDP was project-based and input-focused, rather than being performance and outcome-oriented. The Tenth Plan (2002–2007) recrafted it into APDRP of financial support to lower aggregate technical and commercial (AT&C) losses, improve financial and economic performance of the electricity sector, modernize T&D and improve customer service.

In September 2002, the Deepak Parekh Committee on 'Structuring of APDRP, Reform Framework and Principles of Financial Restructuring of SEBs' recommended 'a composite framework comprising of unbundling and introduction of competition, concentrated zones, multi-year regulation and privatization.' Unfortunately, APDRP achieved only modest results during the Tenth Plan. Most APDRP projects were sanctioned during 2002 and 2003, got delayed and witnessed a diversion of funds for routine operation and maintenance. Funds—with ₹20,000 crore earmarked for investment in modernisation and ₹20,000 crore as incentive for cash loss reduction—remained unutilized. For AT&C loss reduction, only ₹1500 crore of the ₹20,000 crore was earned, and at the national level, such reduction was from 36.8 per cent to only 33.8 per cent.

The Electricity Bill, 2001, introduced in the Lok Sabha in August 2001, aimed at consolidation of the laws relating to the generation, transmission, distribution, trading and use of electricity and measures conducive to the development of electricity industry. The corresponding Electricity Act, 2003, which came two years later, delicensed generation and freed captive generation from all restrictions apart from compliance with technical standards and establishing connectivity to the power grid. Transmission, distribution, and trading of electricity continued to be subject to licensing. Transmission remained reserved for companies owned by the Union or state governments. The Act allowed open access in transmission with a provision for surcharge for taking care of the extant level of cross-subsidy but envisaged a gradual phase-out of the surcharge. The SEBs, owned by state governments, were carrying out generation and T&D. This led to difficulties in diagnosing the relative inefficiencies in the three activities and the root cause of the huge AT&C losses which crippled the financial viability of the SEBs. The Electricity Act, 2003 required unbundling of these three activities by the SEBs. It also made metering mandatory for electricity supply and provisions relating to electricity theft more stringent. It required the setting up of SERC as well as an appellate tribunal to hear appeals against the decision of CERC and SERCs. For rural electrification, it allowed standalone systems for generation and distribution in rural and remote areas, and management of rural distribution by panchayat, cooperative societies, NGOs and franchisees.

In 1994, the National Development Council and the Sharad Pawar Committee had set the target of 100 per cent rural household electrification as 2010. Despite all the financial difficulties in the sector, this target date was brought forward to 2007 in the Conference of Chief Ministers in

2001. In his Budget speech for 2001–02, Finance Minister Yashwant Sinha reported that about 80,000 villages remained unelectrified. In the following year's Budget, he announced a new interest subsidy scheme called the Accelerated Rural Electrification Programme (AREP) with an outlay of ₹164 crore. AREP was introduced in 2003–04 for implementation by state governments through SEBs/Power Utilities.

To electrify all villages and households by 2012 through local renewable energy sources and decentralized technologies, along with the conventional grid connection, the Rural Electricity Supply Technology Mission was initiated on 11 September 2002. The Kutir Jyoti Programme launched under Rajiv Gandhi in 1988–89 was consolidated in the 'Accelerated Electrification of one lakh villages and one crore Households' in May 2004. One of the goals of the Electricity Act, 2003 was electrifying all villages by 2007 and all households by 2012.

Power sector reforms have fallen short of what had been envisaged in 2003 while passing the Electricity Act. Even eighteen years after the Electricity Act was passed, apart from five small states (Arunachal Pradesh, Goa, Mizoram, Nagaland and Sikkim) and three UTs (Jammu and Kashmir, Ladakh and Puducherry) that continued with a vertically integrated power department, there were the six states of Himachal Pradesh, Kerala, Manipur, Punjab, Tamil Nadu and Tripura, which had separated only transmission from 'generation and distribution' which remained together. Metering, particularly of supplies to farmers, has run into—and continues to have— serious problems. AT&C losses were as much as 21.83 per cent in 2019-20.

XXV.6 'India Shining', and NDA voted out in 2004

While the negotiations among the Union and the states about the introduction of VAT were ongoing, the term of the Thirteenth Lok Sabha was coming to an end in late 2004. BJP was buoyed by its clean sweep of the Vidhan Sabha polls in 2003 in Chhattisgarh, Madhya Pradesh and Rajasthan. On 27 January 2004, Prime Minister Vajpayee called on President Narayanan to convey the advice of his Cabinet to dissolve the Thirteenth Lok Sabha on 6 February. Finance Minister Jaswant Singh presented an Interim Budget for 2004–05 on 3 February 2004 and after passage of the vote on accounts, President Narayanan dissolved the Thirteenth Lok Sabha on 6 February. On 29 February 2004, the Election Commission announced election to the Fourteenth Lok Sabha in four phases on: 20 April (141 constituencies), 26 April (137 constituencies), 5 May (eighty-three constituencies) and 10 May (182 constituencies). The NDA under Vajpayee lost the election.

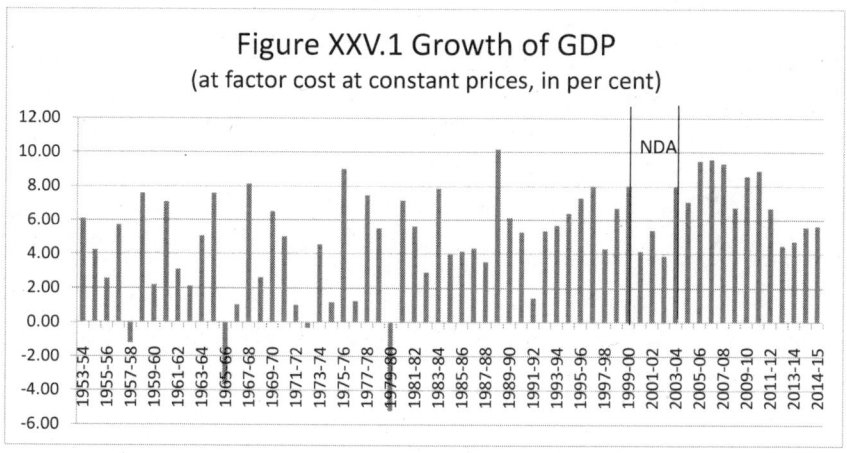

Figure XXV.1 Growth of GDP
(at factor cost at constant prices, in per cent)

Growth in 2014-15 and 2015-16 of Gross Value Added (GVA) at basic prices have been deflated by 27 per cent to approximate growth of GDP at factor cost at constant prices. Growth of both GVA and GDP is available for the two previous years and GVA growth exceeds that of GDP by 21 per cent in 2012-13 and by 33 per cent in 2013-14, yielding an average of 27 per cent.
Source: RBI Handbook of Statistics on the Indian Economy.

The NDA had delivered annual average growth of almost 6 per cent in its five years' rule (Figure XXV.1). Growth was at 8 per cent in the first and last years of its rule, a record surpassed in only four years between 1951–52 and 1998–99. WPI inflation, after declining from 5.9 per cent in 1998–99 to 3.3 per cent in 1999–2000, rose to 7.2 per cent in 2000–01, only to decline to 3.6 per cent in 2001–02 and 3.4 per cent in 2002–03. There was an increase thereafter to 5.5 per cent in such inflation in 2003–04, the last full year under the second NDA government. The buoyant growth was also accompanied by some progress in revenue mobilization and fiscal consolidation. Tax revenue of the Union government, as a proportion of GDP, had gone up mildly from 6.1 per cent in 1997–98 to 6.6 per cent in 2003–04. The corresponding decline in its fiscal deficit as a proportion of GDP was from 5.7 per cent to 4.3 per cent.

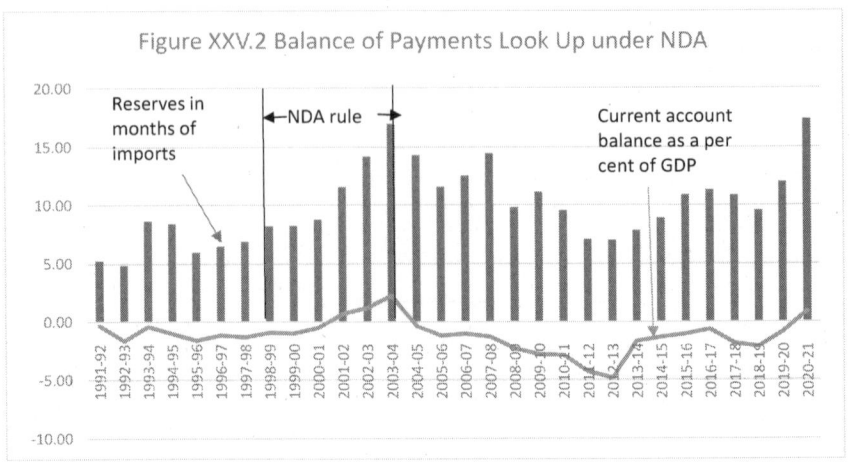

Figure XXV.2 Balance of Payments Look Up under NDA

GDP (at current market prices) refer to 2004-05 series until 2003-04 and 2011-12 series thereafter.
Source: RBI Handbook of Statistics on the Indian Economy

Most dramatic was the change in the balance of payments (Figure XXV.2). The current account deficit, after declining from $5.5 billion in 1997-98 to $2.7 billion in 2000–01, turned into a surplus of $3.4 billion in 2001– 02. After increasing further to $6.3 billion in the next year, it reached a high of $14.1 billion in 2003–04. Net capital flows (both investment and loans), which were $10 billion in 1997–98, remained range bound between $8.1 billion and $11.1 billion in the following three years. In the last full year 2003–04 of the NDA rule, there was a sharp increase in net capital flows to $17.4 billion. Consequently, foreign exchange reserves (inclusive of gold and reserve tranche) went up almost four-fold from $29.4 billion in 1997–98 to $113 billion in 2003–04.

The accumulation of foreign exchange reserves represented the purchase of foreign exchange by the RBI to prevent a sudden appreciation of the rupee and maintain orderly market conditions. However, to avoid inflationary pressures from the rupees released because of such purchases, there was also a need to neutralize the injection of rupees by open market sales of government securities held by the RBI. To conduct its open market operations, the RBI had pursued a policy of converting the entire stock of Union government's non-transferable 4.6 per cent Special Securities to marketable securities by 2003–04. However, even these got depleted. In 2003–04, RBI started using its Liquidity Adjustment Facility (LAF), which was primarily for managing short-term liquidity, for managing capital flows, not a very desirable outcome. Around mid-March 2004, the RBI almost ran out of government securities. On 25 March 2004, the Union government and the RBI formally signed an Memorandum of Understanding (MoU) detailing the rationale and operational modalities of the Market Stabilization Scheme (MSS), which would be effective from April 2004. The surfeit on the foreign exchange front bolstered the 'feel-good factor' and the MSS in a way represented the embarrassment of riches. In fact, the perceived 'feel-good factor' from robust economic growth, reinforced by BJP victory in Chhattisgarh, Madhya Pradesh and Rajasthan Vidhan Sabha elections in December 2003, led Prime Minister Vajpayee to go to the polls six months early on.

India Shining was an advertising campaign to promote India internationally. The media campaign was conducted as part of the India Development Initiative, the budget provision for which was '. . . to support an overall, general and imaginative promotion of India, its trade and foster techno-economic and intellectual cooperation with other countries.'[16] The campaign highlighted the steps the NDA government took to boost growth, slash interest rates, stabilize prices, expand roads, telecom and health networks and offer free basic education. From early December 2003, the advertisements in Indian and international newspapers and TV channels created a controversy about whether it was a ruse to promote the feel-good factor and attracting votes to the ruling NDA in general and BJP in particular. The campaign closed on 20 February 2004 with the Election Commission banning the campaign until the ballot ended on 10 May.

The campaign was, according to the NDA, clearly aspirational—aimed at the emerging middle class with dreams. Projecting colourful images of prosperity and cheer, it did not ask people to do things '. . . for their family and nation, even to sacrifice for them', but urged people 'to do things for themselves'.[17] The opposition parties, particularly the Congress, staged a scathing criticism of the 'India Shining' claim of the campaign. In the poll campaign, for example, Sonia Gandhi, the Congress President, visited the Holambi Kalan area in north-west Delhi where slum dwellers of Yamuna Pushta (embankment) were being relocated. Pointing towards the slum clusters, she asked: 'Where is India Shining?'[18] The campaign was described by some as 'lopsided' with its focus on the urban growth story 'while neglecting the distress and backwardness of the rural landscape'.[19] Some considered it to be the 'worst political advertisement strategies in Indian history' and dubbed it as 'one of the biggest reasons for the NDA government's failure to return to power'.[20] Yet others described the NDA defeat as 'a revolt of rising expectations' and 'set-back to the neo-liberal agenda'.

Was India Shining when India went to the polls in 2004? The answer could be yes and also no. Growth had gained momentum and after growing at 8 per cent in 2003–04, the economy maintained a growth rate of 7.1 per cent, 9.5 per cent, 9.6 per cent and 9.3 per cent in the subsequent four years. Yet, India was still a country with millions of poor, illiterates and people suffering from ill health, and far from its elusive glory. The two critical questions, however, that remain are whether the India Shining campaign was appropriate for gaining votes and was the 2004 vote a vote against the NDA's economic policies.

According to former deputy premier Lal Krishna Advani: 'These phrases, though valid in themselves, were inappropriate for our election campaign . . . By making them verbal icons of our election campaign, we gave our political opponents an opportunity to highlight other aspects of India's contemporary reality—poverty and uneven development, unemployment among the youth, problems faced by the farmers—which questioned our claim. The viciously negative campaign of Congress and Communists, replete with falsehoods, prevailed over the positive campaign of the NDA.'[21] The campaign to highlight a commendable performance was portrayed as a cruel joke on a nation where a third of the people were still below the poverty line.

But, would the BJP-led NDA have won the 2004 election were it not for the India Shining campaign? The answer again is perhaps in the negative. The proportion of popular votes won by the BJP came down only marginally from 23.75 per cent in 1999 to 22.16 per cent in 2004. For the Congress, it came down even more—from 28.30 per cent to 26.53 per cent! Yet, seats won by Congress went up from 114 in 1999 to 145 in 2004, while the BJP's tally went down from 182 to 138. The reason was the adverse distribution of its popular votes across seats. BJP lost votes in critical seats and states where it needed them to retain the seats.

The loss of BJP was particularly pronounced in UP—its tally came down from twenty-nine to ten. BJP's loss of forty-four seats between 1999 and 2004 is more than adequately accounted for by UP (nineteen), Bihar and Jharkhand (seventeen), Andhra Pradesh (seven), and Delhi (six). These states had Muslims accounting for more than 10 per cent of the voters, and the communal riots following the Godhra incident in BJP-ruled Gujarat in 2002 may have played a role in BJP's poor performance in these states. Last but not the least was the break-up of the old NDA alliance and the poor performance of BJP's allies.

In Andhra Pradesh, ally TDP led by Chandrababu Naidu saw its tally come down from twenty-nine to four between 1999 and 2004. In Tamil Nadu, DMK led by M. Karunanidhi had been BJP's partner in the NDA since 1999. It left the NDA in December 2003 and joined the Congress for an electoral alliance. The BJP-led NDA had the AIADMK led by Jayalalitha as a partner. The seats won by Congress's partner DMK went up from twelve to sixteen between 1999 and 2004, while those of AIADMK went down from ten to nil! In West Bengal, BJP's partner AITC saw its tally come down from eight to one. It can be argued that the TDP, AIADMK and AITC lost in their respective states because they were tainted by their alliances with the BJP. But the ascription of such a one-way causality may not be the whole truth.

Was the 2004 electoral mandate a vote against the economic policies of the NDA? It looks unlikely as the Congress led the UPA to victory and the 1.6 percentage points decline in the vote share of the BJP was less than the 1.8 percentage point decline in the vote share of the Congress. The electoral outcome in 2004, particularly the importance of regional parties, once again demonstrated the critical role that identity issues such as language, region, caste/tribe and religion were continuing to play in Indian politics. If a regional party, such as DMK, which had been a constituent of the NDA and bore responsibility for its economic policies, increased its tally from twelve in 1999 to sixteen in 2004 just because it shifted from the NDA to the UPA? The electoral fortunes of regional parties had more to do with local and identity issues than issues of broad economic policy, and the fortunes of a national alliance such as NDA or UPA would partly depend upon which regional parties were hitched to their main wagons.

Even though a voter may have supported the economic policies of the NDA, they may have had a strong preference for the identity politics that a regional party championed. Furthermore, the Congress had a much more effective electoral strategy—or at least it turned out that way post-facto—in consolidating its votes with that of its allies and winning many more seats with fewer votes than before! Because of the Congress leaving a few dozen seats to its allies, its vote share may have suffered a reversal, but the number of seats won went up from 114 to 145. The BJP's seats, on the other hand, came down from 182 to 138. The outcome for the Congress and its pre-poll allies was even more startling—an increase from 136 in 1999 to 221 in 2004 relative to a decline from 299 to 188 for the NDA. At the regional level, the choice of the wrong alliance partners or going it alone could seriously dent the poll fortunes of a coalition. And that is what seems to have happened to the NDA in 2004.

XXVI

The First UPA Government

In 1998, in Panchmarhi, the CWC had announced that it would consider coalitions only when it was absolutely essential. Out of power since 1996, the Congress changed its stance towards coalitions. In 2003, in its fourteen-point Shimla declaration, it called for a joint front of all secular forces against the BJP-led NDA. In many states, such as Gujarat and Maharashtra, where the electoral battle was mainly between the Congress and the BJP, a coalition of non-BJP parties could pay rich dividends. Such coalitions could also be rewarding in states, such as Bihar and Tamil Nadu, where the BJP and a non-Congress party vied for victory, with Congress occupying the third or fourth position. The new approach of the Congress to coalitions was manifest when on 26 December 2003, Congress president Sonia Gandhi said that the would-be Congress-led coalition's partners would collectively decide on the leadership in the event of a victory.

Meanwhile, the NDA was getting fractured. In protest against the communal riots in Gujarat in the wake of the Godhra massacre, on 29 April 2002, Union Coal and Mines Minister Ram Vilas Paswan had resigned from the Cabinet and, with his three other Members of the Lok Sabha from the Lok Janashakti Party (LJP), parted ways with the NDA. The Prevention of Terrorist Act (POTA), 2002 had come into force after the attack on the Indian Parliament on 13 December 2001, and DMK had complained against POTA's misuse by the ruling AIADMK to harass its leaders and workers. It wanted POTA repealed, and when it was not, the

DMK quit the NDA on 20 December 2003. Soon, the traditional allies of the DMK, PMK and MDMK, had followed suit. On 9 February 2004, three days after the dissolution of the Thirteenth Lok Sabha, INLD led by Om Prakash Chautala in Haryana snapped ties, complaining against the NDA's anti-farmer stance and non-implementation of the 2002 Supreme Court judgment on the Sutlej Yamuna Link (SYL) canal. Elections to the Lok Sabha were scheduled for April-May 2014.

Congress managed to stitch together a pre-poll alliance in different states with seventeen parties. Seat sharing among the allies was restricted to only specific states and sometimes to specific seats within a state and hence incomplete. In Andhra Pradesh, it reached an understanding with Telangana Rashtra Samithi (TRS), the party formed by K. Chandrashekar Rao in 2001 over the demand for a separate state of Telangana. It worked out a pre-poll alliance in Bihar with RJD led by Lalu Prasad Yadav and LJP of Paswan. Its alliance partners were NCP led by Sharad Pawar and RPI (Athawale) (RPI(A)) in Goa and Maharashtra; JMM led by Shibu Soren in Jharkhand; DMK, MDMK and PMK in Tamil Nadu. The contrasting postures of the BJP and the Congress were also manifest in the change in the number of seats contested by the two parties between 1999 and 2004: up from 339 to 364 for BJP, down from 453 to 417 for Congress.

Counting had started on May 13, and with only electronic voting machines used for balloting, the outcome was clear by early evening. The newspaper *The Hindu*, in an editorial, commented next morning '. . . this is the first general election since 1977 that has upset every electoral calculation and poll prediction. No pollster or party leader of any significance allowed for a verdict in which the Congress, not the Bharatiya Janata Party, would emerge as the single largest party in the 14th Lok Sabha. Nobody could foresee the Congress-led alliance ending up 30 seats ahead of the BJP-led combine.'[1] Not too many had expected or apprehended that with 'India Shining', the BJP-led NDA would be voted out of power. Neither did the Congress, with its prospective allies, expect to form a government.

The electoral strategy of leaving a few dozen seats to its allies led the vote share of the Congress coming down from 28.3 per cent in 1999 to 26.5 per cent in 2004, while the decline in vote share of the BJP was only from 23.8 per cent to 22.2 per cent. But, in terms of seats, with considerable consolidation of votes from the allies, the dividend for the

Congress was rich—an increase from 114 to 145. The BJP's seats, on the other hand, came down from 182 to 138. The outcome for the Congress and its pre-poll allies was even more startling—an increase from 136 in 1999 to 221 in 2004 relative to a decline from 299 to 188 for the NDA.

In 2004, Sonia Gandhi as the president of the Congress party leading the coalition was a 'natural' choice for the prime minister's post. But controversy arose from her birth as a foreigner. Sonia Gandhi surprised everyone by declaring that, after listening to her inner voice, she would not be the prime minister. Dr Manmohan Singh, a respected technocrat, who had contested Indian elections only once and lost, was Sonia Gandhi's choice for the prime minister's post. Singh, described by one of his former media advisers as the 'accidental prime minister', assumed charge on 22 May 2004.[2] In 1977, Indira Gandhi was the Prime Minister and Devkant Baruah the Congress president. But after that, this was the first time when the Congress Prime Minister was not the party president. Under Indira Gandhi, there were no doubts about where the real power rested, but this time in 2004, it was different at least for some time.

The Congress and its pre-poll allies did not have an absolute majority in the Lok Sabha with 543 members. After the election, Congress went on to form the UPA with Sonia Gandhi as its chairperson. All India Majlis-e-Ittehadul Muslimeen (AIMIM), with Asaduddin Owaisi elected from Hyderabad, joined the UPA, taking its strength to 222. With a general tendency to combine to prevent the BJP from coming to power, the Mulayam Singh-led SJP (with thirty-six seats), Mayawati-led BSP (nineteen), and the left parties, which had fifty-seven seats in the Lok Sabha decided to extend outside support to the UPA. CPI(M) allowed its MP Somnath Chatterjee to become the Lok Sabha Speaker, but along with its other left partners, it was afraid of not being able to exercise sufficient control over economic policies, and declined the offer to join the government. Instead, in return for its support, the left got Congress to agree to protect the extant labour regulations, review the 2003 Electricity Act, which separated the generation and transmission functions of state electricity boards, and generally to desist from privatizing profit-making CPSEs. They got it enshrined as the UPA's National Common Minimum Programme (NCMP), which was released five days after Manmohan Singh assumed office. Soon, the UPA government would have eight flagship programmes: Sarva Shiksha Abhiyan, Mid-day Meal Scheme, Rajiv Gandhi Drinking Water Mission, Total Sanitation Campaign (TSC), National Rural Health Mission (NRHM), ICDS, National Rural Employment Guarantee Scheme (NREGS) and Jawaharlal Nehru National Urban Renewal Mission (JNNURM).

Chidambaram, the former finance minister in the United Front ministries, became the finance minister and continued to be so during the entire tenure of the first Manmohan Singh government. Two significant reforms that had been initiated by the previous NDA government but got implemented by the first UPA government were the VAT policy at the state level and FRBMA.

XXVI.1 Value Added Tax (VAT)

On 18 June 2004, in the meeting of the Empowered Committee of State Finance Ministers, a broad consensus was arrived at among the states to introduce VAT with effect from 1 April 2005. In his Budget Speech for 2004–05, on 8 July 2004, Finance Minister Chidambaram welcomed the decision and went on to add: '. . . I urge all States that have not yet passed the relevant VAT legislation to do so before the end of 2004. International experience, as well as the experience of the State of Haryana, suggests that VAT will lead to an increase in revenue and not a loss in revenue. Nevertheless, in order to give comfort to the States, I propose to evolve a formula for determining the compensation for the loss of revenue, if any.' In this context, the Union government also agreed to compensate any possible revenue loss in the first year, 75 per cent of revenue loss in the second year and 50 per cent of revenue loss in the third year after implementation of VAT. Revenue loss was calculated as the difference between potential sales tax revenue in the absence of VAT and revenue from VAT.

Sixteen states—Andhra Pradesh, Arunachal Pradesh, Bihar, Goa, Himachal Pradesh, Jammu and Kashmir, Karnataka, Kerala, Maharashtra, Mizoram, Nagaland, Odisha, Punjab, Sikkim, Tripura and West Bengal—and three UTs—Delhi, Dadra and Nagar Haveli and Daman and Diu—implemented VAT from 1 April 2005. Assam, Manipur and Meghalaya followed from 1 May 2005, Uttarakhand from 1 October 2005, and the UT of Chandigarh on 1 December 2005. Chattisgarh, Gujarat, Jharkhand, Madhya Pradesh and Rajasthan implemented VAT from 1 April 2006. The last three to join were Tamil Nadu on 1 January 2007, the UT of Puducherry on 1 July 2007 and UP on 1 January 2008. Two UTs, namely, Andaman and Nicobar Islands and Lakshadweep, did not and do not have any sales tax or VAT.

CST at 4 per cent since July 1975 on inter-state sales was a problem in attaining the goal of a destination-based VAT and building a unified Indian market. But its abolition or reduction entailed revenue risks for states. With the promise of compensation for any loss of revenue from the introduction of VAT, there was some attenuation of the resistance from states, and the CST rate was reduced from 4 per cent to 3 per cent with effect from 1 April 2007, further to 2 per cent from 1 June 2008, and thereafter by 1 percentage point in the two succeeding years to nil from 1 April 2010. Some compensation was paid to the states for the loss of 'potential' revenue according to the agreed formula.

XXVI.2 Fiscal Responsibility and Budget Management Act (FRBMA), 2003

Implementation of the FRBMA, enacted by the second NDA government on 26 August 2003, was awaiting the notification of the rules. It was the successor UPA government that notified the rules and brought the FRBMA into force from 5 July 2004. FRBMA was an important institutional expression of Indian democracy to safeguard fiscal prudence and provide support for macroeconomic balance. With the FRBMA in force, traditional annual budgeting moved to a more meaningful medium-term fiscal planning framework.

It took more than three years for the FRBM bill to be passed by Parliament, and to become an act after receiving the President's assent. Some claim that the teeth of the FRBM Bill were removed before being passed. The explicit targets for the reduction of the fiscal and revenue deficits as well as the cap on government borrowing were eliminated from the legislation. Instead of mandating a 0.5 per cent annual cut in deficits, the act said the Centre would take appropriate measures to eliminate revenue deficit by 31 March 2008 and set annual targets for reduction of fiscal and revenue deficits till then. The targeted cap on government borrowings at 50 per cent of GDP by 2010 was removed and left to the discretion of the Centre. The act also provided an escape clause for not meeting the targets on grounds of national calamity, security or other exceptional circumstances. The jurisdiction of civil courts to question the legality of any action taken by the Centre under this act was also removed. Therefore, for its non-justiciability, the FRBMA has been compared to the Directive Principles of State Policy in the Constitution.

XXVI.3 Education Cess, Health, Urban Renewal and Some Other Reforms

Education cess

In his Budget for 2004–05, Chidambaram announced an education cess of 2 per cent to be applicable on all taxes, including personal income tax, as contained in the NCMP. The proceeds of the cess, estimated at ₹4000-5000 crore annually, were to be earmarked for basic education, including the mid-day meal scheme. In 2007-08, he increased the cess to 3 per cent, with the additional 1 per cent earmarked for secondary and higher education and the expansion of capacity by 54 per cent for reservations for socially and educationally backward classes.

Opposition to the NHAI cess on petrol and high-speed diesel during the rule of NDA I had been muted. So was the opposition to the education cess in 2004–05. In a maturing democracy, it showed the people's growing acceptance of the need for adequate public financing of road infrastructure and education and a willingness to pay for it.

Rashtriya Swasthya Bima Yojana and National Rural Health Scheme

The central government launched the Rashtriya Swasthya Bima Yojana (RSBY) or National Health Insurance Scheme on 1 April 2008 to provide health insurance coverage for BPL families of workers in the unorganized sector. The implementation agencies, after verification of the eligibility of beneficiaries, would issue smart cards to them for their identification. The beneficiaries would be eligible for such in-patient care insurance benefits as determined by the respective state governments. But the minimum benefits recommended were: (i) cover for the unorganized sector worker and his family of five members, (ii) total sum insured of ₹30,000 per family per annum on a family floater basis, that is, coverage for the entire family under one insurance policy for the family, (iii) cashless attendance to all covered ailments, (iv) coverage of hospitalization expenses for most common illnesses with as few exclusions as possible, (iv) coverage of all pre-existing diseases, and (v) transportation costs (actual with a maximum limit of ₹100 per visit) within an overall limit of ₹1000. The estimated annual premium per family was ₹750, and the cost sharing for this premium between the Centre and the states was on a 75:25 basis, subject to a maximum of ₹565 per family for the Centre. The beneficiary was liable to pay ₹30 per year as a registration fee.

The National Rural Health Mission (NRHM) was launched by Prime Minister Manmohan Singh in April 2005 to bring about dramatic improvement in the health system and the health status of the people, especially in rural areas. By providing universal access to equitable, affordable and quality healthcare, which is accountable and responsive to people's needs, it aimed to achieve the goals set out under the National Health Policy 2002 and the Millennium Development Goals (MDG) during the Mission period (2005–2012). NRHM aimed to reduce maternal mortality rate from 407 to 100 per 1,00,000 live births, infant mortality rate from 60 to 30 per 1000 live births, and the total fertility rate (TFR)—the average number of children born to a woman over her reproductive lifetime—from 3 to 2.1 by 2012. Along with NRHM, the Janani Suraksha Yojana (JSY) or Safe Motherhood Scheme was launched in April 2005 as a 100 per cent centrally funded scheme to provide cash incentive to pregnant women to register, have a JSY card and a Maternal and Child Health Care card, and go for institutional delivery and post-delivery care.

Special emphasis was put on the eight socio-economically backward states of Bihar, Chhattisgarh, Jharkhand, Madhya Pradesh, Orissa, Rajasthan, Uttaranchal and Uttar Pradesh, referred to as the Empowered Action Group (EAG) states, which lagged in the demographic transition with the highest infant mortality rates in the country. To collect accurate, relevant and up-to-date information to initiate action concerning the gaps in the system, in collaboration with the Registrar General of India, an Annual Health Survey was launched in these eight EAG states and in Assam.

A key component of NRHM was to provide every village with a trained female community health activist called ASHA or Accredited Social Health Activist. ASHA was from the village itself, was trained to work as an interface between the community and the public health system and was accountable to the village. ASHA was over and above Anganwadi Workers under ICDS, who organized supplementary nutrition programmes and other supportive activities.

Dhanalakshmi

Dhanalakshmi or Goddess of Wealth Scheme was a conditional cash transfer scheme for the girl child with insurance cover. Launched on 3 March 2008, it aimed at enhancing the value of life of a girl child rather than treating her as a liability. All girl children born after 8 November 2008 and registered under the scheme were given an initial cash incentive of ₹5000. To eradicate child marriage and encourage parents to educate their children, it offered parents an insurance cover of ₹1 lakh when the girl turned eighteen years and was not married.

Delhi-Mumbai Industrial Corridor

In December 2006, the Union government signed a MoU with the Government of Japan to establish a planned industrial development project between the administrative capital city of Delhi and the commercial capital and port city of Mumbai. Costing about $90 billion, it was an ambitious high-tech industrial zone spread across the six states of Gujarat, Haryana, Madhya Pradesh, Maharashtra, Rajasthan and Uttar Pradesh and along the 1500-km-long Western Dedicated Freight Corridor.

Dereservation of items from the small-scale industry list

For creating space for SSI to grow into medium enterprises, the policy of removing items from the list of items reserved for SSI gathered momentum under the first UPA government. Starting with dereservation of eighty-five items on 20 October 2004, by 10 October 2008, the total number of items reserved for SSI was down from 675 before the UPA rule to twenty-one at the end of the UPA's first term. In 2004–05, the government also announced an increase in the ceiling for loans under the Capital Subsidy Scheme for SSI from ₹40 lakh to ₹1 crore and an increase in the rate of subsidy from 12 per cent to 15 per cent.

Capital markets

Beyond the act of liberalizing the industrial sector from SSI reservations, a second act of liberalization related to foreign investment and capital markets. In 2004–05, the sectoral cap on FDI in telecommunications was raised from 49 per cent to 74 per cent, in civil aviation from 40 per cent to 49 per cent, and in insurance from 26 per cent to 49 per cent. To encourage inflows from FII, the procedures for registration and operations of FIIs were streamlined, and the ceiling on FII investments in debt funds was raised from $1 billion to $1.75 billion in 2004–05.

Credit Information Companies (CICs) can play a useful role in providing banks and financial institutions a one-stop source to get reports on how much a prospective borrower has borrowed from other banks and financial institutions and their track record in making interest payments and repaying loans on time. The Credit Information Companies (Regulation) Act, 2005 in May 2005 strengthened the legal mechanism to enable the CICs to collect, process and share credit information on the borrowers of banks and financial institutions.

With the WPI inflation showing a tendency to rise during the first four years of its rule, the UPA government adopted a cautious stance in monetary policy. Thus, from 4.5 per cent on 14 June 2004, it increased the CRR by 25 basis points each on eight occasions between 18 September 2004 and 28 April 2007 to reach 6.5 per cent. In 2007, it was increased further to 7 per cent and 7.5 per cent on 4 August and 10 November, respectively. The SLR, already at its statutory floor of 25 per cent, was left unchanged. The floor on the SLR was acting as a constraint on the monetary operations of the RBI. The Narasimham Committee had recommended reductions in both the SLR and CRR, which in 1990–91, as proportions of total deposit liabilities, were 38.5 per cent and 15 per cent, respectively. To give more liberty to banks and operational flexibility to the RBI, while retaining the ceiling of 40 per cent, the floor of 25 per cent on the SLR was removed by the Banking Regulation (Amendment) Act, 2007.

To avoid any inconvenience arising from the non-availability of stamp paper like around the time of the Telgi scam in the early 1990s, by the Finance Act of 2004, in an amendment to the Indian Stamp Act, 1899, Chidambaram defined 'stamps' to include any mark, seal or endorsement by any agency or person duly authorized by the state government.

To facilitate institutional investment in infrastructure, the India Infrastructure Finance Limited (IIFCL) was set up as a wholly owned government company in January 2006.

Jawaharlal Nehru National Urban Renewal Mission (JNNURM)

NCMP had stressed urban renewal. To improve the quality of life and infrastructure in the cities, JNNURM was launched in December 2005. With the focus on making the cities economically productive, efficient, equitable and responsive, there were two sub-missions—one on urban infrastructure and governance, and the other on basic services to the urban poor. Beyond asset creation, the focus was also on asset maintenance. The aim was to create economically productive, efficient, equitable and responsive cities. It emphasized public-private partnerships and cost recovery to make service providers financially self-sustaining.

In 2005-06, the JNNURM covered seven mega cities, all cities with more than a million population and some other towns, and had an outlay of ₹5500 crore. Chidambaram mentioned the Mumbai Metro Rail Project, the Mumbai Trans Harbour Link, the Mumbai Western Expressway Sealink and the Bangalore Metro Rail Project as examples of projects which could be supported through the Mission. The outlay on JNNURM was kept at ₹6250 crore in 2007–08 (BE) and ₹6886 crore in 2008–09 (BE).

Bharat Nirman

The UPA government launched Bharat Nirman, a programme for developing rural India (Bharat) by building (*nirman*) rural infrastructure, on 16 May 2005. Phase I of the programme included six components: irrigation, roads (Pradhan Mantri Gram Sadak Yojana), electricity (Rajiv Gandhi Grameen Vidyutikaran Yojana launched on 4 April 2005), housing (Indira Awaas Yojana), drinking water and telecom connectivity, and was to be implemented in the period 2005–06 to 2008–09. By 2009, it aimed to irrigate an additional one crore hectares of land, link all villages of 1000 population and all ST and hilly villages having a population of up to 500 with roads, construct 60 lakh additional houses for the poor, ensure supply of drinking water to all remaining 74,000 villages, electricity to all remaining 1,25,000 villages and provide electricity connection to 2.3 crore houses, and provide telephone facility to all remaining 6,68,22 villages. Pradhan Mantri Gramodaya Yojana, launched in 2000–01, was discontinued from 2005 onwards. The budget allocation for Bharat Nirman was raised from ₹12,160 crore in 2005–06 to ₹18,696 crore in 2006–07 to ₹24,603 crore in 2007–08, and further to ₹31,280 crore in 2008–09.

Efforts to restructure and revive Dabhol Power

After finding that, on behalf of DPC, there was a misrepresentation about the ramp-up of the plant, India rescinded the PPA. A protracted legal battle followed while the DPC was mothballed. Ironically, while the Dabhol plant was mothballed, by the early 2000s, Maharashtra was reeling under long periods of power shortage every day. In the meantime, the UPA I government with Congress in the lead had come to power at the centre in 2004 and Sharad Pawar, who was the CM of Maharashtra when the Dabhol contract had been signed, was the minister for agriculture in the UPA I government.

The Ratnagiri Gas and Power Private Limited was established in July 2005 to rescue the DPC. Its shareholders were mainly public sector undertakings—NTPC and GAIL (25.51 per cent each), MSEB (13.51 per cent), and financial institutions, including IDBI Bank, SBI, ICICI Bank and Canara Bank (total 35.47 per cent). In the same month, a consent award was received from the arbitration court in London for settlement of claims from overseas with a sum of $760 million or ₹3268 crore.

Restructuring the Power Development Programme again

There was insufficient progress from power sector reforms under the APDP launched in February 2000 and its successor APDRP in 2002–03. Dissatisfied with the progress of power sector reforms, in 2006, the Union government appointed a committee under the chairmanship of P. Abraham, former Secretary of the ministry of power, to restructure APDRP. The committee, in its report of October 2006, suggested a Restructured APDRP (R-APDRP) with a focus on actual, demonstrable performance in loss reduction, establishing baseline data on AT&C losses, adopting energy accounting and auditing, and resolute elimination for electricity theft.

R-APDRP would cover urban areas, that is, cities and towns with a population of 30,000 or more (10,000 or more in special category states). In certain high-load-density rural areas, R-APDRP would also take up the separation of agricultural feeders from domestic and industrial ones and implement high voltage (11 kV) distribution systems. For the Eleventh Plan period (2008–2012), R-APDRP was launched in December 2008 as a continuation of APDRP in the Tenth Plan. PFC, a CPSE with Navaratna status from 2007, was the nodal agency for the operationalization and implementation of R-APRDP. Under the overall guidance of the ministry of power, PFC was to take the initiative for the speedy and timely completion of projects and assist the utilities in achieving loss reduction and other targets of the scheme.

Rural electrification

Rural electrification involves the supply of energy for two types of programmes: i) agriculture-related activities, primarily irrigation, etc.; and ii) non-agricultural consumers, including domestic households. Feeder separation refers to the supply of electricity to agricultural consumers and non-agricultural consumers (domestic and non-domestic) separately through dedicated feeders. The separation of feeders helps in flattening of the load curve by shifting the agricultural load to off-peak hours and thus facilitates peak load management. The core objective of the separation of feeders is to a provide regulated supply to agricultural consumers and continuous power supply to non-agricultural consumers in rural areas.

In the meantime, Gujarat's Jyotigram Yojana, or 'village of lights' scheme, had begun on a pilot initiative in 2003 and successfully achieved its two primary goals of improving the quality of electricity supply in rural areas while not adding to fiscal distress. Villages in Gujarat had been 'electrified' a dozen years ago, but supply was interrupted for prolonged periods. Through feeder separation between agriculture, and households and commercial establishments, and reducing electricity theft, Gujarat started supplying electricity twenty-four hours a day without interruptions and the SEB in the state started earning profits from 2006. Some remote villages, where connecting to the grid was difficult or expensive, were provided with solar power.

In 2004, the NCMP of UPA I had announced that 'Household electrification will be completed in five years.' 'Accelerated Electrification of one lakh villages and one crore households' was started in May 2004. It had the provision of 40 per cent grant and 60 per cent loan for projects related to rural electrification. The Kutir Jyoti Yojana was subsumed under it.

In compliance with Section 3 of the Electricity Act of 2003, on 12 February 2005, the Union government notified the National Electricity Policy. It formulated the target of providing minimum lifeline consumption of 1 unit of electricity per day per household as a merit good by 2012. Rajiv Gandhi Grameen Vidyutikaran Yojana (village electrification programme) (RGGVY) was launched by Prime Minister Dr Manmohan Singh on 4 April 2005. All ongoing rural electrification programmes of the Union government—Rural Electrification under Minimum Needs Programme, Kutir Jyoti Scheme and Accelerated Electrification of one lakh villages and more than one crore households—were subsumed under RGGVY and the REC was the nodal agency to implement the programme. In 2006, under the mandate of the Electricity Act, 2003, came the Rural Electrification Policy, which set 2012 as the target for 100 per cent village electrification and 100 per cent BPL household electrification.

Union taxes

In line with the recommendation of the Task Force on Direct Taxes headed by Vijay Kelkar in 2002, Chidambaram raised the exemption limit for personal income tax from ₹50,000 to ₹1 lakh in financial year 2004–05. The limit went up further to ₹1.1 lakh in 2007–08, and ₹1.5 lakh in 2008–09 before the elections to the Fifteenth Lok Sabha in 2009. In 2007–08, the threshold for a woman assessee was increased from ₹1.35 lakh to ₹1.45 lakh, and in case of a senior citizen, from ₹1.85 lakh to ₹1.95 lakh. Furthermore, in 2005–06, the assessees in the tax slab of ₹1 lakh to ₹1.5 lakh, who had been paying tax at the rate of 20 per cent until 2004–05, became liable to tax at the rate of only 10 per cent, those in the tax slab of ₹1.5 lakh to ₹2.5 lakh, who had been paying tax at the rate of 20 per cent until 2004–05, became liable to tax at the rate of only 10 per cent, while those with income between ₹2.5 lakh and ₹3 lakh, who had been paying tax at the rate of 30 per cent, became liable to tax at the rate of only 20 per cent. In the financial year 2008–09, the assessees in the tax slab of ₹1.5 lakh to ₹2.5 lakh, who had been paying tax at the rate of 20 per cent until 2007–08, became liable to tax at the rate of only 10 per cent, while those with income between 2.5 lakh and ₹3 lakh, who had been paying tax at the rate of 20 per cent, became liable to tax at the rate of only 10 per cent, while those in the tax slab of ₹2.5 lakh to ₹3 lakh, who had been paying tax at the rate of 30 per cent until 2007–08, became liable to tax at the rate of only 10 per cent, and those in the tax slab of ₹3 lakh to ₹5 lakh, who had been paying tax at the rate of 30 per cent until 2007–08, became liable to tax at the rate of only 20 per cent.

One prominent exemption from income tax introduced by Rajiv Gandhi in 1987–88 was with respect to the Constituency Allowance of Hon'ble MPs without any monetary ceiling! In 2006–07, Chidambaram extended the benefit to members of state legislatures. In the '2 by 4' criteria of the requirement of filing income tax return introduced first by Chidambaram in 1997–98 and later expanded to '1 by 6' by Yashwant Sinha in 1998–99, the criterion of mobile phone was dropped and replaced by annual electricity bill of more than ₹50,000 in 2005-06.

Finance Minister P. Chidambaram, in 2004–05, abolished the tax on long-term capital gains from securities transactions altogether and replaced it with a Securities Transaction Tax (STT) on transactions in securities on stock exchanges at the rate of 0.15 per cent of the value of security. For discouraging high-value transactions in cash and accumulation of black money, in 2005–06, he introduced a tax on withdrawal of cash on a single day of over ₹10,000 from banks at the rate of 0.1 per cent. This tax, which came to be known as Banking Cash Transaction Tax (BCCT), created a lot of protest, including from bona fide parties such as factory and plantation owners who had to disburse their wages in cash. It was withdrawn at end-March 2009. Fringe benefits, which were fully attributable to the employee, were already taxed in the hands of the employee. Chidambaram introduced a new Fringe Benefit Tax (FBT) in the hands of the employer at the rate of 30 per cent on benefits that are usually enjoyed collectively by the employees and cannot be attributed to individual employees. Transport services for workers and staff and canteen services in an office or factory were left out of FBT. After the STT in 2004–05, in the 2008–09 Budget, Chidambaram introduced the Commodities Transaction Tax (CTT) on the same lines as STT on commodity options and futures.

In 2005–06, Chidambaram replaced the extant rebate for women and senior citizens under personal income tax by higher exemption limits of ₹1.25 lakh and ₹1.5 lakh, respectively. The threshold limit for women was increased to ₹1.35 lakh in 2006–07, ₹1.45 lakh in 2007–08, and ₹1.80 lakh in 2008–09; and the corresponding increase for senior citizens, redefined as those above sixty-five years of age, to ₹1.85 lakh in 2006–07, ₹1.95 lakh in 2007–08, and ₹2.25 lakh in 2008–09. For the shipping industry, in line with the practice in many European countries, a tonnage tax was introduced in 2004–05.

In excise, the policy of granting exemptions to commodities and equipment used in agriculture continued, with the duty rate, for example, on tractors reduced from 16 per cent to nil in 2004–05. Limit for excise exemption for SSI was raised from an annual turnover of ₹3 crore to ₹4 crore in 2005–06, and the exemption for those liable to pay was raised from the first ₹1 crore to ₹1.5 crore in 2007–08. In a controversial move, in 2004–05, Chidambaram also reversed the completion of the CENVAT chain for textiles of the previous year, by exempting the handloom and powerloom sectors from CENVAT and implementing an optional mandatory excise duty regime. In service tax, he increased the coverage of service tax to seventy-five in 2004–05 by including thirteen more services, e.g., airport services, services provided by transport booking agents, transport of goods by air, and pandal and shamiana contractors. By 2008–09, the final full year of the first term of the UPA government, service tax applied to 106 services. The rate for service tax, which was increased from 8 per cent to 10 per cent in 2004–05, went up further to 12 per cent in 2006–07. Service tax on transport of goods by roads was leviable from 10 September 2004. But again, there was a transporters' strike, and the levy was postponed until further notice. A committee was constituted to study the matter, and as per its recommendations, service tax was levied on the transport of goods by road with effect from 1 January 2005.

Given the APM for petroleum products, the final price of LPG to consumers was attributed to the decisions of the Union government. But the VAT rate at the state level also had an impact on the final price of LPG. To rein in any undue state-level levy, in 2006-07, LPG was included under 'declared goods' under the CST Act, 1956. In 2006-07, under the Oil Industries Development Act, the cess per metric ton was increased from ₹1800 to ₹2500.

The peak rate of customs duty, except on agricultural and dairy products, was brought down from 20 per cent in 2004 to 15 per cent in 2005–06, 12.5 per cent in 2006–07, 10.0 per cent in 2007–08. In 2007–08, a duty of ₹300 per metric ton was imposed on export of iron ores and concentrates and ₹2000 per metric ton on export of chrome ores and concentrates.

Transparency in budget-making improved with the addition of Annex 12 entitled 'Tax Expenditure under the Central Tax System: Financial Year 2004–05' to the Receipt Budget of 2006–07. It quantified the foregone revenues because of 'tax preferences' in terms of special tax rates, exemptions, deductions, rebates, deferrals and credits that affect the level and distribution of tax. Tax preferences are spending programmes embedded in the tax statutes and may be viewed as subsidy payments to preferred taxpayers. The quantification of such implicit payments, which are also referred to as 'tax expenditures', is the first step in evaluating the value for money in promoting goals specified for granting such preferences. Tax expenditure went up almost three-fold from ₹1,46,230 crore in 2004–05 to ₹4,18,095 crore in 2008–09 (Table XXVII.1). As we shall see, this was partly in response to the Great Recession in 2008.

Table XXVII.1 Tax Expenditure of the Union Government, 2004-05 to 2008-09

	2004-05	2005-06	2006-07	2007-08	2008-09
Corporate taxes	57,852	34,618	50,075	62,199	68,914
Personal Income Tax	13,229	15,182	15,512	38,057	39,553
Of which: firms, associations of persons, cooperatives, etc.	*1534*	*1632*	*-*	*4779*	*5116*
Excise	18,018	66,760	99,690	87,468	1,28,293
Customs	92,561	1,27,730	1,23,682	1,53,593	2,25,752
Of which input rebate	*35,430*	*37,590*	*53,768*	*56,265*	*44,417*
Total	**1,46,230**	**2,06,700**	**2,35,191**	**2,85,052**	**4,18,095**

Source: Budget Documents, 2006-07 to 2009-10

Disinvestment in Central public sector enterprises

Disinvestment in CPSEs had been a sensitive point between the left parties and the Congress in drawing up the NCMP. Given these limitations, in 2004–05, the government set up a Board for Reconstruction of Public Sector Enterprises to advise on the measures to be taken to restructure CPSEs, including cases where disinvestment or closure or sale is justified, and announcing going ahead with dilution of equity in CPSEs, without affecting their public sector character to raise resources to meet the social sector needs. In 2004–05, while announcing financial support to the ailing Hindustan Antibiotics Limited and ITI, it also indicated that it planned to raise ₹4000 crore through disinvestment, including dilution of a part of its equity through the public issue by NTPC. The issue of CPSE disinvestment remained contentious. The disinvestment agenda stagnated and during the five years between 2003 and 2009, the total receipts from disinvestments were only ₹8516 crore.

Increase in National Old Age Pension Scheme (NOAPS)

Old age pensions granted under NOAPS—a component of NSAP—to destitute persons above the age of sixty-five years, which had been ₹75 per month, was increased to ₹200 per month. From 13 September 2007, the eligibility criterion was changed from being a destitute to a person above sixty-five years of age belonging to a BPL household.

Basic banking 'no frills' accounts

In 2005, for financial inclusion, RBI advised all banks 'to make available a basic banking "no frills" account either with "nil" or very low minimum balances as well as charges that would make such accounts accessible to vast sections of population'.[3] Subsequently, in 2012, all urban primary cooperative banks would be advised to offer 'Basic Savings Bank Deposit Accounts' (BSBDA) without any minimum balance.

XXVI.4 Farm Debt Waiver

In the meantime, farmers' suicides had become an explosive political issue. Such suicides, particularly following droughts in the Vidarbha region comprising eleven districts in eastern Maharashtra, had attracted a lot of public attention from the late 1990s. Vidarbha suffered five years of low rainfall in a row, and there were over 200 suicides in Vidarbha between July 2005 and February 2006. On 1 July 2006, at the end of a two-day visit to the region, Prime Minister Manmohan Singh had announced a ₹3750 crore relief package for farmers in thirty-one districts of the four states of Andhra Pradesh (sixteen), Maharashtra (six), Karnataka (six) and Kerala (three), where the incidence of farmers' suicides was very high.

To investigate the problems of agricultural indebtedness, on 10 August 2006, the government set up an expert group under the chairmanship of R. Radhakrishna. The expert group report in July 2007 pointed out that with limited availability of credit, the farmers' debt was not excessive, and the problem of indebtedness was more a symptom of low returns from agriculture and other structural factors. In his budget speech for 2008-09, Finance Minister Chidambaram noted that the group '. . . had made a number of recommendations but stopped short of recommending waiver of agricultural loans'. Yet, 'sensitive to the difficulties of the farming community, especially the small and marginal farmers', he went ahead with a debt waiver and relief covering all agricultural loans disbursed by scheduled commercial banks, regional rural banks and cooperative credit institutions up to 31 March 2007 and overdue as on 31 December 2007.

Some detractors claimed that the debt waiver was nothing but a populist measure for gathering votes. The partial nature of the measure because of its exclusion of farmers' borrowings from non-bank sources, its iniquity because it penalized farmers who had serviced their debt on time, and its long-term deleterious impact on credit culture, came under severe criticism.

XXVI.5 The NAC and Three Rights

Within a fortnight of the UPA assuming office, on 4 June 2004, the National Advisory Council (NAC) was constituted by a government order. It was meant to provide an interface with civil society and provide inputs to the government on policy and legislative matters with special focus on social sector reforms and their implementation mandated by the NCMP. The NAC consisted of experts ranging from academia to grassroots activists, along with members of the government. While the government had and would continue to have such expert bodies for advice, what was special about NAC was its chairperson Sonia Gandhi, the leader of the largest member of the UPA coalition and the chairperson of the UPA. She got a cabinet rank. It was serviced by the Prime Minister's office and had the power to obtain information from any ministry. Supporters described the NAC as a multi-stakeholder model that embraced civil society in important policymaking. Detractors complained that NAC chairperson Sonia Gandhi was the super prime minister who exercised authority without any accountability.[4]

The NAC played a pivotal role in implementing the rights-based approach to policy. Within the first two years of its setting up, it pushed through three important rights acts. RTI and Right to Work or National Rural Employment Guarantee (NREG Act or NREGA) were enacted on 15 June and 5 September 2005, respectively. Enactment of Recognition of Forest Rights followed on 19 December 2006.

Right to Information Act

A better and stronger RTI was one of the promises in the NCMP. A PIL filed in 2002 by NCPRI demanding an effective law for citizens to access information from civil servants precipitated a response from the government. In August 2004, the NCPRI, after extensive discussions with civil society groups, had forwarded a set of suggested amendments to the Freedom of Information Act to the NAC, which endorsed most of them and sent it to the Prime Minister. The draft rules under the Freedom of Information Act, 2002, finally released on 12 August 2004, were unacceptable to the civil society organization Commonwealth Human Rights Initiative (CHRI). In December 2004, Anna Hazare also warned that he would start an agitation if the government failed to enact the RTI. Arguably, civil society was seen by some as infringing on the rights of the legislature. In the event, the government agreed to the demands of civil society and introduced the RTI Bill recommended by them in Parliament on 22 December 2004.

The Central RTI Act came into force on 12 October 2005. It extended to non-governmental organizations that are 'substantially financed, directly or indirectly' by the government.[5] Expectations about the transformative potential of the new RTI law were very high.

Right to Work or National Rural Employment Guarantee Act (NREGA)

Employment schemes were seen to be serving the important objective of poverty alleviation and have been there from at least 1965. These schemes were all allocation-based schemes and not employment guarantee schemes. There had also been proposals to move to guaranteed employment. For example, the 1989 Lok Sabha election manifesto of the National Front led by V. P. Singh stated that it '. . . believes that every citizen has the right to productive and gainful work in order to live meaningfully and with dignity. The social and economic policy of the National Front will be geared to the realization of the "Right to Work" as a fundamental right of the citizen of India.'[6] V.P. Singh's government did not last for even a year, and what it would have done had it survived longer can only be a matter of speculation.

Guaranteed employment finally came with the National Rural Employment Guarantee Act (NREGA) of September 2005. NREGA aimed '. . . to provide for the enhancement of livelihood security of the households in rural areas of the country by providing at least 100 days of guaranteed wage employment in every financial year to every household whose adult members volunteer to do unskilled manual work and for matters connected therewith or incidental thereto.'[7] It was a labour law and social security measure rolled into one. The implementation of the National Rural Employment Guarantee Scheme (NREGS) in 200 selected districts started on 2 February 2006, was extended to 130 additional districts during 2007–08, and to the entire 596 rural districts of the country by 1 April 2008.

Under NREGA 2005, the Union government could specify the wage rates for different areas independent of the Minimum Wages Act, 1948. It also required payment of unemployment allowance by the state government if an applicant for employment under NREGS is not provided such employment within fifteen days of receipt of their application seeking employment. The entire burden of the wage component was on the Union government, and that of the unemployment allowance on the states. To minimize irregularities in the payment of benefits under NREGA, from October 2008, such payment through accounts of beneficiaries in banks or post offices was made compulsory.

Insufficiency of funds and the late disbursal of NREGA benefits in some states were some of the issues plaguing the scheme. There was also the problem of unemployment benefits that the state governments were obliged to pay if an applicant was not provided such employment in due time. The states pleaded their inability to meet the obligation because of their limited capacity to pay. Furthermore, both the Union's and the states' budgets are allocation-based budgets. To accommodate a demand-based expenditure such as under NREGA—except for assurances of giving as much as is needed—would pose a formidable challenge in the future.

The main difference between NREGA and its predecessors was its justiciability. Awareness about NREGA and their entitlements under it was deficient among the poor, because of their illiteracy and backwardness. Yet, there were several court cases involving the non-fulfilment of the obligation of providing 100 days' employment or in its absence, unemployment benefit and/or delays in payments. These were initiated mainly by civil society organizations.

Recognition of Forest Rights Act

The Recognition of Forest Rights Act (FRA) was a milestone in safeguarding the forest-dwelling tribals' rights. The very weak legal security of the traditional rights of the forest-dwelling tribes had been a problem for decades.

NAC in trouble

Soon, the NAC ran into difficulties with the office-for-profit controversy. On 17 March 2006, the former film star Jaya Bachchan, on her appointment by the government of UP as Chairperson of UP's Film Development Council, was disqualified from being a member of the Rajya Sabha on and from 14 July 2004. The post carried some honorarium, allowances and perquisites. The erstwhile SJP leader Amar Singh, a controversial figure himself, had warned that this expulsion would open up a Pandora's box. And it did. The TDP, then the SJP's ally, filed a complaint against Sonia Gandhi, a member of the Lok Sabha, for being the chairperson of NAC, an office for profit. On 23 March 2006, the day BJP petitioned the President to disqualify Sonia Gandhi from the Lok Sabha for holding an office for profit, she resigned not only from NAC but also from the Lok Sabha. An Opposition leader described it as the politics of revenge recoiling on Sonia Gandhi.

The NAC became headless and non-functional after Sonia's resignation. Even though she got re-elected to the Lok Sabha from Raebareli in May 2006, and the Parliament (Prevention of Disqualification) Amendment Act, 2006 exempted the NAC as an office for profit, Sonia Gandhi did not re-join NAC as chairperson, and NAC remained headless and ineffective until 31 March 2008. When the NAC's term expired on 31 March 2008, it was not reconstituted until 29 March 2010, ten months after the UPA got re-elected in 2009.

XXVI.6 The Great Recession and Stimulus

The year 2003–04 was an agricultural bumper year. Partly because of deficient rainfall adversely affecting agriculture, growth declined from 8 per cent in 2003–04 to 7.1 per cent in 2004–05. There was also a pickup in WPI inflation from 5.5 per cent in 2003–04 to 6.5 per cent in 2004–05. Fiscal deficit of the Union government, again as a proportion of GDP, improved from 4.3 per cent in 2003–04 to 3.9 per cent in 2004–05. The external current account balance, as a proportion of GDP, turned from a surplus of 2.3 per cent into a deficit of 0.4 per cent in 2004–05, but buoyant capital flows continued to augment the foreign exchange reserves from $113.0 billion in 2003–04 to $141.5 billion in 2004–05. Subsequently, growth picked up to 9.5 per cent in 2005–06, 9.6 per cent in 2006–07 and 9.3 per cent in 2007–08. WPI inflation, after coming down to 4.5 per cent in 2005–06, jumped up to 6.6 per cent to 6.6 per cent in 2006–07, only to come down to 4.7 per cent in 2007–08. The current account deficit deteriorated further to 1.2 per cent in 2005–06, 1.0 per cent in 2006–07 and 1.3 per cent in 2006–07, while foreign exchange reserves went up further to $151.6 billion, $199.2 billion, and $309.7 billion. The need for sterilizing the liquidity resulting from exchange market interventions continued.

Budget 2008-09 projected a healthy growth of tax revenue (net to the Union) of 25.6 per cent from ₹4,03,872 crore in 2007–08 (BE) to ₹5,07,150 crore in 2008–09 (BE). Non-debt capital receipts were budgeted to decline by 66 per cent, but with buoyant tax revenues, total revenue was projected to grow by 16.7 per cent from ₹4,47,023 crore in 2007–08 (BE) to ₹5,21,812 crore in 2008–09 (BE). The year 2008–09 was the second year of the Eleventh Five-Year Plan, and there was a large increase of 18.7 per cent in gross budgetary support (GBS) to the Plan.

In the event, in 2008–09, tax revenue (net to the Union) fell short of the budget estimate (BE) by ₹63,831 crore, and total expenditure overshot BE by ₹1,33,072 crore. The fiscal deficit turned out to be ₹3,36,992 crore relative to the BE of ₹1,33,287 crore. As a proportion of GDP, the fiscal deficit in 2008–09 was 6 per cent relative to 2.5 per cent in 2007–08. While a large part of this slippage was no doubt because of unanticipated developments and steps taken to address them during 2008–09, a part of the problem lay in bias in budget making and over-projecting revenue and underestimating expenditure. Some even hint that it was a stimulus package by design, though not presented as such. Many countries, notably

the US and China, had already implemented stimulus packages to deal
with the onset of the Great Recession.

There were unanticipated developments in the deteriorating external
situation with the onset of the Great Recession in 2008. Home prices in
the US, which had risen sharply since the second quarter of 2002, with
excessively permissive mortgage financing, started to fall in the first quarter
of 2007. In the second quarter of 2007, defaults increased sharply, and
some subprime mortgage lenders entered bankruptcy. By the last quarter
of 2008, the subprime mortgage crisis of 2007 in the US was spreading
as the worst recession in over six decades in not only the US but across
Europe as well as in emerging economies around the world. In February
2008, the US had passed the Economic Stimulus Act to grant tax rebates
worth $152 billion to support consumption. Yet, the freeze in credit
markets and the meltdown of house prices continued.

India went through some panic reactions. Market sentiments were
poor after the House of Representatives in the US on 29 September 2008
rejected the $700-billion package to rescue the financial sector. On the
following day, the benchmark Sensex plunged 3.5 per cent to its lowest
levels in two years and panic gripped ICICI Bank customers who queued
up outside ATMs in certain cities to withdraw deposits. Finance Minister
Chidambaram, SEBI and the RBI had to provide assurances before the
market closed 2.1 per cent up.

In October 2008, the US passed the Emergency Economic Stabilization
Act, and launched the Troubled Asset Relief Program. Many other
countries, such as Australia, China, Japan, Korea, Saudi Arabia, South
Africa, Spain and the UK, recognizing the coming crisis, had also launched
stimulus packages. The IMF was calling for concerted and coordinated
action from all countries. In November 2008, at the emergency summit
meeting convened by the leaders of the Group of 20 (G-20) industrialized
and emerging economies, IMF MD Strauss Kahn called for fiscal stimulus
equivalent to 2 per cent of GDP.

In India, many economists believe that fiscal policy had already
turned expansionary with the Budget for 2008–09 in end-February.
Expansionary monetary policies followed from October. RBI has three
important rates in carrying out its monetary policies—the CRR, the SLR
and the repo rate. To fight inflation, in 2008, with six increases of 25 basis

points each, CRR was 9 per cent by end-August. With a change of gears from combating inflation to fighting recession, the CRR was reduced in 2008 to 6.5 per cent on 11 October, and further by 50 basis points each on 25 October and 8 November, and on 17 January 2009 to reach 5 per cent. The SLR's statutory floor of 25 per cent had been removed in 2007, and the SLR was reduced to 24 per cent on 8 November 2008. Repo rate is the rate at which the RBI lends short-term funds to banks against repurchase agreements for securities rendered. The lower the repo rate, the more expansionary is monetary policy. On 20 October 2008, the RBI reduced the repo rate from 9 per cent to 8 per cent, and further to 7.5 per cent on 3 November 2008. On 6 December 2008, the RBI announced a cut in the repo rate by 100 basis points to 6.5 per cent, the lowest in nearly two and a half years. On 5 January 2009, the RBI's repo rate came down further to 5.5 per cent.

On 7 December, the government announced a stimulus package consisting of ₹20,000 crore additional expenditure on social sector schemes, a 4 percentage point reduction in CENVAT rate except on petroleum products, authorizing the newly-established IIFCL to raise ₹10,000 crore through tax-free bonds, interest subvention of 2 per cent on export credit for labour-intensive products, additional allocations for export incentive schemes, zero duty import of naphtha for the power sector, duty-free export of iron ore fines and reduction of duty on export of lumps for the steel industry to 5 per cent, and a full refund of service tax paid by exporters to foreign agents. One estimate put the value of the first stimulus package at ₹30,700 crore.

Within a month of the first, on 2 January 2009 came the second stimulus package consisting of permission for states to borrow an additional 0.5 per cent of their gross state domestic product (GSDP), equivalent to ₹30,000 crore, for capital expenditure, authorizing IIFCL to raise another ₹30,000 crore capital through tax-free bonds, restoration of exporter's DEPB scheme to pre-November levels and extension of the scheme until end-December 2009, and enhanced duty drawback scheme for knitted fabrics, bicycles, agricultural hand tools and specific yarn categories. Under the approval route of the RBI for external commercial borrowing (ECB), the 'all-in-cost' ceilings were removed; to encourage the housing sector, the 'development of integrated townships' was permitted as an eligible end-use; and NBFCs, dealing exclusively with infrastructure financing, were permitted to access ECB from multilateral or bilateral financial institutions. Furthermore, to boost the corporate bond market, FII investment limit in rupee, denominated corporate bonds in India was increased from US$6 billion to US$15 billion. On 2 January, the government clarified that the steps taken so far constituted a substantial counter-cyclical stimulus and it did not envisage any further measures in 2008–09.

Money is shy, and international capital started displaying a marked home bias as well as a desperate search for safety. Growth declined from 9.3 per cent in 2007–08 to 6.7 per cent in 2008–09. Net capital flows declined from US$108 billion in the previous year to only US$8 billion, creating anxieties on the balance of payments front, and the exchange rate of the rupee per US dollar depreciated sharply from ₹39.985 at end-March 2008 to ₹50.945 at end-March 2009.

XXVI.7 Jammu and Kashmir

In Jammu and Kashmir, notwithstanding the continuing underlying trend of decreasing incidence of terrorist violence, there were a few egregious incidents such as the assassination of Education Minister Ghulam Nabi Lone in October 2005.

The PDP-Congress coalition government in the state had been formed in November 2002 with the understanding that after Mufti Mohammad Sayeed of the PDP as CM for the first three years, a leader of the Congress would succeed him for the next three. This change was not easy with Mufti and his PDP arguing for a maintenance of the status quo and Mufti continuing for three more years. The Congress insisted on a change, and Ghulam Nabi Azad, a.k.a Ghulam Nabi Bhatt, of the Congress became CM of the State on 2 November 2005. Azad, fifty-six years old, was the first Congress CM of the state after Syed Mir Qasim in February 1975. An ethnic Kashmiri, he was also from Doda district in Jammu and hence the first CM of the state from the Jammu region.

In its Common Minimum Programme (CMP) 2004, the UPA had announced: 'The UPA government is pledged to respecting the letter and spirit of Article 370 of the Constitution that accords a special status to J&K. Dialogue with all groups and with different shades of opinion in J&K will be pursued on a sustained basis, in consultation with the democratically-elected state government.' These announcements helped in running the Congress-PDP coalition, but problems remained. While sporadic violence by terrorists continued, the flashpoint for the coalition came with the 100-acre land transfer to the Sri Amarnathji Shrine Board (SASB).

The Amarnath cave, located at an altitude of 3888 meters in Pahalgam district in Kashmir, is an ancient shrine revered by Hindus. Annually, about half a million Hindus travel to the shrine through high mountains in a yatra or pilgrimage organized by the government and SASB. There were terrorist attacks on the pilgrims in three successive years from 2000 to 2002. On 26 May 2008, the Union government and state government reached an agreement to transfer 99 acres (0.40 km²) of forest land to the SASB in the main valley to set up temporary shelters and facilities for the pilgrims. From late June, there were violent protests by many Muslims, mainly in the Kashmir valley, who accused the government of planning to build Hindu settlements in the country's only Muslim-majority state to change the demographic balance. There were also objections on ecological grounds. The protests brought Abdullah's National Conference, Mufti Mohammad Sayeed's PDP and the militants together in Kashmir. Counter-protests started in the Hindu-majority Jammu region. Though the PDP had been a part of the state government's land transfer decision to SASB, it withdrew support from the PDP-Congress government under Ghulam Nabi Azad on 28 June. Governor Vora revoked the land allocation to SASB the following day and this led to violent protests, including almost week-long strikes, in the Jammu region, Curfew had to be imposed in Jammu. On 7 July 2008, Ghulam Nabi Azad resigned as CM. Jammu and Kashmir came under Governor's rule.

Elections to the Jammu and Kashmir legislative assembly were scheduled in seven phases between 17 November and 24 December 2008. The voter turnout was up from 43.7 per cent in 2002 to 61.2 per cent in 2008. The contest again was mainly among the National Conference, the PDP, the Congress and the BJP, who won twenty-eight, twenty-one, seventeen and eleven seats, respectively. Omar Abdullah, the president of the National Conference, won back the family's stronghold Ganderbal assembly constituency, which he had lost in 2002 to PDP, and as the leader of the single largest party, staked his claim to form the government. Both the National Conference and PDP were keen to have an alliance with the Congress to form a government. Ultimately, Omar Abdullah, at the head of a Congress-National Conference alliance, was sworn in as the CM of Jammu and Kashmir on 5 January 2009.

XXVI.8 Trauma and the Change of Guard in 2009

Like 2004—the first year of its rule—the year 2008 turned out to be traumatic for the country and for the UPA. In 2004, the first year of the UPA's rule, a tsunami, or high sea wave caused by an earthquake or underwater disturbance, devastated the Andaman and Nicobar Islands and the coastal areas of Andhra Pradesh, Kerala and Tamil Nadu a day after Christmas in 2004. The loss of life was more than 10,000 and houses were destroyed in the thousands. The year 2008, apart from the Great Recession, turned out to be equally troublesome for the country in general and UPA in particular due to five developments.

First, there were allegations against A. Raja of the DMK, who was the minister of communications and IT, of foul play in allotting licences for 2G spectrum. Known as the 2G scam, it would haunt the UPA for years.

Second, there was the strike by the goods transport agents from 2 July 2008. They complained about the hike in diesel prices, higher toll tax and service tax making their operations uneconomical. The All-India Motor Transport Congress (AIMTC) went on an indefinite strike carried out by interstate truckers from 2 July 2008. Their demands included the withdrawal of the Income Tax Department Circular of 16 May 2008 for recovery of tax arrears since 2001. With about three-quarters of the total cargo, including cement, fertilizers, food grains and steel, in the country transported by road, there was anxiety over the disruption of supply chains resulting in shortages. The strike was called off on 3 July 2008 after the Department of Roads, Transport and Highways, Government of India and the AIMTC agreed that the higher toll rates in nine stretches of NH notified by the NHAI between November 2007 and May 2008 would not be levied for a year until 2 July 2009. The postponement of the higher levy was controversial.

The government also agreed to issue a notification exempting certain services, such as packing, cargo handling and warehousing provided to goods transport operators en route.

Third was the US-India Civil Nuclear Agreement or India-US nuclear deal, also known as the '123 Agreement'. US President George Bush and Prime Minister Manmohan Singh, after proposing it at the Washington summit in July 2005, signed the US-India Civil Nuclear Cooperation Agreement on 2 March 2006 in New Delhi. The terms and conditions of this 123 Agreement, which required approval of the US Congress and Indian Cabinet of Ministers, were concluded on 27 July 2007. Under the agreement, in exchange for full civil nuclear cooperation from the US, India agreed to separate its military and civil nuclear facilities and place the civil ones under International Atomic Energy Agency's (IAEA) safeguards. The proposed agreement became controversial in India, and the choice for the UPA became to drop either the deal or the left. But with Manmohan Singh reportedly threatening to resign otherwise, there was no turning back. On 8 July 2008, a day before India submitted its safeguards proposals to the IAEA, the four left parties—ComPI, CPI(M), Forward Block and RSP—announced the withdrawal of their support to the UPA government. There was a vote of confidence on 22 July 2008, which the government won with 275 for and 256 against in a house of 543, eleven abstentions and one non-voting seat. The vote was marred by cross-voting and allegations of vote-buying by the ruling coalition. The 123 Agreement was signed by Indian External Affairs Minister Pranab Mukherjee and his counterpart, the US Secretary of State Condoleezza Rice, on 10 October 2008. The 123 Agreement heralded a new phase of Indo-US cooperation.

Fourth, on 26 November 2008, came the Mumbai attack by Pakistan-based terrorists lasting until the morning of 29 November. It came to be known as 26/11. The death toll of 175 (including nine terrorists), hundreds injured, and destruction of property highlighted the insecurity of the situation and heightened the Indo-Pak tension. On 13 September 2008, a series of bomb blasts around Delhi had already taken place under the charge of Home Minister Shivraj Patil, well-known for his 'painstakingly-tailored suits, mostly matched with same-colour shoes', 'perfectly coiffured and gelled hair' and frequent change of clothes.[8] After 26/11, Patil came under severe criticism and resigned on 30 November 2008. Chidambaram moved from the finance ministry to the home ministry and Prime Minister Manmohan Singh took charge of the finance ministry. On 24 January 2009, Pranab Mukherjee, who had already held the post during 1982–84 under Indira Gandhi, became the finance minister.

Fifth, we will recall that the new state of Andhra Pradesh was formed on 1 November 1956 by merging the Telugu districts of Madras and Telangana, the Telugu-speaking areas of the erstwhile princely state of Hyderabad. While there were demands for a separate Telangana state in the past as well, the demand became particularly strong after the formation of the TRS by K. Chandrashekar Rao in 2001. TRS was an ally of the Congress in the 2004 election. On 9 December 2009, the government announced the process of formation of the Telangana state. Immediately, there were violent protests in the coastal Andhra and Rayalseema regions, and the decision was put on hold on 23 December 2009. Telangana, however, finally came into being in 2014.

XXVI.9 The Run-Up to the Fifteenth Lok Sabha Elections

On 2 March 2009, the Chief Election Commissioner announced elections to the Fifteenth Lok Sabha in five phases between 16 April and 13 May 2009. This election also was to be conducted in constituencies redrawn by the Delimitation Commission of India 2002 based on the 2001 population census. Finance Minister Pranab Mukherjee, who had assumed his new charge on 24 January 2009, presented the Interim Budget on 16 February. Mukherjee reported that, in 2008–09, total expenditure was likely to be ₹9,00,953 crore against the budgeted ₹7,50,884 crore, total revenue ₹5,21,812 crore against the BE of ₹4,65,970 crore, and with non-debt capital receipts more or less on target, the fiscal deficit ₹3,26,515 crore against the BE of ₹1,33,287 crore. Over and above these figures, there were the special bonds issued to the oil marketing and fertilizer companies, which did not figure in the expenditure and deficit figures.

FRBMA 2003 had provided an escape clause on grounds of 'national security, act of war, national calamity, collapse of agriculture severely affecting farm output and incomes, structural reforms in the economy with unanticipated fiscal implications, decline in real output growth of a quarter by at least three per cent. points below its average of the previous four quarters'.[9] In a reference to the escape clause, Mukherjee in the Interim Budget 2009-10 said: 'Extraordinary economic circumstances merit extraordinary measures. Now is the time for such measures. Our Government decided to relax the FRBM targets, in order to provide much needed demand boost to counter the situation created by the global financial meltdown.' As we shall see, the escape clause would operate not for a year or two, but for a series of years in the future.

The announcement of the dates of the election to the Fifteenth Lok Sabha would have triggered the model code of conduct and barred any giveaways. On 25 February 2009, Mukherjee announced the third stimulus package of a 2 percentage point cut in CENVAT and service tax rates from 10 per cent to 8 per cent and from 12 per cent to 10 per cent, respectively. Furthermore, the states could exceed the limit of 3 per cent of GSDP in 2009-10. Some commentators described the third stimulus as putting the economy on steroids, an overdose, and even an unwise step. According to the RBI, the additional stimulus measures worked out to 2.9 per cent of GDP in 2008-09. The RBI reduced the repo rate from 5.5 per cent to 5 per cent on 3 March and further to an all-time low of 4.75 per cent on 21 April 2009.

Unique Identification Numbers

The foundation for Unique Identification Numbers (UID) for the residents of India was laid quietly on 28 January 2009. A gazette notification on that date announced the setting up of the Unique Identification Authority of India (UIDAI) as an attached office of the then Planning Commission (now NITI Aayog). The UID came to be called Aadhaar, meaning base. The first UID number would be issued on 29 September 2010 and by end-February 2020, 90.1 per cent of the population would have Aadhar cards. By being robust enough to eliminate duplicate and fake identities and making verification and authentication easy and cost-effective, in a few years' time, Aadhaar would provide the foundation for the digitization and streamlining of many public services such as Direct Benefit Transfer and online banking.

Extension of New Pension Scheme (NPS)

The newly defined contribution pension scheme for new entrants into Union government's service (except the armed forces), introduced by its predecessor NDA government, was extended to all citizens on a voluntary basis by the first UPA government from 1 May 2009. Beyond the mandatory pillar of contribution by the employer, it also provided for a mandatory and voluntary contribution by the employees. Soon, by end-March 2013, twenty-five state governments—all but Kerala, Tripura, and West Bengal—notified the NPS for its employees. The challenge of spreading the message of NPS and old age income security to people in the private sector across the country remained. It required spreading the NPS distribution network to make it easily accessible to all and spreading awareness about it among the people.

XXVII

The Second UPA Government

The depletion of the NDA coalition continued in the run-up to the 2009 Lok Sabha election. Four major alliance partners from 2004, namely AIADMK, BJD, TDP and AITC, were missing from NDA in 2009. While BJP's tally came down from 138 in 2004 to 116 in 2009, the corresponding decline in the tally of the pre-electoral alliance of the NDA was from 188 to 158.

Relative to the BJP-led NDA, Congress did better in keeping its 2004 flock together and even adding a few important new allies. Thus, while it lost the TRS led by K. Chandrasekhar Rao in Andhra Pradesh, PDP in Jammu and Kashmir, LJP and RJD in Bihar and MDMK and PMK in Tamil Nadu, it added AITC in West Bengal, National Conference in Jammu and Kashmir, Kerala Congress (Mani) in Kerala and Viduthalai Chiruthaigal Katchi in Tamil Nadu. The Congress tally improved from 145 in 2004 to 206 in 2009, and the UPA score was up from 221 to 261. There was an increase in the vote share of the Congress of 2 percentage points to 28.55 per cent, while the BJP's vote share was down 3.4 percentage points to 18.8 per cent in 2009. The UPA was short of a majority in the Lok Sabha by only twelve. Support from other parties—SP (twenty-three), BSP (twenty-one), RJD (four), JD(S) (three), and six other parties with one seat each—was readily forthcoming. On 9 May 2009, Manmohan Singh was again sworn in as Prime Minister.

XXVII.1 More Rights

The Congress took its victory as a vindication by the people of its rights-based approach to setting up a welfare state. It pursued it with renewed vigour, and from end-March 2010, the reappointed NAC under Sonia Gandhi again started to drive the rights-based welfare agenda. The NAC's second term, however, was less spectacular than the first. Strong disagreements with the government as well as with expert committees set up by the government came out in the public domain. Several NAC members resigned because of 'tampering' of the rights acts to reduce them to 'minimalists'. Nevertheless, NAC shepherded three important rights laws—the Right to Education Act, 2009, the National Food Security Act, 2013 and Land Acquisition, Rehabilitation and Resettlement Act (LARR), 2013.

Right to Education Act

The Right of Children to Free and Compulsory Education, more popularly known as Right to Education, stipulated, among other things, 25 per cent reservation for disadvantaged children in private schools, no detention or expulsion from school and no Board examination till the completion of elementary education. Passed in mid-2009, it got notified on 26 August 2009.

Right to Food Act

Combating hunger in the country continued to be a major challenge. The National Food Security Act was passed to provide subsidized food grains to India's 75 per cent rural population and 50 per cent urban population. The National Food Security Bill, having been passed by Parliament, was proclaimed as a 'game changer' and an empowerment revolution by Sonia Gandhi.[1] The bill received Presidential assent on 10 September 2013. The timing of the bill's introduction was such that almost all parties found themselves compelled to endorse it. Some opposition members even called the 'Food Security Bill' a 'Vote Security Bill'.[2]

Right to Fair Compensation and Transparency in Land Acquisition, Rehabilitation and Resettlement Act (LARR)

The Land Acquisition Act was passed after Tata's Singur Nano Car project was shelved in 2006 owing to a vigorous and often violent demonstration, spearheaded by the fiery AITC leader Mamata Banerjee, against involuntary displacement of farmers from fertile land. The act sought to end the historical injustice perpetrated under the Land Acquisition Act of 1894. The provision for paying at least twice the market price for land acquired in urban areas and at least four times the market price for land in rural areas, getting the consent of 70-80 per cent of the to-be-affected landowners, doing a social impact analysis, and liberal resettlement and rehabilitation provisions, were pro-poor and just measures. To critics, provisions like these complicated land acquisitions, made it more time-consuming and expensive, and would inhibit the growth of industry, urban centres and infrastructure. They even saw this as an attempt by the UPA and the Congress party to appease the voters and win the election.

According to one commentator, even if the UPA lost the election, 'The UPA is essentially lobbing a ticking-time bomb in the midst of the next government. The next government would be unable to reverse the Bill as any coalition would have landed vested interests in its composition. In short, the UPA was giving the next government the opportunity to commit suicide: poisoned food in the form of the Food Security Bill, or the option to step onto a landmine in the form of the Land Acquisition Bill.'[3]

XXVII.2 Skill Development

The government set up the National Skill Development Fund (NSDF) in 2009 for raising funds both from government and non-government sources for skill development in the country. The NSDF acted through the National Skill Development Corporation (NSDC), an industry-led 'not for profit company', for building skill development capacity and forging strong linkages with the market. The National Skill Development Agency (NSDA) was set up in June 2013 to subsume the Prime Minister's

National Council on Skill Development (PMNCSD), the National
Skill Development Coordination Board (NSDCB) and the Office of the
Adviser to PM on Skill Development.

XXVII.3 Great Recession and the Continuing Stimulus

The global financial crisis helped the UPA in implementing its rights-
based welfare approach. In response to the crisis, the fiscal and monetary
stance was accommodative not only in India but all over the world. The
rights agenda in India fitted in well with the accommodative stance.

After the election, Pranab Mukherjee presented the regular Budget
for 2009–10 on 6 July 2009. Mukherjee's budget contained expansionary
measures relating to both taxes and expenditure. In personal income tax,
the general exemption threshold was increased from ₹1.5 lakh to ₹1.6 lakh,
and the special exemption threshold for women and senior citizens from
₹1.8 lakh to ₹1.9 lakh, and from ₹2.25 lakh to ₹2.40 lakh, respectively.
Furthermore, the surcharge of 10 per cent applicable to income above
₹10 lakh was withdrawn. In corporate taxes, he extended the availability
of deduction in respect of export profits under Sections 10A and 10B of
the Income Tax Act up to 2009–10 by a year and abolished the FBT. The
only revenue-augmenting measure in direct taxes was an increase in the
rate of MAT from 10 per cent of book profits to 15 per cent. Mukherjee,
following the recommendations of the Prime Minister's Economic
Advisory Council, abolished the CTT that had been introduced just a
year before in 2008–09.

In customs, selectively, the rate was reduced on, or exemptions granted
to, a few items such as LCD panels, accessories, parts and components of
mobile phones, permanent magnets for wind-operated power generators,
and drugs. It was also raised on set-top boxes, gold and silver.

In excise, Mukherjee partly reversed the break in the CENVAT chain
in the textile industry introduced by his predecessor Chidambaram in
2004–05. He restored the rate of 8 per cent CENVAT on manmade fibre
and yarn on a mandatory basis and at that rate on an optional basis on
stages beyond fibre and yarn at that rate on optional basis. These changes,
together with duty changes on intermediates, implied a uniform duty rate

on all types of manmade fibre and yarn and their intermediates without any problem of credit accumulation. He also increased the CENVAT rate on several items from 4 per cent to 8 per cent and granted a exemption or reduction in excise duty on a few items such as vehicles with more than 2000 cc engine capacity and gold jewellery. In service tax, he extended some relief to exporters on tax payable on services, such as road transportation received after the goods are cleared from the factory. He extended the service tax to legal services except where the service provider or the service receiver is an individual.

In the 2009–10 Budget, Mukherjee enhanced the allocation under JNNURM from ₹6886 crore in 2008-09 (BE) to ₹12,887 crore. Allocations for NREGS, already up from ₹12,000 crore in 2007–08 (BE) to ₹16,000 crore in 2008–09 (BE), was increased further to ₹40,100 crore. On Gandhi Jayanti 2009, through an amendment to NREGA 2005, the nomenclature became Mahatma Gandhi National Rural Employment Guarantee Act (MNREGA).

Phase I of Bharat Nirman, which had been launched in May 2005, was followed up by its Phase II from 2009–10 to 2011–12. Rural drinking water was one of its six components. Allocations under Bharat Nirman were increased from ₹31,280 crore in 2008–09 to ₹39,100 crore in 2009–10 and further to ₹48,000 crore in 2010–11. With World Bank support, the National Rural Livelihoods Mission (NRLM) was launched in 2011 to create efficient and effective institutional platforms for the rural poor, enabling them to increase household income through sustainable livelihood enhancements and improved access to financial services.

Pensions of government employees under the old pay-as-you-go unfunded scheme were based on their last salary drawn. With changing pay scale and allowances over time, the last pay drawn by two employees retiring from the same rank at different points of time could differ. There was a long-pending demand for one-rank-one-pension scheme for defence pensioners below officer rank. The acceptance of this demand increased the budgetary outgo for the Union government not only in 2009–10, but for years to come, of more than an annual ₹2100 crore. The regular Budget for 2009–2010 also contained additional policy initiatives like fast-tracking of several infrastructure projects and extended debt-waiver schemes.

With all the tax incentives and extra spending programmes, the expansionary fiscal stance of the Union government was continuing in 2009–10. As already noted, the fiscal position of the Union government in 2008–09 had deteriorated considerably, with fiscal deficit rising to ₹3,26,515 crore in RE. Relative to 2008–09 (RE), in 2009–10 (BE), with revenues increasing from ₹5,62,173 crore to ₹6,14,497 crore, non-debt capital receipts declining from ₹12,265 crore to ₹5345 crore, and expenditure increasing from ₹9,00,953 crore to ₹10,20,838 crore, the fiscal deficit increased from ₹3,26,515 crore to ₹4,00,996 crore.

Mid-way through 2009–10, on 5 November 2009, the government announced a new disinvestment policy requiring all listed CPSEs to plan further stake sales and ensure that public holding in these firms was a minimum of 10 per cent, and all profitable unlisted CPSEs with a positive net worth to list on stock exchanges. With proceeds of disinvestment in companies such as NHPC, NTPC, OIL, REC and National Mineral Development Corporation (NMDC), non-debt capital receipts, which are mainly from disinvestment, were revised upwards from BE of ₹5345 crore to an RE of ₹30,212 crore. Actual disinvestment receipts improved from nil in 2008–09 to ₹23,552 crore in 2009–10, the highest ever since disinvestment started in 1991–92.

In December 2009, the Thirteenth Finance Commission under the chairmanship of Vijay Kelkar presented its report for the award period 2010–11 to 2014–15. It had recommended a calibrated exit strategy from the expansionary fiscal stance of the previous two years and a capping of the combined debt of the Centre and the states at 68 per cent of GDP to be achieved by 2014–15. In the Medium-Term Fiscal Policy Statement presented with Budget 2010–11, the rolling targets for fiscal deficit as a proportion of GDP at 4.8 per cent and 4.1 per cent for 2011–12 and 2012–13, respectively, were at least as ambitious as the corresponding Finance Commission recommended figures of 4.8 per cent and 4.2 per cent. However, the Union government was unable to rein in its expansionary stance and the actual fiscal deficit in 2011–12 and 2012–13 would turn out to be well above the targets indicated by the Thirteenth Finance Commission.

XXVII.4 Swavalamban—A Subsidized Universal Old Age Pension Scheme

In the Union Budget for 2010–11, the finance minister announced the Swavalamban (or self-reliance) Scheme to address the problems of the aged in the poorer sections of the country with enhanced longevity. Under the scheme, which was launched on 26 September 2010, the Union government would contribute ₹1000 to each subscriber account of the NPS during 2010–11 and the next three years, provided the subscriber contributed any amount between ₹1000 to ₹12,000 per annum. The scheme, administered by the PFRDA, targeted an increase in the subscriber base of 10 lakh in each of the four years beginning 2010–11, and enhanced the old-age security of the subscribers, particularly in the unorganized sector.

XXVII.5 Direct Benefit Transfer—Launch and Quick Retreat in LPG

The country was making rapid progress in digitization, and this was manifest in, among others, the areas of tax administration and Aadhaar cards. By 2011–12, assessees were provided with the facility of online preparation and e-filing of income tax returns, e-payment of taxes through banks, electronic clearing of refunds directly in taxpayers' bank accounts and electronic filing of TDS. Income tax returns were being processed at the Centralized Processing Centre (CPC) in Bengaluru, and three more CPCs were proposed to be set up. All these steps reduced the need for direct contact between tax officials and the taxpayer. Customs and Excise were also gearing up their Electronic Data Interchange (EDI) and Indian Customs and Central Excise Electronic Commerce/Electronic Data Interchange Gateway (ICEGATE).

In his Budget for 2010–11, Finance Minister Mukherjee had announced that UIDAI would be issuing the first set of Aadhaar Cards in 2010–11. By end-February 2011, 20 lakh Aadhaar numbers had been issued. The UID Mission took off, Aadhaar numbers were being generated on a large scale and from 1 October 2011, 10 lakh would be generated per day. The stage was set for realizing the potential of Aadhaar for improving service delivery, accountability and transparency in governance of various schemes. In Budget 2012–13, Finance Minister Mukherjee announced that the government had accepted the recommendations of the task force headed by Nandan Nilekani on IT strategy for direct transfer of subsidy. In October 2012, Prime Minister Manmohan Singh set up a High-Powered National Committee on Direct Cash Transfers under his chairmanship. The committee decided to roll out Direct Cash Transfer in forty-three identified districts from 1 January 2013. In due course, the scheme came to be called Direct Benefit Transfer (DBT). In his Budget Speech 2013–14, on 28 February 2013, Chidambaram said, 'We have made a modest and cautious beginning on the 1st of January, 2013. Nearly 11 lakh beneficiaries have received the benefit directly into their bank accounts.' For DBT, there was the catchy slogan of '*Aapka paisa apke haath*' or your money in your hand.

The purpose of DBT was to ensure accurate targeting of the beneficiary, curbing pilferage and duplication, and safeguarding the electronic transfer of benefits to beneficiaries' bank accounts, without tiers involved in fund flow delaying payment. Twenty-eight schemes were identified for DBT rollout in the forty-three identified districts in three phases: (a) in twenty districts from 1 January 2013, (b) in eleven districts after 1 February 2013, and (c) in the remaining twelve districts after 1 March 2013. DBT was facilitated by the progress under UIDAI in enrolling residents in the Aadhaar scheme, solving the problem of duplicate or bogus identities, and seeding or linking their bank accounts to their Aadhaar number. In April 2013, the National Committee on DBT decided to extend the scheme to seventy-eight more districts from July 2013 and add three more pension schemes for old age, widows and disability under its coverage. Subsequently, on 12 December 2014, it was decided to cover the entire country under the DBT scheme.

State-owned oil companies at end-2013 were selling diesel at a loss of ₹10.16 per litre, and the losses were ₹32.17 a litre for kerosene and ₹490.50 per 14.2-kg LPG cylinder. In 2002–03, the NDA government had dismantled APM in the petroleum sector and the oil pool account while continuing the subsidy on LPG, diesel and kerosene 'directly' from the Budget. The subsidies had grown and were rendering fiscal consolidation difficult. An expert panel on fiscal consolidation headed by Vijay Kelkar, in September 2012, had recommended an immediate hike in petroleum prices, complete deregulation of diesel prices by 2014–15 and raising kerosene and LPG rates to keep the subsidy at affordable levels.

LPG subsidies had been mounting over the years, and DBT was potentially a very effective instrument for reining it in. In 2013–14, in terms of streamlining and rationalizing subsidies in LPG, there was what one newspaper described as 'One step forward, two steps back'.[4] In September 2012, the government had capped the number of subsidized cylinders of 14.2 kg at six per family. Just six cylinders in a year, even at the subsidized price, involved an annual outlay of more than ₹2400, and it was difficult to see how an average poor family could afford to buy more than six. Yet, this number was raised to nine in January 2013 and further to twelve in January 2014. Under DBT, in LPG, the consumer would pay to the dealer the full price, while the subsidy amount would be transferred to their Aadhaar-seeded bank account. DBT for LPG was rolled out in 291 districts in the country from 1 June 2013 in six phases, covering nearly 10 crore consumers, with over 3770 distributors across the three state-owned Oil Marketing Companies. An amount of ₹5400 crore was successfully transferred to more than 2.8 crore LPG consumers across the country till 8 March 2014.

According to a Review Committee set up by the ministry of petroleum in March 2014: 'Preliminary results show that the results expected from the scheme in terms of detection of duplicate connections and reduction in diversion of subsidized LPG cylinders were achieved. The scheme was innovative, involved multiple stakeholders and was implemented on a large scale over a short period of time. It invoked both praise and criticism based on the individual experiences of the various stakeholders, particularly the consumers. The scheme was both critiqued and supported by media, consumer forums. It also evoked keen interest of policy makers and business analysts. The scheme implementation was rapidly scaled up from a pilot implementation in 20 districts to 291 districts in a short period of time.'[5]

There were complaints from consumers in districts where Aadhaar penetration was relatively low. There was also resistance from some consumers, including most probably some ineligible beneficiaries from the subsidy, in submitting their Aadhaar cards to the banks for seeding their accounts with the Aadhaar numbers. Rather than pushing ahead with increasing the coverage under Aadhaar, regrettably, the government decided to retreat and keep the scheme in abeyance on 7 March 2014. Coincidentally, on 5 March 2014, Chief Election Commissioner V.S. Sampath had announced the poll schedule of 7 April to 12 May for the Sixteenth Lok Sabha. The state-owned oil companies reverted to the old system of subsidized cylinder supplies in the entire country from 10 March 2014.

XXVII.6 A Hesitant Exit—Too Little, Too Late

2010–11

In Budget 2010–11, in personal income tax, only the rate of tax for income between ₹3 lakh and ₹5 lakh was changed from 20 per cent to 10 per cent. While Finance Minister Mukherjee expressed his hope that the much-discussed Direct Tax Code would be implemented from April 2011, it never came. Mukherjee mobilized ₹22,144 crore by diluting the government's stake in six companies. He provided ₹16,500 crore for the public sector banks to attain a minimum 8 per cent Tier-I capital by end-March 2011 and proposed to provide a further ₹6000 crore for recapitalizing them in 2011-12. He substantially raised allocation under energy, education, health, IAY and women and child development.

Given the lack of transparency in the extant process of allocating captive coal blocks, Mukherjee in Budget 2010–11 proposed to replace it with a competitive bidding process. He also announced the setting up of an apex-level Financial Stability and Development Council to monitor macro-prudential supervision of the economy, including the functioning of large financial conglomerates, and address inter-regulatory coordination issues.

As a proportion of GDP, the fiscal deficit came down sharply from 6.5 per cent in 2009–10 to 4.9 per cent in 2010–11. With the stimulus from 2008–09, economic activity responded positively, and growth accelerated from 6.7 per cent in 2008–09 to 8.6 per cent in 2009–10 and 8.9 per cent in 2010–11.

2011–12

After Independence, to avoid perpetuation of the caste system and deepening of social divisions, the category 'Race, caste or tribe' in Census was replaced by SC and ST. However, by 2011, there were strong demands for enumeration of castes other than SCs and STs in Census 2011. In Budget 2011–12, Mukherjee declared that the government had decided to canvass 'caste' as a separate time-bound exercise between June and September 2011. The Socio-Economic Caste Census (SECC) 2011 would be a comprehensive door-to-door enumeration across the country to generate information on housing conditions, work profile and other indicators of social and economic status of the households, both in urban and rural areas.

Mukherjee's Budget for 2011–12 announced six important structural reforms: (i) a phased move by March 2012 from subsidies on fuel and fertilizer to DBT to BPL people; (ii) enhancement of limit on FII investment in corporate bonds of residual maturity over five years issued by infrastructure companies from $20 billion to $25 billion; (iii) beyond only FIIs and sub-accounts registered with SEBI, permission to Indian mutual funds to accept investments from foreign investors who meet the Know Your Customer (KYC) requirement; (iv) requiring the states to amend or enact their FRBMAs to conform to the recommendations of the Thirteenth Finance Commission to eliminate revenue deficit and achieve a fiscal deficit of 3 per cent of their respective GSDPs latest by 2014–15; (v) suitable amendments to the Banking Regulation Act to facilitate the RBI issuing some additional licenses to private sector players; (vi) after ₹20,157 crore in 2010–11, infusion of a further sum of ₹6000 crore in public sector banks for maintaining their Tier I CRAR at 8 per cent.

The popularity of the Kisan Vikas Patra, the Post Office small savings scheme introduced in 1988, was not restricted to kisan or farmers alone. It was a popular scheme under which, initially, money doubled in five years. It had raised some uncomfortable questions relating to the high cost of the scheme, the certificates having no names, no TDS and their free transferability. It could be a good avenue for laundering black money into white. The Kisan Vikas Patra scheme was discontinued in 2011.

In 2011–12, Mukherjee increased the incentive to farmers repaying short-term crop loans as per schedule of 2 per cent interest subvention available in 2010–11 to 3 per cent. After having implemented the nutrient-based policy for all fertilizers except urea in 2010–11, in the Budget 2011–12, he announced the government's intention to extend it to urea as well. In the Budget for 2012–13, the government announced that it would track the movement of fertilizers from retailers to farmers, and, through DBT, link part of the subsidy payment to manufacturers to sale to farmers by retailers. But, the implementation of DBT for urea—the dominant source of fertilizer subsidy—was still awaited when this book went to print.

In personal income tax, Budget 2011–12 raised the exemption threshold from ₹1.5 lakh to ₹1.8 lakh. Exemption threshold for senior citizens was raised from ₹2.4 lakh to ₹2.5 lakh, the age for qualifying as a senior citizen lowered from sixty-five years to sixty years, and a new category, 'super senior citizens' of above eighty years, introduced with an exemption threshold of ₹5 lakh. The expansionary impact of these tax relief measures was compounded by an expansionary stance in MNREGA, Bharat Nirman, Sarva Shiksha Abhiyan and RSBY.

Disinvestment receipts in 2010–11 had fallen short of the BE of ₹40,000 crore by about ₹18,000 crore, yet the corresponding BE in 2011–12 was maintained at ₹40,000 crore. Again, it fell short of BE by almost ₹25,000 crore. The fiscal deficit, as a proportion of GDP, in 2011–12 turned out to be 5.9 per cent relative to 4.9 per cent in 2010–11. There was also a sizeable deterioration in the external current account, with the deficit as a proportion of GDP increasing from 2.9 per cent in the previous year to 4.3 per cent. Foreign exchange reserves declined by over $10 billion to $294.4 billion. Furthermore, growth also tapered off from 8.9 per cent in 2010–11 to 6.7 per cent in 2011–12, while WPI inflation came down only mildly from 8.9 per cent to 7.4 per cent. With the cap at 51 per cent since 2006, there had been extremely limited FDI inflows in single-brand retail. Partly to bolster the external account, on 10 January 2012, the government allowed 100 per cent FDI in single-brand retail subject to mandatory sourcing of at least 30 per cent from domestic small and cottage industries and FIPB approval.

With elections to the Sixteenth Lok Sabha looming large in 2014, the signals from the macroeconomic developments worried the government. Inflation was known to be a game-spoiler for incumbent governments. FRBMA 2003, as amended in July 2004, had required the Union government to reduce its fiscal deficit as a proportion of GDP at 3 per cent or less and eliminate its revenue deficit by end-March 2009, when the world economy was in the throes of the Great Recession. As we have already noted, Mukherjee, in his Interim Budget 2009–10 before the 2009 Lok Sabha elections, had already invoked the FRBMA escape clause for extraordinary economic circumstances. Clause 4 of FRBMA 2003 containing the provision of the escape clause also required the Government to specify the path of return to annual prescribed targets under the section 'as soon as may be, before both the Houses of Parliament'.

2012–13

Finally, in his Budget for 2012–13—which was presented late on 16 March 2012 and incidentally would prove to be Mukherjee's last Budget before being elevated to President of India—presented an amended version of FRBMA 2003 with his Finance Bill, 2012. There were three important features in the amendments. First, the date for achieving fiscal deficit of no more than 3 per cent of GDP was pushed from end-March 2009 to end-March 2015. Second, he introduced the unique and controversial concept of 'effective revenue deficit' and required its elimination rather than that of the revenue deficit, again by end-March 2015. The effective revenue deficit was the revenue deficit reduced by the grants for creation of capital assets. By end-March 2015, the revenue deficit only had to be reduced to no more than 2 per cent of GDP. Third, the amendment provided for a 'Medium-term Expenditure Framework Statement' and set forth a three-year rolling target for expenditure indicators every year.

In personal income tax, Mukherjee enhanced the general exemption threshold from ₹1.8 lakh to ₹2 lakh and reduced the marginal tax rate for income between ₹8 lakh and ₹10 lakh from 30 per cent to 20 per cent. Simultaneously, he removed the special exemption for women below the age of sixty years. In service tax, where he had reduced the rate from 12 per cent to 10 per cent in 2011–12, he restored the rate at 12 per cent and for preventing disputes, introduced the place of supply rules to define such place of service as the location where services are received.

A major reform was the introduction of a negative list for service tax. From 1 July 2012, any service not mentioned under the negative list became subject to the service tax levy under the provisions of the Finance

Act, 2012. This widened the ambit of service tax considerably. The progressive extension of service tax even with regime changes demonstrated the growing maturity of Indian democracy. If a policy is endorsed by the people, then such a policy, even when it was initiated by a different party in the past, would be continued by the successor governments. Service tax provides a good example. It was introduced under Prime Minister Narasimha Rao of the Congress on 1 July 1994, and extended to more services: by United Front Finance Minister Chidambaram under Prime Minister Deve Gowda in 1996–97 and Prime Minister Inder Gujral in 1997–98, under NDA Prime Minister Atal Bihari Vajpayee during 1998–1999 and 2003–04, and under Congress Prime Minister Manmohan Singh in 2004–09 and 2009–10. And, in 2012, under Prime Minister Manmohan Singh and Finance Minister Pranab Mukherjee came the negative list for services from 1 July. Under NDA's Prime Minister Modi, from 1 July 2017, service tax would be integrated into GST.

Under excise, Mukherjee raised the standard rate from 10 per cent to 12 per cent, merit rate from 5 per cent to 6 per cent and the lower merit rate from 1 per cent to 2 per cent, with few exemptions. While he kept the peak rate of customs duty on non-agricultural goods at 10 per cent unchanged, he reduced the basic rate for certain agricultural equipment and their parts and granted full exemption from customs duty for import of equipment for setting up of fertilizer projects up to end-March 2015. Furthermore, he increased the cess on crude petroleum produced in the country to ₹4500 per metric ton. The fiscal deficit, as a proportion of GDP, in 2012–13, turned out to be 5.9 per cent relative to 4.9 per cent in 2011–12. An important landmark of Budget 2012–13 was the announcement of the establishment of a central KYC depository to avoid multiplicity of registration and data upkeep. This was a major move to bring the country's banking payment structure at par with global standards.

What acted up in the meantime was the 'Vodafone case'. In 2007, in the tax haven of Cayman Islands, for about $11 billion, Vodafone had bought a 67 per cent stake in Hutchison Whampoa, which included its Indian mobile telephony business. In September 2007, the Indian government had raised a demand of ₹7,990 crore in capital gains and withholding tax from Vodafone. Vodafone appealed to the Supreme Court and the apex court, on 20 January 2012, ruled that Vodafone's interpretation of the Income Tax Act, 1961 was correct, and its 2007 deal was not taxable in India. In less than a month, on 17 February, the government filed a review petition against the judgment and, in the Finance Bill 2012, introduced a retrospective clarification to the Income-Tax Act, 1961. This clarification or retrospective amendment became very contentious. On the one hand, there was a need to have provisions to avoid tax revenue losses because of base erosion and profit shifting (BEPS) by multinational companies. Furthermore, tax laws have been retrospectively amended by other countries such as the US, the UK and the Netherlands. On the other hand, some argued that such retrospective amendments would create uncertainties regarding the tax regime, undermine investor confidence and adversely affect foreign investment inflows. On 3 January 2013, the Indian government raised a fresh demand for ₹11,218 crore on Vodafone.

To file his nomination for the Presidential poll on 28 June 2012, Pranab Mukherjee resigned from the cabinet on 26 June 2012 and Prime Minister Manmohan Singh took charge of the finance ministry until 31 July 2012, when Chidambaram was back in his old position. On 14 September 2012, the government decided to allow 51 per cent FDI in multi-brand retail with effect from 20 September 2012. Permission was subject to FIPB's approval, a minimum investment of $100 million (of which a half would be in back-end infrastructure such as processing, manufacturing, cold chains and distribution), and 30 per cent procurement from SSI.·

Growth fell from 6.7 per cent in 2011–12 further to 4.5 per cent in 2012–13. On 6 August 2012, shortly after he assumed office, Chidambaram had listed fiscal consolidation as the most important challenge facing the Indian economy. He appointed a committee under Vijay Kelkar to recommend a roadmap for fiscal consolidation. The Kelkar Committee, in its report in September 2012, had cautioned that a business-as-usual scenario for 2012–13 might lead to the fiscal deficit rising to 6.1 per cent of GDP. The government considered such a high level of fiscal deficit to have adverse consequences for the economy. On 29 October 2012, he announced that the government had targeted the fiscal deficit as a proportion of GDP at 5.3 per cent for 2012–13 and 4.8 per cent for 2013–14. The Kelkar Committee had recommended administrative measures to improve tax revenue, new models of disinvestment to mobilize revenue and, in expenditure, rationalization of schemes and strict control. The government had accepted the recommendations, and Chidambaram on 29 October 2012 announced that there would be disinvestment in eight large CPSEs.

The Twelfth Five-Year Plan was starting from 1 April 2012. The Approach Paper to the Twelfth Plan had talked about an annual average rate of growth of 9 per cent. In July 2012, Montek Singh Ahluwalia, deputy chairman of the Planning Commission, said that 'it was not possible to think of an average of 9 per cent' in the Twelfth Plan. He downgraded the prospect to 8-8.5 per cent. Even with easy fiscal and monetary policies, the growth outlook was not looking bright and inflation, particularly increase in food prices, was a major problem. In each of the twenty-four months from April 2012 to March 2014, CPI inflation (all-India, over the corresponding month of the previous year) was between 8 per cent and 11.2 per cent.

With growth languishing in the world economy as well as in India, the target of fiscal deficit as a proportion of GDP looked daunting, particularly with backtracking in reduction of subsidies and shortfall in receipts from disinvestment. Nevertheless, Chidambaram managed to contain the fiscal deficit as a proportion of GDP at 4.9 per cent, well below the 5.3 per cent he had announced in October 2012.

Railway Budget 2012–13

Mamata Banerjee, the chairperson of AITC, had become the railway minister when UPA II came to power in May 2009. On 19 May 2011, Mamata quit to become the CM of West Bengal, and Dinesh Trivedi from the AITC succeeded her as railway minister on 12 July 2011.

The operating ratio—the ratio between operating expenses and operating revenue—had deteriorated from 91.1 per cent budgeted for 2011–12 to 95 per cent. There was hardly any surplus to invest in new projects and further developments. In his Railway Budget for 2012–13, on 14 March 2012, Minister Dinesh Trivedi announced: 'I propose to rationalise the fares to cause minimal impact on the common man and to keep the burden within tolerance limits in general. I am asking for an extra only 2 paise per km for suburban and ordinary second class. Similarly, increase for mail express second class will be by only 3 paise per km; for sleeper class by only 5 paise per km; for AC Chair Car, AC 3 tier and First Class by only 10 paise per km; AC 2 Tier by only 15 paise per km; and AC I by only 30 paise per km. Corresponding rationalisation in minimum distance and fare chargeable in various classes has also been proposed.'

Trivedi's own party colleagues in Parliament immediately opposed the fare increase and demanded a rollback. On the same day, at a rally in West Bengal's Nandigram—which, in its anti-land acquisition movement, had brought her to power in the state in 2011—she declared that she was not aware of rail minister Trivedi's decision to raise fares. She said her party would oppose the move and committed to block it at any cost. On the same day, she wrote to Prime Minister Manmohan Singh to replace Trivedi by Mukul Roy, another AITC minister in the UPA government. Manmohan Singh had described Trivedi's budget as progressive and modern, but AITC's support was critical for the UPA government's survival. Trivedi was replaced by Mukul Roy as railway minister on 20 March 2012. Roy withdrew the proposed hikes in fares for second-class suburban and non-suburban and sleeper class travel, and rolled back increases in the fares for air-conditioned chair cars and air-conditioned three-tier classes.

Railways 2013

In September 2012, when UPA II decided to limit the number of subsidized LPG cylinders to six per user, Mamata withdrew support for her nineteen members of Lok Sabha from the UPA II and demanded that the number of subsidized LPG cylinders be raised to twenty-four, and also reduce the price of diesel by ₹3-4 per litre, and not proceed with allowing FDI in retail trade. UPA II rejected the demands and AITC left the alliance. On 29 October 2012, Congress's Pawan Kumar Bansal became the railway minister.

Finally, Railway Minister Bansal, on 9 January 2013, ahead of the Railway Budget for 2013–14, announced an across-the-board railway passenger fare increase to take effect from 21 January 2013 and raise about ₹6600 crore. In his Railway Budget for 2013–14, he also introduced marginal increases in several charges—such as supplementary charge for superfast trains, reservation fee, clerkage charge, cancellation charge and *tatkal* (immediate booking) charge—as compensation for the cost actually incurred by railways in rendering relevant services.

Within six months of the departure of AITC, UPA II got further dented on 19 March 2013 when the DMK, with its eighteen Lok Sabha members, withdrew support and pulled out its five ministers on the issue of violations of human rights of Tamils in Sri Lanka.

2013–14

The international crude oil price of the Indian basket per barrel, had gone up steadily from $69.76 in 2009–10 to above $105 in 2012–14. Partly because of the higher import bill for oil and sluggishness of the global economy, the current account deficit as a proportion of GDP had gone up steadily from 2.82 per cent in 2009–10 to 4.82 per cent in 2012–13. WPI inflation, after jumping from 3.8 per cent in 2009–10 to 9.6 per cent in 2010–11, had come down to 7.4 per cent in 2012–13. But the increase in wholesale prices of food articles was particularly worrisome and the decline in food inflation from its perilously high level of 15.3 per cent in 2009–10 and 15.6 per cent in 2010–11 to 7.6 per cent in 2011–12 had proved to be temporary with such inflation increasing to 9.9 per cent in 2012–13. Presenting his Budget for 2013–14 on 28 February 2013, Chidambaram acknowledged that the Indian economy was challenged by 'high fiscal deficit; reliance on foreign inflows to finance the current account deficit; lower savings and lower investment; a tight monetary policy to contain inflation; and strong external headwinds.' He said that the purpose of his Budget was 'to create economic space and find resources to achieve the objective of inclusive development,' and reiterated his resolve to implement the path of fiscal consolidation already laid out in October 2012.

In the US, following the Lehman collapse, the systemic problems had revealed the problem of 'too big to fail' and market failure. Basel III was scheduled to be implemented between 2013 and 2015. In his Budget Speech for 2013–14, Chidambaram announced that India would ensure that public sector banks always met the Basel III regulations as they come into force in a phased manner. In the event, the implementation of Basel III got extended and was still ongoing when this book went to print.

In the Budget for 2013–14, for personal income tax, Chidambaram left the exemption threshold, slabs and rates unchanged. He reduced the STT rate on equity futures and mutual funds and exchange traded funds.

He argued that there was no distinction between derivative trading in the securities market and derivative trading in the commodities market, only the underlying asset was different, and reintroduced the CTT on non-agricultural commodities futures contracts at the same rate of 0.01 per cent of the price of the trade as on equity futures.

For 2013–14, in customs, Chidambaram left the peak rate of duty on non-agricultural commodities unchanged at 10 per cent. He granted some concessions, raised some rates and unified some rates to avoid classification problems. He raised the permissible limit for duty-free imports under baggage rules for incoming passengers, which had remained unchanged since 1991, to ₹50,000 for males and ₹1 lakh for females. In excise, Chidambaram granted some exemptions for industrial promotion, increased some specific rates to align them with higher prices, and extended MRP-based assessment to some products to avoid valuation disputes.

We will recall the completion of the CENVAT chain in textiles in 2003–04, when Jaswant Singh abolished the system of deemed credit to promote compliance, encourage modernization and reduce evasion. And how it was reversed by Chidambaram in 2004–05 and how Pranab Mukherjee partly restored the CENVAT chain in the textile industry by imposing an 8 per cent CENVAT duty on manmade fibre and yarn on a mandatory basis and at the rate on an optional basis on stages beyond fibre and yarn at that rate on an optional basis. In the 2013–14 Budget, describing the readymade garment industry to be in the throes of a crisis, Chidambaram restored the 'zero excise duty route' for cotton and manmade sector (spun yarn) at the yarn, fabric and garment stages. In addition to the CENVAT route, under the optional route, at the fibre stage, cotton would enjoy zero duty and spun yarn a duty of 12 per cent. The two reversals of the completion of the value chain in textiles under CENVAT may have reflected regional political compulsions that leaders faced.

In his Budget speech for 2007–08, Chidambaram had announced the introduction of GST from 1 April 2010. The introduction of GST was still awaited in 2013. Some compensation to the states for the reduction of CST from 4 per cent on 30 March 2007 to 1 per cent on 1 June 2008 was still pending and complicating the introduction of GST. In his Budget for 2013–14, he provided for a sum of ₹9000 crore as the first instalment of the balance CST compensation.

The Fifteenth Lok Sabha was completing its Constitutional mandate on 31 May 2014. On 17 February 2014, Chidambaram presented the Interim Budget for 2014–15. In 2013–14, the year just before the election, growth at 4.7 per cent was only slightly better than 4.5 per cent in 2012–13. Shortly before the end of the term of the Fifteenth Lok Sabha, in April 2014, at the Permanent Court of Arbitration at the Hague, Vodafone served investment treaty arbitration notices under the India-Netherlands Bilateral Investment Treaty (BIT).

Too little, too late

The stimulus had run its course by 2011–12 and more of it was leading to not growth but to inflation and balance of payments problems. From 2011, some economists had started to recommend an exit from the policy of stimulus. The reversal of the stimulus that came was too little and too late.

The effort at fiscal consolidation had succeeded in clawing back the deficit of the Union Government from 5.9 per cent in 2011–12 to 4.9 per cent and 4.5 per cent in the two subsequent years. But this again was too little, too late. The current account deficit as a proportion of GDP, which was 4.3 per cent in 2011–12, remained elevated at 4.8 per cent in 2012–13 and came down to 1.7 per cent only in 2013–14. There was pressure on both the external account and price front. The rupee had depreciated vis-à-vis the US dollar from ₹47.92 in 2011–12 to ₹54.41 in 2012–13 and ₹60.50 in 2013–14. Prices of tradable goods were up, and WPI increase had climbed down from 8.9 per cent in 2011–12 only to 6.9 per cent and 5.2 per cent in the two subsequent years. On 5 March 2014, the Election Commission of India announced that Lok Sabha elections would be held in nine phases between 7 April and 12 May 2014. Given the economic situation, the elections were too close for the UPA's comfort.

The run-up to the 2014 election was rough for the UPA and Congress. Apart from inflation, there were widespread cost and time overruns in project implementation, and allegations of policy paralysis and corruption. Many of these projects were stuck because of problems with land acquisition. Many, including some Congress leaders, considered

Jairam Ramesh, the minister for environment and forest between 2009 and 2011 and the chief architect of LARR2013 responsible for the policy paralysis.

XXVII.7 Policy Paralysis

The policy paralysis was reflected in the inability of the UPA in getting its proposed legislations passed expeditiously or passed at all. This led to economic policy uncertainty (EPU). Investors look for predictability of policies and abhor EPU. A major source of uncertainty arises when the fate of a proposed bill in Parliament hangs in the balance. In such a situation, investors can only speculate whether the old laws will continue or be replaced by new laws.

Economists have constructed EPU indices for different countries by using the frequency of three sets of terms—first, 'uncertain', 'uncertainties', or 'uncertainty'; second, 'economic' or 'economy'; and third, 'regulation', 'central bank', 'monetary policy', 'policymakers', 'deficit', 'legislation' and 'fiscal policy'—in some of the most prominent newspapers. By including seven Indian newspapers, they derived EPU for India for January 2003. The EPU was highly volatile across months in a year, but clearly revealed a tendency to rise along a fluctuating trend from 59.29 in 2003–04 to 142.30 in 2008–09 and then to a high of 182.78 in 2011–12 and 170.79 in 2012–13.

The proposed laws that remained uncertain for long periods during the UPA regime were the Banking Laws (Amendment) Act, Goods and Services Act, Pension Fund Regulatory and Development Authority Act, Direct Tax Code, Companies Act, Land Acquisition Act and Insurance Act.

XXVII.8 Corruption Charges

The UPA Government faced numerous corruption charges from 2010. One high-profile case involved the scam around the Adarsh Housing Society in Colaba, a posh locality in south Mumbai in Congress-ruled Maharashtra. The thirty-one-storey apartment building on land owned by the defence ministry was meant for 1999 Kargil war heroes and their widows. In 2010, it came to light that some politicians, including reportedly Chief Minister Ashok Chavan, bureaucrats and military officials, colluded to violate rules concerning land ownership and other norms to get flats allotted to themselves and their relatives in Adarsh Society. Chavan resigned from chief ministership of Maharashtra on 9 November 2010. The Adarsh Society scam, however, was on a relatively small scale and at the state level, there were the following far bigger alleged scams at the level of the Union government.

The 2G or telecom scam

A. Raja of DMK, minister for communications and IT since 16 May 2007, was tainted by the bizarre and controversial way the 2G spectrum and UASL had been allotted in January 2008 by the Department of Telecommunications (DoT). With memories of the Sukh Ram scandal in the early 1990s still alive, the 2G case evoked déjà vu among the public.

On 16 November 2010, the C&AG's report on the issuance of UASL and allocation of 2G spectrum by DoT was tabled in Parliament. It led to a furore. The report had pointed out that the allocation of 2G telecom licences in 2007 had not followed the UASL policy of the government of 2003. The UASL policy envisaged a second stage wherein while the entry fee would be a nominal sum, the spectrum would be charged separately. It stated that the allocation of spectrum 'at prices determined in 2001 which were based on a totally nascent market despite the sector witnessing substantial transformation and manifold growth' entailed huge losses for the exchequer.[6] It buttressed its argument by citing how licence owners had resold the licences to others at high premia. The amount actually received in 2007–08 was ₹12,386 crore, and under different assumptions, the C&AG estimated the amount under a more efficient allocation scheme could have been between ₹57,666 crore and ₹1,76,645 crore. The figure of ₹1.76 lakh crore made newspaper headlines and triggered virulent attacks by the opposition in Parliament.

What made the 2G scam even more explosive for UPA was the leak of the so-called 'Radia tapes'. Niira Radia was the high-profile owner and promoter of the multi-crore public relations firm called Vaishnavi Group, whose client list included some of India's biggest corporate entities such as the Tata Group and Reliance Industries. The CBI and the income tax department were investigating the telecom spectrum scam. With the necessary permissions, the income tax investigators had been tapping Radia's telephone from 20 August 2008 and recording the conversations. After the 2009 Lok Sabha victory, Manmohan Singh, along with his cabinet members, were going to swear in. The Radia tapes contained conversations in which A. Raja was lobbying hard to remain minister for communications and IT, and Radia was helping him in this. In the new government from 22 May 2009, A. Raja continued as minister for communications and IT. The tapes were leaked. A. Raja resigned from the cabinet on 14 November 2010. One of the fallouts of the 2G scam was the resounding defeat of the DMK, to which the tainted minister A. Raja belonged, in the Vidhan Sabha polls held in Tamil Nadu on 13 April 2011.

The trials in the 2G scam case began in November 2011 in a CBI court. In response to writ petitions filed by the Centre for Public Interest Litigation and others and Janata Party president Subramanian Swamy seeking the cancellation of the licences, on 2 February 2012, a two-member bench of the Supreme Court declared the illegal allocation of 2G spectrum by the Congress-led UPA government as an example of the arbitrary exercise of power, and cancelled all the 122 telecom licences allotted on or after 10 January 2008 to eleven companies during the tenure of the former telecom minister, A. Raja. A fresh auction was conducted in November 2012, and only ₹17,343 crore was received as bids from the sale of spectrum in eighteen circles and a one-time fee. There was some relief in government circles that the figure was nowhere close to the ₹1.76 lakh crore mentioned in the C&AG report. But soon, in about thirty rounds of e-auction for the allocation of 2G licenses for 900 and 1800 MHz in the four circles that had received no bids in the earlier auction, the amount netted was ₹61,162 crore, taking the net income of the government closer to what the C&AG had calculated on a presumptive basis. Five years later, in December 2017, Raja and the others accused in the case would be released for lack of evidence of criminality. But the acquittal came much after the Lok Sabha election in 2014. In the meantime, the alleged 2G scam provided critical fuel for the India Against Corruption movement led by Anna Hazare and was frequently invoked by the BJP in the lead-up to the 2014 polls.

AgustaWestland chopper scam

In August 1999, the Indian Air Force, which is responsible for ferrying the President, Prime Minister and other dignitaries or VVIPs, had proposed the replacement of the Soviet Mi-8 helicopters due to operational constraints. In March 2002, a global request for proposals had been issued. In 2006, the Indian government had floated a proposal for a brand-new set of VVIP helicopters to replace the Soviet Mi-8 helicopters. After a long process, that involved changes in evaluation parameters and negotiations, in January 2010, the Cabinet Committee on Security had cleared the proposal to acquire twelve helicopters. On 8 February 2010, the ministry of defence had concluded a contract for the supply of twelve AW-101 VVIP helicopters with AgustaWestland. The contract was for ₹3600 crore. Controversy over the deal flared up when, on 12 February 2013, the Italian government arrested Giuseppe Orsi, the chief executive of Finmeccanica, AgustaWestland's parent company, over corruption and bribery charges. On the following day, Indian Defence Minister A.K. Antony ordered a probe into the contract. A few days later, the government initiated action for cancellation of contract by issuing a formal show cause notice to AgustaWestland seeking cancellation of contract and taking other actions as per the terms of the contract and the integrity pact.

On 27 February 2013, by a motion passed in the Rajya Sabha after a walkout by most Opposition members, the UPA government proposed to set up a Joint Parliamentary Committee (JPC) to probe the chopper scam. BJP took strong exception to the UPA's JPC decision.

Investigations were handed over to the CBI. In March 2013, CBI registered a first information report (FIR) against Air Marshall S.P. Tyagi, who had been the chief of the Indian Air Force between 31 December 2004 and 31 March 2007, and twelve others for alleged criminal conspiracy and cheating in the chopper deal. Defence Minister A.K. Antony admitted that bribes were paid in the AgustaWestland deal. India cancelled the contract on 1 January 2014 and, by encashing the bank guarantee of the company it had received in Italian banks, recovered 45 per cent of the value of the contract it had paid in advance. The company had delivered only three helicopters.

The AgustaWestland chopper scam became a major weapon in the hands of the opposition, particularly the BJP, in the electoral battle for the Sixteenth Lok Sabha in 2014. Alleged references to 'AP', along with 'BUR', 'AF', and some others—where the abbreviations reportedly were references to the late Ahmed Patel, the all-powerful political secretary to Congress president Sonia Gandhi, bureaucrats and air force, respectively—in the contracts that Finmeccanica (AgustaWestland's parent company) signed with middleman Christian Michel James added to the heat that the UPA and the Congress faced in the run-up to the election.

Commonwealth Games or CWG scam

The Commonwealth Games, which started as British Empire Games in 1930, is a mini-Olympic for members of the Commonwealth every four years. It is conducted by the Commonwealth Games Federation. The Commonwealth of Nations, popularly known as the Commonwealth, is a voluntary association of fifty-four nations, all except two former British colonies.

In November 2003, under the NDA government, the right to host the Commonwealth Games in 2010 (CWG-2010) was awarded to Delhi based on the May 2003 bid of the Indian Olympic Association (IOA), and the guarantee of the Union government, in conjunction with the government of the National Capital Territory of Delhi, to bear the financial liability for hosting the Games, including underwriting any shortfall between revenues and expenditure. CWG-2010 was the first big international sports event India was hosting after the Asian Games in 1982. Some considered the CWG-2010 a wastage of funds for a country such as India, with its challenges of poverty, malnutrition and illiteracy. In December 2004, Suresh Kalmadi was appointed as the chairman of the Organizing Committee for CWG-2010.

Suresh Kalmadi, a former Indian Air Force pilot, was from the Congress Party and an MP for many years, a minister of state, and president of the IOA during 1996–2002. Sunil Dutt, the sports minister in 2004, had objected to the appointment, and Dutt's successor M.S. Gill and Mani Shankar Aiyar, in 2007, had expressed serious reservations about what was going on in the run-up to the CWG-2010 under Kalmadi. In the run-up to the games during 3-14 October 2010, there were also some anxious weeks and months about the lack of preparedness. In the event, the games were successfully hosted in due course.

What created the utmost furore was the evidence of misappropriation of funds in the organization of the games. BJP leaders had been demanding a probe by a JPC from August 2010. Even before the games were hosted, there had been complaints to the Central Vigilance Commissioner (CVC), the anti-graft watchdog, of discrepancies in the work being undertaken by civic agencies like Municipal Corporation of Delhi (MCD), New Delhi Municipal Council (NDMC), Delhi Development Authority (DDA) and Central Public Works Department, among others. The CVC had found irregularities in several construction projects. From August 2010, the Citizen's Forum for Commonwealth Games, with BJP leaders at the forefront, was demanding the resignation of Kalmadi and other officials of the Organizing Committee of CWG. After the games, the C&AG reported that compared to the IOA's estimated all-inclusive cost of just ₹1200 crore in its original bid of May 2003, as of October 2010, for CWG-2010, the budget estimate of Government of India and Delhi government, Municipal Corporation of Delhi and New Delhi Municipal Corporation, and related agencies was ₹18,532 crore. What was originally proposed as a revenue-neutral project turned out to be a costly one. The C&AG also found evidence of irregularities in the award of contracts.

After the games, citing 'unprecedented rise in cases of corruption in high places', the opposition, in particular the BJP, was demanding a JPC to probe into the 2G and CWG scam. In the process, Parliament was stalled for several days. Suresh Kalmadi along with some others were arrested on 25 April 2011. In May 2011, the CBI filed its first chargesheet in a Delhi court against Kalmadi, alleging that he was the 'main accused' in a corruption case pertaining to irregularities in awarding a CWG-2010–related contract to a Swiss firm.[7] In February 2013, in a fast-track court, he and nine others were charged with cheating, forgery and criminal conspiracy. The CWG-2010 scam remained a potent weapon of the opposition parties in their crusade against the Congress in the run-up to the Lok Sabha elections.

Coalgate or the coal allocation scam

The ministry of coal had been mired in serious controversies ever since Shibu Soren, the tribal leader of JMM, became the minister in the UPA Cabinet on 23 May 2004. He was first convicted in the Chirudih massacre of 23 January 1975, and then again for murdering Shashi Nath Jha, his private secretary. Having been in and out of the ministry on account of criminal charges, Soren finally resigned as coal minister.

The woes of the ministry of coal were compounded by allegations of corruption in the allocation of coal blocks during 2007–12. The C&AG, under commercial audit, had carried out a performance audit of such allocation of coal blocks and augmentation of coal production by government-owned Coal India Limited (CIL) during the Eleventh Five-Year Plan, 2007–12. The C&AG pointed out how a note by Secretary (Coal) on 16 July 2004 had pointed out that, given the difference between the price of coal charged by CIL and the cost of coal produced from captive mines, captive mines should be allocated by auction. Allocations based on the recommendations of the Screening Committee would result in windfall gains for the allottees. For the government, allocation by auction would capture a part of this windfall and that was the way forward. Despite this note, the government had not adopted auction as the method of allocation. Between July 2004 and March 2012, 194 coal blocks had been allocated to both public and private entities without competitive bidding. The C&AG estimated financial gains to the allottees of ₹1.86 lakh crore, a part of which could have accrued to the national exchequer under competitive bidding for coal blocks.

The C&AG report was tabled in Parliament on 17 August 2012. The opposition smelled corruption and the 'coalgate' scandal broke. During the five years of UPA I, except for some 460 days in three stints during 2004–2006, the Prime Minister held the Coal portfolio. 'Koyle ki dalali hai, saari Congress Kali hai' (there is a scam in coal allocation, the entire Congress is black) and 'Pradhanmantri istipha do' (PM quit) were some of the slogans raised in both Houses. On 29 May 2012, Prime Minister Manmohan Singh offered to give up his public life if found guilty in the scam. Two days later, based on a complaint from two BJP MPs—Prakash Javadekar and Hansraj Ahir—the CVC ordered a CBI enquiry.

In late-August 2012, the government claimed that the presumptive loss calculated by the C&AG was flawed as no mining had taken place in the allocated coal blocks. In early September 2012, a PIL in the Supreme Court sought cancellation of allotments of the 194 coal blocks, and the Supreme Court started monitoring the CBI probe into the coal field allocations. In March 2013, it asked CBI not to share probe details with the government. In the following month, the Parliamentary Standing Committee on Coal and Steel declared that, between 1993 and 2008, the coal blocks were distributed in an unauthorized manner, and the allotment where production had not yet started should be cancelled. In April 2013, CBI Director Ranjit Sinha in an affidavit said that the investigation report had been shared with Law Minister Ashwani Kumar. Within a fortnight, Ashwani Kumar resigned. CBI registered FIRs against Naveen Jindal and Dasari Narayana Rao in June, and against industrialist Kumar Mangalam Birla and former coal secretary P.C. Parakh in October 2013. The coalgate scam raged in the run-up to the nine-phase Lok Sabha elections in April-May 2014.

India Against Corruption and Anna Hazare

The UPA prepared a draft Lokpal Bill in 2010. A 'Lokpal' or defender of people is an anti-corruption authority or ombudsman representing public interest. There had been nine unsuccessful legislative attempts in the past since 1968 to introduce a Lokpal. In February 2011, the Supreme Court, while sentencing former Congress minister R. Balakrishna Pillai in Kerala to one year's imprisonment, directed all High Courts to monitor the cases of graft and seek quarterly reports. The Lokpal Bill in Parliament came into public prominence.

The anti-corruption activist from Maharashtra, Anna Hazare, who had filed a public interest petition in the Bombay High Court in the Telgi scam around 2003, became active on the Lokpal issue. On 26 February 2011, he announced that he would go on a fast unto death from 5 April if Prime Minister Manmohan Singh did not include civil society in drafting the Lokpal Bill. On 5 April, along with his supporters, Anna paid tribute to Mahatma Gandhi at Rajghat, marched to Jantar Mantar and started his fast. There were protests by his supporters in hundreds of places across the country. On 9 April, Anna broke his fast after the government agreed to notify the formation of a ten-member joint drafting panel, with half the members from civil society, to suggest the anti-corruption bill and introduce it in the monsoon session of Parliament. The India Against Corruption movement was on from April 2011 with Anna in the forefront, and Arvind Kejriwal, an Indian Revenue Service officer-turned-social activist, and Kiran Bedi, a well-known former policewoman and activist, among others, in the core group. The group demanded an ombudsman to investigate corruption in the government and proposed the Jan (People's) Lokpal Bill for enactment. It had been drafted by Santosh Hegde, former Supreme Court judge; Prashant Bhushan, Supreme Court lawyer and Arvind Kejriwal.

India's most famous yoga guru Baba Ramdev had adversely commented on the composition of the civil society members of the drafting committee for the Jan Lokpal Bill, particularly the inclusion of the father and son duo of Shanti Bhushan and Prashant Bhushan. On 14 April 2011, Baba Ramdev appealed to the Union government to arm the Jan Lokpal Bill with punitive powers, including sentencing to death. He also wanted the Prime Minister to be covered under the purview of the Lokpal.

In nine meetings during April-June 2011, the Joint Drafting Committee could not agree on six basic issues: (i) whether there should be a single Lokpal Act for both the Union and the states; whether the act should cover (ii) the Prime Minister, (iii) judges of Supreme and High Courts, (iv) the conduct of MPs inside the Parliament and (v) the members of the civil service; and (vi) whether the Lokpal should exercise judicial powers.

Baba Ramdev announced a mass indefinite fast in Delhi's Ramlila Maidan (ground) from 4 June 2011 to demand reforms, including the death penalty for corrupt officials in an anti-graft campaign. He also demanded bringing back black money stashed abroad and demonetization of ₹500 and ₹1000 notes. On 1 June 2011, Baba Ramdev arrived in Delhi from Ujjain by a chartered flight. Finance Minister Pranab Mukherjee and three of his cabinet colleagues met with him and held talks at the Delhi airport. Baba Ramdev did not relent and went ahead with his planned fast from 4 June.

The permission for the Ramlila Maidan site was for a yoga camp for 5000. The police claimed that they cancelled the permission when it turned out to be an agitation by 65,000 people and asked them to move on. Police surrounded the ground, entered the fast site and showed Baba Ramdev his order for externment. Reportedly, the Baba asked for some time and hid himself after jumping off from the stage. 'About two hours later, he was caught outside the protest site while posing as an injured woman wearing a white-coloured *salwar* suit with his head covered with a *dupatta*. At the time of arrest, he was pretending to be moving with the support of two women around whom he put his arms.'[8] He was quickly deported to Haridwar. While it was a serious matter with political implications, this did not prevent the media from commenting tongue-in-cheek that the salwar suit 'flattered his slender yogic image' and his 'womanly garb appeared more carefully picked out than a last-minute choice'.[9]

The Lok Pal Bill, 2011 was introduced in the Lok Sabha on 4 August 2011 and withdrawn. India Against Corruption restarted the agitation by burning copies of the draft Lokpal Bill. Hazare also declared that if the Jan Lokpal Bill was not passed by the Parliament by 15 August 2011, he would proceed on an indefinite fast from 16 August 2011. Ultimately, it became a question of supremacy of the elected MPs in legislative matters. The Lokpal and Lokayuktas Bill, 2011 was introduced on 22 December 2011, and passed by the Lok Sabha on 27 December 2011. The bill would be applicable to states only if they gave their consent to its application.

Anna Hazare, unhappy with the draft bill, declared that he would be launching a fresh agitation from 27 December in Mumbai and from 30 December in Delhi. The protests continued, but on a declining scale. Fatigue was setting in. Furthermore, Team Anna broke up in September 2012 on the question of forming a political party. Arvind Kejriwal and some of his associates went on to form a political party called Aam Aadmi Party and become chief minister of Delhi on 28 December 2013. After forty-eight days in office, he resigned as chief minister of Delhi after failing to table the Jan Lokpal Bill in the Delhi Assembly because of what he claimed to be opposition from the Congress and the BJP. The India Against Corruption agitations petered out, and the Rajya Sabha passed the Lokpal and Lokayuktas Bill, 2011 with amendments on 17 December 2013. The Bill was passed by the Lok Sabha the following day. It came into force after notification on 16 January 2012. But alleged corruption remained a major poll issue and a liability for the UPA in the 2014 Lok Sabha elections.

XXVIII

The First Modi Government

In 2008, Prime Minister Manmohan Singh had been hailed as 'Singh is King', after the title of a Bollywood film. His image got a further boost when he secured a second consecutive term in office in 2009. The decay set in soon thereafter. 'Two out of three say UPA is corrupt,' reported a national daily on 24 November 2013.[1] Furthermore, his image, which had been boosted by the way he salvaged the US-India Civil Nuclear Agreement in July 2008, also suffered because of the lack of coordination between the government and the Congress. Congress president Sonia Gandhi had to be away for medical treatment for prolonged periods. The appointment of her son Rahul Gandhi as vice president did not ease the coordination problem. For example, there was considerable embarrassment when, in a press conference on 27 September 2013, Rahul denounced and tore up the Representation of the People (Amendment and Validation) Ordinance, 2013 that the Government had issued three days earlier to protect convicted MPs and MLAs from immediate disqualification as per a Supreme Court judgement.

Prior to the 2014 Lok Sabha election, the BJP and the NDA also underwent major changes. In the National Executive Committee meeting of the BJP in Goa during 8-9 June 2013, where several senior leaders, such as Lal Krishna Advani, were absent, Gujarat Chief Minister Narendra Modi was appointed chairman of the party's election campaign committee. Because of the communal riots in Gujarat in 2002 when Modi was its CM, his appointment as BJP's face for the 2014 Lok Sabha election resulted in a rapture of the long-running seventeen-year alliance of JD(U) and its leader Nitish Kumar with BJP and the NDA. On 16 June 2013, Chief Minister Nitish Kumar of Bihar, heading a BJP-JD(U) government, walked out of the NDA. BJP announced Narendra Modi as its prime ministerial candidate in mid-September 2013. By the end of 2013, in the NDA, apart from Ramdas Athawale-led RPI (A), the BJP was left with only two major allies in the SAD and Shiv Sena. The NDA, however, acquired four more constituents before the Lok Sabha polls: MDMK, Rashtriya Lok Samata Party led by Upendra Kushwaha, LJP led by Ram Vilas Paswan, and TDP.

It was a nine-phase election between 7 April and 12 May 2014. In a six-month high-voltage campaign, Modi travelled more than 3,00,000 km, addressed over 430 rallies and over 5800 public events. The campaign was focused on the promise of good governance and development. Modi projected himself as 'Vikas Purush' or Development Man. The slogan was 'Sab ka saath, sab ka vikas', or collective effort and inclusive growth.

Growth had decelerated from over 8.5 per cent in 2009–10 and 2010–11 to 6.7 per cent in 2011–12 and further to around 4.5 per cent in the two subsequent years 2012–13 and 2013–14. WPI inflation (2004–05 series) had climbed up from 3.8 per cent in 2009–10 to 9.6 per cent in 2010–11 before climbing down slowly to 8.9 per cent and 7.4 per cent in the two subsequent years and reach 6 per cent in 2013–14, a somewhat elevated level for a pre-election year. Inflation in India during the UPA regime was also a victim of the rise in crude oil prices in the world markets. Annual average price of Indian crude oil basket (FOB) per barrel had gone up from $27.98 in 2003–04, the last year of NDA rule, to a high of $111.89 in 2011–12 before climbing down mildly to $105.52 in its last year in 2013–14. Macroeconomic conditions did not look propitious for the UPA, but the UPA and its leadership were secure in their belief that their contribution to social welfare through its rights-based approach would bring in rich electoral dividends.

The BJP swept the Hindi heartland of Bihar (forty) and UP (eighty), accounting for 120 of the 543 Lok Sabha seats. In these two states, relative to the preceding Lok Sabha election in 2009, it increased its seats from twelve and ten to twenty-two and seventy-one, respectively. In UP, from the Congress, only Sonia Gandhi and Rahul Gandhi managed to secure victory. The BJP's performance in Bihar was particularly noteworthy in view of the break-up of its seventeen-year-old alliance with JD(U) headed by Nitish Kumar. In the north, BJP's performance was equally impressive in Delhi (all seven seats), Uttarakhand (all five), Haryana (seven out of ten), and Rajasthan (all twenty-five). In the west, the BJP won handsomely in Chhattisgarh (ten out of eleven), Goa (both), Gujarat (all twenty-six), Madhya Pradesh (twenty-seven out of twenty-nine), and Maharashtra (twenty-three out of forty-eight). In Maharashtra, its ally Shiv Sena won eighteen seats.

With its tally going up from thirteen in 2009 to twenty-two, BJP gained nine seats in the eastern major states of Assam, West Bengal, Odisha and Jharkhand, with 91 seats. In the major states in the south, namely Andhra Pradesh, Karnataka, Kerala, and Tamil Nadu, in terms of seats won—twenty-one in 2014 compared to twenty in 2009—the BJP's performance was nothing impressive. But like in Maharashtra where its ally Shiv Sena secured major victories, in Andhra Pradesh, its ally TDP led by Chandrababu Naidu won sixteen of the forty-two seats. In 2014, the BJP obtained a foothold in all the major states except Kerala, which did not return any BJP candidate to the Lok Sabha. While the Telangana state was formed out of Andhra Pradesh on 2 July 2014 when the successor NDA was already in power, the announcement of its imminent creation before the polls resulted in a severe electoral setback for the UPA and Congress in Andhra Pradesh. Its tally in Andhra Pradesh came down from thirty-three in 2009 to two in 2014. People in coastal Andhra and Rayalseema regions resented the break-up of their state, and for the people in Telangana, it came after too much procrastination.

After 1984, it was after a long gap of three decades that a political party commanded an absolute majority in the Lok Sabha. The verdict indicated an unequivocal shift in India's political preferences. BJP's vote share of 31.5 per cent was its best; that of the Congress, 19.6 per cent, its lowest ever, surprisingly similar to that of BJP in 2009. In 2014, the BJP got 64 million more votes than the Congress. The swing away from Congress (9 per cent) was like what it suffered between 1971 and 1977, and 1984 and 1989. But, in 2014, the loss from an already precarious low base took it below the threshold of 20 per cent, when converting votes into seats became an uphill task. The 12.7 per cent swing in favour of BJP was unprecedented in Indian electoral history. It is one-and-a-half times what BJP managed between 1989 and 1991 and lent credence to the 'Modi wave' hypothesis. The NDA's victory was partly based on BJP's good performance in Gujarat under Modi for almost thirteen years. On their own, BJP allies in NDA managed to increase their vote share only marginally, but they more than doubled their seats from twenty-five to fifty-three.

The Congress landed only forty-four seats in the Sixteenth Lok Sabha, less than an eighth of what Rahul's father, the late Rajiv Gandhi, managed (404) in 1984 after the assassination of Indira Gandhi. It was less than a half of the 114 seats that Congress won in 1999 when the NDA first came to power. With its tally at less than 10 per cent of the total seats, the Constitution would not allow the Congress leader to be recognized as Leader of the Opposition!

The election results were announced on 16 May 2014. Sworn in as Prime Minister on 26 May 2014, Modi, unlike Manmohan Singh, was no accidental prime minister. With BJP announcing him as its prime ministerial candidate as early as mid-September 2013, the elevation could not have been more deliberate.

XXVIII.1 Reiteration of Commitment to Fiscal Consolidation and Direct Benefit Transfer

On 10 July, presenting the regular budget for 2014–15, Finance Minister Arun Jaitley said, 'The steps that I will announce in this Budget are only the beginning of a journey towards a sustained growth of 7-8 per cent or above within the next three to four years along with macro-economic stabilization that includes lower levels of inflation, lesser fiscal deficit and a manageable current account deficit.' He pointed out that his predecessor had left him with the difficult task of reducing the fiscal deficit from 4.5 per cent in 2013–14 to 4.1 per cent of GDP in 2014–15, especially with slowing growth, low tax buoyancy and growing subsidy burden. However, he accepted this target for 2014–15 as a challenge, and set the targets for fiscal deficit as a proportion of GDP at 3.6 per cent in 2015–16 and 3.0 per cent for 2016–17. He emphasized the need for generating more revenues for developmental expenditure without leaving behind a legacy of more debt for future generations. Without additional revenues, however, the burden of fiscal consolidation fell on expenditure reduction.

Direct benefit transfer, overhaul of subsidy regime 2014 and electronic payment framework

After rolling out DBT of some subsidies from 1 January 2013, just before the Lok Sabha election, the UPA government had retreated and kept the scheme in abeyance from 7 March 2014. The NDA, shortly after coming to power, reintroduced DBT for LPG in fifty-four districts in mid-November 2014 and rolled it out nationally from January 2015. More and more districts and more and more schemes, for example, those pertaining to scholarships, women, child and labour welfare, were brought under DBT. By 12 December 2014, DBT was expanded across the country. Seven new scholarship schemes and MGNREGA were brought under DBT in 300 identified districts with higher Aadhaar enrolment. From 1 April 2015, LPG subsidies were distributed solely by electronic transfer under DBT. Budget 2014–15 promised to overhaul the subsidy regime, including food and petroleum subsidies, and make it more targeted while providing full protection to the marginalized, poor and SC/STs, and formulate and announce a new urea policy.

Transition to DBT for subsidy schemes helped the government save a considerable amount of money by plugging leakages. For example, 4.23 crore duplicate, fake/non-existent, inactive LPG connections, and 2.98 crore duplicate, and fake/non-existent ration cards were eliminated by end-March 2019. Savings (cumulative) from transition to DBT up to March 2018 amounted to ₹90,013 crore, and ₹51,665 crore in 2018–19.

Direct benefit transfer for fertilizer subsidy—An unfinished agenda

The transition to DBT to farmers for subsidy on urea proved harder. The MRP of urea per ton was only ₹5360 while the cost per ton varied from about ₹15,000 to ₹25,000 across the thirty-one producing firms. The units sold urea at the same price but got paid on the basis of their own respective production costs. The sector suffered from two major problems: the existence of high-cost units in the public sector such as in Barauni, Gorakhpur and Sindri, and the risk of the subsidy not reaching the farmers. According to the government's Economic Survey 2015–16, 'as much as 24 per cent of the subsidy was spent on inefficient producers, 41 per cent was diverted to non-agricultural uses, including smuggling to neighbouring countries, and 24 per cent was consumed by larger, presumably richer farmers. That left a tiny 11 per cent for small and marginal farmers, who, according to Modi, should have been the sole beneficiaries of the subsidy.'

With the e-Fertilizer Monitoring System (e-FMS) extended to the entire country in March 2018, disbursal of the full subsidy to producers became conditional on only their actual sales to farmers and these getting registered on point-of-sale (PoS) machines at the dealer's shop. But, with subsidy continuing to be routed through manufacturers, this was not DBT.

Kisan Vikas Patra

The Kisan Vikas Patra launched in 1988, with its high-interest cost and anonymity, had reportedly become an avenue for laundering black money into white, and was discontinued in 2011. The anonymity problem was addressed by introducing KYC norms regarding all National Savings Schemes from January 2012. Furthermore, from 2012–13, the interest rates on various Small Savings Schemes were recalculated and notified annually in March every year, mitigating the problem of high cost. Given the popularity of the Kisan Vikas Patra, it was reintroduced by the 2014–15 Budget.

Mixed success

The outcome of fiscal consolidation was a mixed one at best, but better than what many of the predecessor governments had achieved. In 2014–15, the fiscal deficit as a proportion of GDP did come down from 4.5 per cent in the previous year to 4.1 per cent. But after the first full year, in 2015–16, relative to the target of 3.6 per cent, the fiscal deficit was 3.9 per cent, and in 2016–17, the actual was 3.5 per cent relative to the target of 3.0 per cent. In the last two years of the first Modi government, the fiscal deficit was 3.5 per cent and 3.4 per cent of GDP.[2]

XXVIII.2 Resolution of the Vodafone Case

The Vodafone tax case had been hanging fire since 2007, and the matter had become very contentious after the 2012 retrospective clarification to the Income-Tax (I-T) Act, 1961 and various court judgments. Finance Minister Jaitley, in his Budget speech 2014–15, promised to introduce any retrospective change in tax laws with extreme caution and judiciousness, and get all possible fresh cases arising out of the retrospective amendments of 2012 in respect of indirect transfers scrutinized by a High-Level Committee under the CBDT before initiating any action. The case was, however, close to resolution only in 2021 after Jaitley's successor, Finance Minister Nirmala Sitharaman, brought into effect the Taxation Law (Amendment) Act. The act made transactions before 28 May 2012 beyond its purview.

XXVIII.3 Promoting Defence Manufacturing and Attracting FDI

Ironically, India, a nuclear power and quite advanced in missile technology, did not have a vibrant indigenous defence industry. It relied largely on the rest of the world for its supplies of arms, ammunition and other defence equipment. According to the Stockholm International Peace Research Institute (SIPRI), India, accounting for 15 per cent of global weapons imports between 2010 and 2014, was the world leader in the import of arms, ammunition and defence equipment. India had allowed private sector participation in the defence industry subject to licensing, and FDI in such enterprises was subject to a composite cap of 26 per cent of its equity. In defence, a technology-intensive industry, there was a need for appropriate technology transfer from global firms. Accordingly, to attract FDI, the Modi government raised the composite cap of 26 per cent on FDI in defence manufacturing to 49 per cent with full Indian management and control through the FIPB route. Similarly, the composite cap of 26 per cent on FDI was also raised to 49 per cent for insurance. To encourage the development of Smart Cities, which would also provide homes for the new middle class, requirement of the built-up area and capital conditions for FDI was reduced from 50,000 square metres to 20,000 square metres and from US$10 million to US$5 million, respectively, with a three-year post-completion lock-in.

XXVIII.4 Abolition of Planning Commission 2014

In his first Independence Day speech from the ramparts of the historic Red Fort in Delhi, Prime Minister Modi announced the scrapping of the

Planning Commission. By a press release on 1 January 2015, the Planning Commission was replaced by the National Institution for Transforming India (NITI) Aayog.

The Planning Commission, established on 15 March 1950 through a Cabinet resolution, not only increased the concentration of economic powers in the hands of the Centre, but also detracted from the powers of the Constitutionally-mandated Finance Commission. The Planning Commission had basically become a channel for transferring funds to the states outside the Finance Commission route, raising allegations about favouritism towards states ruled by the same party as in the centre, and intervening in areas, such as health, which were assigned to the states. The most common method of Centre's intervention in areas constitutionally assigned to the states was through the centrally sponsored plan schemes and central sector schemes. From the Fourth Five-Year Plan, the Gadgil formula and then the Gadgil-Mukherjee formula had removed some of the subjectivity in the inter-se transfer of funds among the states, but not entirely. Furthermore, the Union government's fiscal deterioration had led to the disappearance of BCR after the First Five-Year Plan. From the Second Plan, there was no BCR to support the plans.

The lifespan of the Indian Planning Commission proved to be only seven years shorter than that of the famous Soviet Gosplan. In the former Soviet Union, the State Planning Agency, Gosplan, set up in 1921, was dissolved on 1 April 1991. It can be argued that even the Indian Planning Commission should have been abolished in 1991 with the launch of market-based reforms, or shortly thereafter. Even if all that is set aside as a matter of ancient history, the important question that remains is the optimality of its substitution by the NITI Aayog.

Like its predecessor, the Planning Commission, the NITI Aayog is an extra-Constitutional body, set up by a resolution of the Union Cabinet on 1 January 2015. But, unlike its predecessor, it does not have any powers to distribute funds for development purposes. It is expected to perform two functions: as the premier policy 'think tank' of the Government of India, providing both directional and policy inputs, and 'as the quintessential platform of the Government of India to bring States to act together in national interest, and thereby foster Cooperative Federalism'.[3]

Admittedly, the NITI Aayog has already given some useful advice, such as providing a model Agricultural Land Leasing Law for the states to adopt, organizing three sub-groups of chief ministers of states to produce reports on the way forward in CSS, how to implement skill development, and how to achieve Swachh Bharat; advocating strategic sale of loss-making Air India after hiving off its real estate properties; and proposing reforms to the Medical Council of India. Judging the usefulness of the advice by progress so far on their implementation yields a mixed picture. For example, instead of according a Parliamentary nod to the model Agricultural Land Leasing Law, the central government left it to the states to adopt it. Madhya Pradesh, with its Bhumiswami Evam Bataidar Ke Hiton Ka Sanrakshan Bill, which it passed on 29 July 2016, was the first state to accept the advice. Others such as Uttarakhand, Uttar Pradesh, Maharashtra and Andhra Pradesh followed. But many were yet to adopt the model law. Similarly, CSS has been classified into three groups—core of the core, core and optional, and the number of 'core of the core' and of 'core' have been fixed at six and twenty-two, respectively. But the disproportionate increase in central allocation under core by 32.3 per cent from ₹1722 billion to ₹2278 billion between 2016–17 and 2018–91 (BE), compared to 11.8 per cent increase under 'core of the core' from ₹695 billion to ₹777 billion appears counterintuitive.

Perhaps, not having any substitute after the Planning Commission's sudden death was too much of a jolt to give to the system. Nevertheless, the question still remains whether having a 500-strong government-owned institution is the best way for having a premier 'think tank', or promoting cooperative federalism, or monitoring the progress of flagship schemes. The optimal organizational structure as well as staffing policy of NITI Aayog vis-à-vis those of the Planning Commission—undoubtedly critical issues—have so far attracted limited attention. Also, the relative roles of the Constitutional Inter-state Council and of the ministry of statistics and programme implementation vis-à-vis the NITI Aayog merit scrutiny in the medium term. Under the chairmanship of the Prime Minister and with all the chief ministers in the country and six Union ministers of cabinet rank, the Inter-state Council is potentially a very powerful body.

XXVIII.5 New or Revamped Schemes

On 15 August 2014, apart from abolition of the Planning Commission, Prime Minister Modi emphasized two reforms of fundamental importance—Swachh Bharat Abhiyan (SBA) or Clean India Mission, and PMJDY. Then there were other schemes for rural electrification, female child, immunization, promoting entrepreneurship, skill formation and some others.

Swachh Bharat Abhiyan

As Jean Dreze and Amartya Sen commented in 2013: 'Sometimes the most important things in life are least talked about. For instance, it is hard to think of anything more important than health for human well-being and the quality of life. And yet, health is virtually absent from public debates and democratic politics in India.'[4] Discussing the 'stinking' problem of open defecation in India was a taboo among the well-to-do sections of the country. Modi broke the rule and did the unthinkable. In his speech to the nation on Independence Day 2014, he said: 'Brother and Sisters, we are living in 21st century. Has it ever pained us that our mothers and sisters have to defecate in open? Whether dignity of women is not our collective responsibility? The poor womenfolk of the village wait for the night; until darkness descends, they can't go out to defecate. What bodily torture they must be feeling, how many diseases that act might engender. Can't we just make arrangements for toilets for the dignity of our mothers and sisters? . . . The poor need respect and it begins with cleanliness. I, therefore, have to launch a "clean India" campaign from 2nd October this year and carry it forward in 4 years.'[5]

The SBA was launched on Mahatma Gandhi's 146th birth anniversary on 2 October 2014. It differed from the earlier Nirmal Bharat Abhiyan (NBA) in three respects: first, with two components, SBA (Grameen or rural) and SBA (Urban), SBA, unlike NBA, covered both rural and urban areas; second, subsidy for individual household latrine was raised from ₹10,000 to ₹12,000; and third, there was a lot of emphasis on behavioural change through community involvement and public awareness through information, education and communication. A celebrated example was in Indore, where the municipal corporation introduced '*Roko aur Toko*' or 'stop and punish' campaign. As part of the initiative, the civic body formulated '*dibba* gang', 'mic gang' and 'whistle gang', who shouted or made noise and embarrassed people defecating in the open and even imposed a fine of ₹100.

According to the ministry of drinking water and sanitation, on 3 June 2021, the number of toilets built in rural areas since 2 October 2014 was 17.959 million. A Bill Gates and Melinda Foundation (BMGF) survey found that in ODF villages, the incidence of diarrhoea was significantly less, and measures of undernutrition (stunting and wasting) were also significantly better in the ODF villages than in non-ODF villages. On the 150th birth anniversary of the Mahatma in 2019, Prime Minister Modi declared the country ODF, with more than 110 million toilets having been built in five years and 600 million people being given access to them.

Pradhan Mantri Jan Dhan Yojana (PMJDY)

Financial inclusion, that is, extending financial services to those who typically lack access, has been a goal for the Government of India since the 1950s. There was a major expansion of bank branches in rural and other unbanked areas after the nationalization of banks, yet the Census 2011 estimated that out of 24.67 crore households in the country, only 14.48 crore (58.7 per cent) had access to banking services. Prime Minister Modi, on 15 August 2015, said: 'Even after sixty years of independence; even when the banks were nationalized for the poor, 40% people of the country were without a bank account till the last 15th of August.'[6]

Prime Minister Modi called Independence Day 2014 a festival of freedom, pledged to launch a national financial inclusion mission to connect the poorest citizens of the country with the facility of bank accounts and utilize the resources of the country for their well-being. There would be at least one basic bank account for every household, financial literacy, access to credit, insurance and pension facility. A person not having a savings account could open an account without the requirement of any minimum balance and, in case they self-certified that they did not have any of the officially valid documents required for opening a savings account, they could open a 'small account'. The scheme was called the Pradhan Mantri Jan Dhan Yojana (PMJDY) and launched on 28 August 2015.

The Jan Dhan accounts differed from the no-frills and basic savings bank deposit accounts in the availability of a RuPay debit card, with inbuilt accident insurance cover of ₹2 lakh, and access to the overdraft facility upon satisfactory operation of the account or credit history of six months. After the launch of the various social security schemes on 9 May 2015, the Jan Dhan account holders would also become eligible for Pradhan Mantri Suraksha Bima Yojana (PMSBY) or Prime Minister's Safety Insurance Scheme, life insurance cover under Pradhan Mantri Jeevan Jyoti Bima Yojana (PMJJBY) or Prime Minister's Light of Life Insurance scheme and guaranteed minimum pension to subscribers under Atal Pension Yojana.

To expand the reach of banking services, all of over 6 lakh villages in the country were mapped into 1.59 lakh Sub Service Areas (SSAs), with each SSA typically comprising of 1000 to 1500 households. In the 1.26 lakh SSAs that did not have a bank branch, Bank Mitras—or friends at banks—were deployed for branchless banking on the Aadhaar Enabled Payment System. PMJDY offered not only easy access to banking, but also promoted awareness about financial products through financial literacy programmes.

Under PMJDY, by 26 January 2015, 12.55 crore accounts had been opened. On 27 March 2019, the number grew to 35.27 crore, of which 60 per cent were in rural areas and 53 per cent were owned by women. Initially, there was scepticism about how much money would be deposited in PMJDY accounts. But by 27 March 2019, deposits in PMJDY accounts were ₹96,107 crore, and the average deposit per account had more than doubled to ₹2725 from ₹1064 in end-March 2015. The average number of transactions per Bank Mitra also rose over eightfold from 52 in 2014–15 to 4291 in 2016–17. PMJDY, launched in August 2014 initially for a period of four years, was extended beyond 28 August 2018 with the focus changed from a bank account for every household to a bank account for every adult.

Deen Dayal Upadhyay Gram Jyoti Yojana (DDUGJY)

RGGVY launched by the second UPA Government on 4 April 2005 was restructured and renamed Deen Dayal Upadhyay Gram Jyoti Yojana

(DDUGJY) or village light mission after Deen Dayal Upadhyay, general secretary of the Bharatiya Jan Sangh for fifteen years and also its president for a short while during 1967–1968. Launched by the Prime Minister in November 2014, DDUGJY subsumed the balance work relating to rural electrification with the norms of the ongoing scheme of RGGVY in Twelfth and Thirteenth Plans as a distinct component for rural electrification. Feeder separation between agricultural and non-agricultural users of electricity was a major feature distinguishing DDUGJY from RGGVY. Leisang village in the Senapati district of Manipur became the last Indian village to be electrified. With this, electricity reached all of India's 5,97,464 census villages, thus marking the culmination of the marquee Deen Dayal Upadhyaya Gram Jyoti Yojana (DDUGJY).

Beti Bachao, Beti Padhao

Even without any gender selection during induced abortion of female foetuses, the sex ratio at birth—that is the number of girls born per 1000 of boys born—is known to be biased against girls for biological reasons and is around 935-951. Because of cultural reasons, compounded by the problems of illiteracy, poverty and lack of social security, many developing societies are known to have a male-bias. The imbalance in the sex ratio against females is what Amartya Sen has famously described as the problem of 'missing women'.[7]

Apart from the moral and ethical questions that arise in the context of missing women, there is also the issue of the impact of an adverse sex ratio on society and the economy. Reportedly, however, there are two beneficial effects of a deteriorating sex ratio. First is on polygyny or polygamy, where a man takes on multiple wives. Polygyny tends to diminish with the scarcity that men face in finding spouses. Second is on savings. In a competitive marriage market, single men save more to increase their chance of finding a wife. In a developing economy with immense investment potential, higher savings lead to faster growth. More importantly, however, the net effect is more likely to be negative. A very adverse sex ratio results in millions of young men with few or no prospects of marriage, and unmarried young men are known to be the most crime-prone. Law and order are a prerequisite for economic prosperity and a rising crime rate with a falling sex ratio can hurt the process of development.

The child sex ratio—the number of females per 1000 males in the age group zero to six years—already low at 927 in Census 2001, had come down ominously to 918 in Census 2011. Apart from the problem of missing women and its associated effect on society and law and order, there was also the problem of lack of education among women. The crude literacy rate among females, which from less than 8 per cent at Independence, had increased in every Census to reach 57 per cent in 2011, was still far behind the 71 per cent for males.

On 11 October 2014, the third International Day of the Girl Child, Prime Minister Modi asked the country to pledge to create an atmosphere of equality for the girl child. 'Female foeticide is a matter of deep shame and a cause of great concern. Let's work together to remove this menace from society,' he added.[8] After receiving suggestions from the public, he launched the '*Beti Bachao, Beti Padhao*' or Save the Girl Child and Educate Her campaign on 22 January 2015 in Haryana. It was focused on 100 districts in the country which had a low child-sex ratio. It targeted three groups: (i) primary—pregnant mothers, newly married couples, young married couples and lactating mothers, (ii) secondary—nursing homes, diagnostic centres, private hospitals, adolescents and youth, and (iii) tertiary group—industry, medical associations, media, voluntary organizations, religious leaders, frontline workers, women SGHs, PRIs and officials. There were, however, already some conditional cash transfer schemes in force in various states. For example, the Ladli Lakshmi Scheme in Madhya Pradesh and similar schemes in states like UP, Bihar, Chhattisgarh, Delhi, West Bengal, among others. The Beti Bachao, Beti Padhao scheme was supported by the attractive Sukanya Samriddhi Account announced by Finance Minister Jaitley in the Union Budget 2014–15. There are some signs of India doing better in removing the problem of missing women. NFHS-5 found that, in 2019-21, there were 1020 females per 1000 males.

Mission Indradhanush

Despite the introduction of Extended Programme of Immunization launched in 1978 and the UIP in 1985, only 65 per cent of the children were fully immunized in the first year of their lives by 2014. Mission Indradhanush was launched in December 2014 to ensure full immunization for pregnant women and children up to two years of age with all available vaccines. It was called Indradhanush or the bow (*dhanush*) of Lord Indra, which is a common word used for the rainbow and has seven colours.

The preventable diseases included: (i) diphtheria, (ii) pertussis or whooping cough, (iii) tetanus, (iv) polio, (v) measles, (vi) severe form of childhood tuberculosis, hepatitis B, meningitis and pneumonia (Hemophilus influenza type B infections), and (vii) Japanese encephalitis (JE) in JE endemic districts.

Pradhan Mantri MUDRA Yojana (PMMY)

According to NSSO Survey (2013), the major problem of 5.77 crore small business units, mostly individual proprietorships, was finance. To provide integrated financial and support services to micro-units at the bottom of the pyramid, in his Budget for 2015–16, Finance Minister Arun Jaitley announced the formation of MUDRA Bank—Micro Units Development and Refinance Agency Ltd. (MUDRA). MUDRA was registered as a company in March 2015 and as a Non-Banking Finance Institution with the RBI on 7 April 2015. Prime Minister Modi launched it as a wholly owned subsidiary of Small Industries Development Bank of India (SIDBI) on the following day to provide refinance to banks/MFIs/NBFCs for lending to micro units having loan requirement of up to ₹10 lakh.[9] There were three credit schemes: Shishu or 'child' for loans up to ₹50,000, Kishor or 'teenager' for loans between ₹50,000 and ₹5 lakh, and Tarun or 'young' for loans between ₹5 lakh and ₹10 lakh.

The number of loans sanctioned went up from 3.5 crore in 2015–16 to 5 crore in 2020–21, with the amount disbursed going up from ₹1.33 lakh crore to ₹3.12 lakh crore. For public sector banks, Mudra loans outstanding at the end of 2019–20 were ₹3.82 lakh crore. There was a steady rise in NPA in such loans from 3.42 per cent in 2017–18 to 3.75 per cent in 2018–19 and further to 4.92 per cent in 2019–20. Such loans, which were refinanced by SIDBI, were also guaranteed by the government for about 50 per cent of the NPAs up to 15 per cent of the total size of loans. Thus, the NPA problem for banks was not a very major problem in Mudra.

Pradhan Mantri Suraksha Bima Yojana (PMSBY)

On 28 February 2015, in his Budget Speech for 2015–16, Finance Minister Arun Jaitley had announced a move from Prime Minister's Jan Dhan to Jan Suraksha or from People's Wealth to Peoples' Security. He announced three insurance schemes. The first was PMSBY, covering accidental death of ₹2 lakh for a premium of just ₹12 per year. Prime Minister Modi formally launched it on 8 May 2015 in Kolkata. PMSBY was available to resident Indians and NRIs between eighteen to seventy years of age with bank accounts. Linked to PMJDY, it was administered through general insurance companies. The premium was automatically debited from the bank account. The insured amount was ₹2 lakh for unexpected death or full disability, and ₹1 lakh for partial permanent disability. By end-March 2019, 15.47 crore people had enrolled for this scheme, and 32,176 claims amounting to ₹644 crore had been disbursed. Meanwhile, a high loss ratio led insurance companies to demand an increase in premium rates.[10]

From Swavalamban to Atal Pension Yojana

Concerned about the old age income security of the working poor and for encouraging and enabling them to save for their retirement, the third scheme announced by Finance Minister Jaitley at end-February 2015 was Atal Pension Yojana, named after former Prime Minister Atal Bihari Vajpayee. It was launched by Prime Minister Modi on 9 May 2015 in Kolkata.

The Atal Pension Yojana was open to all citizens between the ages of eighteen to forty years and a minimum period of contribution was twenty years. Atal Pension Yojana superseded the Swavalamban scheme launched under the second UPA government in 2010 and had enhanced benefits. Like its predecessor Swavalamban, it was administered by the PFRDA through the NPS architecture and was focused on all citizens in the unorganized sector. Furthermore, it had a government-guaranteed minimum monthly pension for subscribers, ranging between ₹1000 and ₹5000. Also, for subscribers who were not covered by any Statutory Social Security Schemes and were not income taxpayers, the government would co-contribute 50 per cent of the subscriber's contribution or ₹1000 per annum, whichever was lower. For each eligible subscriber who joined the scheme between 1 June and 31 December 2015, the government would co-contribute for a period of five years. All bank account holders could join Atal Pension Yojana and Aadhaar was the primary document for fulfilling the KYC requirement.

Pradhan Mantri Jeevan Jyoti Bima Yojana (PMJJBY)

The second insurance scheme announced by Finance Minister Jaitley on 28 February 2015 was PMJJBY. Launched again in Kolkata on 9 May 2015, it covered death due to any reason—not only accidents—and for an annual premium of ₹330 (June-May) provided a life cover of ₹2 lakh. It was available to all bank account holders in the age group of eighteen to fifty years. Such account holders had to give their consent for auto-debit of the premium. The scheme was offered by life insurance companies with tie-ups with banks. At end-March 2019, 5.92 crore people had enrolled for PMJJBY, and 1,35,212 claims amounting to a total of ₹2,704.24 crore had been disbursed. PMJBY, according to news reports, could not cope with the large number of deaths from COVID-19 during 2020 and the first half of 2021.

Pradhan Mantri Sahaj Bijli Har Ghar Yojana (SAUBHAGYA)

From the Red Fort, on Independence Day 2015, Prime Minister Modi pointed out that there were still about 18,500 villages which did not have electricity connection. He announced his plan for providing electricity connection to all these villages in 1000 days with the help of states and local bodies. This was the Pradhan Mantri Sahaj Bijli Har Ghar Yojana (Saubhagya), or Prime Minister's Power for All programme. With a total allocation of ₹16,320 crore to subsidize electrical equipment like transformers, meters and wires, the programme aimed at achieving universal household electrification by December 2018.

Unlike in the past, when the households had to bear the cost of last mile connectivity, under Saubhagya, apart from the poor households who got it free, even the not-so-poor households were required to pay a total of only ₹500 in ten equal monthly instalments of ₹50 along with their monthly bills. Under Saubhagya, the focus changed from village electrification to electricity to every household.

Pradhan Mantri Krishi Sinchayee Yojana (PMKSY)

Pradhan Mantri Krishi Sinchayee Yojana (PMKSY) or Prime Minister Farm Irrigation Scheme was launched in 2015 with the objective of achieving convergence of investments in irrigation at the field level, expand cultivable area under assured irrigation, improve on-farm water use efficiency to reduce wastage of water, enhance the adoption of precision irrigation and other water saving technologies (more crop per drop), enhance recharge of aquifers and introduce sustainable water conservation practices by exploring the feasibility of reusing treated municipal waste water for peri-urban agriculture and attract greater private investment in precision irrigation system.

Digital India

On 1 July 2015, Prime Minister Modi launched the Digital India programme to reform governance through technology. The program aimed at providing high-speed internet as a core utility available to every citizen, assigning cradle-to-grave unique, lifelong, online and authenticable identity to every citizen, and making government services available from online and mobile platforms. It would also digitally empower the citizen by opening up to them the knowledge, experience and values that people already have.

Pradhan Mantri Kaushal Vikas Yojana (PMKVY)

Skill was in short supply in many professions such as welders, plumbers and electricians. The utilization of the demographic advantage in the availability of a vast working-age population urgently required effective action in skill formation. According to the Sixty-Eighth Round (July 2011-June 2012) of NSSO, only 4.69 per cent of India's total workforce was estimated to have undergone formal skill training, compared with 52 per cent in the USA, 68 per cent in the UK, 75 per cent in Germany, 80 per cent in Japan and 96 per cent in South Korea. Based on the Census 2011 and NSSO (Sixty-Eighth Round) data, it was estimated that 104 million fresh entrants to the workforce would require skill training by 2022, and 298 million of the existing workforce would require additional skill training over the same period.

In his Budget Speech for 2014–15, Finance Minister Jaitley had announced that a national multi-skill programme called Skill India would be launched with an emphasis on employability and entrepreneur skills. Creation of the dedicated Department of Skill Development and Entrepreneurship was notified on 31 July 2014, and subsequently converted into a full-fledged ministry of skill development and entrepreneurship (MSDE) on 9 November 2014, with NSDA, NSDC and NSDF under its purview. The entire network of Industrial Training Institutes and Apprenticeship Training schemes were transferred from the ministry of labour and employment to MSDE on 16 April 2015.

On 28 February 2015, in his Budget Speech for 2015–16, Jaitley had announced that a National Skills Mission would be launched soon through the MSDE. It would consolidate skill initiatives spread across several ministries and allow standardization of procedures and outcomes across skill councils in 31 sectors. The Pradhan Mantri Kaushal Vikas Yojana (PMKVY) or Prime Minister's Skill Development Mission was launched on 15 July 2015. The number of beneficiaries under PMKVY plus fee-based training by NSDC increased from 22.37 lakh in 2016–17 to 70.13 lakh in 2019–20, to bring the cumulative total of beneficiaries to 185.38 lakh by end-March 2020.

Deen Dayal Upadhyaya Grameen Antyodaya Yojana

The birthday of Deen Dayal Upadhyaya (25 September 1916) was christened as Antyodaya Diwas or day for the upliftment of the poorest of the poor. In 2014, on Antyodaya Diwas, Prime Minister Modi announced the Deen Dayal Upadhyaya Grameen Kaushalya Yojana or rural development programme. It was succeeded by the Deen Dayal Antyodaya Yojana a year later. The basic idea was to equip the rural poor to get skilled wage employment, organize them into self-help groups (SHGs) and encourage self-employment. It was an evolution from the IRDP launched in March 1976 to the SGSY from 1 April 1999, and further to the NRLM in June 2011. NRLM, supported by a World Bank loan of $1 billion, was strengthened and renamed as Deen Dayal Antyodaya—NRLM Yojana. By October 2018, 5054 blocks had been covered under the 'intensive' implementation strategy of Deen Dayal Antyodaya—NRLM. Under the SHG-Bank Linkage programme, during 2018–19, about 17.57 lakh SHGs accessed credit of ₹27,911 crore up to October 2018.

Restructuring Dabhol Power Company and closure of a long-standing problem

Reviving Dabhol faced three difficulties. First was the renovation of the Phase I power plant that had been mothballed for five years, and completion of the Phase II power plant that was under construction when Dabhol closed. Second was, from 2013, the shortage of gas supply allocated to the plant from the KG-D6 gas field operated by Reliance. Third were the claims of the Indian lenders on Dabhol Power Plant. In 2015, the Dabhol power project was split into two separate power and Liquified Natural Gas (LNG) companies, and Ratnagiri Gas and Power Pvt. Ltd was demerged into Ratnagiri Gas and Power Pvt. Ltd and Konkan LNG Pvt. Ltd. In April 2019, the Supreme Court closed the case of alleged corruption involving politicians, bureaucrats and corporates in the Enron-Dabhol power project, noting the inordinate delay in the case since it was filed in 1997.

Ujwal DISCOM Assurance Yojana (UDAY)

UDAY, a financial restructuring package for electricity distribution companies (power) (DISCOMs), was envisaged to financially turn around Discoms with their operational improvement as well as reduction in the cost of generating power and development of renewable energy.

Under UDAY, state governments were to take over 75 per cent of the DISCOM's debt as on 30 September 2015 in a phased manner—50 per cent in 2015–16 and 25 per cent in 2016–17—by issuing non-SLR State Development Loans (SDLs) and transferring the proceeds to the DISCOMs in a mix of grant, loan and equity. The SDLs would have a maturity of ten to fifteen years with a moratorium up to five years and bear an interest rate of G-sec plus 0.5 per cent plus 0.25 per cent spread for non-SLR status. The states were given leeway in borrowings for UDAY without including it under fiscal deficit. As far as future losses of DISCOMs were concerned, under UDAY, respective state governments were also required to take over 5 per cent of such losses in 2016–17, 10 per cent in 2017–18, 25 per cent in 2018–19 and 50 per cent in 2019–20, to the extent of loss trajectory finalized with the ministry of power, and finance them through state bonds or DISCOM bonds backed by state government guarantees. All states except Delhi (a UT with legislature) and West Bengal participated in UDAY.

Pradhan Mantri Ayushman Bharat Yojana

The increasing burden of non-communicable diseases and the robust growth of a private segment in the health sector had changed India's health priorities. With the growing incidence of catastrophic healthcare costs on vulnerable household budgets and changing the fiscal capacity of the government, there was a need to revisit National Health Policy 2002.

In 2017, the Modi government came out with a new National Health Policy targeting health and well-being for all, through a preventive and promotive healthcare orientation in all developmental policies, and universal access to good quality healthcare services without anyone facing financial hardship. It defined health expenditure of 10 per cent of the household's total monthly consumption expenditure or 40 per cent of its monthly non-food consumption expenditure as the limit of affordability. Anything beyond these limits was considered as a catastrophic household health expenditure.

The focus of the new policy was on the assured availability of free and comprehensive PHC services, for all aspects of reproductive, maternal, child and adolescent health and for the most prevalent communicable, non-communicable and occupational diseases. It urged a move from a very selective to a comprehensive PHC package which included geriatric, palliative and rehabilitative healthcare services.

National Health Policy 2017 emphasized financial and performance accountability, transparency in decision-making, and elimination of corruption in healthcare systems, both in public and private. It recommended the optimum use of existing manpower and infrastructure in the health sector and collaboration with non-government sector on pro-bono basis for delivery of healthcare services linked to the family health card. It encouraged enabling private sector contribution to make healthcare systems more effective, efficient, rational, safe, affordable and ethical. Strategic purchases by the government to fill critical gaps in public health facilities could create a demand for the private healthcare sector, in alignment with public health goals. Ayushman Bharat-Pradhan Mantri Jan Arogya Yojana (PMJAY) was expected to help reduce expenditure on hospitalizations and mitigate the financial risk arising out of catastrophic health episodes. The Union government envisaged the creation of 1,50,000 health and wellness centres by transforming existing sub-centres and PHCs as the basic pillar of Ayushman Bharat to deliver comprehensive PHC. PMJAY was designed to subsume the ongoing centrally sponsored schemes RSBY and the Senior Citizen Health Insurance Scheme, which had been implemented from 1 April 2016 as a top-up over the existing RSBY Scheme. States running similar schemes could opt to merge them with PMJAY or run them in a parallel manner.

XXVIII.6 Insolvency and Bankruptcy Code

Industrial sickness—often starkly manifested in the inability of a company to discharge its liabilities including wages, payment for supplies, interest and principal repayment of loans—had been a major problem since the 1960s, for example, in the context of the NTC in 1968. A company, once sick, loses value if it is neither restored to health by restructuring nor closed down if it is beyond redemption. For example, arrears of wages mount and employees suffer, machines become obsolete with lack of care, and interest on past dues increases. The 1991 reforms abolishing the permit-licence raj had removed the restrictions on the entry of business into the economy, but exit continued to be extremely difficult and time-consuming and involved multiple laws and their interpretations. To address the continuing problem of industrial sickness, SICA had been enacted in 1985 and two quasi-judicial bodies, namely the BIFR and AAIFR, were set up in January 1987 and 1989. But progress was tardy at best. There was also the need to prevent the problem of the moral hazard in companies resorting to a declaration of sickness only to escape their legal obligations and to gain concessional access to financial institutions.

To minimize hardship and unnecessary loss of value, including by a speedy rehabilitation under alternate management, there was a need for a streamlined code for determining insolvency and bankruptcy in a time-bound manner while avoiding the moral hazard problem of companies using the rehabilitation code to wilfully default on their debt obligations. Such a code was introduced on 28 May 2016 in the form of the Insolvency and Bankruptcy Code (IBC), 2016.

While IBC covered both individuals and companies, the primary aim of the IBC was to rescue the lives of firms in distress, and where that is not possible, to liquidate them and recover the maximum value of their assets. When loans to the firm turn into NPAs, and the equity-holders of a firm cannot resolve the distress, the creditors could get the firm admitted to the Corporate Insolvency Resolution Process. The creditors, empowered by the IBC, were represented by a Committee of Creditors (COC), which could decide about issues such as haircuts to be taken by the creditors, change of management and disposal of assets. During the pendency of Corporate Insolvency Resolution Process, an Insolvency Professional would run the company as a going concern so that the best value could be recovered from the company in distress. The Insolvency Professional would invite feasible and viable resolution plans from eligible and credible resolution applicants. If the COC approved one of the applicants, then the company would be handed over to it. If the COC did not, then the company would go into liquidation. 'All this is done within a period of six months with a one-time extension up to 90 days.'[11] There were also the Adjudicating Authority, the Insolvency and Bankruptcy Board of India, and valuers. The IBC moved the system from debtor-in-possession to creditors-in-control. On 1 December 2016, the Modi government dissolved BIFR and referred all proceedings to the National Company Law Tribunal (NCLT) and National Company Law Appellate Tribunal (NCLAT) as per the IBC.

At the end of June 2020, of about 4,000 firms admitted to the Corporate Insolvency Resolution Process, about 45 per cent had exited with resolution plans, withdrawals or liquidation or were in the process of doing so.[12] Under IBC, the threat of losing ownership or liquidation itself is believed to have contributed to better performance by firms. In the World Bank's Ease of Doing Business Reports, India's ranking in terms of resolving insolvency moved from 136 in 2017 to 52 in 2020.

XXVIII.7 Goods and Services Tax (GST)

GST had been coming in India since at least 2010. But until 2017, taxes on goods and services continued to be under different statutory provisions, with jurisdiction of state VAT restricted to only goods. A nationwide GST to make India a unified common market for both goods and services required considerable streamlining of bases, rates and procedures and their unification across Union and states. It would involve sacrifice of the Union's monopoly to tax services, and states' prerogative to change provisions under their own tax laws. Lack of a consensus among the states and the Union had held up GST implementation.

The NDA Government introduced the 122nd Constitution Amendment Bill, 2014 in the Sixteenth Lok Sabha on 19 December 2014 and got it passed by the Lok Sabha in May 2015. It was referred to the Select Committee of Rajya Sabha on 12 May 2015. Now with Congress in opposition, it was payback time. It held up the bill in the Rajya Sabha, where it was relatively strong. The amendment required a two-thirds majority in each House, and in the Rajya Sabha, the Congress had more members than the BJP.

The Congress demanded that the GST rate be capped at 18 per cent in the Amendment Bill and scrapping of an additional 1 per cent to compensate manufacturing states that fear losing out on revenue from a switch to the destination principle. The government agreed to drop the 1 per cent additional tax, but not the cap of 18 per cent on the GST rate. The experience with such limits on the rate of tax, for example, in the case of professional tax at ₹250, had not been good. But perhaps it was more politics than anything else.

Finance ministers of states agreed with the Centre to keep the cap on the GST rate out of the Amendment Bill and that came as a setback to the Congress. It softened its stand. The Select Committee of the Rajya Sabha submitted its Report on the Bill on 22 July 2015. The Bill, with certain amendments, was finally passed in the Rajya Sabha and thereafter by Lok

Sabha in August 2016. After ratification by the required number of states and Presidential assent, the Constitution (101st Amendment) Act 2016 came into force from 16 September 2016.

Article 279A was inserted in the Constitution to provide for a GST Council with the Union finance minister as chairman, and minister of state (revenue) and the state finance/taxation ministers as members. Four laws—CGST Act, UTGST Act, IGST Act and GST (Compensation to States) Act—were passed by Parliament and notified on 12 April 2017. After getting the rules notified, the return forms prepared, and the registration process and other formalities nearly complete, GST became effective from 1 July 2017. There were some initial hiccups in making GST function efficiently—the GST website got clogged, forms were not available, and flow of input credit was slow. But these impediments were soon overcome.

XXVIII.8 Raising Revenues by Tapping into Black Money

In December 2013, Global Financial Integrity (GFI), a US thinktank, estimated black money outflow from India during 2002–2011 at $343.93 billion. India ranked fifth in the world in terms of illicit outflows. In the run-up to the 2014 Lok Sabha election, BJP leader Narendra Modi's statement that if all the black money deposited by people from India was brought back, every person would get ₹15-20 lakh, kicked up a huge storm before as well as after the election. Once elected to power, on behalf of the BJP, he promised to try and get the black money back. The Modi government, in line with its electoral promise, came down heavily on black money immediately after coming into power. The idea was not only to throw black money out of circulation but also raise the government's revenue by tapping into it. The BJP government took several steps to deal with black money.

Special Investigation Team (SIT) and Black Money Act

A day after taking charge, the Modi government decided to form an SIT to probe black money mostly stashed abroad. On 20 March 2015, it introduced the Black Money (Undisclosed Foreign Income and Assets) and Imposition of Tax Bill, 2015 as a money bill. It became an Act on 26 May 2015 and came to be known as the Black Money Act, 2015.

Automatic exchange of information with other countries

With a view to sourcing information about the financial accounts maintained by Indian residents abroad, the Government of India, on 3 June 2015, joined the Multilateral Competent Authority Agreement (MCAA) for exchanging such information.

Benami Transaction (Prohibition) Amendment Act

One standard way of concealing black money was to deploy such money in benami transactions or transactions with '*benamidar*' or fictitious names or names of persons who are not aware of such transactions or too poor to carry out such transactions. Benami transactions were mostly in property—both moveable and immovable, tangible and intangible, and company shares and bonds. The Modi government amended the Benami Transaction (Prohibition) Act of 1988 by passing the Benami Transaction (Prohibition) Amendment Act, 2016, to get rid of benami transactions. The new law has greater clarity, stricter provisions and an enhanced punishment for the offence.

Income Disclosure Scheme

To allow domestic taxpayers to declare undisclosed income or income represented in the form of any asset and clear up their past tax transgressions by paying tax at 30 per cent, and surcharge at 7.5 per cent and a penalty at 7.5 per cent, which is a total of 45 per cent of the undisclosed income, the Income Disclosure Scheme 2016 was announced in Budget 2016–17.

Demonetization of 8 November 2016

The most aggressive move to curb black money in India was the demonetization of old ₹500 and ₹1000 notes on 8 November 2016. The demonetization was also aimed at curbing fake Indian currency which financed terrorism. In India, after the demonetizations in 1946 and 1978, the one in 2016 was the third. The sudden move by the government created a massive shortage of cash.

A firm or an individual might have had money in the bank but could not withdraw as much of it as desired in cash. Even for the withdrawal of limited sums, there were long queues outside banks. The demonetization might have encouraged digital payments, but the cash shortage had an adverse impact on the economy. The impact on GDP growth could have been as much as 0.7-1.3 per cent in the last quarter of 2016–17. Did the big painful jolt of demonetization create the right psychological milieu for the war against black money to start? Only time will tell.

Declaration of black money under the PMGKY scheme

A second disclosure scheme, known as the Pradhan Mantri Garib Kalyan Yojana (PMGKY) or the Prime Minister's Poor Welfare Scheme, was introduced from 17 December 2016. The scheme provided an opportunity to declare unaccounted income and wealth in a confidential manner and avoid prosecution after paying a fine.

Fugitive Economic Offenders Act, 2018

The problem of economic offenders charged with large value frauds evading prosecution by remaining outside Indian jurisdiction was proving to be difficult. For instance, there were a few high-profile cases involving fraud and financial irregularities. One involved businessman was Vijay Mallya, also known as the 'King of Good Times' for his flamboyant lifestyle. The other was Nirav Modi, an internationally celebrated jewellery designer also known as the 'diamond king' in India, with many high-end jewellery stores, including in Hong Kong, Macau, Mumbai, New Delhi and New York.

The Fugitive Economic Offenders bill was designed to deal with the problem of persons who have arrest warrants issued in respect of a scheduled offence involving more than ₹100 crore and who leave India to avoid prosecution or refuse to return to India. It authorized officials under PMLA 2002 to apply to Special Courts for declaring persons as fugitive economic offenders and attach their properties. The bill was introduced in the Lok Sabha on 12 March 2018 but could not be passed in the budget session of Parliament. The President of India promulgated the Fugitive Economic Offenders Ordinance on 21 April 2018. Vijay Mallya became the first case that the ED decided to move under the Fugitive Economic Offenders Ordinance. The Ordinance, after following the due processes, became an Act on 31 July 2018.

XXVIII.9 Election to the Seventeenth Lok Sabha in 2019

Growth, after accelerating from 6.4 per cent in 2013–14, the last year of UPA rule, to 7.4 per cent, 8 per cent and 8.3 per cent in the first three years of Modi's rule, came down to 6.8 per cent in 2017–18 and further to 6.5 per cent in 2018–19. With better luck than its predecessor UPA, the NDA government under Modi saw the annual average price of Indian basket of crude oil per barrel come down from $105.52 in 2013–14 to a low of $46.17 in 2015–16, before steadily climbing up to $69.88 in 2018–19, the year before the election. The average price of the Indian basket of crude oil per barrel at $60.84 was only about two-thirds of the corresponding average of $96.05 during UPA II. This favourable development in the international oil market, together with prudent macroeconomic policies, resulted in WPI inflation (2011–12 series) coming down from over 5 per cent in 2013-14 to 1.3 per cent in 2014–15, -3.7 per cent (decline) in 2015–16, and then rising to 1.7 per cent, 2.9 per cent and 4.2 per cent in the three subsequent years. The economic outturn during 2014–19 was much more favourable for Modi the government's election prospects in 2019 than what the outturn during 2009–14 had been for the UPA in the 2014 elections.

After the 2014 Lok Sabha elections, fifteen parties, including TDP, MDMK and PMK, had left the NDA. In the run-up to the Lok Sabha elections in 2019, the NDA with BJP in the lead stitched up an alliance with the AIADMK in Tamil Nadu, JD(U) and LJP in Bihar, Shiv Sena in Maharashtra and SAD in Punjab. Relative to 2014, the NDA was trimmer in 2019: the Congress-led UPA linked up with NCP in Maharashtra, DMK in Tamil Nadu, RJD in Bihar, JD(S) in Karnataka and NC in Jammu and Kashmir. In UP, Akhilesh Yadav's SJP and Mayawati's BSP joined RLD led by Ajit Singh, to form a grand alliance. Other important regional players were AITC in West Bengal, YSRCP and TDP in Andhra Pradesh, TRS in Telangana, BJD in Odisha and the Left Front in Kerala.

Modi-led NDA's campaign was based on its achievement during the first term. During 2014–18, according to the World Bank data, on average, every year, India had grown at 7.4 per cent, which was faster than China's 7 per cent. And this encouraging growth had been delivered with moderate inflation, macroeconomic balance and structural reforms. Among the reform measures, the most noteworthy were GST, IBC and Swachh Bharat Abhiyan. There was a host of measures to promote inclusive growth, which included DDUGJY, PMJDY, Beti Bachao Beti Padhao, and Ayushman Bharat.

The opposition campaign was focused on saving institutions and democracy. They accused NDA under Modi of destroying the independent and unbiased functioning of the Election Commission and using ED and CBI as a caged parrot to victimize leaders and functionaries of opposition parties. Even the new series of national accounts with base 2011–12, which was released in June 2015, became a matter of controversy among economists and technical experts. The Opposition highlighted the pain that the people and small businesses had to suffer with cash shortage after demonetization on 8 November 2016. Even the launch of GST on 1 July 2017 affected many businesses. Demonetization together with the ill-prepared GST launch set back MSMEs' business and led to unemployment and privation.

The 2019 Lok Sabha election saw a major shift in the politics of the country. There was a decline in the salience of caste-based regional parties such as BSP and SJP in UP. BSP's vote share in Lok Sabha polls in UP was down from 27.4 per cent in 2009 to 19.6 per cent in 2014 and further to 19.4 per cent in 2019. The corresponding decline for SJP was from 23.3 per cent to 22.4 per cent and 18.1 per cent. Even in the Vidhan Sabha elections in UP in 2012 and 2017, the seats won by BSP fell from eighty to nineteen, and for SJP from 224 to forty-seven. There was a corresponding increase in BJP's victory in the Vidhan Sabha polls in UP from forty-seven to 312 between 2012 and 2017. It probably reflected the caste consolidation among the Hindus in UP. The Vidhan Sabha polls in 2022 in UP provided further evidence of the sustained nature of this trend.

In the event, the BJP-led NDA swept the polls. It won in 303 seats by securing 37.7 per cent of the valid votes polled, up from 282 seats and 31.3 per cent of votes in 2014. Counting its pre-poll allies in the NDA together with those that joined after the election, it had a strength of over 380 members in the Lok Sabha. Narendra Modi was sworn in again as Prime Minister on 30 May 2019. Soon after he assumed office, the world was hit by the COVID-19 pandemic, which led to not only widespread morbidity, including about half a million deaths, but also with lockdowns for preventing the contagion, major loss of business, jobs and livelihoods with breakdowns of supply chains. The second Modi government is only about halfway through its term. So we shall end the story in 2019.

XXIX

Continuing Story of India's Search for Glory

India and the Indians have made some progress in the seventy-five years after Independence. Per capita income at constant prices has increased more than seven-fold between 1950–51 and 2020–21. Electricity consumption per capita is up more than sixty times from less than 20 kWh in 1950 to around 1200 kWh in 2020. The road network has gone up from about 0.4 million kms in 1950–51 to 6.2 million kms in 2020–21. The number of literates has gone up from less than one in six in 1951 to two in three in 2011. Indians have become healthier and their life expectancy at birth has gone up by two-thirds from 41.4 years in 1960 to 69.4 years in 2018. The proportion of people below the poverty line has halved from 54.9 per cent in 1973–74 to 27.5 per cent in 2004–05. For TFR, 2.1 is called the replacement rate because with such a TFR, the population replaces itself from one generation to the other. TFR dropped from around 6 at the time of Independence to 2, below the replacement rate of 2.1, in 2019–21.

But the shine from the story fades when India is compared with that of the East Asian Tigers and China. It looks good but not good enough. India looks far from the glory it seeks. In terms of institutions, what distinguishes India from its not-so-distant successful eastern neighbours is its pursuit of democratic politics right from Independence. It was, and still is, a country with multiple social cleavages in terms of language, tribal and caste identities, and religious faiths. Social fragmentation has a tendency to result in lower provision of public goods such as educational institutions, healthcare centres, availability of water sources and electricity, transportation facilities and communication infrastructure. A benevolent dictator could have overcome the democratic pulls and pressures and designed policies for accelerated growth. Democracy could have waited, like it did in East Asia for quite a while until they reached a critical level of development, or is still waiting in China.

This book argues that relying on a dictator's benevolence was a risk that should have been, and was indeed, avoided. The debate on whether Indian nationalism is only civic or cultural as well, or in other words whether the Constitution created 'Indians' or a core group of Indians predates the Constitution, is beyond the scope of the book. Yet, it is undeniable that the process of making Indians and integrating the country continues as work in progress. The developments in Jammu and Kashmir, which have been discussed through many of the chapters of this book, illustrate the unfinished nature of the job. Pluralist politics can play a major role in this nation-building. Even the princely states would have been much harder to peacefully integrate into anything but democratic India.

Furthermore, this book argues that perhaps nothing except an assimilative democracy could have worked in effectively dealing with the fissiparous tendencies that, like in many other large countries, cropped up in India. Indian democracy, along with its quasi-federal structure, has been a very effective tool in building both India and the Indians.

In the wake of Independence, the Indians effectively contracted out the formulation of economic policies to the leaders of the freedom movement, particularly Pandit Jawaharlal Nehru. This period from Independence until Nehru's demise in 1964 was a dominant one-party rule characterized by the relative autonomy of the State from society. Though subsequent history may have revealed its faults, the policies followed were in the light of the received wisdom of the times. And notwithstanding its limitations, it did change Indians in terms of income, education and health and opened the way for popular participation. Society started to influence the state. The period between 1964 and 1991 saw a surge in popular participation and it was politics more than economics that guided policies.

From this second period, the Indian story became one of interplay between economic policies and democratic politics. Is politics all about 'the economy, stupid', as the US cliche goes? Do political parties and leaders win and lose elections only on the basis of what they delivered in terms of economic outturn or what they promise to do in terms of economic policies in the future? While good economics, or in simple words, what is 'good for all' in economic terms, play a major role in determining politics, it is far from the complete story. In a cleft society, the attainment of 'identity' goals or assertion of identities can become a goal with electoral dividends. Thus, with the popular upsurge in the 1960s, various caste and regional groups coalesced to form political parties and capture power in their relevant states.

Moreover, in a society with widespread illiteracy and lack of information, vacuous but crisp, simple and catchy slogans such as 'Garibi Hatao' became effective vote-catchers. Abolishing privy purses for the erstwhile princes, even if it saved only an insignificant sum and involved a serious breach of a sacred covenant enshrined in the Constitution, held irresistible electoral appeal. Providing better education and health facilities, and physical infrastructure, such as rural roads, to improve the poor's earning capacity, was not only a hard task but also paid dividends only after a few years. Handouts in the form of subsidies for immediate succour would not remove poverty on a lasting basis, but could buy votes. Populist policies of subsidies, nationalization and indiscriminate expansion of the public sector into areas without strategic significance followed. The need for handouts increased over time and subsidies started pre-empting the government's resources. It resulted in fiscal unsustainability and a government out of control. Societal upsurge in the mid-1970s almost overwhelmed the Indian state, an internal emergency had to be declared and democratic rights suspended. Fortunately, it only lasted nineteen months and the balance between society and state was slowly restored.

Governments in India had been spending on investments in and loans to CPSEs and from the early 1970s, on subsidies. The CPSEs were incurring losses and not giving adequate returns. Spending more always pleases people who are the beneficiaries. Similarly, reducing taxes buys popularity. In personal income tax, the emphasis until the late 1980s was on putting spectacularly high, confiscatory rates on the highest income slab. It encouraged evasion and mobilized little, but the optics were good for political purposes. Simultaneously, there was a tendency to grant high exemption thresholds below which no tax was levied. Similarly, there was, and there is, this tendency to grant exemptions and concessions, in both direct and indirect taxes. Thus, democratic politics in India led to a deficit bias, and consequent pressure on inflation and balance of payments. India had to go to the IMF for exceptional balance of payments support in 1957, 1962, 1963, 1965, 1981 and 1991. Many of these were precipitated by exogenous shocks such as the Suez Crisis in 1957 and the Chinese aggression in 1962, but such shocks were just triggers that unveiled crises that would have probably hit India even otherwise in due course, albeit with a lag.

Until 1991 or at least the early 1980s, politics continued to be Nehruvian, through command and control and planning in letter, but populist in spirit. In conformity with IPR 1948, there were policies to promote SSIs, but they were more for their promotion than for their protection. SSI reservations and restrictions on large-scale units competing with SSI came only in 1967. The number of items reserved for SSI went up rapidly from forty-seven in 1967 to 873 in October 1984! But the appeal of populist policies started waning and politicians also started reading mixed signals from the people. For example, during the Emergency, in 1976, Indira Gandhi, by an amendment to Chapter V-B of the Industrial Disputes Act, 1947, raised the threshold requiring government permission for layoffs, retrenchments and closures from 100 to 300. The same Indira, by an amendment in 1982, which took effect in 1984, restored the threshold again to 100 workers.

The intellectual milieu had changed after Mao's demise and the reforms initiated in China around 1982 by Deng Xiaoping. The change was particularly striking after the crumbling of communism in Eastern Europe from 1989 and the disintegration of the former Soviet Union in 1991. Both India and Indians had been changing in the meanwhile. All that a change in policy orientation required was an external trigger. When such a trigger came in the form of the Gulf War in 1991, India was ready to usher in change. Prime Minister Narasimha Rao, with Dr Manmohan Singh as his finance minister, launched reforms to not only move away from command and control but also make prudent macroeconomic policies a part and parcel of it. The reforms were supported by two standby arrangements and one Contingency Financing Facility from the IMF, and a structural adjustment loan from the World Bank. Such external assistance had conditionalities attached. There had been such programmes with conditionalities even in the past, but the accompanying reforms did not last much beyond the programme periods. This time it was different, and the adjustments were there to stay and accelerate in the future. The reason was that Indians had changed.

These changed Indians are reflected in the increased emphasis on primary education and primary healthcare. The middle classes, which had captured education and health policies in the early years after Independence, are much more appreciative of the importance of these two basic services and supportive of government initiatives such as the Sarva Shiksha Abhiyan from 2001 and Ayushman Bharat-Pradhan Mantri Jan Arogya Yojana in 2018. The changed Indians are also reflected in the added emphasis on the girl child. The Balika Samriddhi Yojana in 1997, the Ladli Laxmi Yojana in Madhya Pradesh in 2007 and in Bihar, Chhattisgarh, Delhi, Goa, Jharkhand and UP, the Kanyashree Prakalpa in 2013 in West Bengal, and the Beti Bachao, Beti Padhao programme of the Union government from 2014, attest to this change.

Indeed, popular appreciation of appropriate policies was and is still far from perfect. Public opinion has not fully factored in the hard challenges of implementation because of the inherent limitations to government capacity. Illustratively, this imperfection is reflected in policies towards prohibition and disinvestment. After the introduction of prohibition in Bihar in 2016, smuggling went up, dozens of people died after consuming spurious liquor, and the courts were overburdened by liquor-related cases. Yet, prohibition continued for six years under two different governments. Similarly, for over seven decades, CPSEs failed to generate adequate returns. Air India, after being taken over by the government from Tata in 1953, had accumulated losses of ₹77,953 crore by end-March 2021. From 2007–08, Air India had been incurring losses every year. Yet, when it was sold back to Tata in 2021, opposition to disinvestment had not disappeared. That running businesses is not the business of the government is still not universally accepted in the country. Similarly, there seems to be insufficient popular support for rationalizing subsidies in the power sector, which is at the root of the festering power sector problem since the late 1960s.

Corruption had plagued India right from the early 1950s and 1960s. Corruption is there almost in every country, only its intensity varies across countries. The extent of it depends on the institutional structure and the voter's attitude to corrupt electoral candidates. Public attitude to corruption has changed but in a somewhat ambivalent manner. While allegations of corruption did not affect electoral results significantly in the beginning, a perceptible change in people's tolerance of corruption was seen from the late 1980s. Alleged corruption is likely to have contributed to the defeat of the Congress under Rajiv Gandhi in 1989, and under Narasimha Rao in 1996, AIADMK under Jayalalitha in Tamil Nadu in 1996, and the UPA in the 2014 Lok Sabha election. The RTI Act in 2005 and the Lokpal and Lokayukta Acts in 2013 have strengthened the institutional structure for combating corruption. People have become less forgiving of corruption, irrespective of the perpetrator's caste, tribe, religion, region or group, and information about alleged corruption has become easier to obtain with the RTI Act. But proving allegations of corruption and getting the perpetrators convicted continues to be problematic. Furthermore, still many candidates who are alleged to be corrupt continue to get elected.

There are several possible answers to the question of why the Indian voter sometimes elects corrupt candidates. Given the huge campaign expenses involved in elections, one answer is provided by the political scientist V.O. Key: 'If the people can only choose among rascals, they are certain to choose a rascal.'[1] The other possibility is the lack of information available to the average poor voter about the candidate's character. Another probable reason is the corrupt candidate 'is the crutch that helps the poor and underprivileged navigate a system that gives them so little access'.[2] Hopefully, apart from the resolution of the problem of election funding, as literacy and media coverage improve further and access to public services becomes easier, the tolerance of the voter for corrupt electoral candidates will also reduce.

The attitude of the voters towards corrupt electoral candidates holds a corollary in the dysfunctional system of name and shame in the field of policies. The non-implementation of FRBMA 2003 in spirit is a good example. Objectives such as elimination of the revenue deficit and reduction of fiscal deficit to no more than 3 per cent of GDP remain unattained even after a decade and a half after the original target date. The same antidote to the problem of the tolerance of the average voter for corrupt candidates, namely a better-informed electorate, will also improve the efficacy of naming and shaming in Indian politics.

The story of India's search for glory is an evolving story of the interplay between changing Indians and changing India, and this interplay holds the key to success in India's search for glory. Indians have changed in terms of education, health and income levels. This socio-economic upliftment, together with urban migration, has reduced the social cleavages, particularly of the caste system. But these cleavages have lessened, not disappeared. Elections are still often fought on the basis of identity politics. 'Only *jats*, not jobs: Intense west UP campaign by all parties is on many things, just not on economic problems'[3] ran the headlines in one newspaper in the run-up to the February 2022 Vidhan Sabha elections in UP. But there is progress, and the fractured verdicts of the 1970s produced by an electorate divided along identity issues have given way to more decisive mandates for single parties, particularly since mid-2000.

The caste consolidation among the Hindus, while a very welcome long-awaited development, may be having an adverse impact on inter-religious conflict. Secularization, like many other socio-economic features, is also an evolving story. The religious conflicts, this book argues, are likely to reduce as caste consolidation among the Hindus nears completion. India is changing and so are Indians, and the two are going to reinforce each other to make India's search for glory less and less elusive over the years.

There were reforms and progressive moves in economic policies even during the first two periods. But such moves were mostly top-down. What changed in the third period was the increasing role of the people and their endorsement in determining policy. It is a manifestation of the maturing of Indian democracy and the socio-economic progress of the Indians. In October 2010, Harvard economist Lawrence Summers, who was Treasury Secretary under President Clinton and economic adviser to President Obama, said '. . . perhaps—in 2040, the discussion will be less about the Washington Consensus or the Beijing Consensus, than about the Mumbai Consensus—a third way not based on ideas of laissez-faire capitalism that have proven obsolete or ideas of authoritarian capitalism that ultimately will prove not to be enduringly successful. Instead, a Mumbai Consensus based on the idea of a democratic developmental state, driven not by a mercantilist emphasis on exports, but a people-centered emphasis on growing levels of consumptions and a widening middle class.'[4] This is the same Summers who, when he was World Bank's vice president and chief economist, in mid-1992, had presciently predicted that the rise of China would be a 'transcendent event', and its economy would overtake the US economy!

Acknowledgements

For comments, guidance and inspiration, I am grateful to Anirban Mitra, Anirudh Krishna, Arjun Thapan, Bhaskar Dutta, Debraj Ray, Devajyoti (Doc) Ghosh, D.P. Sengupta, Dhiren Swarup, Gautam Ray, G. R. Reddy, Joan M. Esteban, K. L. Prasad, Lohit Jagtiani, M Govinda Rao, Manipushpak Mitra, M. S. Sahoo, Niraja Jayal, Pinaki Chakrabarty, Rahul Bedi, Rajat Nag, Rakesh Jayal, Sanjay Mitra, Satish Rao, Saumya Mitra, Souvik Roy, Sudipto Mundle, and Vikram Khanna. I am grateful to my editors Manish Khurana and Shreya Mukherjee of Penguin Random House India for providing excellent editorial guidance and support.

I am grateful to my wife Rita for tolerating long, solitary evenings while I worked away under the same roof trying to finish the book and encouraging me to get over the ordeal. My two daughters, Amrita and Madhumita, never failed to inspire me to finish the book and my three grandsons spent days without the company of their grandfather. My son Arjun not only encouraged me to finish writing the book but also presented me with a high-back, executive swivel chair and a 24-inch computer monitor that made my work so much less strenuous.

To all my benefactors, a big thank you!

The errors and omissions that remain are, of course, mine.

Bibliography

'A Beginning, but Miles to Go.' *Economic and Political Weekly*, vol. 38, no. 7, 2003: 579–580.

'Adieu Time,' *Economic and Political Weekly*, 20 July 1996:1907–1908.

'All Honourable Men.' *Economic and Political Weekly*, vol. 13, no. 48, 1978: 1959–1960.

'Bangla in Disarray,' *Economic and Political Weekly*, vol. 4, no. 5, 1969.

'Legacy of Nehru,' *Economic and Political Weekly*, Vol. 11, No. 46 (Nov. 13, 1976), p. 1773.

'Passing of the Periyar.' *Economic and Political Weekly*, vol. 9, no. 1/2, 1974: 13–15.

'Patnaik in the Dock,' *Economic and Political Weekly*, vol. 3, no. 12, 1968: 480–480.

'The National Advisory Council Experiment,' *Economic and Political Weekly*, Vol. 43, Issue No. 15, April 2008.

'The United Front.' *Economic and Political Weekly*, vol. 2, no. 40, 1967: 1802–1803.

'Unplanned Credit,' *Economic and Political Weekly*, 14 November 1970, Vol. 5, No. 46: 1829–1830.

Abdullah, Sheikh Mohammad. *Flames of the Chinar—An Autobiography*. Abridged, translated from Urdu and introduced by Khushwant Singh. Delhi: Penguin Books, 1993.

Abraham, Amrita. 'Maharashtra's Employment Guarantee Scheme.' *Economic and Political Weekly*, Vol. 15, No. 32 (9 August 1980). 1339–1342.

Acemoglu, Daron and James A. Robinson, *The Narrow Corridor—How Nations Struggle for Liberty*, Penguin Random House 2020.

Acharya. S.S. and N.L. Aggarwal. Tables 7.17–7.19 in *Agricultural Marketing in India*. Delhi. Oxford and IBH Publishing Co. Pvt. Ltd., 1987.

Adelman, I and C. Morris. 'Performance criteria for evaluating economic development potential. An operational approach.' *Quarterly Journal of Economics*, Vol. 82, No. 2, (1968). 260–280.

Ahluwalia, Montek Singh. *Backstage – The story behind India's high growth years*. New Delhi: Rupa Publications India, 2020.

Ahmad, Mukhtar. 'Mufti floats new regional party in Kashmir.' *Rediff*, 28 July 1999.

Ahmed, Akbar S. *Pakistan and Islamic Identity – The search for Saladin*. London: Routledge, 1997.

Ahmed, Farzand. 'Indira Gandhi's visit to Belchhi: A well–calculated political move?' *India Today*, 15 September 1977.

Aiyar ,V. Shankar and Sumit Mitra. 'UTI flagship scheme US–64 pauperised by former chairman by gambling on high–risk shares.' *India Today*, 23 July 2001.

Aiyar, Shankar. *Accidental India: A History of the Nation's Passage Through Crisis and Change*. New Delhi: Aleph Book Company, 2012.

Aiyar, V. Shankar. 'Dubious investments, alleged role in stocks scam point to rot in UTI management.' *India Today*, 30 April 2001.

Alagh, Yoginder K. 'Case for an Agricultural Income Tax.' *The Economic Weekly*, 30 September 1961. 1533–1538.

Alesina, Alberto and Bryony Reich. 'Nation–building.' working paper, Department of Economics, Harvard University, 2015. https.//dash.harvard.edu/handle/1/28652213

Alesina, Alberto and Eliana La Ferrara. 'Ethnic Diversity and Economic Performance.' *Journal of Economic Literature*, Vol. 43, No. 3, (September 2005): 762–800.

Ali, Qurban. 'Rammanohar Lohia.' *Mainstream*, Vol XLVII, No 14, (21 March 2009). https.//www.mainstreamweekly.net/article1241.html.

All Parties Conference. *The Nehru Report. An Anti–Separatist Manifesto*. 1928, New Delhi: Michiko and Panjathan, 1975 (1928).

Allcott, Hunt, Allan Collard–Wexler and Stephen D. O'Connell. 'How Do Electricity Shortages Affect Industry? Evidence from India.' *American Economic Review*, 106 (3) (March 2016). 587–624.

Altman, Michael J. 'Hindoos, Hindu, Spelling and Theory.' *Religion Bulletin*, 3 September 2014. https.//bulletin.equinoxpub.com/2014/09/hindoos–hindu–spelling–and–theory/.

Ambedkar, B. R. *Annihilation of Caste*. New Delhi: Rupa Publications India, 2018.

Ambedkar, Babasaheb. 'Writings and Speeches,' Vol. IX, Edited by Vasant Moon, *Dr. Ambedkar Foundation Ministry of Social Justice & Empowerment*, Government of India, 2014. 67. https.//www.mea.gov.in/Images/attach/amb/Volume_09.pdf.

Ambesh, Paurush and Sushil Prakash Ambesh. 'Open Defecation in India: A Major Health Hazard and Hurdle in Infection Control.' *Journal of Clinical & Diagnostic Research*, July 2016. https.//www.ncbi.nlm.nih.gov/pmc/articles/PMC5020240/.

Anand, Dave. 'History of Punjabi Language & Gurmukhi Alphabet.' *Patch Poster*, 23 May 2013. https.//patch.com/connecticut/trumbull/history–of–punjabi–language—gurmukhi–alphabet.

Anandan, Sujata. 'Enron willing to amend Power Purchase Agreement.' *The Hindustan Times*, 9 February 2001.

Ananth, V. Krishna. 'India since Independence – Making sense of Indian politics.' *Longman*, Delhi, 2011.

Andersen, Walter. 'The Rashtriya Swayamsevak Sangh –III: Participation in Politics.' *Economic and Political Weekly*, 25 March 1972. 673.

Ankit, Rakesh. 'The accession of Junagadh, 1947–48: Colonial Sovereignty, state violence and post–independence India.' *The Indian Economic and Social History Review*, Vol. 53, No. 3, 2016. 371–404.

Ankit, Rakesh. 'The Problem of Poonch,' *Epilogue*, Vol. 4, Issue 8, August 2010. https.//books.google.co.in/books?id=DpQh00eGEB0C&pg=PA8&redir_esc=y#v=onepage&q&f=false.

Annett, A. 'Ethnic and religious divisions, political instability and government consumption,' Department of Economics, Columbia University, 1999.

Arora, Subhash Chander. *President's Rule in Indian States (A Study of Punjab)*. New Delhi: Mittal Publications, 1990.

Arora, Subhash Chander. *Turmoil in Punjab Politics*. New Delhi: Mittal Publications, 1990.

Arora. Amrtansh. 'In a first, India's fertility rate falls below replacement level | What it means.' *India Today*, 25 November 2021.

Arunachalam, R M. 'Reserve Bank's Role in Rural Finance,' *The Economic Weekly*, 7 January 1961.

Aryan, Aashish. 'Retrospective taxation. the Vodafone case, and the Hague court ruling,' *Indian Express*, 27 September 2020.

Awana, Ram Singh. 'Pressure Politics in Congress Party – A Study of the Congress Forum for Socialist Action,' New Delhi: Northern Book Centre, 1988.

Azad, Maulana Abul Kalam. *India Wins Freedom: The Complete Version*,' Delhi: Orient Blackswan, 2009 (1959).

Baader, Gerard. 'The Depressed Classes of India. Their Struggle for Emancipation.' *Studies: An Irish Quarterly Review*, vol. 26, no. 103, 1937: 399–417.

Badhwar, Inderjit. 'Durbar move botches Congress(I)–NC alliance in Jammu & Kashmir,' *India Today*, 15 December 1987.

Badhwar, Inderjit. 'Jammu & Kashmir Assembly poll. NC–Congress(I) alliance sweeps a massive win,' *India Today*, 15 April 1987.

Badhwar, Inderjit. 'Violence–ridden Kashmir begins to heal as people participate in assembly elections,' *India Today*, 30 September 1996.

Bagcchi, Sanjeet. 'India's health minister commits government to improving healthcare access,' *BMJ (British Medical Journal)*, Vol. 348, 9 – 15 June 2014.

Bagchi, Amaresh and Nicholas Stern (ed). *Tax Policy and Planning in Developing Countries*. Oxford University Press, 1994.

Bagchi, Amaresh. 'Inflation and Personal Income Tax: A Note,' *Economic and Political Weekly*, Vol. 17, No. 17/18, 24 April – 1 May 1982: 733–738.

Bajwa, Rupa. '1988: Reduced voting age,' *India Today*, 26 December 2005.

Baker, Scott R., Nicholas Bloom, Steven J. Davis. 'Measuring Economic Policy Uncertainty,' *The Quarterly Journal of Economics*, Volume 131, Issue 4, November 2016.

Bal , S. S. 'Punjab after Independence (1947–1956),' *Proceedings of the Indian History Congress*, vol. 46, 1985: 416–430.

Bala Subrahmanya, M. H. 'Reservation Policy for Small–Scale Industry. Has It Delivered the Goods?' *Economic and Political Weekly*, vol. 30, no. 21, 1995: M51–M54.

Balachandran, G. *The Reserve Bank of India, Vol. 2, 1951–1967*. Delhi: Oxford University Press, 1998.

Balouch, Akhtar. 'How Fatima Jinnah died – and unsolved criminal case,' *The Dawn*. 24 January 2015.

Balouch, Akhtar. 'Jogendra Nath Mandal – chosen by Jinnah, banished by bureaucracy' *The Dawn*, 4 November 2015.

Bandyopadhyay, Sekhar. 'Transfer of Power and the Crisis of Dalit Politics in India, 1945–47.' *Modern Asian Studies*, vol. 34, no. 4, 2000: 893–942.

Banerjee, Abhijit, Donald P. Green, Jeffery McManus, and Rohini Pande. 'Are Poor Voters Indifferent to Whether Elected Leaders Are Criminal or Corrupt? A Vignette Experiment in Rural India,' *Political Communication*, Vol. 31, Issue 3, 2014.

Banerjee, Abhijit, Esther Duflo, and Nancy Qian. 'On the road: Access to transportation infrastructure and economic growth in China,' *Journal of Development Economics*, February 2020.

Banerjee, Abhijit, Lakshmi Iyer and Rohini Somanathan. 'History, Social Divisions, and Public Goods in Rural India,' *Journal of the European Economic Association*, Volume 3, Issue 2–3, 1 May 2005: 639–647.

Banerjee, Sumanta. 'Congress (R), ComPI and CPI (M).' *Economic and Political Weekly*, vol. 5, no. 45, 1970: 1804–1807.

Bardhan, Pranab. 'Political Economy of Development in India,' Delhi: Oxford University Press, 1999 (1984).

Bardhan, Pranab. 'Reflections on Indian Political Economy.' *Economic and Political Weekly*, vol. 50, no. 18, May 2015: 14–17.

Barman, Abheek. 'Air Attacks in Mizoram, 1966 – Our Dirty, Little Secret,' *The Economic Times*, 19 February 2013.

Baro, Aniruddha Kumar. 'Sixth Schedule and its implementation. Understanding the case of Bodoland (BTAD) in Assam,' IOSR *Journal of Humanities and Social Science*, Volume 22, Issue 12, Ver. 3 (December. 2017).

Barro, Robert J. *Macroeconomics: A Modern Approach*. Thomson South–Western, 2008.

Barry, Herbert. 'Gold,' *Virginia Law Review*, Vol. 20, No. 3, January 1934.

Baru, Sanjaya. 'No, Don't Blame the Laptop, It Was a Revolt of Rising Expectations,' *Indian Express*, 12 May 2004.

Baru, Sanjaya. *The Accidental Prime Minister – The Making and Unmaking of Manmohan Singh*. Delhi: Penguin Viking 2014.

Barua, Samir K. and Jayanth R. Varma. 'Securities Scam. Genesis, Mechanics and Impact,' *Vikalpa*, 18(1), January–March 1993: 3–12.

Basu Joyeeta & Navtan Kumar. 'Then Home Minister Mufti Sayeed protected terrorists in Kashmir,' *Sunday Guardian*, 31 August 2019.

Basu, Kaushik. 'The Enigma of India's Arrival: A Review of Arvind Virmani's Propelling India from Socialist Stagnation to Global Power', *Journal of Economic Literature*, Vol 46, No. 2, 2008: 396–406.

Basu, Nayanima. 'When Vajpayee took a bus ride and it seemed peace with Pakistan was possible,' *The Print*, 19 February 2019.

Basu, Saurav. 'Revisiting Nehru–Patel Differences,' *Swarajya*, 12 October 2014.

Baweja, Harinder. 'Facing political crisis created by CBI chief Joginder Singh, PM Gujral wields the axe,' *India Today*, 14 July 1997.

Baweja, Harinder. 'J&K CM Farooq Abdullah tries to play autonomy card, strengthen his hold on Valley,' *India Today*, 10 July 2000.

Baweja, Harinder. 'J&K. Countdown begins for first assembly election in 9 years, National Conference in demand,' *India Today*, 31 August 1996.

Baweja, Harinder. 'PM I. K. Gujral's anti–corruption cell fails to keep its basic promises,' *India Today*, 27 October 1997.

Baweja, Harinder. 'With evidence to indicate worsening situation in Kashmir Valley, EC decides against polls,' *India Today*, 30 November 1995.

BBC. 'Villagers massacred in Kashmir,' *BBC News*, 26 January 1998.

Becker, Gary S. 'A Theory of Competition Among Pressure Groups for Political Influence,' *The Quarterly Journal of Economics*, Vol. 98, No. 3, August 1983:371–400.

Becker, Gary S. 'Competition and Democracy,' *The Journal of Law & Economics*, Vol. 1, October 1958: 105–109.

Bedi, Rahul. 'Steady decline from Simla to Shimla, and now to Shyamala,' *The Citizen*, 22 October 2018.

Benack, Carolin. 'Economists are more like story–tellers than scientists – don't let the Nobel for economic sciences fool you,' *Conversation.com*, 11 October 2020.

Beteille, Andre. *Society and Politics in India – Essays in a Comparative Perspective*. Delhi: Oxford University Press, 1999.

Bhagat–Ganguly, Varsha. 'Revisiting the Nav Nirman Andolan of Gujarat,' *Sociological Bulletin*, Vol. 63, No. 1, January – April 2014: 95–112.

Bhagwati Jagdish and T. N. Srinivasan. 'Foreign Trade Regimes and Economic Development. India,' *NBER*, 1975: 18. http.//www.nber.org/chapters/c4508.pdf.

Bhagwati, Jagdish and T. N. Srinivasan. 'India Economic Reforms,' Associated Chambers of Commerce and Industry of India, 1993.

Bhagwati, Jagdish N. and Sukhamoy Chakravarty. 'Contributions to Indian Economic Analysis – A Survey,' *American Economic Review*, Vol. 59, No. 4, 1969: 1–79.

Bhanu, Dharma. 'The beginnings of famine policy in India,' *Proceedings of the Indian History Congress*, vol. 19, 1956: 328–337.

Bharadwaj, Ajay. 'Punjabi edges out Tamil in Haryana,' *DNA*, 7 March 2010.

Bhasin, Prem. 'The Praja Socialist Party,' in Verinder Grover (ed). *Political Parties and Party System – Political System and Constitution of India – 5*. New Delhi: Deep and Deep Publications, 1997.

Bhaskar, Utpal. 'All villages electrified, but last mile supply a challenge,' *The Mint*, 29 December 2019.

Bhat, K. N. 'Bommai verdict: A law for all time,' *Deccan Herald*, 1 August 2021.

Bhat, Mohmad Aabid. 'Preventive detention in counter–insurgencies: The case of Kashmir,' *Insight*, Vol. 21, No. 4, Fall 2019.

Bhat, T. P. 'Growth and Structural Changes in Indian Industries,' *ISID Working Paper*, February 2013, New Delhi.

Bhatia, Varinder. 'Haryana's South connect: When it made Telugu second language in school,' *Indian Express*, 6 February 2019.

Bhatnagar, Ashwini. 'Rajiv Gandhi had wanted to end impasse in Kashmir and saw Farooq Abdullah as its best bet,' *The Print*, 12 February 2020.

Bhatt, Sheela. 'Baba Ramdev was hiding in a saree. Pillai,' 6 June 2011, https.//www.rediff.com/news/report/the–baba–was–hiding–in–a–saree–pillai/20110605.htm.

Bhatt, Virendra Nath. 'Once upon a time, there was the Jan Morcha,' *Financial Express*, 28 July 2009.

Bhole, L. M. 'Administered Interest Rates in India,' *Economic and Political Weekly*, Vol. 20, No. 25/26, 22–29 June 1985: 1089–1104.

Bhushan, Prashant. 'The Freedom of Information Bill 2002,' 15 December 2002, http.//www.freedominfo.org/2002/12/freedom–of–information–law–approved–in–indi/.

Bhuwania, Anuj. *Courting the people. public interest litigation in post–emergency India.* UK: Cambridge University Press, 2017.

Bijawat, Mahesh C. 'Voluntary Disclosure,' *Journal of the Indian Law Institute*, vol. 21, no. 4, 1979: 443–455. ,

Bisht, Akash. 'The hero of Bastar: Remembering BD Sharma and his efforts for tribals,' *Catchnews*, 9 December 2015.

Blaug, Mark. 'Literacy and Economic Development.' *The School Review*, vol. 74, no. 4, 1966: 393–418.

Bloomberg. 'Nirav Modi Managed to Travel Even as Interpol Flashed Information on Revocation of Passport: CBI,' *Bloomberg*, 18 June 2018.

Bloomberg. 'Undisclosed Assets Cases Worth Rs 14,300 Crore,' *Bloomberg*, 8 February 2021.

BM. 'Fund–Bank's Grand Design for India', *EPW*, Vol. 26, No. 27/28, 6–13 July 1991.

Bohlken, Anjali Thomas and Ernest John Sergenti. 'Economic Growth and Ethnic Violence. An Empirical Investigation of Hindu—Muslim Riots in India.' *Journal of Peace Research*, vol. 47, no. 5, 2010: 589–600.

Borders, William. '4 Gandhi Aides Held on Charges of Graft,' *The New York Times*, 16 August 1977.

Borders, William. 'Mrs. Gandhi Back on Political Trail,' *The New York Times*, 15 October 1977.

Bose, Ajay. *Behenji: A Political Biography of Mayawati*. Delhi: Penguin Viking, 2008.

Bose, Ashish. 'The Sanjay Factor,' *India Today*, 15 February 1978.

Bose, Indranil. 'How did the Indian Forest Rights Act, 2006, emerge?' *IPPJ Discussion Paper Series Thirty–Nine*, May 2010.

Bose, Sumantra. *Kashmir – Roots of Conflict, Paths to Peace*. Cambridge: Harvard University Press, 2003.

Bose, Sumantra. *Transforming India – Challenges to the World's Largest Democracy*. Cambridge: Harvard University Press, 2013.

Boughton, James M. 'Was Suez the First Financial Crisis of the Twenty–First Century?', *Finance & Development*, No. 3, Vol. 38, September 2001. IMF. http.//www.imf.org/external/pubs/ft/fandd/2001/09/boughton.htm.

Boughton, James. 'Silent Revolution. The International Monetary Fund 1979–1989,' *IMF*, October 2001: 710. Available at https.//www.imf.org/external/pubs/ft/ history/2001/ch15.pdf.

Brass, Paul R. 'The Political Uses of Crisis. The Bihar Famine of 1966–1967.' *The Journal of Asian Studies*, vol. 45, no. 2, 1986: 245–267.

Brecher, Michael. 'India's Devaluation of 1966. Linkage Politics and Crisis Decision–Making,' *British Journal of International Studies*, Vol. 3, No. 1, April 1977: 1–25.

Buiter, Willem H., and Urjit R. Patel. 'Debt, Deficits and Inflation. An Application to the Public Finances in India,' *Journal of Public Economics*, Vol. 47, No. 2, March 1992.

Business Standard. 'Aadhaar Cards issued to over 90% population of India as of Feb 2020. Govt,' 19 March 2020.

Business Standard. 'Dabhol power project to be split to revive plant,' 30 September 2015.

Business Standard. 'Jairam Ramesh responsible for policy paralysis during UPA–2: Veerappa Moily,' 28 August 2019.

Business Standard. 'Modi government forms SIT to probe black money,' 27 May 2014.

Business Standard. 'Patil quits, Chidambaram to be home minister,' 1 December 2008.

Business Standard. 'Transport body threatens to strike from July 1,' 12 June 2008.

Business Today. '38 economic offenders fled India in last 5 years,' 15 September 2020.

Butler, David, Ashok Lahiri and Prannoy Roy. *India Decides –1952–1995*. New Delhi: Books and Things,1995.

Byres, Terence. *The State, development planning and liberalisation in India*. New Delhi: Oxford University Press, 1998.

Caro, Robert A. *The Years of Lyndon Johnson – the Passage to Power*. New York: Alfred A. Knopf, 2012.

Carroll, Lucy. 'The Temperance Movement in India. Politics and Social Reform.' *Modern Asian Studies*, vol. 10, no. 3, 1976: 417–447.

Cellular Operators Association of India. 'Telecom Sector Reforms in India,' November 2007.

Chakrabarti, Angana. 'Fear of quota claims, "need to save secular state" — why caste never made it to the census,' *The Print*, 9 March 2020.

Chakrabarty, Bidyut. 'The Left Front's 2009 Lok Sabha Poll Debacle in West Bengal, India. Prospective Causes and Future Implications,' *Asian Survey*, Vol. 51, No. 2 (March/April 2011): 290–310.

Chakrabarty, K. C. 'Two decades of credit management in banks. Looking back and moving ahead,' Speech at Bancon, 18 November 2013. https.//www.rbi.org.in/ SCRIPTs/BS_SpeechesView.aspx?Id=857.

Chakravartty, Nikhil. 'Indira Gandhi installed as president of break–away faction of Congress Party,' *India Today*, 31 January 1978.

Chandra, Bipan, Mridula Mukherjee and Aditya Mukherjee. *India since Independence*. Delhi: Penguin Books, 2007.

Chandra, Bipan. 'Jawaharlal Nehru and the Capitalist Class, 1936,' *Economic and Political Weekly*, Vol. X, No. 33–35, August 6, 1975: 1307–1324.

Chandra, Bipan. *In the name of democracy – JP movement and emergency*. Delhi: Penguin, 2017.

Chatterjee, Partha. 'Secularism and Toleration.' *Economic and Political Weekly*, vol. 29, no. 28, 1994: 1768–1777.

Chatterjee, Sibranjan. 'The Role of Governor in Indian Politics since 1967,' *The Indian Journal of Political Science*, vol. 32, no. 4, 1971: 522–535.

Chatterjee, Somnath. *Keeping the Faith: Memoirs of a Parliamentarian*. Delhi: Harper Collins, 2014.

Chatterjee, Surojit. 'Post trust vote victory, India Govt. to move forward with reforms, nuclear deal,' *International Business Times*, 22 July 2008.

Chattopadhyay, Raghabendra. 'Liaquat Ali Khan's Budget of 1947–48. The Tryst with Destiny,' Social Scientist, June–July, 1988, Vol. 16, No. 6/7: 77–89.

Chaudhuri, Saumitra. 'Nationalisation of Oil Companies in India,' *Economic and Political Weekly*, Vol. 12, No. 10, 5 March 1977: 437–444.

Chaudhuri, Saumitra. 'Some Issues of Growth and Profitability in Indian Public Sector Banks,' *Economic and Political Weekly*, vol. 37, no. 22, 2002: 2155–2162.

Chawla, Prabhu. 'Defence minister V.P. Singh quits office with his image in disarray,' *India Today*, 30 April 1987.

Chawla, Prabhu. 'Farooq Abdullah's dramatic dismissal as CM throws J&K into acute political instability,' *India Today*, 31 July 1984.

Chawla, Prabhu. 'J&K CM Farooq Abdullah expels G.M. Shah from primary membership of the party,' *India Today*, 31 October 1983.

Chawla, Prabhu. 'President Zail Singh questions govt's decisions, much to PM Rajiv Gandhi's embarrassment,' *India Today*, 28 February 1987.

Chawla, Prabhu. 'Rajiv Gandhi killing. Jain Commission report indicts DMK for colluding with LTTE,' *India Today*, 17 November 1997.

Chellappan, Kumar. 'How a Tamil failed to become PM,' *The Pioneer*, 28 April 2019.

Chelliah, Raja J. 'Trends in Taxation in Developing Countries,' *Staff Papers (International Monetary Fund)*, Vol. 18, No. 2, July 1971: 254–331.

Clark, J. C. D. 'Secularization and modernization. the failure of a 'grand narrative',' *The Historical Journal*, vol. 55, no. 1, 2012: 161–194.

CNN–IBN. 'Singh is King. UPA wins Trust Vote,' 22 July 2008.

Cohen, Benjamin I. 'The Stagnation of Indian Exports, 1951–1961,' *The Quarterly Journal of Economics*, 78 (4), 1964: 604–620.

Collier, Paul and Anke Hoeffler. 'Greed and Grievance in Civil War.' *Oxford Economic Papers*, 56 (4): 56.

Comptroller and Auditor General of India. 'Audit Report on XIX Commonwealth Games 2010,' Report of the Comptroller and Auditor General of India, Union Government (Civil), Report No. 6 of 2011–12.

Comptroller and Auditor General of India. 'Report No. 19 of 2010 – Performance Audit of Issue of Licences and Allocation of 2G Spectrum of Union Government,

Ministry of Communications and Information Technology,' Comptroller and Auditor General of India, 16 November 2010.

Comptroller and Auditor General of India. Report on Performance Audit of 'Allocation of Coal Blocks and Augmentation of Coal Production by Coal India Limited, for the year ended March 2012,' Union Government, Ministry of Coal, Report No. 7 of 2012–13 (Performance Audit),

Cooke, Nancy. 'Three Extracts on Public Finance by Adolph Wagner,' in Richard A. Musgrave and Alan T. Peacock. *Classics in the Theory of Public Finance*. London: MacMillan, 1967.

D'souza, Dilip. 'Skulduggery in a time of Enron – remembering Abhay Mehta,' *The Mint*, 3 August 2017.

Daalder, Hans. 'In Search of the Center of European Party Systems.' *The American Political Science Review*, vol. 78, no. 1, 1984: 92–109.

Damodaran, Harish. 'Muddling along on fertilizer subsidies,' *The Business Line*, 27 February 2013.

Dandavate, Madhu. *Jayaprakash Narayan – Struggle with Values*. Mumbai: Allied Publishers, 2002.

Dandekar, Kumudini. 'Mortality and Longevity in India, 1901–1961.' *Economic and Political Weekly*, vol. 7, no. 18, 1972: 889–892.

Dandekar, V. M. 'Making Right to Work Fundamental.' *Economic and Political Weekly*, vol. 26, no. 11/12, 1991: 697–708.

Dantwala, M. L. 'India's progress in agrarian reforms,' *Far Eastern Survey*, vol. 19, no. 22, 1950: 239–244.

Dar, Masrook A. 'Negotiations on Kashmir. A concealed story,' *Foreign Policy Journal*, 5 August 2010.

Das Gupta, Monica. 'Public Health in India. Dangerous Neglect,' *Economic and Political Weekly*, Vol. 40, No. 49, 3–9 December 2005: 5159–5165.

Das, B. M. 'Industrial Outlook—Problems of the Leather Industry in India.' *Current Science*, vol. 5, no. 5, 1936: 259–263.

Das, Jarmani. *Maharani*. Delhi: Penguin Random House, 2008.

Das, Sonali. 'Soren acquitted in '75 massacre case,' *The Times of India*, 7 March 2008.

Dasgupta, A K. 'Socialistic Pattern of Society and the Second Five Year Plan', *The Economic Weekly Annual*, 1957.

Dasgupta, A. K. (1987a). 'Keynesian Economics and Underdeveloped Countries Again', *Economic and Political Weekly*, Vol. 22, No. 38, 19 September 1987: 1601–06.

Dasgupta, A. K. (1987b). 'Keynesian Economics and Underdeveloped Countries Again. Postscript', *Economic and Political Weekly*, Vol. 22, No. 37, 21 November 1987: 2019–20.

Dasgupta, A. K. (1987c). 'Keynesian Economics and Underdeveloped Countries Again. Rejoinder', *Economic and Political Weekly*, Vol. 22, No. 49, 5 December: 2126.

Dasgupta, Arindam. 'Recent Individual Income Tax Reform,' *Economic and Political Weekly*, Vol. 40, No. 14, 2–8 April 2005: 1397–1405.

Dasgupta, Swapan, Javed M. Ansari and Harinder Baweja. 'Sonia Gandhi determined to project herself as key player in national politics,' *India Today*, 3 May 1999.

Dasgupta, Swapan. 'Managing power not be a bed of roses for Congress unaccustomed to coalition politics,' *India Today,* 26 April 1999.

Dash, S. C. 'Government and Politics in Orissa,' *The Indian Journal of Political Science*, vol. 26, no. 4, 1965: 83–100.

Dastidar, Abhishek G. and Shalini Nyar. 'Golden Quadrilateral. Vajpayee's biggest infra effort in roadways,' Indian Express, 17 August 2018.

Datar, Arvind P. 'Who betrayed Sardar Patel?' *The Hindu*, 19 November 2013.

Datta Nonica. *Forming an Identity: A Social History of the Jats*. New York: Oxford University Press, 1999.

Datta, Bhabatosh. *Indian Economic Thought – Twentieth Century Perspectives 1900–1950*. New Delhi: Tata McGraw–Hill Publishing Company Limited, 1978.

Davis, Mike. *Late Victorian Holocausts*. UK: Verso Books, 2000.

De Bendern, Paul. 'Swami Ramdev begins fast against corruption,' *The Mint*, 4 June 2011.

De Vries, Margaret Garritsen. 'The International Monetary Fund. 1966–71—The System Under Stress, Vol. I, Narrative', *International Monetary Fund*, Washington DC, 1976.

Deaton, Angus and Robert Fogel. 'The Great Escape. A Review of Robert Fogel's "The Escape from Hunger and Premature Death, 1700–2100"' *Journal of Economic Literature*, vol. 44, no. 1, 2006: 106–114.

Deccan Herald. 'Sonia diagnosed with cervical cancer,' 5 August 2011.

Deccan Herald. 'Swachh Bharat. laudable progress,' 2 October 2019.

Denoon, David B. H. 'Cycles in Indian Economic Liberalization, 1966–1996,' *Comparative Politics*, Vol. 31, No. 1, October 1998: 43–60.

Deodhar, N. S. 'Primary Health Care in India,' *Journal of Public Health Policy*, March 1982, Vol. 3, No. 1: 76–99.

Desai, Hari. 'Abdication of Maharaja Hari Singh of J & K,' *Asian Voice*, 8 August 2017.

Desai, Meghnad. *Rediscovery of India*. Allan Lane (an imprint of Penguin Books), 2009.

Dev, Arun. 'How Telgi Pulled Off Rs 3,000 Cr Stamp Paper Scam, Until He Didn't,' *The Quint*, 25 October 2017.

Dev, S. Mahendra. 'India's (Maharashtra) Employment Guarantee Scheme. Lessons from Long Experience,' published in Joachim von Braun (edited). 'Employment for Poverty Reduction and Food Security', International Food Policy Research Institute, Washington DC.

Devi, Laxmi. 'Can anyone crack the Dabhol puzzle?' *The Economic Times*, 16 May 2005.

Dhar, P. N. 'The Evolution of Economic Policy in India – Selected Essays', New Delhi: Oxford University Press, 2003.

Dhar, P. N. 'The Nav–Nirman Movement,' *Business Standard*, 19 February 2000.

Dhawan, Himanshi. 'ISI backed Kandahar hijackers. Plane crisis negotiator Ajit Doval,' *Economic Times*, 12 July 2018.

Dheeraj. 'Official Birth of Janata Party,' http.//www.yourarticlelibrary.com/politics/official–birth–of–janata–party/49301.

Dhir, Hiranmay. 'Landlordism without landlord: the UP land reform,' in Ajit Kumar Singh and Santosh Merhotra (ed). *Land policies for equity and growth – transforming the agrarian structure in Uttar Pradesh.* Delhi: Sage Publications India, 2014.

Dholakia, Nikhilesh and Rakesh Khurana. 'Public Policy toward Essential Consumption Items: Generalizations from the Indian Experience,' *Journal of Public Policy & Marketing,* Vol. 2 (1983): 171–182.

Dhume, Sadanand. 'Entering uncharted territory. Under Congress India lacked an accelerator. Under Modi's BJP it lacks brakes,' *The Times of India,* 4 May 2019.

Dixit, J. N. *Liberation and Beyond: Indo–Bangladesh Relations.* Konark Publishers, 1999.

DNA. 'PM Narendra Modi invites ideas on 'Beti Bachao, Beti Padhao,' *DNA,* 11 October 2014.

DNA. 'The Sitaram Kesri case. how dynasty trumped ethics,' *DNA,* 10 July 2011.

Dobson, John. 'A One Trillion Dollar Hidden Treasure Chamber is Discovered at India's Sree Padmanabhaswamy Temple,' *Forbes,* 15 November 2015.

Doctor, Vikram and Writankar Mukherjee. 'The Bitterest Ban. The improbable story of how Bengal tried to ban Bengali sweets,' *The Economic Times,* 25 July 2015.

Dongre, Amol R. and Pradeep R. Deshmukh. 'Farmers' suicides in the Vidarbha region of Maharashtra, India: a qualitative exploration of their causes,' *Journal of Injury and Violence Research,* Vol. 4(1), January 2012.

Donovan, Ned. 'India is holding one of the world's largest – and most corrupt – elections,' *The New Statesman,* 6 September

Doshi, Vidha and Nisar Mehdi. '70 years later, survivors recall the horrors of India–Pakistan partition,' *Washington Post,* 14 August 2017.

Doval, Nikita. 'Babri Masjid demolition. The key political players and their roles,' *The Mint,* 6 December 2017.

Downs, Anthony. 'An Economic Theory of Political Action in a Democracy', *The Journal of Political Economy,* Vol. 65, Issue 2, April 1957: 135–150.

Drèze, Jean and Amartya Sen. *An Uncertain Glory—India and Its Contradictions.* US: Allen Lane, 2013.

Drèze, Jean. 'Right to Food and Public Accountability,' *The Hindu,* 5 December 2001.

Drèze, Jean. 'Universalisation with Quality. ICDS in a Rights Perspective,' *Economic and Political Weekly,* Vol. 41, No. 34, 26 August–1 September 2006: 3706–3715.

Drezner, Daniel W. 'Why can't world leaders ever admit they were wrong?' *The Washington Post,* 9 June 2015.

Drèze, Jean and Amartya Sen. 'Basic Education as a Political Issue,' *Journal of Education Planning and Administration,* Vol. IX(1), 1995.

Drèze, Jean and Amartya Sen. 'Democratic Practice and Social Inequality in India', *Journal of Asian and African Studies,* Vol. 37, No. 6, 2002.

Drèze, Jean and Amartya Sen. *Hunger and Public Action.* Oxford: Oxford University Press, 1989.

Drèze, Jean and Jackie Loh. 'Literacy in India and China.' *Economic and Political Weekly*, vol. 30, no. 45, 1995: 2868–2878.

Dubash, Navroz K. and Sudhir Chella Rajan. 'Power Politics. Process of Power Sector Reform in India,' *Economic and Political Weekly*, Sep. 1–7, 2001, Vol. 36, No. 35. 1–7 September 2001: 3367–3387+3389–3390.

Dubey, Suman. '1981. Rajiv becomes MP,' *India Today*, 26 December 2005.

Dubey, Suman. 'Has India fulfilled any of the goals Jawaharlal Nehru envisaged for it?', *India Today*, 15 June 1984,

Duclos, Jean–Yves, Joan Esteban, and Debraj Ray. 'Polarization. Concepts, Measurement, Estimation.' *Econometrica* 72, no. 6 (2004): 1737–772.

Duncan, Ian. 'New Political Equations in North India: Mayawati, Mulayam, and Government Instability in Uttar Pradesh,' *Asian Survey,* Vol. 37, No. 10 (Oct., 1997): 979–996.

Dutt, Amitava Krishna. 'The Political Economy of Indian Economic Reform,' *Journal of International Affairs*, Vol. 51, No. 1, South Asia. The Challenges of Statehood (Summer 1997): 57–83.

Dutt, Romesh C. *The Economic History of India – Vol Two: In the Victorian Age.* Publications Division, Ministry of Information and Broadcasting, Government of India, 1963.

Dutta, Ananya. 'Mamata withdraws support to UPA government,' *The Hindu*, 18 September 2012.

Dutta, Prabhas K. 'Why Governor's and not President's Rule in Jammu and Kashmir,' *India Today*, 20 June 2018.

Dutta, Prabhash K. '2G spectrum verdict. What happens now to 122 cancelled telecom licences?' *India Today*, 21 December 2017.

Dyson, Tim and Mick Moore. 'On Kinship Structure, Female Autonomy, and Demographic Behavior in India.' *Population and Development Review*, vol. 9, no. 1, 1983: 35–60.

Economic Times. 'Baba Ramdev firm on fast even after meet with Pranab Mukherjee, Kapil Sibal,' *The Economic Times*, 1 June 2011.

Economic Times. 'CVC finds irregularities in several CWG projects,' 28 July 2010.

Economic Times. 'DMK submits letter to President withdrawing its support to UPA,' 19 March 2013.

Economic Times. 'Enron–Dabhol power project. Supreme Court closes case of alleged corruption,' 11 April 2019.

Economic Times. 'PM Modi's promise of 'Rs 15 lakh in each account' an idiom. Amit Shah,' 6 February 2015.

Economic Times. 'RBI governor Raghuram Rajan questions farm debt waiver schemes,' December 27, 2014.

Economic Weekly. 'Conditional Mandate for Congress,' 17 May 1952.

Edlund, Lena, Hongbin Li, Junjian Yi, and Junsen Zhang. 'Sex Ratios and Crime. Evidence from China,' *The Review of Economics and Statistics* 95, no. 5 (2013). 1520–534.

EFSAS. *Pan–Islamism and Radicalization of Kashmiri Youth.* Amsterdam: European Foundation for South Asian Studies (EFSAS), June 2017.

Ehrenpreis, Dag. 'Some Models in Indian Development Planning,' *The Swedish Journal of Economics*, December 1970, Vol. 72, No. 4: 301–319.

Eigner, Richard M. 'Indian Income, Wealth and Expenditure Taxes. Integration and Administration,' *National Tax Journal*, vol. 12, no. 2, 1959: 151–162.

Erdman, H. L. *The Swatantra Party and Indian Conservatism*. Cambridge University Press, 1967.

Erdman, Howard L. 'India's Swatantra Party.' *Pacific Affairs*, vol. 36, no. 4, 1963: 394–410.

Erdman, Howard L. 'The Swatantra Party and Indian Conservatism,' *Cambridge South Asian Studies*, Cambridge at the University Press, 1967.

Esteban, Joan and Debraj Ray. 'On the Salience of Ethnic Conflict,' *American Economic Review*, Vol. 98, No. 5, December 2008: 2185– 2202

Esteban, Joan–Maria and Debraj Ray. 'On the Measurement of Polarization.' *Econometrica*, vol. 62, no. 4, 1994: 819–851.

Evans, Peter B, Dietrich Rueschemeyer and Theda Skocpol (eds.). 'Bringing the State Back In,' New York. Cambridge University Press, 1985.

Fan, Shenggen and Connie Chan–King. 'Road development, economic growth, and poverty reduction in China,' *International Food Policy Research Institute*, 2005.

Federal Reserve Bank of St. Louis. 'The United States Balance of Payments, 1946– 1960', *Review*, Vol. 43, No. 3, March 1961.

Fickett, Lewis P. 'The Praja Socialist Party of India—1952–1972: A Final Assessment.' *Asian Survey*, vol. 13, no. 9, 1973: 826–832.

Field, E, M. Levinson, R. Pande, and S. Visaria. 'Segregation, Rent Control, and Riots: The Economics of Religious Conflict in an Indian City.' *American Economic Review*, 98(2), 2008: 505–510.

Fogel, Robert William. 'A Quantitative Approach to the Study of Railroads in American Economic Growth: A Report of Some Preliminary Findings,' *The Journal of Economic History*, Vol. 22, No. 2, June 1962: 163–197.

Fogel, Robert William. 'Health, nutrition and economic growth,' *Economic Development and Cultural Change*, Vol. 52, No. 3, April 2004.

Fogel, Robert William. *The Escape from Hunger and Premature Death, 1700–2100 – Europe, America and the Third World.* UK: Cambridge University Press, 2004.

French, Howard W. 'Uniting China to Speak Mandarin, the One Official Language: Easier Said Than Done,' *The New York Times*, 10 July 2005.

Friedland, Roger and Richard Hecht. 'The Bodies of Nations: A Comparative Study of Religious Violence in Jerusalem and Ayodhya,' *History of Religions*, Vol. 38, No. 2 (Nov. 1998): 101–149.

Friedlander, Peter. 'Reassessing Religion and Politics in the Life of Jagjivan Ram,' *Religions*. November 2020: 224.

Friedman, Milton. 'A Memorandum to the Government of India' 5 November 1955, http.//www.indiapolicy.org/debate/Notes/friedman.htm, accessed on August 4, 2005.

Frontline. 'Asom Gana Parishad – Rise and Fall,' 2 May 2014.

Frontline. 'Crusading Congressman,' Vol. 18, Issue 19, 15–28 September 2001.

Frontline. 'Let them eat the bomb,' 6 June 1998.

Fukuyama, Francis. *State Building. Governance and World Order in the Twenty First Century*. Cornell University Press, 2004.

Furber , Holden. 'Review of V.P. Menon's "The Story of the Integration of the Indian States"' *Annals of the American Academy of Political and Social Science*, Vol. 309, January 1957.

Furber, Holden. 'The Unification of India, 1947–1951,' *Pacific Affairs*, Vol. 24, No. 4, December 1951: 352–371.

Galanter, Marc. 'Who Are the Other Backward Classes? An Introduction to a Constitutional Puzzle,' *Economic and Political Weekly*, Vol. 13, No. 43/44, 28 October 1978: 1812–1828.

Galbraith, John Kenneth. 'Let Us Begin. An Invitation to Action on Poverty.' *Harper's Magazine*, March 1964.

Galbraith, John Kenneth. *Economic Development in Perspective*. Cambridge: Harvard University Press, 1962.

Gandhi, M. K. *Hind Swaraj*. Delhi Open Books 2019(1909).

Gandhi, Ved P. *Some Aspects of India's Tax Structure – An Economic Analysis*. Bombay: Vora and Company Publishers, 1970.

Ganguli, B. N. *Indian Economic Thought – Nineteenth Century Perspectives*. Delhi: Tata McGraw–Hill Publishing Co. Ltd, 1977.

Ganguly, Dilip. 'Full account: Jayaprakash Narayan's escape from Hazaribagh Central Jail,' *India Today*, 22 April 2015.

Ganjoo, R. C. 'Rise and fall of JKLF,' *India Policy Foundation*, 26 February 2021. https.//www.ipf.org.in/Encyc/2021/2/26/Rise–and–fall–of–JKLF.html.

Ghandikota, Priya. 'When "Power Failures" Undermine International Business Negotiations: A Negotiation Analysis of the Dabhol Power Project A MALD Thesis Presented to Jeswald Salacuse,' *Fletcher School of Law and Diplomacy*, April 2002. https.//citeseerx.ist.psu.edu/viewdoc/download?doi=10.1.1.195.55 47&rep=rep1&type=pdf.

Ghani, Ejaz, Arti Grover Goswami, and William R. Kerr. 'Highway to Success. The Impact of the Golden Quadrilateral Project for the Location and Performance of Indian Manufacturing,' *The Economic Journal*, Volume 126, Issue 591, 1 March 2016: 317–357.

Ghildiyal, Subodh and Swati Mathur. 'From Buddhist texts to East India Company to now, "Dalit" has come a long way.' *The Times of India*, 5 September 2018.

Ghizoni, Sandra Kollen. 'Nixon Ends Convertibility of U.S. Dollars to Gold and Announces Wage/Price Controls', Federal Reserve Bank of Atlanta, August 1971. http.//www.federalreservehistory.org/Events/DetailView/33

Ghosh, S. K. *Indian Democracy Derailed Politics and Politicians*. Delhi: S. B. Nangla, 1997.

Ghosh, Srikanta. *Indian Democracy, Derailed Politics and Politicians*. New Delhi: APH Publishing Corporation, 1997.

Ghunawat, Virendrasingh. 'CBI arrests ex–IDBI Bank boss for Rs 900cr loan to Vijay Mallya's Kingfisher Airlines,' *India Today*, 24 January 2017.

Glinskaya, Elena and Michael Lokshin. 'Wage Differentials between the Public and Private Sectors in India,' *World Bank Policy,* Research Working Paper 3574, April 2005.

Godbole, Madhav. *Unfinished Innings: Recollections and Reflections of a Civil Servant* Hyderabad: Orient Longman, 1996.

Gokarn, Subir and Rajendra Vaidya. 'Deregulation and Industrial Performance. The Indian Cement Industry,' *Economic and Political Weekly,* Vol. 28, No. 8/9, 20–27 February 1993: M33–M41.

Gokarn, Subir. 'Future of Development Finance,' *Economic and Political Weekly,* Vol. 39, No. 26, 26 June – 2 July 2004: 2665–2666.

Golley, Jane. 'Population and the Economy. The Ups and Downs of One and Two,' in Jane Golley, Linda Jaivin, and Tomba Luigi (edited). *China Story Yearbook 2016: Control* (First edition, 75–94. Australia. ANU Press, 2017.

Gomez, Clifford. *Financial Markets, Institutions and Financial Services.* New Delhi: Prentice–Hall of India Private Ltd., 2008.

Goode, Richard. 'Report of the India Taxation Enquiry Commission,' *National Tax Journal,* Vol. 9, No. 2, June 1956: 134–147.

Gopakumar, Gopika and Shaswati Das. 'CBI books billionaire Nirav Modi in Punjab National Bank cheating case,' *The Mint,* 5 February 2018.

Gopal, Sarvepalli (ed.). 'Jawaharlal Nehru: An Anthology,' New Delhi: Oxford University Press, 1980.

Gopal, Sarvepalli. *Jawaharlal Nehru – A Biography, Vol. Three, 1956–1964.* Delhi: Penguin Vintage.

Gopal, Surendra. *Mapping Bihar – from medieval to modern times.* UK: Routledge, 2018.

Gordon, James and Poonam Gupta. 'Nonresident Deposits in India. In Search of Return?' *IMF* Working Paper. WP/04/48. 2004.

Government of India. 'An Overview of Service Tax in India,' Central Board of Indirect Taxes and Customs, Government of India, https.//www.cbic.gov.in/resources// htdocs–servicetax/ovw/ovw4_analysis–st–rev–ason120913.pdf Accessed on 28 December 2020.

Government of India. 'Goods and Services Tax (GST) – Concept and Status,' Central Board of Indirect Taxes and Customs (CBIC), Department of Revenue, Ministry of Finance, Government of India, as on 1 May 2019. https.//www.cbic.gov.in/ resources//htdocs–cbec/gst/GST–Concept%20and%20Status01052019.pdf;jses sionid=E0958E67BC72920FB62897B94DB49AB8.

Government of India. 'Guidelines – Central Rural Sanitation Programme: Total Sanitation Campaign,' Department of Drinking Water and Sanitation, Ministry of Rural Development, Government of India, December 2007. https.//jalshakti–ddws.gov.in/sites/default/files/TSCGuideline2007_0.pdf.

Government of India. 'National Population Policy. A Statement of the Government of India,' *Population and Development Review,* Vol. 2, No. 2, June1976: 309–312.

Government of India. 'Report of the Expert Group – Settlement of SEB Dues,' by Chairman Montek Singh Ahluwalia, Ministry of Power, May 2001. http.// orierc.org/OERCOLD/documents/ahluwalia_report.pdf.

Government of India. 'Report of the Expert Group on Agricultural Indebtedness,' Banking Division, Department of Economic Affairs, Ministry of Finance, Government of India, New Delhi, July 2007.

Government of India. 'Report of the Indian Statutory Commission,' Vol. II—Recommendations, Swati Publications, New Delhi, 1988 (1929).

Government of India. 'Report of the State Reorganisation Commission, 1955.' https.//mha.gov.in/sites/default/files/State%20Reorganisation%20Commisison%20Report%20of%201955_270614.pdf.

Government of India. 'Structuring of APDRP, Reform Framework and Principles of Financial Restructuring of SEBs,' Report of the Expert Committee headed by Deepak Parekh, Ministry of Power, Government of India, September 2002. http.//orierc.org/OERCOLD/documents/Deepak_Parekh_Report.pdf.

Government of India. 'The Lokpal and Lokayuktas Bill, 2011,' *Press Information Bureau*, Government of India, Ministry of Personnel, Public Grievances & Pensions, 18 December 2013.

Government of India. 'The Report of the Industrial Licensing Committee', 1969, chaired by Subimal Dutt, http.//reports.mca.gov.in/Reports/8–Report%20of%20the%20industrial%20licensing%20policy%20inquiry%20committee,%20main%20report,%201969.pdf.

Government of India. 'White Paper on Indian States,' July 1948.

Government of India. *Report of the Environmental Hygiene Committee*. Shimla: Government of India Press, 1949. https.//www.indianculture.gov.in/flipbook/1646.

Government of India. Report on Social, Economic and Educational Status of the Muslim Community of India—Prime Minister's High–Level Committee,' Cabinet Secretariat, Government of India November, 2006.

Government of Maharashtra. 'Report of the Energy Review Committee, Part I,' Maharashtra, Chairman Madhav Godbole, 10 April 2001. Para 5.5. https.//www.it.iitb.ac.in/~damani/enron/Home_files/doc/godbole/godbole–report.html.

Govindacharya, K.N. 'The Emergency started long before 25 June 1975,' *The Mint*, 22 June 2015.

Green, Toby. *Inquisition, The Reign of Fear*. Pan Books 2008 (Macmillan 2007).

Guha, Ramachandra. 'A Mask that was Pierced?' *The Hindu*, 24 April 2005.

Guha, Ramachandra. 'LOYALTY OR COMPETENCE? – Sycophancy has been the very signature of the Congress,' *The Telegraph*, 24 May 2008.

Guha, Ramachandra. 'The battle for Andhra,' *The Hindu*, 30 March 2003

Guha, Ramachandra. *India after Gandhi*. Picador, 2007.

Guha, Ramchandra. 'Nehru and Patel. Rivals or comrades?' *Hindustan Times*, 12 October 2014.

Gupta, Aashish, Nazar Khalid, Devashish Deshpande, Payal Hathi, Avani Kapur, Nikhil Srivastav, Sangita Vyas, Dean Spears, and Diane Coffey. 'Changes in open defecation in rural north India. 2014 – 2018,' https.//www.communityledtotalsanitation.org/resources/changes–open–defecation–rural–north–india–2014–2018.

Gupta, Anand P. 'Central Government Taxes. Have They Reduced Inequality?' *Economic and Political Weekly*, vol. 12, no. 4, 1977: 88–100.

Gupta, Anukriti. 'Understanding Vodafone Tax Dispute & Changing Dynamics of Indian Tax Laws,' *Taxguru*, 17 October 2021.

Gupta, Ranjit. 'Rural Works Programme. Where It Has Gone Astray.' *Economic and Political Weekly*, vol. 6, no. 20, 1971: 995–1004.

Gupta, S., S., H. Davoodi and E.R. Tiongson. 'Corruption and the provision of health care and education services,' in A.K. Jain (ed). *Political Economy of Corruption*. London: Routledge, 2001.

Gupta, Uttam. 'Enough of this Urea Populism', *The Business Line*, 30 January 2014.

Gupta, Uttam. 'Feritiliser DBT an illusion,' *The Pioneer*, 24 November 2020.

Gupta, Uttam. 'One step forward, two steps back,' *The Hindu BusinessLine*, 18 February 2014.

Haithcox, John Patrick. 'Left Wing Unity and the Indian Nationalist Movement. M. N. Roy and the Congress Socialist Party.' *Modern Asian Studies*, vol. 3, no. 1, 1969: 17–56.

Hansmann, Henry B. and John M. Quigley. 'Population Heterogeneity and the Sociogenesis of Homicide.' *Social Forces*, vol. 61, no. 1, 1982: 206–224.

Hardgrave Jr, Robert L. 'Caste and the Kerala Elections,' *The Economic Weekly*, 17 April 1965: 669–672.

Harikumar, A. 'Bribes were taken in the VVIP helicopter deal, admits AK Antony,' *India Today*, 25 March 2013.

Head. Brian. 'The Labor Government and 'Economic Rationalism'.' *The Australian Quarterly*, vol. 60, no. 4, 1988: 466–477.

Healy, Andrew and Neil Malhotra. 'Myopic Voters and Natural Disaster Policy,' *American Political Science Review*, Vol. 103, No. 3 August 2009.

Heath, Oliver. 'Anatomy of BJP's Rise to Power. Social, Regional and Political Expansion in 1990s.' *Economic and Political Weekly*, vol. 34, no. 34/35, 1999: 2511–2517.

Hegde, Sanjay. 'A nation builder's pride of place,' *The Hindu*, 14 April 2015.

Heller, Peter S. and Allan A. Tait. 'Government Employment and Pay – Some International Comparisons,' *International Monetary Fund*, Occasional Paper No. 24, March 1984.

Hicks, Ursula K. 'Official Paper.' *The Economic Journal*, vol. 68, no. 269, 1958: 160–169.

Hill, K, W. Seltzer, J. Leaning, S J Malik, and S.S. Russell. 'The Demographic Impact of Partition. Bengal in 1947,' http.//iussp2005.princeton.edu/download.aspx?submissionId=52236 :19–20.

Hindustan Times. ''God's ornaments not for display', Travancore royal family opposes museum for Padmanabhaswamy temple riches,' *The Hindustan Times*, 9 July 2018.

Hindustan Times. 'AgustaWestland scam. CBI files supplementary charge sheet against middlemen Christian Michel James, Rajiv Saxena and 13 others,' *The Hindustan Times*, 19 September 2020.

Hindustan Times. 'Before Ramdev black money fast, panel set up,' 29 May 2011.

Hindustan Times. 'Blow for Congress as states, Centre agree on GST formula,' 27 July 2016.

Hindustan Times. 'Share info on undisclosed black money with I–T dept, earn up to Rs 5 crore,' 1 June 2018.

Hindustan Times. 'Shibu Soren gets life in prison for murdering secy,' December 9, 2006.

Hindustan Times. 'The RTI Story; Power to the People by Aruna Roy with the MKSS Collective,' 13 April 2018.

Hoda, Najmul. 'Why Hamid Ansari is wrong about Hindu nationalism,' *The Times of India*, 31 January 2022.

Hodson, H V. *The Great Divide: Britain–India–Pakistan*. London Hutchinson: Oxford University Press, 1969.

Horowitz, Donald. *Ethnic Groups in Conflict*. Berkeley: University of California Press, 1985.

Huang, Y. *Capitalism with Chinese Characteristics: Entrepreneurship and the State,*' Cambridge University Press, 2008.

Husain, Zakir. 'Gender Disparities in Completing School Education in India. Explaining Geographical Variations.' *Journal of Population Research*, vol. 28, no. 4, 2011: 325–352.

Hussain, Aljaz. 'Jammu & Kashmir minister Ghulam Nabi Lone shot dead, local militants claim responsibility,' *India Today*, 31 October 2005.

Hussain, Monirul. 'Tribal Movement for Autonomous State in Assam.' *Economic and Political Weekly*, vol. 22, no. 32, 1987: 1329–1332.

Huurdeman, Anton A. *The Worldwide History of Telecommunication*. New Jersey: Wiley Interscience, 2003.

Inden, Ronald. 'A campaign that lost sheen,' *The Hindu*, 3 October 2004.

India Today. 'CWG scam. MS Gill, Sunil Dutt had warned PM on Suresh Kalmadi,' *India Today*, 4 July 2011.

India Today. 'Who is Hassan Ali Khan?' *India Today*, 3 March 2011.

India Today. '1958. Feroze Gandhi reveals LIC conspiracy,' *India Today*, July 2, 2007.

India Today. 'After five days, Kashmiri militants release Home Minister Mufti Mohammed Sayeed's daughter,' *India Today*, 31 December 1989.

India Today. 'Baba Ramdev sports woman's dress to hoodwink police,' 5 June 2011.

India Today. 'Battle for the party,' 15 June 1995.

India Today. 'BJP – Aiming High,' 15 May 1991.

India Today. 'BJP allies. A ready reckoner of who is teaming up with the BJP, why and for what,' 2 August 1999.

India Today. 'Caught in a cleft stick,' 15 January 1994.

India Today. 'Closing In,' 15 January 1995.

India Today. 'Cornered into action,' 31 January 1995.

India Today. 'Government to bring ordinance to protect tainted MPs and MLAs,' 24 September 2013.

India Today. 'HDW submarine deal. The scandal surfaces,' 15 March 1990.

India Today. 'He is back with a bang,' 30 April 1994.

India Today. 'How did Rao blunder?' 31 December 1992.

India Today. 'Leaders–in–waiting. The hopeful three,' 28 February 1993.

India Today. 'Mandal Commission – A Tragic Piece,' 15 October 1990.

India Today. 'Mishra murder case. The plot thickens,' 28 February 2014.

India Today. 'Mother of all weddings,' 30 September 1995.

India Today. 'Netting the big fish,' 14 December 1998.

India Today. 'Power play begins as J&K gets another hung house,' 28 December 2008.

India Today. 'Ripples, not waves,' 15 February 1995

India Today. 'Rot at the top,' 30 June 1996.

India Today. 'Sanjay Gandhi and demolition during Emergency time,' 15 January 1978.

India Today. 'Sikhs in Punjab shed its blind hostility towards Hindi,' 24 April 2015.

India Today. 'Tehelka expose. Jaya Jaitly, 2 others convicted in corruption case,' 26 July 2020.

India Today. 'V. P. Singh's shift. A Political Manoeuvre', 15 February 1987.

India Today. 'What makes NDA's 'India Shining' campaign the 'worst' poll strategy in Indian history,' *India Today*, 14 May 2013.

India Today. 'Who is Adil Shahryar and how does he know Rajiv Gandhi?' 12 April 2015.

Indian Express. 'Farewell Note,' 7 May 2014.

Indian Express. 'Govt. Strike at Black Capitalists: Notes of Rs. 500, Rs. 1,000 and Rs. 10,000 cease to be legal tender,' 13 January 1946.

Indian Express. 'Gujarat. Tension over Church construction in Dangs,' 28 November 2018.

Indian Express. 'Indian Express exposed Michel, Tyagi, note with initials; mentioned in chargesheet,' 6 April 2019.

Indian Express. 'Mamata's Opposition rally top quotes: "One ambition — save India, save democracy"' 19 January 2019.

Indian Express. 'Ordinance on convicted lawmakers: Chronology of events,' 2 October 2013.

Indian Express. 'RBI scotches ICICI Bank rumours, Govt says don't panic, we are watching,' 30 September 2008.

Indian Express. 'Telling Numbers. Enrolment and claims in flagship life, accident insurance schemes,' 11 December 2019.

Iyengar, Jayanthi. 'Windfall gains on VDIS jewellery declarations,' *Business Standard*, 26 August 1997.

Iype, George. 'Sonia relents, returns to head Congress,' *Rediff on net*, 24 May 1999.

Jadhav, Vishal. 'Elite Politics and Maharashtra's Employment Guarantee Scheme.' *Economic and Political Weekly*, vol. 41, no. 50, 2006: 5157–5162.

Jaffrelot, Christophe. 'India's Silent Revolution – the rise of the lower castes in Northern India,' London: Hurst and Company, 2003.

Jaffrelot, Christophe. 'The Fate of Secularism in India,' *Carnegie Endowment for International Peace*, 4 April 2019. https.//carnegieendowment.org/2019/04/04/fate–of–secularism–in–india–pub–78689.

Jaffrelot, Christophe. 'The Hindu nationalist reinterpretation of pilgrimage in India. the limits of *Yatra* politics,' *Nations and Nationalism*, 14 January 2009.

Jafri, N R. 'Pakistan's Trade with India,' *Pakistan Horizon*, Vol. 5, No. 2, June 1952: 86–96.

Jagannathan R. 'UPA's legacy. Disasters like Food Security Bill and Land Acquisition Bill,' 30 August 2013,

Jagannathan R. 'Why even Ramachandra Guha has had to rewrite the Nehru–Patel history,' *First Post*, 13 October 2014.

Jai, Janak Raj. *Commissions and Omissions by Indian Presidents –Vol II, 1977–2001.* Regency Publications, 2001.

Jain, Bharti. 'Serial dresser Patil at Saturday night blasts,' *The Economic Times*, 15 September 2008.

Jain, Sunil and Hardev S. Sanotra. 'Shiv Sena–BJP alliance scraps Enron power project at Dabhol, Congress plays safe,' *India Today*, 31 August 1995.

Jakhar, Deepti. 'Ramdev eviction. Why his salwar kameez looks carefully picked out,' *India Today*, 7 June 2011.

James, Gorton. 'British Preferential Export Taxes.' *American Economic Review*, vol. 14, no. 1, 1924: 56–63.

Jeffrey, Robin. 'Grappling with History: Sikh Politicians and the Past.' *Pacific Affairs*, vol. 60, no. 1, 1987, 59–72.

Jha, Ajit Kumar. '1975 Chirudih massacre: Past catches up with Shibu Soren, arrest warrant issued,' *India Today*, 2 August 2004.

Jha, D. C. 'US Policy Towards India,' *The Indian Journal of Political Science*, Vol. 37, No. 1 (Jan.–March 1976): 41–70.

Jhaveri, N. J. 'Tax Exemption on Personal Savings.' *Economic and Political Weekly*, vol. 5, no. 42, 1970: 1743–1750.

Johar, Roshni. 'Passion royale for pampering pets,' *The Tribune*, 24 May 2003.

John, Priya. 'Beedi Industry and Welfare of Workers in India—Review of Policies and Literature,' Centre for Health & Social Justice, New Delhi. http.//www.chsj.org/ uploads/1/0/2/1/10215849/policy_review.pdf.

Jones, Dawn E. and Rodney W. Jones. 'Urban Upheaval in India. The 1974 Nav Nirman Riots in Gujarat,' *Asian Survey*, Vol. 16, No. 11, November 1976: 1012–1033.

Josey, Ann and N Sreekumar. 'Is Anything Being Learnt from Past Programmes?' *Economic and Political Weekly*, Vol. 50, No. 41, 10 October 2015: 12–16.

Joshi, Lt. Gen Ashok. 'Secured in Dhaka, but squandered in Shimla,' http.//www.rediff. com/news/column/secured–in–dhaka–but–squandered–in–shimla/20160702. htm.

Joshi, Manoj. 'Mufti Mohammad Sayeed (1936–2016): From "soft–separatist" to "collaborator"' *Scroll.in*, 7 January 2016.

Joshi, Sharad. 'Case for total farm loan waiver,' *The Hindu BusinessLine*, 6 February 2008.

Joshi, Vijay and I. M. D. Little. *India – Macroeconomics and Political Economy*. Washington DC: The World Bank, 1994.

Judge, Philip. 'Lessons from the London Gold Pool', Gold–Eagle, 21 May 2001. http.//www.gold–eagle.com/article/lessons–london–gold–pool.

Juneja, Nalini. 'Constitutional Amendment to Make Education a Fundamental Right – Issues for a Follow Up Legislation,' Occasional Paper, *National Institute of Education Planning and Administration*, New Delhi, March 2003.

Kabra, Kamal Nayan. 'Nationalisation of Life Insurance in India', *Economic and Political Weekly*, Vol. 21, No. 47 (22 November 1986): 2045–2053.

Kailash, K. K. 'Alliances and Lessons of Election 2009,' *Economic and Political Weekly* Vol. 44, No. 39, 26 September– 2 October 2009: 52–57.

Kaldor, Nicholas. 'Tax Reform in India,' *The Economic Weekly Annual*, January 1959: 195–198.

Kalyanasundaram, S. 'The MPLAD scheme should be discontinued,' *The Hindu*, 21 April 2020.

Kant, Krishna. '40 years ago..and now: How Tata Steel weathered the MRTP Act storm', *Business Standard*, August 27, 2014.

Kapur, Prithipal Singh. 'Master Tara Singh and partition of the Punjab,' *The Tribune Saturday Plus*, 28 November 1998.

Kar, Dev and Brian LeBlanc. 'Illicit Financial Flows from Developing Countries. 2002–2011,' 11 December 2013. https.//gfintegrity.org/report/2013–global–report–illicit–financial–flows–from–developing–countries–2002–2011/.

Karan. 'Debt restructuring plan for power distribution companies,' *PRS*, 27 July 2012.

Karmakar, Rahul. 'Arunachal shuts down over citizenship to Chakma–Hajong refugees,' *The Hindustan Times*, 19 September 2017.

Kasbekar, Mehak. 'Does loan waiver harm credit culture?' *The Mint*, 2 June 2008.

Katakam, Anupama. 'The Telgi Conviction,' *Frontline*, 10 February 2006.

Kaufman, Michael. 'New Party of Old Backers a Blow To Mrs. Gandhi's Political Future,' *The New York Times*, 6 July, 1979

Kaul, H. N. (1991). *K. D. Malaviya and the Evolution of India's Oil Policy*, New Delhi: Allied Publishers, 1991.

Kaur, Harpreet. 'Diasporic Sikh Organisations,' *The Indian Journal of Political Science*, vol. 70, no. 4, 2009: 1085–1098.

Kaviraj, Sudipta. 'Indira Gandhi and Indian Politics,' *Economic and Political Weekly*, Vol. 21, No. 38/39, 20–27 September 1986: 1697–1708.

Keating, Paul. 'Labor's Commitment to Smaller Government,' https.//ipa.org.au/wp–content/uploads/archive/1213831268_document_review39–3_keating–labor_smallgovernment.pdf.

Kelley, Patrick L. 'Is an Expenditure Tax feasible?' *National Tax Journal*, vol. 23, no. 3, 1970: 237–253.

Kennedy, Paul. *The Rise and Fall of the Great Powers*. Vintage Books, 1989.

Kethineni, Veeranarayana. 'Political Economy of State Intervention in Health Care,' *Economic and Political Weekly*, 19 October 1991, Vol. 26, No. 42: 2427–2433.

Key Jr, Vladimer Orlando. *The Responsible Electorate: Rationality in Presidential Voting 1936–1960*. Cambridge: Belknap Press, 1966. Quoted in B. Douglas Bernheim and Navin Kartik. 'Candidates, Character, and Corruption,' *American Economic Journal*, Microeconomics, May 2014, Vol. 6, No. 2: 205–246.

Khan, S. S. 'Tax Amnesties in India,' *TII Special*, Tax International, 12 March 2012. https.//www.taxindiainternational.com/columnDesc.php?qwer43fcxzt=NzU=.

Khatkhate, Deena. 'Monetary Policy in India. A Command Approach,' *Economic and Political Weekly*, vol. 25, no. 33, 1990: 1856–1858.

Khayal, Ghulam Nabi. 'Resettlement bill continues to draw fire from opposition groups in J&K,' *India Today*, 15 June 1982.

Khetan, Ashish. "Radia lobbied to get Raja telecom ministry',' *India Today*, 5 May 2010.

Khosla, Madhav. *Letters for a Nation from Jawaharlal Nehru to his Chief Ministers, 1947–1963*. UK: Penguin, 2015.

Khurana, J. C. 'Politics of President's Rule in India by J. R. Siwach, a Review,' *Journal of the Indian Law Institute*, vol. 22, no. 3, 1980: 442–444.

Kidwai, Rasheed. 'How Indira faced crises in Congress,' *The Tribune*, 8 June 2019.

Kidwai, Rasheed. 'Why Congress should never forget that Mayawati is a "miracle of democracy"' 11 October 2018.

Kidwai, Rashid. *24 Akbar Lane*. Delhi: Hachette India, 2011.

Kiessling, Hein. *Faith, Unity, Discipline – the ISI of Pakistan*. London: C. Hurst & Company, 2016.

Kipgen, Nehginpao. 'Intricacies of Kuki and Naga Ethnocentrism in Manipur,' *Huffpost*, 30 March 2013.

Kit, Dawnay. 'A history of sterling,' *The Telgraph*, 8 October 2001.

Kling, Arnold. 'The New Commanding Heights,' *National Affairs*, Summer 2011.

Kochanek, Stanley A. 'Briefcase Politics in India. The Congress Party and the Business Elite,' *Asian Survey*, Vol. 27, No. 12 (Dec., 1987): 1278–1301.

Kochanek, Stanley A. 'Post Nehru India. The Emergence of the New Leadership.' *Asian Survey*, vol. 6, no. 5, 1966: 288–299.

Kochanek, Stanley A. 'The Indian National Congress: The Distribution of Power between Party and Government,' *The Journal of Asian Studies*, Vol. 25, No. 4, August 1966: 681–697.

Kochanek, Stanley A. *Business and Politics in India*. Berkeley: University of California Press, 1974.

Kochanek, Stanley A. *The Congress Party of India. The Dynamics of a One–Party Democracy*. Princeton Legacy Library, 1968.

Kochar, Anjini. 'Can Targeted Food Programs Improve Nutrition? An Empirical Analysis of India's Public Distribution System,' *Economic Development and Cultural Change*, Vol. 54, No. 1, October 2005: 203– 235.

Kohli, Atul. 'Centralisation and powerlessness. India's democracy in comparative perspective,' in Joel S. Migdal, Atul Kohli and Vivienne Shu (ed). *State Power and Social Forces – Domination and Transformation in the Third World*. UK: Cambridge Studies in Comparative Politics, Cambridge University Press, 1994.

Kohli, Atul. 'Politics of Economic Growth in India, 1980–2005 Part I. The 1980s,' *Economic and Political Weekly*, 1 April 2006: 1251–1259.

Kolappan, B. 'Banking on Kumaramangalam family legacy', *The Hindu*, 22 March 2014,

Komiya, Ryutaro. 'A Note on Professor Mahalanobis' Model of Indian Economic Planning,' *The Review of Economics and Statistics*, February 1959, Vol. 41, No. 1: 29–35.

Koppikar, Smruti. 'Despite opposition from SJM, Shiv Sena–BJP Govt may bring back Enron project,' *India Today*, 15 December 1995.

Kothari, Rajni. 'India. The Congress System on Trial.' *Asian Survey*, vol. 7, no. 2, 1967: 83–96.

Krugman, Paul. 'America's epidemic of infallibility,' *The New York Times*, 20 March 2017.

Kshirsagar, R. K. *Dalit Movement in India and its Leaders 1857–1956*. New Delhi: M D Publications, 1994.

Kudaisya, Medha M. '"Mighty Adventure": Institutionalising the Idea of Planning in Post–Colonial India, 1947– 60', *Modern Asian Studies*, Vol. 43, No. 4, July 2009: 939–978.

Kudaisya, Medha M. *The Life and Times of G.D. Birla*. New Delhi: Oxford India Paperbacks, 2003.

Kulkarni, Sushant. 'Explained. Who is Hasan Ali Khan, the Pune–based businessman facing money laundering cases?' *Indian Express*, 22 December 2020.

Kumar, Devesh. 'BJP's stand on JPC on VVIP Chopper scam quashes hopes of ending deadlock over insurance, pension bills,' *India Today*, 5 March 2013.

Kumar, Dharma. 'Fiscal System', Chapter XII, i Dharma Kumar (edited). *The Cambridge Economic History of India, Vol. II, c. 1757–2003*. Orient Blackswan in association with Cambridge University Press, 2010.

Kumar, Hari. 'The End of Team Anna?' *The New York Times*, 20 September 2012.

Kumar, Madan. 'Fifth resignation in four and a half years,' *The Hindustan Times*, 12 January 2008.

Kumar, Rajiv. 'Nationalisation by Default. The Case of Coal in India,' *Economic and Political Weekly*, Vol. 16, Issue No. 18, May 2, 1981: 824–831.

Kumar, Sanjay. 'BJP's changing equations with NDA allies, in four charts,' *The Mint*, 5 November 2020.

Kumar, Sudhir. *Political and administrative set up of Union Territories in India*. New Delhi: Mittal Publications, 1991.

Kumar, Vinay. 'CWG scam. Kalmadi named 'main accused' in first CBI charge sheet,' *The Hindu*, 20 May 2011.

Kurien, Verghese. 'India's Milk Revolution – Investing in Rural Producer Organisations,' in Deepa Narayan–Parker and Elena E. Glinskaya. *Ending Poverty in South Asia: Ideas that Work*. World Bank, 2007.

Lacina, Bethany. *Rival Claims: Ethnic Violence and Territorial Autonomy Under Indian Federalism*. University of Michigan Press, Ann Arbor, 2017.

Ladejinsky, Wolf. 'Drought in Maharashtra (Not in a Hundred Years),' *Economic and Political Weekly*, 17 February 1973, Vol. 8, No. 7: 383–396.

Lagassé, Jean. 'A Review of Community Development Experience in the World, 1945–1967,' *Anthropologica*, New Series, Vol. 9, No. 2, 1967: 15–28

Lahiri, Ashok K. 'Budget Deficits and Reforms', *Economic and Political Weekly*, Vol. XXXV, No. 46, 11 November 2000: 4048–4054.

Lahiri, Ashok K. 'End of Identity Politics,' *India Today*, 17 May 2014.

Lahiri, Ashok K. 'FRBM Without Its Teeth,' *Business Standard*, 1 October 2015.

Lahiri, Ashok K. 'Macroeconomic Policy,' in S. Narayan (ed). *Documenting Reforms – Case Studies from India*. Observer Research Foundation in Association with McMillan India Ltd., 2006.

Lahiri, Ashok K. 'Sub–National Public Finance in India,' *Economic and Political Weekly* April 29, 2000: 1539–1549.

Lahiri, Ashok K. 'The Middle Class and Economic Reforms,' *Economic and Political Weekly*, Vol XLIX, No. 11, 15 March 2014: 37–44.

Lahiri, Ashok K. 'The Niti Aayog, the RBI and the Politics of Change' in Niraja Gopal Jayal (ed). *Re–forming India – The Nation Today*. Delhi: Penguin Viking, 2019.

Lahiri, Ashok K. 'West Bengal. A View from Kolkata Trams', *Presidency Alumni Autumn Annual*, Vol XLIII, 2014–15: 89–91.

Lahiri, Ashok K. and R. Kannan. 'Indian Fiscal Deficits and their Sustainability in Perspective', paper presented at Conference on India. Fiscal Policies to Accelerate Economic Growth, New Delhi, 21–22 May 2001, organised by National Institute of Public Finance and Policy, New Delhi, Department for International Development (UK) and the World Bank. Reprinted in Edgardo Favaro and Ashok K. Lahiri (edited). *Fiscal Policy and Sustainable Growth in India*. New Delhi: Oxford University Press, 2004.

Lahiri, Ashok Kumar and Prannoy Roy. 'Is Indian industry demand or supply constrained?' *Economic and Political Weekly*, Vol. 21, No. 6, 8 February 1986: 250–255.

Lal, M. B. *Going Back to Gettysburg – Autobiography of a Corrupt Indian*. Delhi: Partridge, 2014.

Lala, R. M. *Beyond the Last Blue Mountain – A Life of J R D Tata*. London: Penguin, 1980.

Lapierre, Dominique and Larry Collins. *Freedom At Midnight*. Simon & Schuster, 1975.

Leeladhar, V. 'Basel II Accord and its Implications,' 13 April 2005. https.//www.rbi.org.in/scripts/BS_ViewBulletin.aspx?Id=6051.

Lewis, John P. *Quiet Crisis in India: Economic Development and American Policy*. Washington DC: The Brookings Institution, 1962.

Lijphart, Arend. *Patterns of Democracy – Government Forms and Performance in Thirty–Six Countries*. New Haven: Yale University Press, Second Edition, 2012 (First edition 1989).

Liton, Shakhawat. 'The depth of 5th amendment,' *The Daily Star*, 22 July 2010.

Liu, Zhenya . 'Global Energy Development. The Reality and Challenges,' Chapter 1 in *Global Energy Interconnection*. Science Direct, 2015, Pages 1–64.

Lohia, Ram Manohar. *The Caste System*. Hyderabad: Navahind Prakasan, 1964.

Lok Sabha. 'India's Retail Sector and Foreign Direct Investment,' *Research and Information Division*, Lok Sabha Secretariat, LARRDIS (E&F) 2014/IB–08, July 2014.

Lok Sabha. 'Report of the Joint Committee on Stock Market Scam and Matters relating thereto,' Vol 1, Thirteenth Lok Sabha, 19 December 2002.

Lok Sabha. 'The Insurance Laws (Amendment) Bill, 2008,' Forty–first Report, Standing Committee on Finance (2011–12), Fifteenth Lok Sabha, Ministry of Finance, Lok Sabha Secretariat, New Delhi, December 2011.

Lone, Arshid. 'Selective memory: Wasn't Omar Abdullah among the first to ally with BJP? Why the amnesia now?' *Daily O*, 31 January 2019.

Lucas, Jr, Robert E. 'On the Mechanics of Economic Development', *Journal of Monetary Economics*, 22, July 1988: 3–42.

M. H. J. 'Reanointment of the Heir–Apparent.' *Economic and Political Weekly*, vol. 14, no. 12/13, 24–31 March, 1979: 613–613.

Madhok, Balraj. *Bungling in Kashmir*. Hind Pocket Book, Orient Paperback, 1974.

Mahajan Committee. 'Report of the High–Powered Committee on Sugar Industry', Vol. 1, Ministry of Food and Consumer Affairs, Government of India, April 1998.

Mahalanobis, P. C. *The Approach of Operational Research to Planning in India*. Mumbai: Asia Publishing House, 1963.

Mahalingam, Sudha. 'The tip of the iceberg,' *Frontline*, 10 January 1998.

Mahapatra, Debabrata. 'Jagannath Temple invokes Ranjit Singh, stakes claim to Kohinoor,' *The Times of India*, 25 April 2016.

Mahapatra, Dhananjay. '13 banks move SC to stop Vijay Mallya, but he's already left India,' *The Economic Times*, 9 March 2016.

Mahurkar, Uday. 'The oil sheikhs,' *India Today*, 31 March 1990.

Majid, Zulikar. 'Autonomy resolution within 30–days if voted to power,' *Deccan Herald*, 20 December 2018.

Makkar, Sahil, Liz Mathew and Anuja. 'Many top BJP leaders call in sick before Goa conclave,' *The Mint*, 8 June 2013.

Makkar, Sahil. 'Rifts apart, Narendra Modi to steer BJP in 2014 elections,' *The Mint*, 10 June 2013.

Malhotra, Inder. 'A hammerblow to democracy: June 25, 1975—A look back', *The Hindu*, June 25, 2000.

Malhotra, Inder. 'Coffingate, corruption and an escape,' *Indian Express*, 13 July 2015.

Malhotra, Inder. 'Rear View. How Narasimha Rao became PM', *Indian Express*, 6 April 2015.

Malhotra, Inder. 'Run over the banks', *Indian Express*, Friday, 10 July 2009.

Malhotra, Inder. 'The abrupt end of Emergency,' *Indian Express*, 4 August 2014.

Malik, Anil. *Journey of a Common Man born in Independent India*. Lucknow: BFC Publication, 2021.

Malkarnekar, Gauree. 'When the satyagrahis came marching in,' *The Times of India*, 16 August 2015.

Mani, Sunil. 'Growth of India's Telecom Services (1991–2007). Can It Lead to Emergence of a Manufacturing Hub?' *Economic and Political Weekly*, vol. 43, no. 3, 2008: 37–46.

Mankekar, D. R. *Accession to Extinction. A Story of Indian Princes*. New Delhi: Vikas Publishing House, 1974.

Manohar, P. K. and Praveen Bhargav. 'The architect of an omnibus forest–protection case,' *The Hindu*, 5 July 2016.

Manor, James. 'After Fifty Years of Political and Social Change. Caste Associations and Politics in India,' *Pacific Affairs*, Vol. 85, No. 2, June 2012: 355–361.

Manor, James. 'Where Congress Survived. Five States in the Indian General Election of 1977,' *Asian Survey*, vol. 18, no. 8, 1978: 785–803.

Mantri, Rajeev and Harish Gupta. 'The Story of India's Telecom Revolution,' *The Mint*, 8 January 2013.

Martin, Leslie A., Shanthi Nataraj and Ann Harrison. 'In with the big, out with the small. removing small–scale reservations in India,' Working Paper 19942, National Bureau of Economic Research, 2014.

Masani, Zareer. 'Janata Party's electoral debacle provides Indira Gandhi the necessary political leverage,' *India Today*, 31 March 1978.

Masoodi, Ashwaq. 'When sterlization wasn't a matter of choice,' *The Mint*, 22 June 2015.

Mathur, Archana S., and Arvinder S. Sachdeva. 'Customs Tariff Structure in India,' *Economic and Political Weekly*, vol. 40, no. 6, 2005: 535–539.

Maurya, Om Prakash. 'Builders of Modern India – Babu Jagjivan Ram,' Publications Division, Ministry of Information and Broadcasting, 2017.

Maxwell, Neville. 'India's Disintegrating Democracy,' *The Times* (London), 27 January 1967.

Maxwell, Neville. *India's China War*. Dehradun: Natraj Publishers, 1997.

Mehdudia, Sujay. 'Despite hurdles, Centre keen on pushing LPG cash transfer,' *The Hindu*, 29 April 2013.

Mehdudia, Sujay. 'FDI in multi–brand retail with riders,' *The Hindu*, 15 September 2012.

Mehdudia, Sujay. 'Govt notifies 100 p.c. FDI in single brand retail,' *The Hindu*, 10 January 2012.

Mehra, Puja. 'Govt, Left fight out over pension fund reforms via PFRDA Bill,' 19 February 2007.

Mehta, J. L. *Advance Study in the History of Modern India, 1707–1813*. USA: New Dawn Press Group, 2005.

Mehta, Jigar. 'Challenges under Black Money Act, 2015,' *TaxGuru*, 14 June 2020.

Mehta, Nalin and Mona G. Mehta. *Gujarat beyond Gandhi*. Oxford: Routledge, 2011.

Mehta, Pratap Bhanu. *The Burden of Democracy*. Delhi: Penguin, 2003.

Mehta, Rajesh. 'Removal of QRs and Impact on India's Import.' *Economic and Political Weekly*, Vol. 35, No. 19, 2000: 1667–1671.

Mehta, Vinod. *The Sanjay Story*. Delhi: Harper Collins, 2015.

Meltzer, Allan H. '*A History of the Federal Reserve, Volume 2, Book 2; Books 1970–1986*. US: University of Chicago Press, 2004

Mendes, Sushila Sawant. 'Jawaharlal Nehru and the Liberation Struggle of Goa,' Proceedings of the Indian History Congress, Vol 67, 2006–07.

Menon, Aditya. 'Land acquisition bill to get top priority in Parliament,' *Mail Online India*, 4 January 2013.

Menon, Amarnath. 'Victorious Chandrababu Naidu will have to reckon with father–in–law NTR's mass appeal,' *India Today*, 30 September 1995.

Menon, V.P. *The Transfer of Power in India*. India: Orient Longman, 1997 [1957].

Meraj, Zafar. 'Jammu & Kashmir. Militants issue call for election boycott,' *India Today*, 30 November 1989.

Meredith, Robyn. *The Elephant and the Dragon – The Rise of India and China and What it Means for All of Us*. W. W. Norton, 2009

Ministry of Consumer Affairs, Food and Public Distribution. 'Report of the High–Level Committee on Long Term Grain Policy,' Department of Food and Public Distribution 2002.

Ministry of Finance (1990). 'Budget Speeches of Union Finance Ministers. 1947–48 to 1990–91', Second Edition, Department of Economic Affairs, Ministry of Finance, Government of India, New Delhi, October 1990.

Mishra, Neelabh. 'People's Right to Information Movement. Lessons from Rajasthan,' Discussion Paper Series – 4, Human Development Resource Centre (HDRC), UN Development Programme, New Delhi, 2003.

Mishra, Prachee. 'Coal Block Allocations and the 2015 Bill,' 7 March 2015. https://www.prsindia.org/theprsblog/coal–block–allocations–and–2015–bill

Mitra Anirban and Debraj Ray. 'Implications of an Economic Theory of Conflict. Hindu–Muslim Violence in India,' *Journal of Political Economy*, Vol. 122, No. 4 (August 2014): 719–765

Mitra, Sumit. 'Assam movement against 'foreign' nationals in transitional stage,' *India Today*, 31 July 1980.

Mitra, Sumit. 'Sitaram Kesri pulls down UF govt, Deve Gowda goes down fighting,' *India Today*, 30 April 1997.

Mitra, Sumit. 'Sonia Gandhi establishes supremacy over Congress by resigning as party president,' *India Today*, 31 May 1999.

Mo, P.H. 'Corruption and economic growth,' Journal of Comparative Economics Vol. 29, 2001: 66–79.

Mohan, Rakesh. 'Small–Scale Industry Policy in India. A Critical Evaluation', in A O Krueger (ed.), *Economic Policy Reforms and the Indian Economy*. Chicago: University of Chicago Press, 2002.

Mohan, Surendra. 'A Learned History of the Socialist Movement,' *Mainstream*, Vol XLVIII, No. 19, 1 May 2010.

Montalvo, Josè and Marta Reynal–Querol. 'Ethnic Polarization, Potential Conflict, and Civil Wars,' *American Economic Review*, Vol. 95, No. 3, June 2005: 796–816.

Morris–Jones, W. H. 'India Elects for Change—and Stability.' *Asian Survey*, vol. 11, no. 8, 1971: 719–741.

Morris–Jones, W. H. *Parliament in India*. Longmans: Green and Co. 1957.

Mueller, Dennis C. 'Public choice in perspective,' in Dennis C. Mueller (ed). *Perspectives on Public Choice, A Handbook*. Cambridge: Cambridge University Press, 1997.

Mukerjee, Dilip. 'Assam Reorganization.' *Asian Survey*, vol. 9, no. 4, 1969: 297–311.

Mukherjee, Aditya. 'Controversy over Formation of Reserve Bank of India, 1927–35.' *Economic and Political Weekly*, vol. 27, no. 5, 1992: 229–234.

Mukherjee, Jhumpa. *Conflict Resolution in Multicultural Societies – the Indian Experience*. New Delhi: Sage Publications, 2004.

Mukherjee, Mahua. 'Private Participation in the Indian Power Sector,' World Bank 2014.

Mukherjee, Pranab. *The Dramatic Decade – The Indira Gandhi Years*. New Delhi: Rupa Publication India, 2015.

Mukherjee, Pranab. *The Presidential Years, 2012–2017*. New Delhi: Rupa Publication India, 2021.

Mukherjee, Pranab. *The Turbulent Years,1980–1996*. New Delhi: Rupa Publication India, 2016.

Mukherjee, Rudrangshu. 'The Prophet Delayed—The India that Rajiv Gandhi dreamt of is now about to happen,' *The Telegraph*, 8 February 2004.

Mukhopadhyay. Sukumar. 'VAT in an Impasse.' *Economic and Political Weekly*, vol. 38, no. 19, 2003: 1822–1826.

Mukund, Kanakalatha. *The World of the Tamil Merchant – Pioneers of International Trade*. Delhi: Penguin, 2012.

Mundle, Sudipto and M. Govinda Rao. 'Volume and Composition of Government Subsidies in India 1987–88,' *Economic and Political Weekly*, 4 May 1991.

Mundle, Sudipto, M. Govinda Rao and N. R. Bhanumurthy. 'Stimulus, Recovery and Exit Policy. G20 Experience and Indian Strategy.' *Economic and Political Weekly*, vol. 46, no. 29, 2011.

Mustafa, Seema, H. Baweja, Bhaskar Roy, and Prabhu Chawla. 'Dramatic developments that almost led to the fall of the National Front Government,' *India Today*, 15 August 1990.

Myint, Hla. 'An Interpretation of Economic Backwardness', *Oxford Economic Papers*, New Series, Vol. 6, No. 2, June 1954: 132–164.

Nag, Sajal. 'Tribals, Rats, Famine, State and the Nation.' *Economic and Political Weekly*, vol. 36, no. 12, 2001: 1029–1033.

Namboodiri, N. V. 'Pilot Intensive Rural Employment Project – An Assessment of Project Worthiness,' *Indian Journal of Agricultural Economics*, Vol. XXXIII, No. 3, Conference Number, October–December 1978: 245–252

Nandy, Pritish. 'Can Camelot be regained?' *Bangalore Mirror Bureau*, 12 May 2015.

Nanjapaa, Vicky. 'Abu Talha Hazari. The terrorist who introduced fidayeen attacks in Kashmir,' *Oneindia*, 15 February 2019.

Nanjappa, Vicky. 'Swiss black money can take India to the top,' *Rediff.com*, 31 March 2009.

Naoroji, Dadabhai. *Poverty and Un–British Rule in India*. (First published by London: Swan Sonnenschein & Co. Ltd., 1901), Indian Edition published by Publications Division, Ministry of Information and Broadcasting, Government of India, Delhi, 1962.

Naqvi, Sabah. 'There are no Babalogs in Congress,' *Outlook*, 4 February 2013.

Narain, Dharm. 'Combating the wheat lobby,' Cross Section, March 1975, quoted in M. Raghavan. 'Politics of Procurement and Price Support', *Economic and Political Weekly*, Vol. 39, No. 5 (Jan. 31 – Feb. 6, 2004): 506–508

Narain, Dharm. 'Growth and Imbalances in Indian Agriculture,' *Economic and Political Weekly*, Review of Agriculture March 1972: A–6

Narayan, Khushboo. 'Enforcement Directorate to move court against Vijay Mallya in first case under new fugitives law,' *Indian Express*, 18 June 2018.

Nariman, Fali. 'Why did Indira Gandhi call off the Emergency?' *Indian Express*, 8 February 2019.

National Council of Applied Economic Research (NCAER). 'Economic and Policy Reforms in India', *NCAER*, New Delhi, August 2001.

Nayar, Baldev Raj. 'Community Development Programme—Its Political Impact,' *The Economic Weekly*, 17 September 1960.

Nayar, Baldev Raj. 'When did the 'Hindu' Rate of Growth End?', *Economic and Political Weekly*, Vol. 41, No. 19, 13–19 May 2006: 1885–1890.

Nayar, Kuldip. 'Operation Blue Star. How Congress invented a saint,' *India Today*, 8 July 2012.

Nayar, Kuldip. 'The day Shastri dies and other stories,' *Outlook*, 9 July 2012,

Nayudu, A. Sri Hari. Tax Revenue Efficiency of Indian States. The case of Stamp Duty and Registration Fees,' *National Institute of Public Finance and Policy*, Working Paper No. 278, August 2019.

Nayyar, Deepak. 'Birth, Life and Death of Development Finance Institutions in India,' *Economic and Political Weekly*, vol. 50, no. 33, 2015: 51–60.

Neale, Walter C. 'Community Development in India. Progress or Rip–Off?' *Asian Survey*, Vol. 23, No. 11, November 1983: 1209–1219.

Nidheesh M K. 'A Jew's death wakes up Kochi's history,' *The Mint*, 9 September 2019.

Nilekani, Nandan. *Imagining India – Ideas for the New Century*. Delhi: Penguin, 2009.

Ninan, T. N. 'Express Case – Pandora's Box,' *India Today*, 15 April 1987

Niyogi, J. P. *The Evolution of the Indian Income Tax*. Westminster: P. S. King & Son, Ltd., 1929.

Noorani, A. G. 'Communist memories,' *Frontline*, Volume 28, Issue 25, December 2011.

Noorani, A. G. 'Confessions of the real Yashwant,' *Frontline*, 13 July 2007.

Noorani, A. G. 'Legal Aspects to the Issue,' in Sarvepalli Gopal (ed.). *Anatomy of a Confrontation – The Rise of Communal Politics in India*. Delhi: Penguin, 1991.

Noorani, A. G. 'Linguistic Trap,' *Frontline*, 23 April 2010.

Noorani, A. G. 'Questions about the Kashmir Ceasefire,' *Economic and Political Weekly*, Nov. 4–10, 2000, Vol. 35, No. 45, 4–10 November 2000: 3949–3958.

North, Douglas C. *Understanding the Process of Economic Change*. Princeton University Press, 2005.

North, Douglas. 'Economic performance through time,' *American Economic Review*, Vo. 84, No. 3, 1994: 359–368.

Nurkse, Ragnar. *Problems of Capital Formation in Underdeveloped Countries*. New York: Oxford University Press, 1953.

Oberoi, Harjot S. 'From Punjab to 'Khalistan': Territoriality and Metacommentary,' *Pacific Affairs,* Vol. 60, No. 1, Spring, 1987: 26–41.

Okedji, O. 'The dynamics of ethnic fragmentation. a proposal for an expanded measurement index,' *American Journal of Economics and Sociology,* Vol. 64, No. 2, April 2005: 637–662

Oommen, John. 'Politics of Communalism in Kerala.' *Economic and Political Weekly,* vol. 30, no. 11, 1995: 544–547.

Oommen, M. A. 'Differential Interest Rate Scheme. Findings of a Field Study,' *Economic and Political Weekly,* Vol. 15, No. 21, 24 May 1980: 937–943.

Opindia. 'Cannabis. What is it, why is it banned in India and how Rajiv Gandhi played a role in its ban,' *Opindia,* 23 September 2020. https.//www.opindia. com/2020/09/cannabis–what–is–it–how–it–was–banned–in–india–during– rajiv–gandhi–govt/

Outlook. 'Agriculture land will be given on lease in Uttarakhand,' *Outlook,* 23 January 2020.

Outlook. 'Black Money Probe. Supreme Court Appoints SIT,' *Outlook,* 4 July 2011.

Oza, A. N. 'Recent Amendments to the MRTP Act,' *Economic and Political Weekly,* Vol 17, No. 42, 16 October 1982: 1697–1705.

Padmanabhan, Anil. 'Manmohan Singh. A legacy of records,' *The Mint,* 30 May 2013.

Palkhivala, N. A. *The Highest Taxed Nation.* Bombay: Mankatalas, 1965.

Palmer, Norman D. 'India's Fourth General Election.' *Asian Survey,* Vol. 7, No. 5, 1967: 275–291.

Pandey, Munish Chandra. 'Vijay Mallya faces likely extradition in 28 days after UK court rejects plea,' *India Today,* 14 May 2020.

Panekar, S. D. 'Labor unrest in the public sector', *The Economic Weekly,* August 3, 1957.

Pannu, S P S. 'UPA's 10–year report card. Scams, policy paralysis crashes India's economy,' *India Today,* 28 January 2014.

Paranjape, H. K. 'The Vanishing MRTP Act. Will Only the Grin Remain?' *Economic and Political Weekly,* Vol 17, No. 23, 5 June 1982: 955–963.

Parayil, Govindan. 'The Green Revolution in India. A Case Study of Technological Change.' *Technology and Culture,* vol. 33, no. 4, 1992: 737–756.

Parihar, Rohit. 'CBI finds no clue against Om Prakash Chautala being accused in poll–killing,' *India Today,* 21 July 1997.

Pasricha, H. R. *The Swatantra Party – Victory in Defeat.* Rajaji Foundation, 2002

Paswan Sanjay and Paramanshi Jaideva. *Encyclopedia of Dalits in India, Vol 13.* Delhi: Kalpaz Publications, 2003.

Patel, I. G. 'On Taking India into the Twenty–First Century (New Economic Policy in India),' Fifteenth Kingsley Memorial Lecture delivered in Cambridge on November 5, 1986. Published in Modern Asian Studies, Vol. 21, No. 2 (1987): 209–231.

Patel, I. G. *Glimpses of Indian Economic Policy – An Insider's View.* New Delhi: Oxford University Press, 2002.

Patel, Razia. 'Indian Muslim Women, Politics of Muslim Personal Law and Struggle for Life with Dignity and Justice,' *Economic and Political Weekly*, Vol XLIV, No. 44, 31 October 2009.

Pattanaik, R. K. and Amaresh Samantaraya. 'Indian Experience of Inflation. A Review of the Evolving Process,' *Economic and Political Weekly*, Vol. XLI, No. 4, 28 January 2006: 349–357.

Pavaskar, Madhoo. 'Short on Logic and Long on Imagination,' *Economic and Political Weekly*, 6–12 May 2006, Vol. 41, No. 18: 1754–1757.

Pavel, Anthony J. 'Gandhi. Hind Swaraj and Other Writings' edited by Anthony J Pavel, *Cambridge Texts in Modern Politics*. Cambridge University Press, 1997: 14–15.

Pawar, Sharad. *Life on my terms – From the grassroots and corridors of power*. Delhi: Speaking Tiger Publishing Private Limited, 2015.

Peach, Jim. 'Galbraith and the Problem of Uneven Development,' *Journal of Economic Issues*, Vol. 42, No. 1, March 2008: 25–35.

Phadke, Anant. 'End of Drug Control?', *Mainstream*, 25 September 2008. http.//www.india–seminar.com/2000/489/489%20phadke.htm

Phadnis, Aditi. 'The Antulay Papers,' *Business Standard*, 3 December 2014.

Phanjoubam, Pradip. 'Why it matters how Manipur became a state,' *The Telegraph*, 20 February 2019.

Pillai, Ajith and Zafar Meraj. 'Slaughter of The Innocents,' *Outlook*, 29 June 1998.

Pillai, Ajith, Yubaraj Ghimire, and Bhavdeep Kang. 'Patch–up or Polls?' *Outlook*, 23 April 1997.

Pillai, Raman K. 'Jan Sangh—A Rightist Opposition to the Congress Party.' *The Indian Journal of Political Science*, vol. 27, no. 2, 1966: 67–81. P. 70.

Pimpalkhare, Ameya and Paresh Rawal. 'Rationalising fares to prevent the financial derailment of Indian Railways,' *ORF Issue Brief*, 24 May 2018.

Planning Commission. 'Performance Evaluation of Targeted Public Distribution System (TPDS)', Programme Evaluation Organisation, Planning Commission, Government of India, New Delhi, March 2005. Available at http.//planningcommission.nic.in/reports/peoreport/peo/peo_tpds.pdf.

Planning Commission. 'Report of the Village and Small–scale Industries (Second Five Year Plan) Committee,' Government of India, New Delhi, 1955.

Popham, Peter. 'Massacre of 36 Sikhs overshadows Clinton's tour,' *Independent*, 22 March 2000.

Porta, Rafael La, Florencio Lopez–de–Silanes, Andrei Schleifer and Robert Vishny. 'The Quality of Government,' *Journal of Law*, Economics and Organization, Vol. 15, No. 1: 222–279.

Posen, B. R. 'Military Responses to Refugee Disasters'. *International Security*, Vol. 21, No 1, 1996.

Prashad, Vijay. 'Emergency Assessments,' Social Scientist, Vol. 24, No. 9/10, September–October 1996: 36–68.

Praval, K. C. '1971. Making Bangladesh a reality – I', *Indian Defence Review*, 16 December 2012.

Prezeworski, Adam and Fernando Limongi. 'Political Regimes and Economic Growth.' *The Journal of Economic Perspectives*, vol. 7, no. 3, 1993: 51–69. P. 52.

Prezeworski, Adam. 'A Flawed Blueprint. The Covert Politicization of Development Economics.' *Harvard International Review*, vol. 25, no. 1, 2003: 42–47. P. 42.

Priya, Ritu. 'Town Planning, Public Health and Urban Poor. Some Explorations from Delhi.' *Economic and Political Weekly*, Vol. 28, No. 17, 1993: 824–834.

PRS. 'Politics of Defection,' PRS, 1 March 2011. Available at http.//www.prsindia. org/theprsblog/?tag=gaya–lal.

PTI. 'Ramdev on being caught dressed as a woman,' *PTI*, 6 June 2011.

Punj, Sweta. 'Mind the Gap,' *Business Today*, 11 November 2012

Purie, Mandira. 'Indira Gandhi. Travelling as an ordinary citizen on an ordinary flight,' *India Today*, 15 August, 1977.

Qasim, Mir. 'My Life and Times' Allied Publishers Limited, 1992.

Quartz India. 'Raghuram Rajan explains why corrupt politicians win elections in India,' *Quartz India*, 14 August 2014.

Raghavachari, M. V. 'Growth of Budgetary Subsidies of Central Government,' *Economic and Political Weekly*, Vol. 14, No. 9, 3 March 1979: 522–528.

Raghavan, Srikanth. 'Indira Gandhi – India and the World in Transition,' p. 235. In Ramachandra Guha (ed). *Makers of Modern Asia*. Cambridge: The Belknap Press, Harvard University Press, 2014.

Raghavan, Srinath. 'Decoding the Emergency,' Seminar, January 2016,

Raghavan, Srinath. 'Twists & turns of 1969 presidential race still the most sensational,' *The Times of India*, 18 June 2012.

Rahiman, K. K. Abdul. 'History of the Evolution of Muslim Personal Law in India,' *Journal of Dharma*. Dharmaram Journal of Religions and Philosophies, Volume Number. 11 Issue Number. 3, July -September 1986: 249-263.

Rai, Praveen. 'Status of Opinion Polls. Media Gimmick and Political Communication in India', *Economic and Political Weekly*, Vol – XLIX No. 16, 19 April 2014.

Rai, Saritha. 'Disunited opposition fails to block PM Deve Gowda's Rajya Sabha route,' *India Today*, 15 October 1996.

Raj, K. N. 'Foreign Exchange Crisis and the Plan,' *The Economic Weekly*, 23 February 1957.

Raj, K. N. 'Small–Scale Industries. Problem of Technological Change,' *The Economic Weekly*, April 1956.

Raj, K.N. 'Foreign Exchange Crisis and the Plan —Reply', *The Economic Weekly*, 6 April 1957.

Rajagopal, Krishnadas. 'Nagarwala case. mystery returns after three decades,' *Indian Express*, 21 December 2008.

Rajagopalan, R. 'Taxes and Control over Molasses and Alcohol. Legal Sources, Conflict of Interest and Policy Issues,' *Journal of Indian School of Political Economy*, Vol. 5, No. 2, April–June 1993: 300–319.

Ram, Mohan. 'Getting Away with Murder.' *Economic and Political Weekly*, vol. 13, no. 30, 1978: 1209–1210.

Ramakrishnan, N. 'Decade of power reforms—Hardly electrifying,' *The Hindu BusinessLine*, 4 September 2001.

Ramakrishnan, T. 'The 1975 Gujarat Assembly Election,' *The Hindu*, 5 December 2017.

Ramakrishnan, Venkitesh. 'Revolt in Congress(I),' *Frontline*, 22 May 1999.

Ranjana–Chaube. 'Forgotten facets,' *The Indian Express*, 14 April 2010.

Rao, I. Ramamohan. 'V.P Singh. A Prime Minister with promise, but who faded away fast,' *Business Standard*, 25 June 2015.

Rao, M Govinda and Nirvikar Singh. *The Political Economy of Federalism in India*. Delhi: Oxford University Press, 2011 (2005).

Rao, M. Govinda. 'Entry Tax as an Alternative to Octroi,' *National Institute of Public Finance and Policy*, New Delhi, 1984.

Rao, M. Govinda. 'Reform in Central Sales Tax in the Context of VAT.' *Economic and Political Weekly*, Vol. 38, No. 7, 2003: 627–636.

Rao, M. Govinda. 'Tax Reform in India. Achievements and Challenges,' *Asia–Pacific Development Journal*, Vol. 7, No. 2, December 2000.

Rao, T. S. Rama. 'The problem of compensation and its justiciability in Indian law,' *Journal of the Indian Law Institute*, vol. 4, no. 4, 1962: 481–510.

Rao, V. K. R. V. 'India's First Five–Year Plan–A Descriptive Analysis,' *Pacific Affairs*, Vol. 25, No. 1, March 1952: 3–23.

Rao, V. Venkata. 'Reorganization of North East India,' *The Indian Journal of Political Science*, vol. 33, no. 2, 1972: 123–144.

Rao, V.K.R.V. 'Investment, Income and the Multiplier in an Underdeveloped Economy,' *Indian Economic Review*, 1952.

Rashid, Shahidur, Ashok Gulati and S. Mahendra Dev. 'Parastatals and Food Policy – The Indian Case,' in Shahidur Rashid, Ashok Gulati and Ralph Cummings, Jr. (ed) . *From Parastatals to Private Trade – Lessons from Asian Agriculture*. Baltimore: International Food Policy Research Institute, Johns Hopkins Press, 2008.

Rath, Basant. 'Abdul Karim Telgi Is Dead. Can We Exhume the Stamp Paper Scam?' *The Wire*, 30 October 2017.

Rath, Nilkantha. 'Economic Origin of Regional and Caste Parties.' *Economic and Political Weekly*, Vol. 47, No. 30, 2012: 24–28.

Ray, Partha. 'Rise and Fall of Industrial Finance in India,' *Economic and Political Weekly*, Vol. 50, No. 5, 31 January 2015: 61–68.

Raza, Danish. 'Tragedy at Turkman Gate. Witnesses recount horror of Emergency,' *The Hindustan Times*, 29 June 2015.

Reddy, Y. V. 'Evolving Role of Gold – Recent Trends and Future Direction,' Speech at a Conference organised by the World Gold Council at New Delhi on 21 March, 2002. https.//www.rbi.org.in/scripts/BS_SpeechesView.aspx?Id=103

Reddy, G. Ram. 'Revenue Culture in Indian Administration,' *The Indian Journal of Political Science*, Vol. 42, No. 4, October – December 1981: 1–13.

Rediff on the Net. '9 days of political cliff–hanger,' 26 April 1999.

Rediff on the Net. 'Samata Party breaks away from JD (U),' 6 January 2000.

Renan, Ernest. 'What is a Nation?', text of a conference delivered at the Sorbonne on March 11th, 1882, in Ernest Renan, *Qu'est–ce qu'une nation?* Paris: Presses–Pocket, 1992. (translated by Ethan Rundell)

Reserve Bank of India. 'Report of the Committee to Review Arrangements for Institutional Credit for Agriculture and Rural Development,' Reserve Bank of India, Bombay, January 1981.

Reserve Bank of India. 'Reserve Bank of India. Functions and Workings.' https.//rbidocs.rbi.org.in/rdocs/Content/PDFs/FUNCWWE080910.pdf.

Reserve Bank of India. *History of the Reserve Bank of India (1935–51)*. 1970.

Reynal–Querol, Marta. 'Ethnicity, Political Systems, and Civil Wars.' *Journal of Conflict Resolution*, 2002, 46(1): 29–54.

Richter, William L. 'Princes in Indian Politics', *Economic and Political Weekly*, Vol. 6, No. 9 (Feb. 27, 1971): 535+537–542.

Rodrik, Dani and Arvind Subramanian (2005). 'From 'Hindu Growth' to Productivity Surge. The Mystery of the Indian Growth Transition,' *IMF Staff Papers*, Vol. 52, No. 2, 2005.

Rosenstein–Rodan, Paul N. 'Natura Facit Saltum. Analysis of the Disequilibrium Growth Process,' https.//www.rrojasdatabank.info/pioneers8a.pdf.

Rosenstein–Rodan, Paul N. 'Problems of Industrialisation of Eastern and South–eastern Europe.' *Economic Journal*, Vol. 53, June–September 1943: 202–11.

Roy, Ajit. 'Tirupati Congress Session. Some Reflections.' *Economic and Political Weekly*, 9 May 1992.

Roy, Bunker. 'Right to Information. Profile of a Grass Roots Struggle,' *Economic and Political Weekly*, Vol. 31, No. 19, 11 May 1996.

Rubinger, Richard. 'Who Can't Read and Write? Illiteracy in Meiji Japan,' *Monumenta Nipponica*, vol. 55, no. 2, 2000: 163–198.

Rukmini, S. 'Two out of three say UPA is corrupt,' *The Hindu*, 23 July 2013.

Sachdeva, Pradeep. *Local Government in India*. Delhi: Pearson, 2011.

Sahay, Arvind. 'India can become the pharmacy of the world,' *The Hindu BusinessLine*, 7 May 2020.

Sahgal, Priya and Aljaz Hussain. 'Ghulam Nabi Azad becomes first Congress CM of Jammu & Kashmir in 30 years,' *India Today*, 14 November 2005.

Sahoo, M. S. 'A Journey of Endless Hope, in Insolvency and Bankruptcy Code. A Miscellany of Perspectives,' Insolvency and Bankruptcy Board of India (IBBI), 2019.

Sahoo, M. S. 'Insolvency Reforms. A Road Under Construction, in Insolvency and Bankruptcy Regime in India. A Narrative (2020),' Insolvency and Bankruptcy Board of India (IBBI), 2020.

Saikia P. *Ethnic Mobilization and Violence in Northeast India*. New Delhi: Routledge. 2011.

Salisbury, Harrison E. *The New Emperors—China in the Era of Mao and Deng*. Little, Brown and Company, 1992.

Samanta, Pradeepta Kumar. 'A Study of Rural Electrification Infrastructure in India,' *Journal of Business and Management*, Volume 17, Issue 2. Ver. IV, February 2015: 54–59.

Samanta, Pranab Dhal. 'NAC, think–tank and policy watchdog for UPA, is no more,' *Indian Express*, 5 April 2008.

Samuelson, Paul. *Economics. An Introductory Analysis*. McGraw Hill, 1967.

Sanghi, Seema. 'Human Resource Management', Vikas Publishing House Pvt. Ltd., NOIDA, UP, 2014, p. 223.

Sanghvi, Vijay. *The Congress – Indira to Sonia Gandhi*. Delhi: Kalpaz Publications, 2006.

Sanyal, Amal. 'The Curious Case of the Bombay Plan,' *Contemporary Issues and Ideas in Social Sciences*, June 2010.

Sapru, R. K. 'Work Force Restructuring under Liberalised Economy.' *Indian Journal of Industrial Relations*, vol. 34, no. 3, 1999: 348–355.

Saran, Rohit. 'Cabinet reshuffle. Jagmohan finally pays for being a stickler for rules,' *India Today*, 21 June 1999.

Saraswati, Sujan Kumar. 'Civil Aviation Environment in India,' *Economic and Political Weekly*, Vol. 36, No. 19, 12–18 May 2001: 1639–1645.

Sarin, Ritu. 'India wanted to raid IC–814 in Dubai, but Farooq Abdullah opposed swap, says former RAW chief AS Dulat,' *Indian Express*, 3 July 2015.

Sarkar, Goutam K. 'India's Sugar Exports. Re–Assessment of Rationale,' *Economic and Political Weekly*, Vol. 7, No. 18, 29 Apr. 1972: 893+895–897.

Sarkar, P. K. 'A rational drug policy,' *Indian Journal of Medical Ethics*, Vol. 1, No. 1, January–March 2004: 11–12.

Saxena, N C. 'Public Distribution System in India—A few suggestions,' available at http.//www.sccommissioners.org/News/Documents/TPDS_Public–Distribution–in–India–A–few–suggestions.pdf.

Sayeed, Khalid B. 'The Capabilities of Pakistan's Political System.' *Asian Survey*, vol. 7, no. 2, 1967: 102–110.

Schanberg, Sydney H. 'Indian Party Stumps for New Symbol,' *The New York Times*, 17 February, 1971.

Schoenfeld, Benjamin N. 'The Birth of India's Samyukta Socialist Party.' *Pacific Affairs*, Vol. 38, No. 3/4, 1965: 245–268.

Schrage, Michael. 'Potato chips vs. computer chips – high technology any way you slice it,' *Washington Post*, 22 January 1993.

Schumpeter, Joseph. *Capitalism, Socialism and Democracy*. New York: Harper & Row, 1942.

Sehgal, Manjeet. 'Days of terror. Punjab back in 1980s,' *India Today*, 9 June 2014.

Sen Gupta, Bhabani. 'Communism. The Red Predicament,' *India Today*, 30 April 1981.

Sen, Amartya and Jean Drèze. *An Uncertain Glory – India and its Contradictions*. Penguin, Allen Lane, 2013.

Sen, Amartya Kumar. *Choice of Techniques*. Oxford University Press, 1960.

Sen, Amartya. *Poverty and Famines: An Essay on Entitlement and Deprivation*. New York: Clarendon Press, 1981.

Sen, Gita. 'Universal Health Coverage in India. A Long and Winding Road,' *Economic and Political Weekly*, 25 February 2012, Vol. 47, No. 8: 45–52.

Sen, Mohit. 'Coalition and Congress.' *Economic and Political Weekly*, Vol. 2, No. 33/35, 1967: 1499–1502.

Seshan, A. 'Fiscal responsibility & Budget management', http.//www.rediff.com/money/2003/may/15guest.htm.

Sethi, Chitleen K. 'Sukh Ram, who once helped Dhumal form government, is no stranger to BJP,' *The Print*, 16 October 2017.

Sethi, Sunil, Suchitra Behal, Shirley Joshua, and Mandira Purie. 'Rukhsana Sultana: The chief glamour girl of the Emergency,' 14 August 2014. Also see https.//homegrown.co.in/article/30209/rukhsana–sultana–sanjay–gandhis–enigmatic–right–hand–womans–role–in–the–sterilization–campaign.

Shackle, Christopher. *The Sikhs*. The Minority Reports Group, Report No. 65. New Delhi: Amrit Publishing House, 1985.

Shah, Pankaj. 'Ahead of UP polls, Yogi slashes power rates for farmers by 50%,' *Times of India*, 7 January 2002.

Shah, Tushar and Mahendra Singh. 'Accelerated Programmes. What Can the Water Sector Learn from the Power Sector?' *Economic and Political Weekly*, Vol. 46, No. 21, 21–27 May 2011: 25–29.

Shahani, Roshan G. 'Parsis. Exploring Identities,' *Economic and Political Weekly*, Vol. 38, No. 33, 16–22 August 2003: 3463–3466.

Shajahan K. M. 'Priority Sector Bank Lending. Some Important Issues,' *Economic and Political Weekly*, 17–30 October 1998, Vol. 33, No. 42/43: 2749–2756.

Shaji, K. A. 'Congress campaign to harp on symbol of faith,' *The Hindu*, 25 October 2018.

Shamrao, Tanpure Sambhaji. 'A Study of Fertilizer Policy in India,' *International Journal of Agriculture Sciences*, Vol. 3, Issue 3, 2011: 145–149.

Shankar, Sheetal. 'A Decontrol Success Story,' *Economic and Political Weekly*, 1 June 1985: 950–951.

Sharma, Kartikeya. 'Sonia Gandhi's super Cabinet rules,' *India Today*, 13 October 2013.

Sharma, Sadhana (ed). *States Politics in India*. New Delhi: Mittal Publications, 1995.

Sharma, Shruti. 'India Energy Subsidy,' International Institute for Sustainable Development (IISD), 2017.

Sharma, Vijay Paul. 'Food Subsidy in India. Trends, Causes and Policy Reform Options,' W.P. No.2012–08–02, Indian Institute of Management, Ahmedabad, August 2012.

Sherman, Taylor C., William Gould, and Sarah Ansari. *From Subjects to Citizens*. Cambridge University Press, 2014.

Shivam, N. 'Public Finance in India,' https.//www.economicsdiscussion.net/india/public–finance–india/public–finance–in–india/21262.

Shourie, Arun. *Worshipping False Gods: Ambedkar, and the facts which have been erased*. New Delhi: ASA Publications, 1997.

Singh Natwar. *One Life is Not Enough*. New Delhi: Rupa Publication India, 2014.

Singh, Arjun, and Ashok Chopra. *A Grain of Sand in the Hourglass of Time*. Hay House Publishers India Private Ltd, 2012.

Singh, B. K. 'Capital Gains Tax,' *The Economic Weekly*, 6 December 1956.

Singh, Bhupinder. 'Politics of Factionalism in Punjab. A Critical Study of Shiromani Akali Dal,' *The Indian Journal of Political Science*, Vol. 67, No. 4, October–December 2006: 839– 848.

Singh, Birinder Pal. 'Ex–Criminal Tribes of Punjab,' *Economic and Political Weekly*, 20 December 2008.

Singh, Charan. 'Public Debt in India. The Need to Separate Debt from Monetary Management,' *Stanford Center for International Development*, Working Paper No. 240, February 2005.

Singh, Dr. Y. Mohendra. 'The Status of Manipur (1823–1947),' http.//books.e–pao. net/Status_Manipur/epShowChapter.asp?src=Notes_Manipur_Join_India.

Singh, J. P. *Leapfrogging Development – The Political Economy of Telecommunication Restructuring*. Albany, New York: State University of New York Press, 1999.

Singh, Mallika. 'The Promise of the Parsis,' https.//www.soulveda.com/across–cultures/the–promise–of–the–parsis/.

Singh, N. K. 'Elections 1996. Although it lacks a credible plank, BJP capitalises on its opponents' weaknesses,' *India Today*, 30 April 1996.

Singh, N. K. *Portraits of Power – half a century at ringside*. New Delhi: Rupa Publication India, 2020.

Singh, Narendra Kumar and Anand Prakash Singh. 'Congress Socialist Party's Separation from the Congress (1946–48): A socialist point of view,' Proceedings of the Indian History Congress, vol. 63, Indian History Congress, 2002: 819–26.

Singh, Rajesh Kumar. 'UPDATE 1–India to raise passenger rail fares for first time in 9 years,' *Reuters*, 9 January 2013.

Singh, Tripurdaman. *Sixteen stormy days – the story of the first amendment to the Constitution of India*. Delhi: Penguin, 2020.

Singhal, D. P. 'Goa – End of an Epoch,' *The Australian Quarterly*, Vol. 34, No. 1, March 1962: 77–89.

Singhvi, L. M. (ed.). *Devaluation of the Rupee: Its Implications and Consequences*. Delhi: The Institute of Constitutional and Parliamentary Studies, 1968.

Sinha, J. K. P. 'Emerging trends in Bihar Politics,' *The Indian Journal of Political Science*, Vol. 34, No. 4, 1973: 471–481.

Sinha, L. P. 'Socialism in India. Challenges and Responses,' *The Indian Journal of Political Science*, Vol. 31, No. 1, 1970: 1–20.

Sinha, Shishir. 'Plan panel may cut back on growth target for 12th Plan,' *The Hindu BusinessLine*, 6 July 2012.

Sinha, Yashwant. *Confessions of a Swadeshi Reformer: My Years as Finance Minister*. Delhi: Penguin Viking, 2007.

Sitapati, Vinay. *Half Lion – How P. V. Narasimha Rao transformed India*. Delhi: Penguin, 2016.

Sivaramakrishnan, Vidhya and Sangeeta Singh. 'Farm loan waiver success sets the tone for a populist budget,' *The Mint*, 30 June 2009.

Siwach, J. R. 'State Autonomy and the President's Rule,' *The Indian Journal of Political Science*, Vol. 46, No. 2, 1985: 150–166.

Slater, Joanna and Annie Gowen. 'Fear and faith. Inside the last days of an American missionary died on tribe's remote Indian Ocean island'. *Washington Post*. 23 November 2018.

Smith, Wilfred Cantwell. 'Hyderabad. Muslim Tragedy.' *Middle East Journal*, Vol. 4, No. 1, 1950: 27–51.

Snedden, Christopher. *Understanding Kashmir and Kashmiris*. London: Hurst and Company, 2015.

Snow, Edgar. *Red China Today—the Other Side of the River*. UK: Penguin, 1970.

Sreekantaradhya, B. S. *Structure and Reform of Taxation in India*. New Delhi: Deep and Deep Publications Pvt. Ltd., 2000.

Sridhar, V. 'Chronicle of a strike,' *Frontline*, Volume 18 – Issue 19, 15 – 28 September 2001.

Sridhar, V. 'Reviving Dabhol,' *Frontline*, 12 August 2005.

Sridharan, E. 'Electoral Coalitions in 2004 General Elections. Theory and Evidence.' *Economic and Political Weekly*, Vol. 39, No. 51, 2004: 5418–5425.

Srinivasan, T. N. 'Comments on 'From 'Hindu Growth' to Productivity Surge: The Mystery of the Indian Growth Transition'', *IMF Staff Papers*, Vol. 52, No. 2, 2005: 229–233.

Streeton, Paul and Michael Lipton (éd.). *The Crisis of Indian Planning: Economic Planning in the 1960s*. London: Oxford University Press, 1968.

Subrahmaniam, Vidya. 'The divide that never was,' *The Hindu*, 14 November 2013.

Subrahmanyam, Sanjay. 'Before the Leviathan. Sectarian violence and the state in pre-colonial India,' in Kaushik Basu and Sanjay Sunrahmanyam (ed). *Unravelling the Nation – Sectarian conflict and India's secular identity*. Delhi: Penguin, 1996.

Subramanian, Dilip. 'Government Wage Policy in the Public Sector, 1947–1982. Relative Failure of Dirigsme,' *Economic and Political Weekly*, Vol 36, No. 2, 13–19 January 2001: 140–154.

Subramanian, Samanth. 'Long View. India's Very First Corruption Scandal', 9 May, 2012. https://india.blogs.nytimes.com/2012/05/09/long–view–indias–very–first–corruption–scandal/.

Sudarji, Padma Rao. "The riches belong to nobody, certainly not to our family,' *Hindustan Times*, 9 July, 2011.

Sundaram K. and Suresh D. Tendulkar. 'Poverty Among Social and Economic Groups in India in the Nineteen Nineties,' *Centre for Development Economics*, Delhi School of Economics, Working Paper 118, 2003,

Surabhi. 'PM to unveil Sukanya Samriddhi accounts to incentivise girl child,' *Indian Express*, 22 January 2015.

Suri, K. C., 'The Economy and Voting in the 15th Lok Sabha Elections,' *Economic and Political Weekly*, Vol. 44, No. 39, September 2009: 64–70.

Swami, Venkitesh Ramakrishnan Praveen. 'A crisis defused,' *Frontline*, 1 November 1997.

Swami, Venkitesh Ramakrishnan Praveen. 'A turning point,' *Frontline*, 18 November 2005.

Swami, Venkitesh Ramakrishnan Praveen. 'Danger signals from the Valley,' *Frontline*, 10 October 2003.

Swami, Venkitesh Ramakrishnan Praveen. 'The Jaish–e–Mohammad's fidayeen factory: How Masood Azhar set up his industry of terror in Kashmir,' *Firstpost*, 22 February 2019.

Swami, Venkitesh Ramakrishnan Praveen. 'Volte–face in Kashmir,' *Frontline*, 2 March 2002.

Swaminathan, K., and Gouri Puri. 'A Realist's Account of the Bombay High Court's Decision in the Vodafone Case.' *National Law School of India Review*, Vol. 23, No. 1, 2011: 99–107.

Swaminathan, Madhura. 'Tasks on the grain policy front,' *Frontline*, Volume 19 – Issue 17, 17 – 30 August 2002.

Swamy, K. R. N. 'The prince who behaved like a pauper,' *The Tribune*, 14 October 2001. H

Swamy, Subramanian. 'Systems Analysis of Strategic Defence Needs.' *Economic and Political Weekly*, Vol. 4, No. 8, 1969: 401–409.

Swarup, Harihar. *Power Profiles*. New Delhi: Har–Anand Publications Private Ltd., 2010: 34–35.

Syed, Maria. 'Pakistan–India Trade: Rationale and Reality,' *Pakistan Horizon*, Vol. 65, No. 3, July 2012: 85–101.

Talukder, Maniruzzaman. 'Bangladesh in 1975. The Fall of the Mujib Regime and Its Aftermath,' *Asian Survey*, vol. 16, no. 2, 1976: 119–129.

Tanzi, V. and H.R. Davoodi. 'Corruption, growth, and public finances,' in A.K. Jain (ed). *Political Economy of Corruption*. London: Routledge, 2001:89–110.

Taskin, Bismee. 'What is 6th Schedule & why it allows parts of Northeast to be exempt from citizenship bill,' *The Print*, 6 December, 2019.

Tauseef. Shahidi and Manjul Paul. 'What it means to have more women than men in India,' *The Mint*, 3 December 2021.

Taylor, C. and M. Hudson. *World Handbook of Political and Social Indicators*. New Haven: Yale University Press, 1972.

Teltumbde, Anand. 'Supreme Court Judgement On Right To Education. Much Ado For Nothing,' *Countercurrents.org*. 13 May 2012. http.//www.countercurrents.org/teltumbde130512.htm.

Tendulkar, Suresh D. 'Planning Process, Planning Commission and Rollover Planning. Some Basic Issues.' *Economic and Political Weekly*, vol. 12, no. 42, 1977: 1777–1782.

Thakare, Ashish Nareshrao. 'Linguistic States and Formation of Samyukta Maharashtra,' *IOSR Journal of Humanities and Social Science*, Volume 20, Issue 12, Ver. IV, December 2015: 80–82.

Thakur, Pradeep. 'Farm loan waivers won LS polls for Cong,' *Times of India*, 15 December 2009.

Thapar, Romesh. 'A Baba–Log Government,' *Economic and Political Weekly*, Vol. 21, Issue No. 9, 1 Mar 1986.

Tharoor, Shashi. *Nehru – The invention of India*. Delhi: Penguin Viking, 2018.

The Economist. 'India's chaos–as–usual politics,' 24 April 1997.

The Economist. 'India's old man in a hurry,' 3 April 1997.

The Economist. 'Tigers, termites and tenacity,' 11 March, 2004.

The Empowered Committee of State Finance Ministers. 'A White Paper on State–Level Value Added Tax,' New Delhi, 17 January 2005.

The Financial Express. 'State–run insurers seek to increase PMSBY premium,' *The Financial Express*, 23 February 2017.

The Guardian. 'Sting on a shoestring,' The Guardian, 21 March 2001.

The Hindu Business Line. 'DRT orders Mallya to repay Rs 6,203 crore to SBI–led banks consortium,' 12 January 2018.

The Hindu. 'Amended GST Bill gets Parliament green signal,' 9 August 2016.

The Hindu. 'Coal scam. Chronology of events,' 25 August 2014.

The Hindu. 'Corruption in CWG projects. BJP demands JPC probe,' 7 August 2010.

The Hindu. 'He was the king among communists. Gowda,' 18 January 2010.

The Hindu. 'Kalmadi's resignation sought on moral grounds,' 5 August 2010.

The Hindu. 'Left to withdraw support to UPA Government,' 8 July 2008.

The Hindu. 'Pranab's stimulus overdose,' 28 April 2009.

The Mint. 'Air India's accumulated losses climb to ₹ 77,953 cr,' 15 October 2021.

The Mint. 'Aiyar–Kalmadi spat over Commonwealth Games, Congress disapproves,' 28 July 2010.

The Mint. 'IOA sacks Kalmadi, V. K. Malhotra named acting president,' 26 April 2011.

The Mint. 'Mamata says TMC to oppose rail fare hike,' 14 March 2012.

The Mint. 'PM Modi urges states to adopt model farm laws drafted by Centre,' March 17, 2018

The Mint. 'Vijay Mallya arrested, gets bail in ED money laundering case,' 3 October 2017.

The New Indian Express. 'Baba Ramdev seeks sufficient powers for Lokpal,' 14 April 2011.

The New Indian Express. 'Legalism and Government Stand in Black Money Case,' 30 October 2014.

The New Indian Express. 'The dethroned king of good times,' 12 May 2017.

The New York Times. 'Land Transfer to Hindu Site Inflames Kashmir's Muslims,' 28 June 2008.

The News Minute. 'Dravidian chronicles – In 1996, a new party is born and a superstar intervenes,' 9 May 2016.

The Outlook. 'Can Rao survive the urea scam?' 26 June 1996.

The Outlook. 'The Pickle King's Papers,' 17 July 1996

The Outlook. 'The Search for New Power Centres,' 1 January 1997.

The Telegraph. 'George scalp or Mamata exit,' 14 March 2001.

The Telegraph. 'Petrol ignites Mamata resignation,' 30 September 2000.

The Times of India. 'Arun Jaitley resumes charge as finance minister,' 15 February 2019.

The Times of India. 'Controversy over GDP data explained,' 10 May 2019.

The Times of India. 'Enact national right to information. Anna Hazare,' 8 December 2004.

The Times of India. 'JD(U) ends 17–year–old alliance with BJP, quits NDA,' 16 June 2013.

The Times of India. 'Nirav Modi fraud costs PNB Rs 14,357 cr,' 15 May 2018.

The Times of India. 'Only 5,000 crore declared under PMG,' 1 June 2017.

The Times of India. 'Oppn stalls Parliament, demands JPC probe into scams,' 10 November 2010.

The Times of India. 'Rahul Gandhi trashes ordinance, shames government,' 28 September 2013.

The Tribune. 'INLD withdraws support to government,' 17 February 1999.

The Tribune. 'Opposition asks PM to quit,' 16 April 1999.

Thimmaiah, G. 'Evaluation of Tax Reforms in India,' in M. Govinda Rao (ed), *Development, Poverty and Fiscal Policy*. New Delhi: Oxford University Press, 2002.

Thomas, K. M. and M. Govindan Kutty. 'AIADMK chief Jayalalitha's pressure tactics paralyse BJP–led Government,' *India Today*, 4 May 1998.

Thongkholal, Haokip. 'Political Integration of Northeast India. A Historical Analysis.' *Strategic Analysis*. Vol. 36, No. 2, March 2012: 304–314.

Tiwari, Santosh. 'Games loot. CAG report nails Kalmadi,' *India Today*, 11 August 2010.

Torri, Michelguglielmo. 'Factional Politics and Economic Policy. The Case of India's Bank Nationalization.' *Asian Survey*, Vol. 15, No. 12, 1975: 1077–1096.

Triffin, Robert. *Gold and the Dollar Crisis. The Future of Convertibility*. New Haven: Yale University Press, 1960.

Triffin, Robert. *Gold and the Dollar Crisis. Yesterday and Tomorrow*. Essays in International Finance, No. 132, December 1978, International Finance Section, Department of Economics, Princeton University. https.//www.princeton.edu/~ies/IES_Essays/E132.pdf.

Tripathi, Devidutta. 'Police break up Baba Ramdev's anti–graft fast,' *Reuters*, 5 June 2011.

Tripathi, Purnima S. 'Games without rules,' *Frontline*, 8 April 2005.

Tsafos, Nikos and Lachlan Carey. 'Success Story #1. Village Electrification, Energy Transition Strategies—Gujarat's Low–Carbon Development Pathway,' *Center for Strategic and International Studies* (CSIS), 2020.

Tully, Mark and Satish Jacob. *Amritsar: Mrs Gandhi's Last Battle*. Delhi: Rupa Publication India, 1986

Umapathy, M. 'Emerging power pattern in India. Infrastructural elite or ideological elite?' *The Indian Journal of Political Science*, Vol. 29, No. 3, 1968: 197–203.

Upadhyay, Ramesh. 'The Drama of the Arrest,' *Frontline*, 23 November 1990.

Vaasanthi. 'Sonia Gandhi's turn to experience Jayalalitha after AIADMK chief squanders Vajpayee,' *India Today*, 12 April 1999.

Vakil, C. N. Vakil and P. R. Brahmananda. *Planning for an Expanding Economy*. Bombay: Vora & Co., 1956.

Value Research. 'Indian Economy on Steroids?' *Value Research*, 27 May 2009.

Varagur, Krithika. 'Converting to Buddhism as a Form of Political Protest,' *The Atlantic*, 11 April 2018.

Varkey, Ouseph. 'The CPI–Congress Alliance in India.' *Asian Survey*, Vol. 19, No. 9, 1979: 881–895.

Varshney, Ashutosh. 'Democracy, Development and the Countryside – Urban–Rural Struggles in India,' *Cambridge Studies in Comparative Politics*, Cambridge University Press, Cambridge, 1994.

Varshney, Ashutosh. 'Ethnic conflict and civil society – India and beyond,' *World Politics*, 53, April 2001: 362–398.

Vatsa. Aditi. 'H. N. Bahuguna, 'Natwarlal' who refused to take Indira Gandhi's 'son' across Uttar Pradesh,' *The Print*, 17 March 2019.

Velayudham, T. K. 'Credit Policy. Shift Away from Regulation.' *Economic and Political Weekly*, Vol. 24, No. 20, 1989: 1083–1086.

Venkataraman, R. 'Nehru, the Parliamentarian,' Inaugural speech at the Seminar on Nehru and Parliament, New Delhi, November 14, 1985.' *Mainstream*, Vol XLVII, No. 24, 30 May 2009.

Venkatesan, J. 'Supreme Court scraps UPA's 'illegal' 2G sale,' *The Hindu*, 2 February 2012.

Venkatesan, V. and T. S. Subramanian. 'An eight–day ordeal,' *Frontline*, 8 January 2000.

Verghese, S. K. 'International Monetary Crises and the Indian Rupee,' *Economic and Political Weekly, 8*(30), 1342–1348.

Verma, Ragini and Asit Ranjan Mishra. 'The UPA bites the bullet and increases train fares,' *The Mint*, 10 January 2013.

Verma, Sunny. 'Mudra loan disbursals & NPAs rise in tandem at PSBs over last 3 years,' *Indian Express*, 17 September 2020.

Vikraman, Shahji. 'On this day 25 years ago, an invaluable devaluation.' *Indian Express*, 6 July 2016.

Vikraman, Shaji. 'In fact. Glitter of 1993 gold scheme lay in its amnesty clause,' *Indian Express*, 5 April 2017.

Vinayak, Ramesh. 'Kashmir. Despite killing of key militants at Charar shrine, India loses a battle,' *India Today*, 31 May 1995.

Virmani, Arvind. 'India's Economic Growth. From Socialist Rate of Growth to Bharatiya Rate of Growth,' Working Paper No. 122, *Indian Council for Research on International Economic Relations*, February 2004.

Virmani, Arvind. 'Propelling India from Socialist Stagnation to Global Power.' *Academic Foundation*, 2006.

Visaria, Pravin and Leela Visaria. 'Employment Planning for the Weaker Sections in Rural India.' *Economic and Political Weekly*, Vol. 8, No. 4/6, 1973.

Vittal, B. P. R. 'Federal Financial relations – The Plan/Non–Plan Conundrum,' *Economic and Political Weekly*, Vol. 34, No. 7, 13–19 February 1999: 431–36.

Vohra, Pankaj. 'Poll symbols. Lifeline of political parties,' *The Sunday Guardian*, 26 November 2017.

Wahi, Namita. 'Agrarian Reform and the First, Fourth and Seventeenth Amendments [Articles 31(4) and (6) and Articles 31(A) and 31(B)],' in Sujit Choudhri, Madhav Khosla and Pratap Bhanu Mehta (ed). *The Oxford Handbook of the Indian Constitution*. UK: Oxford University Press, 2016.

Wallace, Paul. 'The Dispersion of Political Power,' *Asian Survey*, Vol. 8, No. 2, A Survey of Asia in 1967. Part II (February 1968).

Washington Post. 'Indian Prime Minister wins battle over Deputy's post,' *Washington Post*, 17 July 1990.

Weber, Eugen. *Peasants into Frenchmen – the Modernization of Rural France, 1870–1914*. Stanford University Press, 1976.

Weiner, Myron. *Party Politics in India – the Development of a Multi–party System*. Princeton University Press, 1957.

Weisman, Steven R. 'India's Drought Is Worst in Decades,' *The New York Times*, August 16, 1987.

Wilcox, Wayne. 'The Economic Consequences of Partition. India and Pakistan.' *Journal of International Affairs*, Vol. 18, No. 2, 1964: 188–197.

Windmiller, Marshall. 'The Politics of States Reorganization in India. The Case of Bombay,' *Far Eastern Survey*, Vol. 25, No. 9, 1956: 129–143.

Xaxa, Virginious. 'Politics of Language, Religion and Identity. Tribes in India,' *Economic and Political Weekly*, Vol. 40, No. 13, March 26– April 1, 2005: 1363–1370.

Xaxa, Virginious. 'Tribes in India,' in Veena Das (ed). 'The Oxford India Companion to Sociology and Social Anthropology,' Delhi: Oxford University Press, 2003

Xaxa, Virginius. 'Protective Discrimination. Why Scheduled Tribes Lag behind Scheduled Castes', *Economic and Political Weekly*, Vol. 36, No. 29 July 2001: 2765–2772.

Yadav, Shyamal. 'Uttar Pradesh – A Political History,' *Indian Express*, 11 March 2017.

Yadav, Yogendra. 'On Remembering Lohia.' *Economic and Political Weekly*, Vol. 45, No. 40, 2010: 46–50.

Younger, Coralie. *Wicked Women of the Raj*. Delhi: Harper Collins Publishers India, 2003.

Zacharia, Benjamin. 'Rewriting imperial mythologies: The strange case of Penderel Moon', *South Asia: Journal of South Asian Studies*, 8 May 2007.

Zubrzycki, John. *The Last Nizam*. Australia: Picador, Pan Macmillan, 2006.

Notes

The Backdrop

Chapter I. India in Search of Glory

1　Pranab Mukherjee's speech on sixty-fourth Republic Day, Government Video Portal, 25 January 2013, ttps://webcast.gov.in/events/MTA3OA--/session/MjcwOA--

2　Paul N. Rosenstein-Rodan, *Natura Facit Saltum: Analysis of the Disequilibrium Growth Process*, https://www.rrojasdatabank.info/pioneers8a.pdf

3　Pranab Bardhan, *Political Economy of Development in India*, (Delhi: Oxford University Press, 1999 [1984]), p 73.

4　'Fodder scam cost me dear: Lalu,' The Times of India, 20 December 2006.

5　Robert A. Caro, *The Years of Lyndon Johnson – the Passage to Power*, (New York: Alfred A. Knopf, 2012), p 569.

6　Robert A, Caro, *The Passage to Power: The Years of Lyndon Johnson*, (New York: Alfred A. Knopf, 2012): p 569.

Part I. 1947–1964—Policy Autonomy: Pluralist Politics, Socialist Economics, Integration and the Colossus

Chapter II.　Post-Independence Integration

1　Wikipedia. 2022. "Mao Zedong." Wikimedia Foundation. Last modified September 20, 2022. https://en.wikipedia.org/wiki/Mao_Zedong.

2　Robyn Meredith, *The Elephant and the Dragon: The Rise of India and China and What it Means for All of Us*, (New York: W. W. Norton & Company, 2007): p 55:

3　Padma Rao Sudarji, 'The riches belong to nobody, certainly not to our family,' *Hindustan Times*, 9 July 2011.

4   Jarmani Das, *Maharani*, (Delhi: Penguin, Random House, 2019): pp. 44-45.

5   Ibid.

6   Ramachandra Guha, *India after Gandhi*, (London: Picador, 2007): p 50.

7   Ibid.

8   Ibid.

9   Ibid.

10   John Zubrzycki, *The Last Nizam*, (London, Picador, 2006): pp 244-245.

11   H.V. Hodson, *The Great Divide: Britain-India-Pakistan*, (London: Hutchinson, 1969): p 428.

12   Hamish McDonald, *The Polyester Prince*, (Australia: Allen & Unwen, 1998).

13   Rakesh Ankit, 'The accession of Junagadh, 1947-48: Colonial Sovereignty, state violence and post-independence India,' *The Indian Economic and Social History Review*, Vol. 53, No. 3, (2016): pp 371-404.

14   Sumantra Bose, *Kashmir – Roots of Conflict, Paths to Peace*, (Cambridge: Harvard University Press, 2003): p 56.

15   John Zubrzycki, *The Last Nizam*, (London: Picador, 2006).

16   Wilfred Cantwell Smith, 'Hyderabad: Muslim Tragedy.' *Middle East Journal*, Vol. 4, No. 1, (1950): pp 27–51.

17   John Zubrzycki, *The Last Nizam*, (London: Picador, 2006): pp 190-199.

18   Chandernagore was the French name of Chandannagar.

19   Sushila Sawant Mendes, 'Jawaharlal Nehru and the Liberation Struggle of Goa,' *Proceedings of the Indian History Congress*, Vol 67, (2006-07).

20   D. P. Singhal, 'Goa – End of an Epoch,' *The Australian Quarterly*, Vol. 34, No. 1, (March 1962): pp 77-89.

21   Ibid.

Chapter III. Linguistic Identities

1   Henry B Hansmann and John M. Quigley, 'Population Heterogeneity and the Sociogenesis of Homicide.' *Social Forces*, Vol. 61, No. 1, (1982): pp. 206–224.

2   'The Nehru Report: An Anti-Separatist Manifesto,' The Committee appointed by the All Parties Conference, 1928, Michiko and Panjathan, New Delhi, 1975 (1928), pp. 61-62.

3   'Report of the State Reorganisation Commission, 1955.' p 14, https://www.mha.gov.in/sites/default/files/State%20Reorganisation%20Commisison%20Report%20of%201955_270614.pdf.

4   S.K. Dar, Pana Lall, Jagatnabrain Lal and B.C. Banerjee, 'Report of the Linguistic Provinces Commission, 1948,' Government of India, https://indianculture.gov.in/report-linguistic-provinces-commission-1948.

5   Nalin Mehta and Mona G. Mehta: "Gujarat beyond Gandhi: notes on identity, conflict and society', South Asian History and Culture, 1: 4, 467 — 479. P. 472.

6   Marshall Windmiller, 'The Politics of States Reorganization in India: The Case of Bombay,' *Far Eastern Survey 25*, No. 9 (1956): pp 129–43.

7   Singh, Khushwant, *A History of the Sikhs: Volume 2: 1839-2004*, 2nd edn (Delhi, 2004; online edn, Oxford Academic, 18 Oct. 2012), https://doi.org/10.1093/ac prof:oso/9780195673098,003.0016,

8   Constitution of India, 'Article 3,' https://www.constitutionofindia.net/ constitution_of_india/the_union_and_its_territory/articles/Article%203.

9   Andrew Healy and Neil Malhotra: "Myopic Voters and Natural Disaster Policy," American Political Science Review Vol. 103, No. 3 August 2009. Jean Drèze and Amartya Sen: "Hunger and Public Action," Oxford University Press, Oxford, 1989.

Chapter IV. Fractured Identities: Scheduled Tribes and Castes

1   http://www.tribalzone.net/people/jaipalsingh.htm

2   Constituent Assembly Debates On 17 December 1946, https://indiankanoon. org/doc/1887990/

3   'Gujarat Dalit groom rides horse, his community faces social boycott,' *The Indian Express*, 10 May 2019, https://indianexpress.com/article/india/gujarat-dalit-groom-rides-horse-his-community-faces-social-boycott-5720156/.

4   Arvind Chauhan, 'Body of Nat woman taken off funeral pyre after upper castes object,' *Times of India*, 27 July 2020 https://timesofindia.indiatimes.com/city/ agra/body-of-nat-woman-taken-off-funeral-pyre-after-upper-castes-object/ articleshow/77206355.cms.

5   http://www.tribalzone.net/people/jaipalsingh.htm

6   Constitution of India, 'Special Representation in Services for SC/ST,' https:// dopt.gov.in/sites/default/files/ch-11.pdf.

7   Virginius Xaxa, 'Politics of Language, Religion and Identity: Tribes in India,' *Economic and Political Weekly*, Vol. 40, No. 13, March 26-April 1, 2005, pp. 1363-1370.

8   Government of India (Exluded and Partially Excluded and Partially Excluded areas) Order, 1936. HL Deb 25 February1936 vol 99 cc734-43, https://api.parliament. uk/historic-hansard/lords/1936/feb/25/government-of-india-excluded-and

9   Constituent Assembly Debates, http://164.100.47.194/Loksabha/Debates/ cadebatefiles/C06091949.html

10 Annual Report, 2016-17, Ministry of Tribal Affairs, Government of India, https://www.tribal.nic.in/writereaddata/AnnualReport/AnnualReport2016-17. pdf p.24. Also, Statistical Profile of Scheduled Tribes in India, 2013,Ministry of Tribal Affairs, 2013. https://www.tribal.nic.in/ST/StatisticalProfileofSTs2013. pdf p.166.

11 Subir Bhaumik: "Insurgent Crossfire: North-east India," Chapter 3, https:// books.google.co.in/books?id=iftjFki3fhYC&pg=PA47&lpg=PA47&dq=Naga +Chinese+connection&source=bl&ots=GmBdpfj1UR&sig=ACfU3U3AFdQ 69czWO_0eTVgTsSgO0mExOg&hl=en&sa=X&ved=2ahUKEwjdxKe1wZr oAhUvyDgGHZSDA904ChDoATADegQIBxAB#v=onepage&q=Naga%20 Chinese%20connection&f=false

12   Report of the States Reorganisation Commission, 1955. P. 194. http://14.139.60.114:8080/jspui/bitstream/123456789/958/30/Assam%20%28183-195%29.pdf

13   Government of India Act, 1935. Section 26(1), p. 227. http://www.legislation.gov.uk/ukpga/1935/2/pdfs/ukpga_19350002_en.pdf

14   Arun Shourie, *Worshipping False Gods: Ambedkar, and the facts which have been erased*, (New Delhi: ASA Publications, 1997), p 3.

15   A. K. Biswas, 'A memorable chapter neglected in history: Ambedkar's odyssey to the Constituent Assembly of India through Bengal,' *Mainstream*, Vol. LV, No. 1, 24 December 2016, Annual 2016.

16   Sekhar Bandyopadhyay, 'Transfer of Power and the Crisis of Dalit Politics in India, 1945-47.' *Modern Asian Studies*, Vol. 34, No. 4, 2000, pp. 893–942.

17   Sanjay Hegde, 'A nation builder's pride of place,' *The Hindu*, 14 April 2015.

18   T. J. S. George, 'How Ambedkar makes us richer,' *The New Indian Express*, 23 December 2018.

Chapter V. Religious Conflicts

1   'Sarah Cohen, the oldest Kerala Jew, passes away,' *The Hindu*, 30 August 2019.

2   Debabrata Mahapatra, 'Jagannath Temple invokes Ranjit Singh, stakes claim to Kohinoor,' *The Times of India*, 25 April 2016.

3   http://www.columbia.edu/itc/mealac/pritchett/00islamlinks/txt_jinnah_assembly_1947.html

4   Sir Roland Knyvet Wilson, 'A Digest Preceded by a Historical and Descriptive Introduction of the Special Rules now Applicable to Muhammadans as such by the Courts of British India, with Full References to Modern and Ancient Authorities,' *W. Thackr & Co.*, 2 Creed Lane, E. C. Calcutta, 1903. p 39. https://archive.org/stream/in.ernet.dli.2015.12393/2015.12393.Anglo-muhammadan-Law-A-Digest_djvu.txt

5   Ibid, p. 40.

6   'Constituent Assembly Debates (Official Report),' Vol. VIII, Lok Sabha Secretariat, New Delhi 1989, pp. 540-552, http://164.100.47.194/Loksabha/Debates/Result_Nw_15.aspx?dbsl=182

7   Christophe Jaffrelot, 'The Fate of Secularism in India,' Carnegie Endowment for International Peace, 4 April, 2019. https://carnegieendowment.org/2019/04/04/fate-of-secularism-in-india-pub-78689

8   Partha Chatterjee, 'Secularism and Toleration,' *Economic and Political Weekly*, Vol. 29, No. 28, 1994, pp. 1768–1777.

9   'Legacy of Nehru,' *Economic and Political Weekly*, Vol. 11, No. 46 (Nov. 13, 1976), p. 1773.

10   Walter Andersen, 'The Rashtriya Swayamsevak Sangh –III: Participation in Politics,' *Economic and Political Weekly*, March 25, 1972. p. 673.

11   Walter Andersen, 'The Rashtriya Swayamsevak Sangh–III: Participation in Politics,' *Economic and Political Weekly* (25 March 1972): p 675.

12 A definition offered in 1977 by Francesco Capotorti, Special Rapporteur of the United Nations Sub-Commission on Prevention of Discrimination and Protection of Minorities 1/ E/CN.4/Sub.2/384/Rev.1, para. 568.

13 From a now lost manuscript quoted in George J. Stigler: 'The Effect of Government on Economic Efficiency,' *Business Economics*, vol. 23, no. 1, 1988, pp. 7–13. P. 7.

14 Maulana Abul Kalam Azad, *India Wins Freedom: The Complete Version*, (Delhi: Orient Blackswan, 2009 [1959]), pp. 200-201.

15 Mr Jinnah's presidential address to the Constituency Assembly of Pakistan, 11 August 1947 http://www.pakistani.org/pakistan/legislation/constituent_address_11aug1947.html

16 Ernest Renan, *What is a Nation?* text of a conference delivered at the Sorbonne on March 11th, 1882, in Ernest Renan, 'Qu'est-ce qu'une nation?' Paris, Presses-Pocket, 1992. (translated by Ethan Rundell).

17 Ashutosh Varshney, 'Ethnic conflict and civil society – India and beyond,' *World Politics*, 53, (April 2001): pp 362-398.

18 Anjali Thomas Bohlken and Ernest John Sergenti, 'Economic Growth and Ethnic Violence: An Empirical Investigation of Hindu—Muslim Riots in India,' *Journal of Peace Research*, vol. 47, no. 5, (2010): pp 589–600.

19 Anirban Mitra and Debraj Ray, 'Implications of an Economic Theory of Conflict: Hindu-Muslim Violence in India,' *Journal of Political Economy*, Vol. 122, No. 4 (August 2014), pp. 719-765.

20 B. R. Ambedkar, *Annihilation of Caste*, 1936, First edition of Annihilation of Caste - Annihilation of Caste - Wikipedia

21 Joan-Maria Esteban and Debraj Ray, 'On the Measurement of Polarization,' *Econometrica*, vol. 62, no. 4, (1994): pp 819–851. Jean-Yves Duclos, Joan Esteban, and Debraj Ray, 'Polarization: Concepts, Measurement, Estimation,' *Econometrica* 72, no. 6 (2004): pp 1737–1772.

22 Pratap Bhanu Mehta, *The Burden of Democracy*, (Delhi: Penguin Books India, 2003), p 11.

Part II. 1947-1964 - Policy Autonomy: Pluralist Politics, Socialist Economics, Integration and the Colossus

Chapter VI. Pursuit of Democratic Socialism

1 Maria Syed, 'Pakistan-India Trade: Rationale and Reality,' *Pakistan Horizon*, Vol. 65, No. 3, July 2012, pp 94-95.

2 *History of the Reserve Bank of India (1935-51)*, Reserve Bank of India, 1970, pp. 664-666. India recognised the changed value of the Pakistani rupee only in February 1951.

3 Sankar Ghose, *Jawaharlal Nehru, A Biography*,)Delhi: Allied Publishers, 1993), p 49.

4 Ibid, p. 241.

5   Ibid, p. 240.

6   Ibid, p. 232.

7   Jawaharlal Nehru, 'Presidential Address to the Indian National Congress,' *The Labour Monthly*, Vol. 18, May 1936, No. 5, pp. 282-305

8   Jawaharlal Nehru, 'Presidential Address to the Indian National Congress at Faizpur,' *The Labour Monthly*, Vol. 19, February 1937, No. 2, pp. 98-107

9   *History of the Reserve Bank of India (1935-51)*, Reserve Bank of India, 1970, P. 507.

10   *History of The Reserve Bank of India (1951-67)* Reserve Bank of India, 1998, P. 318.

11   Madhav Khosla, *Letters for a Nation from Jawaharlal Nehru to his Chief Ministers, 1947-1963*, (London: Penguin UK, 2015).

12   Tripurdaman Singh, *Sixteen stormy days – The story of the first amendment to the Constitution of India*, (Delhi, Penguin Random House India, 2020).

13   V. K. R. V. Rao, 'India's First Five-Year Plan-A Descriptive Analysis,' *Pacific Affairs*, March, 1952, Vol. 25, No. 1 (Mar., 1952), pp. 3-23. P. 3.

14   Ibid, p 6.

15   Ryutaro Komiya, 'A Note on Professor Mahalanobis' Model of Indian Economic Planning,' *The Review of Economics and Statistics*, Vol. 41, No. 1, (February 1959): pp 29-35.

16   M. Govinda Rao, 'Central Transfers to States in India Rewarding Performance while Ensuring Equity (Final Report of a Study Submitted to NITI Aayog),' https://www.niti.gov.in/writereaddata/files/document_publication/Final%20 Report_25Sept_2017.pdf.

17   P. N. Rosenstein-Rodan. 'The International Development of Economically Backward Areas,' *International Affairs* (Royal Institute of International Affairs 1944-), vol. 20, no. 2, 1944, pp. 157–65, P. 160.

18   Jagdish Bhagwati and Sukhamoy Chakravarty, 'Contributions to Indian Economic Analysis – A Survey,' *American Economic Review*, Vol. 59, No. 4, (1969): pp 1-79.

19   Baldev Raj Nayar, 'Community Development Programme—Its Political Impact,' *The Economic Weekly*, 17 September 1960.

20   Government of India, Ministry of Food and Agriculture and Ministry of Community Development and Cooperation, 'Report on India's Food Crisis and Steps to Meet It,' April 1959, It was by the Agricultural Team sponsored by the Ford Foundation.

21   Ranjit Gupta, 'Rural Works Programme: Where It Has Gone Astray,' *Economic and Political Weekly*, Vol. 6, No. 20, 1971, pp. 995–1004.

Chapter VII. Industrial Licensing, Public Sector Undertakings and Commanding Heights

1   Medha M. Kudaisya, *The Life and Times of G. D. Birla*, (Delhi: Oxford India Paperbacks, 2003), p 307.

2 N. P. Nawani, 'Indian experience on household food and nutrition security,' *Regional Expert Consultation*, FAO-UN Bangkok, 8-11 August 1994. https://www.fao.org/3/x0172e/x0172e00.htm#TopOfPage, Chapter 6.

3 Bhabatosh Datta, *Indian Economic Thought – Twentieth Century Perspectives 1900-1950*, (New Delhi: Tata McGraw-Hill Publishing Company Limited, 1978), pp. 6, 64, 66.

4 Gary S. Becker, 'Competition and Democracy,' *The Journal of Law & Economics*, Vol. 1, October 1958, pp. 105-109.

5 After setting up the Swatantra Party in 1959, referring to Dr. Harekrushna Mahatab, an old Congress associate and then the Chief Minister of Odisha heading a Congress-Parishad government, Rajaji had said "Not only Dr Mahatab but all the old warriors of the Congress who do not approve of and are not happy with the permit-quota-license raj that goes by the name of socialism, are to join hands with me." Hindustan Times, June 26, 1961. Quoted in H. L. Erdman, *The Swatantra Party and Indian Conservatism*, Cambridge University Press, 1967, p. 131.

6 Milton Friedman, 'A Memorandum to the Government of India,' 5 November 1955, https://www.indiapolicy.org/debate/Notes/friedman.htm.

7 John P. Lewis, 'Quiet Crisis in India. Economic Development and American Policy,' The Brookings Institution, Washington DC, 1962.

8 Planning Commission, 'Second Five-Year Plan,' Government of India, p. 392.

9 'The Report of the Industrial Licensing Committee,' 1969, chaired by Subimal Dutt, p. 29.

10 Planning Commission, 'Report of the Committee on· Distribution of Income and Levels of Living,' Part I, Government of India, (Delhi, 1964): p. 30.

11 Chairman T Swaminathan, 'Interim Report of the Industries Development Procedures Committee,' 17 December 1963, para 5.

Chapter VIII. Tax Regime and Fiscal Devolution

1 Dharma Kumar, 'Fiscal System,' Chapter XII, in Dharma Kumar (edited), *The Cambridge Economic History of India, Vol. II, c. 1757-2003*, Orient Blackswan in association with Cambridge University Press, 2010, p. 905.

2 I. G. Patel, *Glimpses of Indian Economic Policy – An Insider's View*, (Delhi: Oxford University Press, 2002): p 56.

3 G. Thimmaiah, 'Evaluation of Tax Reforms in India,' in M. Govinda Rao (ed), *Development, Poverty and Fiscal Policy*, (New Delhi: Oxford University Press, 2002).

4 'Report of the Taxation Enquiry Commission, 1953-54,' Vol. 1, Ministry of Finance (Department of Economic Affairs), Government of India, P. 149. https://indianculture.gov.in/flipbook/2855

5 https://nipfp.org.in/book/952/

6 '"Warned Nitish about it": Lalu seeks to disown Bihar liquor prohibition,' *New Indian Express*, 22 November 2021.

Chapter IX. Resource Constraint and Neglect of Taxation, Education and Health, and Physical Infrastructure

1   G. M. Young (ed), *Speeches of Lord Macaulay*, (London: Oxford University Press, 1935): p 135

2   John Kenneth Galbraith, *Economic Development in Perspective*, (Cambridge: Harvard University Press, 1962). Quoted in Jim Peach, 'Galbraith and the Problem of Uneven Development,' *Journal of Economic Issues*, Vol. 42, No. 1, (March 2008): pp. 25-35.

3   John Kenneth Galbraith, 'Let Us Begin: An Invitation to Action on Poverty,' *Harper's Magazine*, March 1964. Quoted in Jim Peach, 'Galbraith and the Problem of Uneven Development,' *Journal of Economic Issues*, Vol. 42, No. 1, (March 2008): pp. 25-35.

4   Jean Dreze and Amartya Sen, 'Basic Education as a Political Issue,' *Journal of Education Planning and Administration*, Vol. IX(1), (1995).

5   Pranab Bardhan, 'Reflections on Indian Political Economy.' *Economic and Political Weekly*, vol. 50, no. 18, pp. 14–17.

Chapter X. Balance of Payments Crisis, the Ensuing Debate and Policy Hysteresis

1   Amaresh Bagchi and Nicholas Stern (ed), *Tax Policy and Planning in Developing Countries*, (Oxford University Press, 1994), p 3. Quote from the text: '"Before the decade of the 1980s had drawn to a close it was evident that the government budget in India was in a crisis and this was at the root of the structural imbalances plaguing the economy," they added.'

2   Richard A. Musgrave and Alan T. Peacock, 'Three Extracts on Public Finance by Adolph Wagner,' in *Classics in the Theory of Public Finance*, Translated from German by Nancy Cooke, (London: MacMillan, 1967): p 8. http://desmarais-tremblay.com/Resources/Musgrave%20Peacock%201958%20Classics%20in%20the%20Theory%20of%20Public%20Finance.pdf.

3   A. K. Dasgupta, 'Keynesian Economics and Under-Developed Countries Again: A Rejoinder.' *Economic and Political Weekly*, Vol. 22, no. 49 (1987) p. 2126.

4   Government of India (1965), 'Report of the Fourth Finance Commission, Ministry of Finance, New Delhi, 1965,' para 148.

5   R. K. Pattanaik and Amaresh Samantaraya, 'Indian Experience of Inflation: A Review of the Evolving Process,' *Economic and Political Weekly*, Vol. XLI, No. 4, (28 January 2006): pp. 349-357.

6   RBI, *History of the Reserve Bank of India (1951-1967)*, Chapter 16, "Dealing with Scarcity," pp. 627-628.

7   Paul Krugman, 'America's epidemic of infallibility,' *New York Times*, 20 March 2017.

8   Jamelle Bouie quoted in Daniel W. Drezner, 'Why can't world leaders ever admit they were wrong?' *The Washington Post*, 9 June 2015.

9   Medha M. Kudaisya, *The Life and Times of G. D. Birla*, (New Delhi: Oxford India Paperbacks, 2003): p. 306.

10 'The Report of the Industrial Licensing Committee.' chaired by Subimal Dutt, 1969, p.183.

11 Quoted in Amal Sanyal, 'The Curious Case of the Bombay Plan,' *Contemporary Issues and Ideas in Social Sciences*, (June 2010): p. 27.

12 Sankar Ghose (1993), p.239.

13 'FICCI: Proceedings of the Twenty-Fifth Annual Meeting, 1952,' FICCI, Delhi, 1952, pp. 33-34.

14 B. M. Birla at 'FICCI: Proceedings of the Twenty-Seventh Annual Meeting, 1954,' FICCI, Delhi, 1954, pp. 8-20, 34. Quoted in Stanley A. Kochanek, *Business and Politics in India*, Chapter XIII, (Berkeley: University of California Press): p. 218.

15 Stanley A. Kochanek, *Business and Politics in India*, Chapter XIII, (Berkeley: University of California Press): p 188.

16 Ibid. p 206.

17 'Presidential Address to the Indian National Congress,' *The Labour Monthly*, Vol. 18, No. 5, (May 1936): pp. 282-305.

18 Ramachandra Guha, *India after Gandhi*, (Delhi: Picador, 2007), p 130.

19 Saurav Basu, 'Revisiting Nehru-Patel Differences,' *Swarajya*, 12 October 2014, available at http://swarajyamag.com/politics/revisiting-nehru-patel-differences-alternate-perspectives.

20 Vidya Subrahmaniam, 'The divide that never was,' *The Hindu*, 14 November 2013.

21 A. K. Dasgupta, 'Socialistic Pattern of Society and the Second Five Year Plan,' *The Economic Weekly Annual*, 1957, p. 91.

22 Ibid.

Part III. 1964–1991—More Politics Than Economics: Nehruvian Policies with a Populist Twist

Chapter XI. Passing of an Era and Interregnum of Hope

1   Neville Maxwell, *India's China War*, (Dehradun: Natraj Publishers, 1997), p 72.

2   Ibid. p 364.

3   Sheikh Mohammad Abdullah, *Flames of the Chinar- An Autobiography*, Abridged, translated from Urdu and introduced by Khushwant Singh, (Delhi: Penguin, 1993), pp. 53-54.

4   The Unit Trust of India Act, 1963.

5   Herbert Barry, 'Gold,' *Virginia Law Review*, Vol. 20, No. 3, (January 1934): pp. 263-306. pp. 280-281. It mentions citizens' right to purchase, hold and sell gold, which was legalized only on 31 December 1974 under President Gerald Ford.

6   Quoted in Kanakalatha Mukund, *The World of the Tamil Merchant – Pioneers of International Trade*, (Delhi: Penguin Books, 2012).

7   Shashi Tharoor, *Nehru – The invention of India*, (Penguin Viking, 2018).

8 The Food Corporation Act 1964.

9 Verghese Kurien, 'India's Milk Revolution – Investing in Rural Producer Organisations,' in Deepa Narayan-Parker and Elena E. Glinskaya, 'Ending Poverty in South Asia: Ideas that Work,' *World Bank*, 2007.

10 I. G. Patel, *Glimpses of Indian Economic Policy – An Insider's View*, (Oxford University Press, 2002).

Chapter XII. Indira Gandhi Becomes Prime Minister With Economy in Turmoil

1 David B. H. Denoon, 'Cycles in Indian Economic Liberalization, 1966-1996,' *Comparative Politics*, Vol. 31, No. 1 (October1998): pp. 43-60.

2 Dennis Kux, 'India and the US—Enstranged Democracies,' p. 254, https://books.google.co.in/books?id=zcylFXH9_z8C&pg=PA253&lpg=PA253&dq=sachin+chaudhuri+finance+minister&source=bl&ots=PAHrhf2nA4&sig=AgKeoks66SlyCmf_qvOMcg-b8LY&hl=en&sa=X&ei=1o_rVO7WG5K3uQTBh4II&ved=0CCMQ6AEwATgK#v=onepage&q=sachin%20chaudhuri%20finance%20minister&f=false.

Chapter XIII. The Rise of the Opposition

1 Neville Maxwell, *India's China War*, (Dehradun: Natraj Publishers, 1997), p 90.

2 R. Venkataraman, 'Nehru, the Parliamentarian,' Inaugural speech at the Seminar on Nehru and Parliament, New Delhi on 14 November 1985. Mentioned in *Mainstream*, Vol. XLVII, No. 24, (30 May 2009).

3 The Indian Express, 'SPECIAL REPORT: Amazon launches their newest platform AmazonCoin™ - aims to help familiesbecome wealthier, http://www.forumindia.org/.

4 Howard L Erdman, 'The Swatantra Party and Indian Conservatism,' *Cambridge South Asian Studies*, Cambridge at the University Press, (1967):p 107, https://archive.org/stream/swatantrapartyin00erdm#page/106/mode/2up.

5 Narendra Kumar Singh and Anand Prakash Singh, 'Congress Socialist Party's Separation from the Congress (1946-48): A socialist point of view,' *Proceedings of the Indian History Congress*, vol. 63, Indian History Congress, (2002): pp. 819–26. p 820.

6 John Patrick Haithcox, 'Left Wing Unity and the Indian Nationalist Movement: M. N. Roy and the Congress Socialist Party,' *Modern Asian Studies*, vol. 3, no. 1, (1969): pp. 17–56. p 20.

7 Ram Manohar Lohia, *The Caste System*, (Hyderabad: Navahind Prakasan, 1964), https://archive.org/stream/in.ernet.dli.2015.65344/2015.65344.The-Caste-System_djvu.txt.

8 JP's description of Lohia's views reported in Hindustan Times, 13 June 1964 quoted in Benjamin N. Schoenfeld, 'The Birth of India's Samyukta Socialist Party,' *Pacific Affairs*, vol. 38, no. 3/4, (1965): pp. 245–268. p 261.

Chapter XIV. Troubled Politics and Rapid Left-Turn

1   Akhtar Balouch, 'How Fatima Jinnah died—and unsolved criminal case,' *The Dawn*, 24 January 2015, https://www.dawn.com/news/1159181.

2   Rajni Kothari, 'India: The Congress System on Trial,' *Asian Survey*, vol. 7, no. 2, (1967): pp. 83–96.

3   In a speech at Panjim, Goa on 5 March, 1967 and repeated several times elsewhere, quoted in Norman D. Palmer, 'India's Fourth General Election,' *Asian Survey*, vol. 7, no. 5, (1967): pp. 275–291. p 278.

4   W. H. Morris-Jones, *Parliament in India*, (UK: Longmans, Green and Co., 1957), p 174.

5   Mohit Sen, 'Coalition and Congress,' *Economic and Political Weekly*, vol. 2, no. 33/35, (1967): pp. 1499–1502.

6   Ouseph Varkey, 'The CPI-Congress Alliance in India,' *Asian Survey*, vol. 19, no. 9, (1979): pp. 881–895. p 891.

7   David Lockwood, 'The Communist Party of India and the Indian Emergency,' *Sage* Series in Modern Indian History, Vol. XVII, 2016.

8   Sudipta Kaviraj, 'Indira Gandhi and Indian Politics,' *Economic and Political Weekly*, vol. 21, no. 38/39, (1986): pp. 1697–1708.

Chapter XV. More of Command and Control

1   P. C. Mahalanobis, *The Approach of Operational Research to Planning in India*, (Mumbai: Asia Publishing House, 1963).

2   K. N. Raj, 'Small-Scale Industries: Problem of Technological Change,' *The Economic Weekly*, (April 1956).

3   Legal Services in India.com, 'Priority sector lending in India,' http://www.legalservicesindia.com/article/2417/Priority-Sector-Lending-In-India.html

4   Report on Currency and Finance, 1972-73, p. 110.

5   Verghese Kurien, 'India's Milk Revolution – Investing in Rural Producer Organisations,' in Deepa Narayan-Parker and Elena E. Glinskaya, 'Ending Poverty in South Asia: Ideas that Work,' *World Bank*, 2007.

6   Ibid.

7   Pratik Ahvad, 'The Indian pharmaceutical industry: the 'pharmacy of the world'?', *Deloitte*, 20 March 2020, https://blogs.deloitte.co.uk/health/2020/03/the-indian-pharmaceutical-industry-the-pharmacy-of-the-world.html

8   Arvind P. Datar, 'Who betrayed Sardar Patel?' *The Hindu*, 19 November 2013.

9   Vijay Sanghvi, *The Congress – Indira to Sonia Gandhi*, (Delhi: Kalpaz Publications, 2006), p 70.

10   Sumanta Banerjee, 'Congress (R), CPI and CPI (M),' *Economic and Political Weekly*, vol. 5, no. 45, (1970): pp. 1804–1807.

11   I.G. Patel, *Glimpses of Indian Economic Policy – An Insider's View*, (Oxford University Press, 2002), p 140

12   The underlying assumption is that such wealth yields a return of 10 per cent. Anand P. Gupta, 'Central Government Taxes: Have They Reduced Inequality?' *Economic and Political Weekly*, vol. 12, no. 4, (1977): pp. 88–100. p 88.

13   Rajni Kothari, 'Voting in India: Competitive Politics and Electoral Change: Introduction,' *Economic and Political Weekly*, vol. 6, no. 3/5, (1971): pp. 229–30. p 229.

14   Nikhil Chakravartty, 'Indira Gandhi installed as president of break-away faction of Congress Party,' *India Today*, 31 January 1978.

15   Major K. C. Praval, '1971: Making Bangladesh a reality – I,' *IDR: Indian Defence Review*, 16 December 2012.

Chapter XVI. Boiling in Oil—The Turbulent Seventies

1   Barry Eichengreen, *Exorbitant Privilege: The Rise and Fall of the Dollar and the Future of the International monetary system*, (Oxford University Press, 2012), p 3.

2   Shebonti Ray Dadwal, 'The Current Oil 'Crisis': Implications for India,' *Strategic Analysis (IDSA)*, Vol. XXIV No. 2, (May 2000).

3   David M. Kennedy and Lizabeth Cohen, *The American Pageant, Since 1865, Vol. 2*, (Boston: Wadsworth, 2007): p 876.

4   Sec 2. https://indiacode.nic.in/bitstream/123456789/2118/3/A1951-65.pdf.

5   Dharm Narain, 'Combating the wheat lobby,' *Cross Section*, March 1975, quoted in M. Raghavan, 'Politics of Procurement and Price Support,' *Economic and Political Weekly*, Vol. 39, No. 5 (31 January–6 February 2004): pp. 506-508.

6   Chairman S. R. Sen, 'Committee Report on Cost of Cultivation,' 1979. para 9.29, p. 42. Available at https://cacp.dacnet.nic.in/KeyBullets.aspx?pid=66

7   Dharm Narain, 'Growth and Imbalances in Indian Agriculture,' *Economic and Political Weekly*, Review of Agriculture, (March 1972): A-6

8   Department of Fertilizer, Government of India, 'Report on Optimisation of Fertilzer Usage, 2010,' http://fert.nic.in/sites/default/files/documents/fertusage_19042011.pdf

9   Lakshman H. K. Rao, 'Management of fertilizer marketing systems: a study focusing the logistics,' School of Management, Pondicherry University, April 1994. http://hdl.handle.net/10603/897, p. 152.

Chapter XVII. Mid-Seventies Nightmare and Its End

1   Ramachandra Guha, *India after Gandhi*, (Delhi: Picador, 2007),p 414

2   The Telegraph, 'Clement Attlee attends Lord's debates,' July 1947.

3   Riccardo Orizio, 'Idi Amin's Exile Dream,' *The New York Times*, 21 August 2003,

4   William Case, 'Semi-Democracy in Malaysia: Withstanding the Pressures for Regime Change,' *Pacific Affairs*, Vol. 66, No. 2 (1993): pp. 183-205. p187.

5   Madhav Godbole, *Unfinished Innings: Recollections and Reflections of a Civil Servant*, (Hyderabad: Orient Longman, 1996), pp. 87-88.

6   T. Ramakrishnan, 'The 1975 Gujarat Assembly Election,' *The Hindu*, 5 December 2017.

7   Overseas Hindustan Times, March 18, 1976, p. 2 quoted in Myron Weiner, 'India at the Polls: The Parliamentary Elections of 1977,' p. 119.

8   'National Population Policy: A Statement of the Government of India,' *Population and Development Review*, Vol. 2, No. 2 (June 1976): pp. 309-312.

9   Fali Nariman, 'Why did Indira Gandhi call off the Emergency?' *Indian Express*, 8 February 2019.

Chapter XVIII. The Second Oil Shock and the Demise of the Janata Government

1   Mohan Guruswamy, 'FDI: A good step, but a lot more left to do,' *Deccan Chronicle*, 23 June 2016.

2. The High Denomination Bank Notes (Demonetisation) Act, 1978, 30 March 1978.

3   'Indira calls on JP,' *Indian Express*, 15 August 1977. 'Indira Gandhi meets Jayaprakash Narayan,' *India Today*, 15 September 1977

4   Pranab Mukherjee, *The Dramatic Decade – The Indira Gandhi Years*, (New Delhi: Rupa, 2015), p. 162.

5   Vasant Sathe quoted in Pranab Mukherjee, *The Dramatic Decade – The Indira Gandhi Years*, (New Delhi: Rupa, 2015), p 139.

6   Pranab Mukherjee, *The Dramatic Decade – The Indira Gandhi Years*, (New Delhi: Rupa, 2015), p163.

Chapter XIX. Beyond 'Hindu' Rate of Growth with Ideology in the Backseat

1   James Boughton, 'Silent Revolution: The International Monetary Fund 1979-1989,' *IMF*, October 2001. P. 710. Available at https://www.imf.org/external/pubs/ft/history/2001/ch15.pdf

2   Vijay Joshi and I. M. D. Little, 'India – Macroeconomics and Political Economy,' *The World Bank*, Washington DC, 1994, p 59.

3   Oriental Outpost, 'Black or White Cat Matters Not as Long as It Can Catch Mice,' https://www.orientaloutpost.com/shufa.php?q=black+or+white+cat+matters+not+as+long+as+it+can+catch+mice

4   *The Saturday Review*, 9 August 1975 quoted in Vijay Prashad, 'Emergency Assessments,' *Social Scientist*, Vol. 24, No. 9/10 (September–October 1996): pp. 36-68.

5   Sudipta Kaviraj, 'Indira Gandhi and Indian Politics,' *Economic and Political Weekly*, vol. 21, no. 38/39, (1986): pp. 1697–1708. p 1697.

6   Suman Dubey, 'Has India fulfilled any of the goals Jawaharlal Nehru envisaged for it?' *India Today*, 15 June 1984.

7   Budget Speech 1981-82.

8   Bhabatosh Datta, 'Finance Ministers on Show—Speeches of Union Finance Ministers, 1947-48 to 1984-85,' *Economic and Political Weekly*, Vol. 20, No. 17 (27 April 1985): pp. 755-757.

9   I.G. Patel, *Glimpses of Indian Economic Policy – An Insider's View*, (Oxford University Press, 2002), pp.164-172.

10 Montek Singh Ahluwalia, *Backstage – the story behind India's high growth years*, (New Delhi: Rupa, 2020), pp. 61-62.

11 Atul Kohli, 'Politics of Economic Growth in India, 1980-2005 Part I: The 1980s,' *Economic and Political Weekly*, (1 April 2006): pp. 1251-1259. p 1252.

12 H. K. Paranjape, 'The Vanishing MRTP Act: Will Only the Grin Remain?' *Economic and Political Weekly*, Vol 17, No. 23, June 5, (1982): pp. 955-963.

13 Atul Kohli, 'Politics of Economic Growth in India, 1980-2005 Part I: The 1980s,' *Economic and Political Weekly*, (1 April 2006): pp. 1251-1259. p 1252.

14 Robert E. Lucas, Jr., 'On the Mechanics of Economic Development,' *Journal of Monetary Economics*, 22, (July 1988): pp. 3-42.

15 Robert J. Barro, 'Macroeconomics: A Modern Approach,' *Thomson South-Western*, 2008, p.37.

16 Arvind Virmani, 'India's Economic Growth: From Socialist Rate of Growth to Bharatiya Rate of Growth,' Working Paper No. 122, *Indian Council for Research on International Economic Relations*, (February 2004): p 64

17 Ibid. p 41.

18 Amitava Krishna Dutt, 'The Political Economy of Indian Economic Reform,' *Journal of International Affairs*, Vol. 51, No. 1, South Asia: The Challenges of Statehood (Summer 1997), pp. 57-83.

19 Ghulam Nabi Khayal, 'Resettlement bill continues to draw fire from opposition groups in J&K,' *India Today*, 15 June 1982.

20 Sumantra Bose, *Kashmir – Roots of Conflict, Paths to Peace*, (Cambridge: Harvard University Press, 2003), p 92.

21 Frontline, 'Asom Gana Parishad – Rise and Fall,' 2 May 2014.

22 India Today, April 1988.

Chapter XX. The Camelot Days

1   Inaugural Speech by Congress President Rajiv Gandhi at Congress Centenary Session (Indira Nagar [Brabourne Stadium], Bombay), 28 December 1985. Available at http://indiatoday.intoday.in/story/full-text-of-rajiv-gandhis-famous-1985-speech/1/243106.html.

2   'Rahul echoes Rajiv Gandhi's comment on public funds,' *Rediff.com*, 17 January 2008, available at http://www.rediff.com/news/2008/jan/17rahul.htm.

3   https://southasia.ucla.edu/history-politics/independent-india/rajiv-gandhi/

4   Rudrangshu Mukherjee, 'The Prophet Delayed—The India that Rajiv Gandhi dreamt of is now about to happen,' *The Telegraph*, 8 February 2004, http://www.telegraphindia.com/1040208/asp/opinion/story_2871766.asp#

5   Pranab Mukherjee, *The Turbulent Years,1980-1996*, (New Delhi: Rupa, 2016).

6   David Brewster, *India's Ocean: The story of India's Bid for Regional Leadership*, (Routledge, 2014).

7   Long Term Fiscal Policy, Government of India, 1985.

8   N. A. Palkhivala, *The Highest Taxed Nation*, (Bombay: Mankatalas, 1965), P. 51.

9   V. P. Singh, 'Budget Speech 1985-86,' Government of India.

10   https://www.cbic.gov.in/resources//htdocs-cbec/customs/cst1819-010219/Chap%2021.pdf

11   https://pharmaceuticals.gov.in/sites/default/files/DPCO1979.pdf

12   Dani Rodrik and Arvind Subramanian, 'From "Hindu Growth" to Productivity Surge: The Mystery of the Indian Growth Transition,' *IMF Staff Papers*, Vol. 52, No. 2, (2005).

13   T. N. Srinivasan, 'Comments on "From "Hindu Growth" to Productivity Surge: The Mystery of the Indian Growth Transition,' *IMF Staff Papers*, Vol. 52, No. 2, (2005): pp. 229-233.

14   Atul Kohli, 'Centralisation and powerlessness: India's democracy in comparative perspective,' in Joel S. Migdal, Atul Kohli and Vivienne Shu (ed), 'State Power and Social Forces – Domination and Transformation in the Third World,' *Cambridge Studies in Comparative Politics*, Cambridge University Press, UK, 1994

15   Ibid. p 104.

16   Romesh Thapar, 'A Baba-Log Government,' *Economic and Political Weekly*, Vol. 21, Issue No. 9, (1 March 1986).

17   Ira Pandey, 'In *baba-log* world, small towns don't exist,' *The Tribune*, 17 November 2013. http://www.tribuneindia.com/2013/20131117/edit.htm#2.

18   A. G. Noorani, 'Legal Aspects to the Issue,' in Sarvepalli Gopal (ed.), *Anatomy of a Confrontation – The Rise of Communal Politics in India*, (Delhi: Penguin Books India, 1991).

19   L. M. Koul, *Kashmir – Past and Present, unravelling the mystique*, (Sehyog Prakashan, 2002), Chapter 20. http://ikashmir.net/pastpresent/doc/pastpresent.pdf.

20   Prabhu Chawla, 'President Zail Singh questions govt's decisions, much to PM Rajiv Gandhi's embarrassment,' *India Today*, 28 February 1987.

21   India Today, 'Mounting Inertia,' 30 April 1989.

22   David Butler, Ashok Lahiri and Prannoy Roy, 'India Decides –1952-1995,' *Books and Things*, New Delhi, 1995. p 25.

23   Rohit Parihar, 'CBI finds no clue against Om Prakash Chautala being accused in poll-killing,' *India Today*, 21 July 1997.

24   Christophe Jaffrelot, 'The Hindu nationalist reinterpretation of pilgrimage in India: the limits of *Yatra* politics,' *Nations and Nationalism*, 14 January 2009.

25   Ramachandra Guha, *India after Gandhi*, (Picador, 2007), p 635.

26   Ramesh Upadhyay, 'The Drama of the Arrest,' *Frontline*, 23 November 1990.

27   Inderjit Badhwar, 'Jammu & Kashmir Assembly poll: NC-Congress(I) alliance sweeps a massive win,' *India Today*, 15 April 1987.

28   Sumantra Bose, *Kashmir – Roots of Conflict, Paths to Peace*, (Cambridge: Harvard University Press, 2003), pp. 48-49.

29   Speech of Shri Yashwant Sinha, Minister of Finance, Introducing the Interim
     Budget for the year 1991-92. https://eparlib.nic.in/bitstream/123456789/110/1/
     Budget_speech_1991-92.pdf.

30   Quoted in Willem H.Buiter and Urjit R.Patel, 'Debt, deficits, and inflation: An
     application to the public finances of India,' *Journal of Public Economics*, Volume
     47, Issue 2, (March 1992): pp. 171-205.

Part IV. 1991-2020—Reforms with Its Ups and Downs

Chapter XXI. Crisis and the Launch of 1991 Reforms

1   Lok Sabha proceedings on 15 July 1991, available at https://parliamentofindia.
     nic.in/ls/lsdeb/ls10/ses1/1315079101.htm.

2   https://dpiit.gov.in/sites/default/files/chap001_0_0.pdf.

3   Pranab Mukherjee, *The Turbulent Years, 1980-1996*, (New Delhi: Rupa
     Publications, 2016). p 155.

4   Vinay Sitapati, *Hal Lion – How P. V. Narasimha Rao transformed India*, (Delhi:
     Penguin, India, 2016). p 163.

5   Parliament   of   India,   https://parliamentofindia.nic.in/ls/lsdeb/ls12/ses1/
     0228039813.htm.

6   Navroz K. Dubash and Sudhir Chella Rajan, 'Power Politics: Process of Power
     Sector Reform in India,' *Economic and Political Weekly*, Vol. 36, No. 35 (1–7
     September 2001): pp. 3367-3387+3389-3390. P. 3372.

7   Idbi.

8   Dilip D'souza, 'Skulduggery in a time of Enron – remembering Abhay Mehta,'
     The Mint, 3 August 2017.

9   Ibid.

10   Ronald Reagan, 'Tear down this wall,' http://www.historyplace.com/speeches/
     reagan-tear-down.htm.

11   Parliament   of   India,   https://parliamentofindia.nic.in/ls/lsdeb/ls10/
     ses1/1315079101.htm.

12   Ibid.

13   BM, 'Fund-Bank's Grand Design for India,' *EPW*, Vol. 26, No. 27/28, (6–13
     July 1991).

14   Arun Shourie, 'When spirit is willing, flesh has a way,' *Indian Express*, 4 February
     2004. http://archive.indianexpress.com/oldStory/40417/. DGFT is Directorate
     General of Foreign Trade in the Ministry of Commerce and Industry which is
     involved in the regulation and promotion of foreign trade.

Chapter XXII. End of Narasimha Rao Government

1   Yubaraj Ghimire, 'Dharma Sansad emerges as flagship of Hindutva movement,'
     India Today, 30 April 1994.

2   Vohra Committee Report, Ministry of Home Affairs, 5 October 1993. Available at https://adrindia.org/sites/default/files/VOHRA%20COMMITTEE%20 REPORT_0.pdf

3   Ibid.

4   Nikita Doval, 'Babri Masjid demolition: The key political players and their roles,' *Mint*, 6 December 2017.

5   Ibid.

6   Zafar Agha, 'Babri Masjid demolition: Rao failed to evolve his own plans to counter BJP's strategy,' *India Today*, 20 May 2013.

7   Girilal Jain, 'Narasimha Rao understands, Arjun Singh doesn't,' 14 April 1992. http://www.girilaljainarchive.net/1992/04/narasimha-rao-understands-arjun-singh-doesnt-girilal-jain/

8   Zafar Agha, Yubaraj Ghimire, N K Singh, M Rahman and Dilip Awasthi, 'PM Narasimha Rao in crisis; Arjun Singh, Sharad Pawar, N.D. Tiwari wait for their big chance,' *India Today*, 15 January 1993.

9   Zafar Agha, 'Growing dissent finally galvanises PM Narasimha Rao into tightening his grip on Congress(I),' *India Today*, 31 January 1995.

10   Ramesh Vinayak, 'Kashmir: Despite killing of key militants at Charar shrine, India loses a battle,' *India Today*, 31 May 1995.

11   Harinder Baweja, 'Operation Blunder,' *India Today*, 15 November 1993.

12   Prabhu Chawla, 'Calling to account,' India Today, 28 February 1990.

13   N.K. Singh, 'Narasimha Rao obviously meant that the instructions to get the documents attested had come to him from Prime Minister Rajiv Gandhi himself,' *Rediff on the net*, http://www.rediff.com/news/1996/0310kit6.htm.

14   Samir K. Barua and Jayanth R. Varma, 'Securities Scam: Genesis, Mechanics and Impact,' *Vikalpa*, 18(1), (January-March 1993): pp. 3-12. http://faculty.iima. ac.in/~jrvarma/papers/vik18-1.pdf.

15   Supreme Court of India, 'Vineet Narain & Others vs Union Of India & Another on 18 December, 1997,' https://indiankanoon.org/doc/1203995/

16   Zafar Agha, 'Jain hawala payoffs scandal throws entire political system into a dizzying tailspin,' *India Today*, 15 February 1996.

17   Shefali Rekha Alam Srinivas, 'The Great Sugar Scandal,' *India Today*, 30 June 1994.

18   Outlook, 'The Pickle King's Papers,' 6 February 2022.

19   Ibid.

20   Chitleen K. Sethi, 'Sukh Ram, who once helped Dhumal form government, is no stranger to BJP,' *The Print*, 16 October 2017.

21   Ibid.

22   Aruna Roy, Nikhil Dey, and Shankar Singh, 'Prabhash Joshi and the RTI Movement,' *Mainstream*, Vol XLVIII, No 19, (1 May 2010).

23   "Prime Minister condoles demise of P.V Narasimha Rao", 23 December 2004. https://archivepmo.nic.in/drmanmohansingh/pmmessageappeals. php?nodeid=17

24 K. Natwar Singh, *One Life is Not Enough – An Autobiography*, (New Delhi: Rupa Publications, 2014).

Chapter XXIII. Nineteen Months with Three Governments

1 Zafar Agha, 'War of nerves between Narasimha Rao and Arjun Singh-N.D. Tiwari combine reaches a flashpoint,' *India Today*, 15 June 1995.
2 P. Chidambaram, 'Budget Speech, 1996–97'.
3 The Economist, 'India's old man in a hurry,' 3 April 1997. The term had been used by the conservative Lord Randolph Churchill, Winston Churchill's father, to describe the liberal British Prime Minister Gladstone in the late nineteenth century.
4 George Iype, 'Congress withdraws support to UF govt, stakes claim to power,' *Rediff on the net*, http://www.rediff.com/news/mar/30cong.htm
5 S. S. Khan, 'Tax Amnesties in India,' TII Special, *Tax International*, 12 March 2012. https://www.taxindiainternational.com/columnDesc.php?qwer43fcxzt=NzU=.
6 Ibid.
7 The Hindu, 'NGO points out 'exclusion errors' in PDS,' 2 August 2018
8 Human Rights Watch, 'The Enron Corporation – Corporate complicity in human rights violation,' https://www.hrw.org/reports/1999/enron/enron2-4.htm
9 N. Ramakrishnan, 'Decade of power reforms -- Hardly electrifying,' *The Hindu Business Line*, 4 September 2001, quoting Deepak S. Parekh, Chairman, Infrastructure Development Finance Corporation. Also quoted in https://fsi-live.s3.us-west-1.amazonaws.com/s3fs-public/India_Country_Study__UPDATE.pdf.
10 Venkitesh Ramakrishnan Praveen Swami, 'A Crisis Defused,' *Frontline*, 1 November 1997.
11 Prabhu Chawla, 'Rajiv Gandhi killing: Jain Commission report indicts DMK for colluding with LTTE,' *India Today*, 17 November 1997.
12 Business Standard, 'President Dissolves 11th Lok Sabha,' 5 December 1997.
13 Ministry of Finance, Government of India, 'Economic Survey, 1997-98,' Chapter 6.
14 Inderjit Badhwar, 'Violence-ridden Kashmir begins to heal as people participate in assembly elections, *India Today*, 30 September 1996.
15 Harinder Baweja, 'Seven Pandits killed in Kashmir Valley, incident may trigger second wave of migration,' *India Today*, 15 April 1997.

Chapter XXIV. The First NDA Government

1 N. K. Singh, 'Elections 1996: Although it lacks a credible plank, BJP capitalises on its opponents' weaknesses,' *India Today*, 30 April 1996.
2 Rediff, 'National Agenda for Governance,' https://www.rediff.com/news/agenda.htm.
3 Nayanima Basu, 'When Vajpayee took a bus ride and it seemed peace with Pakistan was possible,' *The Print*, 19 February 2019.

4   Ibid.

5   Frontline, 'Let them eat the bomb,' 6 June 1998.

6   Navroz K. Dubash and Sudhir Chella Rajan, 'Power Politics: Process of Power Sector Reform in India,' *Economic and Political Weekly*, Vol. 36, No. 35 (1–7 September 2001), pp. 3367-3387+3389-3390.

7   Abhishek G. Dastidar and Shalini Nyar, 'Golden Quadrilateral: Vajpayee's biggest infra effort in roadways,' *Indian Express*, 17 August 2018.

8   Rediff on the Net, 'UTI won't be allowed to fail, reassures Sinha,' 8 October 1998. https://www.rediff.com/business/1998/oct/08sinha.htm

Chapter XXV. The Second NDA Government

1   V. Shankar Aiyar and Sumit Mitra, 'UTI flagship scheme US-64 pauperized by former chairman by gambling on high-risk shares,' *India Today*, 23 July 2001.

2   George Iype, 'Sonia relents, returns to head Congress,' *Rediff on the Net*, 24 May 1999, https://www.rediff.com/news/1999/may/24iype1.htm.

3   Mukhtar Ahmad, 'Mufti floats new regional party in Kashmir,' *Rediff on the Net*, 28 July 1999.

4   Praveen Swami, 'The Jaish-e-Mohammad's fidayeen factory: How Masood Azhar set up his industry of terror in Kashmir,' *Firstpost*, 22 February 2019.

5   Zulfikar Majid, 'Autonomy resolution within 30-days if voted to power,' *Deccan Herald*, 20 December 2018.

6   Manoj Joshi, 'Mufti Mohammad Sayeed (1936-2016): From 'soft-separatist' to 'collaborator',' *Scroll.in*, 7 January 2016. https://scroll.in/article/801492/mufti-mohammad-sayeed-1936-2016-from-soft-separatist-to-collaborator.

7   The Constitution (Eighty-eighth Amendment) Bill, 2003.

8   'A Beginning, but Miles to Go,' *Economic and Political Weekly*, Vol. 38, no. 7, (2003): pp. 579–580. p 580, https://www.epw.in/system/files/pdf/index/2003_oct_12_SUBJECT_Index-2003_.pdf.

9   Public Health Engineering Department, Government of Meghalaya, 'Swachh Bharat Mission(SBM)/Total Sanitation Campaign (TSC)'https://megphed.gov.in/tsc.htm#:~:text=From%201999%2C%20a%20%20E2%80%9Cdemand%20driven,of%20demand%20for%20sanitary%20facilities.

10   Cellular Operators Association of India, 'Telecom Sector Reforms in India,' November 2007.

11   N. K. Singh, *Portraits of Power – Half a Century at Ringside*, (New Delhi: Rupa Publications India, 2020): pp. 181-182.

12   Arun Dev, 'How Telgi Pulled Off Rs 3,000 Cr Stamp Paper Scam, Until He Didn't,' *The Quint*, 25 October 2017.

13   Hindustan Times, 'Abdul Karim Telgi, the rise and fall of India's stamp paper scam kingpin,' 27 October 2017.

14   N. Ramakrishnan, 'Decade of power reforms -- Hardly electrifying,' *The Hindu Business Line*, 4 September 2001, quoting Deepak S. Parekh, Chairman,

Infrastructure Development Finance Corporation. Also quoted in https://fsi-live. s3.us-west-1.amazonaws.com/s3fs-public/India_Country_Study__UPDATE.pdf.

15 Report of the Expert Committee headed by Deepak Parekh, Ministry of Power, Government of India, 'Structuring of APDRP, Reform Framework and Principles of Financial Restructuring of SEBs,' September 2002, http://orierc. org/OERCOLD/documents/Deepak_Parekh_Report.pdf.

16 Zee News, 'Expenditure on India Shining campaign figures in Rajya Sabha,' 23 August 2005, https://zeenews.india.com/news/nation/expenditure-on-india-shining-campaign-figures-in-rajya-sabha_236806.html

17 Ronald Inden, 'A campaign that lost sheen,' *The Hindu*, 3 October 2004, http:// www.thehindu.com/mag/2004/10/03/stories/2004100300160200.htm.

18 The Hindu, 25 January 2004, http://www.thehindu.com/2004/01/25/ stories/2004012509030300.htm.

19 Bhuvan Bagga, 'What makes NDA's "India Shining" campaign the "worst" poll strategy in Indian history,' *India Today*, 14 May 2013,

20 Ibid.

21 Debating India, 'India Shining backfired: Advani,' 29 May 2004. http://india. eu.org/1634.html

Chapter XXVI. The First UPA Government

1 Rukmini S., 'How the BJP won this election,' *The Hindu*, 17 May 2014, https://www.thehindu.com/news/national/how-the-bjp-won-this-election/ article6020712.ece.

2 Sanjaya Baru, *The Accidental Prime Minister – The Making and Unmaking of Manmohan Singh*, (Delhi: Penguin Random House India Private Limited, 2015).

3 RBI, 'RBI's Mid-term Review of Annual Policy for the year 2005-06,' para 97.

4 Editorial, 'The National Advisory Council Experiment,' *Economic and Political Weekly*, Vol. 43, Issue No. 15, April 2008.

5 Right to Information Act, Section 2(a). https://rti.gov.in/RTI%20Act,%20 2005%20(Amended)-English%20Version.pdf.

6 V. M. Dandekar, 'Making Right to Work Fundamental.' *Economic and Political Weekly*, vol. 26, no. 11/12, 1991, pp. 697–708.

7 The Gazette of India, 'The National Rural Employment Guarantee Act, 2005,' Extraordinary, 5 September 2005.

8 Bharti Jain, 'Serial dresser Patil at Saturday night blasts,' *The Economic Times*, 15 September 2008.

9 FRBMA, Section 4(2). https://dea.gov.in/sites/default/files/FRBM%20Act%20 2003%20and%20FRBM%20Rules%202004.pdf.

Chapter XXVII. The Second UPA Government

1 The Hindustan Times, 'Sonia's ambitious food bill wins LS vote; UPA gets its 'game-changer',' 27 August 2013.

2   The Times of India, 'Sonia defends Food Security Bill; BJP calls it 'vote security bill,' 26 August 2013.

3   R. Jagannathan, 'UPA's legacy: Disasters like Food Security Bill and Land Acquisition Bill,' *Firstpost*, 30 August 2013, http://www.firstpost.com/business/upas-legacy-disasters-like-food-bill-and-land-acquisition-bill-1071847.html.

4   Uttam Gupta, 'One step forward, two steps back,' *The Hindu Business Line*, 18 February 2014.

5   Ministry of Petroleum, 'Review of the Direct Benefit Transfer for LPG Scheme May 2014,' May 2014, http://petroleum.nic.in/sites/default/files/dhande.pdf.

6   Comptroller and Auditor General of India, 'Report No. 19 of 2010—Performance Audit of Issue of Licences and Allocation of 2G Spectrum of Union Government, Ministry of Communications and Information Technology,' 16 November 2010.

7   Vinay Kumar, 'CWG scam: Kalmadi named 'main accused' in first CBI charge sheet,' *The Hindu*, 20 May 2011.

8   PTI, 'Ramdev on being caught dressed as a woman,' 6 June 2011. https://www.ndtv.com/india-news/ramdev-on-being-caught-dressed-as-a-woman-457723. India Today, 'Baba Ramdev sports woman's dress to hoodwink police,' 5 June 2011.

9   Deepti Jakhar, 'Ramdev eviction: Why his salwar kameez looks carefully picked out,' *India Today*, 7 June 2011.

Chapter XXVIII. The First Modi Government

1   S. Rukmini, 'Two out of three say UPA is corrupt,' *The Hindu*, 23 July 2013.

2   'Budget at a Glance,' Union Budget, Government of India, 2019-20 and 2020-21.

3   NITI Aayog, http://niti.gov.in/content/overview#. 'While designing strategic and long term policies and programmes for the Government of India, NITI Aayog also provides relevant technical advice to the Centre and States.'

4   Jean Dreze and Amartya Sen, *An Uncertain Glory -- India and Its Contradictions*, (UK: Penguin, Allen Lane, 2013): p 143.

5   Narendra Modi, 'Text of PM's speech at the Red Fort,' https://www.narendramodi.in/text-of-pms-speech-at-red-fort-6464.

6   Press Information Bureau, 'English rendering of PM's address to the Nation from the ramparts of the Red Fort on the 69th Independence Day,' https://pib.gov.in/newsite/PrintRelease.aspx?relid=126094

7   Amartya Sen, 'More Than 100 Million Women Are Missing,' *New York Review of Books*, 20 December 1990..

8   DNA, 'PM Narendra Modi invites ideas on 'Beti Bachao, Beti Padhao,' 11 October 2014.

9   SIDBI had been set up in April 1990 to serve as the principal financial institution for finance to the MSME sector.

10 'Telling Numbers: Enrolment and claims in flagship life, accident insurance schemes,' Indian Express, 11 December 2019 and 'State-run insurers seek to increase PMSBY premium,' The Financial Express, 23 February 2017.

11 M. S. Sahoo, 'A Journey of Endless Hope,' in *Insolvency and Bankruptcy Code: A Miscellany of Perspectives*, (Delhi: Insolvency and Bankruptcy Board of India, 2019).

12 M.S. Sahoo, 'Insolvency Reforms—A Road Under Construction,' in *Insolvency and Bankruptcy Regime in India: A Narrative* (2020), Insolvency and Bankruptcy Board of India (IBBI), 2020: p 2.

Chapter XXIX. Continuing Story of India's Search for Glory

1 Vladimer Orlando Key Jr., *The Responsible Electorate: Rationality in Presidential Voting 1936-1960*, (Cambridge: Belknap Press, 1966). Quoted in B. Douglas Bernheim and Navin Kartik, 'Candidates, Character, and Corruption,' *American Economic Journal: Microeconomics*, Vol. 6, No. 2, (May 2014): pp. 205-246.

2 Quartz India, 'Raghuram Rajan explains why corrupt politicians win elections in India,' 14 August 2014.

3 Times of India, 30 January 2022.

4 Remarks at The Asia Society, Mumbai, India, 'India and the Global Economy,' 15 October 2010. Available at https://asiasociety.org/india/india-and-global-economy.